Actors On Guard

Actors On Guard

A Practical Guide for the
Use of the Rapier and Dagger
for Stage and Screen

Dale Anthony Girard
Illustrations by Zina Lee

A Theatre Arts Book
ROUTLEDGE
NEW YORK & LONDON

Published in 1997 by

Routledge/Theatre Arts Books
29 West 35 Street
New York, NY 10001

Published in Great Britain in 1997 by

Routledge
11 New Fetter Lane
London Ec4P 4EE

Library of Congress Cataloging-in-Publication Data

Girard, Dale Anthony, 1964–
    Actors on guard : a practical guide for the use of the rapier and
dagger for stage and screen / Dale Anthony Girard.
        p.   cm.
    Includes bibliographical references and index.
    ISBN 0-87830-057-0 (hb). — ISBN 0-87830-058-9 (pb)
    1. Stage Fighting.   2. Stage Combat.   3. Theatre.   4. Acting.   I. Title.
PN2071.F4G55   1966
792′.928—dc20
                                                                                96-2617
                                                                                  CIP

Table of Contents

Preface

In 1983, while performing a sword fight at the Colorado Renaissance Festival, I had the misfortune of receiving a blow to the face with a seven–pound broadsword (to this day I still bear the scar). Head wounds bleed a great deal, and although the cut wasn't deep it certainly put me on guard. It was then I decided that there must be a better way to perform a stage fight than by the laws of "survival of the fittest." It was this incident that spurred my desire for professional training and, later, the development of this text. I began studying with the Society of American Fight Directors. Under their tutelage I found the safe and dynamic swordplay that I knew existed.

I began reading anything I could on the subject of stage combat and theatrical violence. At first I was surprised at how few books were available on the topic. Conflict in theatre is as old as theatre itself, and stage fights have been performed by actors for centuries. The real surprise, however, came when I actually sat down and read the few books that dealt with stage swordplay. The dangerous practices I was trying to escape were often supported in these misleading texts. Some advocated attacks at the face, and swords pointed directly at the eyes. These methods seemed like haphazard adaptations of fencing strategies to theatre, with no thought of what might happen when the jacket and mask of the fencer were removed. This type of dangerous misinformation is what I was trying to escape. Unfortunately these books and their practices have been adopted by many directors and self-described "fight choreographers," resulting in many minor injuries like mine, more serious injuries, and unfortunately even some deaths.

I started to note what was wrong—and right—with these texts, and couple it with my notes from various classes, tutorials, and workshops. To keep track of my process I found myself constantly organizing and reorganizing my notes. As I began to teach and work professionally my observations from professional experience constantly amended this information. Reading and research also kept adding to my "notes" until they became various files within my computer. Each entry was made to help me clarify specifics and insure that I was constantly aware of the safety issues within the dynamics of the stage fight. Each year the files became larger and more detailed as I grew in my understanding and application of the art. Eventually the files became "Chapters" and the idea of the book was born. Information and insight that I'd been using on the stage, in films and in the classroom were notated and available in a semi-tangible form. My research merely needed to be organized and put into a presentational pattern.

This book was written to put actors "on guard," not only with a sword, but with the knowledge they need in order to protect themselves from unsafe stage combat. It offers a system that thoroughly explains the elements of technique. Detailed movements of the sword, including where the tip should and should not travel, are painstakingly described. It defines the exact location of targets, explains proper distance and footwork, and covers every aspect of the style presented. Hundreds of illustrations have been provided to clarify descriptions of movement and show the proper placement of body and blade.

While nothing can impart the precise, detailed understanding of stage combat that study with a skilled master instills, my hope is that this book will serves as a valuable introduction and guide to the areas of safety, technique, and theatricality. If this helps prevent even one "blow to the face" or other injury on stage, then my time and effort has paid off.

Table of Plates

Acknowledgments

I would first like to acknowledge the work of fight master William Hobbs, whose choreography in Richard Lester's film *The Three Musketeers* first introduced me to the art of swordplay and whose brilliant examples, shown so often on stage and screen, still continue to thrill, challenge, intrigue, and inspire me.

Secondly, I would also like to acknowledge the Society of American Fight Directors who took me under their wing at an early age and taught me the art that is now my life and livelihood. In particular I would like to acknowledge maestro David Boushey who since my induction has been my teacher, my mentor, my friend. I would also like to acknowledge all the masters of the SAFD (J.R. Beardsley, David Boushey, Drew Fracher, Erik Fredricksen, David Leong, J.D. Martinez, Richard Raether, J. Allen Suddeth, Christopher Villa & David Wooley) who spent the time and energy to allow me to grow and blossom, to see my full potential while supporting my efforts to strive to reach it. Without the SAFD this book would not be possible.

Thirdly, this book is for my family, friends, colleagues, and students whose kind words, faith, and encouragement provided the impetus for this project. In particular I would like to acknowledge my teaching assistants (Trent Dawson, Ian Marshal, Timothy Tait and Dane Torbenson) who, in various ways over the years, have contributed to this text. Thank you also to all the members of On Edge Productions that crossed swords with me at various festivals and fairs. All of you played a part in the development of my style and philosophy of stage swordplay.

Special thanks to Zina Lee, my illustrator, who graciously took on the challenge of turning hundreds of photographs into the line drawings that now grace the pages of this text. Acknowledgement is also due to my models (Trent Dawson, Janine Hawley, and Timothy Tait) who patiently posed for hundreds of pictures during the evolution of this text.

Last, but certainly not least, this book is for Janine, who tolerated the months of isolation as I labored to turn notes and ideas into a comprehensive written form.

This book is for her, my sounding board, my proof reader, my best friend, my wife.

Prologue

"One cannot make rules regarding creativity, but only regarding technique and safety." [William Hobbs][1]

Before delving into a manuscript of this scope, I think it is fair to inform the reader that the approach toward stage combat taken in this book—both in its style and its terminology—is idiosyncratic. The process herein is my interpretation and theatricalization of historical swordplay and by no means the only approach to the art. There are many fight choreographers who prefer a less historical and methodical approach to theatrical blade-play. This does not mean that one approach is right and the other is wrong, it only means that they are different. If you are using this text in a classroom, you may find your teacher's personal experiences and approach infringing on the practices of this text. These differences in style are not inappropriate; in fact they help enlarge the art and enrich everyone's skills. After all, the overall effect of stage combat, like so many art-forms, lies in the hands of the artist.

The above quote from the famous English fight director William Hobbs is quite true, and is the founding principle of this text. While there are no "rules regarding creativity" in stage combat, you must still adhere to those concerning safe, effective blade-play. This book will help develop a strong understanding of safe stage mechanics so that you are able to work with a variety of fight directors and apply your own creative aspects of the acting craft to meet the specific needs of each character.

The approach presented herein is based on developing a firm mechanical knowledge and practice of specific techniques. These techniques are taught in a neutral stance, devoid of character or acted conflict. This is a placement of the body that is neither sloppy or stiff, but well-balanced and centered, with a relaxed but powerful energy ready to be discharged in a highly focused way into whatever activity is asked of it. Such a "correct" or neutral placement enables you to approach the building of a character within a fight from a firm, centered base with no personal mannerisms. This is important to this text because I feel there is a great difference between learning "a fight" and learning how to perform stage fights. "Fights" are performed in character. In learning "a fight," you merely learn how a specific character would fight. This is product-, not process-, oriented. If, however, you learn and master specific techniques common to all staged conflicts that themselves "say" nothing, either about your physical or your psychological attitude, you develop a process from which specific acting choices can be made.

Like voice work and stage diction, the mechanics must be mastered before they can appear natural on stage. A firm understanding of good diction allows the actor to create a dialect that sounds distorted and slurred while still communicating the words to the audience. The same is true of the mechanics of a stage fight. The techniques presented in this text are exercises in good physical diction. Their neutrality is devoid of character and conflict, focusing instead on an ideal that can then be molded to the variable circumstances of a production. In embracing the techniques that follow, it is important to know that they are the foundations of stage swordplay, and not the final

---

[1]Hobbs, *Stage Combat*, p. 65.

product. The actions must always remain safe, but they also must come from the character. Perfect stance, posture, movement, and execution are an ideal for the swordsman, not a constant.

It is important, therefore, that you do not become entrapped in the neutral stance of this text. The stance, posture, and mechanics presented in here are the springboard for acting choices and not a character style. If you only learn the neutral stance, you run the risk of that becoming your "habit" rather than your foundation. If you are using this text as apart of a class, your teacher will be able to address these issues in various exercises as you develop your techniques. If, however, you are working on your own, I would suggestt that you read Chapter 20 before working your way through the text. This chapter encapsulates the acting process of a fight and helps provide a better understanding of the entire process as bad technique.

To further help develop a true "actor/combatant," I have laden this text with healthy amounts of rapier lore and history. I do this not only because of the importance of such information to the classical actor, but also because of the fact that it is difficult to understand how to do something if one does not know why it is done. For me, the idea of movement for movement's sake defeats the dramatic significance of stage combat. I found in developing this book that when the mechanics were presented without their history, the truth of the action was unwittingly omitted. I understand that some actors want to "cut to the chase" and cross swords as soon as possible, but in doing so I feel they are robbed of knowledge that will fill the action with meaning and help in making informed choices during a fight.

If you have fenced before, you will find some terms used in this book have different definitions than those of sport fencing. This is due to the fact that the actions in sport fencing are tactical while the actions in stage combat are theatrical. The variables of each action executed on stage are the result of choreography, and not specific to the reactions of an opponent or an intention to hit. The terms and definitions provided herein are specific to theatrical swordplay and are intended to develop a more common language among choreographers, teachers, and students. As new words and techniques are provided in the text, take the time to become familiar with them. This will prove beneficial in later chapters and as you study and work with other fight choreographers.

In your career, I hope you have the opportunity to work with a variety of fight directors and choreographers. They may use different terms and a variety of new and wonderful techniques. Learn from these masters. Add their terms and techniques to the foundation you develop here to grow and create your own style. Stage combat is a living, maturing art. As you read and learn from this text and study with your teacher, director or choreographer, remember anything is possible—there are no boundaries to what can be done with a sword as long as the combatants are safe and the audience believes.

A Note For the South-Paw

Due to the volume of the material covered in this manuscript, space has not allowed for mechanical descriptions of technique for both right and left-handed combatants. Because the greater number of combatants are right-handed, the techniques are presented from that point of view. This does not, however, imply that stage combat should not be executed with the left hand. There is no reason for anyone to take up a sword in any hand other than that with which they are most comfortable.

As a left-hander approaching the techniques in this manuscript, follow all the provided safety rules and invert the described actions. Left and right are switched, as are the directional paths of clockwise and counter-clockwise. Several techniques in this text are taught from the vantage of a clock; in left-handed swordplay the clock becomes a mirror image. Three o'clock now being on the left, nine o'clock on the right and so on. Angles and vertical movements remain the same, although the direction of the angle opposes those described.

Your teacher should be a help clarifying any transitions that may be confusing. Do not get frustrated. Many actors are left-handed and should not be expected to master swordplay with their right-hand until right-handed actors learn to write with their left hand. Besides, a left-handed fencer paired with a right-handed fencer is quite dynamic and effective on the stage. The swords can be placed up stage, opening both actors to the house and presenting an open, unobstructed encounter.

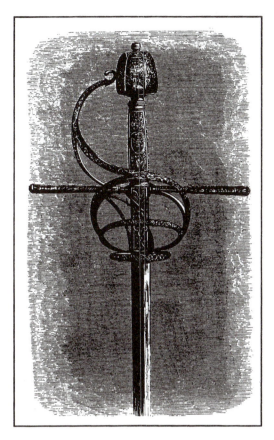

Plate I: Sixteenth–century Italian Swept-Hilt Rapier.

"The exercising of weapons putteth away aches, griefes and diseases, it increaseth strength and sharpeneth the wits, it giveth a perfect judgment, it compelleth melancholy choleric and evil conceits, it keepeth a man in breath, perfect health and long life. It is unto him that hath the man in breath, perfect health and long life. It is unto him that hath the perfection thereof a most friendly and comfortable companion when he is alone, having but only his weapon about him, it putteth him out of all feare."

Chapter 1

Safety First!

"It is good sleeping in a whole skinne." [G. Silver][1]

Until a few years ago stage combat had been an inexact practice handled by just about anyone who felt qualified for the job; however, many were not. Professional and university productions were often staged by local fencing coaches, who had little or no knowledge of the essence of theatre. Fights were generally an incoherent compilation of moves drawn from sport fencing, awkward in the hands of the actor and incomprehensible to the audience.

To solve this problem, directors would often ask actors with fencing experience to set the fight. Even actors who were fairly proficient in fencing couldn't change the fact that the entire practice of sport fencing was to deceive one's opponent and score with a hit. This made the fights confusing to the audience and dangerous to the actor. Dramatically, these fights were either ineffective due to fear and hesitation on the part of the actors, or heart-stoppingly dangerous due to the actors swinging out of control at one another.

Hesitant actors would often be told to "go for it!" long before they were ready to perform. Actors would be told to "do the fight thing" and return with something the director could iron out and plug into the scene. The actor would commit to this, knowing no other way to stage a fight. Unfortunately, actors would often get hurt because they knew nothing about staging a fight—and often neither did the director.

> *"My training and exercise in the art of fence,"* says Laurence Olivier, *"has been largely grounded on the clockwork technique of 'one, two, three; two, one, four;' or 'bish, bash, bosh; bash, bosh, bish; no, no, no, you should not be doing bosh there, it is bash first, then bosh, now then, bosh, bash, bish, then backhand bosh'."*[2]

No one seems excluded from the hazards of the old school as Olivier goes on to tell some dreadful war stories and list a half page of personal injuries due to ineffective stage combat. Needless to say, the art of theatrical swordplay has not been an exact science.

In the past thirty years or so, the theatre has begun to acknowledge this serious problem. As long as there has been theatre, there has been someone to arrange the fights, but not until recently has a specialist class of fight directors existed. In Britain, America and Canada there are established societies of professional fight directors whose goals are to make the physical conflict in the theatre

---

[1]A term used to express safety and caution in Elizabethan swordplay as it appears in several period fencing manuals. Silver, p. 8 and Swetnam, p. 70.

[2]Hobbs, *Stage Combat.*

as safe and exciting as possible. These societies, and other professionals with like interests, have made actors and directors aware that fights not only can be, but need to be, safe and dramatically effective.

MAKE IT SAFE

It is essential that actors protect their most valuable instrument: their body. If ever there is a conflict between safety and someone's notion of "dramatic effectiveness," *safety comes first.* The theatre is illusion. The artist is not Hamlet or Juliet, they do not die at the end of the play; they *ACT!* There is no reason, at any time, that an actor should be put in even the slightest amount of physical danger. A performer should be able to walk away from a fight and any number of fight rehearsals without having experienced pain. Safety is the first of all priorities. If you cannot do the prescribed action safely, do not do it at all.

Many people think stage combat is limited only to the likes of the brawl in *Romeo and Juliet* and the duel in *Hamlet.* In reality, however, it includes any and all physical conflict, armed and unarmed, that takes place in the theatre. From one seemingly simple slap or shove to the mass battle of Bosworth field, each and every physical encounter on stage is serious business. It is not a game or a contest; there are no winners in that frame of mind, only losers. Neither the director nor the performers should ever forget that fact.

There is something utterly bewitching and romantic about a sword fight. Young actors, especially men, tend to carelessly jump into the fray, overcome with machismo and a desire to "sling steel." A sword seems to bring out the swashbuckler in everyone. All too often, it is only *after* an injury occurs that cast and crew realize that stage combat is an art and not a game.

The business of a stage fight calls for concentration, diligence and particularly trust in one's partner. There is no room for someone trying to show how incredibly tough they are. It is certainly not an activity for show-offs or devil-may-cares. Nor is it a game, but rather a precision dance highlighted with *acted* aggression.

The art of stage combat, when approached with professional care, precision and respect, when prepared and practiced with patience and enthusiasm, is a spectacle of stagecraft.

> *"I have always felt very strongly that a stage fight offered the actor a unique opportunity of winning the audience, as great almost as any scene, speech or action. That Shakespeare put it high in his estimation of stage effect is proclaimed by the amount of times he trustingly leaves it to this element to provide him with his dénouements."*[3] [Laurence Olivier]

A stage fight can and should be the highlight of a scene or the climax of the production. It should bring the audience to the edge of its seat or leave them in stunned silence, have them rolling in the aisles or cheering for more, all in perfect safety for everyone involved.

PREPARING FOR COMBAT

How then does one make a fight safe and effective? How do we override the primal instinct and conditioned response system to portray conflict without fighting? How can we bring blood to boil, tears to the eyes and a smile to the face of the audience while keeping it all safe? These are questions the artist must ask continually, for there is no single procedure that will protect an actor from carelessness, ignorance or "horsing around." Only through constant practice and questioning of techniques and procedures can stage combat be made safe for the artist. Only by understanding the entire procedure, both how and why it is safe, can the actor truly be *On Guard.*

---

[3]Hobbs, *Stage Combat.*

Setting the Stage

Before you begin training, rehearsal or performance, it is essential that you make sure you have enough room to comfortably allow for the movement required in the combat. Weapons such as knives, swords and sticks increase the reach of the combatant in height, width and depth. Lights, curtains or scenery can be struck by a weapon raised over the head. Scenery and props, as well as other actors, can be struck by a weapon swung behind the back or from side to side. Be sure that you have no opportunity to stumble or trip on furniture, cords, props or scenery. Keep your blades away from lights and lamps, as well as mirrors and windows. The combat area should be free and clear of any and all obstacles not precisely involved in the combat.

Work Surface

The ideal surface to work on is a sprung wood floor like those in a dance studio. This allows you to commit to footwork without fear of injury. If a sprung wood floor is not available, try to work on a wooden or linoleum floor built over a plywood base. Never work on concrete or asphalt surfaces, even when covered with wood and linoleum; movement on such hard surfaces can be damaging to your feet and legs.

Make sure that the surface is not slippery and that you are aware of any stairs, ramps and risers, and that you work well away from such hazards. If the fight is to be set on stairs or other uneven surfaces, it is best for you to rehearse on the actual set as soon, and as often, as possible. Be sure that the floor is free of loose boards and debris. It is wise to sweep the floor prior to working on it, giving particular attention to tacks, staples, nails, screws and the likes—which can prove hazardous. If the surface is dusty, a good mopping will take care of that risk. If you do mop the floor, wait for it to dry before working on the surface.

Appropriate Lighting

Good lighting is a necessary element to safe stage combat. Whether training, rehearsing or performing a fight, you need sufficient light to make effective eye contact, discern objects around you and clearly see the movement of any weapon involved in the exchange. To work in insufficient light places too many elements outside of your control. Even when designed as "mood lighting" in a production, dim or insufficient lighting is unsafe to perform in, and leaves the audience in the dark.

What to Wear

When training in stage combat, it is best to dress in comfortable, nonrestrictive clothing. Blue jeans, skirts (especially short skirts), dresses and all other types of clothing that can inhibit movement or get caught under the feet should not be worn while training. At all times wear comfortable shoes that won't slip or slide, and if you are in costume ensure that shoes and boots have good, non-slip rubber soles. If you wear glasses and cannot work without them, get a band to keep them on your head. If you will wear contact lenses during a performance, you should wear them throughout the rehearsal process to avoid last minute problems.

If you have long hair, pull it back out of your eyes. Once you start moving this will be a big help, it will keep your sight-lines clear and allow your partner to make eye contact with you. If a wig or long flowing hair is desired in the production, it is best to learn techniques and choreography first, then add the hair to rehearsal once you are comfortable with the movements. Before costumes are added to the rehearsal process be sure that *all* movements set in the fight can be performed safely in the costume. It is best to be aware of the restrictions of costumes before a fight is set, but if this is impossible, you must test the costumes prior to wearing them in the fight. Some costumers love to put whistles, buzzers, buttons and bells all over period costumes, which is fine to a point. If any part of the costume can prove dangerous to the combatant, talk to the fight choreographer about having the decoration moved or removed for safety's sake. For your own safety you should remove all personal jewelry and potentially sharp or dangerous objects. This includes earrings, belt buckles, keys, necklaces, rings, bracelets, pens, pencils or any other object that you might be wearing or carrying prior to training or performance.

Warming Up and Stretching Out

Once you have established a good rehearsal space with plenty of room, a sound floor and good lighting, and changed into comfortable nonrestrictive clothing, it is vitally important that you warmup. Although a good session of stage combat is an excellent physical workout, it is important to prepare through preliminary exercise. The body should be warm and limber prior to the training or rehearsal session. This includes cardiovascular work. To be completely alert and focusing on the work at hand, the brain needs a plentiful supply of blood, fully oxygenated by a warm body. You should also go through a full series of stretches in the legs, arms, back, torso, wrists, feet, head and neck. In stage combat, as in any physical discipline, the warm-up period is important in safeguarding against sprains, strains and pulled or torn muscles. A good warm-up limbers the body and enhances one's kinesthetic awareness, aiding in concentration. If you are unsure about the physical demands of stage combat, due to a past accident or injury, it is recommended that you consult your physician before beginning training. It is also important that you inform you instructor, choreographer or fight director of any personal injuries, physical limitations or problems prior to starting any practice sessions.

Personal Preparation

It has been said more than once that "an ounce of prevention is worth a pound of cure," and although understanding that the business of a stage fight calls for concentration, diligence and trust in one's partner, it isn't enough. Safety is easily preached and easily neglected in foreign terrain. To know you should be safe is not the same as knowing that you are safe, thus it also has been said that "a little knowledge is a dangerous thing." To know that stage combat is a distinct dramatic movement discipline where the artist's safety is paramount does not mean that one also knows how to make it safe. Safety may be the first rule of stage combat, but it is by no means the only rule.

As you progress through this text, you will find that every action has any number of built in safeties. These "safeties" are, however, only effective if you approach the techniques keeping this primary rule in mind: stage combat is acted aggression where "safety comes first." Whether involved in armed or unarmed stage combat, you need to overcome your primal instincts and violent reflex actions. You need to slowly develop a new set of conditioned responses. New habits need to be built where old habits lie. Your body and mind need to learn the art of the stage magician. Misdirection and illusion are the key. What is, and what appears to be, are two separate entities in the stage fight.

In order to redirect the body and mind away from the reality of actual aggression to the process of acted aggression, you must be submerged in the methodology of stage combat. The idea of learning by doing is as old as education. The slow process of trial and error and practiced repetition has taught us how to walk, talk, eat, ride a bicycle and drive a manual transmission. These actions, along with stage diction, dialects and breath support were once foreign to our kinesthetic process and took time and patience to master. Stage combat, as any new process, requires that same time and patience.

Don't Rush

Many actors and directors get frustrated that they don't pick up combat skills quickly. Some actors rush the process, not giving their bodies time to actually learn the mechanics. By rushing the learning process, they may get from point "A" to point "D" but will have no control in the action and will be unable to correctly go through stages "B" and "C." By rushing the learning process, you miss the inherent safety of the technique through an incomplete understanding of the process. This can develop habits that may prove harmful.

Everyone learns at their own rate, what is simple for one person is difficult for others; and conversely, what may seem easy for others may be difficult for you. Take the time to get it right—for you. Find and understand the technique in your body. Master each technique slowly and carefully, without rushing or being rushed, and you'll be fine. If your instructor, director and/or partner try to rush you, and you are not ready to move on, say ''No!'' and stay at slow motion until you are secure. You will be happier in the long run for doing that, and possibly healthier, too.

Kinesthetic Learning

To make stage combat a safe practice, it must be ingrained in the actor's muscle memory through constant repetition. By slowly repeating mechanics, a thin layer of ''potential habit'' is placed in one's physical and mental memory. The mind and the body begin to make the actions more natural; this is known as *kinesthetic learning*.[4] Each time the mechanics of a technique are repeated the layers of potential habit thicken. When a technique is practiced often enough, the action slowly becomes second nature. Eventually the pattern of movement becomes thoroughly ingrained, completely accurate and subject to instantaneous recall. Like riding a bicycle, once you've learned how, you never forget.

Learning stage combat is like riding a bicycle or any other physical discipline. On a bike you start learning the mechanics while being supported by training wheels. After a great deal of patience, practice and repetition, the training wheels are removed and away you go. If you rush the process and remove the trainers too early, you wobble and fall down. Kinesthetic learning takes time. You cannot ride a bike on the first day or dance in the grand ballet with only three weeks of classes, nor can you earn a martial arts black belt without a lot of hard work and dedication. Do not expect to master stage combat quickly. If you do learn quickly, all the better for you, and if you don't, then you are learning at an average pace. Don't worry about how long it takes—look at the results after it has been mastered.

Developing Consistency

Each of the lessons in this text are presented so as to lead you step by step through the techniques of stage combat; from the sheer, simple mechanics to the safe completion of the illusion. You should master the techniques taught in each chapter before moving on to the next sequence of techniques. Like removing the training wheels on the bicycle, when swords are eventually picked up, it is essential that you can rely on the consistency of movement and mechanics established earlier in the process.

It is necessary that you feel confident in the moves and techniques and in your ability to carry them out. If your training is thorough and methodical, you will feel more comfortable and less likely to become fearful or inaccurate, become unwilling to try new things in class or rehearsal, or lose control in a performance. The positive and certain performer is always best, provided that at the same time they act with intention, discipline and control.

Communication

Everyone learns at a different rate and in a slightly different manner. It is therefore important to maintain an open and constructive forum of communication and constructive criticism. Through a process of comparison and contrast, and personal trial and error, combatants can help one another understand and master the techniques offered in this text. By analyzing each other's technique, they

---

[4]The concept of kinesthetic learning has been applied to dance and dramatic movement for years—and hence its application to stage combat. Such an application is noted in Albert M. Katz's text *The Theatre Student: Stage Violence*.

can help one another hone reflexive actions, improve timing and develop a mutual accuracy in executing technique.

Open Dialogue

When allowing actors to analyze the movement of others, everyone must understand the technique from both an internal and external standpoint. This understanding develops a proficient stage combatant. Partners have the responsibility of measuring the amount of force and velocity utilized during any given technique and expressing praise or concern about said technique. It is essential that you feel confident both with the moves you are given, and in your ability to carry them out. Therefore, by keeping an open dialogue, you eventually experience complete trust and relaxation with yourself, your partners, and the stage fight. It is important, however, that you not take on the role of teacher. The objective of open dialogue between combatants is to develop a rapport and mutual understanding, not to provide you with a forum for one-upmanship.

Physical Dialogue

As you learn to relax and trust yourself, your partner and the techniques of stage combat, it is important to remember that what you are learning is a performance art, not competitive fencing. Don't relax into the routine so much that the fight becomes a fast pattern of movements between you and your partner. The objective of the techniques you are learning is to communicate a story to an audience. To accomplish this, connect and communicate with your partner and the audience. A stage fight is not a monologue or showcase for a particular character, it is a physical dialogue specifically designed to further plot and character in a production. It is the job of the choreographer to set that dialogue, and it is the job of the actor to communicate it. Remember ''actions speak louder than words,'' but only if the audience can perceive them.

Groundwork for Training

Once you are warmed-up, mentally and physically, you can begin the process of training in stage combat. Because many of the techniques are new to you, it is important from the beginning for you to establish the habit of ''think and then do.'' What this means is that you visualize and understand a technique or action before physically committing to it. Think about technique, know that what you are about to do is right, and then do the action. All too often the learning process is a series of ''do and then realize.'' The beginning combatant will do a move, and then realize that it was an incorrect action. Aside from being potentially dangerous, the practice of do and then realize works against a healthy training process and the theory of positive reinforcement in learning. Dangerous or incorrect actions tend to provoke negative comments, making the actor perceive their technique as ''wrong'' or ''bad.'' If a little more time is taken in the training and rehearsal process, the actor can complete an action ''correctly'' or ''well'' by thinking through technique or choreography before doing the action.

In the long run, by mastering the ''think and then do'' technique you will also be a much safer combatant. When steel is put in your hands, if you think and then do, you will never release an attack if your partner has not offered the proper response. If you do and then realize, you could swing a sword too soon, only to realize the error too late.

The Victim in Control

It is important to remember that the physical conflict on stage is an *illusion;* at all times each combatant should be fully in control of themselves and their weapons. Each combatant is completely in control of their actions, and the victim is always in control of their reactions. There is no actual force ever exerted on the victim *in any situation.* In swordplay, the victim, in essence, reaches out to meet the attacking blade, while the attacker merely supports the illusion through placing the blade at the correct target, at the correct time, throwing their energy beyond the victim, not into them. By placing the victim in control, it provides that actor with the extra margin of safety to make this kind of stage violence almost foolproof in terms of both illusion and safety.

Allow Adequate Training/Rehearsal Time

Be sure to allow enough time to learn and practice each move before you move on to the next technique. Adequate time must be allowed for the mechanics to become habit, and for you to become confident in those habits. It is impossible to create any worthwhile performance with insufficient rehearsal, and attempts to do so are likely either to prove dangerous, look amateurish, or both.

The Physical Inventory

In the process of learning, it is important to trust your body. When you are engaged in a fight, swords swinging hither and yon, you won't have time to look at your feet or check the placement of other sundry parts of your body. Therefore, as you practice technique, start taking physical inventory. This is a process of looking inside yourself and trying to feel what is right and what is wrong. A check of your physical inventory should tell you where your weight is, where you are centered, what foot is where, and so on. Get into the habit of using your muscles to "look" inside first, and leave your eyes to the business at hand.

Breathe and Relax

While you are trying to remember all these rules and practice the intricate mechanics of the techniques ahead, try to remain relaxed. A relaxed body moves more fluidly, and has less chance of pulling or straining a muscle. Tension and frustration provide obstacles that work against the learning process and can be quite dangerous. Also remember to breathe during this process. There is a tendency among some students to hold their breath while concentrating on technique. This practice is counterproductive to kinesthetic learning. Your brain and muscles need oxygen to function, and by holding your breath the body tenses up and the mind starts to cloud. So breathe and relax. Breathe like you would in a vocal exercise (deep into the diaphragm, in through the nose and out through the mouth. Take things slowly and easily. Everything will come in time.

Safe and Effective

Learning to ride a bike, you started on training wheels and after a certain amount of time you set those aside to ride under your own power and control. Once you were confident and comfortable on two wheels, new obstacles arose. You were confronted by curbs, gravel and dirt roads. Each new step was approached slowly, and eventually mastered. Some of us even went on to ramps and BMX dirt trails. Aside from the insane moments where peer pressure pushed you over the edge, seldom did you try any tricks before you were properly prepared. The same should be true in stage combat. Work with the training wheels, master the mechanics before moving on to other obstacles or tricks. Avoid succumbing to peer pressure. You can't jump a curb if you can't ride a bike, and you can't make effective choices within a fight if you haven't mastered the mechanics.

First and foremost, a stage fight must be safe, but if it is not effective either in choreography or in execution, it's not a good fight. The mechanics need to be mastered so that the training wheels can be removed and you can move on under your own power and control. If all the rules provided in this text are followed to the letter, and you haven't mastered the techniques, the fight can still be a dismal failure. Like Shakespeare, stage combat when performed by an unskilled artist can be a dreadful thing. Yet, in the hands of a trained professional, it is poetry.

RULES IN REVIEW

None of the following rules can protect you from ignorance or carelessness. Only diligence, practice and hard work can prevent accidents.

1. Always keep a healthy, positive, open frame of mind.
2. Be sure you have enough room to comfortably allow for the movement required in combat. Keep the area clear of scenery, props, furniture and uninvolved actors.
3. Always work on a safe surface; never work on asphalt or concrete.
4. Be sure that the surface area is clear of debris and hazards.
5. Make sure that the surface is not slippery and that all combatants are aware of any stairs, ramps, and risers, and that you work well away from such hazards.
6. Always work in good, even lighting.
7. Dress in comfortable, nonrestrictive clothing and wear comfortable shoes that won't slip or slide.
8. Secure your glasses (if you must wear them) and pull your hair back to keep your sight-lines open.
9. Remove all jewelry and sharp or dangerous objects.
10. Always warm up prior to training, rehearsal or performance. Never work a fight cold.
11. THINK and then DO!
12. The victim is *always* in control.
13. Adequate time must be allowed for the mechanics to become habit, and for you to become confident in those habits.
14. Don't look at your feet. Trust your body; take a physical inventory.
15. Relax and breathe.
16. Communicate. Perform a physical dialogue with your partner and tell a story to the audience.
17. Make the fight safe, but effective.
18. Remember, you are the ultimate safety device; you have the power to say "NO!" No part is too special, no role too dear to be worth endangering yourself in any way.

Chapter 2

The Sword and the Stage

" . . . a history of the sword would be a history of humanity, since the latter has ever been a chain of struggles between nations and men decided by violence." [Egerton Castle][1]

From the stone, wood and bone clubs of prehistoric man to the foil, epée and sabre of the modern fencer, one can trace a series of changes in the evolution of the sword. It is not the purpose of this book, however, to trace meticulously the detailed pedigree of the sword. Such information would prove of little use to the actor.

The purpose, then, is to provide the actor and student of stage combat with a general knowledge of the European rapier and the manner in which it was used. This is not done in hopes of making staged combats historically accurate, but to make the actor aware of the social and political relevance of the sword and its relationship to their character.

The relationship of a person to the weapon they carry is characterized by their view of themselves. It is a direct extension of themselves. It is their view of how best they can defend themselves and how best they can manifest their aggression. Without properly understanding the weapon, an actor cannot fully understand the period character. If an actor wishes to project a consistent and coherent image of a character, they must look at the practice and philosophy of swordplay in the period the play takes place, and in which the play was written, since that allows the actor to interpret an author's intentions as successfully as possible. Without clear understanding, the actor cannot make informed choices.

The sword was a crucial element of the class and character of an individual. Shakespeare, Jonson and their contemporaries provide little in the way of stage directions, but will often list the specific weapons of particular characters. The sword was an extension of the man, it was the most important part of their wardrobe. A different coat, shirt or breeches could be worn for a variety of occasions, but a man never went anywhere without his sword.

The sword, says Egerton Castle, was *"the constant companion and support of its master—a friend always at his side when he walked or rode, who kept watch at the head of the bed at night, and rested behind his chair as he took his meals; it was never chosen unless it felt in his hand like a part of himself, and was deemed incapable of turning traitor in the most desperate struggle."*[2]

---

[1]Castle, *Schools and Masters of Fence*, p. 4.
[2]Castle, p. 225.

It is also the intention of this book to acquaint the reader with the sword as a deadly weapon of destruction. How often do we see characters in the background on stage watching the raging battles and life-threatening duels as if they were no more than a match of ping pong? It is important to understand that at each stage of history, the weapons of that period were the most terrifying and deadly weapons imaginable. A drawn sword on stage, whether you are the combatant or simply an observer, should emulate the feeling of terror that a loaded machine-gun in a crowded shopping mall would today. A sword fight was not a sport to watch like modern fencing—it was life or death. More than likely, every character in a Renaissance and Restoration drama had a close friend or loved one die by the sword. It was very real to them and an integral part of their everyday life.

THE AGE OF THE RAPIER (*Circa* 1550–1625)

The second half of the sixteenth century marks the beginning of the "Golden Age of Swordplay." The Golden Age spans the sixteenth to eighteenth century, from the introduction of the rapier to the eventual retirement of the civilian sword.[3] By the end of the sixteenth century firearms were playing an increasingly effective part on battlefields, and the sword found its role limited more and more to personal combat. Before this period, swordplay had mostly been a crude, unscientific affair, and by the end of the eighteenth century it had become so formalized, so hemmed in by restrictive theory, that there was little difference from modern fencing, either in appearance or intention.

Full suits of armor were being used less in military conflicts and various types of half-armor were being employed by the likes of guardsmen, sentries and patrol troops during this period. Full suits were generally being employed for the joust and tournaments, while ceremonial and parade armor became more and more decorative, and less and less practical for actual combat.

The period of the rapier marks the beginning of the abandonment of armor and the clash of station and style in swordplay. The side arm became part of the attire of every gentleman as a status symbol. The fact that the sword was always carried meant it could be used in a flash for self-defense or to settle a matter of honor. Duels and brawls were sometimes fought over no greater pretense than the way someone looked, dressed, spoke or the type of weapon they carried. An example of this is offered in the discourse between Benvolio and Mercutio in Shakespeare's *Romeo and Juliet.*

> *"Why, thou wilt quarrel with a man that hath a hair more or a hair less in his beard than thou hast.*
> *Thou wilt quarrel with a man for cracking nuts, having no other reason but because thou hast hazel eyes*
> *. . . Thou hast quarrelled with a man for coughing in the street, because he hath waked thy dog that hath*
> *lain asleep in the sun. Didst thou not fall out with a tailor for wearing his new doublet before Easter;*
> *with another for tying his new shoes with old riband?"* [III.i.16–29]

Duels, dueling, foreign masters and their foreign blades invaded the traditional sword and style of English heritage. "True" Englishmen took great insult to the imported "scientific" practices of the Italians and Spaniards.

The Rapier

Originally referred to as the *Spanish sword* by sixteenth century Englishmen, the rapier was introduced to the court of Mary Tudor (Mary I, 1553–1558) by fashionable Spanish noblemen. Though quite popular in Spain, the long thrusting *espada ropera* did not sit well with England's

---

[3]The rapier was one of the first swords to be considered primarily a civilian weapon. The Spanish name *espada ropera,* literally means, "dress sword"; and within a few decades of its first appearance in the 1480s the rapier had become an essential part of every Spanish and Italian gentlemen's proper attire, regardless of his actual skill at swordplay.

preferred style of swordplay. The French, as early as 1474, referred to the weapon as the *epée rapiere,* a contemptuous term for the ridiculously long Spanish sword.[4]

The contempt for the rapier and its practice was intensified when the Italian masters came to England to instruct the "true art of defense" to the uneducated Englishmen. While many of the English nobles and gentlemen were quite taken by the new and "scientific" art and masters of the Italian *spada,* the English masters of defense were not impressed. The common Englishman, being a true "sword and buckler man," saw the foreign sword as a threat to their heritage and as an insult to their ideals. It is no wonder that when the rapier finally gained acceptance, they Anglicized the name *rapier,* from the contemptuous *rapiere* of the French.[5]

The Blade

The rapier was originally used for both cut (blow) and thrust attacks (actually being poorly designed for either), but eventually became a weapon chiefly used for thrusting. In comparison to the military sword of the day, the rapier was a lighter weapon with a narrower double-edged blade and sharp point. Through the latter half of the sixteenth century, and into the seventeenth, the blade became narrower and lighter and eventually practical for nothing but point work.

The Hilt of the Rapier

In an attempt to protect the sword hand from a thrust of the adversary's blade, over a hundred distinct forms of the hilt were developed.[6] Different bars, rings, branches and arms were added to the *hilt* at varying angles towards this end. In the mid-seventeenth century the Spanish developed the *cup-hilt* that completely protected the hand.

Defense

Use of the Left Hand

The weight and length of the early rapier made it quite difficult to stop an attack with the sword itself. The awkward weapon restricted the fencer from blocking an attack with any advantage or speed. The rapier needed a second weapon that could move quickly enough to respond defensively to an oncoming attack. This weapon could be a hand shield, dagger, cloak, mail glove, or when all else failed, even the unarmed left hand. The defensive action of the left hand, however, was still not what we would envision a block or *parry* to be today. The combatant used the weapon in the left hand to help deflect the blow as they simultaneously launched a counter attack with the rapier. These actions were taken in order to limit the motion of the sword hand to that of the aggressor. It was

---

[4]Tarassuk, *Arms and Weapons,* p. 402

[5]The rapier itself has been referred to by a sorted collection of names, most derived from previous weapons or those similar in use like the estoc. The rapier also received many other names from phonetic renderings and mispronunciations of foreign terms for the sword and like weapons.

Although the actual name *rapier* is not traceable to one definite source, it is most commonly linked to the French *rapiere,* which itself can be traced to the Spanish *espada ropera.* Some, however, believe that the term is derived from the Spanish *raspar,* which means "to scrape or scratch," while others from the German term *rappen* meaning "to tear out"; the latter being less plausible as the rapier was generally a thrusting weapon and introduced to Germany through Spain. [Tarassuk, *Arms and Weapons*]

[6]The *hilt,* the portion of the sword comprised of the guard, grip and pommel.

The modern term *"To the hilt,"* meaning to "go all the way" or "go all out" comes from swordplay and refers directly to the hilt of the sword. "To the hilt" is a term for a thrusting attack that is delivered and lands in one's opponent and is further driven into the victim's body "all the way" up to its hilt.

"*. . . if he would strike him in the brest, he may thrust his sword up to the hiltes.*" [di Grassi, p. 51]

common practice to remove or *void* the body than to take the full force of an attack with the left hand.

> *" . . . he tilts/ With piercing steel at bold Mercutio's breast,/ Who, all as hot, turns deadly point to point,/ And with a martial scorn, with one hand beats/ Cold death aside, and with the other sends/ It back to Tybalt, whose dexterity/ Retorts it."*[7]

It was not until the seventeenth century that the rapier became lighter and more manageable, making the dagger unnecessary. The single rapier became equally effective for offense and defense. The discarding of the cut as a popular mode of offense made it possible to defend the body against the thrust without the aid of a second weapon. This did not mean that daggers became obsolete or were no longer used. Rather, it meant that they were no longer essential to the defensive action. They were, however, used well into the eighteenth century.

THE AGE OF TRANSITION (*Circa* 1625–1675)

The Transitional Rapier

It is easiest to define the second phase of the Golden Age as "transitional," during which the rapier decidedly tended towards simplification, but had not yet assumed the definite shape that we call the *small sword*. In the early parts of this period, the protective guard started to increase in size until this buffer reached the form of the cup guard or cup-hilt. Many rapiers, however, still used the complex guard of swept rings and counter guards to protect the sword hand. Blades were diminished in size, and although the point was paramount, they still often maintained an edge. This, however, was not as much for use in cutting attacks as to prevent the opponent from executing a disarm by taking hold of the blade. The average blade length of the weapon was generally between thirty to thirty-five inches (in comparison to the thirty-nine to forty-eight inch blade of roughly thirty years earlier).

During the early part of this period, the principles of the Italian schools of fence were the common mode of practice. Rapier play, for the most part, was executed in a linear fashion with the thrust executed on a lunge.[8] Sidestepping and dodging attacks were still effective, as was circular negotiation and the occasional cut on a pass, but in the new schools of fence this was not encouraged.

The dagger had, for the most part, been abandoned, leaving the left hand free for the play of the weapons. Some schools taught the fencer to trust solely in the rapier for defense, others let the left hand continue to function as a defensive weapon, and still others taught a method of fencing with both hands upon the sword. Because of the variance in methods, gentlemen had their choice of masters and techniques, and fenced with the sword of their particular fancy.

THE SWORD AND THE STAGE

> *"A gentleman only needs know the meaning of the words 'hilt, blade, handle and scabbard'; all others are beneath his notice."*[9]

Presently, we live in the "Theatrical Age" of the sword where the largest group of people that

---

[7]Shakespeare, *Romeo and Juliet*, (III.i).

[8]The modern term "rapier wit" comes from the transitional style of rapier play. The term implies a fast, sharp and piercing cleverness or sense of humor.

[9]Unknown writer, 1687. *A Brief Discussion of Sword Nomenclature, The Fight Master,* Vol. XI, #3, Fall 1988, p. 12.

regularly use the sword are actors. Swords are brandished with great regularity on the stage and screen with no more knowledge of the types and parts of sword than the gentleman dilettante had three centuries ago. For safety's sake, however, the theatre can no longer afford to be ignorant of the weapons we use on stage.

SAFE SWORDPLAY STARTS WITH SAFE SWORDS

There are a surprising number of costume houses and "sword-cutlers" that manufacture and rent "stage" swords today. Many of these weapons are no more than decorative wall hangers that are in no way designed, engineered or constructed for stage combat. Built of pot metal parts, these weapons stand a good chance of sending a blade flying of into the wings, the cast or the audience. Other weapons are a collection of "universal" parts that are slapped together in various arrangements to make a great number of "stage swords." These parts are haphazardly stacked and then wrenched together. All this allows for a great deal of slop, which, as the parts loosen, causes metal fatigue and sooner or later sends a blade flying, and assorted parts falling to the stage.

Impractical Sword Blades

> *"I thought it necessary, before I set down any rules for the use of the sword, to premise a few words, not only how to mount a sword, but likewise upon the choice of a blade; for, with a bad sword in hand, bad consequences may ensue, be the person ever so courageous and active."* [Angelo][10]

What was true of swords two hundred years ago is true of swords today: the blade must be dependable. Unfortunately, some stage blades are constructed of soft metal that bends and nicks when used in combat. Blades that are angled easily can break easily, and several nicks along the edge of a blade create a type of serrated edge that can cut through costume and flesh quite easily. Other swords use the modern fencing epée blade; a blade designed *only* for point work. The taper of this blade can make the last third invisible on stage, to the confusion of the audience and terror of the performer. The actual mechanical construction of the epée blade does not sustain the constant edge to edge abuse of stage combat and often breaks both near the tip and at the hilt. The fencing foil and sabre are even worse and therefore seldom used.

Twenty years ago these were the only weapons readily available, but today, among these relics of the stage are weapons specifically designed for the repetitive abuse of stage combat. Many of the swords mentioned above are billed as "combat serviceable," but in reality are unsafe and should be avoided. No matter how safe the practice of stage combat, if the weapons are unsound, the combat is still dangerous. To be ignorant of the weapon one wields on stage today can be as dangerous as playing with a loaded gun.

What Makes a Stage Sword Safe

It is not important that you know all the ancient names of every bar and loop that make up a rapier. It is important that you are aware of what makes a stage weapon safe or dangerous. This is technically the job of the fight master or property department, but when it comes down to your safety, be on guard. The fight master may only be a fencing coach, and the props people may have rented from "Al's Discount Costume and Sword Emporium"; you never know.

Don't Take the Word of Others—Be Sure Yourself

Like the gentleman dilettante of three centuries ago, our lives depend upon the quality of our sword. However, unlike the craftsmen of that period, many of today's sword-cutlers are interested

---

[10]Angelo, *The School of Fencing*, p. 2

in quantity rather than quality. There is no perfect stage weapon, and even the best swords can break. Your awareness of the weapon's limitations and its correct use and maintenance helps make a good stage sword last a long time. You must take as few chances as possible, lowering the risk of accident, injury and lawsuit. Don't stake your life on the word of a sword-cutler, property master, director or fight choreographer, CHECK OUT THE WEAPON.[11] You are the one that is there when it breaks, not them. Be sure the weapon is safe.

The Blade

The first and most important thing to be said about weapons is that they are tools of the performer and not toys! They must be handled carefully and with respect. In dealing with any bladed weapon designed for cut and/or thrust, no matter how dull or how blunted, you are dealing with a potentially lethal weapon. Because of this, we start by looking at the blade.

The Actual Rapier Blade

Although there are more types of rapier blades than there are schools of fence, there are some common properties. The historical rapier blade was long and flat, and generally quite heavy. To help lessen its weight, grooves or channels were often made in the flat of the blade. The *fullers* or *fluting* of the blade were designed to lessen the weight without jeopardizing its structural integrity. They were never intended as "blood grooves" or "blood gutters" as they have been mistakenly called. The idea is basically the same as that of the steel "I" beam in modern construction. Structural weight can be placed on the edges of the beam, supported by the flat strap in the center. The hollow areas, on either side of the flat strap and between the upper and lower surfaces, are like the fullers of a blade.

The flat of the rapier blade should taper to two edges, the fore or *true edge* and the back or *false edge.* The true edge is that part of the blade which, when the weapon is held correctly, is naturally directed towards one's opponent. It is with this edge that most cutting attacks on stage are delivered, and most parries received. The false edge was generally sharp for at least the uppermost third of the blade, and would often be sharp from the point to forte like the true edge.

Anatomy of the Blade

The blade's construction plays a great part in its effectiveness in the stage fight. The blade, the essential part of the cut and/or thrust weapon, actually covers the entire expanse of the sword. It extends from the guard of the weapon to the extreme of the tip. Because of this, and for clarity, the blade of the rapier is broken down into several parts: *tip, foible, middle, forte, shoulders, ricasso* and *tang.* The cutting portion of the blade is divided into the true and false edge and the tip. For the purpose of reference, Figure 1 depicts the common parts of the theatrical rapier blade.

The Edges and Point

All weapons on the stage, whether used for combat or not, must be dulled at the edge and at the point. The audience cannot perceive the difference, but your skin can. The tip of the weapon should be buttoned, or rounded, making penetration difficult. The edge should be flat and dull, free of nicks and burrs that can catch or cut skin. Blades made of wood or plastic can be visually effective, if constructed correctly, but generally are not combat serviceable. These weapons can also be as stiff and sharp as the blunt steel weapons and can penetrate the body just as easily.

---

[11] *"AS AN ACTOR, YOU ARE ULTIMATELY RESPONSIBLE FOR YOUR OWN SAFETY AND THE SAFETY OF YOUR FELLOW CAST MEMBERS. Production management and crew are responsible for creating and maintaining safe conditions, but it is your right and responsibility to double-check the set-up to insure your own safety."* SAG industry-wide safety bulletins.

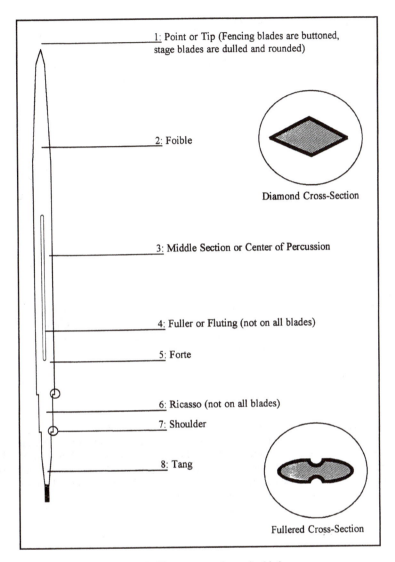

Figure 1. The anatomy of a rapier blade.

The Foible

The foible is the uppermost, and weakest, third of the exposed blade closest to the tip. The word foible, in seventeenth century French, actually means "weak." It is this portion of the blade that is generally used as the offensive part of the weapon. Modern fencing weapons; foil, epée, sabre, all have incredibly flexible foibles, designed to give, or bend, on a hit to avoid penetration.[12] (Fig. 2)

---

[12]The slight bow or bend in the flexible foible of the fencing blade allows the blade to give on the hit rather than pierce. This allows the blade to arch or bend as denoted in the classically executed hit, and is generally referred to as the *avantage*.

This, in theory, seems like a good idea for a stage sword, but since our intent is never to "hit," this function actually works against our purposes. A weak foible, when used in edge to edge play, can whip around the defending parry and still strike your opponent. Through repetitive contact, and bending around the parry, a weak foible will eventually snap; much like a coat hanger bent back and forth too many times. This sends the tip of the blade soaring, and leaves the combatant holding a sword with a sharp tip.

The Middle or Center of Percussion

The middle of the blade is that portion that links the weaker foible to the stronger forte. Generally this section of the blade is not specifically used for offensive or defensive actions. As the center of percussion it is the mediator between the percussive attacks of the foible and percussive blocks of the forte. It is for this reason that some schools exclude this portion, and simply divide the blade in half: foible and forte. Generally in stage combat the middle is still referred to, and is used in the execution of several actions of the blade.

The Forte

The forte of the blade is the widest and strongest third of the exposed blade closest to the hilt of the sword. It is the portion of the weapon used by the combatant to block and parry attacks. The forte, however, although initially the tool for defense, is not what makes the weapon sound for parries on stage. It is the joining, or mounting of the forte to the hilt of the weapon that gives it its strength.

Most stage weapons seat the blade on the uppermost part of the hilt. The blade then narrows and passes through the guard and handle of the sword. This portion of the blade is known as the *tang* or "tongue" of the blade. The narrowing point of the blade, from forte to tang, is referred to as the *shoulders* of the blade. The defensive strength of the sword lies on the shoulders and the tang.

The Shoulders

Parts of a stage weapon must fit together like well-machined parts, there should be no gaps, shims or wedges to make it all fit. If a blade is poorly shouldered on the hilt of a sword, each parry and percussive attack is focused on the forte, slightly shifting its position. Each shift bends the tang just a little, and each bend weakens the entire structure of the sword. Finally, like the wire hanger, the metal fatigues and the tang snaps. The forte of the blade must be securely shouldered to the hilt; wrenching the parts together will not alleviate the problem. The shoulders of the blade must meet flush and flat to the hilt of the sword, and the hole that the tang passes through must be fitted to the tang.

The Tang

The tang itself is another matter of concern. Since the tang is not visible unless a weapon is disassembled (or falls apart) it is often the most neglected part of the sword. Aside from the aesthetic and structural problems of fencing blades, their tangs are not, in any way, shape or form, designed for the edge-play of stage combat. The fencing sabre, a cutting weapon, is not intended for the amount and type of blade-play involved in the run of a stage fight. The tangs of the foil, epée and sabre are generally no bigger than a number two pencil, sometimes tapering to something the size of coat hanger wire. These tangs are designed for the practiced point work of sport fencing, not stage

---

This "bending" of the blade is different than those of the soft metal blades discussed earlier. A tempered fencing blade has a great deal of elasticity in its foible. It bends on the hit, and then springs back to its original shape. This is known as a "trained" blade. Through use the fencing blade can soften, and when it bends and does not return, the blade is retired.

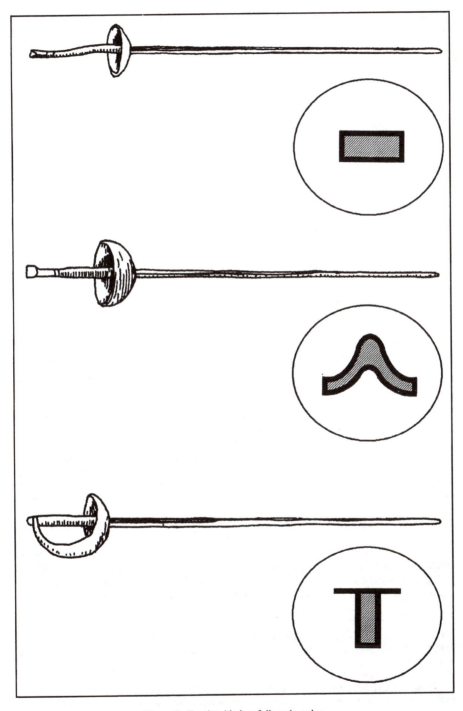

Figure 2. Fencing blades: foil, epée, sabre.

combat. Yet, there are some companies that sell only epée bladed weapons.* These are fine for point work and practiced swordsmen, but in the mind of mass production these already small tangs are often filed down to slip into the hilts of their weapons.

"You must observe not to file or diminish the tongue of the blade," says eighteenth century fencing master Domenico Angelo, *"for on that depends the stability and strength of your sword."*[13]

As stated above, the tang is the strength and stability of the sword, it should be strong enough to withstand the abuse of stage combat, and it must not be diminished or tampered with.

In addition to modern fencing blades, many other "stage" weapons have insufficient tangs. There are companies that advertise "super strong tangs," but even these can be inadequate. The best advice when it comes to the tang is to disassemble the weapon and inspect the tang and all its housings. If the tang is thin or weak, and the fittings allow movement, the weapon is unsafe. If the weapon does not disassemble at all, it is probably not safe for stage.

Types of Blades

Before looking at the hilt of the weapon, there is the matter of the blade itself. As mentioned earlier, the rapier is a weapon meant for both cut and thrust, and to effectively serve this purpose an "edged" blade is best used. Initially, the sport sabre blade seems like the best candidate, but its foible is generally the most flexible of the fencing blades. The foil blade is square and the stiffer epée blade is triangular. Save for the sabre, these fencing blades are designed for nothing other than point work.

The Giant Epée/Musketeer Blade: For stage weapons, there is a "giant epée" blade, or "Musketeer blade" available today. It is basically a standard epée blade that has been widened severely at the forte and tapers to a much stiffer foible. The basic design of the blade is still for point work, being a triangular, fluted blade, and the tang has not been sufficiently enlarged to handle much edge to edge play. This blade is quite popular, but still has the habit of breaking at the tang and foible. All in all, the "Musketeer blade" seems to work best on transitional rapiers, where there is much less edge-play.

The Schlager Blade: At this time, the best blade suited for the needs of the theatre (light, manageable, and incredibly durable) is the German *schlager* blade. The schlager is the weapon that replaced the rapier of German students in the early nineteenth century. The blade of the weapon, still used in student "duels," is long and flat with a rounded point, and is of excellent design for edge to edge play, and is used as a rapier blade in many stage weapons. Along with the strong flat blade, the tang of the schlager also is quite a bit more substantial than that of most other blades available today.[14]

Recently there has been an addition to the schlager family, the *diamond-grind schlager.* Like the regular schlager, it is a strong, stiff blade. In fact, it may actually be stronger than the original schlager. Its difference is in shape. Instead of being flat, the blade is diamond-shaped in cross-section. From the center-line of the blade, the edges are tapered down towards the edges. The taper

---

*There are a variety of epée blades available (electric, "dry", practice, Russian, French, etc.) with various tang, forte, and foible strengths/widths. A trained fight director will know which can be used on stage—and which should not.

[13]Angelo, *The School of Fencing* p. 1

[14]I personally have never heard of a schlager blade *ever* breaking in class or during a performance. As far as I am concerned, they are the best of the light blades for use in edge to edge theatrical rapier play readily available today. Some fight directors do not prefer these blades because they feel they do not "ring" when joined with another sword. This is untrue. A schlager blade, well mounted on a steel hilt, will ring as well as any epée or Musketeer blade.

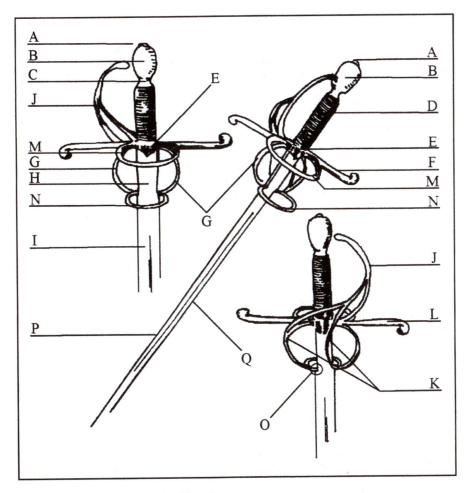

Figure 3. The anatomy of a two-ring hilt rapier
A-Lock-nut or Capstan Rivet; **B**-Pommel; **C**-Neck (some rapiers have a ''neck'' or base to the pommel that acts as a step from the grip to the counterweight; **D**-Grip or Handle; **E**-Quillon Block; **F**-Upper Quillon or Back Quillon (situated on the ''back'' side of the blade); **G**-Pas d'ane or Arms of the Hilt; **H**-Ricasso; **I**-Blade; **J**-Knuckle Bow or Branch; **K**-Counter Guards (bars or rings placed on the inside of the hilt to help protect the combatants hand and wrist); **L**-Lower Quillon or Front Quillon (situated on the true or ''front'' side of the blade); **M**-Upper Side-Ring or Upper Port (the larger ring of the ''two-ring'' hilt, designed to protect the back side of the sword hand); **N**-Lower Side-Ring or Lower Port (the smaller ring of the ''two-ring'' hilt, designed to protect the back side of the sword hand); **O**-Shoulders of the Blade; **P**-True Edge; **Q**-False Edge.

does not sharpen the blade, but the effect on stage is amazing. The tapering of the edges also removes some of the weight from the blade, making it more manageable on theatrical weapons.

The Hilts of the Rapier

When it comes to naming the parts of the rapier, the hilt is where most people get lost. The hilt itself is made up of only three parts: the guard, the grip and the pommel, but it's the pieces' parts that can make the head spin. In stage rapiers, there are basically three types of guards: the two-ring, swept and cup-hilt. Within these, there are a vast variety of configurations, but the audience can make little distinction between them from the stage.

The following are the three most prevalent types of rapier hilts used on stage today. The common elements of the guard configuration at the end of the blade do not vary much, but there are some differences. Although the audience can seldom tell the swords apart, you should become familiar with the general parts of the weapon, as the terms are used throughout the text. You also may find these terms useful if renting or purchasing a sword.

The Two-Ring Hilt

The two-ring rapier hilt is the earliest rapier developed from the medieval cross-hilt, having the beginning forms of protection for the hand. For further hand protection against the thrust, counter guards were added to the standard hilt. The hilt configuration, however, is fairly simple and does not afford a great deal of hand protection in actual rapier play. Following are the component parts of the two-ring rapier hilt.

The Swept-Hilt Rapier

In the swept-hilt rapier, side-rings are rearranged to offer better protection for the back of the hand. More bars and rings are added to the hilt, interconnecting with one another, giving the guard a grace of design matched by few other swords. (Fig. 4)

The names of the parts of the hilt generally remain the same. Although the side-rings have been slightly relocated on the hilt, and branches now stem to the knuckle bow. The larger ring is still referred to as the "Upper Side-Ring," (M) and the smaller as the "Lower Side-Ring" (N).

The Cup-Hilt Rapier

The cup-hilt rapier offers the fencer almost complete protection of the sword hand.[15] The guard assembly is still made up of the basic components, the quillons, pas d'âne and knuckle bow, but unlike the bars and rings of the two-ring and swept-hilted rapiers, there are no gaps or openings through which an offensive thrust can penetrate. The cup-hilt was devised by the Spanish, and was common among rapiers during the latter half of the sixteenth, and throughout the seventeenth and eighteenth centuries. In fact, the cup-hilt worked so effectively that it is the basis of the guard for the modern fencing foil and epée. Following are the variable parts of the cup-hilt.

The Pommel

Locking together the different parts of the weapon and acting[16] as a counter[17] weight to the blade is the *pommel*.[18] Some rapiers have a *neck* or base to the pommel that acts as a step from the grip to the counterweight, but this is not necessary on theatrical rapiers. On historical weapons, the tang is fed through a hole in the pommel, heated and riveted over the end of the pommel permanently securing the parts of the sword together. This is known as the *capstan rivet*. This method is not

---

[15]The cup or bell-shaped guard of the Spanish rapier; possibly deriving its name from not only its bell-like shape, but also the bell-like sound it emits upon being struck.

[16]*Cuscinetto* is an Italian term for the small circular leather cushion often placed on the inside of the cup-hilt to prevent the fingers from jamming against the guard.

[17]The Rim or Lip of the Guard is a rounding of the edge of the cup-hilt designed to deflect attacking blades away from the sword-hand. If there was no lip, a thrust might slide over the curved surface of the guard and wound the hand. (Not on all theatrical cup-hilt rapiers)

[18]The term "*pommel*" has crept into modern usage as *pummel* (old French for "little apple"). The pommel of the sword made an effective bludgeoning weapon in a backhand blow or at close quarters, hence, the term "to pummel" someone is used today to represent pounding, beating or striking repeatedly as with the pommel. The term today, however, is generally applied to the fists.

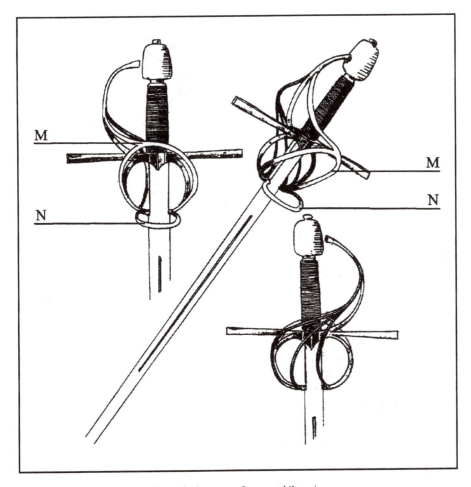

Figure 4. Anatomy of a swept-hilt rapier.

practical in stage weapons for, as the weapon is used, parts can settle, stretch or shift and the hilt becomes loose. Today, the pommel of most stage weapons is threaded like a large nut and screwed onto a threaded tang. This ensures that if pieces settle that the hilt can be tightened to avoid unnecessary metal fatigue. If parts happen to break, this also allows the sword to be easily disassembled for repair.

The best material for the pommel is solid steel. Other materials, when threaded, eventually strip and become useless to the sword. To better ensure the pommel's reliability, it is often drilled completely through, and threaded at the upper end. A small portion of the tang is allowed to stick out, and a small lock-nut can then be screwed onto the threaded tang. This nut serves the dual purpose of being a removable capstan rivet, and helps lock the pommel in place. If the pommel is drilled through, the tang cannot protrude beyond the top of the pommel (or capstan rivet) or the threads may catch costuming or cut the hand.

When working with a screw pommel, it is important to be sure the pommel is tight. This does not mean to wrench down on the poor thing until it's about to snap, because it will! You will find that the disk-shaped pommels of the Middle Ages have a particular problem in tightening. In order to line the pommel up so that it is parallel to the blade, one must leave it a little loose, or wrench it

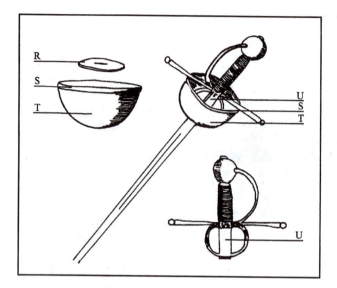

Figure 5. Anatomy of a cup-hilt rapier.

a little too tight. If it is only turned to its snug position, the pommel could sit slightly askew, or completely perpendicular to the blade. This makes the weapon difficult to hold and aesthetically unpleasant. To battle this problem, sword-cutlers have stacked and unstacked washers on the tang to get it to sit just right. But then parts settle, the grip warps and the whole thing is askew again. Because of this problem, a rounded or other form of invariant pommel should be used on stage weapons. From an aesthetic standpoint it is also interesting to note that pommels that are round or uniform in design can be turned to the correct tightness without appearing off center.

The Grip

Mounted between the guard and the pommel is the grip. Seemingly simple enough, the grip can actually play a big part in the effectiveness of the weapon. If the grip is not fitted well to the tang it could slip, turn or shift, putting undue pressure or torque on the tang, and possibly causing the actor to drop the sword. Grips are constructed from a number of materials: wood, metal, bone and plastic. The traditional wood grip (and most reliable) is made of northern hardwoods like beech, ash or maple. Grips of softwoods, like pine and fir, have a tendency to split or crack under pressure, and hardwoods like oak have a tendency to splinter or mushroom between the pommel and the guard. Metal is less frequently used, and generally comes in the form of tubing or pipe, which is difficult to fit to the tang. Bone looks good on a sword, but is generally too costly and too brittle for stage weapons. Plastics seem to be the sure bet for a strong grip. Some sword-cutlers are now supplying their weapons with grips of Lexan, a clear, strong polycarbonate plastic which resists the cracking, shrinking and distortion often associated with wood. Whatever the grip is made of, it should be fitted snugly to the tang and seated flush to the base of the *quillon block*. During combat, a loose grip uses the guard as a fulcrum and can easily snap the tang.

The grip should fit well in the hand; too large or too small a grip can cause the combatant to lose the sword. It is best if the grip of the sword is covered in some no-slip material; preferably leather or wire wrap. A bare wood or metal grip held in a hot, sweaty hand is likely to slip and could possibly fly out of control.

The Quillon Block and Quillons

The defense of the hand, or "guard" of the sword are the variety of branches and bars that extend out and around the sword-hand. The guard of the typical medieval sword consisted merely of a pair of straight or only slightly curved branches sticking out perpendicular to the blade, called *quillons*. The right angle of the blade and quillons created a "t" or cross at the guard, leading to the term *cross-hilt* or *cross-guard*. The quillons provided the sword hand with a protective barrier, preventing the opposing blade from sliding down the sword and striking the hand. In the sixteenth century the quillons were extended with the intent to displace or entangle the opponent's blade. The quillons were either straight as in the medieval swords, recurved in S-form or bent towards the blade.

In some types of hilts one quillon was curved toward the pommel, serving as a guard for the knuckles. This was not a new development, for early in the fifteenth century such a branch of the hilt had been developed. Whether a quillon, or a separate bar, this branch sweeps from the hilt to the pommel in a bow shape, in order to better protect the hand. Hence, the term *knuckle bow*. Previous to this addition, the sword with a cross-shaped hilt could be held with either of the two cutting edges to the front; now, with the development of the guard and the knuckle bow, the sword came to have an outer and inner edge, since it had to be held in a manner predominated by its hilt. Because the sword with a knuckle bow could only be held one way, the sword developed a forward or *true edge* and a back or *false edge*. The addition of the knuckle bow also helped clarify the branches of the hilt. The quillon protruding from the same side as the knuckle bow (or serving as the knuckle bow) came to be known as the "front" or *lower quillon,* while the quillon extending in the plane of the false edge is called the "back" or *upper quillon.*

Each of these branches, quillons, knuckle bow, as well as the variety of other loops and rings of the rapier hilt, extended from a small block of metal called the *quillon block.* This is a sturdy part of the sword's hilt through which the tang passes, placed between the shoulders of the blade and grip, that acts as a base for the sword's guard.

The Pas d'âne and Side-Rings

The common practice of placing one or two fingers over the cross guard of the sword, for better management of the blade, led to the introduction of the *pas d'âne* or *arms of the hilt* in the early fifteenth century.[19] This extra defense for the hand was two half rings branching up from the cross guard to encase the otherwise unprotected fingers. The pas d'âne, once adopted, remained, in conjunction with the quillons, and functioned as the foundation from which the most complicated, and eventually the simplest, guard was constructed.

A variation on this was a large ring on the side of the hilt intended to protect the knuckles. On the early rapier, both the pas d'âne and *side-ring* were utilized to protect the sword hand. The two-ring and swept-hilt rapiers had two distinct side-rings. The larger ring on both hilts is the *upper side-ring* or *upper port* and the smaller ring is the *lower side-ring* or *lower port.* The terms "upper" and "lower" refer to their orientation on the weapon. The parts of the sword generally listed from pommel to tip, situating one ring above the other on the sword. Both rings are intended to protect the back side of the sword hand.

The Ricasso

Shouldered at the top of the pas d'âne, and again at the block where the quillons meet, is a section of the tang called the *ricasso*. The ricasso is a thick portion of the tang, and is used to place the index finger around when holding the rapier. The ricasso is still a part of the stage weapon and is necessary

---

[19]*Pas d'âne* is old French for "donkey step" or "mule foot." Both of these terms fit the horseshoe shape of the protective rings or "arms of the hilt." However, according to Tarassuk, the term is incorrectly used. He believes the term was used in the seventeenth century to describe one of the oval shells that formed the sword's guard and not the arms of the hilt. [*Arms and Weapons,* p. 361]

for the correct handling of the sword. Because of the narrower blade of stage weapons, a ''false ricasso'' has been developed. Instead of shouldering at the pas d'âne and again at the quillon block, the blade is shouldered at the pas d'âne and the tang is passed through a part of the guard mounted in the ricasso's place. Some stage swords use a section of pipe, metal tubing or even stacks of washers, but in order to be effective and prevent shifting and slipping of the tang, the false ricasso must be a fixed and fitted part of the guard.

Counter Guards

Developed in the early sixteenth century, the *counter guards* are bars or rings placed on the inside of the hilt to help protect the combatant's hand and wrist. These bars or rings, especially on the swept-hilt, generally branched from the knuckle bow to join with the quillons or arms of the hilt. Because the common placement of the sword and arm when a combatant was on guard had this portion of the sword turned to the left, it was deemed ''inside'' the sword, and was thus also termed the *inner guard* of the rapier.

Hilt Materials

No matter which hilt you decide to work with, it is important that you consider its construction. Brass hilts look pretty on stage, but, aside from being historically inaccurate, they can easily bend and snap, leaving sharp edges that can cut the hand. Many cast guards are quite brittle and will also snap during regular use on stage.[20] During a regular theatrical fight, weapons are disarmed, dropped and tossed, hilts are brought together in some way or another, or even swung as weapons themselves; brass and brittle metals cannot stand up to this rigorous abuse. All guards should be of cast, or welded, low carbon steel. Low carbon steel works well for stage sword hilts because it is incredibly durable and slightly flexible without being brittle. This gives the hand strong durable protection, but if a sword is dropped or squashed, it will generally bend rather than break. The guard can then be bent back into shape without snapping. Steel can also be polished to a mirror finish, which looks wonderful on stage, but if you absolutely must have a ''gilded'' guard, paint it gold.

Points of the Hilt

Be sure to examine the guard of your rapier for sharp corners, points or barbs. The quillons project from the guard, but they should be well blunted with rounded edges. The knuckle bow should curve down from the quillon block to the pommel, and should have a rounded or dulled end. The pas d'âne should be closed at both ends and should create a protective screen for the index finger. There should be no spikes, spears or points with which you could possibly puncture the skin. The inside of the guard also should be free of burrs and rough edges that may catch or tear the hand. Finally, be sure the hilt and blade are clean and rust free. If skin is broken, you don't want to increase the chance of tetanus. Handle with care.

Balance

Aside from the assembly of the sword, its balance is also very important to the theatrical combatant. A poorly balanced sword can put too much weight into the blade, making it difficult to control safely, and too much weight in the hilt makes the blade feel sluggish and awkward. The *peso,* or point of balance on a sword, should be about two or three inches from the hilt.[21] It is said that

---

[20]Cast hilts are any hilt manufactured by pouring liquid metal into a mold and letting it harden without applied pressure. Some hilts are cast in separate pieces and welded together.

[21]The use of the term *peso* for the balancing point of the sword is used in both Spanish and Italian, and is believed to have derived from the Spanish *peson,* which was a weight used in the balancing of scales. The word *peso* is the Spanish word for ''weight.''

a correctly balanced sword should maintain its equilibrium when the peso is placed on a finger. Italian fencing master Rudolfo Capo Ferro (1610) indicated that, for a rapier to be well balanced, the point of balance had to be 8 cm. (3.1 inches) down the blade from the ricasso. This, however, refers to a real sword. Depending on the sword-cutler and the choreographer's preference, a stage rapier balances somewhere between the peso and the quillon block. This keeps the sword in the scabbard when moving about on stage and the sword in the hand when drawn for combat. A correctly balanced stage sword gives the combatant maximum control of the blade without making the weapon clumsy or unmanageable.

Selecting a Sword

Personal preference plays a great deal in the selection of a sword. Some people want a sword that sparkles and shines, others want a rugged, durable weapon. There are a great variety of hilt configurations and types of finish and decoration available on swords. Where you go and what you want will determine the quality and price of the weapon.[22] No matter what you choose, whether for personal or classroom use, the sword must meet certain criteria. The following is a guide list to selecting a safe stage weapon.

Although there is no perfect stage weapon, you must take as few chances as possible in order to lower the risk of accident and injury. Catalogues and sales personnel can be deceiving. A sword is both a financial and a personal investment, CHECK OUT THE WEAPON. When purchasing or renting a sword, be aware of the following:

I. The Blade

- It must be tempered. If bent, it should snap back to true upon release
- It must be designed to sustain the constant abuse of stage combat.
- It must be dulled at the edge and at the point, free of any nicks and burrs.
- The tip should be buttoned, or rounded, making penetration difficult.
- The foible must be stiff, but flexible.
- The forte must be securely shouldered to the hilt.
- The shoulders must meet flush and flat to the hilt.
- The tang must be substantial, and must not be rounded at the shoulders, filed down or tampered with.
- The giant epée/Musketeer blade is best in swords used mainly for point work. It is not a reliable blade for edge-play.
- The schlager/diamond-grind schlager is a strong durable blade, with a substantial tang. It is excellent for edge-play and point work.

II. The Hilt

- The weapon must be designed to withstand being disarmed, dropped and tossed.
- It should be constructed of cast, or welded low carbon steel.
- The quillons and knuckle bow must be blunt with rounded edges.
- The pas d'âne should closed at both ends, creating a protective screen for the index finger.
- There should be no spikes, spears, burrs or points that could possibly catch or puncture the skin.

---

[22]See Appendix B for a detailed list of suppliers.

III. The Grip

- The grip should be constructed of a durable material such as a northern hardwood or strong polycarbonate plastic.
- The grip must be fitted to the tang and sit flush to the base of the quillon block. It must not slip, turn or shift.
- The grip should fit well in the hand and be covered in some no-slip material.

IV. The Pommel

- The pommel should be solid steel.
- The pommel must be well threaded to avoid stripping.
- It may be drilled completely through, threaded at the upper end and locked in place with a second nut.
- The pommel should be round or uniform in design so that it can be turned to the correct tightness without appearing off center.

V. Fittings

- The weapon should be disassembled to inspect the tang and all its housings.
- Each piece must fit together like well-machined parts, there should be no gaps, shims or wedges to make it all fit.
- The ricasso of the blade must be shouldered at the pas d'âne and again at the quillon block.
- A false ricasso must be a fixed and fitted part of the guard between the quillon block and the top of the pas d'âne.
- If the weapon does not disassemble at all, it may not be safe for stage.

VI. The Weapon

- The point of balance should be about two to three inches from the hilt.
- The hilt and blade must be clean and rust free.

Chapter 3

Stance and Footwork

"Most great is the care and considerations which the paces or footsteps require in this exercise, because from them in a maner more then from anie other thing springeth all offence and defence." [di Grassi][1]

Stance and footwork have always been considered important to the swordsman. Balance and mobility are dependent upon the correctness of stance. From a sound foundation, the combatant can learn to move their body rapidly, giving or taking ground with equal agility and wielding the sword with confidence.

A good grasp of correct body alignment is essential to this understanding. As in dance, proper alignment (sitting or standing) serves as the axis from which all movement begins. Correct alignment (essentially good posture) means the various parts of the body—head, shoulders, arms, ribs, hips, legs, feet—are all in correct relative position to one another. Viewing the profile of a body in good posture one can imagine a straight line. This line is often called the line of gravity. It can be visualized passing through all these points of the body. (Fig. 6)

"Good alignment can also be evaluated from the front or back of the body," says James Penrod, in *The Dancer Prepares.* (Fig. 6) *"From either of these viewpoints, the shoulders and hips should appear level in a well-aligned body. The knees should be at the same level from the floor, with the weight placed evenly on both feet. Rolling in on the arches or to the outer border of the foot should be avoided in any dance movement or position where one or two feet are placed flat on the floor. Generally, a triangular weight placement is recommended with three points—the inner border of the ball of the foot, the outer border of the ball of the foot, and the middle of the heel placed firmly on the floor."*[2]

Bad posture can result in slumping, rounding the shoulders and tipping the head forward, or a sway, with the pelvis released backward, causing a hollowed look to the lower back. These, and any other distortion in alignment are detrimental to an ordinary body, but they are potentially hazardous to the combatant.

---

[1]di Grassi, p. 28.

[2]Penrod, James, and Plastino, Janice Gudde. *The Dancer Prepares.* 2nd ed. Palo Alto, California: Mayfield Publishing Co., 1980, p. 21.

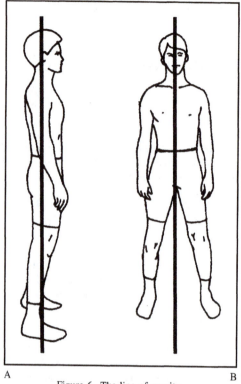

A   B
Figure 6. The line of gravity.

"Any departure from the balanced posture will strain muscles and ligaments and cause undue friction in joints—if one segment of the body is out of line, all others will be affected." [3]

THE ON GUARD STANCE

Correct Placement

To develop a proper understanding of correct placement, stand facing your partner (or a mirror), with your feet placed shoulder width apart, or a little farther and pointing straight ahead in what dancer's call *second-position parallel.* (Fig. 7) Your feet should feel relaxed. The toes are flat, with the weight of your body resting mainly on the three points of the feet: the heel, the base of the big toe and the little toe. In this position, you may check correct alignment by using the line of gravity.

Lead Foot/Lag Foot

In order to adjust the placement of second position parallel to a correct Elizabethan rapier stance, the right foot takes a step, the length of one foot, forward. (Fig. 8) If you imagine an outline of your feet, the right foot advances forward with its heel just in front of where the toe originally was. As the right foot becomes the lead foot, it remains pointing straight forward, while the left foot turns

---

[3]Featherstone, Donald F. *Dancing Without Danger.* South Brunswick and New York: Barnes, 1970, p. 65.

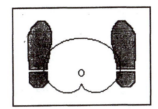

Figure 7. Second position parallel feet shoulder width apart.

slightly to the outside. It is from this placement of the feet that the terms *lead foot* and *lag foot* are set. As the feet move throughout footwork, whichever foot is towards the front will be regarded as the lead foot, and that to the rear, as the lag foot.

Remaining Square with Your Partner

"Alwaies bearing thy full belly towards thy enemie, I mean the one shoulder so neere as the other, for if thou wreathe thy bodie in turning the one side neare to thy enemie then the other, thou dost not stand in thy strength, nor so readie to performe an answere, as where thy whole bodie lieth towards thy enemie." [Swetnam][4]

In correct placement, your "belly" or torso should remain square to your partner. The body does not turn three-quarters away from your partner, as modern fencing dictates. You face your partner full on, so if you were to walk towards each other, would meet belly to belly. (Fig. 9) If you do not have a partner to work with, position yourself so that the flat of your chest is parallel to a wall. You also may face a mirror, so that you are facing chest to chest with your reflection.

This wide base of support may at first seem odd, especially to someone familiar with modern fencing. The wide base of support, however, places your center on a foundation that supports movement of the body both from side to side and forward and back. This "squaring" of the body is sometimes called a *four-point stance.* (Fig. 10) This is done because the squared stance provides equal balance and movement in four directions. The "full front" stance also is safer than the "two-point" fencing stance. (Fig. 11) The wide base allows for the variety of movement required in a stage fight, and provides the necessary balance and support for awkward conditions such as a raked stage, uneven platforms and risers, or the variables of a film location. This placement of the body also allows for the use of the left hand for defense, much like in modern boxing. The wider base allows a greater variety of movement to the fencer having to protect himself from cutting attacks in any direction. This also allows you to move in a greater variety of directions, avoiding and circling your opponent.

Lowering the Center of Gravity

From this position, lower your center of gravity by bending the legs slightly at the knees, making a pentagon with the ground (demi-plié position) (Fig. 12). The knees will travel out over the feet, resting above the instep, but never going beyond that point. Do not allow the knees to bend inward. Your weight should be distributed evenly on both legs and the three points of each foot. This lowered center of gravity makes you a much more stable and centered combatant.

---

[4]Swetnam, p. 97

Figure 8. The lead foot and lag foot. The right foot steps forward the length of one foot into the *lead* position. **A**-The "lead foot"; **B**-The "lag foot."

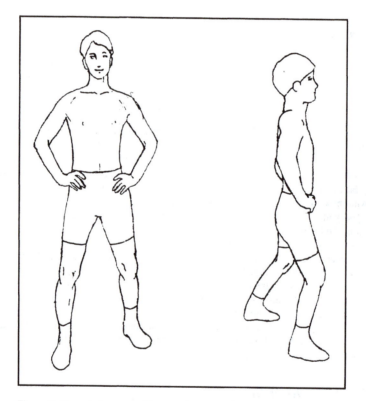

Figure 9. Correct placement. The torso is square, facing your partner full on.

Equilibrium and Readiness

Another requirement of proper placement in the On Guard stance is equilibrium and readiness. This can be ensured with the proper bearing of the trunk and the distribution of weight. The pelvis should be in a midway position, neither tucking under or sticking out. Imagine your pelvis as a bowl brimming with water—if you tip it either forward or backward, the water will be spilled. To check this position, place your right hand on your abdomen, which should feel pulled up and flat, and place your left hand in the small of your back. Your right hand should be perpendicular to the floor and the left hand nearly so.

Although the torso is lowered into the legs, its weight is lifted with the center, away from gravity. The center of the body is the center of gravity. This is the densest point in the body, located in the middle of the pelvic area. (The center of gravity in women is generally lower than in men.) The legs and thighs pull apart the center of gravity in opposite directions while the trunk of the body lifts up the weight of the center. This holds the body in a state of equilibrium, a ready starting position.

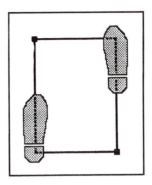

Figure 10. The four-point stance.

Lifting of the Center

It is important at this stage that you do not exaggerate or entirely flatten out the natural curves of the spine, which allow it to be flexible and to absorb shock, when lifting the center. Maintaining a firm abdomen, elongating the spine, stretching up taller and lifting against gravity help achieve correct lifting of the center. Lifting and elongating the spine is safer and more efficient than just "standing up straight."

The rib cage should be directly in line with the hips. Any lift of the ribs should coincide with the lengthening of the spine. At no time should the rib cage feel rigid or forced forward; breathing should remain normal.

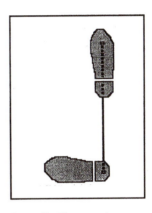

Figure 11. The two-point stance.

The shoulders are relaxed, low, not pulled backward, the arms hanging naturally at your sides. To feel the correct position of the shoulders, lift them up to your ears, hold them a few seconds, and then relax, and *slowly* lower them. You should feel the shoulders blades resting downward, relaxed.

Keep the back of the neck long, making the neck a continuation of the spine on which the head lightly rests. The head must be in alignment with the ribs and hips. The neck muscles should be relaxed as much as possible and should allow free movement of the head without effort. Stiffness in the neck muscles negatively influences the entire body, potentially impairing vision, perception and observation, and affecting both balance and movement. The eyes should be focused forward, directly at your partner, with your chin parallel to the floor.

The Sword Hand

Place the right hand (left handers please follow the "advice for the southpaw" offered at the beginning of the text) in front of you, just above the level of your waist. This hand will eventually become the sword-bearing hand. Your elbow should rest outside your chest, to the right, and roughly two to three inches forward. Your arm is bent at roughly ninety degrees. There should be at least a four-inch gap between your elbow and your side. (Fig. 13) Do not allow the elbow to stick out beyond the plane of your hand. A protruding elbow can lead to possible accident or injury in the future.

To help develop a relaxed grip and fixed and stable sword hand, hold a business or playing card

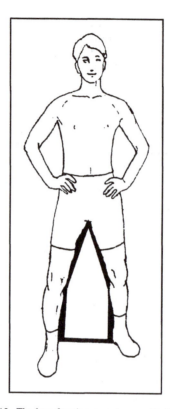

Figure 12. The legs forming a pentagon with the floor.

between the thumb and forefinger. (Fig. 14) The other three fingers should curl up, placing the finger tips loosely to the muscle pad of the thumb. It should be held firmly, but not so tight that it creases the card. A firm, but relaxed grip.

The Left Hand

Place the left hand in front of your chest. Your thumb turned to the right and palm angled slightly out towards your partner. Your elbow should be bent at roughly forty-five degrees, with your upper arm at your side. There should be about a four-inch gap between your arm and your side. The hand should be open and relaxed.

If the left hand and arm have a tendency to relax and hang at your side, try placing the hand on your chest. (Fig. 15) The contact between the hand and body helps develop a feel for when the hand relaxes. Holding the hand on the body develops the muscles and the kinesthetic memory needed to maintain an elevated and active left hand. This will be important as the rapier and eventually the dagger are added to your exercises.

THE FOUNDATION OF GOOD FOOTWORK

The learning of footwork and regulation of safe distance and controlled movement requires a strong foundation. This foundation is the On Guard stance. Practice of footwork should only begin

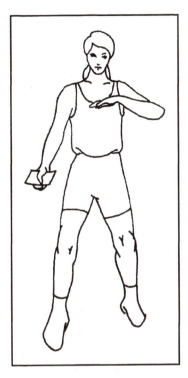

Figure 13. The On Guard Stance: Unarmed placement of the sword arm and left hand.

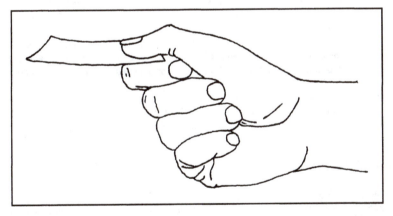

Figure 14. Close up: holding the card. The card rests on the side of the index finger, held in place with the thumb.

after you thoroughly understand and can automatically assume correct placement in the On Guard stance.

The Need for Mobility

An actor needs exceptional dynamism and mobility in order to cope with the increased demands of today's film and theatre. Often a series of footwork or jumps and steps are called for where the

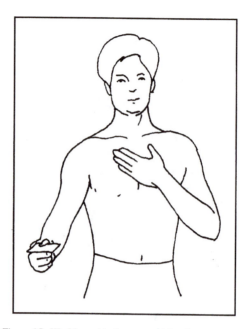

Figure 15. Working with the unarmed hand on the chest.

combatants must turn circles, fight up and down stairs, leap over tables and recreate the "swash-buckling" style of swordplay made popular in motion pictures. For obvious safety reasons ". . . *every step and move should be planned,*" says British fight master William Hobbs, "*and never allowed to vary.*"[5] This can only be achieved through careful planning. The footwork must be unified with the swordplay.

It is essential that you execute each movement precisely, each and every time. Because of this, you should learn the various footwork elements individually since they serve as a base. The final objective, however, is that you be able to combine and connect the individual elements smoothly and effectively.

Each piece of footwork needs to be completed in a ready position to start any other. It is important that you always complete each action with correct, stable placement. Footwork performed in this kind of technique allows you to stop, start and change direction at any time, catering to the demands of today's complex choreography.

The Size of the Step

 "I advise everie man in al his wards to frame a reasonable pace, in such sort that if hee would step forward to strik, he lengthen or increase one foot, and if he would defend himself, he withdraw as much without peril of falling." [di Grassi][6]

Following the above example from sixteenth century Italian fencing master Giacomo di Grassi, the length of a step in stage swordplay, as a rule, is that of your foot. (Fig. 16) This may change, however, depending upon the size of your partner, the character you portray or with the special requirements of a particular fight or fight style.

---

[5]Hobbs, *Stage Combat,* p. 31.
[6]di Grassi, p. 30.

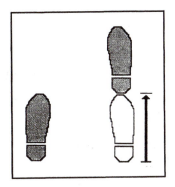

Figure 16. The size of the step.

Steps should be smooth and soundless. An audible slapping of the foot to the floor suggests an improper shift in your center of gravity. This causes your initial foot to be raised too high and your supporting foot to bounce off the floor like a rubber ball.

Sensing the Floor

traverse thy ground so leisurably, that thou mayest be sure to have one foote firme on good ground before thou pluckest up the other; for else, going fast about, thou mayest quickly be downe if the ground be not even. [Swetnam][7]

The advice of the ancient masters is as applicable now as then. Each step of the foot and shifting of weight should be made in a process of sensing and grabbing the ground. Imagine stepping cautiously onto thin ice. You would not shift your full weight to that foot until you were sure the supporting ground was safe.

"The gradual giving and taking of the center of gravity can be illustrated with the example of handing over and receiving a tray," sites fencing master Laszlo Szabo. "The deliverer gradually releases the tray; the receiver, with an ever strengthening grip, smoothly takes it over."[8]

When the feet travel backward, you will push down into the toes of the moving foot and lift the heel off the floor. (Fig. 17) The ball of the foot then travels backward, barely leaving the floor (almost skimming the ground). This is done with any foot traveling backward. The foot skims, or senses the floor, and is not lifted so that the body remains centered and balanced. Although the toes brush the floor the heel is lifted to avoid tripping or stumbling on uneven terrain.

When the feet travel forward, you will lift the toes, then the ball of the moving foot slightly off the ground. (Fig. 18) As the foot moves forward, the heel barely leaves the ground, skimming it in the same manner as the ball of the foot in the movement backward. By lifting the foot in this manner rather than dragging it, you can commit to a forward action of the body without fear of tripping or catching the foot.

All footwork is executed in this manner unless specifically stated otherwise. When traveling backward, you will lift the back of the foot and skim the front along the floor, and vice versa. At this stage, the feet never leave the floor, they are always brushing the ground, sensing the floor. A dragged foot can snag and trip. A removed foot can take you off balance or be set down on unsafe

---

[7]Swetnam, p. 89.
[8]Szabo, Laszlo, p. 126.

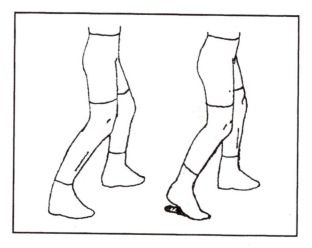

Figure 17. Lifting the heel of the lag foot.

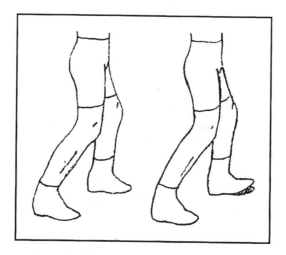

Figure 18. Lifting the toe and ball of the lead foot.

ground (stairs, loose props, edge of platform, etc.). An attached, sensitive foot feels the floor and conducts the body safely to its intended placement.

The Railroad Tracks

In all footwork that involves moving forward or backward in a linear fashion, the feet should be treated as if locked on a set of parallel railroad tracks. (Fig. 19) These tracks keep your feet at the correct distance apart, your torso traveling straight forward. It is very important to condition your feet to stay on these imaginary tracks, especially when traveling backward where your feet extend outside your peripheral vision. As you face your partner your right foot should be on the same track as their left, and your left foot on the same as their right. This will help you remain square to your partner and insure consistent footwork when traveling forward and back.

As you begin to execute footwork, focus first on your lower body by resting your hands on your hips. This allows you to feel if your pelvis twists or rotates during the execution of the actions. The hips, pelvis and torso should remain facing forward, square to your partner and move only in a horizontal plane. Great care must be taken that the center of gravity moves horizontally in one plane. There should be no up or down bobbing of torso and no jerky, leaping motions. The trunk does not twist away from your partner, nor does it bend at the waist; you should start and arrive smoothly.

Once comfortable with the execution of these actions, take your hands from your hips. Bring your hands into the correct placement of the On Guard stance discussed earlier. Move your hands and arms as dictated by the particular action being executed. Using the concept of kinesthetic learning, repeat each exercise this way until it becomes second nature to you, then move on to the next one.

SIMPLE FOOTWORK

The footwork in this chapter is classified as either simple or compound. Simple exercises involve the execution of one element, such as a single motion forward or back. Compound exercises involve the execution of two or more elements, usually designed to cover greater distance. Thus, to accomplish the compound actions of footwork, you must first practice the simple action.

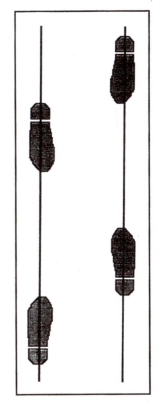

Figure 19. The imaginary railroad tracks that join your feet with those of your partner.

Stationary Movement

The simplest form of footwork requires no foot movement. By merely shifting your center of gravity, your body takes on an offensive or defensive attitude. To achieve this stationary action, press down on one foot and shift your weight (roughly sixty percent) onto the other. As the center of gravity is shifted to one foot, the pushing or shifting leg should be straight. Do not lock the knee of that leg. The knee of the supporting leg should be pointing directly out over the supporting foot and no more than three inches over the supporting foot's toes.

There is no actual movement of the feet. The head, shoulder and chest remain in correct placement, square to your partner. The pelvis does not twist. The shifting leg is straight, but not locked. The supporting knee retains its original position pointing straight forward out over the foot; not angling in or out.

The body "rocked backward" and your center over your lag leg and foot, is the *stationary defensive position*. (Fig. 20) The body "rocked forward" and your center placed over your lead leg and foot, is the *stationary offensive position*. (Fig. 21)

The terms backward and forward in this instance may be slightly misleading. These terms refer to the shift in your center, and not specifically the direction the body travels. You will discover that the action carries the hips and torso from side to side or leg to leg rather than back and forth.

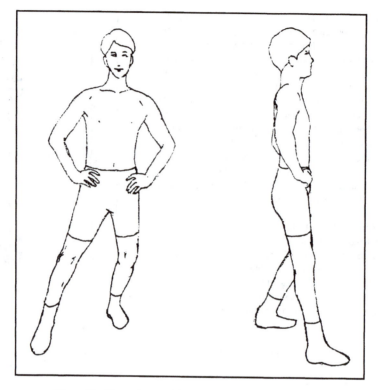

Figure 20. The stationary defensive position—"rocked back."

The Advance

The advance and the *retreat* are the result of the modern style of fence founded by the Italian fencing master Ridolfo Capo Ferro.[9] Prior to the seventeenth century, movement forward or back was generally only made by a walking step,
and not until the development of the *lunge* did linear movement prove useful. From Capo Ferro's work, however, we know these actions existed as early as 1610, and most likely earlier.

The advance, also known as the "fencing step forward," moves or "advances" a combatant towards their partner. You transfer your weight to your lag foot, then lift the toes and ball of the lead foot slightly off the ground and carry the heel of the lead foot forward approximately one foot's length.

Once the heel is securely on the floor your weight begins to shift forward. At the same moment the front heel stops its forward movement, the lag foot should begin to advance in the same toe, ball, heel—heel, ball, toe manner. Leaving the floor, it moves forward and carries the body forward with it.

Both feet cover an equal distance, maintaining the same relationship to one another. The feet should complete the action simultaneously, placing the ball and then the toe of both feet soundly upon the floor. (Figs. 22 & 23)

---

[9]The great sixteenth century Italian master, who, with the invention of the "botta lunga" (the lunge) changed the manner of executing swordplay. See Appendix D for more details.

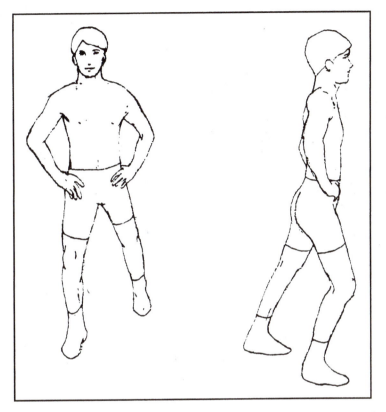

Figure 21. The stationary offensive position—"rocked forward."

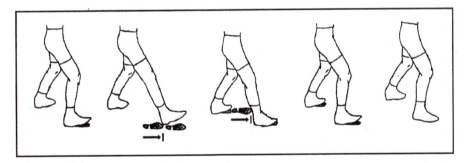

Figure 22. The five stages of the advance.

The Retreat

The retreat, also known as the "fencing step backward," is the reverse of the advance, moving you away from your partner. In the retreat, the lag foot leaves the ground first, shifting your weight forward to the lead foot. Smoothly, with a loose extension, the lag foot stretches backward approximately one foot's length.

As the front foot pushes the body backward, the lag foot grips the floor. First the toes, and then

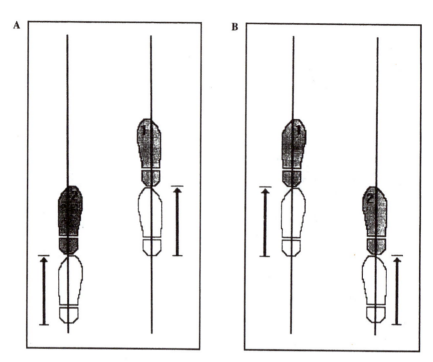

Figure 23. The advancing of the feet. **A**-An advance right foot dominant; **B**-an advance left foot dominant.

the foot and leg take over their share of the body's weight. With this, the unburdened lead foot may begin to leave the ground. Do this in the same heel, ball, toe—toe, ball, heel action. The foot travels backward carrying the body backward with it, taking up the new position.

Both feet should move an equal distance and should finish at approximately the same time. (Figs. 24 & 25)

The Pace/Passing

Passing, or the ''passata,'' was the chief means of gaining and breaking ground prior to the seventeenth century. This form of footwork made up the greater part of offensive and defensive movement before the introduction of the lunge and was most likely the original form of footwork in armed encounters. The pace or pass simply consists of passing one foot by the other. This is unlike the advance or retreat. These later developments of footwork maintain the same position of the feet where the pass changes the placement of lead and lag foot.

The pass, pace, passing, passes, pasada, or passado (to name a few variations) appears in the works of most masters of fence, as well as those of many dramatists well into the nineteenth century and when accompanied by a thrust was probably the ''imortal passado'' of *Romeo and Juliet.*

Pass Forward

The pass forward, also called the ''walking step forward,'' is an action that brings you closer to your partner by passing your lag foot forward past your lead foot into a new lead position. In the pass forward, you initiate the movement with the lag foot. Pointing the lag foot directly forward, your weight is transferred to your lead foot.

With your weight forward, you will lift the toes and then the ball of the lag foot slightly off the

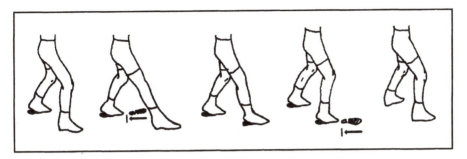

Figure 24. The five stages of the retreat.

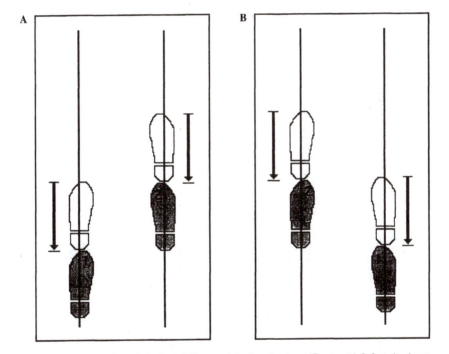

Figure 25. The retreating of the feet. **A**-Retreat right foot dominant; **B**-retreat left foot dominant.

ground, carrying the heel of the lag foot forward along the railroad track, passing the lead foot. The heel comes to rest in a plane just past the toe of the lead foot. This puts the lag foot in the new lead position. The lag foot will travel *over* the length of one foot, or two foot lengths forward. Once the heel is securely on the floor, place the ball and then the toe of the new lag foot soundly upon the floor. (Figs. 26 & 27)

Pass Backward

The pass backward or pass back, also called the "walking step backward," is the reverse of the pass forward. It moves you away from your partner by passing your lead foot backward beyond your lag foot into a new lag position. The movement of the pass back is initiated with the lead foot.

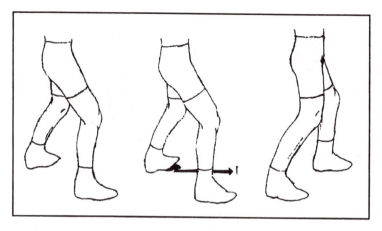

Figure 26. The pass forward.

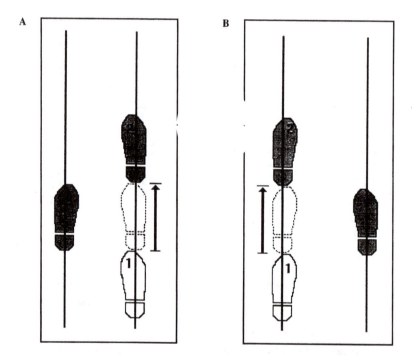

Figure 27. The passing forward of the feet. **A**-Pass forward on the right foot; **B**-pass forward on the left foot.

Transferring your weight to your lag foot, you lift the heel, then the ball, and then the toes of the lead foot and carry them straight backward along the railroad tracks, past the lag foot. The toes stop in a plane just past the heel of the lag foot. This puts the lead foot in the new lag position. The lead foot travels *over* the length of one foot, or two foot lengths backward. Once the toe is securely on the floor, place the ball and then the heel of the new lag foot soundly upon the floor. (Figs. 28 & 29)

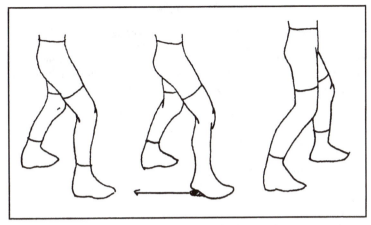

Figure 28. The pass back.

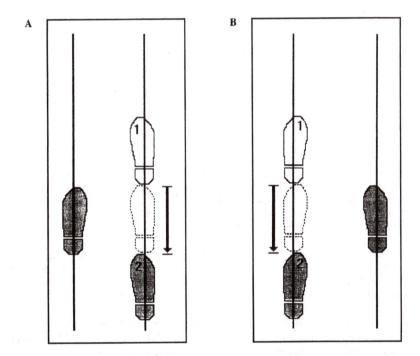

Figure 29. The passing back of the feet. **A**-Pass back on the right foot; **B**-pass back on the left foot.

After passing forward and back several times, try working the advance and the retreat with various lead and lag feet. As you progress in your skills, you will find that the mechanics of a stage fight will call on you to perform the advance and retreat with either foot forward. This may feel awkward at first, but through time you will perceive no difference in your ability to execute these actions with either foot forward.

The Lunge

Unconfined by all the rules and regulations of modern fencing, rapier play had not reaped the benefits of the complete evolution of fencing. The lunge, one of the most commonly used moves in stage combat and fencing today, is a form of footwork that, though often thought to belong to the most ancient forms of swordplay, is actually quite new. As far as documented, it appears the lunge was not developed until the beginning of the seventeenth century.

Before the late sixteenth century, a fencer used the point of the sword to threaten the opponent's face. The cut on a pass, however, was considered the best method of attack. In 1568, the Italian swordsman Camillo Agrippa viewed the point as having offensive potential.[10] He recommended an extended arm thrust to the face or torso, punched out from the shoulder.

Despite the advanced notions of Agrippa's work, however, it was Viggiani's *Lo Schermo* ("The Shield") of 1575 that first proclaims the superiority of the thrust over the cut.[11] Accordingly, he developed the *punta sopramano* ("thrust over the hand"). Viggiani's *demi-lunge,* however, was neglected in this development. The favored technique of fencing at a distance where one's opponent could be hit by simply extending the arm, remained the common practice.

The Italian fencing masters Giganti (1606) and Capo Ferro (1610) developed the lunge as we know it today.[12] The *stocatta lunga* ("elongated thrust") or *botta lunga* ("elongated blow"), respectively, were executed from the position of a bent arm. The arm extended and body traveled forward at the same instant, concluding in what we now call a "lunge." This seemingly simple move changed the execution and manner of swordplay. The old round circling style of footwork was slowly discarded and swordplay evolved to that of the direct linear style of today.

The Standing Lunge

The standing lunge is the theatrical equivalent of Agrippa's "thrust." It is simply a modification of the stationary offensive position adding a thrust from the arm and upper body. The right hand is thrust forward as you shift your center of gravity forward onto the lead foot (The reverse is true if the left arm is the sword-arm).

Deliver the standing lunge by first extending the right arm forward, to your partner's left, or across your body and forward, to your partner's right. As the arm completes its extension, press down on the lag foot, shifting your weight forward onto the lead foot. Your arm should be horizontal to the floor, the lag leg should be straight. Do not lock the knee. The knee of the lead leg points straight forward along the railroad track. It should be no more than three inches in front of the toes of the right foot. Both the extension of the arm and the extension of the knee are completed at the same time.

Without pausing in the action, bring the right shoulder forward, turning slightly at the trunk, so that your chest is about three-quarters on to your partner. As you do this, throw the left elbow back. Keep the hand in front of the chest and the left arm in the same horizontal plane as the right arm. This should create the sense of push to the thrust, and work as a counterweight to the extended right arm. (Fig. 30)

Do not twist or shift the pelvis. The lag leg is straight, but not locked. The lead knee retains its original direction: pointing straight forward. It must not angle in. The center of gravity is balanced between the legs with the weight evenly distributed on the three points of each foot.

To recover from the standing lunge, push down on the lead foot, draw the arms in and bring your

---

[10]Camillo Agrippa was a famous sixteenth century Milanese gentleman who was the first to introduce a reduction in the vast number of fencing guards advocated by the masters of his day. See Appendix D for more detail.

[11]Viggiani was an Italian master of the sixteenth century who first proclaimed the superiority of the thrust over the cut. See Appendix D for more detail.

[12]Giganti was an illustrious Italian master of the sixteenth century who is noted mostly for having first clearly explained the techniques of the "stocatta lunga" (the lunge). See Appendix D for more detail.

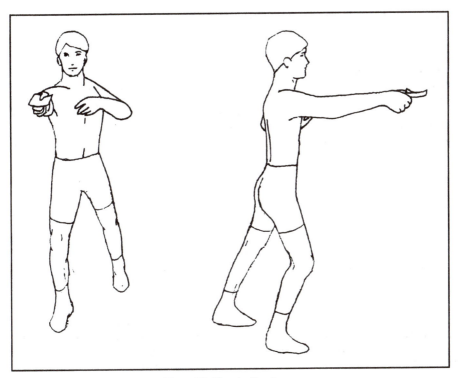

Figure 30. The standing lunge.

upper body back into correct placement. Shift your center of gravity back to where the bent lag leg supports its share of the weight.

Unlike the upcoming demi-lunge and grand lunge, the standing lunge is not necessarily an action designed as a "coup de grace." The standing lunge is constantly used throughout bouts of choreographed blade work.

The Demi-Lunge ("Punta Sopramano")

About 1560, Angelo Viggiani introduced the "punta sopramano." This action suggested the first, clear development toward the "lunge" as we understand it today.

> *"When thou shalt have a mind to deliver a 'punta sopramano,' see that the right foot advances one great step, and immediately let thy left arm fall, and let the right shoulder at the same time press the arm forwards, dropping the point slightly downwards from above, and aiming the while at my chest, without in any way turning the hand. Push thy point as far as ever thou canst."[13]*

Viggiani's teachings show the development of a new school of thought in which "passing"

---

[13](Castle, p. 66) translated from:

—*Lo Schermo d'ANGELO VIGGIANI, dal Montone da Bologna. Nel quale, per via di dialogo si discorre intorno all' eccelenza dell' Armi et delle lettere, et intorno all offesa difesa. Et insegna uno Schermo di Spada sola sicuro e singolare con una tavola copiosissima. 4°. Venetia. 1575*

Appresso Giorgio Angelieri.

tended to be replaced by the "lunge." Unfortunately, in his introduction of the punta sopramano, Viggiani was not bold enough to apply the execution of the "lunge" to all attacks. As such, he missed his chance of being deemed the founder of the modern school of fence.

The punta sopramano, or demi-lunge, is a single action that combines the standing lunge with the initial footwork of the advance. To deliver the demi-lunge, first extend the right arm forward from the shoulder, to your partner's left, or across your body and forward, to your partner's right. Reach, rather than push, the hand forward. As the arm completes its extension, transfer your weight to your lag foot. Then lift the toes, then the ball of the lead foot slightly off the ground. With no resistance from the lead foot remaining, the pushing force of the lag foot begins to take over, driving the heel of the lead foot forward along its railroad track. The lead foot should travel forward approximately one foot's length.

The main force of the demi-lunge is provided by the extension of the lag leg, which drives the body forward. The driving force that propels you forward must push *straight* forward through the hips, rather than up and forward.

Without pausing in the action, bring the right shoulder forward, turning slightly at the trunk, so that your chest is about three-quarters on to your partner. While doing this, do not twist or rock the pelvis. The lag leg is straight, but not locked. The knee of the lead leg retains its original direction: pointing straight forward (it must not angle in).

As the body lunges forward, throw back the left elbow, keeping the left arm in the same horizontal plane as the right arm. This should create a sense of push to the thrust and offer a counterweight to the extended right arm. The head, shoulders, trunk and pelvis maintain the position of correct placement.

The right arm at full extension should be horizontal to the floor. The lag leg is straight, without locking the knee. The knee of the lead leg points straight forward along the railroad track directly over the instep of the lead foot and perpendicular to the floor. (Figs. 31 & 32)

Although your center of gravity is not at the geometrical center of the demi-lunge, try to distribute your weight equally on both legs.

The Recover Backward

This movement starts with the lead foot, from the completed lunge position. Push down into the toes, raise the heel and thrust the body backward along the railroad track. The lag leg takes over the "thrusted" center of gravity. The torso returns to correct placement, withdrawing the extended right arm. The lag leg also helps pull the body backward by bending the knee, bringing it back over the foot. The movement is completed by bringing the lead foot to rest (toe, ball, heel) into the On Guard stance.

The Recover Forward

The movement starts from the completed lunge position with the lag foot. Push down into the toes and lift the heel of the lag foot, then thrust it forward to take up its normal position in the On Guard stance. The lead leg takes over the "thrusted" center of gravity during this recovery and lifting your center (torso) helps pull the lag leg into place. The torso also returns to correct placement, withdrawing the extended right arm. The movement is completed with the lag foot coming to rest (heel, ball, toe) into a correct On Guard stance.

The Grand Lunge ("Botta Lunga")

Early in the seventeenth century Nicoletto Giganti and Ridolfo Capo Ferro, in separate works, both defined the application and advantage of the "lunge." It was applied by both men to most common and practical attacks.

"To deliver the stoccata lunga," says Giganti, "place thyself in a firm attitude, rather collected than otherwise, so as to be capable of further extension. Being thus on guard, extend thy arm and advance the

Figure 31. The demi-lunge.

body at the same time, and bend the right knee as much as possible, so that thy opponent may be hit before he can parry.''[14]

The honor of having first described the grand lunge goes to Giganti, whose work certainly has the priority of date. Capo Ferro, however, who was a contemporary of Giganti, explained the mechanics of the lunge in greater detail. It is his work that fixed the basic principles of the modern science.

The ''botta lunga,'' or grand lunge, is the same as the demi-lunge, varying primarily in the extension of the lead foot and the placement of the left arm. Deliver the grand lunge by first extending the right arm forward from the shoulder, as in the standing and demi-lunge.

Once the arm is fully extended, transfer your weight to your lag foot. First lift the toes and then the ball of the lead foot slightly off the ground. With no resistance from the lead foot remaining, the pushing force of the lag foot begins to take over, pushing the lead foot forward approximately the length of three of your feet. (The lead foot should travel *over* the length of two feet, or three foot lengths forward).

[14]Castle, p. 113. Translated from:

—*Teatro, nel qual sono rappresentate diverse maniere e mode di parare et di ferire di Spada sola, e di Spada e pugnale; dove ogni studioso potra essercitarsi e farsi prattico nella professione dell' Armi.*

Di NICOLETTO GIGANTI, Vinitiano. Oblong 4°. Venetia. 1606.

Appresso Gio. Antonio et G. de Franceschi.

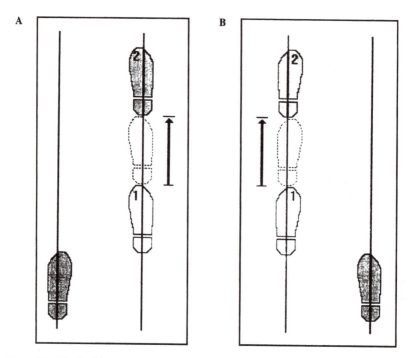

Figure 32. The demi-lunge. **A**-A demi-lunge on the right foot; **B**-a demi-lunge on the left foot.

Plate II: The Botta Lunga as illustrated by Capo Ferro (1610)

As in the demi-lunge, the main force of the grand lunge is provided by the extension of the lag leg. This force must push straight forward through the hips, not up and forward.

The left arm is snapped back, lending force and speed to the lunge. It also serves as a counter-weight for the lunge. The left arm will be completely extended in the same plane as the extended right arm, with the palm up. The left hand and arm may be held slightly lower. Without pausing in the action, bring the right shoulder forward, turning slightly at the trunk, so that your chest is turned about three-quarters to your partner. The pelvis turns slightly with the trunk in order to avoid twisting the knee of the lag leg. (Figs. 33–34)

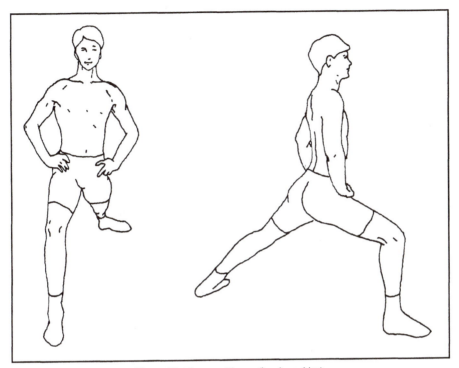

Figure 33. The grand lunge (hands on hips).

Turn the head, shoulders, trunk and pelvis only slightly. Do not lean forward. The torso should maintain correct placement in relation to the line of gravity. On the execution of the lunge, the lag foot pivots roughly ninety degrees, shifting to a placement perpendicular to the linear track of that foot. This is done to relieve strain on the ankle and Achilles tendon. The lag foot should remain flat on the floor with the leg straight, but not locked. The knee of the lead leg retains its original direction, pointing straight forward (it must not angle in).

The right arm at full extension should be horizontal to the floor. The lag foot and knee turned to the side, the leg straight, without locking the knee. The knee of the lead leg points straight forward (along the railroad track) directly over the instep of the lead foot and perpendicular to the floor.

Although your center of gravity is not at the geometrical center of the grand lunge, try to distribute your weight equally onto both legs. This keeps you balanced on stage and facilitates recovery in either direction. (Fig. 35)

Circle Steps

Previous to the linear style of fencing generated by the introduction of the lunge, fencers, especially the Spanish, circled around one another like two animals about to fight.[15]

---

[15]Jeronimo de Carranza is a Spanish master of the late sixteenth century, and ''father'' of the Spanish science of fence. A student of Carranza's, Don Luis Pacheco de Narvaez, verbosely expounded the dignified but unrealistic principles of the Spanish school. Narvaez offered his own reproduction of Carranza's work, basing his system on the ''*imaginary circle.*'' The works of Carranza, which Narvaez's first book embodies, and his later works (and all those about him) form nearly the entire written word on the Spanish school of fence during the seventeenth century.

Figure 34. The grand lunge (arms extended).

"The adversaries are to fall on guard out of measure," explains Egerton Castle, *"and, in order to systematize the general notions of correct distance,* [The Spanish master] *Carranza and his illustrator Narvaez imagine a circle drawn on the ground—'circonferencia imaginata entre los cuerpos contrarios.'*[16]

"The opponents on guard are to be at opposite ends of the diameter, whose length is regulated by the effective length of the arm . . . Tangent to the circle, and at the opposite ends of the diameter, are imagined two parallel lines, which are called infinite—'lineas infinitas'—for the simple reason that both adversaries might travel for ever along these lines together without altering for any practical purpose their relative positions."[17]

After the introduction of the lunge, the "circle steps" were predominantly a feature of the Spanish school. Many masters however, still practiced and taught various forms of evasions and passes on the circle well into the nineteenth century.

The following techniques are theatrical renderings of the Spanish "lineas infinitas." The two parallel lines that, with an imaginary circle on the floor, join your lead and lag foot to your partner's lead and lag foot, respectively. The patterns of stepping on this circle have offensive and defensive purposes in both directions in order to allow correct measure and distance between you and your partner. For the right-handed fencer the right foot generally remains on the inner line of the circle, while the left foot travels on the outer line (except when specifically indicated otherwise).

[16]Castle, p. 113. Translated from

—*Gran simulacro dell'arte e dell uso della Scherma di RIDOLFO CAPO FERRO da Cagli, Maestro dell' eccelsa natione alemanna, nell' inclita Citta di Siena. Oblong 4°. Siena. 1610.*

[17]Castle, pp. 69–70.

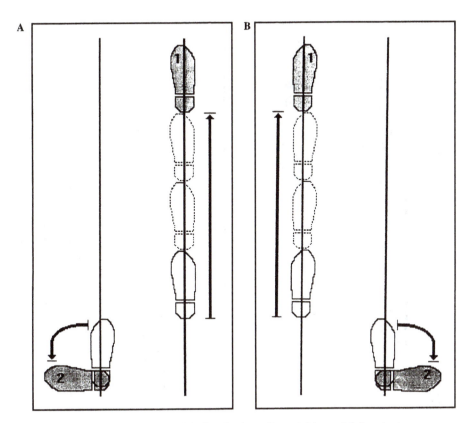

Figure 35. **A**-A grand lunge, right foot dominant; **B**-a grand lunge, left foot dominant.

This imaginary circle, with its two parallel lines, is not unlike the set of railroad tracks you have become accustomed to in the preceding footwork. The difference is that the tracks now bend in a continuous circle instead of traveling straight forward. Your lead foot is now on the same track as your partner's lead foot, and their lag foot is on the same track as yours. Both sets of tracks should be apparent to you at any time during footwork. This offers you the ability to more readily travel back and forth and from side to side on the circle. (Fig. 37)

Circle Step to the Left (Circle Left)

The *circle step left* is an action that carries you around the circle in a clockwise direction. This is achieved by passing one foot past the other on the tracks of the circle. The circle left is very much like the pass forward, differing in the direction traveled and the tracks followed.

Initiate the circle left with the foot in the lag position *in relation to the tracks of the circle.* Once traveling on the circle, your forward foot is still the lead foot and your rear foot is the lag. It is only in the transition from linear to circular tracks where the right foot, as the lead foot, steps "forward" to the left. For example, when in correct placement in the On Guard stance, your right leg is forward. The direction of movement for the circle left is to your left, where your left foot is actually dominant. This puts your left foot in the lead position on the circle. Your right foot, although forward (in what might be called a north-south line), is in the lag position for a circle step to the left.

To execute the circle left, first point the lag foot so that it follows the direction of the circular track on which it now rests. Transfer your weight to your lead foot, then lift the toes and then the ball of

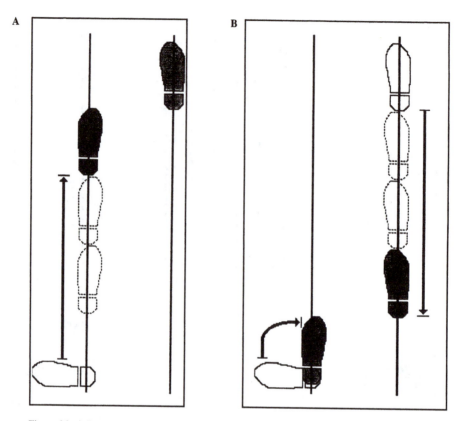

Figure 36. **A-**Recover forward, right foot dominant; **B-**recover backward, right foot dominant.

the lag foot slightly off the ground, and carry the lag foot forward to the left, past the lead foot. Its heel should be parallel to the toe of the lead foot. This puts the lag foot in the new lead position on the circle. Once the heel is securely on the floor, place the ball and then the toe of the new lead foot firmly upon the floor. (Figs. 38 & 39)

Your feet should remain approximately shoulder width apart. Your new stance should be very close to the On Guard stance except you have turned your body roughly sixty degrees from its point of origin. To check and see if you have stepped correctly, turn both of your feet so that they are perpendicular to the linear track from which you just stepped. If you find yourself in correct placement, only facing to the left of where you began, you have stepped correctly. If you have stepped correctly, shift back to the circle, if not, try executing the circle left again.

If the circle step is executed with an attack, you may snap the left arm back as you step on the circle, to serve as a counterweight for the extended sword-arm. The left arm can be completely extended with the hand supinated in the same plane, or slightly lower than the extended right arm.

Your head should look over your right shoulder at your partner. Your shoulders, trunk and pelvis remain in correct placement facing forward on the circular track. The right side of your body faces the inside of the circle, with your shoulder and hip directed toward your partner. The trunk does not lean forward or back, but stays in correct placement over the center of gravity.

The feet do not change from track to track in a circle left. They only travel forward on the circle, one foot passing the other on their separate tracks. (You may find that the left foot takes slightly larger steps than the right. This allows for the variance in size from the inner and outer tracks of the circle.)

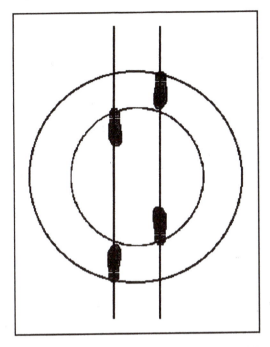

Figure 37. The imaginary circle joining the lead feet and lag feet of the combatants.

The recovery from the circle left can be a simple variation of the recover forward or backward from the demi-lunge. Simply draw yourself back into your original position. You also may pivot on the balls of your feet, turning your body until it is in the On Guard stance. This recovery, however, places the body facing a different direction than your original position.

The left foot may also initiate a circle left. From the standard On Guard stance the action is executed as a demi-lunge out to the left. This is done because the left foot is in a dominant position on the left, and in order for it to move forward on the circle, it must be carried to the side. Thus, if a circle left is to be executed from the linear tracks, it is carried forward on the outer track of the circle by the action of a demi-lunge to the left, otherwise the feet move around the circle in a simple passing action. (Fig. 40)

Circle Step to the Right (Circle Right)

The execution of the *circle step right* is very much like the demi-lunge and grand lunge. The difference is in the direction of the lead foot and the track it follows. It is executed by first transferring your weight to your left foot. Lift the toes and then the ball of the right foot slightly off the ground. With no resistance from the right foot, the pushing force of the left foot begins to take over, driving the right foot forward along the inner track of the circle approximately the distance of one foot length. The lead foot travels to the right and slightly forward the length of one foot.

The left leg should be straight, but not locked. The knee of the right leg angled about forty-five degrees off its original track pointing straight out over the right foot. The knee should be directly above its instep and perpendicular to the floor. The head, shoulders, trunk and pelvis remain facing your partner, and do not turn or lean forward, but stay straight over your center of gravity. (Figs. 41 & 42)

Although your center of gravity is not at the geometrical center of the circle right, equally

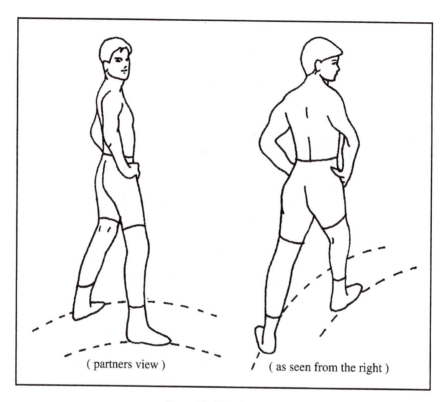

(partners view)   (as seen from the right)

Figure 38. The circle left.

distribute your weight onto both legs as in the demi-lunge. Both the recover backward and recover forward of the demi and grand lunge may be executed from the circle right without variation.

It is important to realize that a passing action, like that of the circle left, initiated to the right, turns the sword arm away from your opponent. Such an action makes an attack or parry quite difficult. It is for this reason that the circle left and circle right are two completely different tactical actions. They are designed to keep the sword-arm forward as one traverses the imaginary circle. If you were to continue around the circle to the right, the footwork would be similar to the pass back—always keeping the sword-arm to the inside.

The recovery from the circle right is the same as that of the demi-lunge; either a recover forward or recover back.

Demi-Volte

The *demi-volte,* or half-volte, is an evasive step, generally to the right removing the body from the line of attack. The lag foot travels backwards on the outer track of the circle. It moves across the straight track of the lead foot to displace the body to the side of the straight track. The lag foot initiates the demi-volte. Transferring your weight to your lead foot, you will lift the lag foot and carry it behind you along the line of the outer ring of the imaginary circle. The toes of the lag foot should be just outside what would be the straight track of the lead foot. Once the toe is securely in place. Set the ball and then the heel of the lag foot firmly upon the floor. (Figs. 43 & 44)

Your feet remain approximately shoulder width apart. Your new stance being very close to the On Guard stance, except you have shifted ninety degrees. If you were to turn your lead foot parallel to your lag foot you should find yourself in correct placement, only facing off to one side (this is

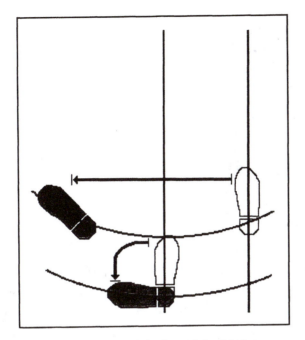

Figure 39. Circle left, leading with the right foot.

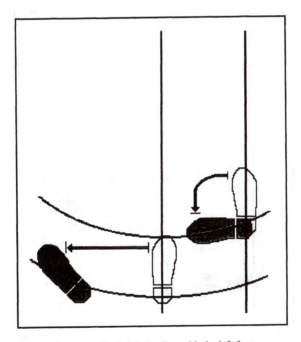

Figure 40. Circle left, leading with the left foot.

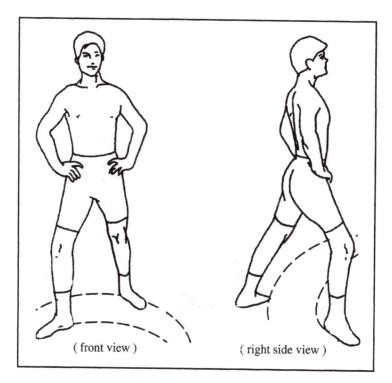

(front view)   (right side view)

Figure 41. The circle right.

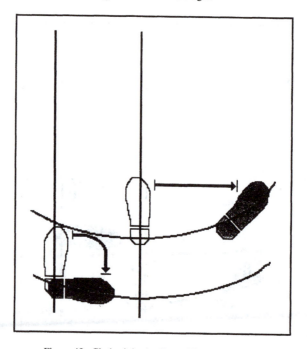

Figure 42. Circle right, leading with the right foot.

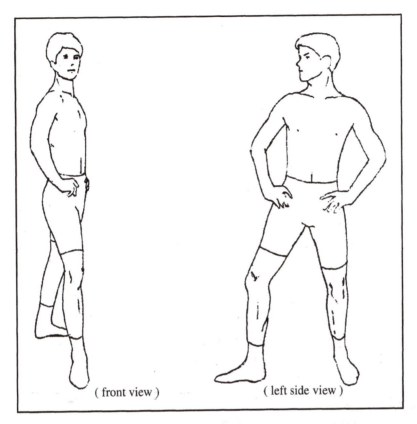

(front view)   (left side view)

Figure 43. Demi-volte to the right.

just a "check," not a part of the volte). As the body turns, your head should turn to look over your weapon-bearing shoulder. Keep your focus on your partner as you move.

You may use the demi-volte as a counter to the circle right, a form of pass back on the circle. This is done in order to travel around the circle in a counter clockwise direction while keeping the sword arm to the inside of the circle.

Grand Volte

The *grand volte* is a large evasive step (generally to the right) in response to an attack. The grand volte is often accompanied by an offensive action with the sword arm. The lag foot vaults backwards in a semicircle to the inner track of the imaginary circle. It travels across the straight track of the lead foot placing both feet on the inner track of the circle. This displaces the body to the side of the straight track.

The lag foot initiates the movement of the grand volte. Pushing down into the toe of the lag foot, lifting the heel, then the ball, and then the toes, transfer your weight to the lead foot. The toes of the lead foot travel behind you, describing a semicircle from the lag position to that of the track of the inner circle, its toes stopping just outside the heel of the lead foot.

As the lag foot vaults back and around to the inner track, the lead foot *relievés* (pushing down into its toes, and lifting its heel off the floor) so that the lead foot can pivot on its ball. The foot pivots in place (like a drafting compass), ninety degrees from its original track. Once the toe of the lag foot

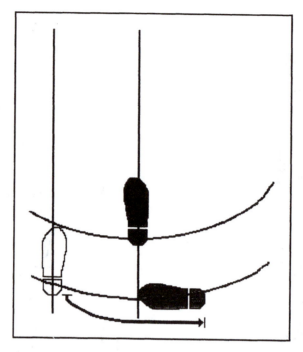

Figure 44. Demi-volte to the right.

is securely in place, simultaneously place the balls and then the heels of both feet firmly upon the floor. (Figs. 45 & 46)

Your feet should remain approximately shoulder width apart. Your new stance should be very close to correct placement except you have shifted 180 degrees. If you were to turn your lead foot parallel to your lag foot you would find yourself in correct placement. You should, however, be facing the opposite direction from where you started.

As in the demi-volte, look over the shoulder of your lead foot, keeping your focus on your partner.

The recovery from the demi and grand volte is a simple reversal of the volte process. Swing the lag foot back to its original position. You also may turn your lead foot so that it is parallel to the new position of the lag foot. This shifts your position either ninety or 180 degrees. At the completion of any of these recoveries, the body should be On Guard with correct placement. The combatant should be balanced and able to move on to any manner of footwork.

COMPOUND FOOTWORK

Crossover Step Forward

The *crossover step forward* is simply a double pass forward. This enables you to close distance on your partner at a much quicker rate. The movement is initiated by passing your lag foot forward, past your lead foot, into a new lead position. The action is then quickly repeated, bringing the original lead foot back into its forward position. (Fig. 47)

Crossover Step Backward

The *crossover step backward* is the reverse of the crossover step forward: a double pass back. This creates distance between you and your partner at a very quick rate. The movement starts with

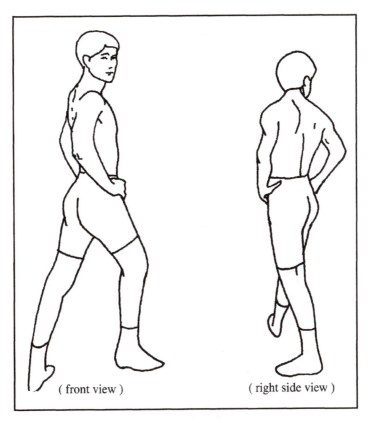

(front view)   (right side view)

Figure 45. Grand volte to the right.

passing your lead foot backward past your lag foot into a new lag position. As before, the action is quickly repeated, bringing the original lag foot back into its rear position. (Fig. 48)

Patinando (Advance-Lunge)

The *patinando* is a quick succession from an advance to the grand lunge. Execute these actions one right after the other, as a means of quickly traveling a great distance and closing measure on your partner. The patinando generally ends with an attack. In the patinando, it is of increased importance to be sure that in the advance, you put down the lead and lag foot simultaneously. This insures correct placement and balance for the bolt forward in the grand lunge. (Fig. 49)

APPLICATION AND PRACTICE

Footwork is the foundation of fencing and stage combat and must be mastered before moving on to the techniques in the following chapters involving the handling of the rapier. Footwork can be practiced alone, with a partner or in a group.

If you are working with a partner or in a group, have someone call out footwork, in any order, and see how smoothly you travel from one to another. If you are working alone, practice in front of a mirror.

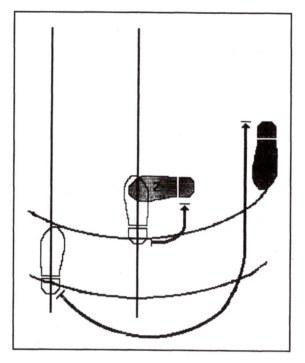

Figure 46. Grand volte to the right.

Perform the movements with your hands on your hips at first. Feeling your pelvis travel directly forward or backward in an unchanging horizontal plane. Imagine you're a statue on wheels, traveling solidly forward or backward by the drive of your legs. Do not rush these activities, it takes time for your kinesthetic memory to become acquainted with new patterns.

Remember to "think and then do": before you initiate the movement, picture the action in your head. Execute the footwork at your own tempo, ending in correct placement, balanced, ready to move again. With time and practice you will acquire efficiency and speed without errors. Hurrying the process provokes mistakes and, when armed, can lead to disaster.

TROUBLE SHOOTING

When first learning the footwork, a bobbing or waving movement in the upper body is a very common problem. In order to correct this, it is necessary to understand the goal of good footwork. Good footwork is the sending of energy either forward or backward with a smooth floating of the torso in a plane horizontal to the floor. The following exercises can help correct this problem, focusing on the goal, not the mechanics.

Bobbing and Weaving

One Card Shuffle

The One Card Shuffle is a practice that often alleviates over-stressed focus on mechanics. Come On Guard, your right hand holding the card with which you have been practicing, and change your

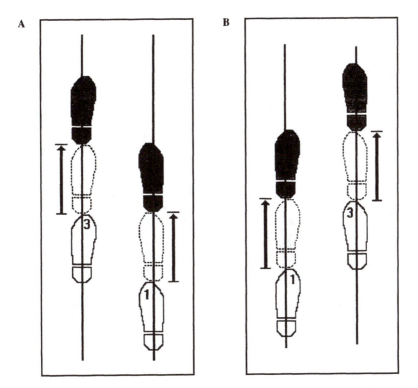

Figure 47. **A**-A crossover step forward leading with the right foot; **B**-a crossover step forward leading with the left foot.

focus from your body to the card. Instead of worrying about the bobbing of your torso, think of the card. Hold the card in place, and make it move forward and backwards in a smooth line horizontal to the floor. The arm should remain relaxed, but should not move from its initial position; your footwork makes the card move, slowly and smoothly forwards and back.

Water Works

Water Works is a variation on the One Card Shuffle. Simply hold a glass full of water in your right hand instead of the card (a small serving tray with a glass of water placed in its center also will do). You should practice stepping forward and back in such a way that not a drop of water spills from the glass. Focusing on the card or the glass of water takes strain off the mechanics of the body. This allows the body to move more freely while insuring that it is controlled and precise. (Fig. 50) Be sure to work with a nonbreakable glass and to promptly clean the floor of any spilled water.

Kicking Foot

For many reasons, when advancing, retreating, lunging, etc., there is an urge to kick the foot off the floor, throwing it forward or back. This causes an awkward weight shift that allows the foot to travel far off the floor. Building a better sensing, or "skimming" across the floor helps alleviate this problem. This may be done in several ways, one of which is the *walking foot*, and another is the *coin carrier* exercises.

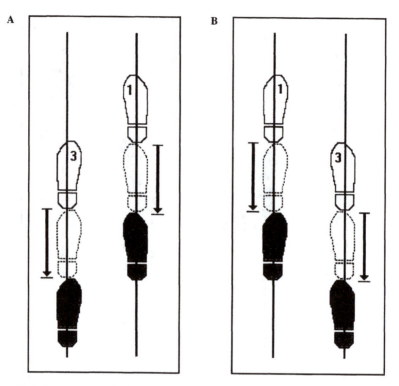

Figure 48. **A-**A crossover step backward leading with the right foot; **B-**a crossover step backward leading with the left foot.

Walking Foot

In the Walking Foot, the advancing or retreating foot is moved in several stages. The center of gravity is slowly shifted to the secondary foot by pressing down into the initiating foot. As this is done, and the foot is lifted, either to its toe or heel, the foot is moved in a walking or "rocking" manner. By slowly guiding the foot in its path, and gently rocking it back and forth, the foot will "skim" the floor. The muscles in the lower body build a better kinesthetic sense of the action in its entirety.

Coin Carrier

In the Coin Carrier, a coin is placed under the heel or toe of the initiating foot before beginning the action. Concentrating on carrying the coin forward or backward with the foot, changes your focus from muscles and movement to a simple coin under your foot. If you execute your advance or retreat correctly, the coin is carried along with the foot. If you execute the footwork incorrectly, the coin is either kicked out in the direction of the action or remains in place.

The "Rearing" Lunge

For a "rearing" lunge, where you rear back like a horse before you spring forward, the blame can often be placed on an over-energetic weight transfer. This causes a thrust up rather than forward from the lag foot and leg. A good gauge of this is to place a coin on the toe of the lunging foot. If you send the coin up or across the room in a high arch, you are rearing too much in your lunge. To

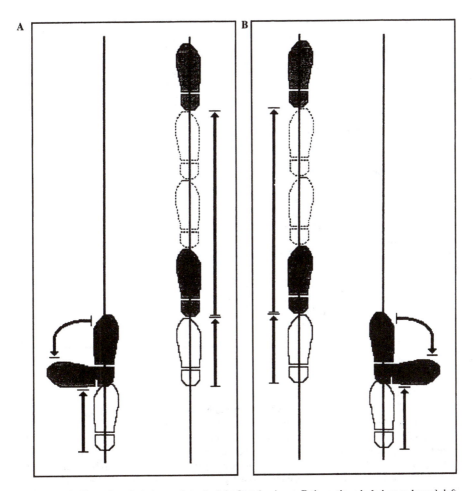

Figure 49. **A-**The patinando [advance-lunge], right foot dominant; **B-**the patinando [advance-lunge], left foot dominant.

correct this, focus on carrying the coin forward on the toe of your shoe. Do not try to kick it or flip it, carry the coin; focus on it traveling forward with your foot. This focus frees your mechanics from personal scrutiny, allowing you to develop quicker. (It is normal for the coin to come off your foot upon the completion of the movement because of the braking action of the foot. It should not, however, travel *up*).

Staying on Track

Other than "bobbing" and "rearing" as one executes footwork, the second-most common problem is staying on track. This problem is more pronounced in actors who have taken even a little fencing, but is quite common in most beginning combatants. Usually one steps off track when traveling backwards, where the feet step out of peripheral field of vision. Another common instance is during circle steps. When first traversing the circle, distance, measure and the relative position of the feet to each other, and to your partner, are not yet completely established. The problem of distance and measure will be explored further on in the chapter. For now, concentrate on keeping the feet on track while traversing linear footwork.

Walking the Line

Walking the Line is, in its simplest form, the process of traversing actual physical lines that represent the imaginary railroad tracks used in footwork. The simplest solution is to find two cracks or lines in the floor upon which to place your feet. If such lines are not available, tape two parallel lines onto the floor to represent the tracks you must travel upon. Practice moving back and forth along these tracks, making sure your feet remain "on track." As you travel backward, see if you can feel the tracks; not the tape on the floor, but the position of the body, and how it feels in relation to the tape on the floor. Trust your physical inventory. Try to step on the tape, looking only after moving to check yourself.

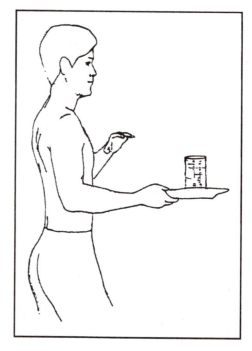

Figure 50. Water works exercise.

Do not rely on the lines; they are a tool that should be discarded as soon as you are physically comfortable. Once you are mentally sure and confident that you can move correctly along the track without needing a check point, remove the tape.

The pass back seems to be the biggest culprit in throwing people off track. In many cases it feels more natural to throw the lead foot back, in an action similar to a volte, placing the foot along the track of the other foot. If you find it difficult to move along the "taped" tracks, and you think you're dead on when actually you have stepped off, do not get frustrated. Any physical discipline involves hurdles for everyone, at one stage or another. Do not get upset and blame yourself—all you need is more practice, or perhaps a greater external focal point.

Walkin' the Plank

Instead of using tape to lay out your tracks, take two 2 × 4 lengths of lumber and lay them out according to the width of your stance. Have a friend at each end of the boards to hold them in place and to let you know when you are reaching the end of the tracks. Placing yourself at one end of the 2 × 4 tracks, slowly take yourself forward, feeling the boards under your feet.

Do not rush this exercise, it is training your kinesthetic sense, not only in your feet but of your entire body in motion. Rushing this exercise also may cause the boards to shift, displacing your track and possibly causing you to fall.

Once you reach the end of the tracks, you may begin to travel backward. As you execute each action, feel the boards and the placement of the feet. Move through the footwork slowly, developing a sense of foot and body placement. Do not look where your feet are going, sense where they are moving to and how they get there. If you should happen to step off the track, correct yourself and move on. You will be surprised how quickly this exercise corrects misplaced footwork. It is important to maintain a sense of lift during this exercise.

Balloon Walk

Many classes and studios cannot allow tape or lumber on the floor, as it would mar the surface. It is for that reason that the following exercise has been developed. It is very effective without jeopardizing the movement surface.

Take an ordinary, round party balloon and inflate it until it is roughly ten inches in diameter. Tie the balloon off and assume the On Guard stance. Once in correct placement, place the balloon between your thighs toward the upper point of the pentagon formed by your legs and the floor. (Fig. 51) With the balloon in place, begin to move through random footwork. You will feel immediately any narrowing of the feet or legs.

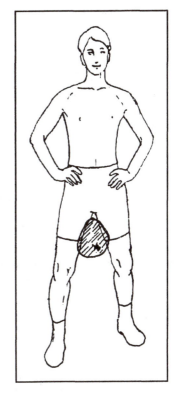

Figure 51. Balloon walk exercise.

THE DRILLS

After becoming comfortable with the footwork and how each action moves from one to another, try practicing the following footwork drills. Make sure that you maintain correct placement and balance. Each action flows smoothly, one into the other. Your feet travel along the corresponding tracks without deviation. The torso glides along without bobbing (move like a chest on wheels). These drills will become a part of further exercises later in the book.

Offensive Footwork Drill

Start in a standing position, bring yourself into the On Guard stance. From the On Guard stance, step through the following pattern:

Advance: Right foot retains the lead foot position.
Pass Forward: Left foot moves to the lead position.
Advance: Left foot retains the lead foot position.
Pass Forward: Right foot moves to the lead position.
Advance: Right foot retains the lead foot position.
Pass Forward: Left foot moves to the lead position.
Pass Forward: Right foot moves to the lead position.
Advance: Right foot retains the lead foot position.
Advance: Right foot retains the lead foot position.
Circle Left: Stepping to the left so that the right foot is in the lead position on the inner track of the imaginary circle.
Circle Left: Left foot moves to the lead position on the outer track of the imaginary circle.
Circle Left: Right foot moves to the lead position on the inner track of the imaginary circle.
Circle Left: Left foot moves to the lead position on the outer track of the imaginary circle.
Recover: Pivot on the balls of your feet so that you face the direction from which you have come. You should be in correct placement in the On Guard stance without having to readjust your feet in any way.
Circle Right: Lunging the right foot to the right on the inner track of the imaginary circle.

Demi-Volte: Stepping back and to the right so that the left foot is just to the outside of the right foot on the outer track of the imaginary circle.

Circle Right: Lunging the right foot to the right on the inner track of the imaginary circle.

Demi-Volte: Left foot stepping back and to the right on the outer track of the imaginary circle.

Recover: Right foot, retaining the lead foot position, lunges out to the right in to correct placement for the On Guard stance. You should be situated on the set of straight tracks on which you began the drill, facing the direction from which you began the drill. You should be in correct placement without having to readjust your feet in any way; your right foot in the lead position, left foot in lag.

Practice this drill until the pattern becomes automatic. All the actions should become one fluid routine.

Defensive Footwork Drill

Start in a standing position, bring yourself into the On Guard stance. From the On Guard stance, step through the following pattern:

Retreat: Left foot retains the lag foot position.
Pass Back: Right foot moves to the lag foot position.
Retreat: Right foot retains the lag foot position.
Pass Back: Left foot moves to the lag foot position.
Retreat: Left foot retains the lag foot position.
Pass Back: Right foot moves to the lag foot position.
Pass Back: Left foot moves to the lag foot position.
Retreat: Left foot retains the lag foot position.
Retreat: Left foot retains the lag foot position.
Circle Left: Stepping to the left so that the right foot is in the lead position on the inner track of the imaginary circle.
Circle Left: Left foot moves to the lead position on the outer track of the imaginary circle.
Circle Left: Right foot moves to the lead position on the inner track of the imaginary circle.
Circle Left: Left foot moves to the lead position on the outer track of the imaginary circle.
Recover: Pivot on the balls of your feet so that you face the direction from which you have come. You should not have to readjust your feet in any way; you should be in correct placement in the On Guard stance.
Demi-Volte: Left foot stepping back and to the right on the outer track of the imaginary circle.
Circle Right: Lunging the right foot to the right on the inner track of the imaginary circle.
Demi-Volte: Stepping back and to the right so that the left foot is just to the outside of the right foot on the outer track of the imaginary circle.
Circle Right: Lunging the right foot to the right on the inner track of the imaginary circle.
Recover Backward: Bring the right foot back into correct placement. Pivot on the balls of your feet so that you face the direction from which you began the drill. You should not have to readjust your feet in any way, you should be in correct placement, your right foot in the lead position, left foot in lag. You should be situated on the set of straight tracks where you began the drill.

Practice this drill until the pattern becomes automatic. All the actions should become one fluid routine.

Once you have gone through the offensive and defensive drills a few times, you may move on to working in opposition with a partner. This is the joining of the two drills so that you become accustomed to moving offensively and defensively in relation to another actor. In the beginning, try to work with someone who is roughly your height with about the same leg length. Working with someone of your same size helps to maintain correct measure.

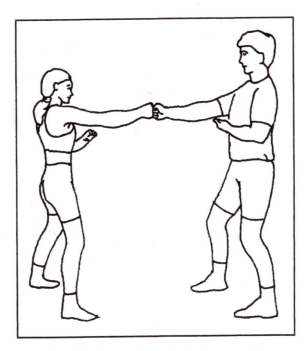

Figure 52. Unarmed distance for the footwork drills.

Fencing Measure

Fencing measure, or "correct distance," is the distance between two fencers that requires extending the sword arm and lunging in order to touch one's partner. In stage combat, we never get close enough to "touch" our partner, except when specifically called for in choreography. There is always a distance of at least six to ten inches from the chest of one combatant to the furthest extension of the sword of the other. Correct distance will be explained in more detail later. For the purposes of the next exercises, we will work with the following measure:

From the point of courtesy and safety, before you ever reach towards your partner, state that you are "checking distance," always letting them know what you are doing. From the On Guard stance, face your partner. Each of you informs the other that you are "checking distance," then extend your sword arm towards one another as if holding the card. Distance yourselves so that with correct placement in the On Guard stance, your arms completely extended, you can just touch the tips of your thumbs. Upon setting this measure, draw your arms back to their original position. You are now in correct distance for executing the offensive/defensive footwork drill (without weapons). (Fig. 52)

Offensive/Defensive Footwork Drill

The following drill, and the offensive and defensive drills, are designed so that they may be repeated without having to readjust your position or stance. Each drill ends in such a way that by executing the opposite drill you travel back to the point you began. This is so that you may concentrate on the drills, your body movement, and relationship to your partner. This should alleviate the constant rearranging of your space in order to execute the movement.

With a partner of roughly your same height and build, assume the On Guard stance, check distance and make any adjustments necessary. With the proper distance set, return to correct placement in the On Guard stance.

Starting in this position, determine who moves on the offensive, and who moves on the defensive. Upon agreeing on these terms, you and your partner step through the offensive and defensive drills together. The offensive initiates the movement, but both offense and defense complete the action at the same time.

When you come to the end of the pattern, you will find that you and your partner have moved to the opposite end of the room. Your placement on the tracks remains the same, but now there is room to trade respective roles. From this position you can begin the pattern again, switching offense and defense. To do this without having to stop the pattern, when offense and defense execute their final recovery, offense and defense switch. At this point, the new offense advances, as called for in the beginning of the offensive drill, and the new defense follows with a retreat. This moves the combatants back down the tracks to where they had begun. This pattern makes it possible to move through the drill as often as desired. You can switch from offense to defense without having to readjust your feet, stance, distance or placement in the room.

As you go through this drill the first couple of times, check your measure every few steps to make sure you retain correct distance during the entire drill. There should only be a fluctuation of about two to three inches during the entire routine. The importance of maintaining correct measure cannot be over-stressed. Once you begin to move with actual swords, and begin to cross steel with your partner, two to three inches will mean much more than just a little distance. Correct measure is an important part of your safety margin.

The perception of correct distance is one of the paramount responsibilities of a stage combatant and is the result of practice and the comprehension of complex interrelationships. Keenness of the eyes, readiness of observation, a sense of tempo, rhythm and space combined with controlled, regulated footwork, are all conditions for good distance perception. Differences in skill levels and body structures of partners make sensing measure and the striving for correct distance more difficult.

More Trouble Shooting

If you find it difficult to maintain correct distance, have trouble moving with a partner, or find yourself paired with a partner who is radically different in body structure, the following exercises may help in the process of sensing measure and correcting distance.

The Tight Rope

For this exercise you need a piece of soft cotton rope. The rope should be no more than a half inch in diameter and four feet in length. Assume the correct On Guard stance, and face off to your partner. Take hold of the ends of the rope with the *manipulators* (thumb and forefinger) of the right hand. Hold the rope as if you were gripping the practice card.

Step back until the rope is tense between the two of you. Remain in a correct On Guard stance. Your right arm is pulled in, bent at the elbow, holding the rope with your palm up.

From this position you and your partner step through the offensive/defensive footwork drill, maintaining the tension on the rope. As before, offensive initiates the action. As soon as the defensive person feels the tension on the rope become relaxed, they should respond with the proper footwork. As both combatants move, tension on the rope should be maintained.

In the circle series of the drill, both combatants must keep their right hands in their original position. This is done in order to maintain correct distance during the entire process of the drill. The tension on the rope constantly ensures the maintenance of correct distance, and helps develop a kinesthetic sense of measure during the changing positions of the bodies.

Hand Over Fist

Assume the correct On Guard stance, and face off to your partner. Check distance by touching thumbs. Instead of bringing your arms back, however, take hold of each other's hand. Lock your fingers around each other's, like thumb wrestlers, in a relaxed but firm grip. (Fig. 53)

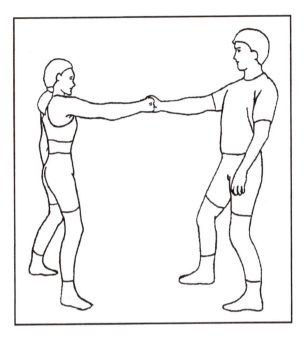

Figure 53. Hand over fist exercise.

From this position, you and your partner step through the offensive/defensive footwork drill, keeping the arms straight, but not locked at the elbow. The offensive initiates the action. As soon as the defensive person senses pressure on their arm, they should respond with the proper footwork. As both combatants move, the arms should be left straight, but relaxed. The grip between the hands constantly ensures the maintenance of correct distance, and helps develop a kinesthetic sense of measure during the changing positions of the bodies. Be sure to keep the hands relaxed: do not white-knuckle your partner.

Once you feel comfortable with this practice, try the drill without holding hands. Place your hands knuckle to knuckle and try to keep them together throughout the entire drill. The hands may come apart during this exercise but the end goal is to maintain a light contact.

Both of these exercises are quite helpful in practicing the circle sequences. The hands are stationed directly over the center of the imaginary circle. The combatants can then walk around the circle as if their hands held a pole at the center.

APPLICATION AND PRACTICE

Practice each of these slowly, following the exercises of application and practice described earlier in this chapter. Once you have accomplished this, and feel confident in your stance and movement, you are ready to move on to the next chapter.

Chapter 4

Getting the Feel of Steel

"The true foundation verily and the true beginning from whence you may learne all things belonging to this art, is the Rapier alone, and from it will I begin." [Saviolo][1]

Before you actually pick up the sword and start "slinging steel," it best to understand the basic safety rules of blade-play. These do not change the rules established in Chapter 1, they add to them. Once steel is added there are a number of new and different problems to consider. You have already explored the first in Chapter 2; selecting a sword. Now, with sword in hand, you are ready to explore the true foundation of the art, the safe handling of a stage weapon.

RULES OF BLADE-PLAY

It is important to remember that a sword is a tool of the theatre, and not a toy. Stage swords, even with dulled blades and blunted tips, are still very real weapons. Because of this, every action with the sword must be completely planned, meticulously rehearsed and ingrained in one's kinesthetic memory before it is inserted in a stage fight. Free sparring and "improvising" with the sword should not be tolerated *at all*. Always, and at all times, handle a stage weapon with care and respect.

When not doing a specific exercise or piece of choreography, put Mom's "scissors rule" into effect: carry it point down and walk don't run. If you should happen to trip or fall and the point is up, or turned in towards you, you may be severely injured. If the point is away from your body, or tucked under your arm, someone around you can wind up with several inches of steel planted somewhere in their anatomy. Even if you are in control, they may trip or fall, or simply back into you; the results are the same. But if the blade is pointed down toward the floor and any of the above things should happen, the sword will be knocked downward into the floor.

During exercises and choreography, be aware of the extra reach the sword gives you. A rapier extends your range by roughly three feet in every direction. Be aware of the greater space necessary for the manipulation of the sword. Keep other actors clear of this area as the combatants move around.

Another basic safety measure is to *never,* whether in offense or defense, let the tip of the blade cross the face or throat of your partner; even when the combatants are out of distance. Any motion

---

[1]Saviolo, p. 12 ff.

of the blade (cut, thrust, slash, stab, etc.) should be directed to a specific, preset, safe target. An unlucky blow in the region of the face or head could be quite serious.

To help build confidence and avoid possible injury, some instructors have their students wear fencing masks or safety goggles during rehearsal. In theory this makes sense, but in practice this generally fosters a false sense of security in the combatants who sooner or later have to remove the masks. It is much better to avoid the possibility of accident and injury through discipline, control and good technique, which, unlike masks, afford real security throughout all performances.

HOW TO HOLD THE RAPIER

In order to first learn how to hold the rapier correctly, take hold of the forte of the blade with your left hand. Your little finger should be resting against the hilt and your thumb toward the middle and foible of the blade. Slowly turn the sword so that the blade is perpendicular to the floor, tip towards the ceiling and hilt towards the floor. Slowly extend the left arm so that it is directly in front of you at roughly chest level. If the blade is not already in this position, turn it so that the false edge faces towards you and the true edge and knuckle bow face away from your body.

Now, reach your right hand forward towards the grip of the sword, as if you were to shake someone's hand. As you are looking at the blade, your thumb should go on the left side of the grip, your fingers on the right. Once inside the guard, guide your index finger (forefinger) above the lower quillon and inside the pas d'âne. Lightly wrap your fingers around the grip, so that you have a firm but relaxed grip. The index finger should be resting on the lower quillon and comfortably wrapped around the ricasso with its pad near the quillon block. Now, place the pad of your thumb onto the false, or back edge of the ricasso, in opposition to the grip of the index finger. Your last three fingers lightly grip the handle, bringing it to bear against the palm of the hand, and very nearly at a right angle to the arm. (Fig. 54) If the thumb in opposition is extremely uncomfortable, try readjusting it on the ricasso, and if all else fails, you may rest it on the index finger. (Fig. 55) Once you are comfortable with the grip, you may release the left hand.

Getting the Feel of Steel

After making sure that there is no other person, prop or obstacle within the range of your extended sword, on all sides, you may try moving the blade about. Get a feel for its weight and balance. Do not slash the sword about, move fluidly and deliberately; become accustomed to the sword.

Take Care of the Sword Hand

While working with a sword it also is a good idea to be aware of your fingernails. Long nails may prevent you from forming a correct grip on a sword and stand a good chance of being torn or broken. For your own comfort they should be cut short and filed smooth before you engage in any rapier play. It is also advisable to wear leather gloves while practicing and performing swordplay. Gloves help protect the hand and help prevent the grip from slipping when the hands begin to sweat. They should be comfortable to the hand, preferably made of soft chamois or doe skin leather. Leather absorbs sweat and as it becomes damp, becoming sticky and improving the hold on the sword. Unless dictated by the choreographer, gloves should always be worn in swordplay.

It's all in the Wrist

Through the movement of the wrist, the thumb and index finger control the movements of the blade. These fingers are often referred to as the manipulators, because where they point, the blade goes. The last three fingers, called the *aids,* help in the management of the blade, keeping the handle snug within the palm of the hand.

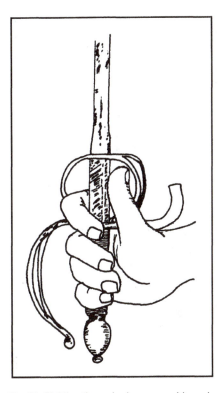

Fig. 54. Holding the rapier in an opposition grip.

Controlling the Point

The aid fingers and the manipulators are the first and primary instruments in controlling the point of the weapon. The technique of controlling the sword with the actions of the fingers is called the *doigté*. The term is used in competitive fencing for the proper use of the thumb and fingers in directing and controlling the energy and precision of one's weapon. The doigté allows the fingers to direct the point in all sorts of movements, circular or lateral, without the stiffening of the arm's muscles. The doigté is the agile turning of the hand on the pivot of the wrist, independent from the arm. The point in fencing should be directed by the principal use of the manipulators (thumb and forefinger), which govern all its movements. The other fingers merely aid by giving the blade steadiness, power, and support in the various actions of blade-play.

Most actors do not naturally have the strength and agility necessary for effectively controlling the point of the weapon. The hand and wrist are generally not exercised in the manner necessary for precision with a sword. Our society has few activities that are similar in style or movement to the mechanics of swordplay. Therefore, exceptional care must be devoted to evolving the strength, agility and dexterity of the hand and wrist because of their obvious significance to safe and effective swordplay. Although exercises for the fingers, hands and arms should be included in your warm-ups, they do not offer development in dexterity and agility with the weapon. The following exercises focus on strengthening the wrist, and its flexibility and ability to fix it at any possible moment.

In working these exercises it is important to remember that the function of each muscle is different. The muscles of your shoulders and the upper arm are capable of exerting great force, whereas those in your forearm serve the purpose of agility. It is important to develop the capabilities

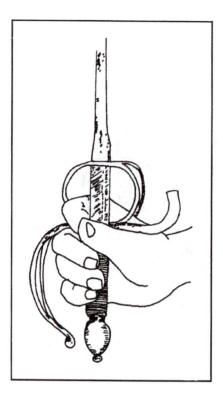

Fig. 55 Holding the rapier in a "relaxed" grip.

of the various muscles to move individually, independent of each other, and yet in necessary harmony. Your shoulders should be loose, relaxed and independent from the actions of the forearm and hand. With the doigté, or hand techniques, the muscles of your forearm are used to support the rapier, while the muscles of your hand control the delicate movements of the fingers and the point of the blade. Your shoulders should hang loosely with your elbow in the most relaxed state possible, even when the arm is extended. The muscles of your hand hold the weapon, your wrist and fingers control it.

Keep a Relaxed But Firm Grip

As you work these exercises, remember to maintain a firm but soft grip. The old rule in fencing is that the handle of the sword is cradled like a small bird: tight enough that it will not fly away, but not so tight that you will crush it. A tight or "Conan" grip is counterproductive to the manipulation of the rapier. The fingers should not be clamped down around the handle. This type of grip tenses the wrist and muscles in the forearm making it difficult to control the weapon. The "Conan" or "battle ax" grip also drains energy out of the sword arm much more quickly than a relaxed grip.

Vertical and Horizontal Blade Movement

The practice of moving the tip of the blade in horizontal and vertical planes seems like a simple enough exercise. There are, however, a few catches to this exercise. The exercise is done with the body in proper placement with your sword arm reached out in front of you, fully extended from the shoulder. Your arm and sword are reached out, horizontal to the floor. The sword arm should not

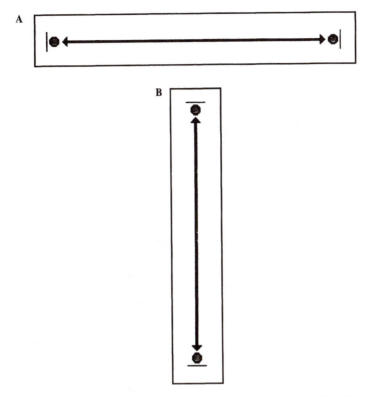

Figure 56. **A-**The horizontal path of the blade; **B-**the vertical path of the blade.

move during this exercise, and the point of the blade must not only travel in a horizontal or vertical plane, but the point must start and stop at a specific point on that plane. The weapon needs to be controlled in its movements, in a specific plane, from point to point at variable speeds. No matter the speed of the blade movement, it must start and stop at a specific point and should be restrained from whipping about. For this exercise try controlling the blade in each plane twenty or thirty times and then switching to the other. (Fig. 56)

In this and the following exercises, your hand may be held with your palm down towards the floor, which is called *pronation;* with your palm up away from the floor, which is called *supination;* or with your palm to the inside with your thumb up, which is called the *vertical* or *middle position of the hand.* These are the three basic positions of the hand in swordplay. Therefore, each exercise is worked in each of these three positions to develop strength and agility with the sword hand. Spend a few minutes on these exercises during your warm-ups each day and the subtlety, strength and freedom of movement in your sword hand will definitely increase. (Fig. 57).

Circles in the Air

Starting in the On Guard stance, reach your sword arm out in front of you until it is fully extended from your shoulder, your arm and sword horizontal to the floor. From this position, try describing a small circle in the air with only the tip of the blade. There is no movement in the arm from the wrist back. The thumb and index finger control the point, the wrist supports the movement.

Starting in pronation, begin to describe a circle in the air. The circle should be roughly the size

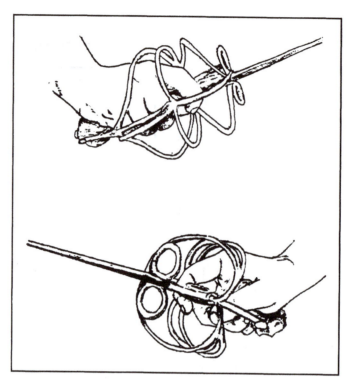

Figure 57. Holding the sword: **A**-Showing the sword hand in pronation.

of a beach ball (two or three feet in diameter). The point of the blade should not waver or slip but should hold strictly to describing the circle. Draw ten or twenty of these circles traveling in a clockwise direction, and then switch to counter-clockwise. Once you have completed this, try the same exercise with a circle the size of a Frisbee, and then an apple, a quarter, a dime. See how precise you can make the command of your weapon's point. (Fig. 58).

The Figure-Eight Drill

As in the Circles in the Air exercise, the Figure-Eight Drill starts in the On Guard stance with your sword arm reached out in front of you, horizontal to the floor. Starting in pronation, describe a figure-eight in the air, with each lobe roughly the size of a beach ball. As before, there should be no movement in the arm from the wrist back. The thumb and index finger steer the point, the wrist supports the movement. (Fig. 59)

Try drawing ten or twenty figure-eights at beach ball size and then work the exercise with smaller circles as in the Circles in the Air exercise. The transfer from clockwise to counter-clockwise should be seamless, without any pauses or displacements of the point. The exercise may also be worked horizontally. The pattern is the number eight laid on its side, or the symbol for infinity, and can be repeated over and over again.

Wrapping the Eights

Wrapping the Eights is an exercise that uses the pattern of the Figure-Eight drill with much larger movements of the blade. The entire arm is involved in this pattern, moving from the shoulder, elbow and wrist. It is called "Wrapping the Eights" because the pattern is carried around on both sides of

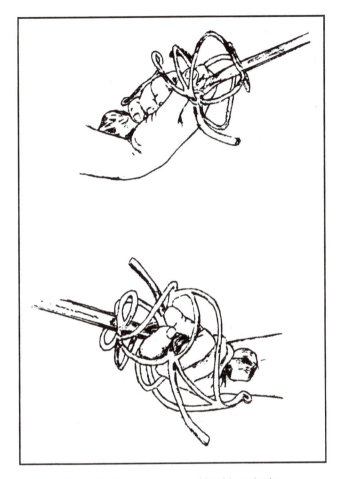

Figure 57. **B-**Showing the sword hand is supination.

the body instead of being drawn in front of the body. Starting with the blade in front of you, turn it towards the floor and carry it back behind you on your right. Moving the blade with the entire arm, compass a large circle with the tip of the sword. Let it travel behind you, up then forward. Your wrist turns clockwise to keep the knuckle bow pointed in the direction of the movement. The circle peaks above your head on the right and begins to descend down in front of you. As the blade descends, guide it across your body to the left, and carry it back behind you by bringing your hand and arm across to your left. Keeping the blade in motion, turn your wrist counter-clockwise to lead with the knuckle bow, compass a large circle up and behind you on the left. The second circle peaks above your head on the left and begins to descend down in front of you across to your right. As the blade drops to the right, carry it back behind you as in the first big circle and repeat the motion. The change from circle to circle takes place directly in front of you as the pattern switches from your right to left and vice versa.

Unlike the Figure-Eight exercise, Wrapping the Eights cannot be done in variable hand placements. Because the action is so large, the hand moves through pronation, supination and middle position throughout the exercise. Because the knuckle bow leads the pattern, however, the most common hand position is the middle/vertical. The knuckle bow is used to lead the action in order to always carry the true edge of the blade forward in the pattern. The pattern of Wrapping the Eights

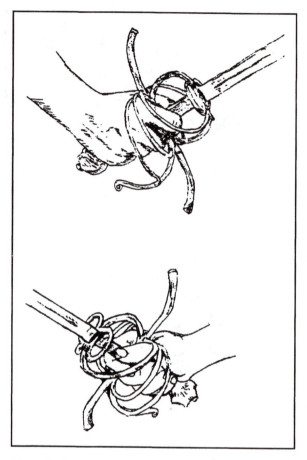

Figure 57. **C**-showing the sword-hand in middle/vertical position.

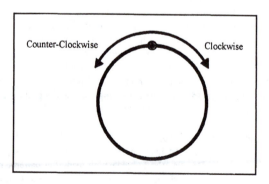

Figure 58. Drawing circles exercise, [clockwise blade path].

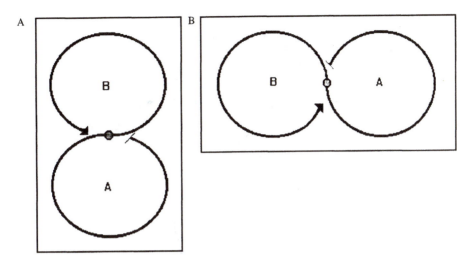

Figure 59. **A**-Figure-eight exercise [vertical]. Circle A is counter-clockwise, circle B is clockwise; **B**-Figure-eight exercise [horizontal]. Circle A is clockwise, circle B is counter-clockwise.

may also be reversed by taking the blade up and back, changing across the body in an ascending instead of descending path of the blade.

The Four-Leaf Clovers

In my experience I have come across two separate fencing exercises entitled the *Four-Leaf Clover*. Both serve roughly the same purpose and differ mostly in the path of the tip in drawing the clover. Both are helpful in developing control of the weapon so I offer them both here. The first seems to be the more traditional pattern, the second being more a variation of the Figure-Eight drill than actually tracing the leaves of the clover. In the first pattern four separate circles are drawn from the blade's same point of origin, differing only in their spatial relationship to one another and in the point the action begins on the circle. One begins from below, the next from its left, the next from above and the final circle from its right. (Fig. 60) Each circle being a leaf on the clover, each leaf being joined by the central placement of the swords point. The exercise may also be executed in a counter-clockwise pattern.

The second four-leaf pattern begins in the same hand and arm placement. The tip of the sword also draws the same four ''leaves,'' only now the blade describes a horizontal and vertical figure-eight. (Fig. 61) The first exercise moves from leaf to leaf around the clover, the second crosses the center point in the manner of the Figure-Eight drill. Both patterns can be repeated without stopping the action of the blade.

There should be no movement in the arm from the wrist back in working either of these patterns. The thumb and index finger steer the point, the wrist supporting the movement. Try drawing ten or twenty clovers at beach ball size and then work the exercise with smaller ''leaves''. The transfer from leaf to leaf, clockwise to counterclockwise, should be seamless. There are no pauses or displacements of the point while describing either of the clovers. The exercises may also be worked in reverse. The first clover is described in a counter-clockwise path, the second working the same pattern only changing clockwise to counter-clockwise and vice versa.

Drawing Diamonds

Along with the horizontal, vertical and circular movements of the blade, there are also diagonal paths of the point. The development of a feel and control of the weapon in all planes of movement

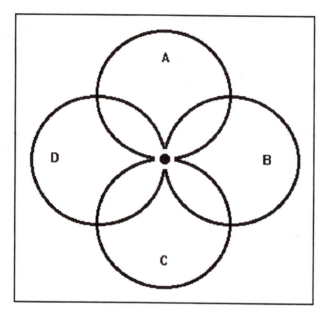

Figure 60. Four-leaf clover exercise [traditional pattern]. Circle A begins at 6 o'clock, circle B begins at 9 o'clock, circle C begins at 12 o'clock, circle D begins at 3 o'clock. The blade path may be executed either clockwise or counter-clockwise.

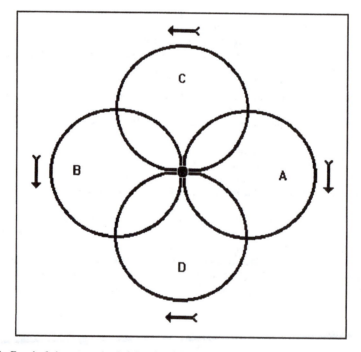

Figure 61. Four-leaf clover exercise [mixing the eights]. A and B are a horizontal figure-eight. C and D are a vertical figure-eight.

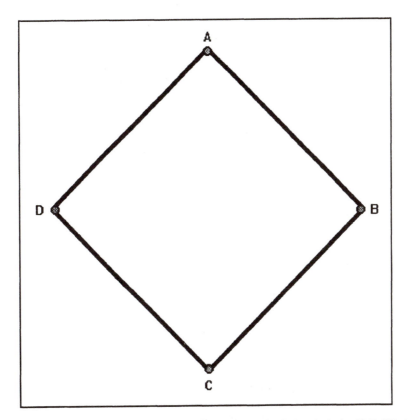

Figure 62. The drawing diamonds exercise. The diamond may be drawn clockwise [A-B-C-D-A] or counterclockwise [A-D-C-B-A].

is essential to grasping the offensive and defensive skills of the sword. The pattern of the diamond allows you to work both ascending and descending movements of the tip toward and away from a central point. (Fig. 62)

For this exercise, start at the top of the diamond and describe the descending diagonal slope to your right. The weapon needs to be controlled in its movement, traveling from point to point in a specific plane. There is no variance. The point travels down and out to the second point of the diamond. It reaches that point and, without any wavering of the blade, redirects its ascension back in toward the third point of the diamond. The third point is situated vertically beneath that of the first. Upon reaching the third point the blade is then guided up and to the left in a path directly opposite to that just drawn. The ascending path terminates at a fourth point situated on the same horizontal plane as the second. From this point the blade begins an inward diagonal ascension back to the original point of the exercise. Thus, describing a diamond in the air with the point of the blade.

No matter the speed or size of these movements, the blade must be able to start and stop at each point on the diamond without any whipping of the blade. This exercise may be done either in a clockwise or counter-clockwise direction. It may also be done in sections like drawing a regular or upside-down "V". In either case, it is important that the exercise focus on controlled ascending and descending diagonal movements of the blade.

The Mark of Zorro

The *mark of Zorro* exercise is based on the trademark "Z" slash of the old swashbuckling hero, Zorro. His mark was a reminder that he could have killed, but instead left a warning. The "Z" of

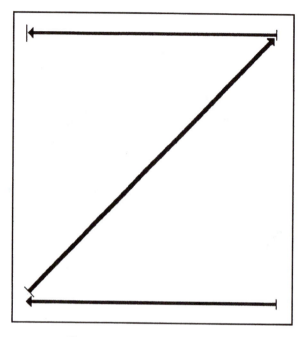

Figure 63. The mark of Zorro exercise.

Zorro was cut into walls, curtains and clothing with the skill and precision of a master swordsman, cutting nothing but what was intended. For this exercise, you will only cut the air, but with the same skill and precision as the famed swashbuckling hero.

The exercise is done with your arm and sword reached out, horizontal to the floor as in the other exercises. The sword arm does not move, and the point of the blade starts at the top of the ''Z'' and cuts the pattern in the air. (Fig. 63) Try leaving the mark of Zorro in a variety of sizes. Always be sure that the ''Z'' is clear and that the point of the blade does not waiver or wander. The mark of Zorro is the mark of an excellent swordsman, and is never sloppy or uncontrolled.

Almost all of these exercises may also be executed with the sword arm relaxed by your side, its forearm directed up and forward from the elbow. The upper arm is at your side, but it does not rest on your body. The activity is still from the wrist, keeping the rest of the arm stationary.

Be Careful—Each Sword is Different

As you work through these exercises and the upcoming techniques of swordplay, get to know your sword, remember which one it is and use it throughout class. When beginning, a slight difference in weight or balance can be a potential danger. In fact, it is best to rehearse with the actual performance weapons from day one, and never change to different weapons without proper rehearsal time.

Further Exercises

If the sword feels heavy in your hand, or if the above exercises tire your hand and wrist easily, you may need further exercises for developing a ''sword arm'' and effective techniques of the doigté. In stage combat, as in fencing, there are a number of physical exercises designed to develop strength and dexterity in the hand and wrist. The following examples are some of the further exercises you can do to help master the sword. They offer splendid preliminary training to develop finger technique, the strengthening of the fingers and the dexterity required for proper hand technique.

Finger Flexing: For this exercise you need one of those "V" shaped spring hand strengtheners. A tennis or racket ball can also serve the purpose if a "grip strengthener" is not available. Place the device in your sword hand and hold it steady with equal pressure from each of your fingers. The device should not touch the palm of your hand, but should be held in place with contact from the pads or first flanges of your fingers. Once in place, press or squeeze the ball or hand strengthener. Do not try to touch your fingers together or to close the "V" of the hand strengthener, but rather to develop a firm and steady grip on the instrument. To do this, practice alternately with the five fingers, with just the manipulators (thumb and index finger), or the thumb and three aid fingers. The rhythm and speed of these "squeezing" exercises are projected to the movement of the point. A slow smooth squeezing movement is more effective. Hard, exaggerated actions of the hand and fingers do not develop the finesse necessary for proper point control. Jerky movements, rather than gentle tension, create uncontrollable acceleration in the point of the weapon. This prevents the stopping of the blade at its proper limit, and also snaps the point away from its intended path or target.

While developing your grip, it is important not to tense up the sword arm and shoulder. With each pressing action, try slowly moving the arm about. Try various degrees of extending, bending and rotating the arm. Its movements should be free and relaxed while the hand maintains a firm grip on the device. The exercise may also be done without the ball or hand strengthener. The squeezing movements of the fingers is done isometrically by flexing the muscles of the hand and fingers. The free and relaxed movement of the arm and shoulder are maintained although the hand and fingers are working.

Finger Waving: The idea of finger waving exercises is to develop strength and agility in the base of the fingers, i.e. the palm. In these exercises the open and closed positions of the hand and fingers are not relaxed, but are flexed with the muscles working. When the hand is open you should feel a stretch through the palm of the hand and down the front of each finger. When the hand is closed it is not balled up into a fist. The pads of the fingers are reached forward toward the inside of the wrist touching the heel of the palm. This should put a focused stretch through the knuckles and along the back of the hand. These exercises are not designed for speed, they are intended to work the muscles of the fingers and hand. Although I am sure there are many forms of finger waving exercises, I offer the three that I have found most useful in the practice of developing strength and dexterity in the hand and fingers for theatrical swordplay.

The first of the three finger waving exercises is called *flying wing.* In the flying wing exercise, hold your hands either out in front of you or out to your sides. Your arms should be straight, parallel to the floor. Your hands starts open with your palm out and fingers up. From this position bend all your fingers forward and down except your thumb. When your fingers reach their maximum stretch, bend your wrist from the upward position down, so that the back of your hand points away from you. Once the peak of the stretch is reached, the pattern is reversed. The wrist is bent back up so that the back of the hand faces you and then the fingers are straightened up again. When the process is repeated over and over again, it looks like a bird waving its wing. Your arms should not move during this exercise. The neck and shoulders should be kept loose and relaxed. Try working this pattern for sixty seconds. The first thirty seconds should be slow and meticulous, the final thirty should be double-timed. The concept of the exercise should be maintained, but the speed of the routine should be increased. There will be a burning in the muscles at the peak of this exercise. In this and the following finger waving exercises it is recommended that you shake out your hands and arms after working the exercise. Relax and release from the shoulders and let the arms and hands swing and shake.

The second of the finger waving exercises is called the *finger wave.* The arms are held out in the same positions as in the flying wing, but this exercise works the hand in supination, pronation and vertical position. In the finger wave you start with an open hand and then bend your fingers forward one after the other except your thumb. Once in the closed position you reverse the process, and straighten them immediately, one after the other. The last finger to close is the first finger to open. Practice starting with both the index and the little finger so that you can do it in either direction. The motion of your fingers should look like an ocean wave. During this exercise your arms should not move and your neck and shoulders should be kept loose and relaxed. Work this pattern in each hand position for sixty seconds. The first thirty seconds of each position should be slow and meticulous, the final thirty should be double-timed.

The final finger waving exercise is called the *finger roll.* Unlike the two prior exercises, the finger roll is executed with the arms relaxed by your side, their elbows bent at ninety degrees, forearms parallel to the floor. The upper arm is at your side, but it does not rest on your body. The hand is open, the palm up. In the finger roll you start by bending your fingers forward one after the other except your thumb. Once in the closed position you reverse the process, and straighten them immediately, one after the other. Unlike the finger wave, however, the first finger to close is the first finger to open in the finger roll. Thus, if the index finger is the first to close the hand, it is also the first to open the hand. The exercise should be worked starting with both the index and little finger. Despite the different arm placement, your arms should not move and your neck and shoulders should remain loose and relaxed. As before, work this pattern for sixty seconds. The first thirty seconds should be slow and meticulous, the final thirty should be double-timed.

The Jug, String & Stick: For this exercise you need an empty one-gallon plastic milk jug (with handle), about three feet of string and a round rod or dowel roughly one-half inch in diameter and two feet in length. Fasten one end of the string to the middle of the rod, and tie the milk jug to the other end. Fill the jug approximately half full of water (this measurement may vary depending on your strength).

The jug, string & stick exercise can be used to strengthen your wrists and your grip. To work your wrists, stand with your feet well apart and hold the bar straight out at shoulder level, holding the rod in your hands. The rod is parallel to the floor and each end is cradled in the palms of both hands. The exercise can be worked both pronated and supinated, but the placement of the hands must match one another. In this position begin turning the rod in your hands and winding the string up around the rod. You should slowly wind the string up until the jug touches the rod, and then unwind it again. Lower the weight by unwinding the cord; and continue winding the cord to lift the weight again in the opposite direction, then lower it again. Work this exercise for three to five minutes each day. As you work the exercise, add a cup or two of water to the jug each week. With this you should also try to increase the number of windings within your set time period. Be sure to try working the exercise both pronated and supinated. (Try alternating the hand placement daily).

To use the jug, string & stick exercise to strengthen your grip hold the rod between your two manipulators with arms relaxed by your side, their elbows bent at ninety degrees, forearms parallel to the floor. Your upper arm is at your side, but it does not rest on your body. The rod is in front of you, parallel to the floor, with each end cradled between your thumb and index finger. The exercise can be worked both pronated and supinated, but the palms do not touch the rod, and the wrists are straight and remain fixed. The jug is raised and lowered as in the above exercise, only here the fingers are used to fix the rod with each twist. This exercise goes more slowly than the wrist exercise, but it works on developing the strength and control in the fingers that actually manipulate the weapon, proving quite beneficial to the theatrical combatant.

RULES IN REVIEW

All rules established in Chapter 1 are applicable to blade-play.

1. Make sure that the weapons you are using are safe and suitable for stage combat.
2. Keep your weapons clean and properly assembled.

3. A stage sword is still a weapon and *must* be treated as one. Handle the sword with care and respect.
4. All movements with the sword *must* be choreographed; there is no improvisational "free play."
5. Unless specifically instructed, *always carry a sword tip down.*
6. A sword adds roughly three feet in all directions to the extension of an actor's arm. Keep this area clear.
7. The tip of the sword should *never* cross or threaten the face or throat; even when the combatants are out of distance.
8. Only discipline, control and good technique build confidence in swordplay.
9. Grip the sword with a firm but relaxed hand.
10. Leather gloves should be worn when practicing or performing swordplay.
11. Do not switch swords without adequate rehearsal time.

Chapter 5

The Guards of the Single Rapier

"Many are the ways of holding the sword, and keeping the arm. Some hold their swords at an angle, and their arm a little forward towards the knee. Others draw their arm back, but have their sword so as to form nearly a straight line from the elbow to the point. Others, again, keep their arm and sword in a straight line from the shoulder." [Salvator Fabris][1]

Being "on guard" is a notion that has greatly changed throughout history. Nowadays, we say a fencer is on guard when they are in a position that enables them to deliver every possible attack and come to every possible parry while expending the least amount of energy. Prior to the seventeenth century, however, the guard was far less comprehensive. Even the term "guard" is relatively new to the science of swordplay. Prior to the Age of Transition, swordsmen used the term *ward* to describe their stances assumed with the sword.[2] A ward was thought of merely as the preliminary stance for an attack, it was not intended to protect any part of the body as much as it was supposed to threaten the enemy.* "The best defense is a good offense," is a strong way to sum up the old philosophy of the ward.

THE GUARD—OFFENSE TO DEFENSE

From its origin as a strictly offensive position to the modern idea, the guard has gone through a variety of transformations. Many of the old wards (and many guards) were impractical, the fancy of a particular master, doing little to advance the science of fence.

Simplifying a Complex Science

The Italian swordsman Camillo Agrippa thought that an effective ward should facilitate every possible combination of attacks. The rapier being held in front of the body, threatening the oppo-

---

[1]Castle, p. 103, Translation from:
—De lo Schermo, overo scienza d'arme, di SALVATOR FABRIS, Capo del Ordine dei sette cuori. Printed by Henrico Waltkirch. 1606.

[2]The English master Joseph Swetnam is the first to use the term "guard" (as reference to the defensive placement of the weapon and body) in an English manuscript on swordplay.

*Both the term ward and guard can be traced to old Germanic origins and mean more "to view" or "to watch/watch over" than postures of offense or defense.

Plate III: The single rapier guard of Terza, as illustrated by Capo Ferro (1610).

nent. Discarding many out-dated and often whimsical wards, (along with their lengthy titles), Agrippa reduced the number of useful wards to four. He gave them simple numerical names: *prima, seconda, terza,* and *quarta.*

Since there was never a guarantee of formality in a fight, being able to draw and to be on guard in one swift and simple action was essential. Agrippa, a man of eminent practicality, efficiently christened the position of a fencer who had just drawn their rapier and turned its point toward their adversary's face, his first ward, "prima." This attitude of practical, efficient guards would later become dominant in the development of swordplay.

di Grassi's Lines of Attack

In 1570 Giacomo di Grassi, a celebrated Italian master, wrote the "*Ragioni di adoprar sicura- mente l'arm*" (reasons to use the sword safely) a work that obtained a great reputation for its simplicity and had the honor of being translated or "Englished by a gentleman" in 1594.[3] His work followed the theory of a very much simpler method than the old schools, much like that of Agrippa.

Giacomo di Grassi was the first to clearly define the different parts of the blade and their properties for both defense and offense. Di Grassi was also the first to consider the question of "lines," dividing them into inside, outside, high and low. He believed that, by placing the armed hand in front of the body in a position approximately equidistant to all parts of the body that could be attacked, those parts above, below, on the right or left of the hand, defined the lines of attack. An attack coming above the hand is in the "high line"; below, in the "low line"; to the right of the hand, in the "outside line"; to the left of the hand, in the "inside line." (Fig. 64)

---

[3]—*Giacomo di Grassi, his true Arte of Defence, plainlie teaching by infallable demonstrations, apt Figures, and perfect Rules the manner and forme how a man, without other Teacher or master may safelie handle all sortes of weapons as well offensive as defensive. With a treatise of Disceit or Falsinge: and with a waie or meane by private industrie to obtaine Strength, Judgment, and Activitie.* First written in Italian by the foresaid Author and Englished by J.G., gentleman. 4°. 1594. London: sold within Temple Barre at the sign of the Hand and Starre.

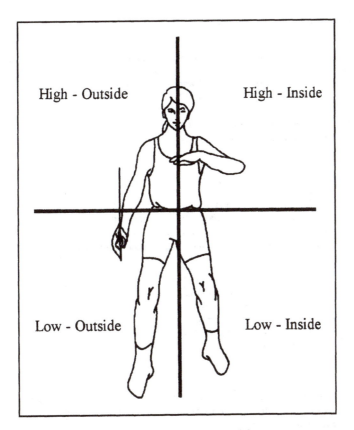

High - Outside

High - Inside

Low - Outside

Low - Inside

Figure 64. The lines of attack and defense.

Closing the Lines

Today a fencer properly assumes a particular guard when the position of their weapon blocks off, or closes, one or more of the lines of attack to their adversary. This placement of the blade should master all attacks in that line unless the adversary somehow displaces the guard. Thus, the expressions high inside (or outside), low outside (or inside) became indispensable parts of later fencing books, modern fencing and stage combat terminology.

In the latter part of the sixteenth century, an appreciation of the rapier's important defensive capabilities was beginning to become apparent. The ward, still thought of mainly as a position to begin an offensive action, was starting to be narrowed down to its simplest forms. Although not specifically intended to "guard," it was being strategically positioned to close certain lines of attack.

A Guard as a Strategic Placement to Launch a Counterattack

In keeping with di Grassi's tendencies towards the end of the sixteenth century, the Italian fencing master Salvator Fabris (1606) promoted the discarding of the cut, and defended the superiority of the thrust. He did however, maintain the old meaning of "ward." The notion of defense was an afterthought. It was secondary to the theory that any attack not met with a counterattack was a mistake.

Fabris' four principal guards are as follows:

> *The first is the position assumed when, the sword being just drawn out of the scabbard, its point is turned towards the adversary, for we think it better that all guards should be formed in that manner; the second is when the hand is slightly lowered; the third, when it is held naturally without being turned, either to one side or the other; the fourth, when it is turned towards the inside,—the left side.*[4]

Fabris directed his fencers to come on guard and assume such a posture with the guard that best suited them. The guard determined the kind of *botta* (attack) to be delivered.

Fabris' "Contra Postura"

His definitions referred only to the position of the rapier, any of which could be assumed with any given *postura*, (position of the body). Fabris believed that against any postura assumed by the opponent, a similar posture taken formed a *contra postura* or *contra guardia*. It is in his definition of the contra postura that the beginning of the modern meaning of "guard" is to be found.

> *"Wishing to form the 'contra postura,'"* says Fabris, *"it is necessary so to place the body and the sword, that without touching the enemy's weapon one should be protected in the straight line which comes from the adversary's point towards the body, and that one should be thus in safety without making any movement whatsoever. In short, that the enemy should not be able to strike the part menaced, but, on the contrary, be obliged—for the purpose of attacking—to carry his sword elsewhere."*[5]

Capo Ferro

Of all the Italian works on fencing, however, none played such a role in fixing the principles of the science as those by Ridollfo Capo Ferro da Cagli (1610). His work went farther in defining the guard than any of its predecessors.

> *"A guard is a posture,"* said Capo Ferro, *"with the arm and the sword extended in a straight line towards the middle of the attackable parts of the adversary, and with the body well established according to its own pace, so as to keep the adversary at a distance, and to strike him should he approach at his peril."*[6]

Believed Terza to be the True Guard

Capo Ferro considered most of Agrippa's guards of little use. Prima and seconda were not equally near all the attackable parts of the body and quarta uncovered too much of the body.[7] He acknowledged terza as the only true guard. This reduced the other guards to special parries, or guards applicable only in certain circumstances.

---

[4]Castle, p. 98. Translated from: De lo Schermo, *overo scienza d'arme, di SALVATOR FABRIS, Capo del Ordine dei sette cuori.* Printed by Henrico Waltkirch. 1606.

[5]Castle, p. 99. Translated from Fabris (1606).

[6]Castle, p. 109. From "Great Simulacrum of the Use of the Sword, by Ridollfo Capo Ferro da Cagli, Master of the most excellent German Nation in the famous City of Sienna." Printed in 1610.

[7]The old definitions of prima and quarta had very flexible meanings. They were referred only to the inside and outside lines and were meant to oppose thrusts in both high and low lines. Capo Ferro's guards, however, were much more defined.

Plate IV: Examples of Fabris' Contra Posturas.

THE HISTORICAL vs. THE THEATRICAL

Not until the eighteenth century did the *colichemarde* and the small sword complete the evolution of the guard to what we now understand.[8] Thus, the guard as a defensive position, completely closing a particular line, is too new an idea to have great historical application to the style of fighting represented in theatrical rapier play. The guards in modern foil literally close a line, preventing *any* successful direct attack to that line. This is not true, however, of the historical and theatrical guards. Foil fencing, as we now understand it, is point work directed only at the opponent's torso. The swordsman of the past, however, defended his entire body from any possible attack, cut or thrust. As such, the combatant was constantly on guard and these guards should be treated as both offensive and defensive positions.

Historically, a wide variety of guard positions may be used, from which offensive or defensive actions can be launched. In practice, you will only be using four defensive positions, and their variations. You will be learning the numerical system originated by Agrippa for the names of the guards. These guards are primarily based on those of Fabris and Capo Ferro, (and to a lesser degree di Grassi and Agrippa). Prima maintains Agrippa's idea of drawing the sword to the first possible guard. All the guards presented are theatrically applicable to the single rapier from the sixteenth through the eighteenth centuries. For reasons of safety and theatricality, alterations have been made to these guards. They have been made larger for the audience, and very specific in their position and target for the safety of the actor.

THE GUARDS OF THE SINGLE RAPIER

In learning the following guards, it is important that you avoid assuming a "fighting" stance and remain in neutral placement. The feet remain shoulder-width apart, the right foot one foot length forward, with a slight bend in the knees. Your knees should not extend out over the toes. Align the head, shoulders, ribs, and hips in their correct relative position with one another. Everything is relaxed. The spine is not straight, but elongated. Center your weight evenly between both legs.

All safety rules apply here. In all the following guards, the tip of the sword must never go above the shoulder level.[9] It must never point toward, or cross the face (even when traveling from one guard to another in any pattern, *ever*). To handle a sword requires rigid discipline and respect. Remember, the point of a sword, even a dull, rounded stage sword, can pierce skin and must never be allowed even the slightest opportunity to do so.

Placing the Unarmed Hand

As you work through the guards, you will find that the position of the unarmed hand may vary from the placement offered in Chapter 3 for the On Guard stance. Although the unarmed hand may move from this position, the hand and arm must still remain in front of the body in such a position that it helps close the lines not specifically closed by the guard of the rapier. Do not remove your hand as you see in modern fencing. In that position the hand is only out of "modern" target. In actual rapier play, however, anything can be attacked, so use your hand to protect what the sword cannot. The position of the left arm will constantly vary according to the ever-shifting position of

---

[8]*Colichemarde, Conichemarde, Konigsmark.* The name "colichemarde" is believed to be a very bad phonetic rendering of its supposed inventor the Swedish Count Konigsmark. In what appears to be a drastic attempt to lighten the blade and bring it to a needle sharp point, the colichemarde was developed around 1680 or 1690. The blade was characteristically wide at the forte, for about eight inches from the hilt and then narrowed quite suddenly. The blade was very light and flexible for the remainder of its length.

[9]In some schools of stage combat the point of the sword is placed above the opponent's hairline when on guard. This will be discussed in Chapter 9, but at this time work as described above—points at armpit level.

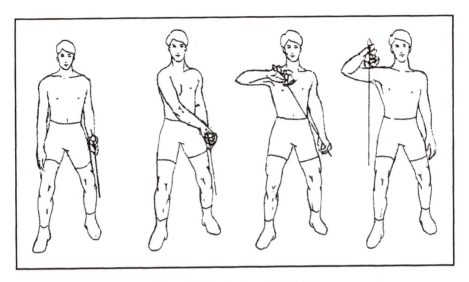

Figure 65. The drawing of the rapier.

your adversary's guard. In upcoming chapters your unarmed hand will be used to beat aside an attacking blade, or even grasp at it in order to gain control of the opposing sword, so keep it in front of you to better facilitate these actions.

No matter the hands placement, there should be about a three-inch gap between your arm and your side. The arm should not rest on your body. If your hand has a tendency to drop to your side, you may begin practicing the guards with your hand resting on your chest as described earlier in Chapter 3. Eventually, however, the hand must be removed and held up on its own accord.

Drawing the Sword

With the sword in its scabbard, reach across the body with the right hand to where the sword is carried on the left hip. Grasp the sword with the right hand (as described in Chapter 4) and hold the scabbard and sword carriage in place with the left hand. If you do not have a sword belt, cradle the forte of the blade in your left hand and let it hang naturally at your side. Do not place the sword through a belt. This puts the hilt too high to effectively be drawn. A sword must hang at arm's length at one's side. Draw the sword from the left hip up and out towards the right shoulder. The sword will travel in a diagonal across the body. The tip of the sword should clear the scabbard with the right hand at roughly shoulder level or just a little above. Now the left hand can release the sword carriage and scabbard. (Fig. 65)

Prima

"This high warde, which also might be called the first, beeinge the very same which every man frameth at the drawing of the sword out of the sheath . . . " [di Grassi][10]

Closing the high outside line, Prima is the first guard that one can safely assume upon drawing the sword. When the tip clears the scabbard (or left hand), allow it to hang, point down. The wrist

---

[10]di Grassi, p. 35.

of the right hand guides the tip from your left hip to your right hip. Do this so that the tip poses no threat to your partner and assures that it will not come anywhere near the face.

Once the tip is on your right side, the right hand continues its motion upward. The tip of the sword and the entire sword assembly is outside your partner's body (on your right, to their left).

When the sword is safely outside your partner's body, raise the tip to the level of your partner's left shoulder. The term "shoulder" means the notch created in the arm where the deltoid and the biceps meet.[11] This junction is roughly a fist and a thumb's length down from the top of the shoulder at roughly armpit level. (Fig. 66)

You are now in Prima. The hilt of the sword is above your head, in front of and outside your body. The knuckle bow is toward the ceiling, with the quillons straight up and down, vertical with the floor. Your knuckles are up and thumb down. Do not angle the sword tip to avoid pointing at your partner. The sword is in one straight line forward from hilt to tip. The tip does not veer in. The blade is parallel to and outside of the imaginary lines on the floor that you and your partner are standing upon. The right arm has a slight crook in it. Do not lock the elbow or let it stick outside the guard. The arm forms a slight curve from the shoulder up and forward.

Seconda

Traveling from Prima to Seconda, the tip of the sword stays at the same point outside your partner's body, at shoulder level. The hilt and arm travel down and forward. Rotate the hilt in a clockwise direction, extending the arm forward from the shoulder. Stop at shoulder level, with the hand pronated, the knuckle bow to the outside, quillons horizontal to the floor. (Fig. 67)

This guard extends straight from the shoulder and is completely horizontal to the floor. The arm is fully extended, but the body remains square to your partner. The right arm has a slight crook in it. Do not lock the elbow or let it stick outside the guard. The arm forms a slight curve from the shoulder out and forward. The tip of the sword always remains outside your partner's body. If you were to walk straight towards your partner without moving your sword, the tip would pass safely outside the body by at least three inches.

Variation A—Low Seconda

Keep the arm at the same level as Seconda proper, but continue rolling the hand in a clockwise position, supinating the hand. The tip of the sword is lowered to the level of your partner's waist. While the blade remains pointing straight forward, it now has a slight downward rake or slope to it. The knuckle bow is to the inside, and the quillons remain horizontal to the floor.

The same guard may be assumed with the hand remaining pronated. However, many combatants find this placement uncomfortable due to the placement of the pommel.

Variation B—High Seconda

From Prima, lower the hilt to the approximate level of your ear. Extend the arm as you did in Seconda proper, turning the hand clockwise until pronated, with the knuckle bow to the outside. The quillons are horizontal with the floor, the tip lowered to the level of your partner's chest. The blade remains pointing straight forward and now has a downward rake to it.

Terza

"This also from the effect is called the base ward or lock: Neither is this name improperlie given by the Professors of this Art, for that it is more strong, sure and commodious then anie other ward, and in the which a man more easilie strike, ward and stand therein with lesse paine." [di Grassi][12]

---

[11]In some schools this target is referred to as "chest," or "chest-level."
[12]di Grassi, p. 38.

Figure 66. The Single Rapier guard of Prima.

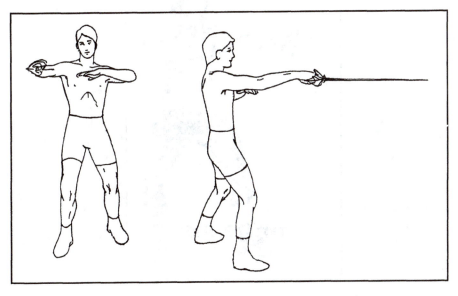

Figure 67. The Single Rapier guard of Seconda.

Plate V: A German ''Rappir'' guard similar to that of Prima (1612).

Plate VI: Seconda Guardia, from the Italian *Scorza* (1803).

Plate VII: The guards of Seconda and Prima according to the Italian fencing master Alfieri (1640). (The lines A and B indicate a separate guard similar to Low Seconda.)

Terza (or as di Grassi called it, the "low ward") is considered the most commodious and practical of the guards. There is less danger of being wounded in the leg, while it theoretically closes the high outside line, (providing suitable, but not complete, protection to the torso and head from attacks to the right side). Like the historical ward, Terza is the attitude most commonly assumed by the theatrical combatant when called "on guard" after drawing the sword.

Assume Terza from Seconda proper by rolling the wrist clockwise and drawing the sword arm in towards you. Keep the tip of the sword at your partner's shoulder level. Your hand and hilt come to rest just above the level of your waist. Your elbow stops outside your body, to the right, roughly two or three inches forward. Your arm is bent at roughly ninety degrees. Without touching your side, your arm should rest outside your frame as if you had a baseball tucked under your armpit. There should be at least a four-inch gap between your elbow and your side. This widening of the arms allows the point of the sword to travel straight forward while avoiding your partner. (Fig. 68)

While in Terza the sword may be held in pronation (palm down), supination (palm up), or vertical/middle position (palm to the inside, towards your body). Any of these are acceptable, and may be used according to arm strength or personal preference. They also may be employed to distinguish characters from one another while in the same guard.

Variation A (Low Terza)

This variation is the same as Terza proper except the tip of the sword is dropped to the level of your partner's belly.

Quarta

The high inside line is that of Quarta from Terza proper, the tip of your sword drops from shoulder level to that of your partner's knees. Keep the action tight so that the right hand does not extend towards your partner. Roll your hand clockwise until supinated. Then move the hilt across your waist line, to the left, keeping the blade pointed down. Stop with your hand about three inches outside your body. The sword is angled down from your waist to your partner's knees.

You may find that, in order for your hand to reach three inches outside your body, you have to turn the right shoulder in a little. This is all right at first, as long as the hips stay square with your

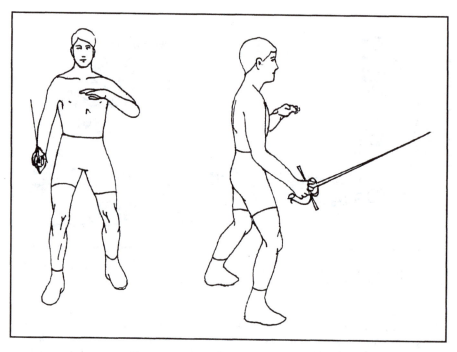

Figure 68. The Single Rapier guard of Terza.

partner and if you don't turn too much to the left. A large rotation to the left exposes your back to your opponent.

Your hand is supinated, with the knuckle bow towards the inside (left). Quillons are horizontal to the floor and your arm is in front of your body, but not resting upon it. The arm is about three inches away from your belly. Once your hand and arm are in place, and your sword is outside your partner's body, you can again raise the tip of your sword to the outside of the notch in your partner's right shoulder, roughly armpit level. (Fig. 69) While in Quarta, the left arm is brought across the torso to the outside (right) of the guard.

Variation A—Low Quarta

Low Quarta is the same as Quarta proper except that you drop the tip of the sword to the level of your partner's belly.

APPLICATION AND PRACTICE

"... when thou hast thy guard it is not enough to know it, but to keep it so long as thou art within reach or danger of thy enemy." [J. Swetnam][13]

---
[13]Swetnam, p. 74.

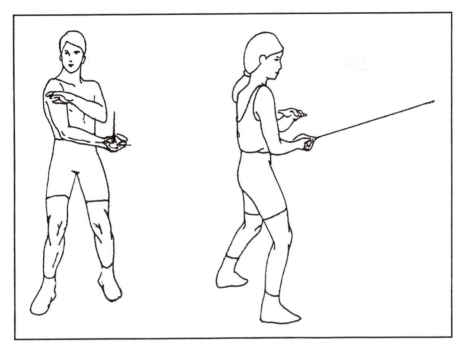

Figure 69. The Single Rapier guard of Quarta.

Plate VIII: The Italian fencing master Vincentio Saviolo's guard with the Single Rapier (1595). Similar to the theatrical guard of Terza.

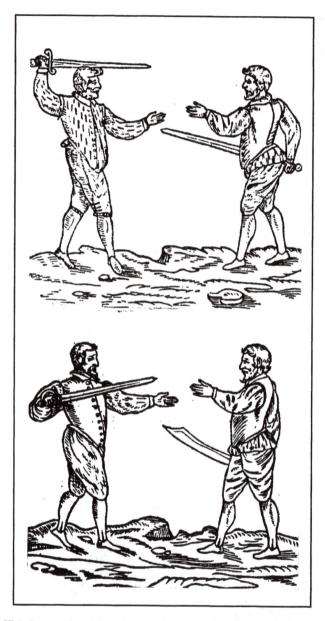

Plate IX: The High, Low and Broad "wards" of di Grassi. The High Ward is similar to Prima, the Low to Terza and the Broad Ward is slightly akin to Seconda, except with the arm drawn back.

Each of the four guards must be practiced until they can be assumed quickly and held correctly. It is best, therefore, to review them slowly. The names of the guards should come to represent in your mind an accurate position of the blade in relation to the body. A good practice drill is to have a friend call the names of the guards, in any order, and see how smoothly you travel to and from each guard.

Do not rush yourself. It takes time for your kinesthetic memory to become effective. Never try to hurry the process. Picture the guard in your head, then slowly move from your present guard to the one called. With time and practice, you will acquire efficiency and speed without errors. Trying to hurry the process only provokes mistakes and mistakes can lead to disaster. Decide where you are going, and then determine how you will most effectively get there. Remember the rules of safety and adhere to them.

After you are comfortable with each guard position and can assume them with some proficiency, try stepping through the footwork drill, (as covered in Chapter 3). When the right leg is forward you may assume either Prima, Seconda or Terza, and when the left leg is forward you can assume Quarta. This is done since one would never advance their leg without some form of protection. As Quarta is the only guard to be assumed on the inside line, it is generally taken when the left leg is forward.

Any guard may be assumed when either foot is forward. The practice of assuming Quarta when the left foot is dominant is much like assuming Terza when coming On Guard. It is a common practice and by no means a steadfast rule. As different characters can come On Guard in different guards, different combatants may assume different guards as they move.

Practice these positions slowly until you become used to moving the lower body and the upper body simultaneously. You may also try the various doigté exercises in each of the guard positions. This may be done both stationary and with accompanied footwork.

CROSS BODY GUARDS

"Let the teacher also put himselfe in the same ward, and hold his Rapier against the middlest of his schollers Rapier, so that the pointe be directlye against the face of his scholler." [Saviolo][14]

Although each of the preceding guards "closes" its line and puts the combatant in a ready position for both offensive and defensive actions, there is another way of assuming them. Because the rapier was in reality held on line, directed "against the face" of the adversary, there was a good possibility that the weapons could cross as the point vied for the best position for offensive and defensive actions. In the sixteenth and early seventeenth century there was some discussion concerning the crossing or joining of the blades, and it was generally discouraged. In swordplay of that period weapons rarely touched, and even then only when one was beaten aside by the other.

Keeping the Blade Free

The common practice of Elizabethan rapier fence was to keep the blade free of the opponent's weapon. Earlier we had the example of Fabris instructing his reader to assume the contra postura *"without touching the enemy's weapon,"* and Capo Ferro speaks against the joining of the blades. In the preceding example from Saviolo's work, however, he does have his teacher *"hold his Rapier against the middlest of his schollers Rapier,"* and di Grassi also talks of joining the blades.[15] He suggests that the "feel" of an opponent's blade might give one important clues as to how they were likely to use it.

---

[14]Saviolo, p. 16.

[15]Vincentio Saviolo's book (*His Practices*) was the first text on swordplay originally written in English. His work represents the basic mode of rapier play in practice while most of Shakespeare's plays were written.

Plate X: English fight master Joseph Swetnam's "Back-Sword" Guard (1617). This guard is similar to the theatrical guard of Terza, and shows the blades joined.

Joining the Blades

The idea of joining blades and feeling the opponent's blade did not readily catch on. It was not until the mid-seventeenth century that the masters of fence found the advantages of joining the blades. Weapons became lighter and faster with the introduction of the transitional rapier, the colichemarde and small sword, making attacks quicker and much more difficult to perceive. By joining the weapons, both combatants could "feel" the blade, sensing their opponent's strengths, weaknesses and movements. This led to the development of the *sentiment de fer* (sensing or feeling of the steel) in the French school of fence, a common practice in blade-play still used in sport fencing today.

The Historical vs. the Theatrical

Although joined blades and cross body guards seem to be the exception rather than the rule, being more a product of the transitional rapier and small sword, they still have their place in theatrical rapier play. Because the old school of stage combat and the early film industry based their swordplay on the principles of modern fencing, "engaged" blades are part of the popular misconception of period fencing. This, along with the variety of actions that accompany such guards, makes them quite adaptable to film and stage, and acceptable to the modern audience.

What is historically accurate is not as important as what the audience believes and what is effective on the stage. It is the job of the actor to understand what a sword fight was, in order to present that understanding, not that reality, to the audience. Today's audiences do not know what a rapier fight was actually like, but they know what they believe. For these reasons, the cross body guards and engaged blades are explored along with the more historical stances. For reasons of safety and theatricality, these guards also have been altered from their "real" placement. Like the four guards presented earlier in this chapter, they have been made larger for the audience, and very specific in their position and target for the safety of the actor.

The Language of Swordplay

Stage combat is a blend of historical swordplay and modern fencing, peppered with varying amounts of artistic license. Because fencing is based on strategy and stage combat on dramatic effectiveness, the exacting definitions of the sport can be confusing. For the purposes of this text, however, certain definitions must be set in order to better present techniques offered later in this book. You have already been exposed to the terminology for the parts of the sword, various forms of footwork, the doigté exercises and the preceding guard positions. Now that you are starting to manipulate the blade, however, you will be presented with a great number of terms and definitions that will make up the language of swordplay. As you begin practicing the cross body guards and the techniques that follow, take a moment to become familiar with the prescribed terminology. By becoming conversant with the language of swordplay, you can more readily grasp the techniques presented later in the book. If, as you progress through the book a certain term seems to have lost its meaning, you can turn to Appendix D in the back of the book and review the definition at a glance in the glossary.

Assuming the Cross Body Guards

The cross body guards may be assumed in two ways, either with the blades joined and *engaged*; or with the blades separated and *free*. When blades are engaged the two swords lightly touch, without shock or force. In order for the swords to be engaged, they must be placed at opposing angles forming an "X" or open "V" with the foibles of the blades. The aim of joining the blades is to guard a specific line with the blade's placement, while slightly opening a line on the opponent by applying a little pressure on their blade. The touching of the blades also tells the combatant when the opponent's blade is at rest and when it is in motion. The action of engaging the blades must be supple, yet firm, the blades joining without knocking one another aside. When the blades are "free," they can be in any guard placement, either cross body or standard, but the blades cannot touch. The guards presented earlier in this chapter are all free, the blades not being joined.

For the purpose of these exercises the following guards are presented as engagements whenever applicable. When the blades are engaged, they meet on the upper third of the blade, foible to foible on the outside of your partner's blade. Not all guards may be engaged. If you wish to work these guards free, simply follow the instructions on the placement of the blades without joining the swords. Both are acceptable guards on stage, although the engagement is more common.

Like the guards discussed before, it is important to maintain a neutral stance and carriage of the body. Unlike the guards discussed before, these guards are best if practiced with a partner. As always, all safety rules apply here. Remember, in all these guards the tip of the sword must never go above the level of your partner's armpits. It must *never* point toward, or cross the face.

SETTING MEASURE

Because these guards are the first "crossing of swords" offered in this text, it is important to understand proper measure. For these exercises, and in most instances in stage combat, the engagement of the blades is executed out of distance, so that you *cannot* actually reach one another. For our purposes there should always be a distance of at least six to ten inches from the chest of one combatant to the furthest extension of the sword of the other.

Checking Distance

From the On Guard stance, face your partner. The combatant with the longer reach sets the measure. That combatant informs the other that they are "checking distance" and then raises their sword

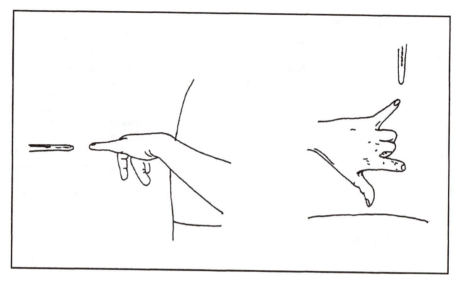

Figure 70. Checking measure (combatants neutral).

outside of the other's body to the level of their chest. The tip of the sword is then *slowly* guided to their partner's center line with the sword arm fully extended in the manner of Seconda. In the practice of guards, the combatant checking distance should be at *full extension* with both combatants' bodies aligned correctly in the proper stance and placement of On Guard. Neither combatant should be reaching forward or leaning back, but should maintain the proper On Guard stance during the execution of the guards. In this position, the tip of the sword should be roughly six to ten inches from the opponent's chest. *The blade should never be any closer than six inches.* (Fig. 70) Upon setting this measure, draw the sword back to your selected guard, without letting the tip cross your partner's throat or face. You are now in correct distance to safely cross swords.

Keeping Measure

Although in these exercises you are not actively moving about the room as in a sword fight, it is still important to set and maintain proper measure with your partner. When working these exercises with footwork, take the time to check distance after every couple of moves to insure that measure is neither gained or lost. The habit of maintaining measure is essential to safe, effective swordplay and must be mastered before you cross steel in offensive and defensive play. Take the time now to develop this skill as it will benefit you greatly as you move on in your training.

Prima Across the Body

Prima Across the Body guards the high outside line. Like standard Prima, it is the first guard that can safely be assumed upon drawing the sword. The movement of the sword hand is the same as standard Prima except the wrist does not guide the tip from your left hip to your right hip. The tip of the sword stays on the left side of your body. The right hand executes the same motion upward, this time with the hilt of the weapon on your right, its blade across your body with the tip to your left. As you raise the right hand to the placement of Prima, you will keep the tip of the sword outside your partner's body, on their right. The tip of the sword is be raised to the level of your partner's right shoulder or armpit. (Fig. 71)

You are now in Prima Across the Body. The hilt of the sword is above your head, in front of and outside your body on your right with the blade in a diagonal line forward across the body to the level of your partner's right shoulder. The blade crosses the imaginary tracks that you and your partner are standing upon, its tip directed at least four inches outside your partner's body.

Prima Across the Body may be engaged against itself, Seconda (Standard and Across), High Seconda (Standard and Across) and standard Prima.

Seconda Across the Body

Traveling from Prima Across the Body to Seconda Across the Body is identical to the mechanics of standard Prima to Seconda. In both cases the tip of the sword stays at the same point during the transition. In this case the point of the blade is across the body at the level of your partner's right shoulder. Your hilt and arm travel down and forward in a clockwise direction, extending the arm forward from the shoulder. (Fig. 72)

The guard is assumed with hand pronated, the knuckle bow to the outside, quillons horizontal to the floor. Seconda Across the Body is be extended from the shoulder across the body in a plane horizontal to the floor. The arm is fully extended with the body remaining square to your partner. Without locking the elbow, the right arm should be fairly straight with the hand placed roughly at mid-torso. The angle of this guard is a line from your right shoulder to your partner's right shoulder. There is no break in the wrist. The tip of the sword always remains outside your partner's body, on their right.

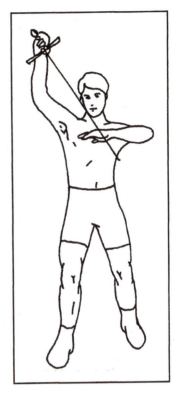

Figure 71. The Single Rapier guard of Prima Across the Body.

Due to the high horizontal plane of Seconda Across the Body, it may only be engaged against Prima (Standard and Across), High Seconda (Standard and Across) and standard Terza.

Variation A—Low Seconda Across the Body

This is done in the same manner as standard Low Seconda with hand supinated and the tip of the sword lowered to the level of your partner's right waist. The blade remains pointed forward and across the body, having a slight downward rake or slope to it. The knuckle bow is to the inside and the quillons remain horizontal to the floor.

Low Seconda Across the Body may be engaged against itself, Seconda (Standard and Across), standard Low Seconda and depending on the slope of the weapons, sometimes against Terza (Standard and Across).

Variation B—High Seconda Across the Body

From Prima Across the Body, the hilt is lowered to the approximate level of your ear with the hand and arm extended as in Seconda Across the Body. The quillons are horizontal with the floor, the tip remaining across the body, now lowered to the level of your partner's right chest.

High Seconda Across the Body may be engaged against itself, Prima (Standard and Across), Seconda (Standard and Across), and standard High Seconda.

Terza Across the Body

Terza, whether Across the Body or Standard, is considered the most practical of the guards. Although standard Terza is the attitude most commonly assumed by the theatrical combatant, Terza Across the Body is used with great effect by many fight directors.

From Seconda Across the Body keep the tip of the sword at the level of your partner's right shoulder and roll the wrist clockwise while drawing the sword arm in towards you. Your hand and arm come to rest in the same placement as standard Terza only with the blade directed across the body with the tip outside your partner's right shoulder. The hand may be held in pronation, supination or vertical/middle position. (Fig. 73)

Terza Across the Body may be engaged against itself, Low Seconda (Standard and Across), standard Terza, and in some instances, although awkward, Quarta Across the Body.

Variation A (Low Terza Across the Body)

This is the same as standard Low Terza, with the tip of the sword dropped to the level of your partner's belly. Only in this particular guard, the tip is on your left, at the level of your partner's right flank.

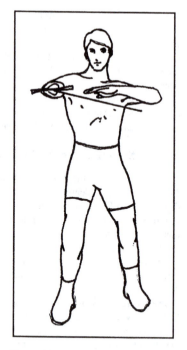

Figure 72. The Single Rapier guard of Seconda Across the Body.

Due to the horizontal placement of Low Terza Across the Body, there are no guards that can effectively join with it. In some instances Low Seconda (Standard and Across) can be used, but the tip of that guard would then need to be dropped below your partner's waist.

Quarta Across the Body

As in all the other guards, Quarta Across the Body is assumed with the same hand placement, differing only in the angle of the blade and the position of its point. From the guard of Terza Across the Body, lower the tip of your sword to the level of your partner's waist. Keep the action tight so that the right hand does not extend towards your partner. Describe a semicircle with the point of your weapon from your partner's right to their left, dropping down to the level of their knees. This is done as you roll your hand into supinated and move the hilt across your waist line, to your left. The point of the weapon moves in the opposite direction of your hand. Stop your hand about three inches outside your body on your left, with the point of the weapon directed across to your right. Your hand is supinated, with the knuckle bow towards the inside, quillons horizontal to the floor. Once your hand and arm are in place, and your sword is outside your partner's body on their left, you can again raise the tip of your sword to the level of your partner's left shoulder. (Fig. 74)

Quarta Across the Body may be engaged against itself and standard Quarta. In rare instances it may also be joined with Terza Across the Body.

Variation A—Low Quarta Across the Body

This is the same as standard Low Quarta, with the tip of the sword dropped to the level of your partner's belly. Only in this particular guard the tip is on your right, at the level of your partner's left flank.

Due to the horizontal placement of Low Quarta Across the Body, there are no guards that can effectively join with it.

CHANGING OF THE GUARDS

Unlike the application and practice of the standard guards where you can move from one guard to another without the interference of the opponent's blade, the addition of the cross body guard makes for more difficult practice. The "J" like movement of the four standard guards can now be obstructed by the point of a cross body guard. Because of this, the practice of changing, joining and freeing of blades becomes a series of removing and replacing the blades known as *changements*. Each type of changement has a particular name and function.

The Changement

In the exercises earlier in this chapter, the free movements of the blade from one guard to another are called *simple changements*. These transfers of guard position move without obstruction, neither over or under, the opposing blade. If, however, the path of the changement is obstructed, the point of the weapon and the blade need to be directed around the opposing guard in order to effectively execute the changing of the guard. This is

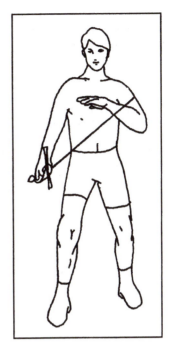

Figure 73. The Single Rapier guard of Terza Across the Body.

where the mechanics of the doigté (Chapter 4) and the practice of manipulating the point come into play.

Changing Under the Opponent's Blade

In both the standard and cross guards of Prima, Seconda and Terza, the point of the weapon stays in place, either at your partner's right or left shoulder. Only in the changement to Quarta (Standard and Across) does the point of the weapon move. The combination of the two guard styles presents the problem of not only moving the guard hand, but the point of the weapon as well. The movement of the tip of the weapon is called *passing the point,* and can be performed in two ways. The first passes the point under the opposing guard, like the action from Terza to Quarta or vice versa. The second passes the point above the opposing guard, and will be discussed later.

There are two ways of effectively passing the point under the opposing guard, either from a free guard or an engagement. The mechanics of the two actions are identical, varying only in the starting postion. To pass the point under the hilt of an opposing weapon from a free guard is called a *change under* and from an engaged guard, a *disengage* or *disengagement.*

The action of passing the point under the opposing guard, although still an intricate part of sport fencing today, has a long history in swordplay. It is speculated in the *Pallas Armata: The Gentleman's Armorie* (1639) that Agrippa developed the movement of the disengage in the mid-sixteenth century. The author of the Armata puts forth that it developed from studying cock-fighting.[16]

[16]G.A., *Pallas Armata: The Gentleman's Armorie.* The Crane in St. Paul's Churchyard: John Williams, bookseller, 1659(39?). From Aylward, *English Masters,* p. 88.

Whether this is true or not, the action of passing the point under the opposing guard (free or engaged) was a common occurrence is swordplay and appeared in most treatises on the topic.

> Saviolo in 1595 tells his student to *"turne his Rapier hand, that the pointe bee conveighed under his masters weapon, which being done, promptly and readily his point will be towards the belly of his master"* [Saviolo][17]

In the manual of English fight master Joseph Swetnam, he clearly describes the action of a disengage.

> *"so soon as you have joyned, turne the heele of your hand upward, and your point downeward, and so bring your point, compassing under your enemies right elbow; and then with the strength of the thumb turne it into his breast."*[18]

But it was not until Fabris that the action and all its intricacies were fully developed. He absolutely defined the rules and actions of engagement and disengagement. He developed a variety of disengages to fulfill the variables of point work and the ever-changing contra postura that are still practiced today.

The Change Under and Disengage

Whether blades are engaged or free, if a line is closed and your opponent is covered in their contra postura, your blade must be moved before you can effectively launch

Figure 74. The Single Rapier guard of Quarta Across the Body.

an attack. The action of passing the point under the opposing guard, known as the "change under and disengage," was called the *cavatione* by Fabris. Historically this was probably a removing of the blade backward from the guard as the term "cavatione" literally means "drawing away," and more than likely was applied to the action of the sword. For the purposes of theatrical swordplay, however, the change under and disengage are executed from the hand and wrist with a semicircular motion of the point. The rest of the movement of the arm and weapon do not vary from the mechanics dictated earlier in this chapter.

Because the mechanics of the change under and disengage are identical save for the engagement of the blades at the beginning of the action, the following techniques are presented from blade engagement. Using the circular doigté techniques of the four-leaf clover and figure-eight drills from Chapter 4, the point is passed under the opposing guard. In the change under, the point is always passed in a semicircular path, either from shoulder to shoulder or waist to waist. This path may also be a large "U" or "J" shape when the point passes from opposite shoulder to waist. (Fig. 75)

In actual fencing and competitive swordplay, the point of the weapon would be carried under the opposing weapon and directed at the opponent's body, generally poised to launch an attack. This makes the change one action, from the guarded placement to free position for attack. At this level of stage combat, however, the blade is not to be directed at one's partner, and only to either side. For these safety reasons, there are two forms of passing the point under the blade. The change around the hilt of the opponent's rapier, remaining on the same side of the body, and the change under the hilt that carries the point to the opposite side of the body. In both instances the point of

---

[17]Saviolo, p. 28.
[18]Swetnam, pp. 121–122.

Plate XI: Joining the Rapiers. From Saviolo (1595).

the weapon completes its action outside your partner's body. The point of the weapon never crosses your partner's face or throat and is never directed towards their body. Your body remains in correct placement, the point of the weapon is lowered down, below the opposing guard with movement from the hand and wrist. The sword arm does not aid in the passing of the point and only moves when changing guard position.

You may practice passing the point below in each of the four guard positions, their variations, both standard and across. In each position, come on guard and work both the circular and semi-circular passage of the point. Starting in Prima Standard, trace a semicircle with the point traveling low and across the body coming back up on the outside of your partner's standard guard of Prima engaging the blades. The placement of the sword arm does not change; the blade, however, is now across the body with the point outside your partner's body at the level of their right shoulder. You are in Prima Across the Body. From this position reverse the action and disengage back to standard Prima. Repeat this action several times.

Once you have passed the point across the body, under the tip of the opposing guard several times, try passing it under the guard on the same side of the body. This action can only be executed from guard positions where the blades can be engaged. If both combatants are in standard Prima, there is no blade to pass under on that side of the body and therefore no changement. The blades need not be engaged for this exercise, but they must be in a placement where they can be joined.

The action of passing the point under the blade to the same side of the body is smaller than the semicircle that passes across the body. It is a circle or "U" shape no longer than the size of a Frisbee. The point of the sword passes under the opposing sword from one side to the other. The tip of the sword must move in a clear and smooth path ending at the same level it began, outside the

Plate XII: Various Contra Posturas of Fabris, showing free and engaged guards (1606).

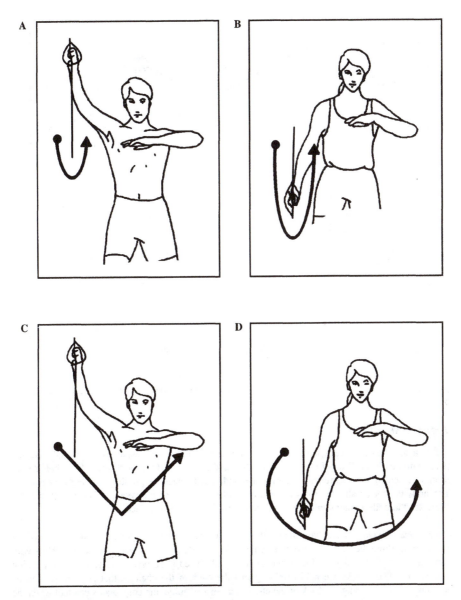

Figure 75. The change under
A-Passing the point under the opposing guard of Prima, to the same side of the body; **B**-Passing the point under the opposing guard of Terza, to the same side of the body; **C**-Passing the point under the opposing guard of Prima, across the body; **D**-Passing the point under the opposing guard of Terza, across the body.

opponent's body but on the opposite side of their weapon. This exercise should be repeated several times in each guard until control and proficiency are gained.

The only time in these exercises where the hand should move is in the cross body passing of the point between standard Seconda and Seconda Across, and vice versa. Here the arm moves from the line forward in the standard guard to the line across the body in Seconda Across. The passing of the

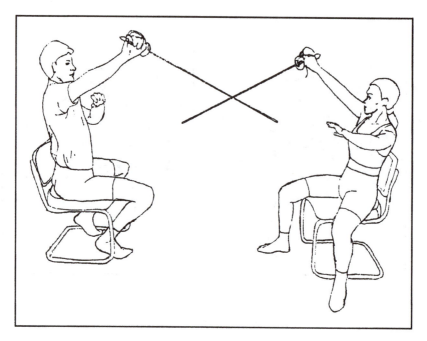

Figure 76. Sitting This One Out exercise.

point is still controlled by the hand and wrist, the arm only moves to complement the line of the blade.

Trouble Shooting

It is a common practice when first working the change under and disengage to try and steer the point with the arm and torso instead of just the hand and wrist. This habit, aside from being poor mechanics, changes measure and can bring the blade inside measure, possibly striking your partner. The body cannot be allowed to sway or move with the point of the weapon. During all of these exercises the body remains in correct placement in the On Guard stance.

Sitting This One Out: If you have the habit of turning or leaning while practicing the passing of the point, try working the exercise seated in a chair. (Fig. 76) Both combatants are placed in chairs with straight backs. The chairs are facing one another and placed at correct measure for the practicing combatants. Their backs are held firmly against the back of the chair so that any release can be instantly detected. Using the back of the chair as a sensory guide, the combatants can feel when the torso reaches or leans forward during the exercise. This helps keep safe measure and shift focus to the management of the point with the hand and wrist and not the arm and torso.

Sitting in the chair can also prove useful if you find your shoulders stiffening during the exercises. Focus is sometimes placed so much on not moving the arm and torso that it can cause extra tension in the neck and shoulders. By sitting in the chair you can relax and place your focus on the movement of the hand and wrist instead of on maintaining correct stance and placement. The sitting position requires less work because you do not need to support your body and may therefore relax the muscles of the shoulders and the trunk.

Wall Bound: An alternative to sitting in the chair is to have the initiator of the changements work with their back up against a wall. As in the chair exercise, the combatant's back is held firmly against the wall so that any release can be instantly detected. This helps maintain measure and places the combatant's focus on the management of the point with the hand and wrist and not the arm and torso.

Changing Over the Opponent's Blade

Like the passing of the point under the opposing blade, there are also two ways of effectively passing the point over the opposing guard. As before, the mechanics of the two actions are identical, varying only in their starting from a free guard or an engagement. To pass the point over an opposing weapon from a free guard is called a *change over* and from an engaged guard, a *coupé*. The term "coupé" literally means "cut over," and the English phrase is often used in place of the French term. However, the fencing term coupé will be used for this action, as the term "cut over" is reserved for another technique to be presented later in the book.

The Change Over and Coupé

Unlike passing the point under, the change over and coupé are executed from the hand, wrist and forearm in the pattern of a regular or inverted "U" or "V" with the point. The size and scope of the movement are dictated by the guard position the point is passed from and over. The body remains removed from the action, the passing of the point over the blade taking place from the elbow down.

Because the mechanics of the change over and coupé vary only in blade placement at the beginning of the action, the following techniques are presented from a free guard. This is done because there are two different ways of executing a coupé from the engaged position. The first is to free the point and to follow the mechanics of the change over and the second is to remain engaged as you travel up the blade. If contact is maintained during the coupé, it is known as an *engaged coupé*, and is characterized by a sliding or scraping noise as the engaged blades quickly rub against one another. The engagement, however, is only maintained until the blade clears the point of the opposing blade, and then it is freely brought to rest at its intended target.

Using the mechanics of the circular and diamond patterns from the doigté techniques, begin passing the point over the opposing blade. As mentioned earlier, the point is always passed in the pattern of a regular or inverted "U" or "V." Although traveling up, over the opposing blade, the point of the weapon is never to cross your partner's face or throat. The "U" or "V" must always take the blade in a path outside the body and above the head. The point must be either passed directly over the tip of the opponent's rapier, returning to the same side of the body, or over the opponent's sword and head to the opposite side of their body. In both instances the point of the weapon completes its action outside your partner's body. Your body remains in correct placement, the point of the weapon is over the opposing blade with movement from the hand, wrist and forearm. The upper arm does not aid in the passing of the point and only moves when changing guard position.

The change over is achieved by stabilizing the point with pressure from the thumb and index finger, lifting the point with a vertical motion of the wrist, drawing back the sword hand toward the shoulder until the tip clears the opponent's point. Here it is either lowered to the same point of origin, except on the opposite side of their blade; or it is carried over the head and lowered to the appropriate guard on the opposite side of the body. If the engaged coupé is being executed, the blades remain engaged until the foible of your blade quits the point of the opposing blade. In all three cases, after the point has bypassed the opponent's blade (and body), it must immediately be lowered to its next placement. (Fig. 77)

You may practice the action of passing the point above in each of the four guard positions, their variations, both standard and across. Like the exercises for passing under the blade, come on guard in each position and work the mechanics of same side and cross body changements. Starting in Prima Standard, draw an inverted "V" up over your partner's head, down to the outside of their standard guard of Prima. Once there, you may engage the blades. The forearm is only drawn back far enough for your point to effectively clear the opposing weapon, and to safely maneuver around

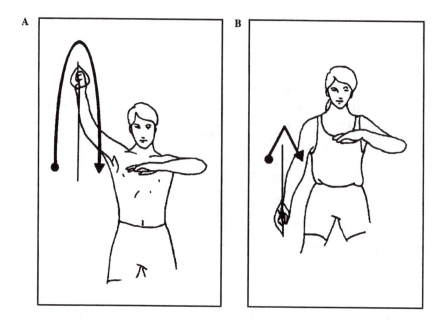

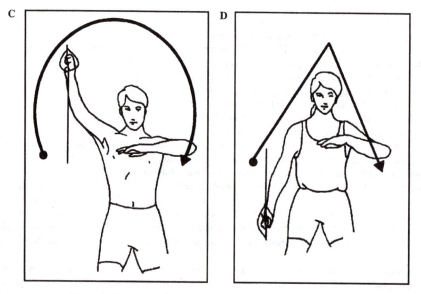

Figure 77. The change over
A-Passing the point over the opposing guard of Prima, to the same side of the body; **B**-Passing the point over the opposing guard of Terza, to the same side of the body; **C**-Passing the point over the opposing guard of Prima, across the body; **D**-Passing the point over the opposing guard of Terza, across the body.

your partner's head. It is not a gigantic action, merely one of necessity. The size of the action does, of course, vary from one combatant to another. What is important is that the action is efficient and that it is executed from the elbow down.

Upon completing the change from standard to cross guard, the arm should return to its normal placement with the blade now across the body with the point outside your partner's body at the level of their right shoulder. From this position reverse the action and change over back to standard Prima. Repeat this action several times and then move on through all the guard positions. Remember, not all guards may be engaged or passed over. If there is no opposing blade in the transition from one guard to another, the action is a simple changement.

After you have worked on passing the point across the body over the tip of the opposing sword, try the same exercise again, only this time passing it over the blade on the same side of the body. This action can only be executed from guard positions where the blade can be engaged. If both combatants are in standard Prima, there is no blade to pass over on that side of the body and therefore no changement.

The process of passing the point over the opposing blade, from one side of the weapon to the other changes little from the action of carrying the point across the body. The largest variance is in the width of the opening on the inverted "U" or "V." Because this action must clear the point of the opposing weapon the peak of the "U" or "V" remains the same, except that the point of the sword is immediately lowered on the opposite side of the opposing weapon. The tip of the sword must move up and over in a clear and smooth path, ending at the same level it began, outside the opponent's body but on the opposite side of the weapon. This exercise should be repeated several times in each of the suitable guards until control and proficiency are gained.

Clarification for Future Practice

At this time it is important to establish common definitions of the disengage and the coupé is that "it is what you are doing and not how you are doing it." In the purest form, a disengage travels *around the guard or hilt* of the opposing weapon and a coupé *passes over the tip of the opposing blade*. Although this seems similar to what we have already learned, there is a variance. If both combatants are guarded in Prima (Standard or Across), the upward action that is characteristic of a change over is termed a disengage because it travels around the hilt of the weapon rather than over its point (see Figs. 75 b & d, 77 a & c). From the same guard, the downward passage of the point that is characteristic of a change under is termed a coupé because it travels around the point of the opposing weapon and not its hilt (see Figs. 75 a & c, 77 b & d). What you are doing is either traveling around the hilt or over the point. That is what determines the term for the action, not the movement above or below. This process is applied to all engagements of the blades. If the passing of the point travels either over or under the hilt of the opposing weapon it is termed a disengage. If the passing of the point travels either above or below the point of the opposing blade it is termed a coupé.

These terms, once again, are only applied to blades that are engaged. If the blades are free and the changement travels up and over, either hilt or point, it is still a change over, as the blade is taken over the opposing weapon. If a free blade travels under the hilt or point of the opposing weapon it is still a change under, as the blade is taken under the opposing weapon. The difference is in whether the blades are engaged or free. Although these changes may be confusing at first, understanding them will prove beneficial in later chapters and as you study and work with other fight choreographers.

Application and Practice

It is important that you work through each of the guard positions and get comfortable with the passing of the point in all the variations. The changements need to be practiced in each of the guard positions. Now that you are working with a partner you must review the actions slowly. All the new guard positions and the different ways of passing the point must come to represent specific positions and movements of the blade in relation to you and your partner's body.

A good exercise in reviewing the various guards, engagements and passages of the point is to have one combatant assume a single guard, and for the other to work their way around it in as many ways as possible. For the purpose of this exercise, each changement can be completed free or with an engagement. Remember, however, not every guard can engage another. In order for the swords to join, they must be placed at opposing angles forming an "X" or open "V" with the upper third of the blade. The swords must cross and touch in order for them to be engaged. The engagement takes place on the foibles of the weapons, on the outside of the blade.

Engagements in Review

If a standard guard engages an across guard, the cross is formed on the outside of the body where the tip is shown. For example, if a standard Terza (tip directed to your partner's left shoulder) engages Seconda Across (tip directed to your partner's right shoulder), the cross of the blades is outside Terza's right shoulder and Seconda's left. The line of the blades forces the cross outside the body. If two across guards are engaged, the cross of the blade is at roughly the center line of the combatants. Because the blades are directed across the body, the foibles of the weapons can only meet between the bodies. This presents a defensive wall not only outside, but in front of the combatant as well.

Although there are a wide variety of possible engagements between guards of the single rapier, the most common on stage are the joining of like across guards: Prima to Prima, Terza to Terza and so on. Take a few minutes and explore what other guards can be joined. It is important to note that to effectively reach these engagements the angles of the blades may need to be altered slightly. This is due in part to the height variance and difference in reach between the combatants. The readjustments of the blade may be either up or down, but *never* at the body, above the shoulders, or toward the face.

Now go through the exercise. One combatant assumes a fixed guard and the other tries the variable contra posturas with the rapier. Take the time to develop an effective kinesthetic memory. There are a great many more variables than the simple changements practiced earlier in this chapter. Efficiency and speed can only be accomplished with time and practice. Now that you are working with a partner you must be aware of your blade and their body at all times. Moving slowly allows you the time to decide where you are going, and how you can most effectively get there. Remember the rules of safety and adhere to them.

If you have trouble moving your torso or arm in this exercise, or if your shoulders stiffen and tense up, you may try "Sitting This One Out." The exercise offered earlier in this chapter is quite helpful in developing a sense of when the body leans or turns, keeping safe measure. It may also be used to shift focus solely to the upper body, relaxing the On Guard stance. Do not shift to your normal "standing" posture during these exercises. You must either remain in the On Guard stance, or sit down. Do not develop the bad habit of losing correct placement as you work the weapon. It will seriously affect your work in later chapters.

Taking it Moving

After you have worked this exercise for a while and are comfortable with all the guard positions, transitions and passages of the point, try adding footwork to the exercise. The objective here is to maintain correct distance and proper control of the blade. This exercise is done in the same manner as the one before only this time both combatants add footwork.

Measure is maintained in the following manner: The combatants begin at correct distance; the initiator of the changement moves their blade first; the combatant in the fixed guard passes back or retreats as they perceive the movement of the blade; the initiator only moves forward with a pass or advance after they see their partner moving back. This process is referred to as *Action-Reaction-Action,* and is a fundamental part of all stage combat and is explained in greater detail later in the book. For right now it is simply applied to this exercise. The changement is the first action, followed by the perception of the action and the second combatant's reaction of footwork, ending with the first combatant's final action of an advance or pass forward.

In this exercise any guard may be assumed when either foot is forward. The common practice of assuming Quarta with the left foot dominant is by no means a steadfast rule. You should, however, try working passes, advances and retreats with both feet forward in this exercise. Don't get locked into moving only with the right foot forward.

Variations and Modifications

Passing of the Point Vertically

In the preceding changements the passing of the point was executed in lateral planes moving from side to side, whether changing actual sides of the body or sides of the blade. The point, however, may also be passed to an open line by moving either up or down. This passing of the point is called a *vertical changement* when the blades are free, and a *half disengage* when the blades are joined. The action was first introduced by Fabris and was called the *meggia cavatione*, literally meaning "half disengage."

> "We call meggia cavatione one in which the sword does not complete its passage from one side to another, but remains under the opponent's blade." [Fabris][19]

The action may now be made from the high to low line or vice versa. The term *mezza cavazione*, however, is still used by the Italian school of fencing for an attack on a half disengagement from a high to a low line on the same side of the opponent's body.

In theatrical swordplay the vertical passage of the point is actually a slightly curved line that moves out from its point of origin in a shallow arc that rounds back into its point of completion. (Fig. 78) Both the vertical changement and the half disengage travel in this path from the high to low line on the same side of the body, and vice versa. This movement is like a change from standard Quarta to standard Low Quarta, standard Low Quarta to Prima Across, standard Low Seconda to standard Terza and so on. The placement of the hand may switch sides of the body, but the tip can only be raised and lowered on the same side of the body. The action must also bring the point around the guard of the opposing weapon for it to be a vertical changement or half disengage. If the action is not a deliberate manipulation around an opposing blade, it is merely a Simple Changement.

Regaining the Contra Postura

Up until this point we have had only one combatant changing their guards while the other remained in a fixed position. In swordplay this movement is generally to one combatant's advantage as they seek the best placement of their weapon for both offensive and defensive action. Changements may, however, be used against changements in order to regain equilibrium, or even the upper hand in guarding the body.

The Counter Changement

A *counter changement* is a responsive action to a changement where a similar changement is executed to bring the opposing blade back to its original placement. In other words, if one combatant executes a disengage, the second combatant instantly responds with a disengage of their own that brings the first combatant's blade full circle back to its point of origin. This action is used quite often in fencing today, but the counter disengage or *contra cavatione* was a common practice in the

---

[19]Fabris, from Castle, p. 101.

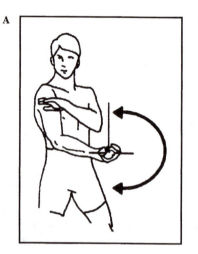 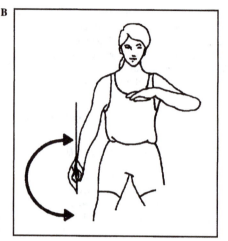

Figure 78. Passing the point vertically
A-The half disengage around Quarta; **B**-The half disengage around Terza.

mid-seventeenth century, and possibly earlier. In his explanation of engagements and disengages, Fabris spells out the specifics of this action.

> *"A contra cavatione is that which can be done, during the time that the enemy disengages, by disengaging yourself, so that he shall find himself situated as before. . . ."* [Fabris][20]

Of course today the action may as easily be a coupé as a disengage. In the response to a changement, the general rule is that what can be achieved by disengagement can also be achieved by coupé. The coupé can therefore be considered a kind of disengagement because in both cases the blade and the point quits one line to move to another.

For the purposes of stage combat, the counter changement is executed when the initial changement is near completion. This is done so the audience can see the action. As soon as the first changement is near completion, the counter changement is executed around the opposing blade, bringing it back to the starting line. The opposing blade is returned to its point of origin because it changed sides in its initial action and the counter brought it back again.

Try this exercise first with the complementary cross body guards (Prima, High Seconda, Low Seconda, Terza and Quarta). Let the initial disengage or coupé carry the point to the opposite side of the sword, on the same side of the body. The counter carries the blade back to its point of origin.

The blades quit one another at the initial changement and re-engage with the counter changement. The re-engagement is not an offensive action that strikes or beats the opposing blade. It is a light joining of the blades, applying only enough pressure to steer the opposing blade back to its original line. Once re-engaged, the blades remain joined until the completion of the action. There is no hard resistance between the combatant's blades in the re-engagement and movement back to the original line. You both know where it is going and should work together to get it there safely.

Once you have worked the complementary cross body guards you may try the counter changements with other guard placements. In the execution of counter changement the guards chosen must

---

[20]Fabris, from Castle p. 101.

be engaged so that the re-engagement brings the blades back to the original line. Each time the first changement is offered, the combatant who presented the fixed guard can now execute a counter changement.

If in this exercise the initial changement moves the combatant's hand to a new guard position, it is the blade and point that are returned to the original line and not the hilt of the weapon. Be extra careful in this exercise as the counter changement may drag the point of the opposing blade across the face. In this case the combatant who initiated the original changement must help steer their point either up or down to make sure it travels safely across the body.

Like the changements offered earlier, the counter changement may also be practiced with footwork. This is done in the same manner as before, with both combatants adding footwork. Measure must be maintained during this exercise using the process of Action-Reaction-Action. The initial changement is the first action, followed by the second combatant's reaction of a pass back or retreat and a counter changement, ending with the first combatant's final action of an advance or pass forward. The reaction of the pass back or retreat and the counter changement are executed simultaneously, as soon as the initial changement is perceived.

Double Changement

As the counter changement managed to put the opposing blade back in line, the *double changement* allows the combatant who initiated the action to continue with their original intent. This is done by making a second disengage or coupé off of the opponent's counter changement. This action, like the counter disengage, is still used in competitive fencing but finds its roots in seventeenth century rapier play. The action was originally called a *ricavatione* by Fabris, and was used then as it is today, as a second disengagement to deceive the counter disengage of the opponent.

> *"A ricavatione is what you may do after the first cavatione, and whilst your adversary makes a contra cavatione. . . ."* [Fabris][21]

Like the counter changement, the double changement may be either a coupé or a disengage. It begins like the counter changement, only as soon as the blades are re-engaged by the opponent's counter, the second changement is initiated. This quits the opponent's blade and takes the blade to its intended placement.

As in the exercise for the counter changement, start practicing the double changement from the complementary cross body guards (Prima, High Seconda, Low Seconda, Terza and Quarta). Let the initial disengage or coupé carry the point to the opposite side of the sword, on the same side of the body. When the counter changement re-engages the blade, execute the second changement across the body to the standard guard. The blades should quit one another at the initial changement and re-engage with the counter changement. The second changement quits the opposing blade once they make contact. The blades do not knock together on the reengagement, but like that of the counter changement, this contact is a light joining of the blades.

After working the double changements in the complementary cross body guards, you may try them with other guard placements. In the execution of this exercise the blades must be engaged in both the initial guard placement and in the counter changement. Be aware of your points in these exercises as they can move quickly around one another. At no time is safety sacrificed for speed. Control and accuracy are the key to handling a weapon safely on stage and they only come from practice and concentration.

Footwork may also be added to this exercise. This is done in the same manner as before, using the process of Action-Reaction-Action. The initial changement is the first action, followed by the second combatant's reaction of a pass back or retreat and a counter changement, ending with the first combatant's final action of a second changement accompanied by an advance or pass forward. The

---

[21]Fabris, from Castle, p. 101.

final action of footwork and second changement are executed simultaneously, as soon as the counter changement engages the blade. Be sure to check measure after every two or three movements to make sure you are not closing distance. Safe distance must be maintained in all these exercises.

Refusing the Blade

The last two changements deal specifically with engaged blades. But as we discussed earlier not all Elizabethan schools of fence practiced the joining of blades. Some masters instructed their students to avoid such actions as they could prove dangerous or deadly. From an engaged position one's opponent could force or beat the blade aside, thrust the blade down or push it aside as they hit home. Because of this a variety of actions were employed to avoid crossing swords with the opponent. Most of the actions were similar to the Change Under, Change Over and Vertical Change. The idea was to execute the changement as the opponent attempted to engage the blades. This action is known as *refusing the blade* or the *time changement*.

> "When the enemy tries to engage your sword, or to beat it aside: without letting him engage or beat it, you must take a cavatione di tempo." [Fabris][22]

The *cavatione di tempo* or "time disengagement" was the action offered by Fabris to deny the opponent an engagement of the blades. The term "time" refers to timing the action so that it is executed at the last possible moment prior to engagement and therefore gaining the advantage. If the action was executed as a standard changement the opponent would not be caught off guard by the action. The timing of the changement is what makes it advantageous to the combatant executing it. The anticipated point of contact on the part of the opponent and the lack of finding the blade at that moment is referred to as *absence of blade*. If you intended to engage the opponent's blade and you execute a changement to join with them and upon completion of that action the blades do not meet, the opponent's blade is "absent" and they have "refused" the engagement.

This technique may be practiced in the same manner as the counter changement, except with the blades free in the complementary standard guards. The first combatant initiates a changement either under, over or vertically in an attempt to engage the opponent's blade. The time changement may also be under, over or vertical, depending on the guard placement to which the blade is being transferred. Do not make the attempt at engagement an offensive action. The time changement is executed at the last possible moment, after the opposing blade has changed lines and is about to touch the blade.

Once you have refused the blade in the complementary standard guards, you may try the time changement with other guard placements. In this exercise, the primary guard you assume must be one that can be engaged, or there will be no blade to be refused. Although there is no contact of blades in this exercise, there must at least be potential for engagement or the exercise is wasted.

The refusing of the blade may also be taken moving. This is done in the same manner as before, using the process of Action-Reaction-Action. The initial changement is the first action, followed by the perception of the action and the second combatant's reaction of a pass back or retreat, the final action is executed by both combatants. The first combatant's final action is an advance or pass forward as they see their partner move back. The second combatant's final action is to wait for the moment the opposing blade is about to engage theirs and, no matter where they are in their footwork, execute a time changement, thus refusing their partner's blade.

The reaction of the second combatant must be immediate upon perceiving the changement of their partner or they will have executed the blade work prior to moving their feet. For this reason it is important to work this exercise slowly to find the appropriate timing of the actions. You must watch your partner and respond efficiently to their actions. Do not jump the gun and respond early. Wait for the correct action or reaction before you begin.

---

[22]Fabris, from Castle, p. 101.

Sensing the Steel

When working on blade engagements, so much of the combatant's technique depends on when the blades touch or quit one another. In the counter changement you feel your opponent's blade leave yours as it begins to execute its changement. When they are joined you know where the opposing blade is. In the double changement you cannot execute the second changement until you feel the blades touch. If you anticipate the action and go early, you can be engaged with a counter changement. The process of refusing the blade denies your opponent information concerning the whereabouts of your blade, its absence meaning it could be anywhere but where it is expected.

The process of sensing or feeling the opponent's blade is known as *sentiment de fer*, and it is an important practice in the sport of fencing today. A fencer well practiced in sentiment de fer develops a kind of intuition, or "sixth-sense," that stretches their tactile sensibility up to the very point of the blade. A good sense of the steel grants the fencer's hand a special guessing instinct that warns them of the intentions and the will of their opponent, allowing the fencer to anticipate them. This process of feeling the blade and reading the opponent's attack may well have been the reason blades were originally engaged in combat. As early as the works of di Grassi, the idea of joining the blades to "feel" the opponent's movements was suggested.

Although you do not need to develop a sense of the blade to second guess your partner's actions in stage combat, you will still need to develop a strong sense of yours and your partner's blade. This is quite beneficial to you as you learn new skills with the sword. As you develop the techniques that make up a stage fight you may not always have the opportunity to watch the contact of the blades and must trust your sense of feel. Even in the earlier exercises you probably could feel the movement of the blade before you saw it. In the double changement you had to feel the engagement of the blades before you could execute the second changement and so on.

Developing a strong sentiment de fer is an invisible, but essential, part of the art of stage combat. For that reason, go back and review the preceding exercises and make sure you not only understand the mechanics, but that you have a good sense of the blade. Without bumping or knocking the blades you should sense when they are together, apart and the direction in which they are going when they quit one another.

A good way of "testing" your sense of the blade is to practice your engagements and variable changements in the complementary cross body guards (Prima, High Seconda, Low Seconda, Terza and Quarta). For this exercise the changements may be the disengage, coupé, counter changement and double changement, but they may only travel to the other side of the blade. Do not pass the point to the opposite side of the body in this exercise, keep it across the body. One combatant is the initiator, the other the responder. The initiator may execute any of the above changements and the responder tries to re-engage the blades. The initiator may be re-engaged, deceive the engagement with a double changement or refuse the engagement with a time changement. Work the exercise this way several times, trying a variety of changements in several different guards.

Once you feel you have a good sense of the blade, try the exercise with your eyes closed. Both combatants must now solely trust their sense of touch. You must feel when the blades are engaged and apart, and you must try to feel the direction of the changement in order to execute the correct counter. The objective of this exercise is not to fool your partner, but for both combatants to work on feeling and sensing the blades. Do not quit the blade and then execute a changement, this provides no tactile sensation for your partner. Quit the blade while executing the changement and trust your sixth sense. For obvious safety reasons, this exercise can only be executed in a stationary position. There can be no footwork during this exercise.

MOVING ON

Take the time to practice all the guards, engagements and changements, and to develop a strong sense of the blade. Gaining a working relationship between yourself, the weapon and a partner is crucial in the further development of safe and effective stage combat. The guards of the rapier are the beginning and ending positions of swordplay and they should be assumed with ease and understanding so that both offensive and defensive actions can be initiated effectively from these positions without confusion or error. Becoming comfortable with the weapon is the first step in making it all come alive. Once you are comfortable with the guards, engagements and changements of the rapier, and feel you have developed a good sentiment de fer, you are ready to move on to the next chapter.

Chapter 6

The Parries of the Single Rapier

"Jussac was, as was then said, a fine blade, and had much practice; nevertheless, it required all his skill to defend himself against an adversary, who, active and energetic, departed every instant from received rules, attacking him on all sides at once, and yet parrying like a man who had the greatest respect for his own epidermis.

This contest at length exhausted Jussac's patience. Furious at being held in check by him who he had considered a boy, he became warm, and began to commit faults. D'Artagnan, who, though wanting in practice, had a profound theory, redoubled his agility. Jussac, anxious to put an end to this, springing forward, aimed a terrible thrust at his adversary, but the latter parried it; and while Jussac was recovering himself, glided like a serpent beneath his blade, and passed his sword through his body. Jussac fell like a dead mass." [Alexander Dumas][1]

The number of misconceptions on defensive actions in rapier play is truly overwhelming. Many historical painters, and such writers as Edmond Rostand, Walter Scott and even Alexander Dumas, describe seventeenth–century duels that are in keeping with the practices of a modern fencing school rather than any form relevant to the actual period. Although these tales of swashbuckling and daring-deeds are exciting, they are not accurate to the period.

The media also perpetuates this wellspring of anachronisms. The duels presented in any Flynn or Fairbanks movie is nothing more than theatricalized versions of modern fencing. They offer defensive moves that were not only impractical to weapons of the period, but had not even been conceived. In classic and recent motion pictures, there are some excellently executed duels, but the combatants, although on open ground, fence as if restricted to a modern fencing strip. Breaking from this pattern only to offer the cliché fight up and down stairs and the dash about the set, the combatants finish their bout by returning once again to the "strip." Many of these "sword and sorcerer" and swashbuckler movies create not only their own swords, but entire forms of swordplay that never existed, in any period.

These falsehoods are no doubt partially due to the lack of information about swordplay, and specifically the parry. Even in the works of Agrippa, di Grassi, Fabris and Capo Ferro, very little is offered as a true definition of a parry. Not until the mid-seventeenth century, with the advent of

---

[1]Dumas, Alexander. *The Three Musketeers*. New York: Airmont Publishing Co., Inc., 1966. (pp. 51–52)

the small sword, do we begin to hear of parries as we now understand them. In the older manuscripts, combatants are told to "cross," "void," "ward" and "break" opposing weapons without any full explanation or definition.

WHAT IS A PARRY?

The definition of a parry today is simply a defensive action of a bladed weapon where the forte opposes the foible of the attacking weapon. In short, a parry is an action that stops the attacking blade at its weakest point with the strongest point of the defending blade.

There are generally two recognized ways of parrying:

• The Blocking Parry

A *blocking parry*, (also known as a standard parry and opposition parry) made by moving the sword to block the line in which the opponent makes an attack. This action also may be called "opposition." The blocking parry is performed two times. This means that the parry is one action, separate from the second action of a counterattack. The defensive action, being separate, may be performed alone, without a counterattack.

• The Beat Parry

A *beat parry*, made by striking the opponent's blade sharply aside, is a much quicker action. It removes the attacking blade while freeing your blade so that you may immediately counter the attack after your defense. When the parry and counterattack are executed in one action, it is called single time. This form of parry and immediate riposte seems to be in keeping with the references to the voiding and warding the blade offered in period fencing manuals.

Simple and obvious as these parries may appear, over three hundred years of practical experiments were required for their reduction to the smallest practical movements of the hand and weapon. There are, of course, several variations on these parries that differ mainly in the motion of the sword and how it arrives at the parry. These variations, however, are merely different actions of the sword that terminate at the same end, either in a blocking or beating parry.

The Historical Parry

Although we are accustomed to seeing the blocking parry in theatrical re-creations, the beat parry is the closest modern equivalent to what a parry might have been with the single rapier. There is no way to be certain what a parry actually was, however, because all books of fence written during the sixteenth century never once defined the action. Parries were always referred to as part of the counterattack (as we understand single time) and never as an independent action (as we understand two times).

Whether it was better to adopt the method of making two distinct motions in parrying and riposting had been questioned, debated and decided in the negative by nearly all masters of that age and earlier. Fabris expresses himself even more decidedly than others in favor of the Italian "stesso tempo," (single time), and advised against "dui tempi," (two times or double time). The common thought was that to parry without attacking simultaneously was a grave mistake.

Capo Ferro addresses the issue of the parry and of the "dui tempi" almost as a note. He concerned himself more with the counterattack than with the actual mechanics of the parry.

"Parries are made sometimes with the right edge, sometimes, though very rarely, with the false; in a straight line as well as obliquely; now with the point high, now with the point low; now under, now over, according as the attack is cut or thrust. But it is to be borne in mind that all parries ought to be done with a straight arm, and must be accompanied by the right leg, followed by the left. When the 'dui tempi'

are observed, as the parry is made, the left foot must first be brought up against the right, and then, as the attack is returned, the right foot must be moved forward." [2]

While this may sound like a lengthy and confusing description of a parry, the straight arm and footwork indicated was the preliminary, if not the actual, movement on the offensive. This "parry" was not solely a defensive action.

The weight and length of the early rapier made it quite difficult to parry with the sword itself. The awkward weapon restricted the fencer from blocking an attack with any advantage or speed. Attacks were, therefore, parried in the same action as the counterattack. Previous to Capo Ferro, the left hand had fulfilled this aspect of swordplay. Attacks were deflected or beaten aside with the left hand, or avoided by escaping backwards or sideways. These actions were taken in order to limit the motion of the sword hand to that of the attack. A good way to sum up the overriding principle of Elizabethan rapier play is "do unto others, *before* they do unto you."

The Left Hand

By the sixteenth and early seventeenth centuries, the rapier and dagger had become the "educated gentleman's" weapon. Both weapons were capable of offensive and defensive actions. The dagger, held in the left hand, however, functioned primarily as a defensive weapon. The rapier alone was looked upon in the best fencing schools as the foundation of the science of arms. As the intervention of the left hand was absolutely necessary for the complete defensive action, the rapier and dagger always went together.

The defensive action of the left hand, however, was still not what we would envision a block or parry to be today. The body of the combatant dodged, weaved and pivoted the oncoming attack. The weapon in the left hand was used to help deflect the blow as a counterattack was launched with the rapier. It was common practice to remove or "void" the body rather than to take the full force of an attack with the left hand.

It was not until Capo Ferro and the Age of Transition that the rapier became lighter and more manageable, making the dagger completely unnecessary. The single rapier became equally effective for offense and defense. The discarding of the cut as a popular mode of offense made it possible to defend the body against the thrust without the aid of a second weapon.

While the discarding of a strictly defensive weapon freed the left hand, the hand was still not removed from the action as is mistakenly portrayed in some movies and is the practice in modern fencing. The position of the left arm would constantly vary according to the ever-shifting position of the adversary's guard. The hand would be used to beat aside an attacking blade, or even grasp at it, in order to facilitate a more expedient counterattack.

"*. . . men do much use at this weapon, to beate off the poynt of the sworde with their handes."* [di Grassi][3]

The transition of the rapier into the small sword forcibly re-addressed the much debated question of "stesso tempo" or "dui tempi." With the long, heavy rapier, rapid action of the hand and sword to allow an independent parry was impossible. Defensive actions, therefore, had to be executed in such a way that would protect the body and act as a riposte, in one action. As swords became lighter and shorter, parrying first and riposting afterwards became more advantageous.

The rapier play of Fabris and Capo Ferro did not seem to transform suitably to the lighter and faster small sword. The lighter weapon allowed for extreme precision and lightning swift management of the blade and its point. This maneuverability of the defensive weapon made the parry and

---

[2]Castle, p. 112. Translated from: *Gran simulacro dell'arte e dell uso della Scherma di RIDOLFO CAPO FERRO da Cagli, Maestro dell' eccelsa natione alemanna, nell' inclita Citta di Siena.* Oblong 4°. Siena. 1610.
[3]di Grassi, p. 148.

Plate XIII: A parry with the left hand. From an eighteenth century French treatise on the science of fence.

counterattack in single time much more of a risk. The agile attacks that the lighter weapon allowed required an equally precise parry that insured prevention of the attack before attempting a counterattack.

The science of defense, which had been the great specialty of the Italians during the sixteenth and seventeenth centuries, seems to have been completely obscured by the transitional stage of the weapon. Clinging to old ideals, and the teaching of the likes of Fabris and Capo Ferro, had nothing but a retarding effect on the Italian science during the next century. It was the French school of fence that picked up the torch and developed the parry, and the science of fence to what we see it as today.[4]

The Theatrical Parry

It is, however, not these delicate parries of "puncture play" that we see presented on stage and screen today. All but the trained eye of a fencer would lose sight of these lightning quick parries. Although they are performed in double time, the actions have become so small and quick that offense and defense become a blur. It is most likely that for these reasons parries of sabre play, although completely foreign to the rapier, were introduced to stage combat.

Although the sabre retains the principles of the cutting attack, its parries, as they have developed, are in no way comparable to those of the rapier. Modern sabre play is performed with an incredibly light and flexible blade. This blade allows movements, both on the offensive and defensive, that could never be performed with the rapier. Yet it is the parries of the modern fencing sabre that we now associate with the rapier.

Parries on the Silver Screen

Errol Flynn, Douglas Fairbanks, Cornell Wilde, Basil Rathbone and many other "swashbuckling" stars of the cinema (or their stunt doubles) were accomplished fencers. Their performances intrigued audiences, and through time, this fast and flashy sabre play transformed into the theatrical versions of broadsword, cross-hilt and rapier play.

Since that time, the audience has come to think the swashbuckling of the silver screen to be real

---

[4]Nowadays there is very little noticeable difference between the parries of the two schools, and their execution has become so minute and precise that the action would be lost to all but the eye of a trained fencer.

swordplay. This has been reinforced time and again until that "romantic ideal" has become a reality to all but the true specialists and fanatics who cling to what is left of the ancient art.

The Historical vs. Theatrical Parry

These early efforts at recreating sword fights obviously made no real attempt at historical accuracy. Focus was placed instead on spectacle and the dramatic impact. Audiences became familiar with this style of blade work and soon would settle for nothing else. The attempt to present a "historically accurate" rapier fight on stage today would more than likely be met with failure. With the best disciplined actors, countless hours of training and rehearsal and a flawless performance, the response would, at best, be mediocre. The modern audience would see that fight, compare it to what they "know," and leave unsatisfied. We cannot recondition our audiences; many prefer the romantic ideal over the historical reality, so the theatre today concerns itself with theatrical effectiveness and not with true historical accuracy.

This is not, however, for the worse. Although the parries are almost entirely historically inaccurate, they do work incredibly well as theatrical tools. An actual parry of the rapier would be visually and dramatically lost to the audience. It would offer a blur of motion that would be as incomprehensible as a dramatic scene where the characters all speak at once. Since action takes focus on stage, strong definite parries, that the audience can see, help to give the physical conflict subtextual nuance and character motivation. In order to communicate the most information, strong stage pictures must be presented in a manner that allows the audience to perceive and interpret them.

THE PARRIES

Before you begin to practice the parries, following are the principals of technique you will need to better execute the actions. These are explained beforehand in order to avoid repetition within the mechanics.

Working with the Face of a Clock

The description of the following parries refers to the position of the blade in relation to the face of a clock. The wrist or hand is always at the center of the clock, treating the blade as a hand of that clock. (Fig. 79) The tip of the blade points towards the designated numbers. *The instructions will always assume you are facing the clock,* and are therefore explained from the perspective of the defender. Although the hand may vary in position, it remains the center. Just as you can move a clock from room to room without the relation of the hands to the center altering, so are you able to move the "clock" from parry to parry. The parries have been listed in a specific order and are described in transition from one to another only. Once familiar with the positions of the parries, it is possible to go from any guard or parry to any other.

Always Travel *Out* to a Parry

It is always essential to travel out towards a parry. The forte of your blade travels through your center in the same plane as the attack. Also keep in mind that everyone's arms are built, and move, slightly differently. If you find that your arm or wrist has great difficulty executing any of the described moves, a slight alteration may be necessary to adapt to your physique. Just remember to carry the forte of the blade through your center line and out towards the attack.

Several of the moves may be awkward at first, but they should never be painful. Difficulty in the execution of these parries often comes from a desperately tight grip on the rapier. Work to relax the grip as described in Chapter 4, before making any adjustments.

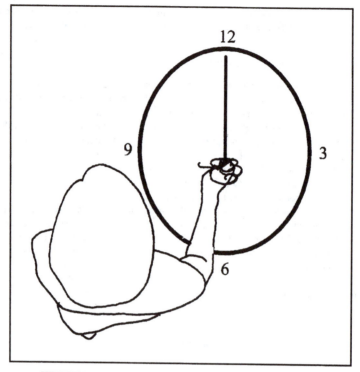

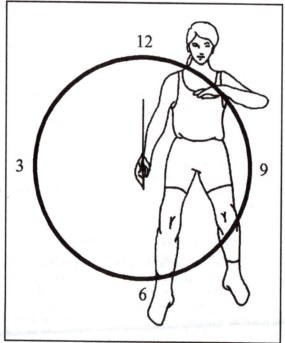

Figure 79. Using the clock-face.

A Parry is an Action of the Blade

"You must be very careful that you doe not over-carry your Rapier in the defence of anie maner of thrust beare him but halfe a foot towards the left side, for that will cleare the bodie from danger of his thrust, and so quicke backe againe in his place, whereby to meet the weapon on the other side." [Swetnam][5]

The action of the parry is, for the most part, an action of the blade. Do not "over-carry your Rapier," keep your hand and arm near the body. Make the large theatrical movements with the sword itself. These are meant to look like last-second defensive actions. It should not appear that you have the time to take "the long road" to any of the parries.

Parry Outside and In Front of Your Body

All parries are made with the blade outside and in front of your body. This protects you from any accidental attack that might be in distance. Placing the blade outside your body is not enough. Since you work in a specific fencing measure that is out of actual striking distance, the parry also must be placed in front of you to meet your partner's blade. This gives the illusion of being in distance without an actual threat to life and limb.

If your partner stands directly in front of you, they are at ninety degrees from your extreme right and extreme left. Placing your rapier outside and in front of you puts the sword at roughly forty-five degrees. (Fig. 80) This is the position of the sword when correctly placed in a parry. This placement should be referred to whenever the text calls for the sword to be outside and in front of your body.

Only Parry with the Edge of the Blade

". . . as the thrust cometh, that he encounter it without, with the edge of the sword . . ." [di Grassi][6]

Always make your parries with the edge of the blade. The construction of the weapon allows for the greatest breadth of the blade to absorb the shock. A parry made with the edge of the blade, correctly shouldered on the hilt, prevents it from bending the tang and eventually breaking the weapon. Also, keeping the edge turned out allows the extra protection of the knuckle bow. This portion of the guard protects the hand if an attack is accidentally off-target. To parry with the flat of the blade not only exposes the hand to possible danger, but also offers the narrowest point of the blade to absorb the shock without any support in the hilt. If you think about it, a wooden ruler breaks more easily across its width than its edge—and so does a sword. There are no exceptions to this rule: thus you encounter all attacks with the edge of the sword.

Forte to Foible

The placement of the blade during a parry is crucial. The forte of the weapon should be used to protect specific targets from specific attacks. *"A horizontal parry meets a vertical attack,"* states British fight master William Hobbs, *"and a horizontal attack meets a vertical parry, which insures that both parties know exactly the angle at which a stroke is coming, and that the attacking blade does not ricochet off the parry."*[7] The planes of the blades must meet at ninety degrees. It is, therefore, very important that the defending blade be placed exactly where instructed, protecting a definite target. Ambiguity is excessively dangerous to the stage combatant. (Fig. 81)

---

[5]Swetnam, pp. 120–121.
[6]di Grassi, p. 50.
[7]Hobbs, pp. 24–25.

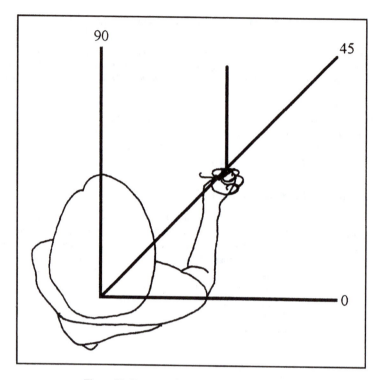

Figure 80. Parry outside and in front of the body.

Preparation and Removal of the Body

As you "wind up," or travel from one parry preparing for the next, rock forward into the stationary offensive position. Then, as you complete the parry, rock the body backward into the stationary defensive position (as described in Chapter 3). This is done to give the impression that the body is being removed from the threat of an attack without having to step out of the way. To achieve this, straighten the lead leg and bend the knee of the lag leg so that it travels out over the foot (the knee never goes beyond the toes). This action moves the upper body away from the attack. The line created by the straightening of the lead leg presents a stage picture of removal or avoidance.

At times you may feel that you are "leaning into an attack" or rocking toward the defended side of the body. Any parry executed on the left side of the body with a right lead foot (and vice-versa) has this sensation. It is the illusion of removal that we are creating, and when the parries become second nature to you, then footwork is added and used to remove your body from the threat. Until that time, "rocking" is be applied to all the parries except where specific lower body movement is dictated. *All safety rules apply here.*

What About the Left Hand?

As you learn these parries, you may find in the transition from one parry to the other that the position of the left hand may vary from the illustrated examples. The main principle is to remove the hand and arm from the side of the body threatened, while keeping it in such a position that it may ward off an attack to the side opposite that being parried. The placement of the left hand does not need to match the illustration, but *it must be removed from the attack.* Do not, however, remove your hand from play as you see in modern fencing. In that position the hand is only out of "modern"

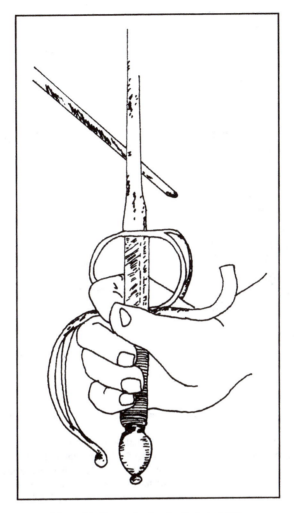

Figure 81. Parry edge to edge/forte to foible.

target. In the period being represented, however, anything is in target, so use your hand to protect what the sword cannot. Let the left hand counter the actions of the parry, protecting the lines opened by the movement of the blade. Although you know what is happening next, your character does not. Use the illustrations as guides and move the left hand to best protect your body from an anticipated attack.

The Parry of 1: Defense for an attack to the left hip

From the guard of Terza, rotate your wrist so that it is pronated (if you are not already in that position of the hand) and guide the tip of the sword down towards six o'clock. Stop the tip of the weapon roughly four inches from the floor. As the tip reaches six o'clock, draw the hilt up so that it is just above the level of your waist. The blade hangs straight down, vertical to the floor.

Leading with the wrist (the sword remains hanging straight down at six o'clock) the hand and sword begin to travel across the body. Guide the arm with an action much like traveling from Terza to Quarta.

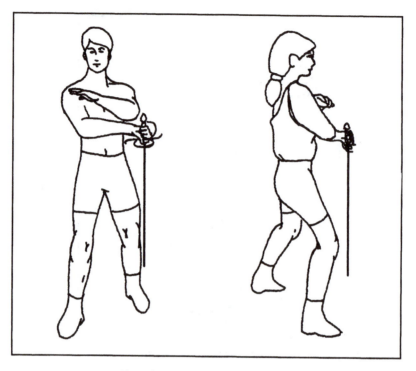

Figure 82. The single rapier parry of 1.

As the motion across the body begins, turn your palm clockwise towards your partner, knuckle bow to the inside (left).

Stop the hand and sword about six inches to the left of, and about eight inches in front of your body. The hilt remains just above waist level, the hand relaxed, with its palm turned towards your partner, thumb down. There is a slight bend in the wrist so the knuckle bow can face out to the left. The sword remains at six o'clock with the blade hanging straight down from the hilt. Your arm is in front of your body, not resting on it. The forte of the blade is at the level of your left hip. (Fig. 82)

The Parry of 2: Defense for an attack to the right hip

From the parry of 1 you move on to the parry of 2. Roll your wrist so that your palm faces you, knuckle bow directed toward the outside (right). Angling the tip slightly forward, draw your hand and sword across your body from left to right. Stop with the right arm outside the body, extended down and slightly forward, with the rapier closing the low outside line.

Your arm is drawn up and bent at roughly forty-five degrees, with your elbow angled behind you, and your hand just above waist level with the knuckle bow turned to the outside (right). The blade of the sword is a solid wall; it does not angle either to the inside or the outside, but travels straight down and slightly forward. The tip is at six o'clock. The forte of the blade at the level of your right hip. (Fig. 83)

The Parry of 3: Defense for a horizontal attack to the right shoulder

From the parry of 2, turn the tip of the sword to the position of nine o'clock. The blade is in line with your waist and horizontal to the floor. As you do this, pronate your hand, turning the knuckle

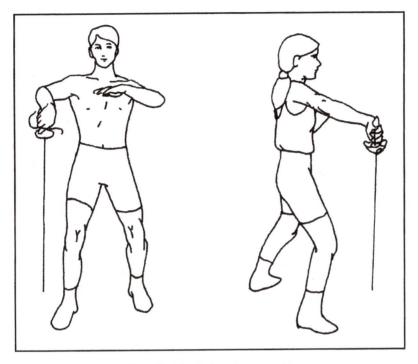

Figure 83. The single rapier parry of 2.

bow towards your partner. Keep your wrist pronated, at waist level, and raise the tip of the sword to eleven o'clock. Once at eleven o'clock, begin to turn your palm towards your partner, keeping it at waist level.

Stop the tip at twelve o'clock. Continue the action by guiding the sword and hand horizontally across the waist towards the right. Stop about ten inches outside and in front of the body. The knuckle bow is towards the outside (right), your palm facing your partner and the tip at twelve o'clock. The forte of the blade will be at the level of the notch in your right arm where your deltoid and biceps meet. (Fig. 84)

The Parry of 4: Defense for a **horizontal** *attack to the left shoulder*

To travel from 3 to 4, turn your knuckle bow to the inside (left) and guide your arm across your waistline from right to left. Keep the tip of the sword at twelve o'clock. As the sword passes the middle of your body, rotating at the waist, turn your right shoulder towards your partner.

Stop your hand and sword about eight inches to the left of, and in front of your body. Your right shoulder is turned slightly towards your partner. Do not turn the upper body sideways, your shoulder should go no farther than your right leg. An extreme sideways position tends to cause your right foot and knee to turn inward (which could possibly dislocate an ankle or knee), but also exposes the back, a target not easily defended.

Your sword hand is at waist level with the knuckle bow to the inside (left). The tip is at twelve o'clock. Your forte is at the level of the muscular notch in your left arm. This notch is where the deltoid and biceps meet. (Fig. 85)

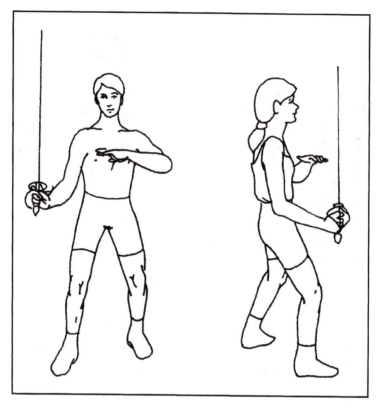

Figure 84. The single rapier parry of 3.

The Parry of 5: Defense for a **vertical** *attack to the head*

From the parry of 4 you will move on to the parry of 5, or "High 5" as it is often called. American fight master David Boushey calls this parry "Muscle Beach," the right arm position being similar to the biceps flex of a body-builder.

From the parry of 4, guide the tip of the sword counter clockwise to the position of seven o'clock. Extend the arm and drop the hand below the level of the waist. Your palm faces towards you, knuckle bow towards the floor, with the tip about three inches from the floor.

From your left, draw the sword across the body to where the hilt is on your right, keeping the tip at seven o'clock. Once the hand is on the right of the body, keep it there, and bring it back up to waist level.

With your wrist, guide the tip in a clockwise direction to the position of nine o'clock. The sword will be horizontal to the floor. Pronate your hand, rolling the knuckle bow towards your partner (much like operating the throttle of a motorcycle). Continuing the rotation of the wrist, raise the sword above your head, keeping it horizontal to the floor and in front of your body.

Your hand continues its "throttle" rotation turning your palm to face your partner. The knuckle bow turns straight up, the tip at nine o'clock and the blade above you and in front of you, horizontal to the floor. The sword does not angle behind you or forward towards your partner. It points straight off to your left. Your arm is to the right of your body and about twelve inches in front of you. Do not lock the elbow. The arm should form a slight curve up and forward. The forte is in front of and

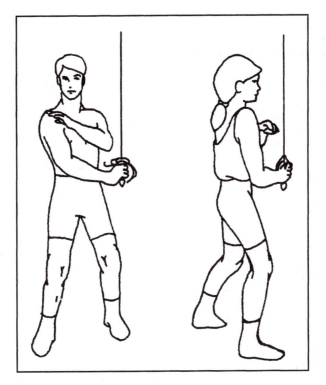

Figure 85. The single rapier parry of 4.

above the center of your head. The parry of 5 defends a vertical cutting attack to the centerline at the head. (Fig. 86)

In the parry of 5, the lower body does not "rock" to the left or the right. It keeps its weight centered between both legs and will slightly increase the plié. The legs (not the arm) should act like shock absorbers for the vertical attack to the head.

The Parry of High 3: Defense for a diagonal attack to the right shoulder

From the parry of 5, pronate your hand and turn the knuckle bow towards your partner. Guide the sword down to the level of your waist. Keep the blade horizontal to the floor and the tip at nine o'clock. The arm stays to the right of your body.

From this position, begin to describe a clockwise circle with the tip of the sword. When the tip reaches eleven o'clock, turn your palm towards your partner, knuckle bow to the outside (right). As you do this, keep the upper arm in place. Pivot at the elbow and bring the hand to the outside (right) of the arm at the level of the elbow.

Your hand is to the right of your body and in front of it. Your palm is towards your partner, knuckle bow to the outside (right) and angled up at roughly forty-five degrees. The blade is at a forty-five degree angle to the floor, outside and in front of your body and above your head. The tip is at eleven o'clock, the forte of the blade protecting the notch in the right shoulder where the deltoid and biceps meet. The sword does not angle off behind you or forward towards your partner, it is in one plane, pointing up and to your left. (Fig. 87)

Figure 86. The single rapier parry of High 5.

The Parry of High 4: Defense for a diagonal attack to the left shoulder

From the parry of High 3, guide the tip of the sword to the position of twelve o'clock. Turn the wrist so that your palm is towards you, knuckle bow to the inside (left). Keep the upper arm in place and pivot from the elbow. This brings the hand to the left of the arm at the level of the elbow. As your hand reaches the center of your body begin rotating at the waist. This turns your right shoulder towards your partner.

Guide the tip to the position of one o'clock. Keep your palm towards you, knuckle bow to the inside (left). Bring your upper arm in until your elbow is centered on your body (in front of your bellybutton). Your right shoulder should be turned slightly towards your partner as in the parry of 4.

Your arm reaches across your body with the elbow at approximately the mid section of your torso. The forearm is angled up slightly, with the hand just above the level of your right elbow. It is to the left of your body and in front of it. Your palm is facing towards you, with the knuckle bow to the inside (left), angled up at roughly forty-five degrees.

The blade is at a forty-five degree angle to the floor, outside and in front of your body and above your head. The tip is at one o'clock, with the forte of the blade protecting the notch in the left shoulder where the deltoid and biceps meet. The sword does not angle off behind you or forward towards your partner, it is in one plane, pointing up and to your right. (Fig. 88)

The Parry of 6: Defense for a thrust to the mid torso

From the parry of High 4, keep the hand on your left. Guide the tip of the sword from one o'clock to the position of twelve o'clock. Once you do this, bring the hand and sword down until you are

Figure 87. The single rapier parry of High 3.

in the guard of Low Quarta. Once you are in Low Quarta (keep the tip outside your partner), raise the tip again, so that it is above your partner's head.

Keeping the upper arm in place, pivot from the elbow and bring the hand and sword straight across the body. The hand travels at roughly waist level. The hand is supinated. The blade is in a straight line forward and the tip *above* your partner's head. The hand comes to rest at the outside of the right arm (Fig. 89)

As the hand passes the arm the pommel is guided above the forearm to rest on the inside of the wrist. In order to do this the hand must be relaxed, allowing the pommel to pass naturally to the top. This position of the hand, pommel and wrist is often called the "broken wrist" of 6.

It is not a good practice to let the pommel pass under or against the wrist. This placement of the pommel, if met with a strong attack, could torque the wrist of the combatant. It is best to let the pommel travel on top of the wrist, alleviating tension against the hand and wrist in an accidental power play.

The sword remains directed in a straight line forward during the entire transition. The tip remains above your partner's head, your hand at waist level, supinated with the knuckle bow to the inside (left). (Fig. 90)

A common mistake in executing this parry is to try to parry with the tip of the sword, hitting an attack aside. This is a contained parry, only the hand, sword and forearm move. The upper arm remains stationary, operating only as a pivot point. This action is sometimes referred to as the "windshield wiper parry" because of the traveling action of the arm. The rapier is in front of and

Figure 88. The single rapier parry of High 4.

outside your body, the forte brought across your chest to protect your mid torso with the false edge of the blade. The tip remains at roughly twelve o'clock.

The Parry of 7: Defense for an attack to the left thigh

From the parry of 6, lower the tip of the sword from its forward twelve o'clock position to that of a forward six o'clock. Lower the hand to the level just below the waist-line, so your palm faces your partner. The thumb is down and the knuckle bow to the inside (left). The sword is directed forward with the tip at six o'clock, about three inches from the floor.

Leading with the wrist, the hand and sword travel across the body. The action is guided by the arm, much like traveling from Terza to the parry of 1. The sword remains hanging with the tip at six o'clock.

As the sword passes the middle of your body begin rotating the upper torso. If necessary, your right shoulder can be turned slightly towards your partner as in the parry of 4 and High 4.

Stop with the sword about six inches to the left of your body and about six inches in front of your body. Your hilt remains below waist level with your hand relaxed. Your palm faces your partner, its thumb turned down and knuckle bow to the inside (left). The tip is at six o'clock. Your arm is in front of and across your body, not resting on it.

The blade of the sword is a solid wall, it does not angle either to the inside or the outside, but travels straight down and slightly forward. The tip is at six o'clock, roughly three inches from the floor. The forte is at the level of the left quadriceps, just above the knee. (Fig. 91)

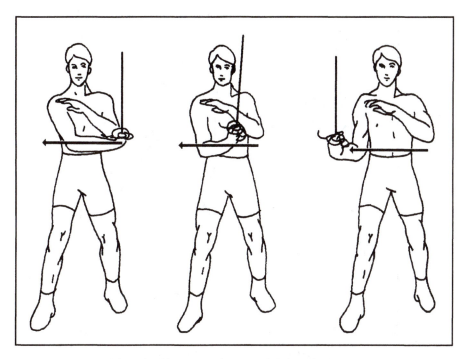

Figure 89. The single rapier parry of 6 (frame by frame).

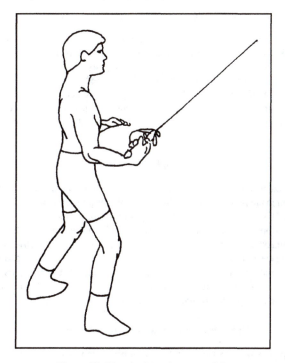

Figure 90. The single rapier parry of 6.

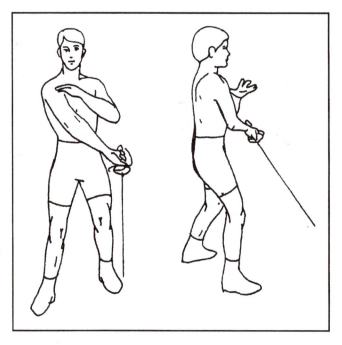

Figure 91. The single rapier parry of 7.

The Parry of 8: Defense for an attack to the right thigh

From the parry of 7, keep the tip at six o'clock. Take the hand back across the body from left towards the right. Keep your palm turned towards your partner and stop your hand approximately six inches outside and in front of your body. Your arm is slightly bowed (elbow directed behind you) with your palm facing toward you and the knuckle bow turned toward the inside (left). The blade hangs straight down and slightly forward with its tip at six o'clock. The tip is about three inches from the floor. The forte is at the level of the right quadriceps, just above the knee. This parry, like the parry of 6, is made with the hand supinated, turning the false edge of the blade towards the attack. (Fig. 92)

The Defensive Box

The ten parries you have just learned are designed to protect the entire body. Each parry protects a specific target, and in the process of executing all the parries you create a wall or "defensive box" around your body. This box, or shield, leaves no portion of the combatant unprotected. (Fig. 93)

Each parry makes up a separate part of this wall and its placement is definite. The aggressor generally aims its attacks at openings in this box and it is the job of the defensive combatant to close those openings. In stage combat the targets are specific. This means not only specific to the area of the body being attacked, but also what parry blocks or protects that target. This box is the combatant's guarantee that no part of the body is left unprotected. Thus, each parry is presented as a "solid wall," making up a portion of the entire defensive box.

The Paths of the Various Parries

Although these parries were explained in transition from one to the other, they can be performed in any variation of combinations. There are no hard and fast rules dealing with the order parries must

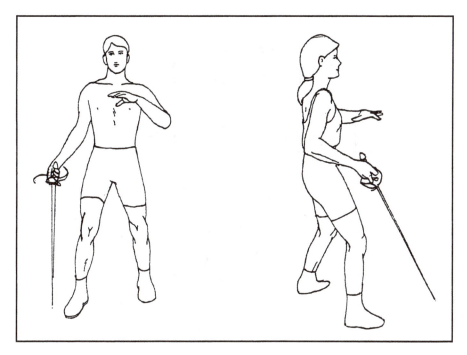

Figure 92. The single rapier parry of 8.

be executed, only guidelines to their effectiveness. A parry must always travel out, away from your center, to meet the attack. The forte travels out to oppose the offending blade, protecting the plane of the target designated by both the parry and the attack. This is extremely important because it is possible for the attack to strike the foible of your blade where there is no strength in the parry or the attack may arrive at the target before the parry and strike your hand. The attack also may miss the hand and sword and possibly strike your body.

The path the blade travels through your center and out to the parry determines the type of parry being executed. Although the end position is the same, parries are classified according to the path followed by the blade. In fencing, and stage combat, the path of the parries are divided into the following types:

- direct parries;
- semicircular parries;
- diagonal parries;
- circular parries.

Direct Parries

Direct parries, also called *instinctive* and *simple parries,* are defensive actions of the blade where both the hand and blade move from one position to another along the shortest possible route in either a horizontal or vertical plane. In the pattern you learned earlier, the transition from 1-2, 3-4, 7-8 and even High 4 to 6 are direct parries. Other direct parries include the reverse of these, 2-1, 4-3, etc. as well as 1-8, 7-2 and vice versa. Even High 3-High 4 are considered direct parries (Fig. 94)

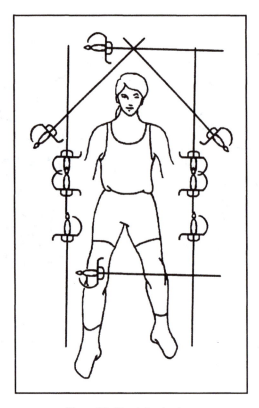

Figure 93. The defensive box.

Semicircular Parries

The *semicircular parry* is a defensive action of the blade where the hand maintains its same relative placement and the blade moves from one position to another in a semicircular path. The starting and ending point of the blade are in the same vertical plane, changing high and low lines but remaining on the same side of the body. The point of the blade describes an arc, not a straight line, as the parrying movement follows a semicircular path from one position to another. In the parries learned so far, the transition from 2-3 is a semicircular parry. Other semicircular parries would include the reverse of that, as well as 4-7, 4-1, High 4-7, High 4-1, 2-6, 2-High 3, 8-6 or 8-High 3, and vice versa. Even 5-2 or 5-8 are considered semicircular parries. (Fig. 95)

Diagonal Parries

Diagonal parries or *half counter parries* are a form of semicircular parry where the hand and blade move from one position to another in a semicircular path. During the execution of this type of parry the hand and blade travel diagonally across the body from the high to low line or vice versa. Although traveling in a diagonal, the point of the blade describes an arc, not a diagonal line. The parrying movement follows a semicircular path from one line to the other and from one side of the body to another. (Fig. 96)

This type of parry was considered quite valuable as point work became dominant in blade-play. In his book on the art of fencing (1765), Domenico Angelo stressed the importance of this action.

Plate XIV: A Marxbruder trains a student in swordplay.[8] The ward being demonstrated is quite similar to the parry of 7.

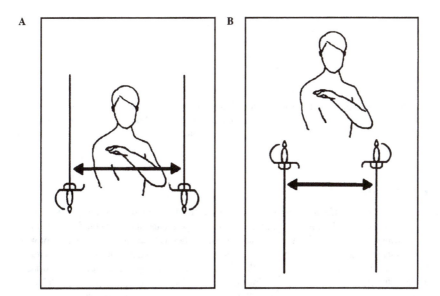

Figure 94. **A-**The path of a direct parry, parries 3 and 4; **B-**the path of a direct parry, parries 1 and 2.

---

[8]The oldest recorded fighting guild or sword-masters was the ''Brothers of St. Mark,'' or *Marxbruders* of Germany founded in 1350. This illustration comes from a late sixteenth century manuscript.

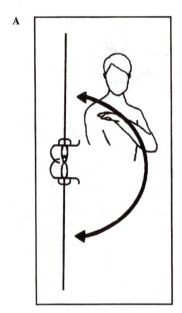 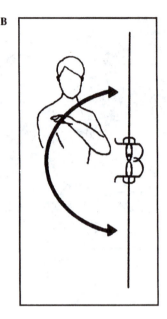

Figure 95. **A**-The path of a semicircular parry between the parries of 3 and 2; **B**-The path of a semicircular parry between the parries of 4 and 7.

> "*This parade* [parry], *which is chief defensive parade of the sword, parries not only all the thrusts, but also obstructs all the feints that can be made; and, to execute it well, you should straighten your arm, keep your wrist in a line with your shoulder, your nails upward, and, by a close and quick motion of the wrist, the point should form a circle from the right to the left, large enough to be under cover from the head to knee*" [Angelo][9]

Of the parries covered earlier, only the transition from 6-7 traveled diagonally across the body from a high to a low line. Other diagonal parries include the reverse of that, as well as 4-2, 4-8, High 4-2, High 4-8, 1-6, 1-3, 1-High 3, 7-6, 7-3, 7-High 3; and vice versa. Even 5-7 or 5-1 are considered a Diagonal Parry.

Circular Parries

The *Circular Parry* or *Counter Parry* (sometimes called the "Twiddle") is any parry in which the point of the weapon describes a complete circle with the hand and weapon finishing in the position in which they started. The point of the blade describes a circle during the movement while the guard remains in the same position. The blade finishes the parry in the same position as that from which it started. Like the Diagonal Parry, the Circular Parry was one of the principle forms of defense in historical swordplay. The sweeping action of the blade was believed to defend the entire body from the aspects of a thrust, a form of "universal parry." In the same passage from Angelo's detailed manuscript, he goes on to explain the process of continuing the circle.

---

[9]Angelo, p. 42.

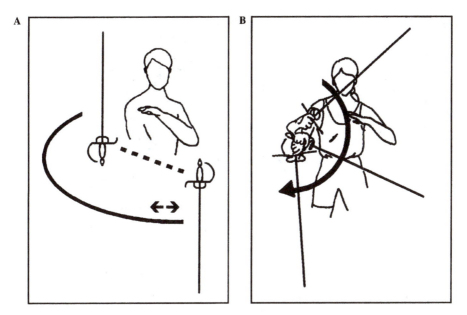

Figure 96. **A**-The path of a diagonal parry executed between parries 3 and 1 (or 7); **B**-The path of a diagonal parry executed between parries 4 and 2.

"The point should form a circle from the right to the left, large enough to be under cover from the head to knee; in this manner, by doubling your circle till you have found the adversary's blade, your parade will be formed." [Angelo][10]

The doubling or duplicating of the Diagonal Parry creates a whole circle with the tip of the blade carrying it back to its point of origin. None of the parries covered above are described as Circular Parries, although any parry can be circular. The blade must describe 360 degrees and the hand must withdraw to the center and then push the parry out again. (Fig. 97)

Although all parries may be executed as Circular Parries, the most common are those of 2, 6 and 8. The parry of 1 is probably the least common Circular Parry due to the awkward rotation of the wrist. For our purposes, we will look at the mechanics of the most common form of this parry: the circular parry of 2.

The Circular Parry of 2: Defense for an Attack to the Right Hip

This is probably the most common form of Circular Parry used in film and theatre. It is so common, in fact, that it is generally known as the *Actor's Parry*. This is the parry you see so many swashbucklers, like Errol Flynn, demonstrate with such dexterity time and time again. It is the same as the parry of 2; only the circular motion adds greater dynamics to the parry. This parry must be carefully practiced and slowly picked up in speed, to become one complete action. Do not try rushing the process.

From the guard of Terza, or a completed parry of 2, supinate your hand and turn the knuckle bow to the inside (left). Place the tip at six o'clock. From six o'clock, begin a counterclockwise circle with the tip of the sword turning just your wrist, keeping your arm as stationary as possible. The tip does not angle away from you, but stays in line with the imaginary clock that you are facing.

---

[10]Angelo, p. 42.

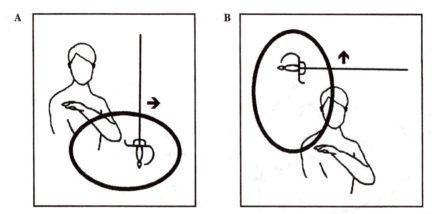

Figure 97. **A-**The path of a circular parry of 4; **B-**The path of a circular parry of 5.

When you reach one o'clock, turn your knuckle bow back towards the inside (left), so your palm faces towards you. Do not stop the action of the circle while doing this; keep moving.

When the tip reaches ten o'clock the arm completes the circle with the hand and sword. From seven o'clock complete the action as described in the parry of 2. The rest of the mechanics are the same; protecting the low outside line. This action defends the right hip. (Fig. 98)

Working the Circular Parries

Work this parry and then try circling the others. Try executing the standard parry and then its circle (i.e., parry 1, circle 1; parry 2, circle 2; parry 3, circle 3; and so on). Remember, circle 1 is difficult (and probably the least used circular parry) so if it is proving awkward, start the series with parry 2 and practice the other parries before returning to 1. Work the mechanics slowly to make sure that the forte travels out in the plane of the attack, and that the parry is made with the true edge of the blade (except in 6 and 8). As you practice, it is easy to let the circular parries become wild and sloppy. They should not. These parries do not swing from the shoulder or affect the rest of your body. They must end in the same controlled placement as that of the standard parries described earlier. If you find yourself drawing huge circles with the arm, try working the parries holding your upper arm against your side with your unarmed hand. This forces the movement to be executed from the hand, wrist and elbow rather than from the arm and shoulder. If you are moving your torso as you execute these parries, try working them using the Wall Bound exercise offered in the last chapter. Your arm needs to operate independently from your body, and the sword needs to operate independently from your arm.

Cutting the Lines

A variation on the circular parry is the action known as *cutting the lines.* This is a circular parry made other than in the line of engagement. It is really the combination of a direct parry and a circular parry. The action begins with a direct parry where the hand and blade move from one position to another in either a horizontal or vertical plane; as in the transition from 1–2, 3–4 or 7–8. As the blade travels across the body, it also executes a circular parry for the line it is moving towards. Thus the action is a circular parry that cuts across the center line of the body, starting on one side, ending on the other. This is like a transition from 1 to 2, ending in a circular parry of 2, or from 7 to 8, ending in a circular parry of 8, and so on. Although not particularly common in fencing today, the process of cutting the lines is used quite frequently on stage due to the dynamics of the circular parry.

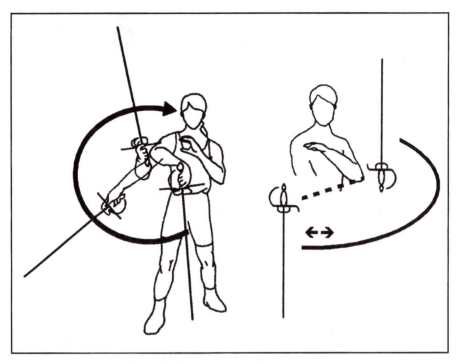

Figure 98. The Actor's Parry (frame by frame).

APPLICATION and PRACTICE

"A good parade is as necessary and useful when well executed, as it is dangerous and fatal if done without judgement, and made wide and rambling."

Practice each of the parries slowly many times to avoid wide and rambling execution. Go slow; keep things safe. Let the names represent an accurate picture in your mind of the exact blade position in relation to the angle of the attack and the areas of the body being defended.

Going from Parry to Parry

A good practice drill for this is to have someone call the numbers of the parries, in any order, and test how smoothly you travel to and from each parry. Do not rush yourself. It takes time for your kinesthetic memory to become effective. Never try to hurry the process. Picture the parry in your head and how you should move to it, then slowly move from your present guard or parry to the next one called. Think, and then Do.

If you find it difficult moving from one random parry to another, try moving to each of the parries, one at a time, from the guard of Terza. Move the tip of the sword on the face of the clock until it coincides with the placement for the particular parry being executed. Try to find a position on the clock with the tip of the sword that is close to the beginning motions of the parry.

Once you are adept at moving to each parry from Terza, try it from one or more of the other guard positions (standard and across). Always keep in mind the position of the sword and the placement of its point. Make sure to follow safety rules. When you are comfortable with this, have someone drill you in traveling from one parry to the next.

---

*Angelo, p. 35.

This process may take a while, but with time and practice you will acquire efficiency and speed without errors. Trying to hurry the process only provokes mistakes and mistakes can lead to disaster. Remember the words of Angelo and avoid danger through good technique and the application of all the aforesaid safety rules.

Trouble Shooting

For Low Line Parries

If you find that the point of your sword strikes the floor as you execute your low line parries. The common solution to this is to raise the hand, but this removes your forte from the plane of the intended target. In order to keep the hand at the proper placement for the parry and keep the blade roughly three inches off the floor, it may be necessary to angle the blade forward towards one's opponent. The tip remains at six o'clock, but the blade is not kept at a right angle to the floor.

Scooping the Parries

When first learning the parries it is common to lead the blade more with the arm than the hand and wrist. This enlarges the path of the parry and can carry the hand through the plane of the intended attack. This movement is known as *scooping*. The increased arc in the blade's path (especially in semicircular and circular parries) scoops the hand into place rather than pushing it out. This is a dangerous practice because the attack may arrive at the target before the hand has finished scooping into place and strike your hand. Work now to avoid developing this bad habit. Set the hand, and then push the parry out, away from your center, to meet the attack. Be sure that only the forte travels out to meet the attack, and that your hand never travels towards the intended attack.

THE DRILL

After becoming comfortable with variables of movement between each of the parries, try practicing this drill on the parries 1 through 8.

From the guard of Terza travel to the parry of 1.

From 1 to the parry of 2. (direct or cutting the lines)

From 2 to the parry of 3.

From 3 to the parry of 4. (direct or cutting the lines)

From 4 to the parry of High 5.

From High 5 to the parry of High 3.

From High 3 to the parry of High 4. (direct or cutting the lines)

From High 4 to the parry of 6.

From 6 to the parry of 7.

From 7 to the parry of 8. (direct or cutting the lines)

Adding the Defensive Footwork Drill

Now, try stepping through the *linear* defensive footwork drill, (as covered in Chapter 3). When you parry on the left of your body, the left leg is to the rear, removed from the attack. When you parry on the right side, the right leg is to the rear, removed from the attack. The traveling of the lower body does not replace the "rocking" action of the legs to remove the body from the attack. The "rocking" just becomes smaller as the focus of the legs shifts to moving the entire body instead of just moving the upper body away from the attack.

Parry Variations and Modifications

Before learning the following variations, practice each of the above described parries slowly. When you have acquired the ability to perform the techniques in and out of order, you can progress to these variations, which provide a greater variety and flourish to the parries.

The Parry of High 1: Defense for a horizontal attack to the left shoulder

Although the parry of 4 is used most often to protect the left shoulder, the parry of High 1 also may be used to defend this target. The parry is often referred to as the ''watch parry'' due to the placement of the hand and wrist; as if you were looking at your watch.[11]

From the guard of Terza, drop the tip of the sword down towards six o'clock, roughly four inches from the floor. As the tip of the sword reaches six o'clock, draw the hilt of the sword up so that it is just above the level of your waist. The blade hangs straight down, its tip to the floor.

Turning your wrist counterclockwise, roll your palm towards your partner, knuckle bow to the inside (left). Leading with the wrist the hand and the sword travel up and across the body. They move from the level of the right hip to above that of your left shoulder. The sword remains vertical, its tip at six o'clock.

Figure 99. The single rapier parry of High 1.

Stop your hand at the approximate level of your neck, and about six inches to the left of your body and about eight inches in front of your body. Your forearm is above your shoulders, horizontal to the floor, hand relaxed, its palm turned towards your partner, thumb down, knuckle bow to the inside (left). The blade is hanging straight down from the hand and hilt, with the tip at six o'clock. Your arm is in front of your body, not resting on it. The forte of the blade is at the level of the notch in your left shoulder where the deltoid meets the biceps. (Fig. 99)

High 2: Defense against an attack to the right shoulder

Although the parry of 3 is generally used to protect the right shoulder, the parry of High 2 can also be used to good effect on stage. Because of the need to push the blade out through the center at shoulder level, High 2 is most commonly executed as a diagonal or circular parry.

From the guard of Terza, supinate your hand and turn the knuckle bow to the inside (left). Place the tip at six o'clock. From six o'clock, begin a counterclockwise circle with the tip of the sword turning your wrist, and extending your arm. Although the arm is now moving with the parry, the tip does not angle away from you.

As the blade and arm reach one o'clock, your elbow is at roughly chest level, your hand above the level of the shoulder. From one o'clock turn your knuckle bow back towards the inside (left), your palm towards you. Do not stop the action of the circle while doing this; keep moving.

---

[11]Some schools apply the term ''watch parry'' to the standard parry of 1, though this is incorrect; the image of looking at one's watch is cleaner in the parry of High 1.

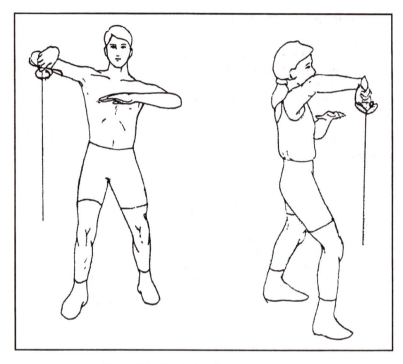

Figure 100. The single rapier parry of High 2.

When the tip reaches ten o'clock the elbow is at the level of your ear. From this placement the circle is completed with rotation to six o'clock from elbow, hand and sword.

Your arm is angled up, elbow at ear level, your hand just above shoulder level, the wrist bent down, knuckle bow turned to the outside (right). The blade of the sword travels straight down and slightly forward, the tip at six o'clock. The forte of the blade is at armpit level. This is the parry of High 2. The high, angled placement of the right arm has earned the parry of High 2 the nickname of the "Chicken-Wing Parry." (Fig. 100)

The Parry of Low 2: Defense for an Attack to the Right Knee

The parry of Low 2 is exactly the same as the standard parry of 2, only the sword hand is lowered to protect the right knee. This parry is used quite often in the theatre in order to avoid using the sometimes awkward supinated position of the parry of 8. The parry also turns the true edge towards the attack, making for a better parry against an aggressive edge blow.

The parry is executed in the same manner as the standard parry of 2, and the "Actor's Parry." Your palm is turned towards you, your hand approximately six inches outside and in front of your body. Your arm is straight with your palm facing toward you and the knuckle bow turned toward the outside (right). The blade hangs straight down and slightly forward with its tip at six o'clock. The tip is about three inches from the floor, the forte at the level of the right quadriceps, just above the knee. (Fig. 101)

"Window Parry": A Variation on the Parry of High 5

As in the parry of 5, this parry gets its name from American fight master David Boushey. He refers to this parry as the "Window Parry" because the reversed position of the right arm and blade

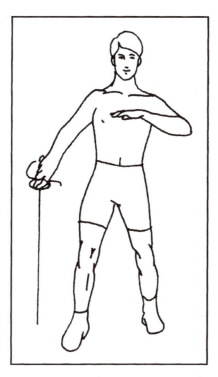

Figure 101. The single rapier parry of Low 2.

form a sort of frame around the face, a little window on the world. The parry is also referred to as 5A; the A standing for *alternate*. In any case, this parry is an alternative defense for the head.

From the guard of Quarta, guide the tip counterclockwise to the position of seven o'clock. Extend your arm and drop your hand below the level of the waist, your palm facing toward you, knuckle bow towards the ground. The tip is about three inches from the floor.

Keeping the tip at seven o'clock, draw the hand and sword across the body from the left until the hilt is on your right. From this point guide the tip from the left out towards your partner and over to your right. Describe a half circle, keeping the tip towards the floor, to the position of five o'clock.

Without stopping the motion, guide the tip to three o'clock and turn the wrist so that your palm faces towards you. The knuckle bow should be turned up. Leading with the wrist, the sword (remaining at three o'clock) travels at a diagonal up and across the body. It moves from the level of the right hip to above your head on your left. The right hand is on the inside (left) of the body at roughly your shoulder level. Do not let your sword hand travel up your center line and through the plane of the oncoming attack. The forte of the blade must travel up through your center line to meet the attack.

As the sword passes the middle of your body begin rotating at the waist, turning your right shoulder towards your partner.

Stop the sword so that your upper arm is horizontal to the floor at the level of your shoulder. Your elbow is bent at roughly forty-five degrees with your forearm to the inside (left) of your body and vertical to the floor.

Your right shoulder is turned slightly towards your partner. Your palm is towards you, knuckle bow up, tip at three o'clock. The arm is bent at roughly ninety degrees with the upper arm parallel to the floor. The sword is horizontal to the floor, above your head and in front of your body. The forte of the sword is in front of and above the center of your head. The sword does not angle behind

Figure 102. The Window Parry.

you or forward towards your partner, but points straight off to your right. This placement forms the window you look through at your partner. (Fig. 102)

The Parry of Low 5: Defense for a vertical attack to the groin

Low 5 is the defensive position to a vertical uppercut to the groin. This parry is often used in farce, much like Charlie Chaplin's "arse-kick," for comic reactions or interaction between characters. Low 5 also is used in defense to a flourish of attacks, or alone, for comic or dramatic affect.

From the guard of Terza guide the tip of the sword up to the position of twelve o'clock. Your palm is facing you, the knuckle bow turned to the inside (left).

Guide the tip in a counterclockwise direction to the position of nine o'clock. Extend your arm and lower your hand below your waist line. Keep your hand to the outside of your right leg.

Slightly increase the depth of your plié, which opens your legs just a little wider. If the blade is still too close to the groin, bend slightly forward from the waist.

Your arm is extended and to the right of your body with your palm towards you. The hilt is outside (right) of the right leg, knuckle bow down. The sword is in front of you, horizontal to the floor and below your crotch. The tip is at nine o'clock with the forte protecting the groin. (Fig. 103)

Parries of the Transitional Age

All of the parries covered so far are those designed to fit the style of the cut and thrust attacks of the early rapier, where the blade is held out like a wall, stopping the blow of the sword. For some choreographers, and some productions, however, this style of "slash and bash" swordplay does not

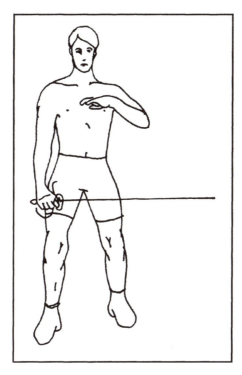

Figure 103. The single rapier parry of Low 5.

fit the bill. Many directors and choreographers prefer a style of rapier play that favors a quick exchange of point work rather than edge to edge play. For this type of ''fencing,'' the vertical parries offered earlier can be slow and ineffective. The blade does not need to be drawn back in order to deflect a thrust, and may be kept angled slightly forward. This type of parry is referred to as a *transitional parry* because it represents the form of defense that complements the thrusting style of the transitional rapier.

For the theatrical combatant, the shift from the standard rapier parries to the transitional parries is quite simple. The hand placement and general mechanics of the parry remain the same, except for the angle of the defending blade. In high line parries like 3 and 4, instead of directing the points straight up, they are angled forward roughly forty-five degrees. The points are also angled slightly away from the body, at one instead of twelve o'clock in the outside high, and eleven instead of twelve in the inside high line. In the low lines the same principal applies. The blades are angled forward towards the opponent. (Fig. 104) In all the transitional parries the hand must still travel out to the parry and the forte still defends the intended target. The blade is kept forward as a threat to one's opponent and to facilitate a quicker thrust after successfully parrying an attack.

It is important to note that transitional parries should not be used in sequences that involve a good deal of edge work. The angling of the blades creates a plane for the offending blade to strike and off of which it may possibly ricochet. In the high line this could harmlessly send a blade down towards the floor, but if the blade happens to bounce up from the low line, it could strike the body or face. It is for this reason that these parries are generally used in sequences that use a great deal of point work and little edge-play.

Both forms of parries are effective, and work well in their specific medium. Neither is better or worse than the other, and it is advisable for you to become familiar with both. Depending on the director, choreographer or period of the production, you will likely be called upon to use both. As

A

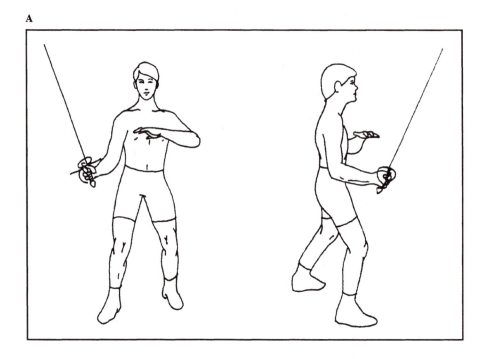

B

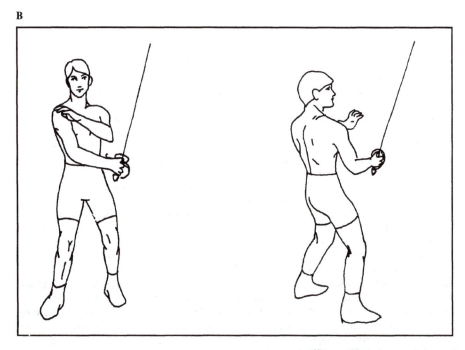

Figure 104. **A**-Transitional parry of 3. **B**-Transitional parry of 4.

long as the parries are safe, there is no rule pertaining to what should be used when. This is really an artistic choice because the parries used on stage are not based on historical swordplay, but on theatrical effectiveness.

Parries with the Left Hand

". . men do much use at this weapon, to beate off the poynt of the sworde with their hands" [di Grassi][12]

The principal of using the left hand for parries is fairly simple. For obvious safety reasons we use the hand to "beat off the point of the sword," only parrying thrusting attacks. The hand is open, presenting only the palm. The fingers and thumb are drawn back out of the way. The hand always travels across the body in a horizontal line to the target of the attack. The hand is presented so that the palm is toward the attacking blade and meets it on the foible, below the tip. The action is usually a "beat" parry, almost like swatting the blade aside, but remains contained and controlled.

MOVING ON

Once you are fluent with the all the parries, their variations and modifications, and their application to the defensive footwork drill, you are ready to move on to the next chapter.

THE PARRIES IN REVIEW

I. At this stage, two ways of executing a parry have been covered:

- The Blocking Parry: made by moving the sword to block the line in which the opponent makes an attack.
- The Beat Parry: made by striking the opponent's blade sharply aside in a much quicker action.

II. There are eleven standard parries in single rapier fence that create a "defensive box" around the body:

- Parry of 1: Defense for any attack to the left hip;
- Parry of 2: Defense for any attack to the right hip;
- Parry of 3: Defense for a *horizontal* attack or thrust to the right shoulder;
- Parry of 4: Defense for a *horizontal* attack or thrust to the left shoulder;
- Parry of 5: Defense for a descending *vertical* attack to the head;
- Parry of High 3: Defense for a descending *diagonal* attack to the right shoulder;
- Parry of High 4: Defense for a descending *diagonal* attack to the left shoulder;
- Parry of 6: Defense for a thrust to the mid torso;
- Parry of 7: Defense for any attack to the left thigh;
- Parry of 8: Defense for any attack to the right thigh.
- Parry Low 5: Defense for a rising vertical attack to the groin.

III. There are four ways of executing these parries:

- Direct Parry: where the hand and blade cross the body remaining in the same line;

---

[12]di Grassi, p. 148.

- Semicircular Parry: where the hand maintains its same relative placement and the blade moves from one position to another in a semicircular path;
- Diagonal Parry: where the hand and blade travel diagonally across the body from a high to a low line or vice versa;
- Circular Parry: where the point describes a complete circle, finishing with the hand and weapon in the original position.

IV. There are two theatrical styles for presenting rapier parries:

- Standard Parries: parries used in sequences that use a great deal of cutting attacks where the blade is held in a strong vertical plane;
- Transitional Parries: parries generally used in sequences that use a great deal of point work and little edge-play where the blade is angled slightly forward and out.

RULES IN REVIEW

1. The Principle of Defense: Defending forte against offending foible.
2. Always travel *OUT* to a parry: The forte travels in the same plane as the attack.
3. Only the forte travels out to meet the attack. The hand never travels out through the plane of an attack.
4. A parry is an action of the blade; keep the hand and arm near the body.
5. Always parry outside and in front of your body.
6. Only parry with the edge of the blade; parries are made with the true edge of the blade (except in 6 and 8).
7. Blades must meet at ninety degrees. A horizontal parry meets a vertical attack. A vertical parry meets a horizontal attack. A diagonal parry meets a diagonal attack.
8. Any parry is achievable from any guard.
9. The blade should not strike the floor in the execution of any parry.
10. Execute all parries with a firm, but relaxed grip.

Chapter 7

Cut and Thrust

"The cut is more natural, that is, the easiest action; the thrust is the result of a complicated and carefully regulated combination of movements." [Egerton Castle][1]

Since the introduction of the rapier, the conflict between "cut" and "thrust" has been constant. While the Italian school proclaimed the superiority of the point, the English populace clung to their rustic ideals and traditional sword and buckler play. The sword that proceeded the rapier and managed to rival it, at least in England, was a stout, short blade, roughly the length of a man's arm, furnished with a simple cross hilt, pas d'âne, side ring and often a knuckle bow. It was meant to be used with a small hand shield called a buckler for defense and the strong and swift cut on the offense. Before the mid to late sixteenth century the cut, on a pass, was thought the best method of attack possible.

The traditional English weapon of sword and buckler and the technique of the cutting attack was stoutly defended even at the end of the sixteenth century. In George Silver's *Paradoxes of Defence* (1599) he attacks what he considers the "foolhardy" Italian weapon, and supports, with examples, how the edge is the only proper attack.

> *"The Rapier fight, whether it be single or accompanied with Poinard* [Dagger], *Buckler, cloke, or glove of male, is still by reason of the insufficiencie or imperfection of the Rapier, an imperfect fight: unperfect instruments can make no perfect musicke, neither can unperfect weapons make perfect fight."*[2]
>
> Silver then goes on to condemn the practice of the "thrust," pointing out that *"a blow commeth continually as near a way as a thrust, and most commonly nearer, stronger, more swifter, and is sooner done.*[3]
>
> *"Perfect fight,"* he states, *"standeth upon both blow and thrust, therefore the thrust is not only to be used."*[4]

At the turn of the century however, the English gave in, and the edge slowly gave way to the superiority and efficiency of the point. It was found and proven that as one swordsman began to deliver a cut, their opponent could "beat their time" by thrusting home upon the preparation of the cut.

---

[1]Castle, p. 45.
[2]Silver, *Paradoxes,* p. 53.
[3]Silver, *Paradoxes,* p. 18.
[4]Silver, *Paradoxes,* p. 19.

Through the evolution of the rapier however, the point did not immediately reign superior and the cut was used in addition to the thrusting attack. Generally when a thrust was unsuccessful, or the blade had been beaten aside, a combatant would attempt to maneuver their blade so that they might cut at their opponent's face or wrist. The edge was considered superior in these instances:

> *"For no other cause, the edge is preferred before the poynt, then for the time: the shortness whereof, is so to be esteemed above all other things in the Arte, that (ommiting the point and edge) it ought to be given for the best and chiefe counsell, that same to be the better blowe, in which a man spendeth least time. And therfore when this happeneth and may be done with the edg, then the edg is to be preferred before the point."* [di Grassi][5]

The Historical vs. the Theatrical Sword Fight

Cutting, to a rapier fencer, was actually a controlled action from the elbow and the wrist, almost flicking the blade towards its target. The large sweeping motions we see on stage and screen today were practically out of the question. This sweeping cut was not only incredibly slow, exposing the body to a counterattack, but the heavy, unbalanced rapier of the period could not be effectively controlled in such a move.

Stock Fights

But, as with the parry, the stage and screen have created another popular misconception in the offensive actions of swordplay. In Victorian times "stock" fights were created to be plugged into productions, and varied in style according to the requirements of the play. These various routines were a series of whacking cuts at the opponent's blade, repeated as required around the set. Stock fight scenes were often passed on from actor to actor allowing for minimal rehearsal (and creativity) and maximal confidence and fury. Other stage fights, such as the duel in *The Dead Heart,* between Henry Irving and Squire Bancroft, planned out only the final thrust, leaving the actors to fence for themselves until they felt the appropriate climactic moment.[6]

Fencing as an Actor's Necessary Skill

During the mid-Victorian period, Felix Bertrand, the renowned master of fence, had in his company of pupils many predominant actors (Tree, Forbes Robertson, Fred Terry, Ben Greet, Henry Irving, Bancroft and Lewis Waller, as well as such writers as Thackeray and Dickens) and set many stage fights.

Flying Sparks and the Clash of Steel

Before the advent of sound movies and the "ring of steel," sparks flying from the clashing blades were considered an important feature to a fight. Flint was attached to blades, and with the advent of electricity, some swords were actually wired so as to throw off even greater showers of sparks.

Sport Fencing as Dramatic Conflict

At the turn of the century, stage and screen duels were nothing more than elaborate fencing exhibitions where even the likes of the great nineteenth century Shakespearean actor Edmund Kean, an accomplished fencer, had little knowledge of historical swordplay and allowed the stage matches to take the form of modern fencing bouts. In 1905 we see the first fencing manual for actors appear, *Sword Play for Actors: A Manual of Stage Fencing* by Fred Gilbert Blakeslee. It is an interesting text that in all simplicity removes the jacket and mask and has the actors "fence." This trend

---

[5]di Grassi, Giacomo. *His True Arte of Defence.* "When it is better to strike with the edge." London: 1594.
[6]Bertrand, M.B. *"Fencing for Everybody." Pall Mall Gazette.* Oct. 17, 1889.

continued into the cinema, where fencing masters staged the duels between Hollywood's dashing heroes. In the pre-1920 films, broad actions and flamboyant gestures enlivened the fencing routines, but no thought was given towards the presentation of technically correct or dramatically effective swordplay.

Fencing Masters as Fight Choreographers

Fencing coaches were brought in to stage the duels and train actors in the finer points of fencing, although many swashbuckling heroes were accomplished fencers (Basil Rathbone was said to have made a success in competitive fencing; Cornel, Wilde, Douglas Fairbanks, Sr. and Jr., John Derek and Robert Douglas all also had several years of sport fencing among their lists of attributes.) Henry J. Uyttenhove, fencing coach at the Los Angeles Athletic Club and graduate of the Belgium Military Institute of Physical Education, staged the silver screen's early fencing matches. But his works were technically stagings of "dramatic" fencing, and he was soon succeeded by a fellow graduate of the Belgian Military Institute, Fred Cavens. Cavens brought style and flair to the cinematic duels, enlarging movement and offering the great spectacle of attacks and parries in a logical context to the fight, disregarding at times classically correct lunges and guards. His aim was to make the "match" a "fight" magnifying correct fencing, leaving the impression of "skill, strength and manly grace." This new form of swordplay became the rule, and Cavens's successors followed it emphatically, and thus conditioned generations of audiences to believe the "magnified" fencing we recognize as swordplay today.

STAGE TECHNIQUES

Although the offensive principle in a real sword fight is to hit your opponent before they realize you have moved, this is ineffective in the theatre. In stage combat every action needs to be telegraphed to the audience so that the audience can follow the action in logical progression. This is one of the many reasons why modern fencing is not suitable for the stage. Without Cavens's "magnification," the action happens so quickly, the movements being so tight and precise, that no one watching can honestly tell what has taken place.

The Physical Dialogue

In everyday conversations, people can speak fast and sloppily, overlap each other and even speak at the same time. On stage however, this is rarely the case. Things must be scripted in such a way that the illusion of reality is created but in actuality there is a give and take as one person takes focus with their lines and another is silent. This principle must also be applied to stage combat. On stage, "action takes focus," and in a fight where all is action, it is essential to give and take focus so the audience can follow the line of intention, just as in scripted dialogue.

Action Takes Focus

Most books on directing state that movement draws the audience's attention, which is why the speaking actor moves and the others listen. If this is the case, then should a fight be a blur of activity that ends in a wound or kill? NO! (except in those instances where such confusion is a specific choice made by the director and choreographer). A play is an audio-visual experience orchestrating the words and intentions of the playwright, the talent and voice of the actor and a variety of visual pictures; a fight is an integral part of this arrangement. In this orchestration, focus is given and taken on stage through careful planning and blocking of movement. If a cast all moved together, the audience would have no idea where or when to look. This disfocus becomes annoying to an audience and eventually either bores them, causing them to lose interest in the scene, or leaves them wondering what happened.

Action-Reaction-Action

The principle of a real cutting attack is to move quickly and efficiently so that the edge may deliver a blow before one's opponent has time to perceive or defend the attack. On stage, however, it is quite a different matter. If you were to move on stage with the tempo, intention and scope of a real fight, not only would your partner have no idea what was going on (and no real time to safely respond) but the audience would be lost as well. Thus, the historical tactics and mechanics of edge play must be sacrificed, in the same way straight lines become curved crosses in blocking on stage, so that the audience is allowed to perceive and understand the story being told. As mentioned in Chapter 6, actions the audience can see help give the physical conflict subtextual nuance and character motivation.

In order to communicate the most information, strong stage pictures must be presented in a manner that allows the audience to perceive and interpret them. Thus, every offensive and defensive movement is broken down into the three distinct motions presented earlier in this text: Action-Reaction-Action. The first *"Action"* is the preparation and cue for an attack. The *"Reaction"* is the acted response to the cue offered by the aggressor. This may be the *beginning* of a parry, evasion or footwork on the part of the victim. The final *"Action"* is the completion of the offensive and defensive movements *together*. Each movement should flow smoothly from one into the other and not appear awkward or "staged."

The First Action

To avoid the dilemma of two characters "speaking" at once in physical dialogue, we must allow each to "say" their piece before the other jumps in. In this, we lead to the first action of an attack ending in a cue, readable to our partner and drawing a strong stage picture for the audience.

For the purpose of theatrical "magnification," the following cutting attacks are executed with a large sweeping wind up; not just a cocking of the arm. This wind up is a fluid action that generally takes the longest path back and around to a "cocked" position. It is this position that ends the first action, and is our cue to our partner and a point of control prior to the completion of the attack.

The Cue

The cue is a placement of the sword and arm that reads to one's partner as a specific attack to a specific target, leaving no question as to the direction of the attack from its point of origin to its intended target. This is incredibly important in combat, for just as we depend upon cues in vocal dialogue, we depend upon them in the physical as well. If you forget a line in dialogue, a strong cue often puts you back on track, and so a cue in a fight is a helpful reminder of where you are and where you are going in the routine.

The Control Point

As one is given a cue in dialogue, one responds and offers the next line. In stage combat, as one is given a cue, one would "react" to the forthcoming attack and begin to defend oneself. It is in this process that our point of control is essential.

The point of control, or "control point," is that point in an attack that reads as a cue to your partner. This allows you to observe your partner's reaction to the cue, and abort the attack before it is launched if for some reason your partner forgets the next move or begins to parry the wrong target.

The control point is essential to safe stage combat because if a combatant just swings without checking, assuming their partner is ready, their partner may step into an attack, place their hand in line with the incoming blade or not react at all. Any of which could lead to possible injury, and if nothing else, an entirely embarrassing stage picture. So, as always, "think" and then "do."

Of the Cut

There is an underlying principle of mechanics that is applicable to all cutting attacks in stage combat. There are some who teach a "pulled" hit, which in all actuality can hyperextend the elbow and possibly cause whiplash to the attacker, not to mention the actual lack of control in the attacking blade. There are others who teach the "just swing" principal, and if your partner happens to miss a parry, it's their own fault. Both of these attacks can actually whip a flexible blade around a successful parry (referred to as "cutting through steel" in modern sabre play) and strike your partner. These attacks, along with other archaic principles of stage swordplay, actually send the energy of an attack towards the actor and are, unfortunately, still being taught and used today.

The principle of mechanics applied to the cutting attacks herein is known as *pistoning*. It is a method of creating the illusion of the arc of a full cutting attack, while actually sending the energy of the edge beyond your partner, not into them. This technique reads incredibly well for camera as well as for stage, and insures absolute control on the part of the aggressor.

Pistoning the Cut

In order to best begin to understand the mechanics of pistoning, start by placing your sword at your left shoulder, tip pointing directly behind you, blade horizontal (parallel) to the floor, knuckle bow facing away from the body (to the left), quillons parallel to the floor with the hand pronated. The blade of the sword forms a ninety degree angle with your forearm. (Fig. 105.a)

From this starting position, begin the "cutting" action by leading the blade forward with an extension from the right elbow. The sword must remain ninety degrees off the arm, and travel forward, describing an arc with its tip, in a plane horizontal to the floor. The blade should be traveling in this plane towards your imaginary partner's right shoulder. (Fig. 105.b)

When the tip of the sword has traveled approximately one third of the arc from your shoulder to your imaginary partner's, the arm stops extending from the elbow, and the wrist will continue the path of the blade, so that the tip points behind you and to the left.

Keep the arm in place. The wrist guides the tip of the sword forward, continuing to describe the cutting arc until the wrist comes to a natural stop, with the tip of the sword pointed forward and out to the left. The tip of the sword should have traveled another third of the arc from shoulder to shoulder, compassing one-half of a circle from beginning to completion. (Fig. 105.c)

If the range of motion in your arm or wrist stops the blade before it has completed one-third of the arc, do not try to force it. The movement of the arm and wrist should feel comfortable. If your body says "stop," then stop, the angles of the hand to the blade are approximate; it is the targets and control of the blade that must be exact.

Once the wrist guides the tip forward in its circle to where it points forward and to your left (or behind your imaginary partner and off to their right), begin to straighten the arm and push the tip of the blade forward. The tip and the blade of the sword extends straight forward, like a piston, completing the final third of the arc without giving any energy to the attack. The extension of the arm redirects the inertia of the attack and thrusts the energy of the arm beyond your opponent rather than into them. Upon completion, the tip of the sword should be at your imaginary partner's shoulder level, about six inches outside their body. For this particular cut, the arm must be extended across yours and your imaginary partner's body, much like Seconda Across the Body. The arm should be straight but not locked at the elbow, your hand remaining pronated, directing the sword forward, outside your partner's body. (Fig. 105.d)

The three distinct motions of the wrist and arm are what makes this attack safe and controlled, while reading to an audience as a full cutting attack without pulling the blade. One does not have to pull the energy of the attack or worry about their partner parrying a full blow. While the blade describes a full cutting arc, the actual energy is channeled forward so that the attacking blade ricochets past an opponent's blade once the blades have met. The real effort of a cutting attack is thrust past one's opponent and is not directed at them at all.

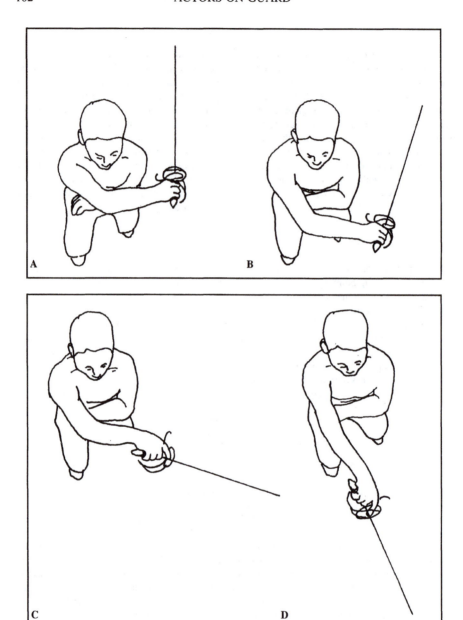

Figure 105. The Piston Cut
A-The chambered or cocked position for the cut; **B**-the first action of the cut: extended from the elbow; **C**-the second action of the cut: extended from the wrist; **D**-the final action of the piston cut: the thrusting of the energy forward.

Practice this technique slowly, initiating the action with the arm, then the wrist, and the completing the action again with the arm. Make one action flow into the other. Do not blur them all together, but make one action fluidly lead into the next, always sending the energy beyond, thrusting the hand on sword forward like a piston.

Once this action becomes comfortable, try overlapping the action of the wrist with the final action of the arm, so that just before the tip completes its half circle (pointing beyond one's partner), the arm begins to push it forward. Practice this action several times for it is the principle for all cutting attacks.

Of the True Edge

For reasons of sheer practicality, all cutting attacks will be delivered with the true edge of the blade. Because the quillons are generally at a right angle to the blade, pointing in the direction of the edges (both lower and upper), they give the combatant a comprehensible gauge to judge the position of the blade; the quillons can be used as the "rudder" of the sword. If an attack is horizontal, the quillons should remain parallel to the floor, and if the attack is on the diagonal, the quillons should be at an angle approximately forty five degrees with the floor. Upon completion of a cutting attack, the tip should be directed straight forward, outside one's opponent. The quillons should be in line with the target, matching the plane of the attack.

As in the wrapping the eights exercise, always lead an attack with the knuckle bow. Since the true edge of the blade is positioned to face the same direction as the knuckle bow, cutting with the knuckle bow towards the target will assure an attack with the true edge.

THE CUTTING ATTACKS

To better grasp the placement of the blade in a cutting attack, it is best to work with an unarmed partner. Be sure your partner is far enough removed so that there is *no possibility* of the attacking blade reaching them. Your partner stands on guard, facing you, and "reacts" by letting you know when they are given the correct cue (responding with a simple "YES" or "No"). They also remain stationary during the exercise, providing you with specific targets and body space to work with. If you are working without a partner, facing a full length mirror, outside of distance, serves as a valid reference point.

First Action into Reaction

During this exercise, the "wind up" is added to the attacks, which adds stationary movement to the lower body. As you wind up, traveling to the cue and control point, rock back to the defensive attitude of stationary footwork (as described in Chapter 3). When your partner acknowledges the cue, you then rock forward into the offensive attitude of stationary footwork. From this position, you perform the mechanics of a correctly pistoned cut towards the specified target on your partner. Be sure to make eye contact with your partner to see them respond to the cue, then look at the target of the attack.

Although a cutting attack may be delivered from any guard position to any of the specified body targets, the offensive actions are presented in an order that corresponds to the defensive sequence or "drill" covered at the end of Chapter 6. It is important to remember that the focus of the attack is the body target, not a defensive blade or number. You do not attack a 1 or 3, you attack the left hip or right shoulder. Different parries can protect the same target; numbers are not consistent, body parts are. Therefore, the attack is to the target, not to the parry (Fig. 106).

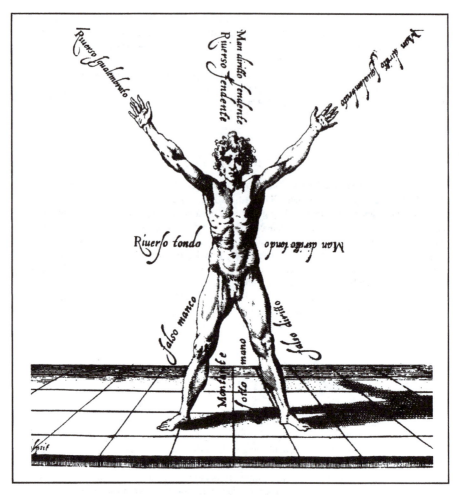

Plate XV: A plate from Fabris' *Sienza e practicia d'Arme,* showing the principal directions of attack (1606).

MAN DRITTO TONDO (Mezzo):
Horizontal Cutting Attack to the Left Hip[7]

The First Action and Cue

From the guard of Terza, rock back, and with the wrist and arm guide the tip of the sword down and behind you on the right (in a manner similar to the wrapping the eights exercise covered in Chapter 4) and raise the tip of the sword to the level of your waist, the blade horizontal to the floor, tip pointed directly behind you, knuckle bow to the outside (right) and your hand supinated at waist

---

[7]The term "Man Dritto Tondo Mezzo" is an old Italian fencing expression for a horizontal cutting attack to the left hip or flank. *Man Dritto* means "right hand" or "forehand," and is applied to any cutting attack delivered from the right side of the body. Much like a forehand stroke in tennis. *Tondo* means "round" or "circular" and refers to the cutting arc of the blade (in contrast to the straight plane of a thrusting attack). *Mezzo* means "middle" and refers to the target at the middle of the opponent's body.

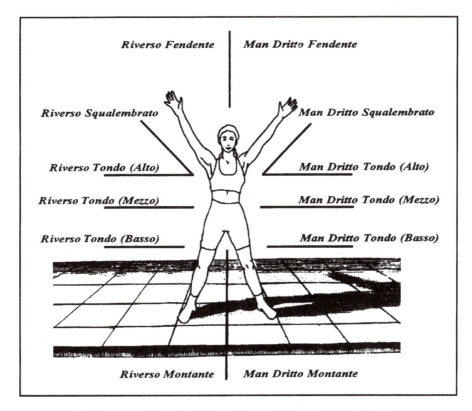

Figure 106. Types of cutting attacks and their specific targets; after Fabris.

level. This position of the sword, with the body rocked back, is the cue for an attack to the left hip. (Fig. 107)

This position may seem awkward, until range of motion and strength in the wrist develops. (A tight grip on the sword also adds to the difficulty of this action; be sure you have a relaxed grip.)

Beware of "Wrapping" your Cue

In this, and all following cutting attacks, be sure the sword does not "wrap around" your torso, masking it from your partner. The blade should be held in a plane parallel to the imaginary tracks on which your feet are placed. Wrapping the blade around you makes the cue difficult for your partner to read and places the blade and tip in a gray area outside your peripheral vision. Keep the blade safely at your side where your partner can see the cue.

Looking for the Reaction

From the cue for a horizontal cut to the left hip, the body begins to rock forward, the hand and blade remaining stationary, until you have rocked forward into the offensive position of stationary footwork. This transition from the stationary defensive to offensive position is your *control point.* This keeps the body moving so that there is no dead time on stage, but allows your partner to read the attack and allows you to perceive your partner's reaction. This gives you the time to decide whether to complete the action or to abort for safety reasons. You are in control.

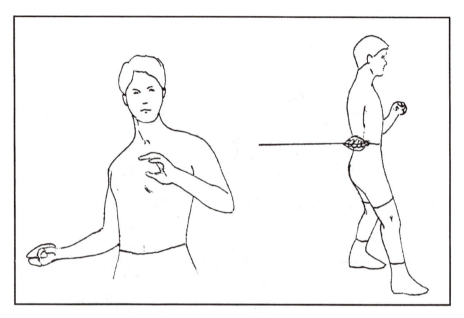

Figure 107. Man Dritto Tondo (mezzo): the cue for a cut to the left hip.

The Training Reaction

When your partner sees the correct cue given for the attack being practiced they should say "YES." If for some reason there is something wrong in the cue, they should say "NO." These are the reactions you are working with at this time, if there is a problem, fix it. Do not come close to a cue, it must be exact. There should be no doubt in the mind of your partner what the cue means. In this case it is a horizontal attack to the left hip, so it should be a horizontal cue from the right waist.

In this, and all following exercises, present the correct cue *as* you rock forward. Stop your body in the offensive position of stationary footwork, and if the correct reaction is given, continue the attack using the mechanics of a pistoned cut to guide the sword to the intended target.

The Second Action

The second action is the pistoning of the cut. Traveling in a plane horizontal to the floor, the blade comes to rest at your partner's waist-level, about six inches outside their body. The hand remains supinated, so that the cut may be completed with the true edge of the blade.

RIVERSO TONDO (Mezzo):
Horizontal Cutting Attack to the Right Hip[8]

The First Action and Cue

From the completed attack to your opponent's left hip, carry the sword across your body to the left, much like the transition from Terza to Quarta. As the sword is carried across the body, begin

---

[8]The term "Riverso Tondo Mezzo" is the old Italian fencing expression for the horizontal cutting attack to the right hip or flank. *Riverso* (also sometimes *Rovescio*) means "wrong" or "other side," "reverse side" or "backhand," and is applied to any cutting attack delivered from the left side of the body. Much like a backhand stroke in tennis.

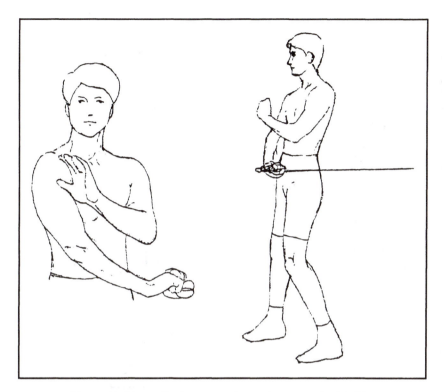

Figure 108. Riverso Tondo (mezzo): the cue for a cut to the right hip.

to rock back to the defensive stationary position. As this is done, guide the tip of the sword up and directly behind you on your left side, hilt at waist-level, blade parallel to the floor, hand pronated with the knuckle bow facing the inside (left). This position of the sword is the cue for a horizontal cutting attack to the right hip. (Fig. 108)

The Final Action

After rocking forward and receiving the correct reaction, the blade travels in a horizontal plane towards the hip, the hand remains pronated completing the action with the tip at the level of your partner's waist, just above the hip bone, blade about six inches outside your partner's body.

RIVERSO TONDO (Alto):
Horizontal Cutting Attack to the Right Shoulder[9]

The First Action and Cue

From the completed attack to your opponent's right hip, begin to rock back, and at the same time draw the sword back and behind you, on your left, similar to the pattern of wrapping the eights. Your

---

[9]The term *alto* means "high," "top" or "upper part" and refers to the target at the upper part of the opponent's body, in this case the shoulder or chest.

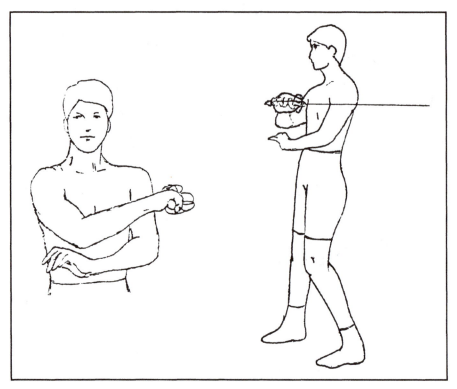

Figure 109. Riverso Tondo (alto): the cue for a cut to the right shoulder.

hand should come to rest at the level of your shoulder, the tip pointing directly behind you, blade horizontal and parallel to the floor, knuckle bow facing away from the body (to the left), quillons parallel to the floor with the hand pronated. This placement of the hand and sword, with the body rocked back, is the cue for a horizontal cutting attack to the right shoulder. (Fig. 109)

The Final Action

After rocking forward and receiving the correct reaction, the blade travels forward in a horizontal plane, the hand remaining pronated, completing the action with the tip at the level of the junction of the deltoid and biceps/triceps muscles in the right arm, the blade about six inches outside your partner's body.

MAN DRITTO TONDO (Alto):
Horizontal Cutting Attack to the Left Shoulder

The First Action

From the completed attack to the right shoulder, roll your wrist counterclockwise and lower the tip of your sword so that it is at six o'clock, the tip directed straight down towards the floor. Your knuckle bow is to the outside (left), thumb down and your palm turned towards your partner, much like the parry of High 1 discussed in Chapter 6.

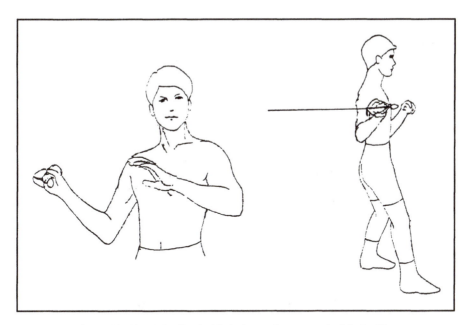

Figure 110. Man Dritto Tondo (alto): the cue for a cut to the left shoulder.

The Mollinello

As the sword and hand reach this position, begin to rock back, at the same time begin to lift your sword hand so that it is above your head, tip still hanging down towards the floor. Guide the sword around behind you in this manner. Keep the blade in close to your body, but be aware of the quillons. If your sword is not held high enough or if it is carried around to close too the body, you could possibly strike yourself in the head. This circular transfer behind the head is known as a *mollinello*.[10] It is best to take the mollinello quite slowly at first.

Keeping the blade vertical and close to your body during the mollinello maintains a sound control over the tip of the weapon as it travels behind you. In class, or on stage where there are many bodies working in a confined space, this allows for maximum efficiency with minimum danger.

Once the blade is behind your right shoulder, begin lowering your arm and guiding the blade the rest of the way around to your right side, turning your wrist so that the palm is supinated with the knuckle bow to the outside (right). The sword hand should come to rest at shoulder level, and the wrist should be used to lift the blade to a position where it is horizontal to the floor, tip pointed directly behind you.

The Cue

This position of the sword, tip straight behind you, blade horizontal to the floor at shoulder level on the right side of your body, with the body rocked back, is the cue for a horizontal attack to the left shoulder. (Fig. 110)

---

[10]*Mollinello* means "like a little wind-mill," and describes the action of pivoting the blade in a circle, in either a clockwise or counterclockwise direction, over the head or on either the inside or outside lines. The wrapping the eights exercise introduced in Chapter 4 practices both inside (on the left) and outside (on the right) mollinellos.

The Final Action

After rocking forward and receiving the correct reaction, the blade travels forward in a horizontal plane, parallel to the floor. The hand remains supinated, completing the action with the tip at the level of the junction of the deltoid and biceps/triceps muscles in the left arm, blade about six inches outside your partner's body.

The transition from a horizontal cut to the right shoulder to a horizontal cut to the left shoulder (and vice versa) may also be performed in a larger sweeping action if space and distance allows. From the completed attack to the right shoulder, begin to draw your arm back in toward you, keeping the blade horizontal, hand pronated. As your arm is drawn back, also begin to rock backward, to the stationary defensive position.

Once the tip is pointing directly out to your left, begin to raise your arm, roll your wrist counterclockwise so that it is supinated, and guide your sword hand and sword around and behind your head. The blade should remain parallel to the floor and the tip should describe a large circle around your body. When the blade is behind your right shoulder, begin lowering your arm and guiding the blade the rest of the way around to your right side, into the cue for a man dritto tondo alto (cut left shoulder).

FENDENTE: Vertical Cutting Attack to the Head[11]

The cut to the head can be executed from either the right side of the body (*Man dritto fendente*) or from the left (*Riverso fendente*). For the purpose of the drill the head cut will be executed from the right, but for the sake of further practice the technique from the left is included.

The First Action and Cue for the MAN DRITTO FENDENTE

Rock back, and with an outside mollinello guide your sword around and behind your right shoulder by bending at the elbow and raising the sword arm to the approximate level of your ear. Complete the action with the sword on the right side of your head, directly behind your right shoulder blade, hilt and sword hand at the level of your ear, blade vertical, hanging straight down behind your back, tip at six o'clock, the palm turned in towards the ear with the knuckle bow directed straight behind you. This position of the blade is the cue for a vertical cutting attack to your partner's head, from your right side. (Fig. 111)

The Reaction and Final Action

Once you have rocked forward, and have received the correct reaction, complete the attack by using the mechanics of a pistoned attack. Extend your sword arm toward your partner's head, letting the blade trail behind you. Extend your arm to the level of your partner's forehead, never any lower.

Positioning the sword hand at your partner's forehead assures that the cut is always directed up and beyond them. If your partner happens to be a good bit shorter than you, shoulder level or more, direct your wrist to a point approximately six inches above your partner's head rather than at their forehead. This allows you to send the energy of the attack safely over and beyond your partner's head.

Then initiate the action of the wrist bringing the blade forward, and complete the action by channeling the energy of the cut forward, above your partner's head, thrusting up and beyond them towards the ceiling. The action should complete with the blade positioned on the center line of your

---

[11]*Fendente* means "a downward stroke of the sword" or "to strike a cleaving blow" and is applied to a descending vertical cutting attack to the head.

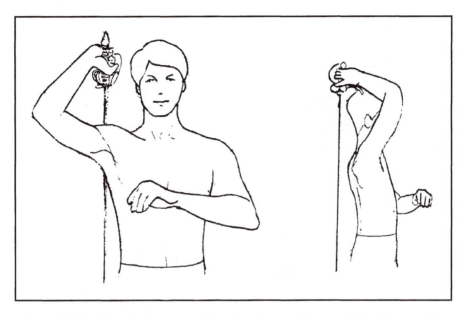

Figure 111. Man Dritto Fendente: the cue for a descending vertical cut to the head from the right.

partner, about six to ten inches above their head, your sword hand at the level of their forehead and the sword arm and sword in a straight line angling up from your shoulder.

The First Action and Cue of the RIVERSO FENDENTE

Begin to rock back to the defensive stationary position, and at the same time carry your sword behind you and to your left with an inside mollinello. Completing the action, the sword should come to rest on the left side of your head, directly behind your left shoulder blade, hilt and sword hand above the level of your head, blade vertical, hanging straight down behind your back, tip at six o'clock, the palm turned out away from your head, with the knuckle bow directed straight behind you. This position of the blade is the cue for a vertical cutting attack to your partner's head, from the left. (Fig. 112)

The Reaction and Final Action

The mechanics for the cut are identical to those from the right.

RIVERSO SQUALEMBRATO:
Diagonal Cutting Attack to the Right Shoulder[12]

The First Action and Cue

From the completed vertical attack to your opponent's head, lift the sword and sword arm up, and carry them outside your partner's body, to your right. (The blade may also be cleared to the left, but

---

[12]There is no direct translation for the term *squalembrato*, although Fabris' text and illustrations seem to indicate that it is a descending diagonal cutting attack. The Italian word *squilibrato* means "unbalanced" and may indicate the oblique angle of the original cutting attack.

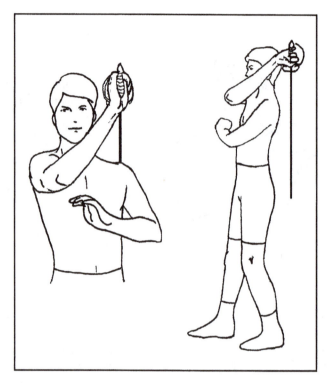

Figure 112. Riverso Fendente: the cue for a descending vertical cut to the head from the left.

for the purposes of the drill, carry the blade to the right.) Once the sword is outside your partner's body, begin to rock back to the stationary defensive position and draw your sword hand in and behind you to the right by bending at the elbow. Guide the blade behind you, much like the mollinello from riverso tondo alto (cut right shoulder) to man dritto tondo alto (cut left shoulder), only from the right to the left, with your sword hand behind you and your arm above your head. Once on the left side of your head, the sword should come to rest on your left side, hilt at shoulder level, blade pointing straight behind you and angled up at approximately forty-five degrees, hand pronated with the knuckle bow facing the inside (left). This position of the sword is the cue for a diagonal cutting attack to the right shoulder. (Fig. 113)

The Final Action

Once you have rocked forward, and have received the correct reaction, complete the attack using the mechanics of a piston cut. The blade will travel down from this position to the shoulder at an angle of roughly forty-five degrees, the hand remains pronated, completing the action with the tip at the level of the junction of the deltoid and biceps/triceps muscles in the right arm, blade about six inches outside your partner's body, quillons diagonal to the floor.

MAN DRITTO SQUALEMBRATO:
Diagonal Cutting Attack to the Left Shoulder

The First Action and Cue

From the completed diagonal attack to the right shoulder, begin to rock back, and at the same time begin to execute a mollinello, from left to right, guiding the sword around behind you. Keep the blade in close to your body, but be aware of the quillons so you do not strike yourself in the head.

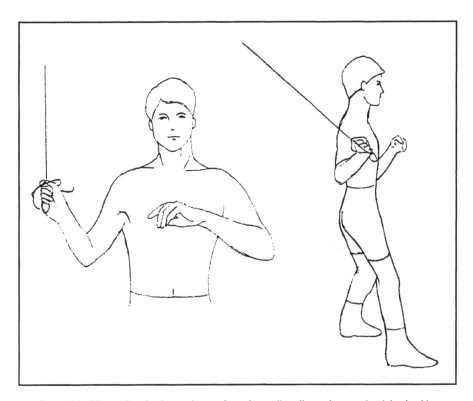

Figure 113. Riverso Squalembrato: the cue for a descending diagonal cut to the right shoulder.

The sword should come to rest on your right side, hilt at shoulder level, blade pointing straight behind you and angled up at approximately forty-five degrees, hand supinated with the knuckle bow facing the outside (right). This position of the sword is the cue for a diagonal cutting attack to the left shoulder. (Fig. 114)

Reaction and Final Action

Once you have rocked forward, and have received the correct reaction, complete the attack using the mechanics of a piston cut. The blade travels down from the control point to the shoulder at an angle of roughly forty-five degrees, the hand remains supinated completing the action with the tip at the level of the junction of the deltoid and biceps/triceps muscles in the right arm, blade about six inches outside our partner's body, quillons diagonal to the floor.

If space and distance allow, the transition between the diagonal cutting attacks may also be executed in the larger sweeping mollinello described earlier.

MAN DRITTO TONDO (Basso):
Diagonal Cutting Attack to the Left Thigh[13]

The First Action and Cue

From the completed diagonal attack to your opponent's left shoulder, begin to rock back, and at the same time guide the tip of the sword behind you on your left side, and mollinello behind you

---

[13]The term *basso* means "low" or "lowered" and refers to the lowest immediate target of the opponent's body, in this case the thigh or knee.

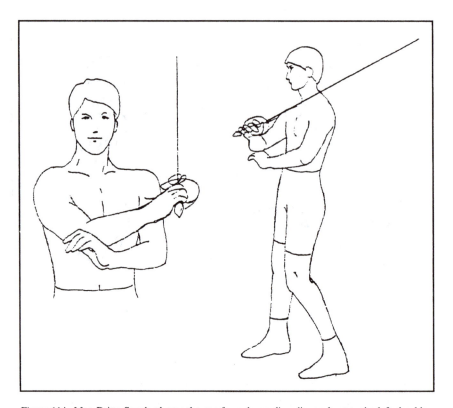

Figure 114. Man Dritto Squalembrato: the cue for a descending diagonal cut to the left shoulder.

as in the transition from riverso tondo alto (cut right shoulder) to man dritto tondo alto (cut left shoulder). The sword should come to rest on your right side, hilt at waist level, blade angled at approximately forty-five degrees with the tip just above the level of your shoulder, hand supinated with the knuckle bow facing the outside (right). (A tight grip on the sword will add to the difficulty of this action. Be sure you have a relaxed grip.) This position of the sword is the cue for a diagonal cutting attack to the left thigh. (Fig. 115)

Reaction and Final Action

Once you have rocked forward, and have received the correct reaction, complete the attack using the mechanics of a piston cut. The blade travels down to the thigh at roughly a forty-five degree angle, the hand remaining supinated. The action is completed with the tip at the level of the quadriceps just above the knee bone, blade angled down and about six inches outside your partner's body.

RIVERSO TONDO (Basso):
Diagonal Cutting Attack to the Right Thigh

The First Action and Cue

From the completed attack to your opponent's left thigh, begin to rock back and, with the sword tip down, guide the sword across your body as in the transition from man dritto tondo mezzo (cut

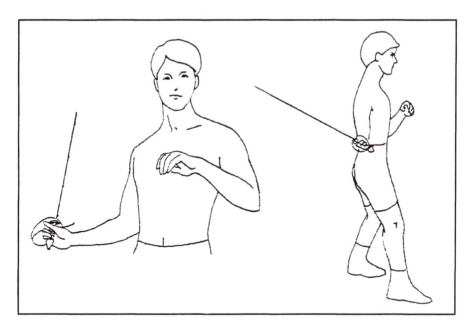

Figure 115. Man Dritto Tondo (basso): the cue for a cut to the left thigh.

left hip) to riverso tondo mezzo (cut right hip). The sword should come to rest on your left side, hilt at waist level, blade angled at approximately forty-five degrees with the tip just above the level of your shoulder, hand pronated with the knuckle bow facing the inside (left). This position of the sword is the cue for a diagonal cutting attack to the right thigh. (Fig. 116)

Reaction and Final Action

Once you have rocked forward, and have received the correct reaction, complete the attack using the mechanics of a piston cut. The blade travels down to the thigh at a forty-five degree angle, the hand remaining pronated. The action is completed with the tip at the level of the quadriceps just above the knee bone, blade angled down and about six inches outside our partner's body, quillons parallel to the floor.

You may also make a diagonal cutting attack at the right thigh by carrying the blade around and behind the body with a mollinello, much like the transition from man dritto fendente (cut to the head from the right) to riverso squalembrato (diagonal cut to the right shoulder).

MONTANTE: Vertical Cutting Attack to the Groin[14]

The First Action

Although the montante can be executed both man dritto and riverso, at this time we will only explore the riverso; the man dritto will be discussed later. Leading with the wrist, lower the tip of

---

[14]*Montante* is Italian, literally meaning "rising, mounting; an uppercut." The French *montant* literally means "rising." Both refer to specific cutting attacks generally delivered upward to the groin or under the arms. The latter is referred to in Shakespeare in such works as *Much Ado About Nothing* (I.i.30), *Merry Wives of Windsor* (II.iii.27) and in Ben Jonson's *Every Man in His Humor* (IV.v)

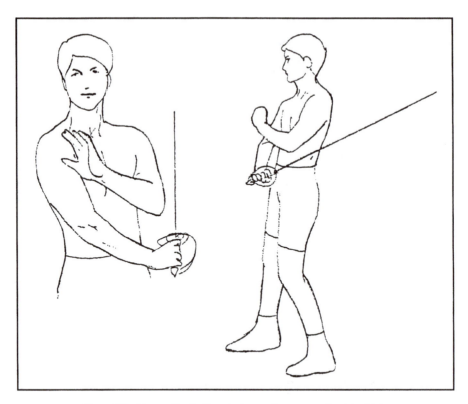

Figure 116. Riverso Tondo (basso): the cue for a cut to the right thigh.

your sword so that the tip is just off the floor, and guide the sword across your body. Once the hand and the sword are outside, rock back to the defensive stationary position. As this is done, guide the tip of the sword up and directly behind you on your left side. Do not raise the hand above the level of your waist, but by rotating the wrist, let the tip of the sword angle up behind you so that the tip points roughly towards the ceiling.

The Cue

For the riverso montante, the sword is on your left side, hilt at waist level, blade angled up toward the ceiling, hand in middle or vertical position, palm towards the body, with the knuckle bow facing directly behind you. This position of the sword is the cue for the montante, a vertical cut up into the groin. (Fig. 117)

Reaction and Final Action

Once you have rocked forward, and have received the correct reaction, complete the attack using the mechanics of a pistoned cut. Extend your sword arm toward your partner's groin, letting the blade trail behind you. Extend your arm to the level of your partner's groin, *never any higher*.

Positioning the sword hand at the level of your partner's groin assures that the cut is always directed down and below them. If your partner happens to be a good bit shorter than you, shoulder level or more, direct your wrist to a point approximately six inches below your partner's groin. This allows you to send the energy of the attack down, safely below your partner's groin. If your partner

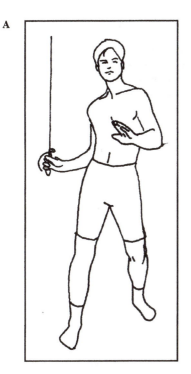 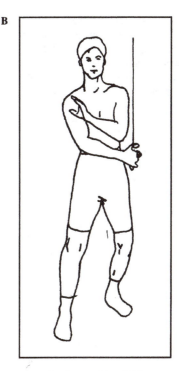

Figure 117. Montante: the cue for a rising vertical cut to the groin. **A**-man dritto; **B**-Riverso.

is not tall enough to execute this technique, or if your blade strikes the ground during the attack, you may angle the blade slightly outside to facilitate the cutting arc. If there is still a problem with the attack, the montante may not be a practical technique for you.

From the first one-third of the attack, the extended arm position of the piston cut, initiate the action of the wrist, bringing the blade forward, and complete the action by channeling the energy of the cut forward, below your partner's groin, thrusting down and beyond them towards the floor. The action completes with the blade positioned on the center line of your partner, about six to ten inches below their groin, your hand at the level of their groin and the sword arm and sword in a straight line angling down from your shoulder. This attack is generally parried in Low 5.

OF THE THRUST

". . . the right or streight Line is of all other the shortest: wherefore if a man would strike in the shortest lyne, it is requisite that he strike in the streightline." [di Grassi][15]

There is no question of the superiority of the thrust over the cut since an attack with the point travels forward in a straight line, having the advantage of time and distance over an attack with the edge. This, however, poses a difficult problem for the theatrical sword fight. The actual mechanics of the thrust are such that one's opponent should not perceive its execution until they are hit. How

---

[15]di Grassi, p. 16 ff.

then can such an action be executed safely and effectively in the process of physical dialogue in a stage fight? The straight line of the thrust cannot be magnified in the manner of the cutting arc. The large sweeping actions of an edge blow read well to the combatants and the audience, but the strong visual cue of a safe stage thrust is not readily apparent. It is for these, as well as many other reasons, that some styles of stage combat teach the principal of thrusting *on-line* with the center of the opponent's body, so the target is apparent, and letting them parry as a modern fencer would, actually removing a threatening blade.

Point work, the most dangerous and effective form of actual swordplay, is not something that should be loosely adapted from modern fencing, or left to the mechanics of an actual parry on the part of an untrained actor. Professional fencers, who also depend on the mechanics of an actual parry, miss; why then should a beginning combatant do any better?

Action-Reaction-Action

As you know, "action-reaction-action" makes cutting attacks safe; it also allows for the giving and taking focus in point work while cueing one's partner as to exactly where the thrust will be directed. As described earlier, the cue in a cutting attack is the visible chambering of the weapon after the wind up and prior to releasing the attack. Because a thrust does not always have a "wind up," the first action and cue of theatrical puncture play is known as *showing the point.*

Showing the Point

Once you are comfortable with the mechanics of giving and taking focus in the cutting attacks, the principle of point work is actually quite simple. Showing the point is exactly what it says. You draw back your sword, much like the retracting of a needle by a sewing machine, while rocking back into the stationary defensive position. Once there, you extend your sword toward its target, *off-line* about three to six inches outside the body. This extension from the rocked back position is the cue and control point of the thrusting attack. You actually show your partner where you will be attacking with the point of your sword, while the rocked back position keeps you out of distance. Being out of distance you can be fully extended and observe your partner's reaction so you can safely complete the attack. (Fig. 118)

As discussed in Chapter 6, there are only eight points of the body where an attack with a sword can safely be directed. Although any one of these points, or targets, may be attacked with the edge of the sword, only six of these can safely be attacked with a thrust. This is because the tip of the sword, although varying in origin, does not vary in angle and plunges straight forward, limiting the areas it may advance toward safely.

THE THRUSTS

Beginning the Techniques

The Cue and Reaction

These exercises, like those of the cutting attacks, should first be worked with an unarmed partner, who is far enough removed that there is no possibility of the attacking blade reaching them. Your partner stands on guard, facing you, and lets you know when they are given the correct cue, responding as before with a simple "YES" or "NO." They also remain stationary during the exercise, providing you with specific targets and body space to work with. If you are working without a partner, facing a full length mirror, out of distance, serves as a valid reference point.

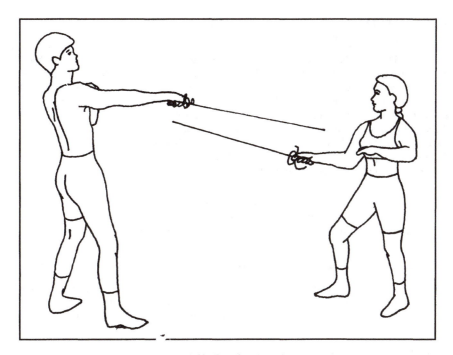

Figure 118. Showing the point.

Targets

All of the following attacks are *off-line,* meaning that they are directed three to six inches outside the body. A dulled or buttoned sword is still quite lethal and can, with little effort, easily penetrate flesh. As always, a threatening blade should never cross the face or throat, for any reason.

It is important to remember that the *focus* of the attack is the body target, not a defensive blade or number. The thrust is made in the plane of a specific point on the body, not to a defensive position of a blade. For example, the parry of 6 defends against a thrust to the mid torso, the attack is actually a thrust at the level of the torso, three to six inches to the right of your partner's body, at chest level, not to number 6. Focusing on body targets serves two purposes; one, it forces the combatant to concentrate on specifics and two, it provides clear objectives to which a character can commit.

Footwork

Although every guard position allows for several possible thrusts and may be accompanied by the standing, demi or grand lunge, for the purposes of this exercise, all thrusts are executed with a *demi-lunge,* and delivered in the manner described in the exercises below. Be aware: this will change your measure with your partner. Set your measure so that the demi-lunge keeps you outside measure. Be sure to make eye contact with your partner to see them respond to the cue, then look at the target of the attack.

The Control Point

In these thrust attacks, the sword advances first. The extended arm and sword show your partner the intended target of the attack without actually threatening it. Your body remains rocked back in the defensive position of stationary footwork. This "removed" extension is your control point. You have shown your partner the cue for the attack, but you have not yet committed to the footwork. This allows your partner to read the attack and allows you to perceive your partner's reaction. By extending the arm prior to executing any footwork, you have the time to decide whether to complete the action or to abort for safety reasons. Remember, although the victim controls the action on stage—you must never be out of control. The control point is an added safety in the mechanics of theatrical swordplay. *You must always be in control.*

The extension of the arm does several things:

- It provides a controlled, visible cue for your partner;
- It provides a line of intent for the audience;
- It makes the sword and arm a "spear" that the body drives forward for the attack.

All Thrusts Must Travel in a Straight Line

All thrusts must travel in a straight line from start to finish. A wavering or floating blade or arm is a hazard and must be avoided. The extension of the sword arm is like pushing a drawer closed. The wrist, arm and shoulder work together to push the hand forward in an even horizontal plane.

The First Action and Cue of the Thrusting Attack

From the prescribed guard, rock back into the stationary footwork defensive position. Guide the tip of the sword (so that it in no way threatens your partner) to the intended target. Be sure the sword is directed off-line, outside your partner's body at the exact level of the intended target. From the rocked back position the arm is fully extended, showing your partner the line and target of the attack. The extended arm, with the body rocked back in the stationary defensive stance, point showing a specific target, is the first action and cue for a safe thrusting attack.

The Reaction and Final Action

In these exercises, when your partner sees the correct cue given for the thrust being practiced, they say "YES." If for some reason there is something wrong in the cue, they say "NO." These are the reactions you are working with at this time. If there is a problem, fix it. There should be no doubt what the cue means. The blade *must be off-line,* outside the body roughly three to six inches and at the exact level of the intended target.

From this cue, providing your partner says "YES," begin the specified footwork, the hand and blade remaining stationary through its completion. You will find that the rocked back position serves as an effective weight shift, allowing the lead foot to be lifted and extended forward into the demi-lunge. The nature of these mechanics are as if the body were being pulled forward by the tip of the blade. The point is drawn forward, pulling the hand, the hand pulls the arm, the arm the shoulder, the shoulder pulls the torso and the torso pulls the body. Each part of the body is reached forward before the next. The point drawing the body forward into the attack.

At the completion of the demi-lunge, the blade comes to rest at the level of the intended target, about three to six inches outside their body. The hand and sword remain in the same placement (supinated, pronated, etc.) as the specified cue. The position of the hand does not change.

The following thrusts are theatrical representations of the most common thrusting attacks made with the Elizabethan rapier. As in the cutting attacks, the mechanics of the historical attacks have been adapted for the specific demands of theatrical swordplay.

IMBROCCATTA: A pronated thrust from Prima to either the right or left shoulder[16]

Historically, the *imbroccatta* was a descending thrust directed to the face, breast or shoulder. It was a thrust punched down at the opponent from above their guard, often keeping the hand in the same placement as the guard of Prima. For the purposes of safe stage swordplay, the action is directed down from Prima to your partner's shoulders, and should be completed with the hand pronated.

STOCCATA: A pronated thrust from Terza to either the right or left shoulder[17]

The *stoccata* would generally be a rising thrust directed towards the opponent's torso or throat underneath their sword hand or guard. Because such an action would prove exceedingly dangerous, the theatrical version of the stoccata is a rising thrust from Terza to your partner's right or left shoulder.

In Elizabethan England the term stoccata became the common reference for all thrusts and was often used with disdain by English swordsmen who preferred the use of the edge. In Shakespeare's *The Merry Wives of Windsor* he has Shallow proclaim:

> *"In these times you stand on distances, your passes, stoccadoes, and I know not what. 'Tis the heart, Master Page, 'tis here. I have seen the time, with my long sword I would have made you four tall fellows skip like rats."* (II.i.213–218)

Further, in *Romeo and Juliet,* Mercutio singles out the stoccata as the very essence of the detested foreign school of fence. When Romeo refuses to fight Tybalt, Mercutio sees it as a slap in the face.

> *"O calm, dishonourable, vile submission:*
> *Alla stoccata carries it away!"* (III.i.72–73)

---

[16]There is no direct modern translation for the Italian *imbroccatta,* the term however was quite common in period fencing manuals, both Italian and English. The information from these manuscripts allows us to develop a general concept of the attack. Although he never defines the action, Saviolo does state that the thrust was to be directed at the opponent's face. (p. 18 ff) George Silver defines the "imbrocata" in his *Bref Instructions,* as an attack where the combatant is to *"lye w^t yor hylt hyer then yor hed, beringe yor knuckles upwarde, & yor point depending towarde yor Enemys face or brest."* (p. 88). This describes our guard of Prima as the point of origin for the attack. Joseph Swetnam adds that *"there is a falling thrust that may hit any man which lies open with his points by following it into his face or brest,"* and later defines the "imbrokata" as a *"falsifying thrust, first to proffer it towards the ground, so low as your enemies knee, and then presently put it home unto your enemies Dagger-shoulder, or unto anie part of his Dagger-arme . . . "* (p. 89 & 113) Other texts imply that the thrust traveled in a downward direction, reached the opponent over their sword, hand or dagger, and concur with Silver that the attack was delivered with the knuckles up. The terms *imbraccio* which means "to bring to the shoulder"; *imbracciatura,* meaning "placing on the arm"; and *imbrocco,* meaning "to strike, to hit the target," also help indicate the nature of the word.

[17]The term *stoccata* is the most common fencing reference used in Elizabethan theatre. It is Anglicized into such expressions as "stuck," "stock" and "tuck" and appears throughout the plays of Shakespeare, Jonson and their contemporaries (*Merry Wives*—II.i.214, II.iii.24; *R&J*—III.i.73; *Madame Fickle*—V.ii; *Antonio's Revels*—I.ii(iii); and so on.) The term literally means "to thrust" or "stab" and is therefore often applied to any thrust with the sword. Di Grassi, Saviolo Fabris and the like do not literally define the action, but they do imply that it is the direct opposite of the imbroccatta. The stoccata seems to be a rising thrust, reaching the opponent under their guard, sword or dagger. This is exemplified in Swetnam's manuscript as he states that *"A Right Stock, or Stockata, is to bee put in upwards with strength and quicknesse of the bodie."* (p. 113)

Mercutio's comment can be taken further when it is understood that some schools taught the stoccata as a thrust executed with the sword held only by the pommel.[18] To let someone who used such a foolish practice carry the day was surely an insult not to be borne.

Although the practice of grasping the sword by the pommel was a "common" practice according to Swetnam, the stoccata of the stage is executed with a standard grip and represents only the thrust, not the manner of holding the sword.

PUNTA DRITTA: A pronated thrust from Seconda or Terza to either the right or left hip or thigh[19]

Because the imbroccatta was a descending thrust and the stoccata was a rising thrust, there needed to be a clarification between them and the straight thrusts delivered from the right. The *punta dritta* is the thrusting attack delivered to the hips and thighs from the guards of Seconda or Terza. It is a straight thrust punched forward with a pronated hand, directly at the intended target.

PUNTA ROVESCIO: A supinated thrust from the left[20]

The *punta rovescio* ("reversed thrust") is a thrust delivered from the reverse, or left side of the body. The thrust is always supinated, in comparison to that of the imbrocatta, stoccata and punta dritta, that were delivered in pronation. The punta rovescio is generally delivered from the guard of Quarta to the opponent's right. In stage combat, however, the term is applied to all supinated thrusts delivered from the left.

No matter from what guard the action begins, the punta rovescio theoretically passes through the guard of Quarta. You may, however, move to this position from any of the other guards. For example, if you were in Prima, you would pass through Seconda and Terza to get to Quarta and launch a punta rovescio, and so on.

THE PISTON THRUST: A thrust from a withdrawn arm position

The *piston thrust* is a thrust much like the stoccata, punta dritta and punta rovercio, only it is delivered from an exaggerated wind up rather than a standard guard position. It may be targeted to either the right or left shoulder, hip or thigh and is generally executed from a drawn back position of the hand and arm on the right side of the body. Starting in any guard position, rock back into the stationary footwork defensive position. As the body is rocked back, the hand and hilt of the sword are drawn to the waist and back. The hand and blade placement is similar to that of Low Terza, only with the sword hand and arm drawn back behind the body. From this drawn back position the arm is pushed forward into a thrusting cue. As in all other thrusting attacks, the tip is directed at least three inches outside your partner's body. The extended arm position from this exaggerated wind-up is the cue for the attack and should indicate the specific target in the same manner as all other thrusting attacks. (Fig. 119)

---

[18]*"The third* [way of holding the sword] *is but to have onelie the fore-finger and thy thumbe within the pummell of thy Rapier, and thy other three fingers about thy pummell, and beare the button of thy pummell against the in-side of thy little finger; this is called the Stokata fashion"* [Swetnam, p. 93]

[19] The Italian term *punta* means "point" or "thrust with the point" and the term dritta means "right," "right side" or "forehand." A thrust with the sword from the right side.

[20]Most period fencing manuals use the term punta rovescio in some variation of spelling. Swetnam, however, uses the term *Slope Stocke* to represent the same action. (Swetnam, p. 113)

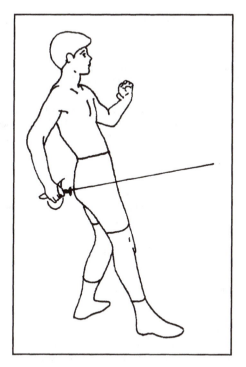

Figure 119. The piston thrust.

The piston thrust is generally executed with a pronated hand, but it may be supinated if being executed as a punta rovescio. The large preparation may be executed from either a guard position, or from a completed attack where the arm is quickly drawn back and then shot forward again—much like the direct in and out action of the needle on a sewing machine or the piston of an engine.

APPLICATION AND PRACTICE

Show and then Go

The underlying principles of offensive actions, both cut and thrust, are to cue your partner, perceive the correct response, and complete the action. As always, you must "think" and then "do," and in these actions you must also "show" and then "go." You must show the cue, and then go to the target. The two actions should eventually flow from one into the other, but they should never become one action. By joining the action of the cue with the attack, you remove your control point and an essential safety mechanism. The mechanics should appear as one movement, but never be executed as anything other than an initiating *action*, waiting for a *reaction*, completing with the final *action*.

Practice each of the attacks, both cut and thrust, slowly many times. The timing of your partner's reaction is essential to developing a fluid transition from action to action. As soon as the proper cue is perceived the reaction must begin in order to effectively complete the final action. Repetition of the techniques to develop proper timing needs to be stressed.

Methods of Practice

The cutting attacks have been listed in a specific order and are described in transition from one to the next. Once familiar with the mechanics of the attacks, it will be possible to go from any guard or attack to any other. A good practice for this, and for thrusts as well, is to have someone call out the name of the attack and its target, in any order, and see how smoothly you move to and from each attack. Do not rush yourself.

If you find it difficult moving from one random attack to another, first try moving to each of the attacks from the guard of Terza. Remember that the weapon should never pose any possible threat to your partner, and that the point must never cross the plane of their face or throat. Once you are adept at moving to each attack from Terza, try it from one or more of the other guard positions. Always keep in mind the position of the sword and the placement of the point. Make sure that all safety rules are followed.

This process may take a while, but with time and practice you will acquire efficiency and speed without errors. Trying to hurry the proces only provokes mistakes and mistakes can lead to injury. Be sure to ''think'' and then ''do,'' and ''show'' and then ''go.''

Flash Cards

The purpose of this exercise is two-fold. First it is designed as a training tool for cueing and cue response in blade-play; and second it works on the actor's focus and perception abilities of a partner's actions.

The exercise can be done with two or more combatants. (All combatants need to be armed for this exercise.) One combatant is the ''*Leader,*'' and all others are ''*Players.*'' The Players line up across the room so that they all may clearly see the Leader. The Leader positions himself facing the Players several feet outside measure. Everyone comes On Guard. Once everyone is ready the Players close their eyes and the Leader moves to the cue position of a cutting attack. Once there, the Leader calls ''FLASH'' and the Players blink their eyes open and closed again. The Players should open their eyes only long enough to perceive the cue for the attack. Once their eyes are closed again they should go to the correct parry that corresponds to the cue offered by the Leader. The Player who first misses three parries takes over the Leader position and the Leader becomes a Player.

The exercise may be worked with single rapier as well as rapier and dagger (to be covered later). To avoid confusion at this stage, all parries should be the defensive action offered against the cue in the following offensive and defensive blade-play exercises.

Flash Cards may also be orchestrated by a Referee. The Referee would make sure everyone is ready, and instead of calling ''FLASH'' they would clap their hands for the Players to open their eyes, and again for them to close them. The Referee could then monitor the time spent concentrating on the presented cue. Starting the exercise at ten seconds and then in degrees bringing it down to one. The students may rotate from Player, to Leader, to Referee, back to Player.

THE OFFENSIVE DRILL

After you become comfortable with each of the attacks, and how they interrelate to one another, try practicing the following drill. Note that the attacks offered in this exercise correspond to the defensive drill of parries offered in the preceding chapter.

From the guard of Terza, man dritto tondo mezzo (cut left hip).
From the left hip, riverso tondo mezzo (cut right hip).
From the right hip, riverso tondo alto (horizontal cut right shoulder).
From the right shoulder, mollinello, man dritto tondo alto (horizontal cut left shoulder).
From the left shoulder, outside mollinello, man dritto fendente (cut to the head).
From the head, mollinello from your right to left, riverso squalembrato (diagonal cut right shoulder).

From the right shoulder, mollinello from your left to right, man dritto squalembrato (diagonal cut left shoulder).

From the left shoulder, recover to Terza, stoccata (thrust right chest).

From the thrust right chest, mollinello left to right, man dritto tondo basso (cut left thigh).

From the left thigh, riverso tondo basso (cut right thigh).

Adding Footwork

After you are comfortable with the above drill, try stepping through the *linear* portion of the offensive footwork drill (as covered in Chapter 3). Treat the footwork as the "rock forward" or demi-lunge practiced with your control point. The traveling of the lower body does not replace the "rocking," however, the rock back is still necessary for the preparation, and the rock forward, with the footwork, is necessary for the element of reach in an attack. Remember when thrusting that the rock back position is the control point. In this exercise, when you attack from the right, your right foot is forward, and when you attack from the left, your left foot is forward. This helps lend support to the attacking arm while keeping the open or exposed leg to the rear, removed from a possible counterattack. When working thrusts, try executing them with a standing, demi, and grand lunge. You also may try the offensive footwork drill with thrusts instead of cuts.

Although you should not yet be crossing swords in these exercises, you must still be aware that there are no thrusting attacks to High Five (the head), and as such, when running the drill with point work, retain the man dritto fendente, cut to the head or thrust between the legs (parried in Low 5). Be sure to agree with your partner prior to executing the attack. There are a good number of combinations that may be explored, just be sure that the target of the thrust corresponds to the parry set in the defensive drill. Remember, "show" and then "go."

MOVING ON

Once you are fluent with all the attacks, both cut and thrust, and are comfortable with them both stationary and moving across the floor with the offensive footwork drill, you are ready to move on to the next chapter and cross swords.

Chapter 8

Crossing Swords

"Thoughts fast, Blades slow
Points low, Fight light
Create an illusion, Not a real fight."
[Patrick Crean][1]

Now, with sword in hand, we must face our partner and put the practice of the past seven chapters to work. Prior to this chapter you have been more a threat to yourself than anyone else, but here you take the safety of another in your hands. It is important, therefore, that you have actually practiced and understand the mechanics of footwork, parries and attacks. No matter how many techniques and rules for your safety are established in this text, there is no procedure devised by man that will protect you from carelessness or under-rehearsed techniques. Be sure that you are comfortable and confident, and that you have established safe techniques and habits before you try crossing swords with another actor.

SETTING MEASURE

In a stage combat, where safety is the first concern, most blade-play is executed out of distance, so that combatants *cannot* hit each other. That is to say, when you make an attack, your partner's body is always out of reach. The blades are just able to make contact, but the attacking sword is unable to hit your partner. This not only means that the point of a blade is short of the target but it forces the aggressor to reach with the body (rocking forward) in order to make blade contact, thereby creating far more dynamic movements and images.

Fencing Measure vs. Theatrical Measure

Fencing measure, is the distance between two fencers that requires extending the sword arm and lunging in order to touch one's partner. This is only good if you wish to hit your partner in theatrical swordplay. In stage combat, there should always be a distance of at least six to ten inches from the

---

[1]The quote is from Patrick Crean. Maestro (Paddy) Crean is called "the Dean" of stage combat by his colleagues. He is a respected Fight Master in the Society of British Fight Directors, Fight Directors Canada and an honorary member of the Society of American Fight Directors. The final line of the quote "create an illusion, not a real fight" is an addition by the author.

chest of one combatant to the furthest extension of the sword of the other at the completion of any attack and/or any footwork, including a lunge.

Complementary Footwork

Your footwork in a fight should always complement that of your partner, always keeping correct distance as you move across the floor. If you take a single step forward, your partner must take a step back; two steps forward is complemented by two steps back and so on. Choreography, at times, may bring fencers inside distance, but in this chapter you always work at correct measure. Before you ever reach towards your partner to check your measure, state that you are "checking distance," always letting them know what you are doing.

Checking Distance

Now that you and your partner are armed, you must learn to check distance with swords. The extended reach of the sword makes the process of checking distance learned in Chapter 3 too close for safe swordplay. Here then is the process to check distance with the rapier.

The combatant with the longer reach will set the measure. That combatant informs the other that they are "checking distance." Both combatants face one another in the On Guard stance, then the combatant with the longer reach rocks forward into a standing lunge and raises their sword *outside of the other's body* to the level of their chest. The tip of the sword is then *slowly* guided in to the opponent's center line, with the sword arm fully extended. The combatant checking distance should be at *full extension* and makes sure they do not reach beyond this mark during swordplay. The combatant with the shorter reach rocks back, and then moves to properly distance themselves. Distance should be set with the tip of the extended sword roughly six to ten inches from their chest; the aggressor rocked forward (with sword, arm and body at full extension) and the opponent rocked back. At this time *the blade is never any closer than six inches.* Upon setting this measure, draw the sword back to your selected guard (without letting the tip cross the combatant's throat or face) and bring your bodies back to correct placement in the On Guard stance. You are now in correct distance for crossing steel. (Fig. 120)

Distance may be set on a pass, advance, lunge, etc. This is done by checking measure with the completed footwork and then recovering back to On Guard. This sets the measure for specific offensive footwork. For example, if you needed to begin an action or routine at grand lunge measure, you would execute a grand lunge, check distance with your partner, and then recover backward to an On Guard stance. This positions the body at a distance where a grand lunge can be safely executed. Correct distance is not how far the combatants are from one another, it is how far the blade is from the body at the completion of an attack.

Keeping Measure

The perception of correct distance is one of the paramount responsibilities of a stage combatant and is the result of practice and the comprehension of complex interrelationships. The keenness of the eyes, the readiness of observation, the sense of tempo, rhythm and space combined with controlled, regulated footwork, are all conditions for good distance perception. So be alert, as keeping measure is an essential safety technique in the execution of stage combat.

Start Out of Measure

It is best that in the exercises presented in this chapter that you *always* begin practicing out of measure. At the beginning, set a distance where there is no possibility of swords crossing and work at keeping that measure. By removing any fear of accident or injury, you are able to concentrate on the task at hand. Only after you are comfortable with the exercise should you then move into correct measure for safe stage combat.

Figure 120. Setting measure for offensive/defensive interaction.

TECHNIQUES FOR CROSSING STEEL

Timing and Rhythm

The first step in joining offensive and defensive blade-play is the synchronization of the opposing footwork with the various movements of the sword. From the beginning it is possible to work to a definite, well-defined, rhythm. The establishment of such a rhythm is of tremendous importance, for no matter how fast the fight eventually becomes, it always is firmly supported by a built-in feeling of timing. A fight is a physical dialogue where each actor is completely dependent on the timing and rhythm of the other. Each actor's movements cannot be thought of as individual, but must merge together to resemble an incredibly well-oiled machine, where the different cogs work together in unison.

Action-Reaction-Action

If you think of a fight as a conversation with steel, you begin to see its internal rhythm. Theatrical timing requires a sort of pause or enunciation of movement for the audience to appreciate the action as it is happening; otherwise the action may happen too quickly for the audience to follow. The rhythm or "pause" in physical dialogue is established through a technique in active listening—the process of Action-Reaction-Action. As discussed earlier, every offensive and defensive movement is broken down into these three distinct motions. The first "action" is the preparation and cue for an attack. Now that the swords are to be crossed, the "reaction" changes. Instead of the "Yes" or "No" response the reaction is now the defendant's acted response to the cue offered by the aggressor. This may be the *beginning* of a parry or footwork on the part of the defensive partner. The final "action" is the completion of the offensive and defensive movements *together*. Each movement should flow smoothly from one into the other and not appear awkward or "staged."

Eye Contact

During the execution of these mechanics, it is important that you stay connected with your partner. It is a good idea to talk to one another during the early stages of any engagement of blades and you should always stay connected with *eye contact*. Eye contact, or "*eyes*," is a strong line of defense against accidents. You should always look into your partner's eyes to establish a mutual awareness and readiness to perform any technique prior to its execution. Eye contact should be a natural part of your control point, it only needs to last a moment; then you should return your concentration to what you are doing. The attacker must focus on their target in order to be accurate, and the victim must focus on the movement of the blades to correctly time the prescribed reaction. Do not make the mistake of maintaining constant eye contact during a fight. This habit forces attacks and parries to be executed in the peripheral field of vision and limits the actor's physical response to the moment to moment actions of the fight. For safety's sake it is always best to look at where your weapons are being placed. Dramatically your point of focus also helps tell the audience what is important to the character. Recognition of your opponent is important, but you as a combatant need to see what is happening to insure safe and proper execution, and your character needs to see what is happening so that they may truthfully "discover" or "react" to it within the fray. Therefore, you should always look at what you are doing after you have made eye contact with your partner and you are sure it is safe to move on.

Be Sure Blades Meet Edge to Edge

As you begin to cross steel, be sure that the offensive and defensive blades meet edge to edge and at approximately ninety degrees. A vertical attack should always meet a horizontal party, and a horizontal attack should always meet a vertical parry. The forte of the parrying blade should meet the foible of the attacking blade. Here you have the fullest command of your opponent's blade. Because the parry is near your hand, it has more strength and support for those instances where an attack accidentally comes in hard or heavy. By parrying with the forte of the blade you have more control of the weapons. (Fig. 121)

Spot Your Targets

Be sure that all your attacks are aimed exactly at their intended target, and that they stop three to six inches outside your opponent's body. The defensive blade should move out to meet the attacking blade. Remember that a parry must be outside and in front of your body. If the parry is too near your body, the force of a poorly executed attack could knock the parry back into you.

It's Better to be Too Slow Than Two Pieces

Mark through each of the drills slowly, finding the timing in each technique. The parry should not be waiting for an attack, nor should an attack stop shy of the body and wait for a parry. The attack and parry should be completed together. The parry should appear to stop a cut intended for the body or deflect a thrust aimed at the body and not just meet a blade outside the body. As you find your timing, slowly pick up the tempo. Do not rush this process, because even though you may feel entirely comfortable, your partner may not. Both combatants must be ready to move on before any routine is picked up in speed.

Kissing Steel

The meeting of the blades in stage combat is not a contest. The aggressor does not pound the parry of the victim, smashing the blades together. A fight is *acted* aggression. Energy is sent beyond, not

A   B

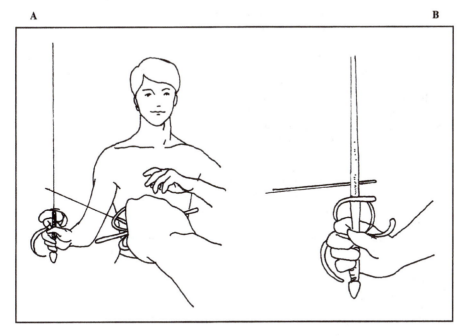

Figure 121. Edge to edge/forte to foible. **A**-offensive prospective; **B**-close up of blades.

into a parry. The victim should act the impact, not react to an impact. The blades can meet with passion, but always with care. The kissing of steel is the soft light touch of offensive and defensive blades. Aside from making the fight less abusive on the blades and actors, the kissing of steel allows the blades to ring on contact where pounding blows stifle the ring in the same manner as suppressing the clapper on a bell. There is no real fight, so let the blades kiss and make up.

Remember, Seeing is Believing

If the following techniques are performed with skill, they are extremely effective. In stage and film, seeing is believing. If fully acted intention is put behind the attack and the reaction is properly timed and appropriate to the attack, an audience believes they are witnessing a "real" fight. A relaxed body, cool head, technical skill and acted aggression makes the fight seem real while keeping you perfectly safe.

RULES IN REVIEW

All rules concerning safety *must* be applied here. Please review the rules regarding the management of the blade, especially those in Chapters 1 and 3.

1. *Know* your mechanics, footwork, parries and attacks prior to engaging blades with another combatant.
2. Proper measure in stage combat is a distance of at least six to ten inches from the chest of one combatant to the tip of the other's fully extended sword at the completion of any attack.
3. No combat (unless specifically staged that way) takes place inside proper measure.
4. Always check your distance prior to engaging steel.

5. The mechanics of a fight are broken down into three distinct motions: **Action**—the cue; **Reaction**—control point and response; **Action**—completion of offensive and defensive motions.

6. Always get eye contact prior to executing an attack.

7. Always spot the target of the attack. Do not cut or thrust towards the body without looking at where the blade is being placed.

8. Be sure that the offensive and defensive blades meet edge to edge and at approximately ninety degrees.

9. The forte of the parrying blade should meet the foible of the attacking blade.

10. All attacks must be directed to their exact target and stop three to six inches outside your opponent's body.

11. A parry moves out to meet the attacking blade.

12. A parry must be outside and in front of your body.

13. Offensive and defensive actions must be completed at the same time.

14. The tip of the sword must never cross the face or throat, whether in attack or in defense, even when out of distance.

15. Be particularly aware of the space around the action when the combatants move together.

16. The engagement of blades *is not* a contest; it is a choreographed piece of business and should be respected as such.

17. Start learning all routines slowly, and *out of measure* to develop proper timing.

18. Once comfortable with the routine out of measure, practice the drills at correct distance in slow motion.

19. Make any adjustments to keep the routine safe, comfortable and workable for both parties; then *set it* and do not let it vary.

20. Do not shortcut the learning process! That is how people get hurt.

THE DRILLS

In all the following exercises the combatants will be listed as ''A'' and ''B.'' Decide which combatant you are and move through the entire exercise as that combatant. A always initiates a routine, but both combatants have a chance at all the techniques worked in the exercise.

Stationary Drill

A: From the guard of Terza, Man Dritto Tondo mezzo (cut left hip).

B: From the guard of Terza travel to the parry of 1, left hip.

A: From the left hip, Riverso Tondo mezzo (cut right hip).

B: From the parry of 1, go on to the Actor's Parry of 2, right hip.

A: From the right hip, Riverso Tondo alto (horizontal cut right shoulder).

B: From the parry of 2, go on to the parry of 3, right shoulder.

A: From the right shoulder, mollinello, Man Dritto Tondo alto (horizontal cut left shoulder).

B: From the parry of 3, to the parry of 4, left shoulder.

A: From the left shoulder, outside mollinello, Man Dritto Fendente (cut to the head).

B: From the parry of 4, to the parry of High 5, head parry.

A: From the head, mollinello from right to left, Riverso Squalembrato (diagonal cut right shoulder).

B: From the parry of High 5, to the parry of High 3, right shoulder.

A: From the right shoulder, mollinello left to right, Man Dritto Squalembrato (diagonal cut left shoulder).

B: From the parry of High 3, to the parry of High 4, left shoulder.

A: From the left shoulder, recover to Terza, Stoccata (thrust right chest).

B: From the parry of High 4, to the parry of 6, right chest.

A: From the thrust right chest, mollinello left to right, Man Dritto Tondo basso (cut left thigh).

B: From the parry of 6, to the parry of 7, left thigh.

A: From the left knee, Riverso Tondo basso (cut right thigh).

B: From the parry of 7, to the Parry of 8, right thigh. From the parry of 8, bring the blade back on the right, switch sides on the drill and Man Dritto Tondo mezzo (cut left hip).

Repeat the drill as many times as you like. At the completion of each series A and B switch, the defender begins the offensive sequence and the offender shifts to the defensive part.

Traveling Drill

A: From the guard of Terza, show to the left hip, *Advance,* Man Dritto Tondo mezzo (cut left hip).

B: From the guard of Terza, *Retreat,* and parry 1, left hip.

A: From the left hip, *Pass Forward,* Riverso Tondo mezzo (cut right hip).

B: From the parry of 1, *Pass Back,* and parry right hip, Actor's Parry of 2.

A: From the right hip, *Advance,* Riverso Tondo alto (horizontal cut right shoulder).

B: From the parry of 2, *Retreat,* parry 3, right shoulder.

A: From the right shoulder, mollinello as you *Pass Forward,* Man Dritto Tondo alto (horizontal cut left shoulder).

B: From the parry of 3, *Pass Back,* parry 4, left shoulder.

A: From the left shoulder, *Advance* outside mollinello, Man Dritto Fendente (cut to the head).

B: From the parry of 4, *Retreat,* parry High 5, head parry.

A: From the head, mollinello as you *Pass Forward,* Riverso Squalembrato (diagonal cut right shoulder).

B: From the parry of High 5, *Pass Back,* parry High 3, right shoulder.

A: From the right shoulder, mollinello as you *Pass Forward,* Man Dritto Squalembrato (diagonal cut left shoulder).

B: From the parry of High 3, *Pass Back,* parry High 4, left shoulder.

A: From the left shoulder, recover to Terza, Stoccata show to the right chest, *Advance* (thrust right chest).

B: From the parry of High 4, *Retreat,* parry 6, right chest.

A: From the thrust right chest, mollinello as you *Advance,* Man Dritto Tondo basso (cut left thigh).

B: From the parry of 6, *Retreat,* parry 7, left thigh.

A: From the left knee, *Circle Step Left,* Riverso Tondo basso (cut right thigh).

B: From the parry of 7, *Circle Step Left,* parry right thigh, parry of 8.

From the parry of 8, A and B will *Recover* back to their original placements. B will bring their blade back on the right, and switch sides of the drill. At the completion of each series the defender will begin the offensive sequence and the offender will shift to the defensive part.

Adding the Riposte

Before moving on to the cut and thrust exercises on the circle, it is important to introduce a new technique in swordplay, the riposte. Up to this point you have been offering a series of attacks that have been met by the corresponding parries. On these circle exercises, and many further exercises and techniques of blade-play, the attacks are on the exchange. This is where combatant B parries an attack, and then offers a counterattack of their own and vice versa. The riposte is the counterattack launched by the combatant after successfully completing a parry.

Be careful as you begin practicing the riposte. The manipulation of the blade from a parry to an attack must still be controlled and safe. From the parry the sword must be carried to its cue and control point. Do not go from the parry directly into the attack. The mechanics of cue and response must be adhered to during the exchange of blades.

An exercise for the riposte is to use the pattern of the Stationary Drill, but to take it on the exchange. In this exercise, from the guard of Terza, combatant A cuts left hip. Combatant B parries 1, and then ripostes with a cut to the left hip. Combatant A parries 1, and then ripostes with a cut to the right hip, and so on. Each combatant has a chance to parry and riposte in all lines and each of the ten parries. The exercise may also be practiced with thrusts instead of cuts. In this exercise however, there are no thrusting attacks above the armpits (High 3, High 4 and 5), these attacks must be executed as cuts. If you wish to thrust 5, you may thrust Low 5.

The addition of footwork to this exercise is fairly simple. The process of Action-Reaction-Action is still adhered to, except the role of the aggressor constantly switches throughout the exercise. The switch takes place in the transition from the rocked back position of the parry to the cue for the riposte.

Cutting on the Circle

A: From the guard of Terza, *Circle Step Left* (passing with the right foot), Riverso Tondo basso (cut right thigh).

B: From Terza, *Circle Step Left* (passing with the right foot), parry 8, right thigh.

B: From parry 8, *Circle Step Left* (passing with the left foot), riposte Riverso Tondo alto, (horizontal cut right shoulder).

A: From the cut to the right knee, *Circle Step Left* (passing with the left foot), parry 3, right shoulder.

A: From parry 3, *Circle Step Left* (passing with the right foot), riposte Riverso Tondo alto, (horizontal cut right shoulder).

B: From the cut to the right shoulder, *Circle Step Left* (passing with the right foot), parry 3, right shoulder.

B: From parry 3, *Circle Step Left* (passing with the left foot), riposte Riverso Tondo basso, (cut right thigh).

A: From the cut to the right shoulder, *Circle Step Left* (passing with the left foot), parry 8, right thigh.

A & B: *Recover:* Pivot on the balls of your feet so that you face the direction from which you have come. You should not have to readjust your feet in any way and should be in correct placement in the On Guard stance, standing roughly where your partner *was* at the beginning of the exercise.

A: From the recovery, *Circle Right* (lunging the right foot to the right on the inner track of the imaginary circle), Man Dritto Tondo basso (cut left thigh).

B: From the recovery, *Demi-Volte* (stepping back and to the right so that the left foot is just to the outside of the right foot on the outer track of the imaginary circle), parry 7, left thigh.

B: From parry 7, *Circle Right*, riposte Man Dritto Tondo alto, (horizontal cut left shoulder).

A: From the cut to the left knee, *Demi-Volte*, parry 4, left shoulder.

A: From parry 4, *Circle Right*, riposte Man Dritto Tondo alto, (horizontal cut left shoulder).

B: From the cut to the left shoulder, *Demi-Volte*, parry 4, left shoulder.

B: From parry 4, *Circle Right*, riposte Man Dritto Tondo basso (cut left thigh).

A: From the cut to the left shoulder, *Demi-Volte*, parry 7, left thigh.

A & B: *Recover,* right foot, retaining the lead foot position, lunges out to the right into correct placement for the On Guard stance. You should be facing the direction from which you began the drill. Your feet do not have to be adjusted in any way. You are in correct placement, your right foot in the lead position and left foot in lag. You are situated on the set of straight tracks on which you began the drill. At the completion of this exercise A and B may switch roles and repeat the routines as often as desired.

The pattern of this drill (8, 3, 3, 8, [turn] 7, 4, 4, 7) may be varied as the combatants see fit. The thing to keep in mind is that the pattern *must* be established prior to execution, and that all attacks during the circle left are to the right of the body, and all attacks on the circle right are to the left of the body.

Thrusting on the Circle

A: From the guard of Terza, *Circle Step Left* (passing with the right foot), Punta Rovescio (thrust right thigh).

B: From Terza, *Circle Step Left* (passing with the right foot), parry 8, right thigh.

B: From parry 8, *Circle Step Left* (passing with the left foot), riposte Punta Rovescio, thrust right shoulder.

A: From the thrust to the right knee, *Circle Step Left* (passing with the left foot), parry 3, right shoulder.

A: From parry 3, *Circle Step Left* (passing with the right foot), riposte Punta Rovescio, thrust right shoulder.

B: From the thrust to the right shoulder, *Circle Step Left* (passing with the right foot), parry 3, right shoulder.

B: From the parry 3, *Circle Step Left* (passing with the left foot), riposte Punta Rovescio, thrust right knee.

A: From the thrust to the right shoulder, *Circle Step Left* (passing with the left foot), parry 8, right thigh.

A & B: *Recover:* Pivot on the balls of your feet so that you face the direction from which you have come. You should not have to adjust your feet in any way and should be in correct placement in the On Guard stance facing your partner.

A: From the recovery, *Circle Right* (lunging the right foot to the right on the inner track of the imaginary circle), Punta Dritta (thrust left thigh).

B: From the recovery, *Demi-Volte* (stepping back and to the right so that the left foot is just to the outside of the right foot on the outer track of the imaginary circle), parry 7, left thigh.

B: From the parry 7, *Circle Right,* riposte Stoccata, (thrust left shoulder).

A: From the thrust to the left thigh, *Demi-Volte,* parry 4, left shoulder.

A: From parry 4, *Circle Right,* riposte Stoccata, (thrust left shoulder).

B: From the thrust to the left shoulder, *Demi-Volte,* parry 4, left shoulder.

B: From parry 4, *Circle Right,* riposte Punta Dritta (thrust left thigh).

A: From the thrust to the left shoulder, *Demi-Volte,* parry 7, left thigh.

A & B: *Recover,* as directed in the circular footwork drill in Chapter 3.

At the completion of this exercise A and B may switch roles and repeat the routines as often as desired. As in the "cutting on the circle" drill, the pattern of this drill may be varied as the combatants see fit.

Trouble Shooting

As combatants begin to cross swords, there is a natural tendency to "reach" for your partner with the sword and body. Proper fencing measure and the delivery of attacks outside the body can make some combatants feel the need to extend the arm on a parry or to bend at the waist in order to get closer. Both of these practices are unnecessary, and the latter can even prove dangerous. Your body cannot be allowed to randomly change measure. During all of these exercises your body remains in correct placement in the On Guard stance. Thus, if you ever feel the need to "reach" your partner, either with attack or parry, stop and check your measure. A simple variance in distance can easily affect your mechanics. If distance is the problem, work the drills slowly and check measure after every couple of moves. If the problem continues, go back and work on the Tight Rope and Hand Over Fist exercises offered in Chapter 3.

The Guiding Hand

If you have a habit of breaking at the waist, and bending forward to reach your partner during these drills, be careful; this can seriously affect your measure. Aside from developing a habit that will be hard to break, bending at the waist can bring your point in distance where it could possibly strike your partner. The exercises offered in Chapter 5, Sitting This One Out and Wall Bound, designed to deal with the habit of turning or leaning while passing the point, are not effective here. This is because of the work in the low lines and the need for mobility when the exercises are taken moving. When the entire body is used and mobile, the combatant cannot effectively work from a chair or up against a wall.

To deal with this problem try placing a fencing glove on your head. The glove should lay across the top of your head with the fingers toward one ear, the cuff towards the other. Using the glove as a sensory guide, you can feel when you bend or reach forward during the exercises. A slight bend causes the glove to shift. A dramatic lean in the torso will cause the glove to fall. This "guiding hand" helps keep safe measure and proper stance during the execution of these drills and exercises.

Dealing with Wide Parries

There are generally two reasons a combatant reaches out with their parry if measure is not a problem. The first is if the attack is delivered more than eight inches outside the body. Attacks that are too wide force the defender to reach out to meet the blade, seriously affecting their technique. In this case the aggressor must work their technique slowly to be sure they are not stopping the blade short of its intended placement. Remember, six inches are as good as a mile. If a blade is properly directed outside the body by six inches, it will be safe. Attacks at proper distance delivered outside the body cannot hit the defending combatant. Do not pull them short for fear of hitting someone. If you are unsure of your technique, work the mechanics alone before crossing steel. The second reason for wide parries is due to a sense of displacement on the part of the defender. For some reason the attacking blade seems either too far away or that it will be missed with a standard parry. This may be a habit developed from working with a hesitant partner or from trying to cross swords while outside of measure. It is important to remember that the blades are not supposed to meet in the middle, but that the foible of the attacking blade should contact the forte of the defending blade. The practice may also come from insecurity in the mechanics of the parries. If this is the case, the parries should be reviewed prior to working these exercises.

Touch & Go: This exercise is designed to work both on wide attacks and parries. It uses the offensive and defensive pattern of the Stationary Drill described earlier in this chapter. From the guard of Terza, combatant A cuts (or thrusts) to the left hip. Combatant B does not begin the parry until the attack is correctly completed. Cuts should stop roughly six inches outside the body, thrusts three to six inches. All attacks must stop at the exact level of the intended target. Once the attack is completed, combatant B executes a parry of 1. The mechanics of the parry must be correct, and the parry should just touch the opposing blade. As soon as the blades touch, A goes on to the next attack. At each target the attack is checked, the parry executed, the blades touch, and then they move on. Because the reaction of the parry is delayed in this exercise, use the vocal reaction "yes" in response to the cue. This exercise allows the combatants to look at the blades and to see how tight the attack can be while remaining safe. It also allows the defending combatant the time to see the opposing blade and move towards it correctly, without reaching. Remember, a parry is a defensive action that stops an attack intended for the body. The attack comes to you, you do not reach for the attack.

OTHER EXERCISES IN SWORDPLAY

Practicing the Scales

This exercise consists of running both the linear and circular patterns together in one drill. By combining the cutting attacks on a pass and the thrusts on the circle, you run the entire range of offensive and defensive actions of the single rapier most often used on stage. Running the "scales" is an effective warm-up of mechanics prior to class or rehearsal of a fight and should be constantly practiced in order to maintain maximum efficiency in technique and execution. This exercise received its name from comparison to the constant practicing of scales by musicians.

The footwork of this drill should be executed in the same manner as the Offensive/Defensive footwork drill described in Chapter 3. For the best mix of cut and thrust, start the drill with the pattern set in the Traveling Drill, switching to the Thrusting on the Circle after the circle step left, cut right knee at the end of the Traveling Drill. The attack to the right knee may be executed either as a cut (as in the final action of the Traveling Drill) or as a thrust (as in the first action of Thrusting on the Circle). From the final parry of 7, A and B recover back to their original placement on the linear tracks, but should be on the opposite sides of the room. B then brings the blade back on the right, and switches roles in the drill. At the completion of each series, the defender begins the offensive sequence and the offender shifts to the defensive part. In this manner the drill may be repeated over and over again without having to readjust in the room.

Renewing the Attack: The Reprise

The riposte, and the exchange of offensive and defensive actions is part of the fundamental basis of theatrical combat. Having the ability to parry an attack and launch a counter attack supplies the give and take necessary to build dramatic tension in a fight. Despite this, the constant exchange of parry and riposte can become boring or detached from a production. This can easily become an ''I go, you go, I go, you go'' exchange if further techniques of swordplay are not interjected into the routine. One technique that breaks the pattern up further is the *reprise*. This is the process of renewing a parried attack when the opponent fails to offer a riposte. Generally the arm is drawn back to the cue position, and then the renewed attack is made in the same line as the original. A reprise may be the renewal of an initial attack, on a riposte if the opponent fails to offer a counter-riposte.

The following is a good exercise for working both the reprise, and the counter parries. Using the pattern established in the Stationary Drill, combatant A cuts left hip. Combatant B parries 1, but does not riposte. A then draws the arm back in preparation for a piston thrust, and executes a second attack, thrusting to the left hip. B executes a counter parry of 1 (B may also execute a counter parry of 7 if the mechanics of a counter 1 are too awkward). Combatant A then moves on to cut right hip. B parries 2. A then draws back into a piston thrust, and reprises the attack with a thrust to the right hip. Combatant B executes a counter parry 2, and so on.

For the parries of High 3, High 4 and High 5, the reprise alternates the preparation for the attack. The first attack to High 5 should be an outside mollinello (on the right) with a Man Dritto Fendente (head cut from the right). The reprised attack mollinellos around to the left for a Riverso Fendente (head cut from the left). The first attack to High 3 mollinellos around from the outside (right), while the reprised attack is delivered from a mollinello on the inside (left), and so on. On an attack to the right chest, the first attack is a stoccata, the reprise a punta rovescio.

Practice this exercise in a stationary position at first. Once you are comfortable with the blade pattern of the reprised attacks and the corresponding counter parries, try adding footwork. Because this exercise parallels the Stationary Drill, the footwork of the Traveling Drill can be applied. Work the exercise first with no footwork on the reprise, the reprised attacks being executed in a stationary position. Movement only takes place during the execution of the initial attacks. Once you have done this several times with proper measure and good blade control, you may try adding footwork to the reprised attacks. Thrusts may either be delivered with an advance with the right foot in a dominant position, or you may pass the left foot forward when delivered from the left, and pass the right foot forward when delivered from the right.

Around the Clock

Another exercise is to run through the cutting or thrusting attacks on the exchange, either in numerical order or around your partner's body like the numbers on the face of a clock. If you are running the drill in numerical order, A initiates with a cut to ''one'' (the left hip), B parries 1 and ripostes cutting back to ''one.'' A parries 1 and ripostes cutting to ''two'' (right hip), B parries 2 and ripostes cutting back to "two," and so on. If you are running the drill around the face of a clock, the pattern starts with an attack to High 4 (one o'clock) and moves around the body in a clockwise fashion. Upon completion, A and B switch so that both combatants have a chance to initiate the routine. Remember, if you are working this drill with point work, there are no thrusting attacks above the arm-pits (High 3, High 4 or High 5).

This drill should at first be attempted in a stationary position. Once you are comfortable with the blade pattern try adding footwork. Cutting attacks delivered from the right are executed with the right foot dominant, cutting attacks from the left, with the left foot dominant. Point work also may follow this rule, or may be executed on the advance with either the right or left foot forward.

Parries with the Left Hand

The principle of using the left hand for parries was covered in Chapter 6 and may now be applied here. The unarmed hand cannot effectively stop a cutting attack, the hand, therefore, can only be used to parry thrusting attacks. The hand is open, presenting only the palm. The fingers and thumb are drawn back out of the way. The hand always travels across the body in a horizontal line to the target of the attack. The hand is presented so that the palm is toward the attacking blade and meets it on the foible, below the tip. The hand parry is made either by opposition or a beat, swatting the blade aside. (Figs. 122–124)

Working the Parries

In Chapter 6 you were introduced to two forms of parry the standard/opposition parry and the beat parry. These along with the following *detached parry* form the three distinct forms of parry in standard and transitional rapier play. Until swords are crossed, however, the distinct mechanics of these three parries are difficult to practice. The mechanics and movements are so similar that there is hardly a difference in the execution of the various types of parry. In most instances the response of the opposing blade is the real variance, and that cannot be practiced until the parry meets the offending blade.

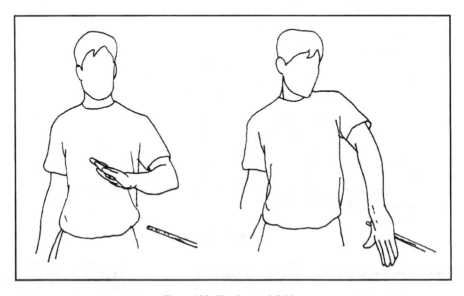

Figure 122. Hand parry left hip.

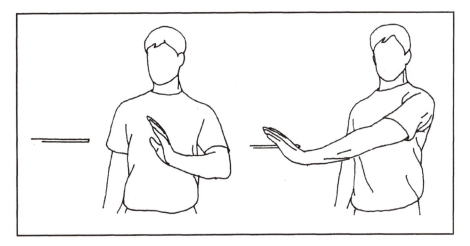

Figure 123. Hand parry right shoulder.

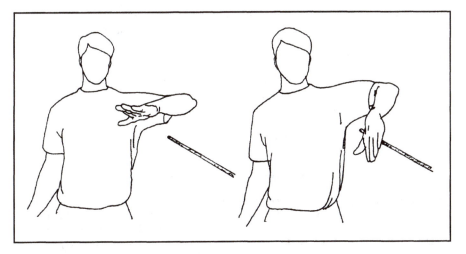

Figure 124. Hand parry left shoulder.

The Opposition Parry

So far in these exercises you have mostly been working the mechanics of the opposition or "blocking" parry. This is where the parry is one distinct action, blocking the opposing blade, providing a solid wall of defense until the threat is removed.

The Beat Parry

Now that you have had a chance to work all the exercises using the blocking parry, you may try applying the beat parry to the same routines. This type of parry is probably the closest theatrical equivalent to what a parry with the rapier may have been like. Although this action is often mentioned in treatises of the period, exactly how it was executed is neglected.

"If the sworde come with a thrust, he must finde it and beat it aside: for every litle motion is sufficient to drive the poynt farre enough from danger of hurte." [di Grassi][2]

For the purposes of theatrical swordplay, the advice of di Grassi will be followed, making the beat parry a small "litle motion" of the blade. The general mechanics of the parry remain the same, changing only the meeting of the blades. As the blades are about to join, the hand and wrist of the parry punches out about two to four inches, deflecting the opposing blade by "striking" it sharply aside. The strike should be out to the side, and not forward towards your partner, up or down. This "litle" action removes the attacking blade while freeing your blade so that you may immediately riposte after your defense.

The beat must be executed at the last possible moment. If a beat is executed early, the parry is made wide, or with a straight arm. This makes both the parry and beat ineffective. The motion of the hand and wrist that strikes the opposing blade aside should keep the hand in the same relative placement of a standard blocking parry. A beat parry against a thrust only needs to punch out about two inches, a beat against a cut, about four. The punching motion of the wrist should forcefully slap the forte of the blade against the opposing blade's foible, knocking the attacking blade aside and freeing your blade for an immediate riposte or further defensive action.

It is important to note that the aggressor must give in the hand and wrist upon receiving a beat parry. The beat parry must not be met with a stiff or rigid arm. The moment the blade is struck, the opposing blade must be released and allowed to be deflected aside. The reaction needs to be larger than that of a "fencing" beat parry because the audience needs to understand the cause and effect of the action. If the knocking aside of the blade is unclear, the audience loses the reason for the action.

The Detached Parry

The detached parry is an action of the blade that mixes the defensive wall of a blocking parry with the quick release of the beat. It is a crisp action of the blade that blocks the opposing blade and then immediately leaves the parried blade as soon as contact is made. The action does not beat the blade aside, it merely taps it to confirm the parry and then moves on to the next action with all haste. Because this is not a "strong" parry, the detached parry is only used against thrusts, and generally in the transitional style.

Application and Practice

Work each of these parries through the preceding exercises and drills, both standard and transitional. You will find that the beat and detached parry work well in those exercises that call for an exchange of attack and riposte. Go slow at first to be sure you understand the mechanics and execution of the various forms of parries. The immediate riposte of the beat and detached parry must still follow the procedure of the riposte dictated earlier. The safe mechanics of the riposte are not bypassed, the action of the parry merely allows you to move to the cue much more quickly.

MOVING ON

In the past eight chapters you have become familiar with the fundamental language and mechanics of the theatrical rapier fight. You have gone from the preliminary stages of selecting a sword to the actual mechanics of "slinging steel" with a partner. The practice of the preceding drills and exercises by now should have made you comfortable with the sword and the prospects of offense and defense. With this foundation built, you are now ready to move on to learn further techniques of the threatrical swashbuckler.

---

[2]di Grassi, p. 45.

Chapter 9

Further Techniques of the
Theatrical Swashbuckler

*"He that perswads himself that he can learn this Art by the exercise
of a few perticuler stroks of the point and edg is utterlie deceived."*
[di Grassi][1]

The preceding eight chapters have established the groundwork of theatrical swordplay. The understanding and mastery of the history, guards, parries, attacks, offensive and defensive interplay and safety techniques therein are the synthesis of the art. Like all artistic endeavors, however, there is more than one way to skin a cat. Or in our case, there is more than one way to swing a sword. This chapter is designed to offer a variety of philosophies and techniques that can provide more depth and color to a stage fight. Building on the "perticuler stroks of the point and edg" offered earlier, these techniques allow greater variety to your repertoire of dramatic movement.

FOOTWORK: BEYOND THE BASICS

Although the footwork offered in Chapter 3 is the premise for almost all movement of the feet in a staged sword fight, the actions can become restrictive in terms of a dramatic encounter. Because there are so many variables within a fight and all actions do not have the same weight or value to the combatant, the length of the step in regulated footwork can be restricting. A desperate or enraged character would not necessarily advance and retreat the length of one foot. The situation or the character might necessitate more dynamic footwork. This is known as *active movement* or *active footwork*. Active footwork is the process of amplifying the distance a standard or *passive* piece of footwork would cover.

In Chapter 3, most footwork carried the combatant the length of one foot either forward or back. In active footwork this can be amplified to two or three foot lengths. Stationary footwork now moves the body forward and backward much like an advance and retreat. Passing and circle steps become deeper, and the advance and retreat can now cover twice as much ground. (Figs. 125–126)

In active footwork there are no hard and fast rules concerning the exact length of the step, as long as both combatants keep relative measure. The fundamental mechanics of the footwork should not change. Placement on linear or circular tracks should not shift. Active footwork should only affect the depth of the step and the distance the action covers. The movement should be comfortable for the combatants and must be able to facilitate further footwork. An active pass forward for example, should not be so deep that another pass cannot be initiated, and so on.

---

[1]di Grassi, p. 43

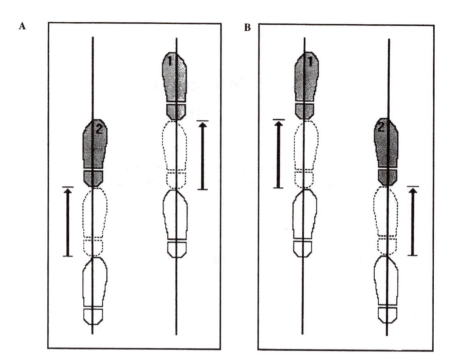

Figure 125. **A-**An Active Advance right foot dominant; **B-**An Active Advance left foot dominant.

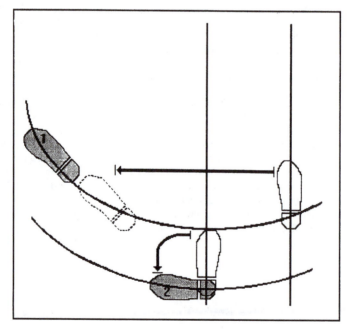

Figure 126. An Active Circle Step Left leading with the right foot.

Active footwork may be taken through all the drills and exercises of the previous chapters. Be careful that you match the depth of your partner's step. It is best when you start working active footwork to practice keeping measure by using the Tight Rope exercise from Chapter 3. This helps you and your partner keep distance by matching the size of your steps. If you are working circle steps, it is important to remember that active footwork carries further around the circle. The circle right and circle left exercises now carry you beyond the half-way point, possibly all the way around the circle. There is nothing wrong with this, as long as the reversed sequence carries you back to your point of origin. This allows you to repeat the drills in the same manner as presented in Chapter 8. A fluency in both passive and active footwork allows for a larger spectrum of choices in a physical encounter.

Additional Footwork

Jump Forward

The *jump forward* (sometimes called an active advance), can be defined as a forceful hop or glide forward. The action is executed quickly but remains close to the ground. The feet do not begin movement at the same time but do finish simultaneously. Action for the jump forward is initiated by the lead foot. Transfer your weight to your lag foot, then lift the toes and then the ball of the lead foot slightly off the ground. With no remaining resistance on the lead foot, the pushing force of the lag foot takes over. The lead foot kicks forward, propelled by the lag foot and leg, approximately two lengths of your foot. The lead foot should travel *over* the length of one foot, or two foot lengths forward.

The main force of the jump forward is provided by the extension of the lag leg. This action drives you forward. This force must push straight forward through the hips. Do not push the body up and forward.

When the lead leg has reached peak extension, it is snapped down toward the floor quickly. Before the lead foot touches the ground, the lag leg should be energetically accelerated and pulled forward under the body. This should be done so that both feet land on the floor at the same time. Upon completion of the jump forward you should be in correct placement in the On Guard stance.

Jump Back

The *jump back* (sometimes called an active retreat) is simply the reverse of jump forward, removing you backward from your partner. In the jump back the lag foot leaves the ground first. This shifts your weight forward to the lead foot. The lag foot raises its heel, then ball and toes, and kicks straight backward approximately the length of two feet. The lag foot should travel *over* the length of one foot, or two foot lengths backward.

The main force of the jump back is provided by a push down into the lead leg and its extension. This action drives the body backward. The driving force must push straight back through the hips. Do not push the body up and back.

When the lag leg has reached peak extension, it is quickly snapped down toward the floor. Before the lag foot touches the ground, the lead leg is energetically accelerated and pushed backward under the body. This is done so that both feet land on the floor at the same time. Upon completion of the jump backwards you are in correct placement in the On Guard stance.

Passing Jumps, Forward and Back

A variation on the jump is the *passing jump*. These actions are initiated as a pass, but as the passing foot transfers to the new lead or lag position it propels the body in that direction with a much greater force (and much further, too!). The supporting foot follows the action as if it were a jump. Both feet, as in the jump, complete the action at the same time. One can jump forward or backward in this manner.

Turning

From the linear planes of movement dictated by the preceding footwork, both in this chapter and in Chapter 3, a combatant can and should be able to break free. Characters such as Cyrano or D'Artagnon should be able to freely turn and spin during swordplay while others such as Andrew Aguecheek or Falstaff can be sent whirling out of the fray. Such actions help break the line of the fight and can provide valuable information about the character or their actions. The problem is that just about anything that spins the combatant falls under the heading of "Turning." Thus, there is an endless variety of spins and turns that can be used in swordplay. The primary concern in executing these actions is that they are controlled and the combatants balanced, centered, and safe. Keeping these rules in mind, any turn is possible. Following are examples of two types of turns, but they are by no means the only turns for the theatrical swashbuckler.

The Turn

From the On Guard stance, transfer your weight to your lag foot. The toes and then the ball of the lead foot are then lifted slightly off the ground. Barely leaving the floor (almost skimming the floor), the heel of the lead foot advances approximately one foot length forward.

Once the heel is securely on the floor your weight begins to shift forward, placing the ball and then the toe of the foot soundly upon the floor. At the same moment the front foot contacts the floor, transfer your weight to your lead foot.

Skimming the floor, the toes of the lag foot travel behind you. The foot should outline a semicircle from the lag position to that of the track of the inner circle. The placement of its toes should be just outside the heel of the lead foot (just as in a grand volte).

As the lag foot travels back and around to the inner track, the lead foot relevés (pushing down into its toes, lifting its heel off the floor) so that the lead foot can pivot in place on its ball. The lead foot should turn ninety degrees from its original placement.

Once the toe of the lag foot is securely in place, the foot is placed firmly upon the floor. Shift your weight to the volted foot. Direct your lead foot in the direction exactly opposite its point of origin. Lift the toes and then the ball of the lead foot slightly off the ground. Barely leaving the floor (almost skimming the floor), the heel of the lead foot advances approximately one foot length forward.

Once the heel is securely on the floor, your weight begins to shift forward, placing the ball and then the toe of the foot firmly upon the floor. The lag foot turns slightly to the outside and the lead foot takes over its share of the body's weight. Both feet are in correct placement. The entire body, however, has been turned one hundred and eighty degrees from its point of origin. (Fig. 127)

Forward Turn

From the On Guard stance, transfer your weight to your lead foot. The toes and then the ball of the lag foot are lifted slightly off the ground. Barely leaving the floor (almost skimming the floor), the heel of the lag foot is passed forward onto the track of the lead foot. The lag foot comes to rest on the same track as the lead foot, approximately one foot length forward.

Once the heel is securely on the floor your weight begins to shift forward, placing the ball and then the toe soundly upon the floor. At the same moment the foot contacts the floor, transfer your weight to the new lead foot.

On the weight shift, the heel of the new lag foot is lifted off the floor (almost skimming the floor), its toes carried around and forward, outlining a semicircle from the its lag position to a new lead position on the same track. The circular pass of the foot should turn the body 180 degrees. If the left foot is passed forward first, the body turns counterclockwise, and vice versa with the right foot. The turn of the body should pivot on the ball of the lead foot, just as in a grand volte. The pivoting foot turns one hundred-eighty degrees from its original placement, along with the body.

Shift your weight to the volted foot, once it has been placed firmly upon the floor. Continue the

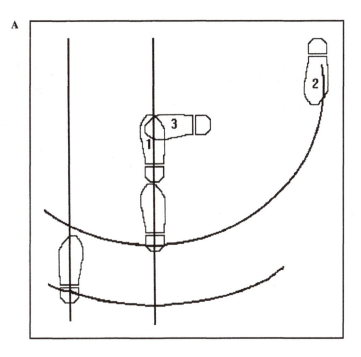

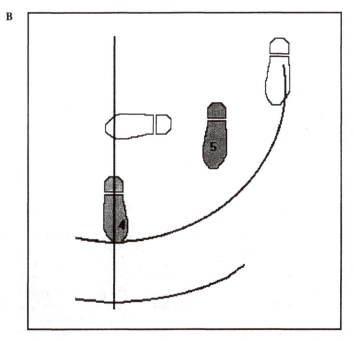

Figure 127. **A**-The Turn. 1—A step forward with the right foot. 2—A grand-volte to the right with the left foot. 3—Ninety degree pivot on the ball of the right foot. **B**-4—The right foot is turned and carried forward. 5—The left foot moves back to On Guard.

turning of your body, completing a 360 degree turn. As the body completes the turn, bring the new lag foot out, off the line of the lead foot and back to proper placement on the parallel track. Your body ends in the same placement as the action began. The forward turn should cover the same ground as two standard pass forwards. (Fig. 128)

Balestra (Jump Forward-Lunge)

The *balestra* is an immediate succession from a jump forward to the grand lunge. The action travels a great distance and quickly closes measure on your partner. The balestra is an aggressive action meant to end with an attack.

In the balestra, the lag leg is drawn in from the jump forward. The lag foot meets the lead foot, narrowing your base for a split second. The lead foot, however, is not brought in contact with the floor, but hangs ready. This affords a greater reach in the bolt forward for the grand lunge.

Full Pass (Pass Forward-Lunge)

The *full pass* is a compound action in footwork that combines the walking action of the pass with the extended leg position of the lunge. The action moves from one action to the other without stopping the forward motion of the leg. This is a fast and furious movement often completed with the upper torso extended beyond the lead leg with the unarmed hand used for support. Generally, however, it is a pass forward taken into a grand lunge.

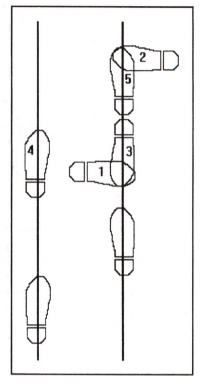

Figure 128. The Forward Turn. 1—Left foot forward to right track. 2—Right foot compass forward on right track. 3—Pivot on left foot, turn 90 degrees. 4—Left foot steps out onto left track. 5—Right foot pivots back to lead position.

Half Pass

"Halfe pace: and that is, when the hinder-foote being brought nere the fore foote, doth even there rest: or when from thence the same foote goeth forwardes." [di Grassi][2]

The *half pass,* also sometimes called the "cheat" or "paused" step, is an action of the feet that carries the lag foot forward in the same manner as a pass, only bringing the foot to rest parallel to the lead foot rather than one foot length forward. The half pass is a simple form of footwork generally executed in conjunction with a similar action of the foot, making the movement compound in execution. The first step to parallel is the half pass, and at this point an offensive or defensive action can be executed without committing the body forward or changing measure. Once the action is complete, the body can be carried forward on an attack. The pause between the first and second action of the feet is quite short, and is followed immediately by another half pass forward. (Fig. 129)

Because both feet are parallel during the pause, you have the option of continuing the initiating

---

[2]di Grassi, p. 31

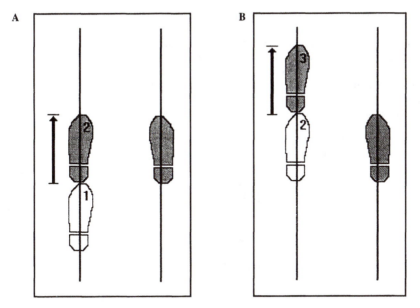

Figure 129. **A**-Primary half pass; **B**-Secondary half pass.

foot forward, or moving the original lead foot forward into the lead position. The half step is a tactical action for effectively closing measure on one's opponent. For this reason there are seldom half passes to the rear. The cheating of the step forward moves the combatant forward, hopefully without notice by the adversary. Movements backward are generally defensive in nature and require quick rather than subtle movement.

Fleche (Running Attack)

The direct translation of *fleche* is arrow or dart, and as a means of offensive footwork the translation holds true. The fleche is an explosive running attack designed to cover great distances quickly and to afford an attack even on the fastest retreating opponent. The movement begins with the lag leg pushing the body forward beyond the point where your center of gravity begins to tip forward.

At this point, the lead leg vigorously joins in with a pushing motion much like running. The lag leg, having spent its energy, is passed forward in a long reaching step to help regain balance as soon as possible. The body continues to move forward in this manner, and usually overcomes your partner, passing them either on the right or the left. Due to the nature and speed of this action, never direct the fleche towards your partner. The attack is always delivered to one side or the other.

During the fleche, the feet step off their tracks and travel much more like a sprinter's feet. They travel along the same track, reaching forward.

Once you regain your balance, you can easily turn yourself to face your partner by executing the turn described earlier.

Footwork of the Transitional Age

The footwork covered up to this point is that designed for the cut and thrust swordplay of the rapier, and the rapier and dagger. The positions and placement of the body during footwork being designed to keep a strong wide stance with the left hand forward for necessary defensive actions. The strong use of cutting attacks required a wider base that allowed for a greater variety of movement to the swordsman who had to protect himself from attacks coming from any direction. As rapier fence changed, however, so did the physical needs of the combatant. Because the transitional rapier was primarily a thrusting weapon, the footwork began to mimic the actions of the blade. The combatant needed to shoot in and out of the play as quickly as the point of the rapier.

The thrust comes much quicker and requires agility in movement rather than strength. The square, four-point stance of the early rapier did not provide the speed necessary to gain or break ground in the fast action puncture-play of the transitional rapier. Because the left hand was no longer essential for defensive actions, it could be drawn back, turning the torso slightly away from the opponent. This turn narrowed the stance and target, making it more difficult for the opponent to thrust home while facilitating quicker footwork.

The transitional style of rapier play preferred by many directors and choreographer's requires a style of footwork that supports quick detached parries and rapid-fire exchange of point work. For this type of "fencing," a narrower stance and base are needed. Start with the toes of the right foot directed straight forward, towards the opponent, with the toes of the left foot directed straight off to the left. Your feet at ninety degrees to one another with the heels touching. Your right shoulder is aligned with the toes of the right foot, your left shoulder with the left foot. Unlike the standard placement, your trunk and torso are turned roughly forty-five degrees off to the left. A half turn away from the square "chest to chest" placement with your partner.

From this placement, the left foot is carried forward, in the direction it points, one foot length. Once the left foot is set on the floor, the right foot may be carried forward, in the direction it points, almost two foot lengths. The trunk and torso remain on a diagonal with the body retaining correct alignment. With the feet in this position the weight of your body rests equally between your feet. This is a *three-point stance*. (Fig. 130)

The three-point stance, in comparison to the standard four-point stance, consists of an increased depth and reduced width. The feet remain approximately shoulder width apart, only now on a diagonal. This narrows the parallel tracks of linear and circular footwork from shoulder width to approximately one foot. Because the parallel tracks are closer, the push and pull of the legs in footwork is focused on a tighter area, allowing for a greater concentration of effort. Such a stance allows for strong, quick movements of the feet such as the advance and retreat.

This narrower base of support allows for stability and balance in this quick linear movement. It does not, however, supply much support in side to side movement. The three-point stance supports the fencer during defensive movements to the inside, but lacks an effective brace for the outside. For this reason the transitional rapier is generally carried in Terza or Seconda, closing the outside line, forcing all attacks to the inside where there is greater strength and stability.

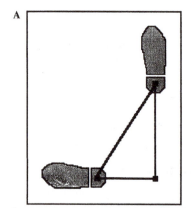 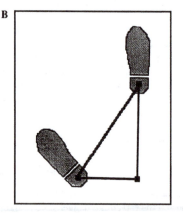

Figure 130. The On Guard position of the feet during transitional rapier play. **A**-The Three-Point Stance. **B**-A variation on the Three-Point Stance with the left foot angled forward at roughly forty-five degrees.

The transitional guard position calls for the same bending in the legs at the knees, to form a pentagon with the floor as the standard on guard position. The knees travel out over the feet, resting above the instep. The pelvis is in a midway position, neither tucking under or sticking out. The trunk and torso are half turned to the left, the right arm and chest aligned with the leading right foot. The torso is lowered into the legs, its weight is lifted with the center, away from gravity. The legs and thighs pull apart the center of gravity in opposite directions while the trunk of the body lifts up the weight of the center. This holds the body in a state of equilibrium, a ready starting position.

In theatrical swordplay, the transfer from standard to transitional footwork is quite simple. Aside from the change in placement, the mechanics remain the same. The drills and exercises offered in the previous chapters may be executed in transitional footwork as easily as standard. This style of footwork is most often accompanied by the transitional parry covered in Chapter 6. Both forms of footwork are widely used by today's fight choreographers. Some prefer one form or the other, while others use both effectively, often mixing them within a single fight. It is important to remember, however, that this type of stance is intended for fights that contain a large amount of point work and little edge-play. Be sure that you are properly centered for the activities within the fight, and that the activities within the fight are safe for your chosen movement.

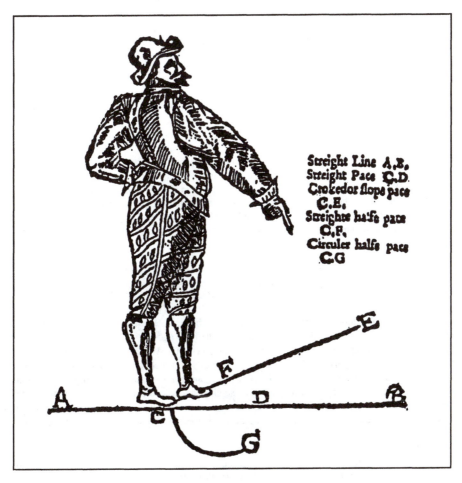

Plate XVI: di Grassi's variable planes of footwork (1594).

The Variable Planes of Footwork

Since the introduction of footwork in Chapter 3, you have been practicing your footwork and blade-play on two sets of railroad tracks. Footwork has either taken you forward and backward, in a line much like competitive fencing, or on a circle with your partner. Although the pass was the most common form of gaining and breaking ground in rapier fence, the line of the pass was not solely limited to the linear and circular tracks previously covered.

Treatises such as di Grassi's and Saviolo's talk of a variety of "paces" with the feet, and the Spanish "imaginary circle" also contained a great many variable planes of footwork. Each action of the foot was mathematically divided and subdivided into its proper angle and tangents for attack and defense. This is illustrated in the work of the French fencing master Thibaust, who produced one of the most extravagant treatises on the art of fence ever published.[3] Based on the works of Carranza and Narvaez, his book brilliantly illustrates the art and science of the Spanish school of fence. Unfortunately, by the time the manuscript was printed, the French science of fence had greatly surpassed the practice of the Spanish school. His illustrations, however, are remarkable. The plate detailing the imaginary circle and its variable planes of footwork, although detailed, looked more like a map for complex dance steps than anything we've worked on so far. This is because rapier fence was not limited to the competitive fencing strip. Fights could, and did cover a good deal of ground from a wide variety of angles.

Aside from the historical truth of variable planes of footwork, there is the theatrical necessity for variety. Linear swordplay can appear repetitious, more like an exhibition than a dramatic encounter. The characters must be free to move about in their environment, using their surroundings to their advantage, and to their opponent's disadvantage. A theatrical sword fight should be able to be taken off the linear tracks and in any direction. It needs the options of traveling backwards, forwards, in a circle, up and over a table, down stairs, around furniture, as well as to one side or the other. For this reason the ten directions of footwork have been developed.

The Ten Directions of Footwork

During the course of a stage fight there are ten directions that any piece of footwork can take the combatant. Each of these directions generates out from a central position, like the points on a compass, or like the parries moving in relation to the face of a clock. As the wrist or hand is always the center of the clock, the combatant is always the center of the compass. Positioned in the center, the instructions for the ten directions of footwork will always assume that you are facing "north." Although you may turn and twist about the stage, the compass is always below you, and your chest and torso are always facing north.

> *"It is to be knowen that the feete move either streightly, either circularly: If streitly, then either forwardes or backwards . . . [if circular] they are made thus: When one hath framed his pace, he must fetch a compasse with his hinder foote or fore foote, on the right or lefte side"* [di Grassi][4]

The first four directions were previously covered in Chapter 3. These are the linear movements on the parallel tracks, and the circular movements to the right and left. (Fig. 131) Any movement that carries you forward on the linear tracks carries you north. As exemplified above, these are known as *straight paces forward.* If the movement carries you straight backward, or "south," these are known as *straight paces backward.* Circular paces are another matter. A compass has eight points, north, northeast, east, southeast, south, southwest, west and northwest. At first glance circular steps travel northeast and northwest, but this is actually not the case. Circle steps are the ninth and tenth direction of movement on the compass. Each of the other eight points travel out,

---

[3]The "Academi de l'Espee" (1626) written by Girard Thibault provided advanced theories and detailed illustrations concerning Spanish rapier styles and advocated their use and superiority.

[4]di Grassi, p. 30–31

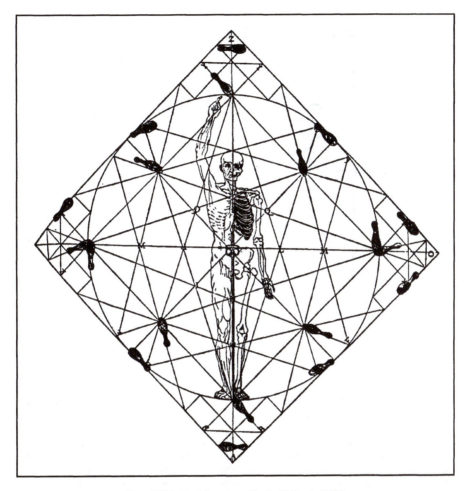

Plate XVII: The Mysterious Circle. Thibault (1626)

away from the center. Circle steps, however, cross each of the angular planes and eventually return to the center. Therefore circular steps are referred to as *circular pace right* and *circular pace left*. (Fig. 132) These match the pattern of the theatre's "mysterious circle" covered in Chapter 3. There are, however, six other directions for the execution of footwork.

> *"By croked or slope pace is understood, when the hinderfoot is brought also forewards, but yet a thwarte or crossing: and as it groweth forwardes, it carrieth the body with it, out of the straight line"* [di Grassi][5]

Pertaining to the points on a compass, you have practiced your movements only as straight paces, moving north and south. There is still east, west and diagonals. (Fig. 133) In footwork, actions may be taken to either side, right or left. These are planes of movement that run perpendicular to the straight paces, and that line is called a *traverse*. Actions taken to the right, or east, are called *traverse*

---

[5]di Grassi, pp. 30–31.

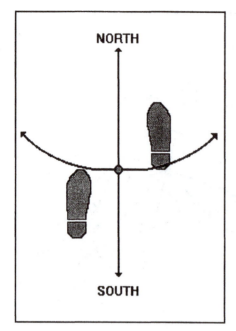

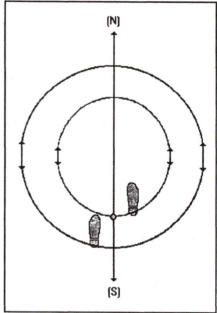

Figure 131. The direction of Straight and Circular Paces.

Figure 132. Straight and Circular Paces aligned on a compass.

right, and action to the left, or west, are called *traverse left.* This set of tracks runs through the middle of each foot as they are placed in the on guard position on the north-south tracks of the straight pace. They are the same width apart and may be traveled in the same manner as their counterpart. The diagonals of the footwork compass, northeast (NE), southeast (SE), southwest (SW) and northwest (NW) are known as *sloped paces.* Sloped paces may be taken forward to the right (NE), backward to the right (SE), backward to the left (SW), and forward to the left (NW). The railroad tracks of the sloped paces run at a forty-five degree angle to the north-south, east-west tracks. All tracks of the feet are the same width apart, and may be moved upon in the same manner as the tracks of the straight pace and circle steps. (Fig. 135)

All the footwork expressed in Chapter 3, and earlier in this chapter, may be applied to the ten planes of movement. Advances and retreats may be taken on the circle, as well as on a sloped pace or traverse. You may pass, volte and lunge on either foot, on any track, in any direction. These planes open the field of footwork and allow for a greater variety of direction in the course of a fight on stage. You should practice various forms of footwork on these different tracks, and experiment with the variety of drills that can be adapted to the alternate planes of movement. Explore how measure can be maintained and changed through different combinations of footwork. There are no hard and fast rules concerning this exploration other than movements must complement one another in some manner in order to maintain proper measure. These planes of movement are commonly used on stage and should be practiced in order to effectively execute footwork in any direction.

GUARDS: BEYOND THE BASICS

In Chapter 5 you learned the most common guards for the single rapier, standard and cross body. In that chapter all guards were assumed with the points at armpit level or below. Some fight

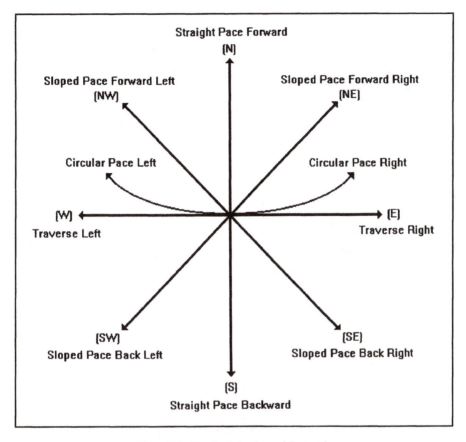

Figure 133. The Ten Directions of Footwork.

directors, however, have their combatants come on guard with their sword points at the level of their partner's hairline (especially in transitional rapier play). The idea for this guard is twofold: one, it is believed that if the combatants should accidentally close measure the points would be brought safely above the head rather than down into the body; and two, it gives the illusion of threatening the exposed face with the point of the sword. The concept behind the placement of this guard is sound, and many fight directors have their beginning students come on guard with their points directed at hairline. Experience has shown, however, that until a combatant becomes familiar with handling a sword and some strength has been developed in the sword arm, a rapier can become heavy in the hand, allowing the point to wander or drop towards the face. This is the danger of such a guard and the reason that it was not addressed until now. To make this guard placement truly safe, it requires the observation of a good teacher and the steady hand of a practiced student.

If you wish to assume this guard placement, the mechanics offered in Chapter 5 need not be altered. The only variance in this type of guard is that the point of the weapon is angled up above the eyes, at the opposing combatant's hairline or the top of their head. The blade is still directed outside the body—only the level of the point is changed. It is imperative that the point not drift downward towards the face and it is advised that such a guard only be practiced under the tutelage of a qualified instructor. If, for some reason, you should close measure with your partner, the points of your swords should be directed up (towards the ceiling) rather than down into the floor.

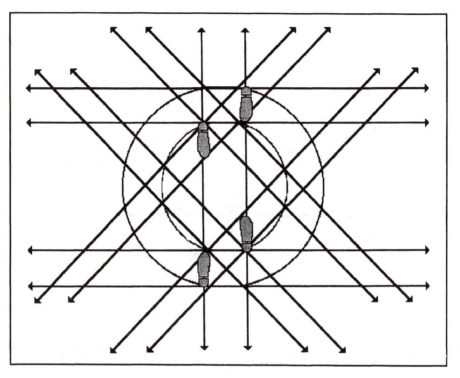

Figure 134. The Variable Planes of Footwork.

PARRIES: BEYOND THE BASICS

Although Chapter 6 covered a complete series of parries that adequately defend the entire body, there are still some variations and modifications that are commonly used on stage. Defense is not always the primary concern in a theatrical encounter. As the flourish of the Actor's Parry is a testament to the theory of dynamics versus practicality, there are further parries that when executed do more to tell a story than defend the body. In this field there are a great many of these theatrical parries. I have included some of the more common variations, but there are many more used on the stage today. In practice, any parry is safe as long as it passes through the center of the body, meets the opposing blade edge to edge, and blocks or deflects the opposing blade away from the hand and body. If you are ever in doubt, review the rules for safe stage parries offered at the end of Chapter 7.

The Beat Away

The *beat away* or *quillon bash,* is a delayed form of beat parry that knocks the opposing blade away after the successful completion of a blocking parry. Unlike the beat parry, the beat away is an aggressive action with the hilt of the sword and not the forte of the blade. After the opposing blade has been stopped by a successful parry, and while it remains engaged, punch the hilt of the sword towards the parried blade. The marked action of the hand and hilt deflects the opposing blade by "bashing" or knocking it aside. The beat with the hilt should always be out, away from you and your partner.

As a general rule, beat aways always knock the opposing blade in the direction the defending blade points. Beat aways from the parry of 3 and 4 knock the blade up and out; from 1, 2, 7, 8, High 1 and High 2 the blade is knocked down and out; horizontal parries such as 5 and Low 5 knock the blade to either the right or left, and so on. The beat must be executed after the parry is completed. Movement of the hand prior to stopping the opposing blade can bring the hand into the attack, possibly striking the hand. The motion of the hand and hilt that knocks the opposing blade aside should keep the hand in the same relative placement as the parry. The hand should travel no more than six inches to strike the blade aside. The punching motion of the hilt should force the opposing blade down the forte of the defending blade and knock the hilt of the sword against the opposing blade's foible. This punch or beat with the hilt knocks the attacking blade aside and frees your blade for an immediate riposte or further defensive action.

It is important to note that the aggressor must remain engaged during the beat away, and must maintain a certain amount of pressure on the defending blade. There is a characteristic "scraping" noise as the blades slide along one another. This can only be achieved when light pressure is applied by the aggressive weapon. The pressure should be enough to keep the blades engaged during the action, but not so much that the action becomes labored or difficult. Once the hilt strikes the sword, the pressure must be released and the hand and wrist of the aggressive blade must give as in a beat parry.

Beat-Aside

The *beat-aside* or *rising parry* is a defensive action that beats the offensive blade aside during the execution of an attack. For this reason it is sometimes also called the "intercept parry." The beat-aside is generally used in defense against a vertical or diagonal cutting attack, called a *swipe*. Unlike the attacks offered in Chapter 7, however, swipes are not pistoned, but swing clear through the plane of the body. The diagonal attacks are delivered from either the right or the left, traveling in a descending plane outside the body at roughly forty-five degrees. The diagonal swipe is cued with the blade pointing up and behind you at roughly forty-five degrees and the hilt above the shoulder at roughly ear level. (Figs. 135–136) From this position the blade travels down, from either right to left, or vice versa, in a diagonal plane starting from the cue and descending to the opposite side of the body. The descending diagonal crosses your partner's center line above their head, never across the body. (Fig. 137) Vertical cutting attacks, like diagonals, may be delivered from either the right or the left, and are never aimed at your partner, but travel six to eight inches outside the body in a plane perpendicular to the floor. (Fig. 138) The cue for the descending attack is identical to the cut to the head (Chapter 7), either man dritto or riverso. From this position the blade travels straight down, in a vertical plane outside your partner's body. None of these attacks are terminated by striking the ground. They should be carried off into a molinello or similar action. These attacks must be delivered with a full extension of the weapon and arm traveling in a full arc from head to toe. The defending blade is brought up to intercept the attacking blade and knock it aside before it lands on its "intended" target.

Beat-Aside to the Right

To beat an attack aside to the right, bring your sword hand to your center, the tip of the sword to the position of nine o'clock. The blade is in line with your waist and horizontal to the floor. As you do this, pronate your hand, turning the knuckle bow towards your partner. Keep the tip at roughly nine o'clock with your wrist pronated, and raise your hand up and to the left. Once at the level of your left shoulder, reach the hand forward and up, while at the same time sharply flicking the point of the blade in a clockwise path from nine to three o'clock. This whipping action of the blade intercepts the opposing blade, beating it aside while still above the head. The hand and arm move together to the right, not stopping at three o'clock, but continuing to descend off to the right. This action works both with a diagonal and vertical cutting attack to the right.

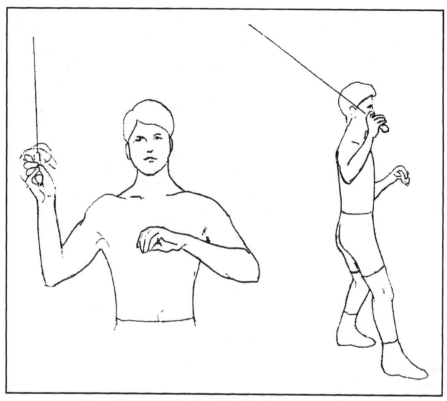

Figure 135. Cue for the descending diagonal attack, right to left.

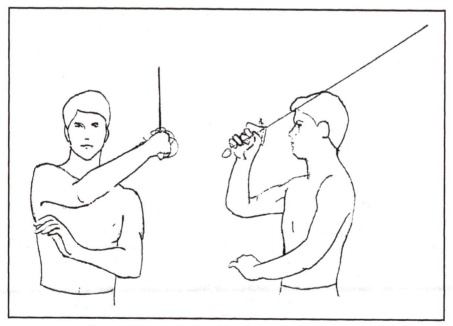

Figure 136. Cue for the descending diagonal attack, left to right.

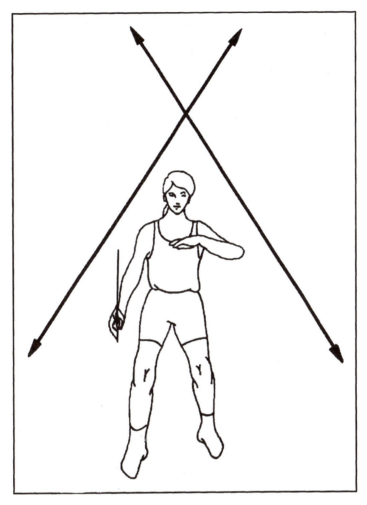

Figure 137. Paths of a Diagonal Swipe.

Beat-Aside to the Left

A beat-aside to the left is executed by bringing the sword hand to your right, the tip of the sword to the position of two o'clock. Your sword hand is at roughly waist level, supinated with the knuckle bow towards your partner. Keep the tip at roughly two o'clock with your hand supinated, and raise your hand up to the level of your right shoulder. Once there, reach the hand forward and up, while at the same time sharply turning your palm towards you and flicking the point of the blade in a counterclockwise arc from two to eight o'clock. This whipping action of the blade intercepts the opposing blade, beating it aside while still above the head. The hand and arm move together to the left, not stopping at eight o'clock, but continuing down and to the left. This action works both with a diagonal and vertical cutting attack to the left.

The beat-aside is an action of both the hand and arm that reaches the blade up to meet the attack above the head and between the combatants. It is an action executed with the true edge of the defending blade being beaten against the false or back edge of the attacking sword. Timing between the combatants is incredibly important in the execution of this action. If the aggressor changes the rhythm or tempo of their attack, the blades could easily miss in the air, or meet on the side of the

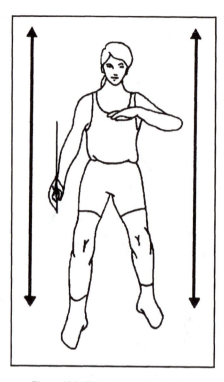

Figure 138. Paths of a vertical swipe.

body and not above the heads. The preliminary movements of the defending arm start at roughly the same time as the attacking blade gives its cue. The flick of the wrist for the beat begins as the offending blade begins to reach forward, the beat taking place above and between the combatants. The action should be practiced slowly between the combatants in order to develop a sense of timing.

Hanging Parries

Hanging or *sloped parries* are defensive actions against diagonal and vertical swipes as those described above. Unlike the beat-asides, the hanging parries deflect rather than intercept the offending blade. They present a sloped or angled blade that meets the attacks and causes it to sheer or ricochet off to the side.

Hang Left

The hanging parry for the left shoulder or *hang left* is executed from the guard of Terza by dropping the tip of the sword to the position of seven o'clock and turning the wrist counterclockwise so that your palm is toward your partner, knuckle bow to the inside (left). From this position move your hand in line with your center and the tip to roughly eight o'clock. Keeping the hand and blade in this position, raise the sword above your head. The blade is diagonal to the floor in front of and outside your body to the left.

Your hand is above your head, with your palm facing your partner. The knuckle bow angles up and to the left, the blade sloping down with the tip at roughly eight o'clock. The blade is above and in front of you, in a diagonal plane similar to that of High 4. The sword does not angle behind you or forward towards your partner, but angles down and off to your left. Although your hand is directly above your head, your arm is to the right of your body and about twelve inches in front of you. The arm needs to be bent in this parry, do not lock the elbow. The arm is lifted up at the shoulder and forms a ninety degree bend at the elbow, angling up and back to your center. The middle of the blade is in front of and above the notch in your left shoulder. If no footwork is executed with the hang left, the lower body will "rock" to the right, away from the attack. (Fig. 139)

Hang Right

Hang right or the *sword arm protect parry* is executed from the guard of Terza by dropping the tip towards the floor, to the position of six o'clock. Your palm faces toward you, knuckle bow towards the outside (right). Leading with the wrist, the sword travels at a diagonal up and across the body. It should move from the level of the right hip to above your head on your left. As the hand is raised it is turned clockwise, turning your palm back in towards you. With the turning of the wrist, the tip of the sword is guided out to the right to the position of four o'clock. Your sword hand travels up your center line and just off to the

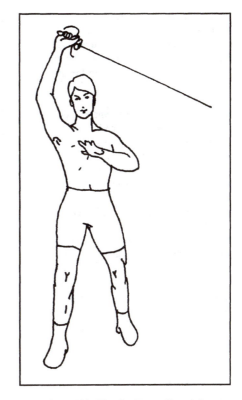

Figure 139. Hanging Parry: Hang left.

left of your head, the forte of the blade traveling up past your right shoulder. As the sword passes the middle of your body, begin rotating at the waist, turning your right shoulder slightly towards your partner.

Stop the sword so that your upper arm is horizontal to the floor at the level of your shoulder. Your elbow should be bent up at roughly ninety degrees, your forearm to the inside (left) of your body, vertical to the floor. Your right shoulder is turned slightly towards your partner. Your hand is above your head on the left, palm towards you, knuckle bow up and to the right, blade sloped down with the tip at roughly four o'clock. Although the placement of the arm is similar to the window parry, the slope of the blade makes the parry more difficult. This is an awkward hand and wrist position and will take some practice to master comfortably. It should not hurt however. The sword is sloped down and to the right with the middle of the blade in front of and above the notch in your right shoulder. If no footwork is executed with the hang right, the lower body "rocks" to the left, away from the attack. (Fig. 140)

A variation on this parry, what many fight choreographers call the "true" sword arm protect, is to drop the tip to six o'clock and to raise the hand and sword up on the right side of the body. The hand is carried from the right hip up above the head on your right. The hand is turned clockwise as the sword is raised, turning your thumb down and palm towards you. As the blade is raised and the wrist turned, the tip of the sword is guided out to the right to roughly four o'clock. The sword hand travels up in a straight line ending at approximately ear level with the forte of the blade outside your right shoulder. Your elbow is directed forward, with the forearm bent back towards you. Your hand is at roughly ear level, palm towards you, knuckle bow angled up and to the right. The blade is outside and in front of the body, sloped down with the tip at roughly four o'clock. If no footwork is executed with the sword arm protect, the lower body "rocks" to the left, away from the attack.

All hanging parries are intended to deflect and not block the offending blade. Unlike other parries the opposing blade meets the middle of the defending blade, not the forte. Vertical swipes meet the blade and skid down the remaining two-thirds. The sliding down the blade is characterized by a fast scraping noise. This sheering of the blades has given this type of parry the nick-name "waterfall parry." Diagonal swipes generally ricochet off the defending blade rather than slide down the parry. The angle of the attack allows the blades to meet, and then avert the attacking blade off to the side. In this type of parry the blades still meet edge to edge, but at a more drastic angle than standard parries.

Reinforced Parry

The *reinforced* or *split parry* is a defensive action of the sword and unarmed

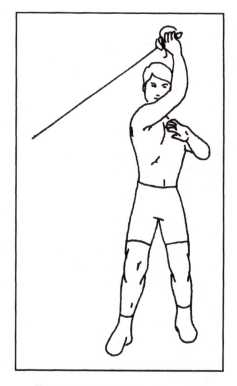

Figure 140. Hanging Parry: Hang right.

hand, usually against what appears to be a hard cutting blow. The term "reinforced" is used to represent the addition of the left hand on the foible of the blade to strengthen and brace the parry against the opposing blade. These parries use the mechanics of several standard parries, reinforced by the left hand. The placement and mechanics of the right hand and sword do not change, the left hand merely takes hold of the rapier's blade approximately one third of the way from the tip, and then both hands push the parry out from the center of the body to meet the attack. There are four standard reinforced parries, one for the head, right shoulder, left shoulder and groin. To help maintain the illusion of a "sharp" blade, these parries are usually only executed with a gloved hand.

Reinforced 5

For the reinforced parry of 5, the sword is pushed up towards the attack like someone lifting a set of barbells. The hands and blade remain parallel with the floor, moving up and out in complete unison. The forte of the blade still defends the center line, allowing the opposing blade to meet the parry at an even split between the two hands. (Fig. 141)

Reinforced 3

The right shoulder is defended with a reinforced parry of 3. The left hand joins the rapier as the point begins its rotation towards twelve o'clock. It will take hold of the foible somewhere between nine and ten o'clock. The hand is then carried above your eye line as the blade reaches twelve o'clock. Once perpendicular to the floor, the hands and blade move in unison, out to the right to meet an attack to the right shoulder. (Fig. 142)

Reinforced High 1

For the left shoulder, you reinforce a parry of High 1. The left hand joins the rapier as the sword hand is raised towards twelve o'clock. It takes hold of the foible near the center or right side of the body with the blade roughly parallel to the floor. The right hand is then carried up in a counterclockwise path, above your eye line. This puts the point at six o'clock and the hilt at twelve. Once perpendicular to the floor, the hands and blade move together, out from the center to meet an attack to the left shoulder. (Fig. 143)

Reinforced High 3

For a diagonal cutting attack to the right shoulder, you reinforce a parry of High 3. The left hand joins the rapier when the point is directed at nine o'clock. It takes hold of the foible and travels with the blade

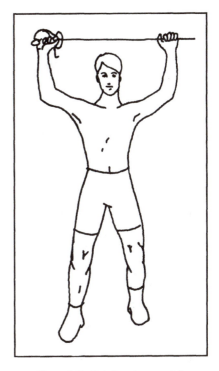

Figure 141. Reinforced parry of 5.

as it is carried to eleven o'clock. The hand is then carried above your head and to the right as the right hand carries the sword to the standard position of High 3. Once the sword matches the diagonal plane of the cutting attack, the hands and blade move in unison, up and out to the right to meet a diagonal attack to the right shoulder. (Fig. 144)

Reinforced Hang Left

For a diagonal cutting attack to the left shoulder (not a swipe), you reinforce the hang left. The left hand joins the rapier as the tip is placed at roughly eight o'clock. It takes hold of the foible near the center or right side of the body with the blade diagonal to the floor. Both hands then move together, pushing the blade up at a diagonal, the sword hand carried above your head, the left hand to roughly armpit level, with both palms facing your partner. The blade is above and in front of you, in a diagonal plane. The middle of the blade is in front of and above the notch in your left shoulder, with the right hand above and to the left of the head, the left hand in front of the body at armpit level, and the opposing blade splitting the parry between the two hands. (Fig. 145)

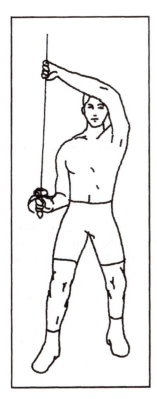

Figure 142. Reinforced parry of 3.

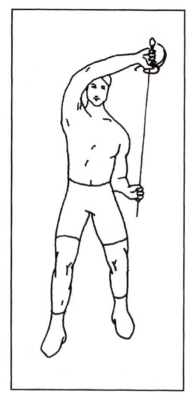

Figure 143. Reinforced parry of High 1.   Figure 144. Reinforced parry of High 3.

Reinforced Low 5

The reinforced parry of Low 5, is the direct opposite of reinforced 5. The sword is pushed down towards the attack, as if barbells were too heavy and needed to be put down. The hands and blade remain parallel with the floor, moving together, down and out. The forte of the blade defends the groin from a Montante, with the right hand in front of the right leg, the left hand in front of the left leg, and the opposing blade splitting the parry between the two hands. (Fig. 146)

All reinforced parries must be executed in the same manner as the standard parry. The blade must come to rest outside and in front of the body. The blades must meet edge to edge, perpendicular to one another, forte to foible. Although the right shoulder could be defended with a reinforced High 2, and the left with a reinforced 4 and High 4, both of these actions carry the elbow through the plane of the attack. This exposes the arm to possibly being struck during the execution of the parry.

BEYOND THE BASIC ATTACKS

Up until this point in the text you have concentrated on cutting attacks delivered with the whole arm from the shoulder. These whole arm attacks communicate action and intention to the audience so that they can follow the movements of the fight in logical progression. Theatrical sword fights, however, like historical rapier play, need a variety of cuts to become completely effective.

The broad movement of a cut from the shoulder primes the audience for the attack, informing them of the action and its intention. This type of attack by itself however, can convey too much information at certain times during the fight. As mentioned in Chapter 7, the dramatic story is told through vocal intensities and patterns as well as with physical postures, placement and movement. Smaller and faster patterns of movement communicate different meanings to an audience just as various vocal patterns do. A series of actions, or the intensity and speed of a particular action, communicates as much to an audience as specific, broad movements. Variations in size, speed and intensity counterbalance one another. Each offers a point of reference to the others to make their particular value clear. Without the use of other cuts, the dynamic action of the shoulder cut would become monotonous, much like an actor only using one vocal tone. Variance enhances and colors the fight while helping to further inform the audience.

In Chapter 7 the principle of action taking focus was discussed, pointing out that the audience's eye is drawn towards activity. It was also made clear that fast, tight movement in a fight loses the audience and provides your partner with no real cue

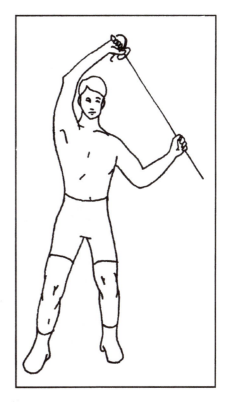

Figure 145. Reinforcement of the hang left parry.

and limited time to safely respond. This remains true in the following cutting attacks. The reference to "quick" and "efficient" attacks was applied to actual attacks with the blade, actions intended to hit, not those designed to portray that intention.

The Three Types of Edge Blows

"The Arme likewise is not in everie part of equall force and swiftness, but differeth in everie bowing thereof, that is to saie in the wrist, in the elbow and in the shoulder: for the blowes of the wrist as they are more swift, so they are lesse strong: And the other two, as they are more strong, so they are more slow, because they performe a greater compas." [di Grassi][6]

In the practice of Elizabethan rapier play there were a variety of ways to attack with the edge of the sword. In the above example from di Grassi's treatise, he offers the example of three distinct types of "blow" with the rapier: from the wrist, elbow and shoulder. This practice was not limited only to his work, but was a common practice in both the Italian and Spanish schools of fence. The schools of Carranza and Narvaez divide their cuts into those from the wrist with a flip of the point, the *mandoble;* those delivered from the elbow, the *mediotajo;* and those cuts delivered with the whole arm from the shoulder, the *arrebatar.* You have already practiced the techniques of the cut delivered from the shoulder, thus we will now explore the elbow and wrist cuts.

---

[6]di Grassi, p. 23.

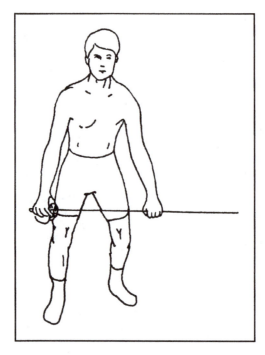

Figure 146. Reinforced parry of Low 5.

Cutting from the Elbow

In theatrical swordplay, the cut from the elbow is simply an abbreviation of the full or standard cut. In the standard cut, there are three stages of the arm as it pistons the blade forward. The first stage is an extension from the elbow, the second a continuation of the cutting arc from the wrist, and the third stage is a straightening of the arm and pushing of the foible forward past the target. Cutting from the elbow uses the same mechanics, only it begins the attack from the completion of the first stage of a full cut. The attack then, literally cuts from the elbow, completing the final two-thirds of the cutting arc. For this reason the elbow cut is sometimes called a two-thirds attack or two-thirds *cut*. The elbow cut can be executed to all twelve targets to which standard cuts are delivered. (Fig. 147)

The two distinct motions of the wrist and arm are what keep this attack safe and controlled. Despite the reduced wind up and cutting arc, you do not have to "pull" the energy of the attack, because the actual energy of the cut is still channeled forward. By maintaining the push of the arm at the end of the cutting arc, the attacking blade ricochets past your partner's parry once the blades meet. The effort of the cut is thrust past one's opponent, not directed at them. This allows you to safely attack all the targets offered in Chapter 7.

Action-Reaction-Action

The principles of safe cutting attacks offered in Chapters 7 and 8 are applied to the elbow cut. Each offensive and defensive movement is still broken down into the three distinct motions of Action-Reaction-Action. As you wind up, traveling to the cue and control point, rock back to the defensive attitude of stationary footwork. Rock forward in the cue, looking for your partner's acknowledgment of the cue. Upon perceiving the correct reaction, you may execute an elbow cut at the specified target on your partner.

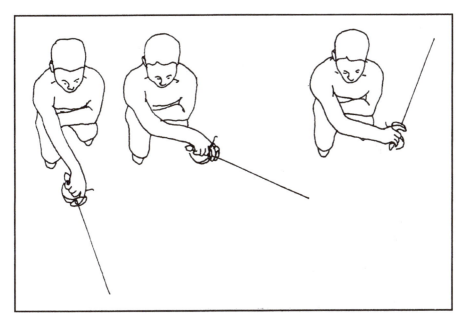

Figure 147. The elbow cut.

The elbow cut travels in a shorter arc and therefore moves much more quickly. Be sure that all your attacks are aimed exactly at their intended target, and that they stop three to six inches outside your opponent's body. During the execution of these mechanics, it is important that you get "eyes" and connect with your partner before moving on to the task at hand. Be sure that the offensive and defensive blades meet forte to foible, edge to edge and at approximately ninety degrees. Remember, a vertical attack always meets a horizontal parry, and a horizontal attack always meets a vertical parry. If you are unsure of all the procedures involved in the cutting attack, review the rules offered in Chapter 8.

The Cues

When cueing an elbow cut, the placement of the arm and the sword is similar to that of the shoulder cut. The position of the hand and sword should read as a specific attack to a specific target. Although the arm is extended from the elbow, there should be no question as to the direction of the attack and where it should land.

Working the Elbow Cut

Because elbow cuts move faster than shoulder cuts, it is a natural habit for beginning combatants to rush past the control point of the cut. The point of control, however, is the cue to your partner and your check point for safety. It allows you to observe your partner's reaction, and to abort the attack if anything goes wrong. The control point is essential to safe stage combat, especially as the blades move faster and there is less margin for error. Remember to always "think" and then "do."

Although the mechanics of the elbow cuts are similar to those of the shoulder cut, it is recommended that you work through each of the attacks several times on your own. You need to become familiar with stopping the blade at the correct point, offering the proper cue and executing a safe, effective cut. Once you are competent in moving from cut to cut, you may practice the attacks with a partner. The cut from the elbow can be taken through all the exercises offered in Chapter 8 that

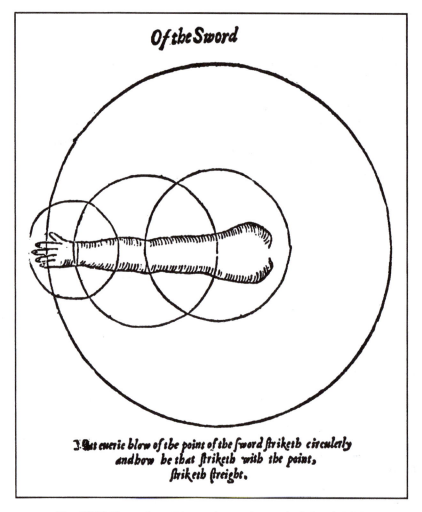

Plate XVIII: The motions of the arm in a cutting attack. di Grassi (1594)

utilize the cutting attack. These include both traveling and stationary drills and work with the blocking, beat and detached parries. Be aware that the reduced cut affects the timing of your partner's parries. The time from the cue to cut is less, and requires a faster reaction from your partner. To find this timing it is best to first mark through the drills slowly, talking through the Action-Reaction-Action process. Your partner can then say "YES" or "NO" in response to your cue. This helps them spot the cue, and corrects possible faults in your execution. The flash card exercise may also be used to further help in this process.

The Cut from the Wrist

The wrist cut is the fastest and tightest cut delivered in theatrical swordplay, and is more akin to competitive sabre fencing than historical rapier play. Like the elbow cut, the wrist cut is an abbreviation of the full or standard cut. Cutting from the wrist begins the attack from the completion of the second stage of a full cut. The attack consists of the final third of the cutting arc. For this reason the wrist cut is sometimes called a one-third attack or *one-third cut*. Unlike the other cuts, however, this cut is supplemented by a flicking action of the wrist and fingers. This flicking action allows the blade to travel in a succinct cutting arc while still controlling the power of the attack.

The "flicking" of the wrist cut is the result of relaxation and tension of the fingers and hand during the thrusting of the blade forward. The wrist along with the manipulators (thumb and index finger) steer the attack while the last three fingers or aids loosen and tighten on the grip of the sword, flicking the blade forward. To practice these mechanics, hold your rapier in Terza standard, your hand in middle/vertical position. With the unarmed hand, reach across the body and in front of the blade, taking hold of the rapier's foible. From this starting position, pull the blade back towards you with your unarmed hand, and at the same time release your grip with the aid fingers. It is important to note that the word "release" does not mean that fingers totally release or leave the grip, but rather maintain contact, while the handle of the weapon leaves the cushion of the hand. When you reach the limit of movement, with the grip pressing out against the pads of the aid fingers, pull the grip back into the palm of the hand with the aid fingers. (Figs. 148–149)

When you pull the blade back to Terza, apply some opposition with your unarmed hand. This helps develop the muscles necessary for delivering this cut and will prevent you from accidentally letting go of the grip with the aid fingers at the release.

Practice this release-pullback exercise several times. Work in supination, pulling the blade horizontally to the right and in pronation, pulling the blade horizontally to the left. Once you are comfortable with the release-pullback in the three hand positions, try moving from one hand position into another while simultaneously pulling the blade back with the unarmed hand. For example, start pulling the blade back in middle/vertical position and as the hand releases the grip, rotate the hand to a supinated placement. The rotation of the hand carries the tip of the sword from a position of

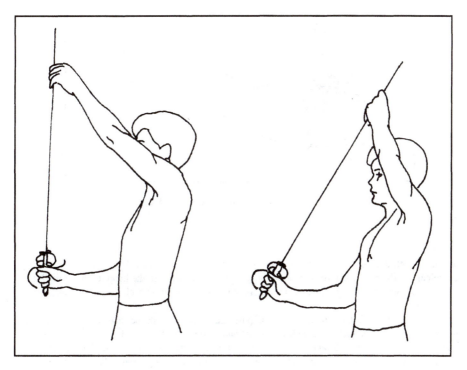

Figure 148. Practicing the flick cut.

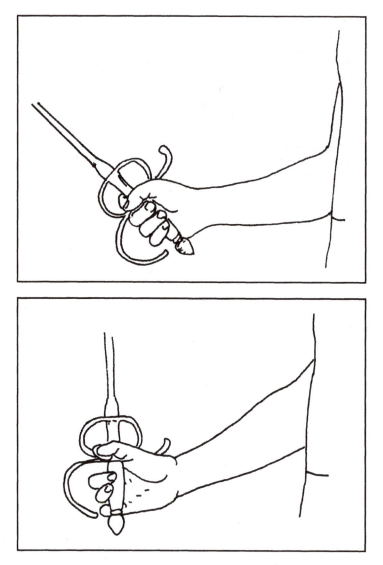

Figure 149. Close up of the hand in a flick cut.

twelve o'clock to a position of three o'clock. The rotation of the hand and blade takes place during the release of the grip. Once in supination the grip is pulled back into the hand, carrying the blade forward in a horizontal plane. This technique should be practiced from each position of the hand to the others.

Once you are comfortable with the release-pullback exercises with the unarmed hand applying resistance, practice the technique with the sword hand alone. Try this first in one plane, then with transitions from one plane to another, and then with a soft extension of the arm from Terza.

Like the elbow cut, the wrist cut can be executed to all twelve body targets. The "flick" returns the blade to the placement of a standard cut as the thrust of the arm safely guides the blade past your partner. Despite the size and speed of the cut, the extended arm pushes the blade forward three to six inches outside your opponent's body.

The Cues

Reading the cue of a wrist cut can prove difficult at first. It is like trying to read shorthand after working solely with typewritten text. All the information is there, however, it just takes a trained eye to effectively grasp the presented information. As in the shoulder and elbow cuts, the hand and blade placement provide the defender with the cue concerning the angle and target of the attack. A hand at shoulder level with the blade flat to the floor is a horizontal shoulder cut; at waist level with a diagonal blade is a cut to the thigh and so on. The cues come quickly, but there should still be no question as to the direction of the attack and where it is intended to land.

In these cues, the grip is in the released position. This allows the blade to form nearly a ninety degree angle with the arm, making the cut effective even from the position of the extended arm. The actual cut is executed from the cue by pulling the grip back into the hand while simultaneously completing the extension of the arm. The extension of the arm and the action of the aids and wrist finish at the moment the blade meets the opposing parry.

Working the Wrist Cut

Although the wrist cut is not executed from the elbow, the joint maintains a central role in manipulating the blade, acting much like a control tower. The elbow steers the hand and sword to the appropriate side of the body and allows for fluid rotation from supinated to pronated hand positions. The slight bend in the elbow allows for the final punch of the attack forward and for the quick removal of the blade after an attack is parried. For this reason the elbow must be relaxed, even when the arm is extended forward at the completion of the attack. A stiff elbow or arm can seriously affect the speed and mechanics of the wrist cut. To practice working a relaxed arm in the execution of wrist cuts, try running through the around the clock exercise offered in Chapter 8. Cut around the clock with small mollinellos executed from the wrist and elbow. Working this exercise alone helps build speed in execution and working with a partner facilitates better focus on targets and the proper communication between combatants.

It is recommended that you first work through each of the wrist cuts without a partner. The mechanics of these cuts are new and you need to become familiar with movement of the extended arm, the proper placement of the cues and the flicking of the cut. Once you have worked the cuts around the clock and feel comfortable with the mechanics of the sword and arm, practice the exercise with a partner. Be aware that this cut seriously affects the reaction time of your partner. If your partner has trouble reading the cues of the wrist cuts, take the time to work the flash card exercise from Chapter 7. Once you are comfortable with the wrist cuts, you can work them in all the exercises offered in Chapter 8 that utilize the cutting attack.

Trouble Shooting

Relaxing the Cut

If your blade tends to "stick" in the cut rather than returning after completing the action, you are probably locking the arm muscles as you tighten your grip on the sword. Your grip needs to be fairly relaxed to ensure fluid movement of the hand and arm. Pressure should be applied only to bring the blade forward in the cut. Once the cut is completed, the grip must once again be relaxed. To help release the hand after executing a cut, try executing two or three cuts in succession. This should help you feel and understand how the tension and relaxation of the fingers, thumb and wrist work in the final stage of the cut.

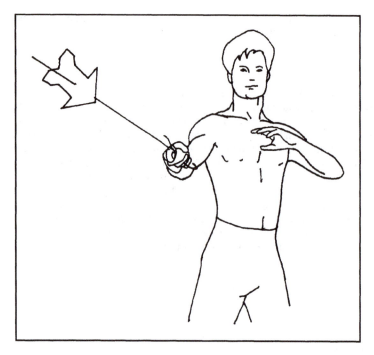

Figure 150. **A**-Pointing the way exercise.

Pointing the Way

While delivering these attacks, some combatants have trouble directing the blade effectively towards the intended target. The point seems to wander or flip up or down, missing the parry or striking the blade closer to the foible than the forte. This is a sign that the mechanics have probably been rushed and that the pulling of the grip back to the palm has become a clenching of the fist rather than a pulling back of the grip to its point of origin. The best way to solve this problem is to go back to the release-pullback exercise and slowly review the mechanics. When the unarmed hand is removed from the process, go directly to working the cuts around the clock. In practicing these cuts, place a cardboard ''arrow'' or a triangle on the foible of the blade. (Fig. 150) The point of the arrow or triangle should represent the direction of the cutting edge and should allow the combatant to better focus on the exact placement of their cut. A partner can then stand outside measure and each attack can be given, using the arrow to be sure that all attacks are aimed exactly at their intended target. This exercise can be used in any cutting attack (standard, elbow, wrist) where there is a question of targeting.

Strengthening the Manipulators

If you find the rapier too heavy, and the wrist cut difficult, you should continue working the doigté exercises offered in Chapter 4. If the ''flicking'' of the cut is awkward, or if the hand tends to drift or punch the cut forward, you may try the following exercise. Extend your sword arm forward into Seconda. With your unarmed hand, take hold of the forte of the blade and work the mechanics of the release-pullback exercise offered earlier. To develop the strength and agility of the fingers, your arm and wrist must be held motionless, in a fixed state. Movements of the point which span a large area are done by allowing the grip to move away from the palm. Opposition with the

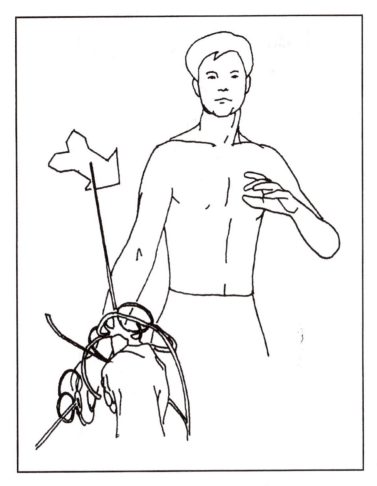

Figure 150. **B**-Pointing the way exercise.

unarmed hand is important in this exercise as the pressure of the grip against the fingers is what exercises the manipulators.

Thrusting On-Line

Now that distance and measure are a practiced part of swordplay you can safely explore the method of *on-line fencing*. This is the mode of theatrical swordplay where attacks are aimed directly at the combatant's body. In Chapter 7 you only learned off-line attacks. These are the safest form of point work and recommended for beginning combatants because the attacks are directed safely outside the body. There are however, instances where off-line fencing can appear staged, proving ineffective to the audience. Such instances are fights staged in the round, on a thrust or any other staging situation where the observers can easily see if the blade is directed towards the opponent or safely outside their body. This is quite evident in film fighting when the action is filmed over a combatant's shoulder. The line of the blade is easily visible and if the attacks are off-line, there is no apparent danger in the fight. For these reasons, a system of fencing on-line had to be developed for safe stage swordplay.

Figure 151. The Triangle Target of On-Line Attacks.

On-Line Targets

There are three "target" systems most often used in on-line attacks, these are the *triangle target,* *box target* and the *hour-glass* system. The triangle target is a system of three on-line body targets; one center chest (at the zyfoid process) and the other two located on opposite thighs at approximately groin level. The chest target is parried by 3,4 and 6, the thigh targets work for both the parries of 2 and 8 as well as 1 and 7. (Fig. 151) The box target isolates four points on the body of the victim that when joined with imaginary lines form a box. These targets are generally right and left chest (at armpit level) and right and left thigh. As in the triangle target, the thighs may be parried on the right by 2 or 8, and on the left by 1 or 7. (Fig. 152) The hour-glass system is the most common, and the least confusing in reading cues. It offers five on-line body targets. These are the right and left chest, center line at waist level and the right and left thigh. (Fig. 153) In this system the addition of the center target makes the cues of shoulder, waist and thigh transfer to on-line fencing without having to alter the mechanics of the cue or the reading of the attack by the victim. It is for this reason that when working on-line, it is best to work the hour-glass system.

Beginning the Techniques

In these exercises you will work with the hour-glass target system. Shoulder thrusts are directed at the right or left chest roughly two inches inside the torso at armpit level. Thrusts to the right and left hip are directed at the center of the body, approximately at the belly-button. Thrusts to the knees

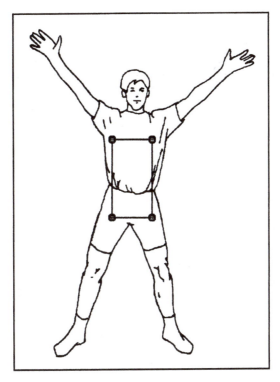

Figure 152. The Box Target of On-Line Attacks.

are delivered to the center of the upper leg, between the knee and the groin. *No on-line attacks can be executed inside measure.* There are no exceptions to this rule.

Distance and measure, along with the practiced mechanics of Action-Reaction-Action make on-line fencing possible. Once a combatant is comfortable with the mechanics of off-line point work, the principle of on-line fencing is actually quite simple, although it usually takes a while for most combatants to become used to directing a blade at their partner. You will draw back your sword and rock back into the stationary defensive position. Once there, extend your sword toward the intended body target. As in off-line fencing, this extension is the cue and control point of the thrusting attack. With the tip of your sword, point to the target being attacked. The rocked back position keeps you safely out of distance. Being out of distance you can be fully extended and observe your partner's reaction so you can safely complete the attack.

You can work the on-line attacks in the same exercise offered in Chapters 7 and 8. These exercises, however, should be first worked with your partner far enough removed that there is no possibility of the attacking blade reaching the parry. Starting with the exercises in Chapter 7, your partner stands on guard facing you, and lets you know if they are given the correct cue by responding with a simple "YES" or "NO." They also remain stationary during these exercises, providing you with specific body targets. When the thrust is carried forward it must travel in a straight line. A wavering or floating blade in this type of attack is a hazard and must be avoided.

Once both you and your partner are comfortable with the on-line cues, you can try joining blades and working through the point work exercises. It is incredibly important that you work these exercises slowly. When the blades make contact, the aggressor must give in the wrist and allow the blade to be carried outside the body. There cannot be resistance in the point of the weapon. Although

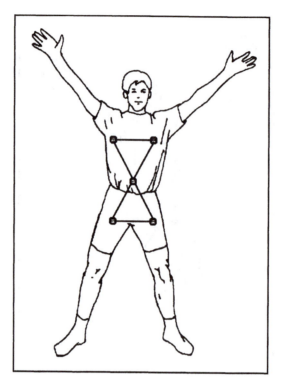

Figure 153. The Hour-Glass System of On-Line Attacks.

the attack is directed towards the body, the attack is in no way directed at the body. Whether the parry is a block, beat or detached action the thrust must not resist the parry. Remember, a dulled, rebated or buttoned sword is still dangerous and can with little effort, easily penetrate flesh. As always, a threatening blade should never cross the face for any reason.

As long as the correct mechanics of the thrust and proper distance are maintained, there should be no danger to the combatants. It is best therefore, that when first practicing these techniques you check measure every couple of moves. If you close measure inside six inches from the torso, stop. Measure problems must be worked out prior to executing on-line attacks. If you are finding problems with maintaining correct distance take the time to work the distance exercises offered in Chapter 3.

Although on-line fencing is safe when handled correctly, it is a style of theatrical swordplay that should not be attempted by beginners. Generally, the audience cannot tell the difference between on-line and off-line attacks and therefore there is little reason to remove the added safety of attacking outside the body. Some fight directors and choreographers however, work solely in this mode. It is presented herein as a solution to difficult staging problems and to provide you with a working understanding of the techniques used on the stage and screen today.

MOVING ON

The techniques presented in this chapter demonstrate the great variety of actions available to the theatrical swashbuckler. These are by no means the only techniques that may be attempted with the sword. The list of "further techniques" is virtually endless. In your classwork, or in the productions in which you perform fights, there is a never-ending supply of variations upon the fundamental techniques set forth in this text. Each new technique provides an additional hue to the artistic palate of stage combat, providing more depth and color to the fight and greater variety to the repertoire of dramatic movement. As long as these actions are safe for the artist and believable to the audience, there are no boundaries to what can be done. With this knowledge and these skills in hand, you are ready to "color outside the lines" and apply yourself to the actions of swordplay that step outside the boundaries of standard offensive and defensive play. You can now attack, parry and move in a variety of different ways and thus you are ready to learn the variables that turn simple swordplay into a dramatic sword fight.

Chapter 10

Evasive Actions

"You must therefore labour and take paines, which beeing joyned to the great desire and love you beare to this arte, will bring you to perfection thereof. Insomuch that you shall bee able to turne and winde your bodie which waye you will, and therewithall know how and which waie you ought to turne it." [Saviolo][1]

Within the various philosophies of defense, there was a fairly common principal in schools of rapier play: to get in and get out quick, and to never trust the defense of the weapon completely. Because an attack could be falsed or a thrust that had been effectively removed could then come back as a cut or redoubled as another thrust, the defensive action often consisted of some type of twist or turn of the body to remove it from the threat of the attacking blade. These maneuvers could be an execution of some type of footwork or the complex turning and winding of the body causing an attack to miss its intended target without moving the feet.

Vincentio Saviolo tells his readers that they *"shall be able to turne and winde your bodie which way you will . . . If your enemie make to wardes your right side, and offer a thrust, happilie pressing too much forward, you shall immediatlie turne your body on the left side, so that the point of his Rapier passing beside your bodie, you may give him a stoccata: or you may play with your bodie, and beate his Rapier pointe outward . . ."* [Saviolo][2]

To this philosophy di Grassi adds that *"There is great regarde to be taken in warding of thrusts, to wit: to beare the bodie out of the straight lyne, because this is the safest waie that may be found to void them."* He explains this further than Saviolo, in stating that the displacement of the body makes it easier to find the opponent's blade without danger of being hit. He explains that removing the body is necessary *"because it is verie difficult to meete with them* [the opponent's blade], *when they come barred and closed in, and are forciblie discharged."* [3]

The idea of dodging and manipulating the body to avoid the opponent's blade was a large part of the defensive strategy. In Saviolo's example, the use of the weapons for any type of defense seems to be an option. These practices are similar to the medieval foot soldiers who used agility and dexterity to fight against their armored opponents. But this practice was against the cutting attack

---

[1]Saviolo, p. 80.
[2]Saviolo, p. 80.
[3]di Grassi, p. 70.

of the broad bladed swords of the period, not against the fast and deadly thrust of the rapier. It is no wonder that so many gentlemen fell by this sword; two men of good skill and practice could, and often did, run one another through as they attempted to void their adversary's attack.

Evasions Were a Common Practice

If the fencing manuals of the sixteenth century are any indication, the use of the body to avoid and dodge attacks seems to have been the practice in almost all the schools of that time. It would seem that the only manual of fence in this period that did not approve of the voiding and slipping of the body was George Silver's *Paradoxes of Defence.* His manual attacked the foreign schools, noting well the chance of both men being killed by this "imperfect fight." Like Mercutio in Shakespeare's *Romeo and Juliet,* George Silver rails on about these foreign "masters" and their practices.

> *"Now, o you Italian teachers of Defence, where are your Stocatas, Imbrocatas, Mandritas, Puntas, & Puynta reversas, & playing with your bodies, removing with your feet a little aside, circle wise winding your bodies . . ."*[4]

Silver was an Englishman who fought with the true English short sword and found the foreign rapier play to be foolish, impractical and deadly. He was of course mistaken on a great many grounds in his *Paradoxes,* and seemed to be clinging to a dying art, but in his observance of trusting to the voiding of the body for defense he may well have been right. It is interesting to note however, that in his second book, *Bref Instruction,* Silver instructs his reader at various times to *"slippe alyttle backe"* or to *"slyde a lyttle back"* in order to *"endangr him & go free yorself."*

It would seem, therefore that in actual "life or death" swordplay, avoidances and evasions were of common practice in almost all schools. During the sixteenth and seventeenth century, more reliance was placed on the agility and mobility of the body than on any form of guard or parry. It was thought better to "remove the body" than to test your life on some unsettled principles.

Historical Evasions Unsafe on Stage

As these "evasions" were practiced, the idea was to avoid the oncoming attack while simultaneously extending the sword arm into the path of the assailant. This action was made in hopes that the opponent would impale themselves on the extended sword. This evasion with the thrusting of the arm is called a *stop thrust,* literally a thrust that stops an oncoming attack.

Because of the speed and timing of these actions, the stop thrust as part of an evasive action can be very unsafe on stage. The quickness of their actions also does not play well on stage, happening too fast for the audience to acknowledge and understand the action. Such movements should be considered very carefully before being used, and taught only by a professional fight choreographer.

For the purposes of stage combat, the single action evasion can be very effective as a reactionary part of a theatrical sequence. The circle steps covered in Chapter 3 are used as evasions, but are just a few of the possible slips and twists of the body, made available through the variable planes of footwork.

Don't Look Away from Your Partner

In any evasion be sure not to look down or away from your partner. Keep track of their actions and always be aware of where their sword travels. It is not good enough to assume or generalize; you must know exactly what is happening, and the only way to insure that is to see it happen!

---

[4]Silver, *Paradoxes,* p. 55.

First Action into Reaction

In the beginning stages of these techniques, use the "wind up" for the attack as covered in Chapter 7. As you wind up, traveling to the cue and control point, rock back to the defensive attitude of stationary footwork. Be sure to make eye contact with your partner to see them respond to the cue, then look at the exact path of the attacking blade. You should see the evasion being executed as you rock forward into the offensive attitude of stationary footwork. Once the evasion has begun, you can swipe completely through the plane of the attack, in the same manner of cutting the air used in the diagonal and vertical swipes covered in the last chapter.

The Cue

The cues for evasive actions are primarily the same as those provided for offensive actions in Chapter 7. Attacks may be thrusts or cuts delivered in a horizontal, diagonal or vertical plane. Depending on the nature of the evasion, the attacks may be delivered from either the right or the left. When working these evasions, the proper attacks will be specified. If more than one attack is possible, you must decide ahead of time which attack will be executed and initiate the proper cue.

The Reaction

By now your cues with the rapier should be effective enough that we can dispense with the verbal reactions used in the training of cuts. However, if for some reason there is a problem with the cue, the victim should say "NO," and all action stops until the problem is fixed. If there is no problem with the cue, the attack is completed as described above.

Timing the Action and Evasion

In the beginning, evading prior to the motion of the blade may feel awkward, but it is for your own safety. A fully committed attack with the sword will move many times faster than your body, and if you wait for the blade to begin the attack, it will be completed before you execute the evasion. The evasion must come first, followed immediately by the attacking blade. The speed of the offensive action covers the unnatural timing making the action appear tight and dangerous while remaining safe.

Timing is important. The final action of the offense cannot be delivered *after* the evasion is complete, it must be executed upon the perception of the appropriate reaction. Just like parrying an attack, the evasion cannot be completed prior to the attack, the two must appear simultaneous.

Cutting the Air: The Second Action

Unlike the diagonal and vertical swipes covered in the last chapter, several of the evaded attacks forcefully cross the plane of your partner's body. The targets and timing, therefore, must be exact. The arm begins the cut, bringing the blade forward as in a piston cut, and when the wrist generally takes over, the arm is extended and released from the shoulder. The energy of the swipe is accelerated by the action of the wrist combined with the swinging motion of the arm. The blade travels in a specific path and does not waiver. The hand completes the action in the same orientation as the attack was begun; either pronated or supinated.

Air Doesn't Bleed!

If evasive actions are executed correctly, there is no danger of striking one's partner, even when the blade crosses the plane of their body. The final cutting action of the attack is not executed until your partner has correctly reacted and begun the evasion. Because of this you can commit completely to the cutting attack, swinging the blade quickly and furiously. These actions need to be strong because they help tell the audience how much "force" is in the other attacks that are parried.

Therefore, commit to these actions. If there is only air where you are swinging, really cut the air. No matter how hard you hit it, air doesn't bleed.

Commitment and Control of the Attack

In executing these attacks, do not get carried away. Committing to an action is not the same as over-committing to an action. Remember, *you must always be in control of every action in a stage fight.* When cutting the air, do not allow the swipe to throw you off-balance. You must remain grounded and centered in your stance. If you are off-balance even slightly, the trajectory of your blade can change, possibly bringing it inside measure or across the plane of your partner's face, or both. Relax from the shoulder and let the arm swing. Do not throw it out to the side. The peak of the cut should be when the arm is directly in front of you, at the apex of the cutting arc.

It is also important to note that if you are practicing in slow motion, be sure that the swipe travels at the same tempo as the evasion. Do not change tempos on your partner (unless specifically dictated within this text), executing a fast swipe at a slow evasion. Control the actions of the blade so that the commitment to the attack matches that of the evasion.

Measure

During all of the following evasions the attacks are executed at proper measure. Measure is not changed by the aggressor. At this time, the victim executes any footwork to affect measure.

Keep Your Hands and Weapons Clear of the Attack

In the execution of all the following evasions, it is important to remember to always remove your hands and weapons from the path of the attacking blade. Do not let them travel forward or outside where the attack is directed. Even if executed in proper measure, your hand can extend into the space between you and your partner's blade and possibly be struck. Safely remove the hands and weapons as part of the evasion to avoid any accident or injury.

Using the Ten Directions of Footwork

To better understand the variable planes of movement used in the following evasions the compass points utilized in the last chapter's ten directions of footwork will be employed. If you are not yet wholly familiar with these planes of movement, you may wish to review that portion of the chapter and use Figure 133 as a guide.

EVADING HORIZONTAL SWIPES

The Cue

Horizontal cutting attacks are delivered from either the right or the left, and are generally targeted across the chest or belly. If a chest cut is delivered, it must never travel higher than the victim's arm-pits. The cue for the chest cuts are identical to those for horizontal attacks to either the right or left shoulder. Cuts across the belly are cued in the same manner as attacks to the right or left hip. (Fig. 154)

Backward Lunge (Echappement)

The *backward lunge* is an evasive action that removes the body from a swipe across the belly or chest. Because the torso is slightly lowered in the evasive action, it is best to start working this evasion with a belly swipe. The action is executed without lowering the body into a duck or surrendering ground to one's opponent. The backward lunge is executed as a grand lunge, only with

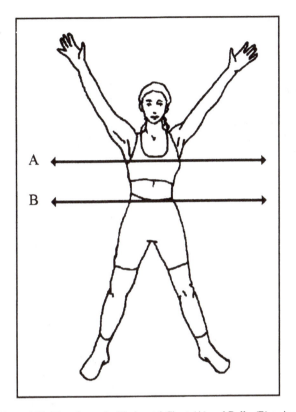

Figure 154. The plane of a Horizontal Chest (A) and Belly (B) swipe.

a straight pace back (south). The backward lunge is performed by first transferring weight to your lead foot. The heel and then the ball of the lag foot are lifted slightly off the ground. With no resistance remaining on the lag foot, the pushing force of the lead foot begins to take over. Skimming the floor, the toes of the lag foot are propelled backward by the lead foot and leg covering three foot lengths.

The main force of the backward lunge is provided by the extension of the lead leg, which drives you backward. This force must push straight back through the hips and not up and backward.

It is important that the torso move backward, not down. There will be some lowering due to the expanding of the legs, but it should not be too much. The more the body is lowered, the more the face and head are brought into the path of the sword. Use the evasion to draw you backward, not down.

As the center of gravity moves backward, both hands may drop down in front of you and travel safely out to your sides, and slightly behind you. They may also travel up and back. This is to remove your hands and arms from the path of the attacking blade. For this reason, it is imperative that the hands do not travel out and around, but either down and back or up and back.

As the lag leg completes the lunge, turn the hips slightly (about three quarters from your partner) so that the lead leg is straightened, but not locked. The knee of the lag leg travels in the same line as its toes (which are between forty-five and ninety degrees off the line of the lead foot) in order to avoid twisting or straining the knee.

Turn the head, shoulders and trunk only slightly. They should be tilted backward, matching the angle of the straightened lead leg. The lead leg is straight, without locking the knee. The knee of the lag leg is pointing in the direction of its toe. The knee is directly over the instep of the lag foot and perpendicular to the floor. Although your center of gravity is not at the geometrical center of the backward lunge, try to distribute your weight equally onto both legs. (Fig. 155)

To recover from the backward lunge, simply execute a pass, either back or forward. This puts you into correct placement. You also may re-center your torso between your legs and execute a "reverse" of the standard recover backward for the demi and grand lunge.

Evade Back

The *evade back* can be in response to a belly and chest swipe and is initiated in the same manner as a pass back. The lead foot travels backward (south) along its track, passing the other foot, and coming to rest in the new lag foot position. It is from this terminating point that the evade back differs from a pass back. The new lag foot travels about a foot's length farther backward, much like an active pass back. The

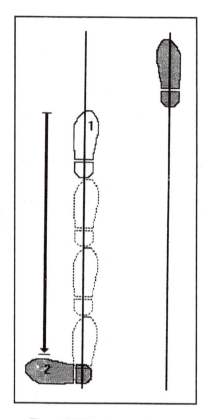

Figure 155. The Backward Lunge.

lag foot remains on its original track, with your center of gravity continuing to shift backward onto the new lag leg.

This transfer from "pass" to "rock back" happens without a pause or break in execution. It is done by pushing down into the new lead foot and straightening its leg as the new lag foot is placed firmly onto the floor. (Fig. 156)

As you shift your center of gravity over your lag leg, bend the knee so that it travels straight out over the toes. Your torso remains facing your partner, but now leans slightly backward. Your right and left arm may be lowered below your waist line or lifted above your head or carried behind you to avoid being hit by an attacking blade.

In this, and most evasions, the evaded attack is a swipe across the belly. The stomach is contracted backward at the onset of the evasion, "removing" it from the threat of the blade. If the attack is to the chest, the head and face are drawn back in reaction. Playing the response in the head and face makes the

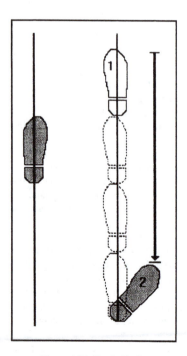

Figure 156. Evade Back.

attack appear higher than it really is. In either case, the evasion is not just the footwork, it is the removal of a specific threatened target by contraction and displacement of the body.

To recover from the evade back simply take another pass back that puts you into correct placement. You also may bring the torso back into line and pass forward to your original position.

Jump Back

The *jump back* described in Chapter 9 may also be used as an evasive action, removing the body backward from a horizontal swipe. Upon completion of the jump back as an evasion, you should be in correct placement in the On Guard stance and your upper body should be rocked back into the stationary footwork defensive position.

Passing Jump Back

Like the jump back, the *passing jump back* of Chapter 9 may also be used as an effective evasive action. This evasion is executed as the jump back, only the lead foot begins the action as in an evade back. The lead foot is passed back on the evasion, but as it transfers to the lag position it propels the body backward with a much greater force. The new lead foot follows the action as if it were a jump back. Both feet, as in the jump back, will complete the action at the same time with body rocked back into the stationary footwork defensive position. (Fig. 157)

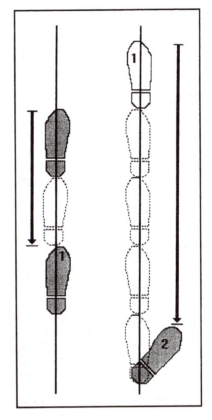

Figure 157. Passing Jump Back.

Vertical Jumps

Vertical jumps, or the ''jump,'' is the classic cliché for the dashing swordsman to jump over an adversary's attack at the feet. This action is listed as number seven in William Hobbs' list of top ten fight clichés. He warns his readers to ''*think again before using any* [cliché] *in a serious combat situation.*''[5] There is, however, a place for such an action. The jump is still called for in fight choreography, and therefore should be part of the trained actor's repertoire.

The Cue

Horizontal swipes under the feet are delivered from either the right or the left, cued in the same manner as a cut to either the right or left thigh. When executing this swipe the weapon is directed towards the floor with its point no higher than the level of your partner's ankles. The cut is made to where the ankles *were,* prior to the jump.

---

[5]Hobbs, *Stage Combat,* p. 95.

Figure 158. The jump over the blade.

It is important to note that when you are cutting under someone's feet, the blade must be swiped in real time. Your partner cannot jump in slow motion, therefore the cutting action must be executed at proper speed in order to insure safe passage before the feet re-enter the offensive path of the blade. Even though the attack is done out of measure, this is important because it maintains the illusion and provides for the possibility of your partner accidentally jumping forward inside measure.

The Jump

Initiate the jump with a deep plié. Bend the knees directly over the feet as deeply as the Achilles' tendons safely allow, coiled like springs. Then shift your weight to your lag leg. With resistance removed, shoot the lead foot up off the floor by an upward motion of the knee. At the same time, shoot the energy of the coiled spring of the lag leg down into the floor. The thigh muscles contract, and the lag leg straightens as its foot leaves the floor by a strong push down into the toes.

In the air the upper body is in correct alignment. The lead foot is raised to a level just below the knee of the lag leg. This gives the illusion of greater height. The lag leg is slightly bent with toes extended towards the floor. (Fig. 158)

The landing from this jump must be smooth. As the body reaches its peak, the lead foot should reach down so that the toes of both feet touch the floor at the same time. Do not anticipate the floor by relaxing the point of the feet until the toes touch the ground. Then roll down through the balls of the feet until the heels come to rest on the floor. As the heels touch the floor the legs act as giant shock absorbers. Allow the knees to bend into a demiplié or even grand plié. This action cushions the downward action of the center of gravity. Your feet touch down in proper placement, and upon rising from the plié, at the end of the jump, you are in correct placement, standing in the On Guard stance where the action began.

Jumping Inside Measure

There are, of course, variations on the jump. Many variations depend on the execution of the attack to be avoided by a jump. I find the preceding jump to be the most practical in most circumstances. No matter how high the jump, one foot is always close to the ground for support and the other is quite removed from any attack. In the unlikely case that during a performance an actor cannot execute a choreographed jump, they are safe and can still avoid the attack by lifting their lead foot from the threat of the attack without having to execute the leap with the lag leg.

The following variation is offered for those instances where the blade of the attacking sword is in distance and needs to actually pass under both feet. Measure is generally closed by the attacker, lunging or passing inside measure on the preparation of the attack. In this jump both legs begin the action by taking a deep plié, knees bent directly over the feet and as deeply as the Achilles' tendons comfortably allow. The feet are firmly on the ground; head, shoulders, chest and pelvis in correct alignment. From the preparatory action, push down into the floor, the thigh muscles contract and the knees straighten as the feet leave the floor. (Fig. 159)

Once off the floor the legs are slightly drawn up towards the body. This gives greater clearance and insures missing the attacking blade. The toes are pointed towards the floor.

The landing from the jump must be smooth. As the body reaches its peak, the legs extend and the feet reach down so that the toes of both feet touch the floor at the same time. Do not anticipate hitting the floor by relaxing the point of the feet until the toes touch the ground. Once on the ground, roll down through the balls of the feet until the heels come to rest on the floor. As the heels touch the floor, the legs act as giant shock absorbers, the knees bending into a demi or grand plié. This action cushions the downward action of the center of gravity. Your feet touch down in proper placement, and upon rising from the plié at the end of the jump, you are in correct placement, standing in the On Guard stance where the action began. In all cuts under the feet the blade travels in a constant horizontal plane four or five inches off the floor where your partner's ankles *were*. Do not strike or hit the floor with the attacking blade. Such an action could bend, damage or break the blade.

Figure 159. Jumping over the blade, inside measure.

Ducks

There are basically two ways to avoid an attack by ducking: the first, the squat, is the most common; while the second, a low line evasion, is particular to fencers in conjunction with a stop thrust. Both "ducking" actions are used to avoid a horizontal head swipe.

The Cue

The mechanics for this attack are identical to those of a horizontal cut to either the right or left shoulder. The cue, however, is placed above the shoulder, with the hand and hilt at roughly ear level, and the blade travels from either right to left, or vice versa, in a plane horizontal to the floor at the level of where your partner's head *was*. (Figs. 160–161)

When cutting "over" the head, be sure that you do not carry the blade in a semicircular arc above where the head was but in a horizontal plane where your partner's ears were. Also beware of *tracking* your cut. This is the practice of following your partner down with your eyes and weapon.

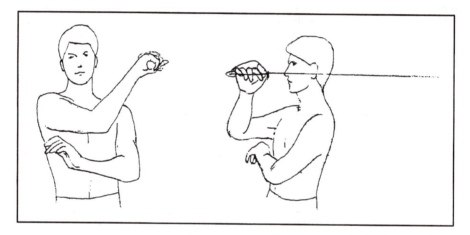

Figure 160. The cue for a swipe over the head, left to right.

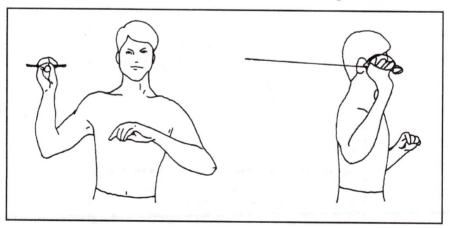

Figure 161. The cue for a swipe over the head, right to left.

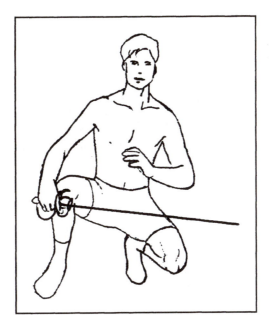

Figure 162. The squat duck.

Watch your partner and place the cut exactly where they were, not down where they are going. Go slow, be exact.

Squat Duck

The *squat duck* is just that, a squat. This duck is simply a deep bend in the knees that displaces the head from being a target by a movement downward. This is accomplished by dropping your trunk and center of gravity by increasing the bend in the knees. When executing the squat duck, keep your torso up in a vertical plane and do not bend forward using your back. This causes you to lose visual contact with your partner and their weapon, and can injure your back. The muscles in the small of your back are not designed to quickly drop and raise the torso, and can be injured if forced to do so. Use the large muscle groupings of the legs to raise and lower the trunk and keep your torso facing your partner, in correct placement, with your head directed forward, eyes always focused on your partner and their weapon. (Fig. 162)

The left hand remains in correct placement or can be placed on the floor for additional balance. The sword and sword arm must be lowered with the body, removing the possibility of being struck by the attacking blade.

To recover from the squat duck, lift your center of gravity and push down into your feet to straighten your legs and raise your torso to the correct level of the On Guard stance.

Passata Sotto (Low Line Evasion)

The *passata sotto* or "pass beneath" is a low line evasion that is generally executed in two ways. The first is like a cross between a reversed lunge and a demi-volte and the second is like a squat duck blended with a reversed lunge. Both actions vertically remove the body from the plane of attack by expanding the base and lowering the physical center.

Plate XIX: The passata sotto to the rear as taught in the Italian *Scorza* (1803).

The Passata Sotto to the Side: The Passata Sotto to the side is executed by first transferring weight to your lead foot and lifting the heel of the lag foot slightly off the ground. With no remaining resistance on the lag foot, the foot extends backward and across the path of the lead foot traversing to the right (east). The foot skims the floor. (Fig. 163)

The toe of the lag foot is propelled backward by the dropping of the torso. The main force of this evasion (and the passata sotto to the rear) is provided by the sudden drop of the center of gravity and the bending of the lead leg's knee. This action shoots the lag leg out, traversing to the right (east).

Without pausing in the action, bring the left hand to rest on the floor for stability and balance during the quickly executed move. Do not use the left hand to "catch" the weight of the dropping torso, use it for balance and stability only. The bones and muscles of the wrist are not designed to take the weight and stress of the falling body. Your legs must control the duck. As the hand is placed on the floor, the pelvis turns slightly with the trunk in order to avoid twisting the knee of the lag leg. (Fig. 164)

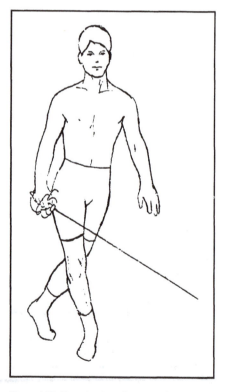

Figure 163. Stepping into the passata sotto to the side.

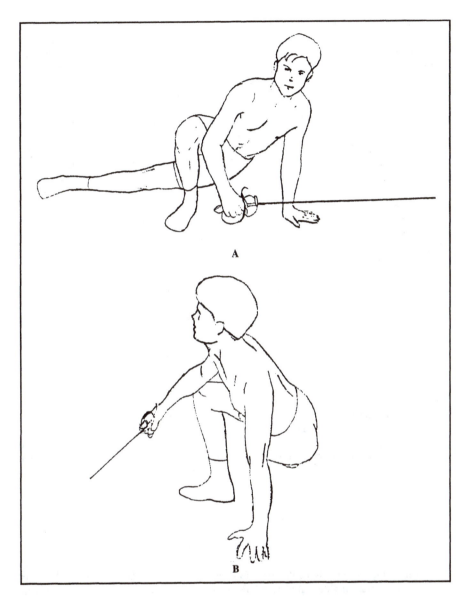

Figure 164. The passata sotto to the side. **A**-Front view; **B**-left side view.

The lag leg is behind the lead leg and extended to the right (east). The outside of the leg is towards the floor with the side of the foot and ankle resting on the floor. The lag leg is straight, but not locked. The knee of the lead leg retains its original direction, pointing straight forward (north) along the railroad track. In this position the right foot is flat on the floor with the knee perpendicular to the floor, situated between the instep and the toes of the lead. Your right hand and weapon are lowered and removed from the plane of attack. The trunk of your body is angled forward and to the left, creating a line with the extended lag leg.

The Passata Sotto to the Rear: The passata sotto to the rear is executed in basically the same manner as to the side, except the lag leg is taken south in a straight pace back instead of being traversed to the right (east). The move is initiated by first transferring your weight to your lead foot and lifting the heel of the lag foot slightly off the ground. The toe of the lag foot is propelled straight backward by the dropping of the torso. As the lag leg reaches its full extension backward, bring the left hand to rest on the floor, for stability and balance during the quickly executed move. As in the other passata sotto, do not use the left hand to ''catch'' the weight of the dropping torso, use it for balance and stability only. Your legs must control the duck. As the hand is placed on the floor, the pelvis and torso tip forward to accommodate the backward extension of the left leg.

The lag leg should be fully extended to the south on its imaginary track. It should not shift to the right (east) as in the other passata sotto. Due to the extension backward, the left foot remains poised on the ball, its heel elevated. The left knee is towards the floor, but not touching it. Do not drop to the knee, as impact can be painful and dangerous. The lag leg is straight, but not locked. Only the left foot, right foot and left hand are in contact with the floor. The knee of the lead leg retains its original direction, pointing north along the railroad track. The right foot is flat on the floor with the knee perpendicular to the floor, situated between the instep and the toes of the lead foot. Your sword and right arm are lowered from the plane of attack. Your pelvis and trunk angle directly forward, creating a line with the extended lag leg. (Fig. 165)

It is important to remember in executing both of the passata sottos, that although the torso tips forward, you never take your eyes off your partner or their weapon. Be sure that as your body tips forward that you do not lock your neck and shift your focus to the floor. Release your neck and allow your head to tip back and remain with the action.

Although your center of gravity is not at the geometrical center in either of the passata sottos, your weight must be equally distributed between both legs and the left hand. This placement has given the passata sotto the names *three feet* and *three leg* evasion.

The passata sotto is meant as a coup de grace, executed with a stop thrust. As a finishing move in a fight, a quick and easy recovery from the move is not the initial concern. A recovery from this position, however, is possible. Initiate this action with a push from the left hand. The torso must be righted with this push. Energy is then pressed down into the lead leg. Lift your center of gravity and push down into your foot to straighten your legs and raise your torso to the correct level of the On Guard stance.

EVADING DIAGONAL SWIPES

The Cue

Diagonal cutting attacks may be delivered from either the right or the left, and can be either descending or ascending in nature. Both types of diagonal swipes travel outside the body in the same forty-five degree plane used in the diagonal swipes used with the beat-away parries covered in Chapter 9.

Descending: The cue for the descending attack is identical to those for the beat-away and hanging parries. Here, as before, the descending diagonal crosses the victim's center line above their head, never crossing the body.

When executing the descending diagonal attack, do not ''cut into the floor.'' The attack is not terminated by striking the ground. It is carried off into a mollinello on the side opposite that of the cue.

Ascending: The cue for the ascending attack is similar to the montante (Chapter 7), with the sword on your right or left side, hilt at waist level, blade angled up toward the ceiling, hand in middle

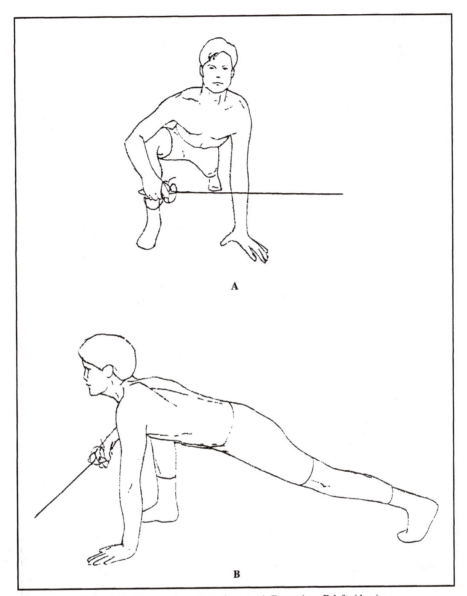

Figure 165. The passata sotto to the rear. **A**-Front view; **B**-left side view.

position, with the knuckle bow facing directly behind you. This is the position of the sword for an ascending diagonal swipe. The blade travels up on the same forty-five degree plane as the descending, crossing your partner's center line above their head.

Whether delivering a descending or ascending swipe, it is important to reach out on the attack with the full extent of the weapon and arm. Do not hold the cut back, but at the same time do not over-extend the attack by breaking at the waist and leaning forward. The arm and blade must travel in a full arc from head to toe or vice versa.

Slipping Right and Left

The slip "evasion" to the left and right can be used to avoid both ascending and descending diagonal cuts. The evasive action is a simple modification of the stationary footwork (Chapter 3). The lower body action remains the same. In the slip, however, the upper body leans in the direction in which the body is "rocking," creating a diagonal at roughly forty-five degrees to the floor in line with the straightened leg. Be sure that you do not lean forward in this action. Your torso is in the same plane as the extended leg, both diagonally (either right or left) and vertically. In order to remove your sword arm as a threat, lower the right hand below the level of your waist. (Figs. 166–167)

You recover from the slip evasions by first bringing the upper body back to correct placement. The torso and center of gravity are then distributed between your legs.

Side Step Evasion or Traverse Right/Left

The traverse evasions may be used to avoid both the descending and ascending diagonal cutting attacks. The evasive step to the right or left is executed much like a standard lunge, except along the east-west linear tracks that run perpendicular to the north-south tracks that connect you with your partner. The action is initiated with the foot dominant to the evasive side. The right foot is taken to the east or left foot to the west, whether in the lead or lag position. The foot is lunged out to the side, as if executing a demi- or grand lunge. The trunk of your body remains facing forward but leans into the lunge following the line of the straightened lag leg. Be sure that you do not lean forward in this action. Your torso is in the same plane as the extended lag leg, both diagonally and vertically. The toes of the lead foot are usually directed towards the lunge. This avoids undue torque in the knee joint. In order to remove your sword arm from the plane of attack, lower the right hand below the level of your waist. (Figs. 168–169)

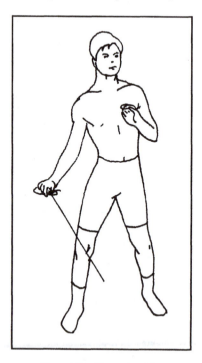

Figure 166. Slip to the right.

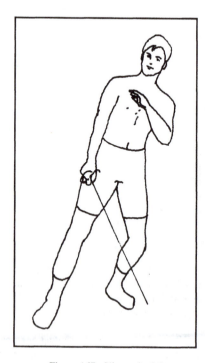

Figure 167. Slip to the left.

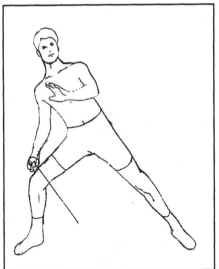

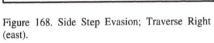

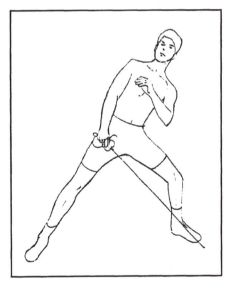

Figure 168. Side Step Evasion; Traverse Right (east).

Figure 169. Side Step Evasion; Traverse Left (west).

Plate XX: A North East Diagonal Avoid on the right foot. Avoiding a descending cut while offering a counter attack. From a seventeenth century German fencing treatise.

The recovery of the sidestep is the same as the recovery backward for the lunge. The action draws you straight back to your original position. As the body is drawn back, return your trunk to correct placement.

Forward Diagonal Avoid

The diagonal avoid is identical to the sidestep or traverse evasions, only differing in the angle of execution. The side steps remove the body in a traverse while the diagonal avoid forward removes the body with a sloped pace on the NE and NW diagonal, roughly forty-five degrees off the parallel tracks of the standard north-south linear footwork. The diagonal avoid to the front, however, although effective for avoiding both ascending and descending swipes, is generally used to avoid the descending attack. The evasion is initiated with the lunging foot, whether in the lead or lag position. The lunge is executed on the NE or NW tracks of footwork. If you lunge to your right (NE), leading with the right foot, or to your left (NW) leading with the left foot, the trunk of your body turns to the inside slightly, facing diagonally in toward your partner. If you lunge with the opposing foot (left foot, to the NE or right foot to the NW) the trunk of your body is turned out and away from your partner. In both cases your torso should lean into the lunge following the line of the straightened back leg. Be sure that you do not bend forward with the waist in these evasions. Your torso should be in the same plane as the extended leg, both diagonally and vertically. In order to remove your sword arm from the plane of attack, lower the right hand below the level of your waist. (Figs. 170–177)

If your torso is turned away from your partner, be sure that you maintain visual contact. Do not lose sight of your partner or their weapon during the execution of these evasions.

The recovery from the forward diagonal evasion is the same as the recover backward of the side step evasion. The action should draw you straight back to your original position. As you draw the body back, your trunk returns to correct placement.

Backward Diagonal Avoid

The backward diagonal avoid is executed in the same manner as the backward lunge only on the diagonal of the SE or SW sloped pace instead of directly backward. The backward diagonal evasion is essentially a backward lunge executed on the forty-five degrees plane of the SE or SW tracks of footwork. There are two differences between the backward lunge and diagonal avoid to the rear. The first is that the forward or lag foot can initiate the evasive action. The second is that the torso is drawn diagonally off to the side in the direction of the evading leg, rather than being carried vertically backward. Because the body is removed backward and to the side, the backward diagonal evasion is generally used to avoid the ascending diagonal cut, although it may be effective for avoiding both diagonal swipes and horizontal swipes across the belly.

The evasion is initiated with the lunging foot, whether in the lead or lag position. The lunge is executed on the sloped pace backward either to the SE or SW. The trunk of your body turns slightly to either the inside or outside, depending on the lunging foot and diagonal taken. If you evade to the SE with the right foot back, you will face off to your right. If your left foot is carried back to the SE you will be facing back and to your left. If you evade to the SW with the left foot back, you will face off to your left. If your right foot is carried back to the SW you will be facing back and to your right. As in the diagonal evasions to the front, your torso should lean into the lunge following the line of the straightened lead leg. Be sure that you do not lean forward toward your partner in this action. Your torso should be in the same plane as the extended leg, both diagonally and vertically. In order to remove your sword arm from the plane of attack, lower the right hand below the level of your waist. (Figs. 178–185)

Although the torso is turned slightly away from your partner, be sure to maintain eye contact. Do not turn your head with the body and lose sight of your partner and their weapon.

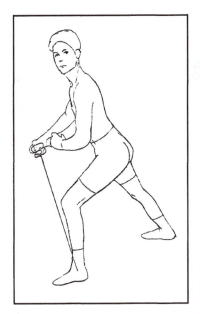

Figure 170. North East Diagonal Avoid made with the left foot. (Front View)

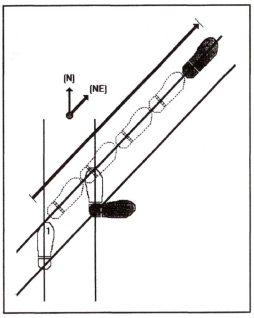

Figure 171. North East Diagonal Avoid made with the left foot.

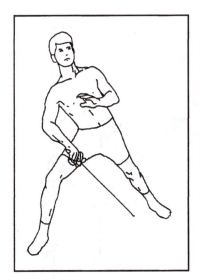

Figure 172. North East Diagonal Avoid made with the right foot. (Front view).

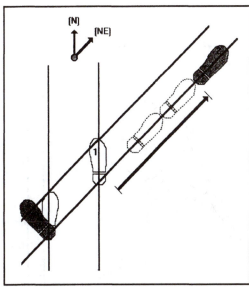

Figure 173. North East Diagonal Avoid made with the right foot.

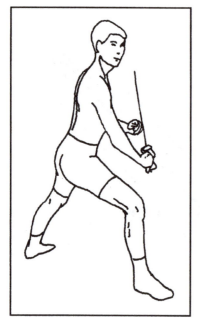

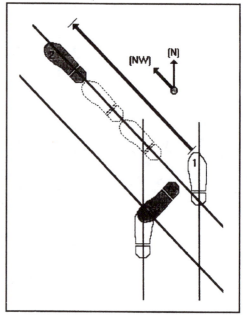

Figure 174. North West Diagonal Avoid made with the right foot. (Front view).

Figure 175. North West Diagonal Avoid made with right foot.

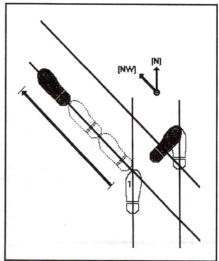

Figure 176. North West Diagonal Avoid made with the left foot. (Front view).

Figure 177. North West Diagonal Avoid made with the left foot.

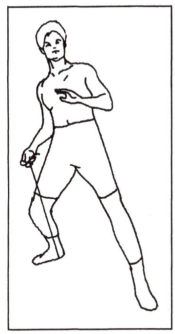

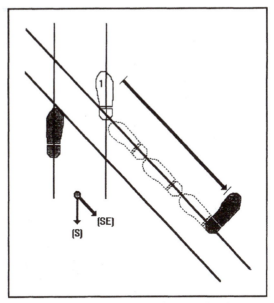

Figure 179. South East Diagonal Avoid made with the right foot.

Figure 178. South East Diagonal Avoid made with the right foot. (Front view).

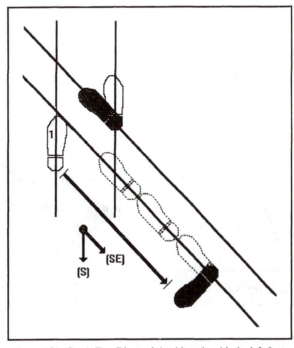

Figure 180. South East Diagonal Avoid made with the left foot. (Front view).

Figure 181. South East Diagonal Avoid made with the left foot.

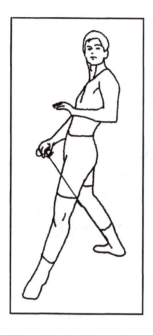

Figure 182. South West Diagonal Avoid made with the right
foot. (Front view).

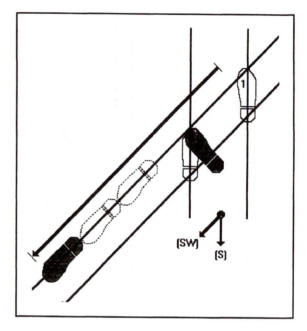

Figure 183. South West Diagonal Avoid made with the right foot.

Figure 184. South West Diagonal
Avoid made with the left foot.
(Front view).

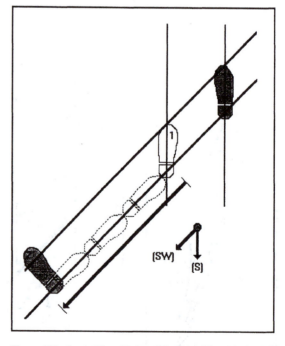

Figure 185. South West Diagonal Avoid made with the left
foot.

To recover from a backward diagonal evasion, simply execute a pass, either backward or forward back onto the north-south tracks of footwork. This puts you into correct placement. You also may return to the linear tracks with the recovery backward of the backward lunge, or you may continue to work on the diagonal plane of footwork.

EVADING VERTICAL SWIPES

The Cue

Vertical swipes, like the diagonals, may be delivered from either the right or the left, and can be either descending or ascending in nature. As discussed in Chapter 9, neither type of vertical cut is aimed at the victim, but travels six to eight inches outside the body in a plane perpendicular to the floor. The cue and mechanics for the descending attack are the same as those applied to the beat-aside and hanging parry in the last chapter. Remember, these cuts should not terminate in the floor. The cue for the ascending attack is similar to the montante (Chapter 7), with the sword on your right or left side. From this cue the blade will travel straight up, along the side of your partner's body in the same vertical plane as the descending cut, roughly six to eight inches outside the body.

There are no evasions specific to the vertical swipe. On stage the action of the blade reads close to a diagonal swipe and the speed of the attack makes it difficult to discern the difference. Primarily it is a choice of the choreographer whether they want a vertical or diagonal swipe. The vertical attack is most often used when the cue and the completion of the attack need to be on the same side of the body. Of the previously described evasions, the slips, the diagonal avoid (front and back), traverse (right and left) and the demi and grand voltes (covered in Chapter 3 and reviewed below) can be used to good effect with the vertical swipe. Evasions like the jump back and backward lunge may be used but they do not appear as dynamic on stage.

EVADING THE THRUST

The process of avoiding a thrust is similar to that of avoiding a swipe, differing mainly in the execution of the attack. The cut is practiced with stationary footwork, but the thrust is taken moving. The thrust, being a strong linear attack, is much more perceptible to the audience than the blur of a fast moving cut and therefore its intent must be made clear with the commitment of the body.

The Cue

The cues for evaded thrusts are the same as those for parried thrusts. From the rocked back stationary defensive position show your point to the intended target. This extension from the rocked back position is the cue and control point of the thrusting attack. Thrusts made to your partner's left will be responded to with an evasion to their right and vice versa.

Footwork

Although any evasion can be set at appropriate measure to function safely and effectively with a variety of offensive actions of footwork, at this stage all thrusts will be executed with a *demi-lunge* and delivered in the manner described in the exercises below. Be sure to make eye contact with your partner to see the correct response to the cue, then look at the "intended" target of the attack.

The Control Point

From the rocked back position of stationary footwork, show your partner the cue for the attack *before* committing to the offensive footwork. Extending the arm prior to executing any footwork allows your partner time to read the attack and begin the proper evasion, and it allows you to perceive your partner's reaction. You are in control. Once the evasion has begun, the offensive footwork may be executed, driving the blade and body forward with a demi-lunge.

Both you and your partner have to be aware that the cue or "control point" is not a point that is held; it is a point that can be held if need be. The aggressor should not sit back in this position and watch the victim move before they themselves move. The control point is merely a check point for safety before committing to an action. The victim responds as soon as they perceive a "threat," and the aggressor attacks as soon as the correct response has begun. The actions flow immediately from one to the other; they should never appear as three separate actions. Remember, Action-Reaction-Action.

Avoid Thrusts with Evasions by Displacement

Out of the evasions we have covered so far, the following may be used for evasions of cuts as well as thrusts. These are the squat duck, passata sotto, diagonal avoid (front and back), and the traverse (right and left). Although the backward lunge, jump back and passing jump back can be used to safely evade a thrust, the action is generally ineffective in a choreographical routine. Evasions by displacement are the most common form of avoiding a thrust, removing the target from the path of the intended attack both safely and effectively.

> "Or the better avoiding of the hurts . . . it is requisite to fetch a compass with the foot backwards on the right side. In like case to turne the bodie the same waie, to the intent, to carrie it out of the straight lyne (in which the blowe commeth) and to drive a reversed thrust at the face." [di Grassi][6]

Demi-Volte

The demi-volte (covered in Chapter 3) is an effective evasive step, generally to the right, removing the body from a thrust to the left side. The demi-volte may also be executed to the left, although not done as often, to avoid a thrust to the right side. If the evasion is to the right, the left foot travels backwards to the right on the outer track of the imaginary circle, and vice versa. The action of the foot turns the body roughly ninety degrees, displacing the leg, hips and torso to the side of the straight track. The body pivots on the lead foot, swinging to the side. The opening allows the thrust to pass where the body was.

Whether volting to the left (clockwise) or right (counterclockwise) your feet complete the action approximately shoulder width apart, with the toes of your lag foot in line with the heel of your lead foot. Your head is turned to look over your shoulder at your partner. Your hands and arms are removed from the opening and the intended path of the offensive blade. Do not let the weapon, hand or arm trail in the opening to possibly get hit. Remove everything from the plane of attack. (Figs. 186–187)

Grand Volte

The grand volte (covered in Chapter 3), like the demi-volte, is a large evasive step (generally to the right) in response to a thrust, or even a diagonal or vertical cutting attack. The grand volte is more often executed to the right because it is generally accompanied by a counterattack with the

---

[6]di Grassi, p. 76.

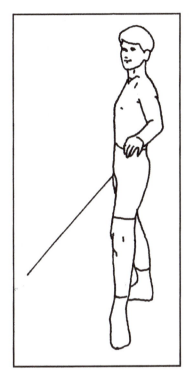

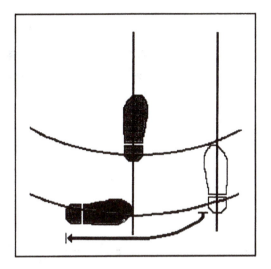

Figure 187. The demi-volte to the left.

Figure 186. The demi-volte to the left.

sword arm. A removal to the left draws the weapon and arm away from the conflict, making it more difficult to launch a counterattack. For theatre, however, the grand volte may be effectively taken to either the right or the left. If the attack is to the left, the action is taken to the right, with the left foot vaulting backwards across the north-south tracks of the lead foot in a semicircle to the inner track of the imaginary circle, and if the attack is to the right, vice versa. The action is completed with your feet roughly shoulder width apart. This action turns the body roughly one hundred-eighty degrees, displacing the body and creating an opening in the same manner as the demi-volte. The scope of this evasion, basically turning your backside to your opponent, has given the grand volte the nickname *bum in your face*.[7] Your head looks back over your shoulder, keeping your focus on your partner as you move. (Figs. 188–189)

The recovery from the demi and grand volte can be a simple reversal of the volte process or further footwork on the variable planes of movement. At the completion of any of these recoveries the body should be On Guard with correct placement.

The Standing Volte, Right and Left

The standing volte is a simple variation on the slip to the left and right. The lower body action remains the same as the slip, but in the standing volte the upper body pivots ninety degrees as the lower body "rocks" away from the attack. If a thrust comes to the left, the body rocks to the right and the torso will be turned counterclockwise, rotating the left shoulder back and to the right. At the

[7]The term is believed to have been coined by famed Brithish fight master Henry Marshall.

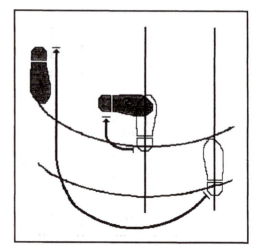

Figure 189. The grand volte to the left. Executed from a left dominant stance.

Figure 188. The grand volte to the left.

completion of this action your torso should be facing to your left and leaning slightly backward in the same plane as the extended left leg. To avoid a thrust to the right, the action is simply reversed, rocking and turning to the left. In both cases be sure that the weapon, hand and arm, are removed from the plane of attack. (Figs. 190–191)

To recover from the standing volte, bring the upper body back to correct placement and then rock back in, re-centering your torso between your legs.

THE UNIVERSAL EVASION or "COBB'S TRAVERSE"

Each of the preceding evasions specifies what attacks it should and should not avoid, making them limited in their effectiveness. A duck executed in response to a vertical attack could prove fatal, as could a volte to a horizontal swipe. Thus, an Elizabethan fencer and well-known brawler by the name of Cobb made the common practice of a universal evasive action now called "Cobb's Traverse." It is certain that he did not invent the action, but he is one of the few fencers noted to have used it with regularity and skill. George Silver explains:

> "This Cob was a great quareller, and did delight in great braverie to give foule words to his betters, and would not refuse to go into the field to fight with any man, and when he came into the field, would draw his Sword to fight, for he was sure by the cunning of his Traverse, not to be hurt by anie man: for

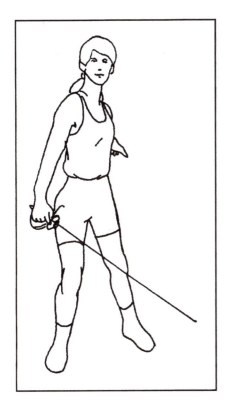

Figure 190. The standing volte to the right.   Figure 191. The standing volte to the left.

at anie time finding himselfe overmatched would suddenly turne his back and runne away with such swiftnesse, that it was thought a good horse would scarce take him." [Silver][8]

In short, Cobb's Traverse is an avoidance or parry by distance that effectively removes the body by running away. The term is generally used as a euphemism for running away from a fight; or sometimes running backward; or back-pedaling from an encounter.

VARIATIONS

There are as many evasions as there are possible combinations of footwork and attacks—these are but a few examples. In all these cases, and in any other evasion, the body must be removed from the line of attack. This may be done by distance, displacement or both. In most cases the face is generally kept towards the action to observe your partner, but not always. The jump forward (Chapter 9) can be executed away from, instead of towards the opponent, as an evasive action from a horizontal cut across the back. Such an evasion is difficult to execute while keeping an eye on one's partner. As a general rule, if the evasion can be executed with visual contact maintained between the combatants, it should be done so.

If you decide to explore further evasions, remember that you must always be in control of the

---

[8]Silver, p. 61.

action. Evasions are executed with one simple action of the foot rather than by a hopping or shuffling of the feet that places the combatant off balance and out of measure for any following movement. It should be possible for the combatant to avoid any attack and return to the On Guard stance by merely reversing the action in one clean and swift movement.

Adding Footwork

Although all the preceeding swipes have been practiced with the aggressor executing only stationary footwork, they may be done a variety of ways. The type of evasion generally determines the possible footwork of the aggressor. If the evasion is a parry by distance (removing the body backward but remaining in line) like the evade back or backward lunge, then the footwork can only be executed in proportion to those of the evasive action. Since the attack crosses the plane of the body, it can never travel within correct distance. So if the evasion is a backward lunge, and the victim's lunge travels just over three feet, the aggressor's pass or lunge cannot exceed three feet in length, thus maintaining measure. If the evasion is by displacement (removing the body from the plane of the attack) like a traverse or volte, then the completion of the attack can be made inside measure. Because the attack never crosses the physical plane of the body, the attack can travel within correct distance. So if the evasion is a forward diagonal evasion, the aggressor may pass or lunge toward their partner as long as the attack is carried safely outside their body. In both cases the aggressive action of the blade is executed after the footwork is completed. The cue and control point of the attack is set on the preparation and weight shift (Action) and maintained during the footwork (Reaction) and released upon arrival (Action). At this time these should be the only attacks executed inside measure—and they should be practiced slowly to insure safety.

Adding Parries

All of the preceding evasive actions have been presented without the joining of blades, the defense being in the removal of the target from the attack. This does not mean that a parry cannot accompany some of these evasions. As discussed earlier in this chapter, the evasion was usually a twisting or turning of the body executed in combination with a parry in order to help guarantee the effective defense of the attack. This concept, however, cannot be applied to all evasions. Ducks and jumps cannot be executed with parries nor can evasions by distance. Basically, no evasion where the blade crosses the physical plane of the body (or where the body actually was) can be accompanied by a parry. If a parry is to accompany an evasion it must be an evasion by displacement.

Parries are most effectively executed in conjunction with the diagonal evasions, traverses, and voltes. The unarmed hand can beat thrusts aside, beat-away parries can easily accompany the slip, diagonal avoids, and traverses while beat and standard parries can be used with the voltes. Hanging parries may be executed with diagonal evasions and voltes, defending against diagonal and vertical swipes. If the cut is pistoned and met with a parry, the evasion should remove the body away from the attack. If an attack is to your left side, the body evades to the right and vice versa.

EXERCISES

Playing the Numbers

This exercise is designed to work evasive actions into short patterns of offensive and defensive blade-play. The pattern for the exercise should be a short series of familiar numbers. This can be your phone number, address, locker number, social security number, historical dates and so on. Attacks in this drill are on the exchange, just as in Around the Clock exercise (Chapter 8). The targets in the drill correspond to those set forth in Chapters 6 and 7. Number nine and zero are where evasions are worked into the routine.

Number Nine: So far we have only learned the eight recognized parries in the French classical school of fencing, and all their variations. There is, however, a ninth parry, the parry by distance. The ninth, or *coward's parry* is an ignoble term given to the avoidance of an attack by removing the body backwards. Fencing in its classical heyday was thought a skillful and dexterous display of blade-play, and to retreat or remove the body was thought unstylish and cowardly. Therefore, when the pattern calls for the number nine, execute a "parry by distance." This may be an evade back, backward lunge, jump back, etc. What this means is that the combatant executing the attack cues for a belly or chest swipe and the victim executes an evasion by distance as their reaction, letting the attacking blade travel safely in front of the body in a horizontal plane parallel to the floor.

Number Zero: The number zero represents nothing, therefore that's what is attacked. When the pattern calls for the number zero, the victim executes an evasion by displacement, removing the target from the plane of attack. This may be a duck, jump, slip, diagonal avoid, traverse, volte, etc. The appropriate cue is presented and the victim executes the evasion as their reaction, letting the attacking blade travel safely outside their body.

For Point Work: Because evasions by distance are so seldom used in theatrical point work, the evasions for number nine do not apply to avoiding the thrust. If you wish to run the exercise with thrusts instead of cuts, apply the following rules. If the number nine is called for, the victim executes an evasion to the right, avoiding a thrust to the left side. When the pattern calls for the number zero, the victim evades to the left, avoiding a thrust to the right side. If the pattern calls for the number five, you may either execute a cut to the head parried in High 5, or you may thrust Low 5. Do not thrust High 5, ever!

In all these exercises, the evasive action and their attacks must be decided upon prior to beginning. Several different evasions may be experimented with, one at a time, with both combatants completely aware of the actions being executed. The numbers may be random, but the actions must be specific.

EVASION RULES IN REVIEW

• ACTION I:

1. All evasions are properly cued and controlled. The cue and control point of the attack is set on the preparation and weight shift (Action I); maintained while awaiting the correct response (Reaction); and released upon completion of footwork (Action II).
2. You must see your partner respond to the cue.
3. All attacks and evasions must be decided ahead of time.
4. The attack must be controlled. There must be time to decide if it is safe before it leaves the control point.
5. The cue or "control point" is not a point to be held; it is a point that can be held if need be.

• REACTION:

1. No evasion can begin until the proper cue is presented.
2. All evasions remove the body from the line of attack, either by distance, displacement or both.
   (a) Evasions by distance remove the body backward away from the attack, but remain in the plane of the attack.
   (b) Evasions by displacement remove the body outside the plane of the attack; either to the sides, up or down.

3. If the evasion can be executed with visual contact maintained between the combatants, it should be done so. The combatants must always be aware of each other and their weapons.
4. Always remove your hands and weapons from the path of the attacking blade. Do not let them travel forward or outside where the attack is directed.
5. Evasions are executed with simple actions of footwork (active or passive) allowing the combatant to return to the On Guard stance by merely reversing the action.
6. No evasion where the blade crosses the physical plane of the body (or where the body was) can be accompanied by a parry. If a parry is to accompany an evasion it must be an evasion by displacement.
7. If the cut is pistoned and met with a parry, the evasion should remove the body away from the attack. If an attack is to your left side, the body evades to the right and vice versa.

- ACTION II:

1. The victim *must* have begun the evasive action prior to executing the attack, or the attack should never leave its control point.
2. The attack must immediately follow the perception of the evasive reaction.
3. Targets and timing must be exact.
4. Horizontal swipes are delivered from either right or left, and are targeted across the chest or belly, over the head or under the feet.
5. Diagonal swipes are delivered from either right or left, either descending or ascending. All diagonal cuts travel outside the body in a forty-five degree plane.
6. Vertical swipes are delivered from either right or left, either descending or ascending. All vertical cuts travel six to eight inches outside the body in a plane perpendicular to the floor.
7. Thrusts for evasions are generally made at chest or waist and sometimes to the thighs.
8. Thrusts made to your partner's left are evaded to their right and vice versa.
9. In all swipes, watch the exact path of the attacking blade.
10. Reach out on the attack with the full extent of the weapon and arm.
11. Air doesn't bleed! The attack to a correctly executed evasion is either out of distance or outside the body and can be completely committed to.
12. Committing to an action is not the same as over-committing to an action. *You must always be in control of every action in a stage fight.*
13. Do not cut into the floor. No attacks are terminated by striking the ground.
14. In an evasion by distance, duck or jump, cut the air where the body *was.*
15. Never follow the victim with the blade. Do not track the attack.
16. In an evasion by distance, the offensive footwork can only be executed in proportion to those of the evasive action. Correct distance must be maintained.
17. In an evasion by displacement, if the attack is carried safely outside the physical plane of the body, it can be executed within distance.

Chapter 11

Attacking the Blade

"Make a narrow space upon him wt your poynt & sodainly & strongely stryke or bere his poynt towarde his right syde, indyrecting the same, & instantly strike or thrust" [Silver][1]

In Chapter 5 you learned the guards of the rapier and the principle of closing lines of attack. The standard and cross body guard were used to establish walls of defense that the adversary had to pass their point around before launching an effective attack. The idea of the "guard" however, presented a further barrier that had to be thwarted before any attack could hit home. Although a changement could manipulate the weapon into an open line, the point of the guarding weapon still posed a threat to the opponent. Any attack launched without removing the point of the guarding blade could impale the aggressor. Thus, the point of the opponent's weapon needs to be "struck" or "borne" aside before one can effectively strike or thrust.

Although in theatrical swordplay the point of the guarding weapon is generally not held on-line, the principal of the guard is maintained. The danger of the fight is acted and must not be neglected in the reality of the stage fight. Therefore the blade, although safe for the artist, must still be treated as a dangerous and deadly weapon by the character. The point of the weapon must be removed by the character or they risk being impaled upon it.

The actions used to remove or displace the opponent's blade are generally known as *attacks on the blade.* The attacks on the blade (also known as *attacks of force*) are a variety of offensive actions executed on the opponent's blade with more or less strength according to the aims of the attacker. Attacks on the blade are generally broken into three major categories: *beats, pressures* and *flowing.* Beats are attacks on the blade that utilize shock to laterally remove the opposing blade. Pressures are attacks on the blade that utilize lateral pressure to displace the blade. There are two common forms of pressure attacks: the *press* and the *froissement.* Flowing attacks are actions of the blade that use a sliding or grazing motion down the opposing weapon in order to displace it. The most common form of flowing attack is the *glissade* or *coulé.*

Although these actions are still a standard part of sport fencing, they have been enlarged for safety and the audience's benefit. They have been broken down into more readable actions. The fast, single action of the modern fencer has been magnified so that the audience can perceive what is happening. However, many of the moves still carry the same name as they do in fencing, although any fencer would cringe at some of the horrid bastardizations of their most loved moves. The action, however, is intended to suit the same purpose, only now it is large enough for the audience to share its intention.

---

[1]Silver, *Brief Instruction.* p. 105.

The Meeting Angle

In the following attacks on the blade, there must be a *meeting angle* for the attack to be effective. As in Chapter 5, when we spoke of the possibilities of engaging blades, in order for swords to join, they must be placed at opposing angles forming an ''X'' or open ''V'' with blades. The same rules for engaging the blades also apply here. In order for any attack on the blade to be effective, the planes of the swords must cross. This is the meeting angle of the blades. (Fig. 192)

The Beat Attack

The beating or *battrement* is probably the most common form of attack on the blade used in rapier play. The *pressure* and the *froissement* are more developments of the small sword than of the rapier. The hitting aside of the opposing blade to open a line of attack, however, was taught in most treatises on fencing during the age of the rapier. di Grassi, Saviolo, Silver, Fabris and Capo Ferro all taught forms of beating the blade.

> *''You may joine your sword within you enemies sword,''* instructs Joseph Swetnam, '' . . . *but presentlie so soone as you have joyned, strike it downe to his legge''* [Swetnam][2]

The battrement was, and still is, a controlled tap against the middle or weak part of the opponent's blade to remove a threat, open a line for attack, or to provoke a reaction. The battrement is a dry shock effectuated with the middle or foible part of one's blade on the foible of the opponent's blade. The beat is generally not a wild action that removes both yours and your opponent's blades from the lines of attack, but rather an action that, like the beat parry, deflects the opponent's weapon while preparing yours for either an offensive or defensive action.

In executing an effective battrement, the ''beating'' is an energetic movement that must be done with vigor and dryness. The term ''dry'' expresses the fact that the contact is made at one point only and that the blades do not scrape or slide. The contact between the two blades provides a short knock-like sound just as in the beat parry. In stage combat there are generally two ways of executing a beat attack. The first is executed from a guard position, like the changements in Chapter 4; the second involves the use of extended parries to displace the offending blade, and is discussed later.

> *''The beat on the sword is done by engaging the blade* . . . [then] *you must leave the blade about four inches, and beat on it in a smart and lively manner''* [Angelo][3]

Because the mechanics of the beat attack executed from a guard position are the same whether joined or free, the following techniques are presented with the blades engaged. From the point of engagement, the blade is drawn back, away from your partner's blade, about four to six inches. Moving the blade with the hand and wrist only, the blade is then quickly snapped back against your partner's foible. Your body remains in correct placement, the attack of the blade being executed from the hand and wrist. The sword arm does not aid in the beat and only moves once the beat is completed and the attack is begun.

In actual fencing and competitive swordplay, after a beat attack the point of the weapon would then be directed at the opponent's body, generally poised to launch an attack. This makes the beat one action, from the guarded placement to the open position for an attack. For the learning of the beat, however, the blade is not to be directed on-line. The point of the weapon completes the beat, showing a cue for a thrusting attack directed outside your partner's body either to their right or left. The point of the weapon never crosses your partner's face or throat.

---

[2]Swetnam, p. 129.

[3]Angelo, p. 24.

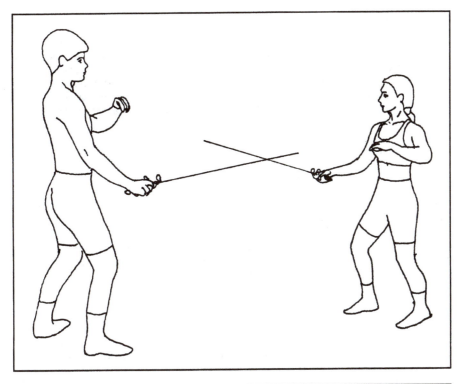

Figure 192. The meeting angle of the blade.

Working the Beat

Beats may be practiced in each of the four guard positions, their variations, both standard and across. Starting in Prima Across, beat your partner's blade off to their left. The placement of your sword arm does not change, the point however, may now be directed either across the body, outside your partner at the level of their right shoulder or straight forward outside your partner at the level of their left shoulder. The beat may take you either to Prima Across or into Prima Standard. Just as in receiving a beat parry, the person being beat needs to give in the wrist and allow their blade to be removed.

The Return Beat

The exercise may be reversed, allowing both parties to work on the beat attack. Yielding to the force of the blow, your partner releases and at the endpoint of the reaction they reverse the action of their wrist and deliver a light blow to the blade of the initiator of the beat. This is called a *return beat,* and it can be used in combat to remove the threat of the new offending blade before an attack can be launched. These blade actions can only be executed from guard positions where the blades can be engaged. The blades need not be engaged for these exercises, but they must be in a placement where they can be joined. For our purposes the beat and return beat may be repeated several times in each guard until control and proficiency are gained.

The Change Beat

The beat attack delivered in the same line of engagement is generally called a beat or *direct beat,* because the attacking blade executes the action without changing lines. An indirect, or *change beat* is a beat attack that is executed after the successful completion of a changement. The beat, accompanied by a changement allows the initiator of the action to manipulate the direction their partner's blade is knocked. From the point of engagement, the blade is carried either over or under the opposing blade with a coupé or disengage and brought to the other side of the weapon. Once on the other side the hand and wrist instantly snap the blade against your partner's foible. Your body remains in correct placement, with the changement and the attack of the blade only being executed from the hand and wrist. In this same vein, it is possible to offer a return beat both directly and indirectly with changements.

A change beat may also be executed from a parry as well as a guard. After a successful parry, a reverse counter parry (cutting the lines) with a beat can be instantly executed to knock the opposing blade to the opposite side of the body. The "reverse counter parry" serves as the changement, bringing your blade over or under their sword. The counter parry then terminates in a beat, displacing the opposing blade. For example, if a blade is parried in 2, a reverse counter parry or cutting the lines with a counter parry of 7 is then instantly executed. This would be a counter parry of 7. The counter of 7 would be executed as a beat parry, picking up the offending blade on the right side of the body and knocking away to the left. This action may be executed in all parries that have an effective counter parry. In beating the blade across the body it is important to keep your distance and to make sure the blade never crosses the face or throat. Because of this, no change beats can be executed from the parries of High 3, High 4, 5, 5 A, and Low 5. The change beat on a parry is different than a beat parry because the latter is defensive and the former offensive.

Beating with an Extended Parry

When blades are not engaged, or cannot be engaged as in the case of Seconda, the threatening point must still be removed before an effective attack can be launched. This can be done by executing a lateral beat parry out in front of the body. Instead of carrying a parry eight to ten inches in front of you, fully extend the arm in order to meet the foible of your partner's weapon. In this beat attack the middle or forte of your weapon must still strike the foible of your partner's. (Fig. 193)

Because the mechanics of this type of beat attack are executed from a guard position where the

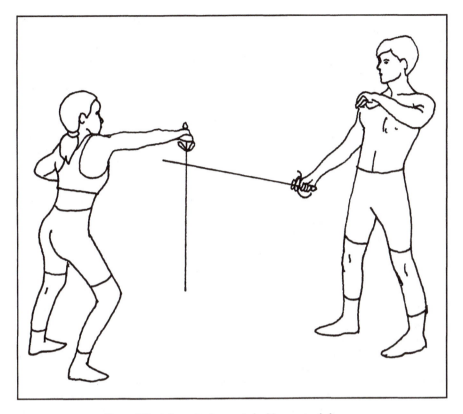

Figure 193. A beat attack executed with an extended parry.

blades are not engaged, the extended parry can be delivered from any guard and to either side. For example, from the guard of Quarta Across, an opposing guard of Seconda can be removed to your left by an extended beat parry of 4; or it can be removed to your right with an extended counter parry of 3. From the guard of Terza, an opposing guard of Prima can be removed to your left by an extended beat parry of 4 or High 1; or it can be removed to your right with an extended counter parry of 3 or High 2; and so on. Simply put, if an opposing guard threatens a certain line, any parry that protects that may be extended in order to beat the guard aside as long as the points of the weapons never cross the face or throat.

Pressure Attacks

Although the beat attack applies pressure to the opposing blade, it is a short burst of pressure rather than applied pressure. The pressure attacks utilize consistent lateral pressure to displace the blade. The contact with the blades is longer and may utilize more than one point on the opposing blade.

The Press

The press, in simplest terms, is the application of pressure against the opposing blade to push it aside and open a line of attack. Because the blades must be joined in order to execute a press, it can only be delivered from guards where the blades are engaged. Moving the hand and wrist, the foible or middle of your blade is pressed against the opposing guard. As in beating, the pressure is done with the middle or forte of one's blade pushing on the part of the opponent's blade near their point.

Just the blade, hand and wrist move. Your body remains in correct placement. The sword arm does not aid in the Press and only moves once the line is open for an attack.

The push is forced, but it may be done either quickly or slowly depending on the desired effect. A quick press instantly removes the blade opening a line for an attack. A slow press may be met with *counter press,* where the opponent presses back in order to keep their blade in place. The action of the press, and the counter press were common in Elizabethan rapier play and are exemplified in Swetnam's treatise.

> *"If your enemie doe joyne his Rapier with yours, and do beare him strongly against you, thinking to over-beare you by strength of arme, then so soone as hee beginneth to charge you strongly, beare your rapier alittle against him, and then sodainely let fall your point so low, as your gerdle-steed, and thrust it home withall, and so you may hit him, for by letting his rapier goe away sodainely, he swayeth away beyond the compasse of defence."* [Swetnam][4]

In rapier play and in competitive fencing today, the bearing down on the sword, and the resistance of pushing back creates a great deal of force between the blades that can easily be mastered. As in Swetnam's example above, if the opponent applies too much pressure on their counter press it can be deceived with a disengage or coupé, quickly taking the blade to the opposite side. The change-ment removes the opposition to their press and so lets the opposing blade carry itself out of line. In either case the opposing blade is removed enough to direct the point of the sword at the opponent, generally poised to launch an attack.

Working the Press

The press may be practiced in all engaged guard positions, both standard and across. Starting in Prima Across, press your partner's blade over to their left, opening their high outside line. Once a strong opening has been created, allow your partner to press you back. There should be some resistance against the counter press. Do not make it a fight, but allow a sensible amount of opposition to be developed between the weapons. Once the blades are pressed back to their original point of engagement, execute a disengage or coupé. This removes the opposition, displacing their point and opening the line. From this opening, move on to another guard and let your partner re-engage you. Once engaged in a new guard, begin the exercise again.

The Froissement

> *"If slang were allowed, this ought to be called the 'scrooge'; but there is no English word which reproduces the French froisse."* [Castle][5]

Because there is no direct English translation to capture the image and action of the "froisse," the froissement has earned a great many nicknames. Some of its more common terms are the ruffling, scrape, effort and *pressure glide.* The term froissement and pressure glide are generally the most common, with pressure glide now becoming the norm in the modern schools of stage combat.

The froissement or pressure glide is the most violent of the attacks on the blade. In actual swordplay it can disarm the opponent. It is a combination of beat and pressure attacks that consists of violently "pressing and sliding" down the opposing blade. The action starts as a sharp beat or press on the opposing blade that remains engaged sliding from the foible of their blade and to forte. It goes from one end to the other with a continuous and energetic friction accentuated by pressure from the wrist. The pressure glide is generally the most common attack on the blade executed from a successful parry as part of the riposte. The froissement on the riposte may be executed in two ways: a cut or thrust.

For the purpose of exercising the pressure glide, and because its mechanics (cut or thrust) can be executed from a free or joined placement of the blades, the following example is described starting from a completed parry of 3. When executed from a guard position, the engagement techniques of

---

[4]Swetnam, p. 122–123
[5]Castle, *Badminton,* p. 52.

the beat are followed. In riposting with a thrust, keep your point in its completed position from the parry (for parry 3 this is straight up at twelve o'clock) and begin extending the arm (Fig. 194-a). The extension of the arm is a strong, sharp, accentuated glide down the opposing blade with your forte. The action moves their foible laterally to the side while moving your hand and sword forward (Fig. 194-b). To achieve the popular "scraping" sound of the pressure glide, your partner needs to apply a bit of resistance and give in the wrist, not the arm. As your arm is extended, a twist or rotation in the wrist guides your point towards its target without releasing the pressure on the blade (Fig. 194-c). The forte of your blade must maintain contact with the opposing blade, your point however, may now be directed either across the body, thrusting outside your partner at their right shoulder or straight forward outside your partner at the level of their left shoulder (Fig. 194-d). Although the sword arm maintains the pressure to the outside, the thrust may be made either to your partner's right or left side. (Fig. 194)

If a cut is to be executed on a pressure glide, the initial mechanics are the same. As the blade is sharply extended out and forward, it remains in the same position as it was in the parry, and instead of dropping the point to execute a thrust, turn the wrist and execute a wrist cut to your partner's right or left side. The forte of your blade must maintain contact with the opposing blade sliding from their foible to their forte. Just as in the thrust from a froissement, the sword arm must maintain lateral pressure to displace the opposing weapon, but the cut may be made either to your partner's right or left side. In either case, the action of the arm and wrist does not intentionally push the opposing blade up or down, but only to the side.

Working the Froissement

The best way to work the pressure glide with all the parries is to take them through the Offensive/ Defensive drill or the Around the Clock exercise offered in Chapter 8. Working with a partner, try each of the parries a few times to get the feel of how the mechanics differ in each position. Then go through the pattern with one person attacking and the other executing a pressure glide and riposte. The froissement can be executed from any free guard position that can engage another. These are any of the guards covered in Chapter 5 that provides a suitable meeting angle of the blades, allowing them to be joined. To practice the pressure glide from a free guard position you simply execute a sharp, crisp engagement of the blades, and apply lateral pressure that displaces your partner's blade to the side while extending your arm forward and gliding your blade down theirs. You can practice these actions in the same manner that you practiced blade engagements in Chapter 5. Be sure your partner is prepared for the action, however, as the "aggressive" attack on the blade can actually disarm an unprepared combatant.

Yielding into a Parry from the Froissement

It is important to note that because the blades remain joined during the pressure glide that it affects the execution of the defending parry. The continued engagement limits the number of possible parries and how they may be executed. When a riposte is parried without the blades separating after the initial attack, the parry is called a *ceding* or *yield parry*. The ceding or yielding parries are a particular method of execution used against thrusts and cuts off a froissement. It's unclear when these parries were first used in swordplay, but they were popular by the late seventeenth century. The French fencing master Labat found the practice indispensable and insisted upon them in his teachings.[6] The yield consists of not resisting the pressure, but waiting to parry until the final stage of the attack when the focus shifts from the pressure to the attack. At that time, without

---

[6]Labat [Maitre fait d'armes de la ville et Academie de Toulouse].—L'art en fait d'armes, ou de l'epee seule, avec les atitudes; dedie a Monseigneur le Comte d'Armaignac, Grand Ecuyer de France, &C. 8°. 1696. Toulouse: J. Boude. (*accents are missing).

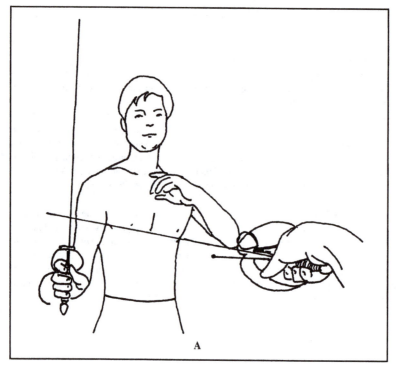

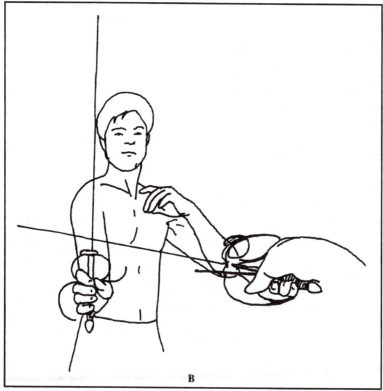

Figure 194. Showing a pressure glide.

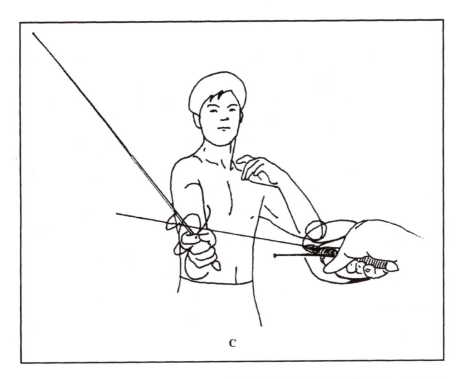

C

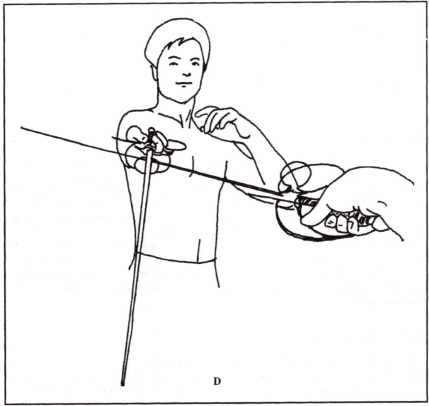

D

Figure 194 (Continued).

losing contact, the pressured blade is quickly drawn back, pressing its forte against the offending blade's foible. Thus, you have yielded your blade into a parry.

The limitations of the yield parry come from the necessity of remaining engaged. For example, when a thrust is returned from your partner's right hip or thigh to your right side, you may only yield into a parry of 2 (High, Standard or Low 8). An attempt to yield into the parry of 3 either separates the blades or carries the offending point to the inside of the parry, towards your body. Conversely, if a thrust is returned from your partner's left hip or thigh to your right side, you may only yield into a parry of 3 (Standard or Low). An attempt to yield into the parry of 2 has the same effect as the parry of 3 earlier. The same limitations are true for the left side of the body. A thrust from your partner's right hip or thigh to your left side, may only be yielded into a parry of 4 (Standard or Low).

In several yield parries your blade pivots around the offending blade from the outside where it was parried, to the inside where it parries. If your opponent presses back in a straight line (i.e., from their right to your left or vice versa) you will need to pivot around the offending blade to make the parry. The pivot is executed with the forte of your blade around the foible of the opponent. The pivot of your blade and the drawing back of the hand and arm carries your rapier into a proper parry. If the riposte off the Froissement is executed across the body, however, their blade remains on the outside of yours and there is no need to pivot the sword. (Fig. 196)

The pressure glide and yield parry can now be taken through the Offensive/Defensive drill or the Around the Clock exercise offered in Chapter 7. One person attacks, and the other executes the pressure glide and riposte. It is important to note that because straight line ripostes can only be yielded into high line parries, do not offer a straight line riposte to the hip or thigh. Low line attacks can be delivered across the body where your partner's yield parry can effectively pick it up.

The Flowing Attack

The other category of attacks on the blade is the encounter with the opposing blade without shock or pressure. This is called a flowing attack. These attacks use a sliding or grazing action down the opposing blade in order to create an opening for attack. Unlike the froissement, flowing attacks do not use excessive pressure on the opposing weapon. They use a gentle, but continuing amount of opposition to move the blade aside. Flowing attacks are much more delicate and gentle than the pressure glide.

The Glissade

The most common form of flowing attack in stage combat is the glissade or coulé. It is the action of sliding the blade all along the opposing weapon by extending the sword arm in order to prepare or lodge an attack. The glissade is executed by extending the sword arm as you would for a thrust, making your blade slide against your partner's, keeping continually in contact without pressure or intensity. Excessive force is not needed in the glissade because it is generally executed against an opponent whose guard insufficiently closes the line of attack.

The glissade must be executed from an engaged guard position, as it can only be delivered from guards where the blades are joined. Using the mechanics of the thrusts offered in Chapter 6, you simply slide down the opposing blade, applying just enough lateral pressure to expose the intended target. The glissade is executed with the middle or forte of your blade sliding down your partner's blade foible to forte.

Working the Glissade

The glissade may be practiced in all engaged guard positions, both standard and across, but it is most practical in cross body guards. Starting in Prima Across, execute an imbroccatta to the right shoulder. Work this a few times and then try a botta dritta from Terza Across, and then a punta dritta, and so on. This exercise can be worked with the glissade alone, or it may be taken into a yield parry.

Figure 195. A pressure glide executed from a parry of three attacking the left shoulder yielded into a parry of High 1 (the parry pivoting around the offending blade).

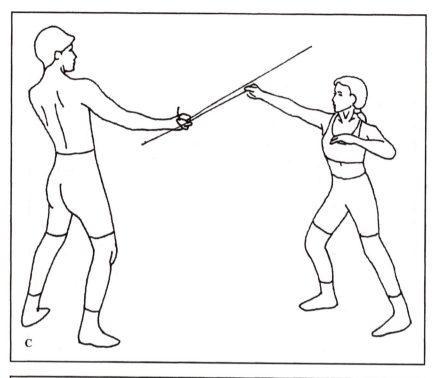

Figure 195 (Continued).

Figure 195 (Continued).

If the yield parry is used, be careful not to let the glissade become a pressure glide. Let the blade flow to its intended target.

The Pris d'Fer

As the thrust became a greater threat in swordplay, the concept of commanding the opponent's blade rather than just displacing it came into practice. A blade beaten or pushed aside could easily be brought back to hit home or to deflect the counterattack. The other combatant could also remove their body from the line of attack while simultaneously launching a counter thrust. Because of this, and the manageability of the lighter rapier, several methods of taking the opponent's blade were developed. These actions removed the opposing blade in a variety of directions, momentarily paralyzing the opponent's defense. These types of actions were referred to as *controlling the point* in sixteenth century swordplay and are now known as the *pris d'fer*.

The pris d'fer, or "taking of the blade," are attacks on the blade that catch the opposing blade, master it, and hold it or remove it to the final attack. There are three generally accepted pris d'fer: the *croisé*, which commands the blade either up or down on one side of the body; the *bind*, which commands the blade either up or down across the body; and the *envelopment*, which carries the blade in a circle back to its point of origin. The froissement is said to be a part of these actions because it generally commands the blade either to the right or left, laterally across the body. In stage combat, however, the pris d'fer are most commonly recognized as the croisé, bind and envelopment.

The Croisé

The croisé, sometimes called the "twist" or "cut down," is an attack on the blade that carries the opposing weapon from a high line to a low line, or vice versa, on the same side of the body as the engagement. The original object of this action was to disarm, or thoroughly overwhelm the

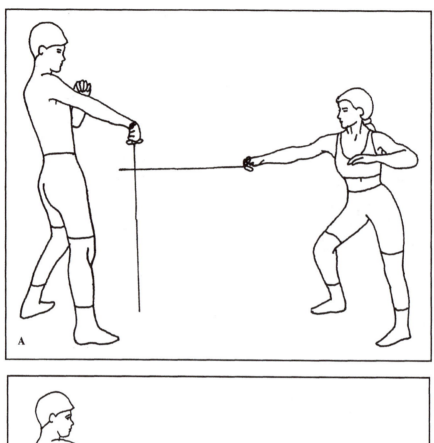

Figure 196. The yield parry executed across the body in the same line.

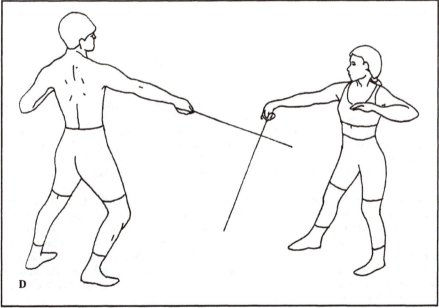

Figure 196 (Continued).

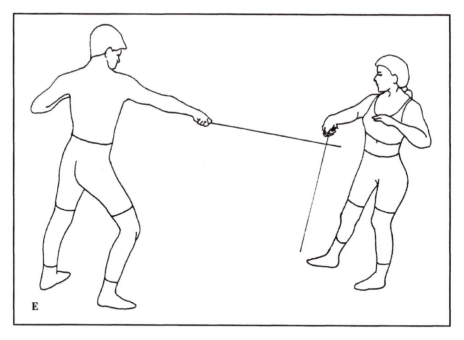

E

Figure 196 (Continued).

opponent for a moment. Called *crossing* in the eighteenth century, the technique was not popular, but did prove effective.

> *"Very few masters teach the crossing of the blade; this operation is the more necessary, being not only useful to put the adversary's blade from the wrist to the knee, but will often throw his sword out of his hand."* [Angelo][7]

As Angelo describes, the results of the croisé are similar to that of the froissement; displacing or disarming the opposing blade. The action can be executed from either an engaged guard position, or from a successful parry as part of the riposte. The attack delivered from the croisé may be executed two ways; either as a cut or thrust. From an engaged guard position the foible of the opposing blade is seized with the forte and is quickly forced either up or down by an opposing semi-circular movement of the hand and wrist. This action forces the blade aside, creating an opening for the attack.

The best descriptions of the croisé are a elbow cut or a reversed semicircular parry delivered against an engaged blade. In reality it is a combination of the two. Starting in a parry of 3 (if you are engaged in Terza Across, extend your arm and raise your point so that the middle or forte of your blade encounters the opposing foibleas in a parry of 3), instantly begin pressing the blade out and down in the manner of a diagonal parry from 3 to 7. At the same time, extend your arm and turn your wrist as if you were delivering an elbow or wrist cut to your partner's left thigh. The action of the blade does not continue through to the parry of 7, it stops at least ten inches outside the body at this target. The extension of the arm is a firm glide down the opposing blade, moving their foible out and down while moving your hand and sword forward. (Fig. 197) In this, and in the following pris d'fer, it is important that your partner not try to "help" the action by lending the movement.

[7]Angelo, D. p. 53.

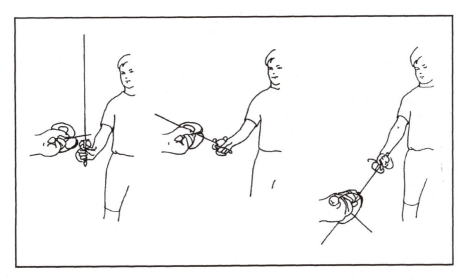

Figure 197. Showing a Croisé from the parry of 3.

The instigator of the croisé must lead the action by pressing against the opposing blade. As in the pressure glide, your partner needs to apply some resistance to make the move effective on stage. The combination of the semicircular movement of the blade with the extension of the arm and cut from the wrist, carries the opposing sword down into the low-line. Be sure that the opposing blade is displaced by the combined actions of the blade, hand and wrist and not by lowering the arm. The hand must remain at roughly waist level or the advantage of the action is lost. If both weapons are removed below, there is no purpose in the action.

Your hand, wrist and elbow must remain relaxed while executing these movements. Tension adversely affects the actions of the blade. Be sure your shoulders hang loosely, even when extending the arm. A stiff or rigid joint makes these movements choppy and awkward. The same applies to the bind and envelopment. The pris d'fer are not moves of strength, they are moves of timing and skill.

In the execution of the croisé, and all the following pris d'fer, you have two options for how you can complete the blade taking action. You may either remain engaged and *command the blade* or you may fling it aside with and *expulsion*. To command the blade you complete the action in the same manner that you would a standard oppostion parry. The hand and blade stop with a clean crisp motion, keeping the opposing blade engaged. This is the common form of a pris d'fer as it maintains control of the opposing sword and allows you the option of a variety of other attacks on the blade. To fling the blade away with an expulsion (as is done so often on stage and screen), the action is completed with an extra punch like that of a beat parry. This extra action of the sword and hand allows you to remove the opposing weapon from the field of play. Some schools add to the expulsion the action of a glissade, sliding down the blade as it is thrown aside. This addition is not necessary to the action, but it does add a little more force to the expulsion and the grazing sound of the glissade.

When you execute a pris d'fer with an expulsion, your partner needs to be sure they're holding their sword properly. Even a theatrical expulsion, when done correctly, can disarm an unprepared combatant. Once the blade is removed, an attack can instantly follow. This may be in the form of a cut or thrust.

If the croisé is to be executed from a guard, the technique is almost exactly the same as from a parry. From the guard position the hand and sword are brought forward to the placement of an extended parry (and if free, joined with the blade), setting you in an ideal position to execute a croisé. A parry of 3 has the same mechanics as Terza, 4 as Quarta and so on. The difference in parries versus guards is that there are many more parries than engaged guards. This is especially true of the low line. If an attack is parried in 1, you instantly begin pressing the blade out and up in the manner of a diagonal parry from 1 to 3. At the same time, the arm is extended as if you were delivering an elbow or wrist cut to your partner's right shoulder. Like before, the action of the blade does not continue across the body into the parry; it stops with the action of the cut, at least ten inches outside the body. The combination of the upward movement of the blade with the extension of the arm and cut from the wrist can carry the opposing sword up and into the high line or fling it away with an expulsion.

It is important to note that the croisé on stage is generally executed from the high line to the low line. This general practice is to avoid bringing the blade up as in the previous example. This is the reason the action has received the name the *cut down*. It is feared that the upward action of the blade brings the point up and into the face. In some instances this is true. In the engaged guard of Prima, the path of the ascending blades are dangerously close to the face and the croisé should not be attempted. The cut up from the low line parries should not be viewed the same way. If practiced slowly, the upward action is no more threatening to the face than a standard cut to the shoulder. The mechanics are similar, the targets the same and the croisé stops the blade further outside the body. There is no threat or danger to the face as long as both combatants are in control of their points and the proper techniques are followed.

Working the Croisé

To work the croisé, start by practicing in the engaged guard positions (avoiding high line guards such as Prima and High Seconda). Perform the action from both the right and left side of the body, getting a feel for its timing. This allows you to practice the croisé by taking the blade down and away from the face. Once comfortable with the mechanics of the cut down, try a few cut ups. Working with a partner, try a croisé from a parry of 2 and then from a parry of 1. Go through these a few times to get a feel of how the mechanics differ from the cut down. Upon reaching a fluid and safe delivery of these techniques, take them through the Offensive/Defensive drill or the Around the Clock exercise offered in Chapter 7. Go through the pattern with one person attacking and the other parrying then executing a croisé.

After successfully working the croisé (command and expulsion) in all the parries, a riposte may be added to the pris d'fer. Whether cut or thrust, the action and target of the riposte must be determined ahead of time. The defender of the riposte has the option of parrying the attack in the standard fashion or, when applicable, executing a yield parry. Remember, yield parries can only be executed if the blades remain engaged and that straight line ripostes can only be yielded into high line parries.

The Bind

The bind is probably the most common of the pris d'fer used in rapier play on stage. It is an attack on the blade that carries the opposing weapon from a high line to a low line, and vice versa, diagonally across the line of engagement. The result of the extended carriage of the opposing blade is a longer paralysis of their defense and a greater variety of possible attacks. In competitive swordplay binds are usually used against opponents who tend to hold their weapons firmly or rigidly, thus offering resistance. An action like a beat would be more effective against blades which are loosely held. On stage, however, the bind is a dynamic sweeping action of the blades that effectively conveys its intent to the audience.

The bind can be executed from either a successful parry as part of the riposte or an engaged guard position, but it is most often from a parry. Like the croisé, the attack delivered from the bind may either be a cut or thrust. Unlike the croisé, and the previously offered attacks on the blade, the bind can be executed both in a passive and active form. In both cases the foible of the opposing blade is instantly seized by the forte and forced up or down across the body by an opposing movement of the hand and wrist. This contact between the blades is maintained for a relatively long time and is characterized by a scraping sound caused by the pushing action of the weapon. The bind may be executed with a command or with an explosion, flinging the blade aside, and uncovering the opponent.

Figure 198. Showing a passive bind from the guard of Quarta.

The Passive Bind: Because the passive bind is more contained and controlled, it is generally used in transitional rapier play or from engaged guard positions. The movement of this bind is merely a confined diagonal parry delivered against an engaged blade. Starting in an engaged guard of Quarta, instantly begin pressing the blade out and down in the manner of a diagonal parry from 4 to 2. At the same time, extend your arm slightly so as not to lose the foible of the opposing blade. The action of the blade continues across the body to the placement of parry 2. (Fig. 198) Be sure that as the blade is guided across your partner's body, that the tip stays low and close to their guard. Your point should circle their hand as in a changement. During this action the foible of the opposing blade is kept on your forte, close to the hilt. In binds to the high line, you and your partner need to work out the amount of resistance necessary to keep their point from crossing your face while maintaining the relative placement of the blades.

Depending on the execution of the passive bind, the opposing blade may be kept engaged for a further command (such as a glissade) or flung out and away with an expulsion. In either case the opposing blade must be displaced by the action of the blade, hand and wrist and not by swinging the arm. As in the croisé, your hand must remain at roughly waist level or the advantage of the action is lost. Once the blade is removed, an attack can instantly follow. This may be in the form of a cut or thrust.

The Active Bind: Active binds are more common on stage because the size and scope of the action read well to the audience. The dynamic action of the active bind is an exaggeration of the movement for a diagonal parry. Starting in a parry of 1, instantly begin pressing the blade out and up in the manner of a diagonal parry from 1 to 3. At the same time, extend your arm so that the blades are crossed in their middles. The action of the blade continues up and across the body to the right, but instead of moving to the placement of parry of 3, the hand describes an exaggerated arc above shoulder level. (Fig. 199)

The blades remain crossed at their middles, forming an "X" as they travel. The points of the blades are directed outside the body and carried up and over the head. The active bind is truly a partnering technique. You and your partner need to work out the amount of resistance necessary to keep the "X" of the blades consistent while remaining joined.

A common mistake in practicing the active bind is to direct the blades straight up, causing them to lose contact. The cross of the blades must be maintained. Another common error is to swing the blade from the shoulder with a virtually straight arm. Although the move is exaggerated, the

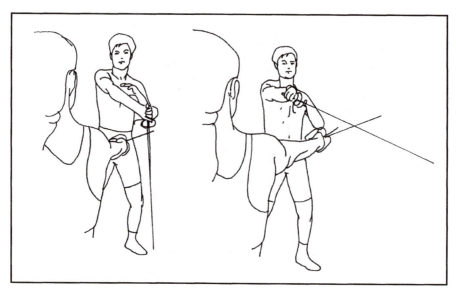

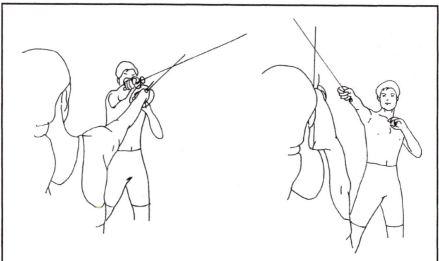

Figure 199. Showing an active bind from the parry of 1.

mechanics still must be practical. The movement of the hand, wrist, elbow and arm are quite similar to a diagonal shoulder cut, only off to your right rather than towards your partner. The similarity in these mechanics also helps you stop your blade in the opposing line instead of just swinging your arm. If you use the mechanics of the cut, your blade will stop in a position ready to launch an effective attack. As in the passive bind, your blades can remain engaged, commanding the blade, or with a crisp action of the wrist you can expel your partner's blade.

Working the Binds

To work the binds, start by practicing the passive binds in the engaged guard positions. Perform the action in each of the guards, getting a feel for its timing. Once comfortable with the mechanics of the passive bind (command and expulsion), try working active binds with a variety of parries or in exercises like the Offensive/Defensive drill or the Around the Clock exercise. You can go through the pattern with one person attacking and the other executing a parry and Bind, or you can try going around the clock on an exchange. This is where one person attacks one o'clock (diagonal cut left shoulder), the other parries, executes a bind and ripostes to one o'clock. The pattern continues with the cut being parried, a bind and a riposte to two o'clock, and so on. If the passive bind is worked in this type of exercise the defender of the riposte has the option of parrying the attack in the standard fashion or, when applicable, executing a yield parry.

The Bind Over

The *bind over* is a form of the active bind that commands the opposing blade down to the floor. The action generally begins with a low line parry, followed by a dynamic bind that carries the blades up, over and down to the floor on the opposite side. The objective of this action is to disarm the opponent or to pin their weapon, making its immediate use impossible.

The bind to the floor is just that, to the floor. The action is not a real power play where the blades are driven into the floor. It is a partnered action where both combatants guide the blades over in an ''X'' and bring the points of the weapons to rest upon the floor. There should be no hard impact or whipping of the blades into the floor.

The Bind Away

The *bind away* or *throw off* is a variation on the active bind and expulsion. This apparently forceful action not only flings the opposing blade away, but also the combatant who wields it. In its execution there is really no difference from an active bind with an expulsion, other than the acting value of the movement. The apparent force must be greater, but the reaction is what sells the move. The recipient of the bind away needs to act as if the bind is strong enough to throw them off balance and out of the way. This can be accented by the aggressor by passing forward into the bind as the blades pass twelve o'clock. The victim can react using the turn or forward turn in Chapter 9, or they can fling themselves in any number of other ways. The important thing is that the victim needs to be in control, even when they throw themselves. They should never actually be thrown or off balance, they should act it. If you are working in a class, it is incredibly important to work slowly and be aware of other couples. Even if you and your partner are in control of what you are doing, two completely safe couples can have a very unsafe collision. Go slowly.

Beating the Bind

Beating the bind or the *change bind* is an offensive move executed by the victim of a bind. Like the press and counter press, if a combatant opposes the bind, a great deal of resistance between the blades can easily be developed. If the aggressor applies too much pressure on their bind, it can be deceived with a changement, quickly taking the blade to the opposite side. The changement removes the opposition to the bind, letting the blade carry itself off line. The disengaged blade is then brought around the opposing blade and executes either a beat attack or bind. In either case, when on the opposite side, the victim launches an attack on the opponent's blade.

The action of beating the bind is similar to a change beat executed out of a bind. At the initial point of being bound, opposition is offered by the victim. The bind is allowed to begin, but requires more effort on the part of the aggressor. Once the blades begin motion and the aggressor is committed to the action, execute a disengage around their guard, in the same direction you are being bound, bringing your blade to the other side of their weapon. Once on the other side, the hand and wrist instantly snap the blade against the middle or foible of your partner's blade. The changement and the attack on the blade must be quickly executed from the hand and wrist.

The Change Bind

The change bind is a defensive action that ends in an offensive pris d'fer. Like the action of beating the bind, the change bind uses a disengage or coupé to surpass the original bind. Here, however, the similarity ends. Instead of knocking the offending blade away in the path it was traveling, the change bind picks up the blade and carries it back to the originating line. The bind is allowed to begin as before, and once the blades begin motion, a disengage is executed around their guard, in the same direction as the bind or a coupé over the point against the bind. The blade then continues around and re-engages the aggressor's blade, binding it back to the line of origin. In essence, the action consists of two binds. For example, if you are bound from a parry of 3, you are bound to your low outside line; their parry of 7. That bind is deceived while in motion, and picked up again in your low outside line with an extended parry of 2. From your low outside line their blade is carried up and across to your high inside line, matching their point of origin. Two binds diagonally across the body bring the blades back to their original line.

The Envelopment

The final pris d'fer is the envelopment. It is an attack on the opponent's blade which, by describing a circle with both blades in contact, returns to the original line of engagement. Because of this circular action, the envelopment is sometimes referred to as "Wrapping it Up," or the "Wrap Up." The envelopment is executed from both an engaged guard position and a successful parry as part of the riposte. The attack delivered after the envelopment may either be a cut or thrust, but is usually a thrust. As in the bind, the envelopment can be executed both in a passive and active form and can be completed with a command or an expulsion. In both cases the foible of the opposing blade is captured by the forte and carried in a circular path by combined movement of the hand and wrist. The envelopment maintains the longest contact between blades of any of the blade-taking actions. In competitive fencing the object of the action is to find an open line during the circular process where an attack can be launched. On stage, the action is carried in the entire circle and is used to illustrate a mastering of the opponent's blade.

The Passive Envelopment: The passive envelopment, like the passive bind, is a contained and controlled manipulation of the blade. Because of this it is generally used in engaged guard positions or transitional rapier play. The movement is merely a confined circular parry delivered against an engaged blade. Starting in an engaged guard of Terza, begin pressing the blade out and down in the manner of a circular parry of 3. As you do this, slightly extend your arm to keep the foible of the opposing blade on your middle or forte. The action of the blade continues its clockwise path, returning to the placement of parry 3. (Fig. 200) It is important to make sure that as your blade is guided across your partner's body, that your tip stays low and close to their guard. Your point should circle outside their hand by only six inches. During this action the foible of the opposing blade is kept on your forte, close to the hilt. Be sure that their point doesn't get caught on your quillons. Long quillons can catch blades quite easily, entangling blades, losing the envelopment, and if forced they can possibly break the tip of your partner's rapier. When working the envelopment there is a give and take of energy that needs to be practiced between you and your partner to avoid slipping or catching blades. You and your partner need to work this out in order to safely maintain the relative placement of the blades. If the envelopment is not executed properly, the controlling arm tends to extend or "pump" forward in an attempt to manipulate the blade. Aside from the slight extension forward at the beginning of the envelopment, the arm should be stationary and still.

The intent of the aggressor in a passive envelopment determines if the opposing blade is expelled or kept engaged for a pressure glide or other attack on the blade. In either case the opposing blade must be displaced by the turning action of the blade, hand and wrist and not by a circle of the arm. Your hand must remain at roughly waist level or the blades can become disconnected or travel up toward the face. Once the blade is removed, an attack can instantly follow, generally in the form of a thrust. The blades do not need to remain engaged during the attack.

The Active Envelopment: Active envelopments are basically enlarged counter parries executed with the blades engaged. Starting in a parry of 8, the opposing blade is instantly pressed out and up in the manner of a counter parry of 8. As you do this the arm is extended so that the blades cross in

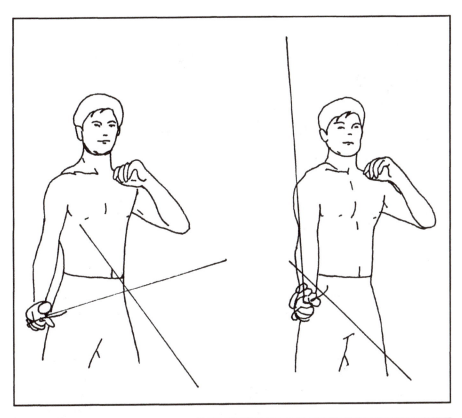

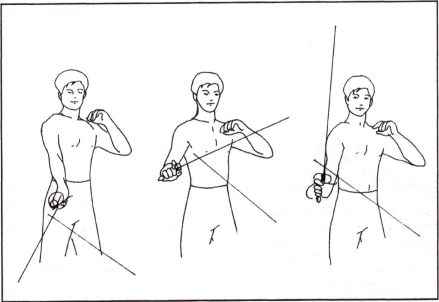

Figure 200. Showing a passive envelopment from the guard of Terza.

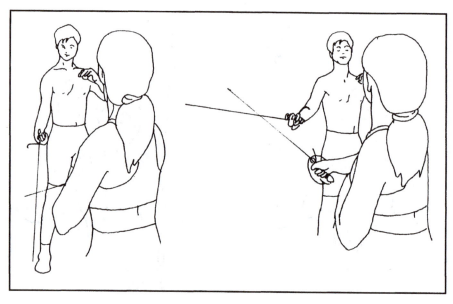

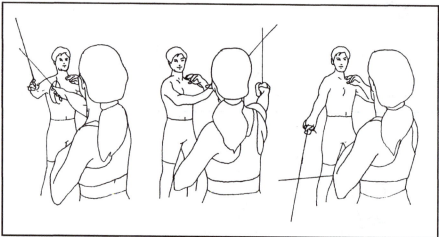

Figure 201. Showing an active envelopment from the parry of 8.

the middle. Do not go beyond the middle of your blade however, as you have no control in this action with the foible of the blade. The circular action of the blades is controlled by the wrist and elbow, not by the shoulder. The blade is carried up and across the body to the right, the hand describing a large arc above shoulder level. The arc of the arm continues its path, descending on the right side of the body and swinging low and back to the left and the parry of 8. (Fig. 201) As in the active bind, the blades remain crossed at their middles, forming an "X" as they travel. The give and take of pressure needs to be practiced between you and your partner in order to avoid the blades separating or scissoring in towards the body. Also, be aware of the "jump rope" envelopment. This is an action where the movement of the blades is instigated from the shoulders instead of the elbows. The straight arms and circling blades tend to look more like a child's game of jump rope than an offensive action of swordplay. Relax the arm and shoulder.

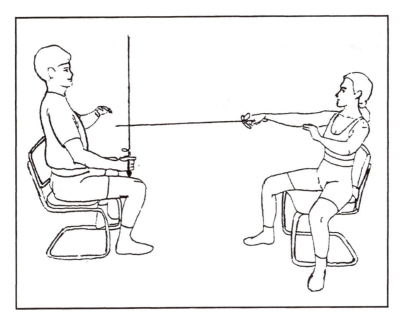

Figure 202. Sitting This One Out Exercise.

Working the Envelopments

To work the envelopments, start by practicing the passive techniques in the engaged guard positions (excluding high line guards such as Prima and Low Seconda, as the points can be brought near the face). Work through the action in each of the guards until the action is comfortable to you. Once you get a feel for the mechanics of the passive envelopment (command and expulsion), try working Active techniques in exercises like the Offensive/Defensive drill or the Around the Clock exercise. This may be done with one person attacking and the other executing a parry and envelopment, or try going on an exchange as described in the bind techniques. If the blades are kept engaged during the attack, yield parries may be used.

Trouble Shooting

When first learning the attacks on the blade and pris d'fer, it is a common practice to try and steer or control the point with the arm and torso instead of just the hand and wrist. This can dramatically change your distance, bringing the blade inside measure, possibly striking your partner. If you find yourself with these problems, try working the technique using the Sitting This One Out or Wall Bound exercises offered in Chapter 4. (Fig. 202) You may also try The Guiding Hand exercise from Chapter 8. Any of these help keep safe measure and shift focus to the management of the point with the hand and wrist and not the arm and torso.

Taking it Moving

After you have practiced these techniques and are comfortable with their mechanics, try adding footwork to the exercise. The objective is to maintain correct distance and proper control of the point. The exercises can be worked as before, only now footwork is added on the attack *after* the blade taking action. Do not move on the attack on the blade or pris d'fer, move on the attack immediately following the action.

If you are working the offensive/defensive drill, then your footwork is already set. If you are working another exercise, be sure to set a pattern of footwork for both combatants prior to taking the routine moving. Try working passes, advances and retreats so that you can practice the techniques with either foot in the lead position. Don't get locked into only moving with the right foot forward.

MOVING ON

Once you are comfortable with the all the attacks on the blade, their variations and modifications, and have worked them both stationary and moving, you are ready to move on to the next chapter.

Chapter 12

Deceits and False Play

"For Disceit or Falsing is no other thing, than a blow or thrust delivered, not to the intent to hurt or hitt home, but to cause the enemie to discover himselfe in some parte, by means whereof a man maie safely hurt him in the same part." [di Grassi][1]

Up until this point you have been working in the *True Art* of fence, attacking and defending one line at a time, with a single action of the blade. Tactically and theatrically, however, this has its limitations. Historically the science of fence was divided into two arts, the True Art and the *False Art*. The True Art was the philosophy of superior practice and skill in the techniques of striking the opponent while safely defending one's self. The False Art was the process of using tricks and misleading movements of the sword and body to dupe the opponent into unwittingly opening a line for attack. Of course the honorable practitioners of the Noble Science found these tricks distasteful and uncalled-for. Various schools had different opinions of these false actions of the blade. di Grassi took the time to define the two arts, and then explain to the reader his strong opinion against the False Art.

"I am constrayned to divide this Arte into two Arts or Sciences, callinge thone the True, the other, the False art: But with-all giving everie man to understand, that falsehood hath no advauntage against true Art, but rather is most hurtfull and deadlie to him that useth it." [di Grassi][2]

To this, Capo Ferro adds that false attacks, *"are no good, for they cause loss of time and distance."*[3] Saviolo, however, felt that mastery of both the True and False Art was a sign of a skilled fencer.

"For if your enemie have skill in fence, and should not finde you to stand surely upon your gard in this assault, he might deliver a straight stoccata to your face, not purposing fully to hit him, which if you should break with your Rapier, he might put his under yours, comming forward aside toward your right hande, and might give you a stoccata in the face." [Saviolo][4]

---

[1]di Grassi, p. 146.
[2]di Grassi, p. 18.
[3]Capo Ferro; translated by Castle, p. 111.
[4]Saviolo, p. 39.

Although considered by many as an ungentlemanly or unsafe practice, the delivering of attacks "not purposing fully to hit," was a common practice in Elizabethan swordplay. Although many of the practices of rapier fence fell by the wayside as fencing developed, the False Art flourished. The idea of faking an attack or deceiving the opponent into error became a common and accepted practice in the art of swordplay. Because these actions were eventually accepted, the "false" movements all became part of the tactics of the true art of fence. The single actions of the true art became known as *simple attacks,* and the tricks and fakes of the false art as *compound attacks.* Both simple and compound attacks are still a great part of the tactics in modern fencing and play a big part in the staging of theatrical fights.

Theatrically, deceptions and faked attacks help in the rhythm and flow of the fight. They offer variance to the "I go, you go, I go, you go" delivery of the True Art's simple attacks. False actions and their reactions can be quite telling to the audience in regards to a character's intentions, frame of mind and emotional state. The true personality and makeup of the character can be disclosed in how they use the arts of fence. For example, in the duel in the final act of Christopher Hampton's *Les Liaisons Dangereuses,* the cold, manipulative character of Valmont is more than likely to take full advantage of the False Arts against the straightforward, naive Danceny. The contrast between the arts could also be helpful in depicting the satirical, witty nature of Mercutio against the officious, arrogant Tybalt. It is for these reasons that the tactical actions of both arts are transposed to the art of stage combat.

THE TRUE ART

The attacks covered in Chapter 7, and their exercises and variations up until this point have been the rudimentary offensive actions of the true art of defense. Simply put, each action from its control point to its target has traveled in one direct path. All of these attacks are delivered in one blade movement without the relative position of the blades changing. These actions by themselves are referred to as *direct attacks.* Every attack covered so far, cut and thrust, when executed by themselves, are direct attacks.

Indirect Attacks

The attacks on the blade and the pris d'fer offered in the previous chapter are aggressive actions that in their execution do not immediately threaten the body. In order to hit the opponent, any of these actions must be followed by another attack. Simply put, these actions attack the blade, not the combatant. Thus, for clarification, attacks on the blade and pris d'fer are known as an *indirect attacks.*

Simple Attacks

When a direct attack is executed after successfully completing an indirect attack, such as an attack on the blade or pris d'fer, this combination of actions is called a *simple attack.* Although this action is comprised of two separate attacks, indirect and direct, it is assumed to be the simplest attack possible in swordplay and thus the true art. This assumption is made on the fact that a direct attack launched on an effective guard either meets the defending blade or impales the aggressor. Thus, the simplest attack is to displace the opposing blade and then strike in one swift motion. The exercises in the last chapter where you displaced the opposing blade and then attacked your partner were simple attacks.

In theatrical swordplay any single offensive movement of the blade, together with a direct attack, composes a simple attack. Thus, the attacks on the blade are not the only indirect attacks that may be used in the execution of a simple attack. Along with the attack on the blade and the pris d'fer, there are six other simple attacks. Each of these simple attacks uses the indirect actions of the changements offered in Chapter 5. The actions of changing from one guard position to a new contra postura may also be used to manipulate around the opposing blade to make a direct attack. These are the *straight attack,* change under, disengage, change over, the coupé and the half disengage. Although these are not attacks on the blade, Each of these single offensive movements may be used to manipulate around the opposing guard to an open line, facilitating a direct attack.

The Straight Attack

The straight attack is the natural, unadorned attack, a direct attack. It can only be executed from an open guard position where the opposing blade is neither an immediate threat and does not close your immediate line of attack. This is where a direct, or straight attack may be effectively launched. The opposing blade neither needs to be displaced or avoided in order to effectively launch this attack. It may be launched from any free guard position, offering the correct circumstances, to any immediately open target.

The Changement as an Indirect Attack

In the True Art, or simple attacks of stage combat, the changements taught in Chapter 5 play a key role in finding an open line for attack. When assuming standard or cross body guards where your opponent closes the immediate line of attack with their contra postura, your blade must be moved before you can effectively launch an attack. Changements such as the change under, change over, disengage, coupé and half disengage assist in avoiding the opposing blade and moving to an open line where a direct attack can be effectively executed.

To practice the simple attack with a changement, review the actions in Chapter 5 and execute them in conjunction with a direct attack. Starting with both combatants in Prima Across, execute a changement around the opposing weapon, although your blade can be directed to either side of the body, begin by returning your point to the inside of the opposing guard on the same side of the body. Once the changement is complete, offer an imbroccata to the right shoulder. Although the imbroccata (and all other direct attacks offered with a changement) is part of the action of a simple attack, the action must follow the proper mechanics of cue and response established in Chapter 7. Your partner then needs to parry for their right shoulder.

Once you have practiced the change under with a direct attack on the right side of the body, try the change under to the opposite side of the body. Although the placement of the sword arm does not change, the blade is now across the body with the point outside your partner's body at the level of their left shoulder. The tip of the sword must move in a clear and smooth path ending at the same level it began, outside the opponent's body but on the opposite side of the weapon. As before, once the changement is complete, offer an imbroccatta, now to the left shoulder. Your partner then needs to parry either with a direct parry of High 1 or a diagonal parry of 4.

This exercise should be repeated several times with all the changements, attacking each open target from each guard until control and proficiency are gained. Each attack, cut, thrust and target must be determined prior to working the exercise. Your partner should execute an appropriate parry to the target being threatened.

When changing across the body, you may attack any target that is exposed or open in that line. For example, if you change from the right to the left side of your partner's body, a cut or thrust may be directly delivered to either their left shoulder, hip or knee and vice versa. The head and groin are also often exposed in a changement, but the guard position from which you changed determines if they are accessible for direct attacks. If a cutting attack is offered from a changement, it generally is an elbow or wrist cut. Cutting attacks from the shoulder are generally too broad an action to accompany the "tactics" of the changement for an attack. The large wind up is too telling to the audience and your partner. The actions need to be large enough for the audience to perceive, but not so large that the surprise of the changement and attack is lost dramatically.

No matter which side of the body the changement is delivered toward, the change under can only be executed from guard positions where the blades can be engaged. If both combatants are in standard guards, the opposing blade provides no obstacle, and therefore no reason to change lines.

Taking the Simple Attacks Moving

After you have worked these exercises for a while, and are comfortable with all the different simple attacks, try adding footwork. The objective here is to maintain control of the point and weapon during the execution of the changement and attack while also executing footwork. It is important that while focusing on the movements of the blade, you do not lose correct distance. Measure is maintained in the following manner: The combatants begin at correct distance; the initiator of the attack, A, moves their blade first; the defending combatant, B, remains stationary throughout the changement, and only begins to pass back or retreat as they perceive the cue for the predetermined attack. Combatant A only moves forward with a pass or advance after they have properly shown the cue for the attack and see their partner moving back. The changement and cue for the attack is the first action, followed by the perception of the attack and Combatant B's reaction of footwork and parry, ending with Combatant A's final action of an attack and advance or pass forward. The attack and parry meet together at the same time.

In this exercise you may work with either foot in the lead position. You should, however, try working the simple attacks with passes, advances and retreats with both feet forward. This practice helps avoid the "fencing" look of only moving with the right foot forward.

Countering a Simple Attack

As the changements of Chapter 5 are used to facilitate the simple attack, the counter changement of that same chapter may be used to foil the attack before it is executed. Thus, if one combatant executes a disengage, the second combatant instantly responds with a changement of their own, bringing the first combatant's blade full circle back to its point of origin prior to executing the attack. As in the exercises in Chapter 5, once the first changement is perceived, the counter changement is executed around the opposing blade, bringing it back to the starting line.

As the counter changement can be used to foil the changement of a simple attack, the double changement can be used to continue with the original intent. This is done by making a second changement off of the opponent's counter changement. The double changement begins like the counter changement, except as soon as the blades are re-engaged by the opponent's counter, the second changement is initiated, quitting the opponent's blade and taking the blade to the open line of attack. The second changement quits the opposing blade the moment they make contact.

The double changement, in conjunction with the counter changement, may be worked into the preceding exercises. The initial changement is offered, the counter executed and followed by the double changement and direct attack. All this does is change the beginning of the exercise; the final actions remain the same.

The Remise

In Chapter 8 you had a chance to work through redoubled attacks in the process of the reprise. With the addition of the changement as part of the simple attack, a direct attack may now be immediately renewed without withdrawal of the weapon arm. This uninterrupted continuation of the attack is known as a *remise*. If a riposte is not immediately offered by the defensive combatant, a disengage, coupé or half-disengage may be immediately executed, allowing for a continuation of the attack. Because the weapon-bearing arm is almost completely extended during this changement and redoubled attack, the remise is generally executed with a thrust or cutting from the wrist.

After a simple attack is successfully parried, a changement may be offered to the inside of the defending sword or across their body in the continuation of the attack. The half-disengage may also be used to offer a thrust or cut either above or below the parry.

In executing a changement with an extended arm you must maintain control of your weapon. If the point seems to waiver or float in towards the body, go back and practice some of the straight arm point work exercises offered in Chapter 4. Although executed from the straight arm position of a completed attack, these changements must still be executed with the same safety precautions described earlier.

A good exercise for practicing the remise is within the Offensive/Defensive blade-play drill. Combatant A attacks and Combatant B parries as in the drill, Combatant A then executes a remise with a disengage or coupé and reattacks the target, B counter parries and after the successful parry A moves on to the next attack within the drill. This exercise may also be taken on the exchange, around the clock, or from each of the engaged guard positions. The attack and the remise may be offered to all open targets on either side of the body.

The addition of footwork to this exercise is quite simple. On Combatant A's initial attack the footwork parallels that of the previous exercise. When A continues the attack, the Offensive/Defensive drill is repeated. On the remise, A shows, B reacts, A completes the attack. A variation on this is to remain stationary on either the initial attack or on the remise.

Simple Attacks on the Riposte

The riposte, or counterattack discussed in Chapter 8, may now be offered with a changement as part of the simple attack. The straight attack was explained as the primary form of counterattack, but now the disengage, coupé and half-disengage may also be used to execute effective ripostes. From the engaged placement of a successful parry, the defender may offer a changement to the inside of the offending sword or across the body, expanding the possibilities of the riposte. The half-disengage may also be used to offer a riposte either above or below the offending blade.

A good exercise for working the simple attacks and the riposte with a simple attack is to have both combatants come on guard in an engaged guard position. Combatant A executes a selected changement and direct attack. Combatant B parries the attack and offers a prearranged changement and riposte, the riposte being parried by A. This exercise can be taken from all the engaged guard positions and be riposted to all open targets on either side of the body.

The addition of footwork to this exercise is quite simple. On Combatant A's initial changement and attack the footwork parallels that of the exercise described above. When B offers the riposte, the pattern reverses. On the riposte, B is the offensive combatant, A the defensive.

Trouble Shooting

If you have a tendency during these changements to reach forward with the torso, especially during a remise, try the Sitting This One Out exercise offered in Chapter 4. You may also try the Guiding Hand exercise of Chapter 8. Both exercises are quite helpful in developing a sense of when you bend forward at the waist. This is quite important in the execution of these techniques because a leaning in of the torso can bring the point of the weapon inside measure. It is important that you maintain correct placement and a good On Guard stance as you work the weapon.

THE FALSE ART

The simple attacks of the true art are the fundamental actions of swordplay. The idea of attacking the open lines in the quickest and shortest path possible was believed to encompass the science of fence. Anything beyond the rudimentary actions were often considered base or false practices of the true science. These false actions went beyond the scope of simple changements and used tricks and extraneous movements of the blade to fool or set up the opponent in order to make a hit.

Although the false art was frowned upon by many schools of fence, its practices flourished. Apparently many swordsmen either didn't trust their own skills in the true art, or found holes in its theory, for deception and false actions were widely practiced despite the teachings of the true art of fence. The extraneous movements of the false art became known as compound attacks. The term "compound" was used because the actions require the combined movements of at least one false attack and a changement before the execution of the direct attack. Simply put, the false art consists of the combination of at least one faked attacked with the sword followed by whatever movements are necessary to avoid the parry of the opponent.

Although the tactics of fencing are not necessary on the stage, the concept and presentation are. Theatrical swordplay, no matter how distant from the sport, still needs to parallel it in a great many ways. There is never a point where one combatant is actually trying to "fool" or "set up" their partner in order to make a hit. Every action and reaction is pre-planned and rehearsed in order to avoid accident and injury. Yet, the presentation of "tactical" actions is imperative to a dynamic, theatrical sword fight. The aim of these actions is not to fool or deceive your partner, but to appear to deceive a character. These actions develop further skills with the sword that help in telling the story necessary to further character and plot. Thus, the tactics of fencing are the tools of the theatrical combatant.

FEINT ATTACKS

"A feint is, to shew the appearance of a thrust on one side, and execute it on the other. In this you should lead the adversary's wrist so much astray as to obtain an opening sufficient to throw in the thrust you have premeditated." [Angelo][5]

In the fencing world, *feint attacks* are any actions susceptible to misinterpretation by the opponent as to the nature and sincerity of their intentions. In a wide sense, feint attacks, or *feints,* may consist of movements of the arm, body, legs, or various actions of the blade aiming to upset, keep off balance, and disconcert the opponent. Their intent is generally to provoke the opponent's reflex reactions in order to take advantage of their responses. In stage combat, Feints are any action of the body or blade choreographed not to be met by a parry, avoided or land on the body. These are movements staged to appear as if they distract one's partner, test their reactions, or to draw an unnecessary parry and open a line for attack. They come in three basic forms: feints with the body, feints with the edge and feints with the point.

Feints With the Body

"Some, when making feints, move more with their feet than their swords, stamping as much as they can, trying to frighten the enemy and disturb him before striking him." [Fabris][6]

The Appel

Feints with the body are actions of footwork, physical movement or even sounds intended to frighten or disturb the enemy. The most common of these is the *appel.* This is a stamping or slapping of the floor with the sole of the lead foot. The action is highly characteristic of both the historic and modern Italian school of fence. The appel is generally executed immediately before an attack and is often accompanied by a loud shout. The "Hay" exclaimed in *Romeo and Juliet,* in regards to Tybalt's foreign fencing practices, is speculated to be an Appel. The "Hay" being the shout taught with the Italian practice of fence.

It is debatable that this action had any real effect on anyone but the most timid swordsman. In his text on the art of fencing Egerton Castle had this to say about the appel.

"In the days when idiocy played so large a part in fencing it was thought that the appel frightened the adversary. Of course it never frightened anybody over five, and served no purpose but to put the antagonist on his guard and to retard the attack of the booby who made it." [Castle][7]

---

[5]Angelo, p. 46.
[6]Fabris, translated by Castle, p. 101–102.
[7]Castle, E. *Badminton,* p. 42.

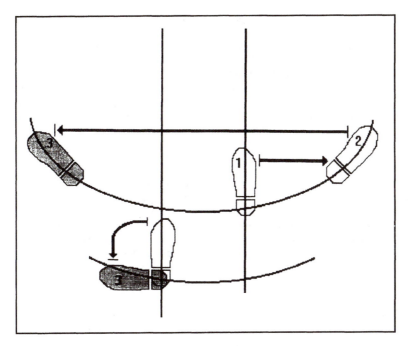

Figure 203. A Circular Feint. 1–2 a feint of a circle right. 2–3 a circle right pushed into a circle left.

Be that as it may, the appel is a common action of theatrical swordplay; especially transitional rapier play. The action is an audible and visual action that effectively communicates the intentions of the combatant. Whether executed with the "Hey" or not, the appel is a falsing action that often is used with a feint of the blade to frighten the adversary. Whether it has an effect is determined by the characters and the choreography.

Feinting with the Feet

Physical feints can be any false action executed by the body. These can be anything from a bob of the head to a twitch in the shoulder. The most common form of physical feints are usually some form of footwork that is initiated, but either drawn back or stopped short of its full execution. These can be advances, passes, lunges and so on, that are slightly exaggerated in preparation and initiation. The actions, however, are restrained or redirected once the desired response is gained. For example, a circle right could be initiated, the opponent perceiving the supposed threat removes themselves with a demi-volte. This being anticipated, the right foot is merely placed on the floor in the circle right to spring another action into motion. The foot was never intended to rest in that position. Instead, it is pushed off in the opposite direction into a circle left. The opponent, falling for the feint, completes their demi-volte, actually turning their back towards the real attack. This is known as a *circular feint.* (Fig 203) Feints with footwork may also be executed on the straight pace, sloped pace and traverse. Feints with the feet are generally accompanied with a feint attack with the blade.

Feints with the Edge

Feints with the edge are offensive movements made to resemble cutting attacks or the beginning of an attack with the edge. In theatrical rapier play there are two types of feint cuts: the *stop short* and the *set up*. The stop short involves a wind up, cue and first third of a full arm cutting attack. The action is then abruptly brought to a halt, prior to executing the final two-thirds of the cut. A set up is a feint cut aimed at a target on one's partner other than that which is the real object of the attack. Its aim is to set up the opponent, provoking a reaction or parry that opens the desired line. This type of feint cut contains the first two-thirds of the cutting arc prior to its redirection. The attack should be pushed sufficiently for the audience and thus your partner to take notice of it. It is generally directed against targets that are obviously uncovered, so as to appear really threatening. The redirection of the cut only takes place when the adversary acknowledges and begins to respond to the attack. Any cutting attack may be executed as either a stop short or a set up.

The Glissade Feint

Another form of feint with the edge is the *glissade feint*. This is the feint of a flowing attack on the blade. Basically it is the same as a regular glissade, only the action stops with the extension of the arm, the body remaining stationary. It is meant to draw a parry against which an attack may be made with a redirection of the point. The other attacks on the blade and pris d'fer cannot technically be falsed. The actions themselves are surprise attacks and therefore difficult to falsify. One could feint a beat, but the action and its intent would be lost to an audience. Therefore the flowing attack of the glissade is the only practical feint of attacks on the blade for the stage.

Feint with the Point

"Step not forth with your foote when you faine a thrust, but with the second thrust which you meane to speed your enemie withall, let then your foote and hand go together." [Swetnam][8]

The feint of a thrusting attack is the simplest of the theatrical feints. As explained by Joseph Swetnam, it's simply all show, no go. The body is rocked back in preparation of an attack, the arm punches the blade forward towards it target, but there is no extension made to hit. An appel or footwork may accompany this action, but the rock forward and physical "reach" is reserved for redirected attack. Feint thrusts may be executed in any line or manner that an actual thrust can safely be executed on stage.

Reacting to a Feint

All of the above feints—body, edge and point—must be executed in such a way that the audience, and your partner, can perceive the intended threat. If the "fake" attack does not appear real and dangerous, and its stop or change does not catch the audience by surprise, the intention of the feint is lost both dynamically and theatrically. If the intent is to fool the character, the entire body must be committed to the false action from its initiation until its termination or redirection. The feints must be mistaken by the audience for a real attack so as to provoke the desired defensive reactions from the opponent. The audience needs to believe and respond to the feint, or the character's reactions are incongruous and therefore unbelievable.

Of course, not every feint is successful, nor is every character going to respond in the same way. How a feint is executed and a character's reaction are dictated by the character and choreography. The way Macbeth responds to a feint delivered by Young Seward is completely different than Oswald's reaction if Edgar or Kent feinted an attack.[9] Generally a defending character has four options to a feint attack. They can remove themselves from the threat; remain unmoved without reacting; launch a counterattack into the feint; or make a parry to protect themselves from the threatening movement. If the person being attacked tries to parry, the aggressor must then initiate the second part of the compound attack and *deceive* the parry.

---

[8]Swetnam, p. 102.

[9]Shakespeare's *Macbeth* and *King Lear*, respectively.

Deceptions

The two major components of the False Art are the feint attack and deception of the parry. The deception, however, is the most crucial part of the compound attack. For if a false attack is parried, there is no deception and therefore no compound attack. The deceive, also called the *tromper,* is a changement executed during the final stage of a feint attack which avoids blade to blade contact with the opponent's parry, or parries. If the blade deceives only one parry, the attack is a *single feint attack.* Attacks which deceive two or more parries are double or *multiple feint attacks.*

Single Feint Attacks

Single feint attacks are the feint of a direct attack, followed by a deception of parry and ending with an actual direct attack in a different line. These consist of any of the feints of the blade described above coupled with a simple attack. Because the blades are not engaged in this technique, the deception is either a change under or change over. With the arm almost fully extended, the changement used to deceive the parry and the final attack, are executed in the manner of a remise attack.

Falsing the Cut

"And in all these ways to remember, that the blowe be continually different from the false: That is, if the thrust be falsed above to drive it home belowe: If within, yet to strike it without, [etc.]." [di Grassi][10]

Four hundred years after being written, di Grassi's tactics are still valuable instruction to the fencer and stage combatant. In offering feint cuts with deceptions, it is important to offer the feint in a completely opposite line for which the actual attack is intended. If you feint an attack to the head, deliver the real attack to the knees or groin. If you feint cut to the left shoulder, deliver the actual cut to the right thigh, hip or shoulder, and so on. The deception must set up your partner, and clearly open the other lines of attack.

For our purposes, when a feint cut is offered with a deception, it is generally a set up. The feint is aimed at a target on one's partner other than that which is the real object of the attack. As described earlier, the attack should be pushed sufficiently for the audience to take notice of the action. The changement only takes place after the parry is initiated by your partner.

Further Deceptions

The actions of the change under and change over are generally associated with transferring guard positions or changements in simple attacks. In feinted attacks with the edge, there are two other possible changements, the *cut over* and *cut under.* Both of these actions mimic the change under and over, but the deception is executed by pulling the blade and arm back from the false attack into the cue position for the actual cutting attack. This is generally done with wrist and elbow cuts because the broad action of the shoulder cut is too slow to effectively present a deception on stage. Once the parry is deceived, the true cutting attack is launched to the now open target.

Falsing the Thrust

"Likewise, you may proffer or faine a thrust two foot wide of your enemie his right side, and presently thrust it home to his breast, for hee will beare his rapier beyond the compasse of true defence." [Swetnam][11]

---

[10]di Grassi, p. 152.

[11]Swetnam, p. 120.

In historical swordplay, it was a common practice to feint a thrust outside the body in order to force a wide parry on the part of the defender. The parry being carried outside the body, "beyond the compass of true defense," would then be difficult to recover from in time to defend against the real attack. As described earlier, the body is rocked back while the blade is punched forward towards its false target. The thrust is made outside the body, and as the parry is executed the blade is refused, deceived with a change over or under and brought in line with the actual target. The body then rocks forward and the blade reaches towards the target. Feint thrusts are generally delivered to one side of the body while intended for the other. The deception however, may be taken to the inside of the blade on the same side of the body. The false thrust must be far enough outside the body that it effectively deceives the parry, but not so far outside the body that there is no appearance of threat: roughly six to ten inches. The thrusts may be executed in any line or manner that an actual thrust can safely be executed on stage.

Using the Piston Thrust to Deceive a Parry

"Some, when making feints . . . feign to carry their point forward, and when the adversary comes to parry, first draw in their sword and then hurl back the thrust." [Fabris][12]

Along with the change under and change over, the historical swordsman also used an action similar to the piston thrust to deceive a parry. Although this action was condemned by Fabris, it adds variety and dynamics on the stage. From a rocked back position, the blade is punched forward towards its false target. As the parry is executed, the blade is refused by jerking the sword backward away from the parry. Once deceived, the blade is shot back forward again with the body rocked forward and the blade extended towards the real target. The in and out action of the blade is much like the needle on a sewing machine. This, like other false thrusts, may be executed in any line or manner that an actual thrust can safely be executed on stage.

Parrying a Feint Attack

"For no man can tell whether the fained thrust will come home or not, but he which doth thrust it." [Swetnam][13]

Unless specified by character and choreography, most feint attacks bring about a parry. If the false attack appears real to the audience, the deception is true and the response of the character must fit what is happening on stage. What was true in actual rapier play should appear true on stage today, no one except the person who executes the feint should be able to tell whether it will hit. Therefore, although the feint is a choreographed action, the combatant must appear to respond to the implied threat of the attack and attempt to parry it.

The timing of a parry in this type of blade-play is quite important. A parry executed in the regular process of Action-Reaction-Action could accidentally meet the false attack, or appear like an actor's error to the audience. In the execution of feint attacks, the parry must be "late." It must be executed at the peak of the false attack so that the story of the movements is clear. The audience must clearly see the false attack, and believe its intention. The character then responds at the peak of the attack and begins the parry. The deception is initiated, allowing the parry to travel into an open line while bringing the offending blade around in preparation for the real attack. For an effective deception, the first "Action" should be the execution of the feint attack, not its preparation. The "Reaction" is the late parry, and the final "Action" is the deception and cue for the ensuing attack.

To further help in conveying the story to the audience, deceived parries are made roughly four to six inches wider than regular parries. This is done to illustrate the deception and the opening created for the real hit. The character's anticipation of meeting the offending blade generates movement

---

[12]Fabris; translated by Castle, pp. 101–102.
[13]Swetnam, pp. 102–103.

designed to stop an attack. The absence of the blade forces the energy of the intended parry to be released outside the body, sending the defending blade "outside the compass of true defense." It is important not to swing the blade out of line during a deceived parry. The misdirected blade could accidently strike the opposing weapon.

On stage the rhythm and duration of a feint is determined by the defending character's nervous condition, temperament and speed of reaction, not by the intention of the aggressor. If the defender is a nervous type, they can be induced to react with the slightest indication or simulation of an attack such as a stop short or an appel. If the character is calm or patient in nature, only a strong, committed attack can provoke their defensive reflexes. Obviously, many different characters exist between these two extremes.

Practicing the Single Feint Attack

When working on the feint attack, it is important to remember that the deception is executed at the last possible moment prior to engaging the parry. The timing of the deception is what makes the feint believable to the audience. The anticipated contact of the blades is replaced by a wide parry and relocation of the offending blade.

The changement after the feint is executed in the same manner as the changement in the simple attacks. For this reason, you may practice single feint attacks as you did the changements in the simple attacks, working both sides of the body and all open targets.

Taking the Feint Attacks Moving

After practicing the timing of the single feint, both cut and thrust, and the deceived parries, try adding footwork to the exercises. It is important that while focusing on the movements of the blade you do not lose correct distance. Measure is maintained in the following manner: The combatants will begin at correct distance; the initiator of the feint, A, begins the feint attack; the defending combatant, B, begins to pass back or retreat as they perceive the feint attack is in motion. B initiates their response with footwork, and as they move back they begin to parry. Combatant A does not move forward until the deception of the parry. For the purposes of this exercise, the deceive should be executed at the last possible moment, just before the opposing parry touches the blade (although character and circumstances may dictate otherwise in a production). As the parry is deceived, A moves forward with a pass or advance, as they deceive the parry. The feint attack is the first action, followed by Combatant B's reaction of footwork and attempt at parry, ending with Combatant A's final action of a deception of parry and advance or pass forward. Combatant A should complete the exercise in the cue position for a direct attack. This may be taken moving, or executed in stationary position. If the exercise is taken moving, the direct attack follows the standard rules of footwork combined with blade-play.

Multiple Feints

The second category of feint attacks are the multiple feints. Multiple feints are a combination of two or more single feint attacks. Because each feint and deception opens a variety of new lines, there are an infinite number of feints that may be executed together. Each feint must deceive its intended parry (or an appropriate defensive reaction such as an evasion). Once an attack is parried, the series of feints is ended.

The Doublé

Although there are a great variety of multiple feint attacks, there is one that is used with great regularity on the stage and screen, this is the *doublé* or double deception. The doublé is a multiple feint attack which deceives a direct parry and a counter-parry. For example, Combatant A feints a thrust to the left shoulder, Combatant B responds from Terza with a direct parry of 4. A deceives the parry of 4 with a change under and redirects the attack back to the left shoulder. With A's point now inside the sword, B responds with a counter-parry 4. Combatant A also deceives the counter-parry with another change under and redirects the attack to the right shoulder. Combatant B then executes a direct parry of 3 and finds the opposing blade outside the right shoulder. The doublé can be executed in any open line and with any combination of changements on the deception—but it must deceive a direct and counter parry. If the action is taken moving, the same rules apply as in a single feint. The aggressor's footwork is usually executed on the deception but may be performed during footwork such as a demi or grand lunge.

The Remise with a Feint Attack

If a riposte is not immediately offered by the defensive combatant, a single or multiple feint attack may be immediately executed as a remise. After an attack is successfully parried, a single or multiple feint attack can be executed to draw the defending blade to another line, creating an opening for a redoubled attack. Because these feints are executed from the straight arm position of a completed attack, the initial feint must either be of a thrust or cut from the wrist. If more feints follow, they may be either cut or thrust and of any variety.

Feints on the Riposte

After a successful parry, a feint attack may be immediately launched as a riposte. The feint may be either single or multiple. The initial feint should represent a straight attack to draw the parry. Once that parry is deceived the real attack may be launched or further feints may follow.

CHAPTER IN REVIEW

1. All actions of the blade (attacks and parries) must be determined prior to working any exercise.
2. In a simple attack, the transition from an indirect to a direct attack is immediate. Once the indirect attack is complete and the blade is safely directed to its cue position, the action is made.
3. All attacks must follow the proper mechanics of cue and response established in Chapter 7.
4. Changements can be executed in two ways; rounding the opposing weapon on the same side of the body; and across the body to the side opposite that of the engagement.
5. When changing across the body, any target that is exposed or open may be attacked.
6. Cutting attacks offered from a changement are generally an elbow or wrist cut.
7. Feints must be mistaken by the audience for a real attack, or the character's reactions are incongruous and therefore unbelievable.
8. Feints should be offered in a completely opposite line than for which the actual attack is intended.
9. Feints must clearly open other lines of attack.
10. Feint thrusts must be delivered off-line so that it may effectively deceive the parry.
11. Feint thrusts may be executed in any line or manner that an actual thrust can safely be executed on stage.
12. There are four options to a feint attack; to withdraw from the threat; to remain unmoved; to launch a counterattack; or to make a parry.
13. A deception of parry only takes place after the parry is initiated by your partner.
14. With parries of feint attacks, the parry must be "late," executed at the peak of the false attack.
15. Deceived parries are made slightly wider than regular parries.
16. Deceptions are generally executed at the last possible moment prior to engaging the parry.
17. Offensive footwork during the execution of deceptions is not executed until the deception of the parry.

Chapter 13

Closes and Gripes

"There is no manner of teaching comparable to the old ancient teaching, that is first quarters, then their wardes, blowes, thrusts and breaking of thrustes, then their Closes and Gripes, striking with the hilts, Daggers, Bucklers, Wrastlings, striking with the foote or knee in the Coddes [groin], *and all these perfectly defended in learning perfectly of the Gripes."* [Silver, p. 25]

As a swordsman you have now learned and practiced your stance, footwork, guards, cuts, thrusts and parries, and now in the manner of the "ancient teaching" you will move on to the *closes* and *gripes*. This is the rough and tumble portion of swordplay. Closes or "Close Quarter" fighting is when two combatants are inside normal measure, by accident, design or confines of fencing space, but can still wield their swords correctly. In this position they can strike with the unarmed hand, kick and punch their opponent. This type of swordplay is mentioned in the works of Shakespeare and his contemporaries and is referred to as "the close," "foot-to-foot" and fighting "at the half-sword."

Gripes on the other hand are techniques of swordplay that favor the locks, holds, grips and throws of wrestling. This practice is mentioned in disfavor by di Grassi and Saviolo, yet both masters point out that it is a common practice. The same examples are true in George Silver's *Paradoxes of Defence.*

"When two valiant men of skill at single Rapier do fight, one or both of them most comonly standing upon their strength or skill in wrestling, will presently seeke to run into the close . . . that being done, no skil with Rapiers availeth, they presently grapple fast their hilts, wrists, armes, bodies or necks, as in lustring, wrestling, or striving together, they may best find for their advantages." [Silver][1]

Despite the scholarly practices of the true art of defense, Elizabethan swordplay was probably anything but a polite encounter. Despite the rules of conduct and codes of honor that gentlemen followed to mount the field of honor, a sword fight was still a fight. The practiced techniques of the swordsman were only as good as their temperament. Social facades and feigned graces fell by the wayside as blood boiled or fear took the heart. Because of this the codes of dueling established in this period had gentlemen meet at dawn, after they had rested and were in their right mind and cold blood. With the heat of the moment passed, they could then rationally come to terms or settle their differences as gentlemen. Be this as it may, whether in the heat of the moment, or in cold blood, the

---

[1]Silver, p. 25.

fact that the combatants were in a life or death situation still removed the affected air of the fencing school. Emotions generally overrode logic and in the fray they would do what they had to in order to survive. For this reason Joseph Swetnam passed this advice on to his readers.

"For everie one will, in a quarrell, do what his affection leadeth him best to" [Swetnam][2]

There are no rules on the field of "honor." A classic example of this is the duel between the playwright Richard Sheridan and Captain Matthews. Sheridan, a close friend of the English master Angelo, fought two duels of honor against a Captain Matthews. It would seem that Matthews, a married man, was making advances toward a young singer named Elizabeth Anne Linley. Sheridan took it upon himself to protect her. Outraged by Sheridan's interference, Matthews publicly besmirched his character, forcing Sheridan to make a challenge.

Despite Matthews' years of experience in the army and in the fencing schools, the twenty-year-old Sheridan easily won the first encounter with a disarm. To save face, Matthews was forced to challenge Sheridan again. The second encounter, like the first, started with the proper punctilio of a meeting of honor, but after the first few exchanges it quickly went awry. It would seem that, despite all the rules, codes and procedures of gentlemanly conduct, when a man's honor and life are at stake, the only rule is survival.

Matthews tripped up Sheridan and the two men fell into a rough and tumble upon the ground. The fall broke both their blades as the two grappled and wrestled in the dirt. Neither Sheridan's nor Matthews' seconds[3] interrupted the combat and Matthews took the day by finally pinning Sheridan to the ground, with his broken blade, through the skin of the neck. Despite the wound and injuries received during the fight, Sheridan recovered, married Miss Linley, and settled in London becoming quite a popular playwright and member of Parliament.

In this affair of honor their swords were broken and the two men wrestled and grappled on the ground without any interference from their seconds. Notwithstanding the teachings of the True Art, the close and gripes of the ancient school obviously remained a common practice of swordsmen.

Knowing that a sword fight was more than just a fencing match opens the door to a great many possibilities concerning character and choreography. The choices a character makes during the fight can be quite telling to an audience. The degeneration of a sword fight to the "down-and-dirty" techniques of kicking and punching can depict the extremes of the situation and the state of the character's emotion. The contrast between these techniques can also be quite effective on stage. If one character insists on base combat and coming to the close while the other remains composed and ethical, their true nature is exposed for all to see. Take, for example, the fight at the end of Shakespeare's *King Lear*. Edgar may be incensed with Edmond, but he would probably never kick Edmond when he was down: it is not ethical and it is not in his nature.

Because this book deals specifically with the use of the rapier, and later the rapier and dagger, this type of rough-and-tumble "swordplay" needs to be addressed. The truth of the matter, however, is that the wrestling techniques of the gripes are more *hand to hand* combat techniques than swordplay. Hand to hand is the term for the unarmed fight techniques used in theatre and film and is a style of stage combat that would take a book of this size just to teach the basics. For this reason, this chapter can only touch on the basics of is part of swordplay.[4]

---

[2]Swetnam, p. 160.

[3]In a formal duel, most combatants had friends whose duties were to convey the challenge and see to arranging the details of the actual encounter. These friends were referred to as *seconds*. During the heyday of dueling, several conventions concerning the second developed, notably seconds were often expected to engage one another in combat, sometimes in an orderly fashion, sometimes like a brawl where any victorious member could then come to the aid of anyone he chooses. In more "civilized" duels a second could be expected to face the opposing principal, as well as his second(s) if his friend should not be able to continue.

[4]If you wish to explore unarmed combat further, you may consider reading Joseph Martinez's *Combat Mime*.

COMING TO THE CLOSE

"we/Have us'd to conquer standing on the earth,/And fighting foot to foot."[5]

Poop-Deck Fighting

Now that you have spent so many hours practicing swordplay at proper measure, it may seem a little odd to move inside correct distance and cross swords. There are however, some schools of theatrical combat that always work inside measure. This is done under the belief that the tip of the sword only shows a true threat when the blade is actually in the plane of the body. However, this is only true in film fights and intimate theatrical productions. On stage the points of the weapons are generally difficult to see and the reaching and removing of the combatants' bodies tell the story of offensive and defensive intentions. In film, however, the camera can be right on top of the action. If the shot calls for the profile of both combatants, the fights may need to be executed inside measure in order to see the blades and get both combatants in frame. This tight type of swordplay has been nick-named *poop-deck fighting* by famed fight master Patrick Crean. He coined the phrase when he worked with the likes of Errol Flynn in the swashbuckling films of the 1930s and 1940s.

When the combat is brought inside measure for this reason, it is a technical rather than tactical execution of blade-play. What this means is that if the fight is choreographed at the close because of the confines of the set or the needs of the camera, measure is closed not by the character, but by the choreographer. In these instances your fight director will explain exactly what they need in order to fit the specific demands of the set or shot. If you are working on a film, you may have to work the fight in a variety of ways depending on the camera angle. Measure and targets are two of the things most often affected by film fighting.

Closing measure in a fight for tactical rather than technical reasons is what makes close quarters combat exciting and dynamic to the audience. If the combatants are already inside measure, the immediate danger and contrast of the action is not apparent. The closes of rapier fence were tactical actions where the fencer deliberately closed measure with their opponent in an effort to enable them to execute specific offensive or defensive actions. The action could come from desperation or from practice, but in either case the idea was to get inside the point of the opposing weapon and surprise the opponent.

Close Measure

Combatants usually come to the close in two ways, either from an offensive or defensive position. On the offensive, the combatant either attacks the opposing blade with a beat or pressure, or removes it with a form of pris d'fer. This displaces the threat of the point and allows the combatant to move safely within measure. From a defensive position the fencer either parries and then closes measure with a blade-taking action, or executes a *step-in parry*. The step-in parry is a defensive action against a cutting attack that combines the mechanics of a standard parry while moving in to the close. All of the techniques are safe and acceptable as long as the blades are off-line and outside the body as the combatants close measure.

When you work in close quarters with the rapier, measure is generally closed by an action of simple footwork. This can be a pass forward, advance and so on. The actions must be active or you merely move forward a foot and do not effectively close with your partner.

Offensive Actions Inside Measure

When working offensive/defensive blade-play in the close, your blade should extend beyond your partner by no more than three inches. When checking measure, do not bring the point on line, but

---

Chicago: Nelson-Hall Publishers, 1988. Although unarmed combat cannot be learned from a book, it is a good, safe introduction to the art form.

[5]Shakespeare, *Antony and Cleopatra* III.vii.64–66.

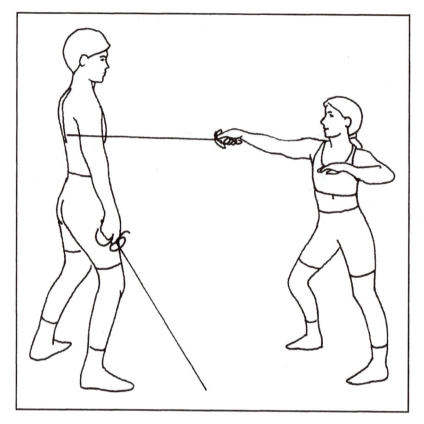

Figure 204. Measure for fencing at close-quarters.

rather bring it up outside your partner's body. If you were to guide the blade in, maintaining an extended arm, the foible of the blade would contact the side of their body. Your torsos should be no closer than four feet apart. If you move in any closer, it will be difficult to safely continue blade-play. (Fig. 204)

Cutting it Close

Inside the close, the most common form of offensive blade action is the cut. Point work proves difficult because the extended arm cue reads as a deliberate miss to the audience. Of the three cutting attacks, it is advisable to use only shoulder and elbow cuts. The extended arm of the wrist cut makes timing the parry quite difficult in the limited space. The cues of these attacks are also more awkward to read. In delivering shoulder and elbow cuts inside measure, your attacks must now be directed twelve to fourteen inches outside the body. This increase allows for the close-in parry to safely meet the middle of the attacking blade without force or opposition.

Now that you are inside measure, be sure that your wind ups are clear and outside the body and that any actions of the blade that cross in front of you stay within a foot of your body. It is also a good idea to check your parries, as any blade angled forward could become a threat to your partner. Be sure your parries are not wide and that your tip isn't angled toward your partner. When transferring the blade from side to side for various attacks, it is usually better to carry the blade behind you with a molinello than to cross in front of you. Remember, you and your partner are now only four feet apart; large actions in front of your body may accidentally strike your partner or their weapon. Be conservative in your actions in order to avoid possible accident or injury.

The Thrust

The practiced art of puncture play is contrary to the physical drive of coming to the close. Point work, however, is still used in this position by many fight directors and is necessary in some film work. Whether used on stage or screen, all thrusts must be delivered off-line. Any time you are inside measure, the point of the weapon must never travel towards the body. When working inside measure, the thrust's extended arm cue is ineffective. The extension of the arm, even in the rocked back position, carries the blade outside and past your partner before they parry. Such an action remains safe on stage, but it never appears as anything other than an intended miss.

To effectively launch a thrusting attack in close quarters you must draw the blade back in the manner of a piston thrust. From this withdrawn position of the blade the cue is issued. Unlike thrust cues at correct measure, the close proximity of the combatants allows for withdrawn arm cues to be adequately read. In the drawn back position of the piston thrust, a straight line with the blade from your right to your partner's left indicates a thrust to the left. If the blade is across the body to your partner's right, it is a thrust to the right. The position of the point of the blade denotes the target. If the point is angled up, it is a thrust to the shoulder; horizontal with the floor, it is a thrust to the hip; and angled down, it is a thrust to the knee. These cues are much like those of the wrist cut, the control point must be held during the rock forward, but the time between cue and reaction is extremely limited. Both the aggressor and defendant must concentrate on the actions to make sure that the cue, reaction and final action all work together. It is also important to note that thrusts can still be delivered three to six inches outside the body, but the aggressor must give in the wrist in the manner of an on-line thrust so that the blade can be carried outside the body with an in-distance parry. Do not resist the parry. The closer you are to your partner, the further your blade is carried to the outside by the parry.

Footwork in the Close

Although measure has changed and the practice of technique is altered in the close, the principles of footwork do not change. The size, scope and mechanics remain the same. The actions, however, are generally passive because active footwork is generally incongruous to the tight measure.

Parrying Inside Measure

While working inside measure the defensive actions of the hand, blade and arm do not change. The mechanics remain the same, but the parries are now made with the forte of the blade against the middle of the opposing blade. (Fig. 205) The parry is made "at the half-sword," hence the name.[6] If the attack meets the parry with too much force, the aggressor needs to deliver their cut further outside your body. It is important that you look at a parry prior to closing distance. Although all parries should be executed no more than fourteen inches from the body, some counter parries and other actions may travel out, towards the aggressor. If this is the case, you need to review the mechanics of these parries. If you are unsure of any parry, you can practice the technique facing a wall. This practice can be used to identify possible problems before an accident takes place. Reaching forward can cause an accidental collision of hands, swords or worse.

COMING TO THE GRIPES

The gripes are the real rough and tumble part of swordplay. As discussed earlier by Silver, they are "striking with the hilts, Daggers, Bucklers, Wrastlings, striking with the foote or knee." The

---

[6]Shakespeare, *Henry 4 Part 1* II.iv.164(182).

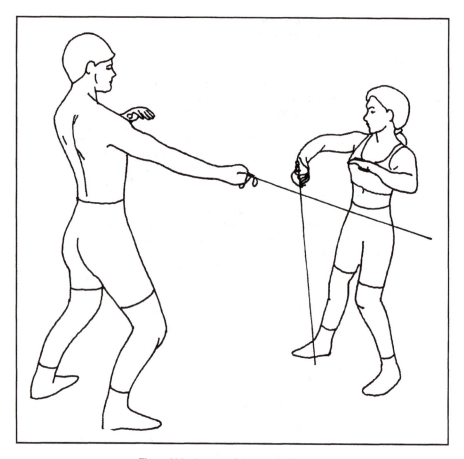

Figure 205. A parry of 1 at the half-sword.

punches, kicks and sundry body blows of the gripes are something that must be staged by your fight director. Hand to hand techniques are as exacting and meticulous in execution as swordplay. The actions must be safe, controlled, choreographed and rehearsed. Whether the actions are executed with or without a sword, they must be acted, not real.

In the techniques of this book, and in all physical encounters on stage, the victim must be in control of what is happening. It is important to remember that the physical conflict on stage is an *illusion*. You must be in full control of yourself and your weapons. A real push or shove, even a little one, can possibly get out of hand. Any time you are responding to a real physical action, you have ceased to act. When you are pushed, shoved, grabbed or made to fall, the immediate physical responses are yours, not your character's. Your reflex responses may well be out of place in the scheme of the play and scene, especially if you are injured in the tussle. By specifically staging each action, you are given the room to act because the environment is free of personal danger. Fear of accident or injury, or the accident itself, creates physical tension which in turn affects your movement and acting. For this reason, there is no actual force ever exerted on the victim in any of these actions.

The Corps-à-Corps

With this in mind, you will now work your first physical contact techniques. The most common form of gripes used in theatrical swordplay are known as clinches, or the *corps-à-corps*. The corps-à-corps (literally "body-to-body") is an action in which there is body contact or where the blades are locked together and distance is closed so that normal fencing action becomes impossible.

Although there are a great many forms and variations of the corps-à-corps, there are two specific forms used on the stage today; the corps-à-corps to the *hilts* and to the *grasp*.

To the Hilts

The corps-à-corps to the hilts is an active form of coming to the close. In this action the four foot barrier between combatants is eliminated and the initiator of the action moves right up against their partner. The hilts may be executed either from an offensive or defensive position. If you are on the attack, begin moving forward the moment you have been parried. You may close measure in any number of ways. The key to the action is to keep the blade engaged as you close measure. As you move in on your partner, they must keep their parry in place, allowing you to glide forward from your foible to forte. Be careful as you close measure, you need to be aware of your partner's feet and knees. Also, if you are attacking in a low line, be aware of the defending weapon's point as you come to the close. If your partner's parry is too tight, the point could possible stick you in the foot or shin. The completed action should find the rapiers hilt to hilt, and the initiator of the action at a measure where they can comfortably lean against their partner. Generally, if the right foot is forward, the right shoulder is brought against your partner and vice versa. The bodies must not strike one another. The attacking body needs to remain centered and balanced. The energy of the attack must be terminated into the floor with the forward foot. With a gap of two or three inches between the combatants at the completion of the action, they can safely lean in and touch one another without danger.

Although the hilts is meant to be an explosion of activity ending in a physical encounter, it must be practiced slowly. You and your partner need to walk through the movements to make sure that the footwork safely carries the body to the close and that the path of the weapons does not interfere with the physical movement. When working in the high lines it is important to keep the hilts outside the body and away from the face. Although this action can be executed in all manner of parries, the following example shows the process of the corps-à-corps to the hilts from a thrust to the right shoulder.

From a right dominant position, Combatant A shows a thrust to B's right shoulder. Combatant B reacts with a parry 3, and A completes their attack meeting B's parry. Immediately upon making contact with the parry, A initiates an active crossover step forward, passing left then right. The blades remain engaged and A's blade glides from foible to forte as they move forward, where their hilt comes to rest against B's forte. A is right dominant with their right shoulder about four inches from B's chest. The two combatants then lean in against one another applying controlled pressure. The controlled pressure allows the bodies to work against one another without pushing. From this position A can then deliver the line: "You've come to Nottingham once tòo often!" (Fig. 206)

Coming to the hilts can also be executed from a parry. The action is identical, only the action is initiated immediately upon completing the parry. Once you have parried the blade, instantly move in to the close. The blades remain engaged, sliding up the opposing blade to its hilt and into the corps-à-corps.

To the Grasp

The transition between the two forms of corps-à-corps, coming to the hilts and to the grasp, is as simple as taking hold of your partner's hilt with your unarmed hand. To the "grasp" is a sixteenth and seventeenth century term for seizing and wrenching the opponent's hilt or arm in order to take their weapon or break their wrist in the attempt. The action of coming to the close and the corps-à-corps remains the same and can be executed from both offensive and defensive positions. As the bodies come together you grasp your partner's hilt. (Fig. 207)

> *"but looke that you laie not holde of his arme, for if your enemie perceive it, hee maie change his Rapier sodainly into his other hand, & so have you at a great advantage, & therefore I teach you to laie hold on the hilts, because you have then commanded his sword surely."* [Saviolo][7]

---

[7]Saviolo, p. 51.

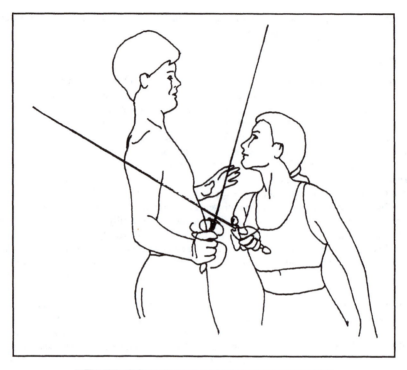

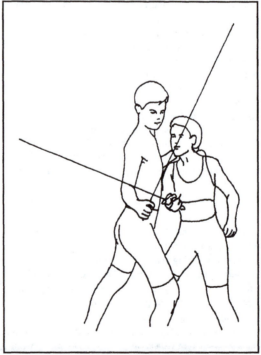

Figure 206. To the hilts, from a parry of 3.

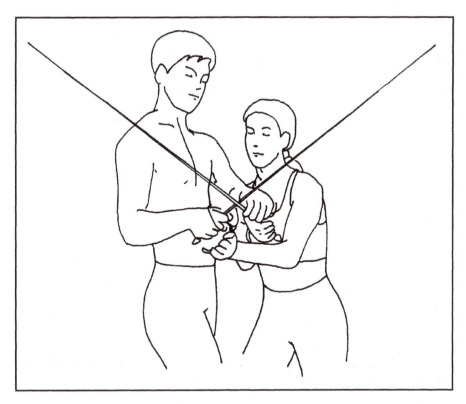

Figure 207. The grasp in a corps-à-corps.

Although this is good advice to the Elizabethan swordsman, in stage combat you must grasp either the hilt or forearm of your partnèr.

It is important, however, that you do not grasp their hilt too early. This could possibly knock or redirect their weapon as you come together. Generally, once you have grasped your partner's sword, they reply in kind and take hold of
your hilt. In this "struggle" both combatants must keep from manipulating the placement of their partner's weapon after they have made the grasp. Remember, there is no real struggle.

The grasp, and the ensuing struggle can end in a *disarm,* break or throw. The disarm is explained later; the break or throw uses the same idea as the reaction to a bind-away. One combatant can act as if they shove or throw away the other from the struggle. The victim can then react using a spin or turn like those offered in Chapter 9, or they can fling themselves in any number of other ways. The important thing is that the victim needs to be in control, even when throwing themselves. It is also very important to make sure that the blades safely clear both combatants during this action. The aggressor must physically "follow" the victim with their hands and arms to maintain the illusion of the shove, but there should be no actual opposition between the combatants. The presentation of proper physics is important in these stage shoves and throws; the action that initiates the victim's movement must be apparent and the force of the throw must match the size of the reaction. Remember, to every action there is an equal and opposite reaction. To keeps these actions safe, let the victim lead the movement. The aggressor then follows the action, allowing the victim to freely act the shove.

Variations and Modifications

The corps-à-corps can be executed in a great many ways in a large variety of postures and placements. A pris d'fer can be used to manipulate the opposing blade to a better vantage while initiating a corps-à-corps. The grasp can be executed with or without the bodies touching, the physical contact taking place in the grasp and not with the shoulders or torso. A classic example of this is the old "rabbit ears" or "scissors" grasp. This corps-à-corps is executed from the parry of High 5. Both combatants grasp hilts above the heads and then create an "X" with the blades and bring the hilts down to chest level. The blades point up and out to the side, each combatant's sword directed up, and off to their left. The cross of the swords is at chest level, and the combatants can lean in towards one another, glaring into each other's eyes. (Fig. 208)

DISARMS

A disarm is an action of the blade or body that forces the weapon from the hand of one's opponent in combat. The action is no longer valid in modern fencing, but it was taught by most of the old masters, and was a feature of swordplay until late into the eighteenth century. Stage disarms can be done in two ways, either by *securing the sword* or by *loosing the sword*. Both types of disarms can be used with good effect in theatrical combat, and have an endless supply of variations and styles. The following are some examples of this action.

Securing the Sword

To secure the sword is to wrench it out of the hand from a physical action such as the gripes. The weapon stays in the hand of the aggressor and is never free or loose on the stage. This is the safest disarm to be executed on stage because the blade is contained and controlled. In the gripes offered earlier, the combatants had the opportunity of executing a throw or a disarm from the struggle. If a disarm is executed, it is a securing of the sword, as each combatant retains the weapon of the other as they break apart. In these actions, as in all disarms where the sword is secured, it is very important that the victim remove their index finger from the ricasso prior to surrendering the sword. If the finger is not removed, it has the possibility of being wrenched inside the hilt as the blade is removed. It is equally as important that the aggressor have a firm grip on the sword prior to trying to remove the weapon. If this process is rushed in either way, the sword can be dropped or someone can get hurt. Go slowly in these disarms, be sure that both of you are ready before transferring from the grasp to securing the sword.

The Hamlet/Laertes Switch

> *"Laertes wounds Hamlet; then in scuffling, they change rapiers."*[8]

The scuffle and change of rapiers in the fight in the final act of Shakespeare's *Hamlet* is an example of a secured disarm. It is difficult to say what actually happened in period performance, but the common practice of grappling in close quarters and coming to the gripes indicates that this action could quite possibly be a transfer of blades such as a securing of the swords from a corps-à-corps. The mutual disarm and exchange of rapiers was a technique taught by di Grassi, the French Master Sainct Didier (1573) as well as other masters and schools of fence at this time, and could quite possibly be the action used in the original production. (Fig. 209)

Disarm by Beat Away

A secured disarm can be executed from a grasp by using the mechanics of the beat away offered in Chapter 9. The grasp is executed in the same manner with the swords coming to the hilts and your unarmed hand grasping the hilt of your partner's sword. Once the grasp is complete, you immediately draw your blade back about six inches, remaining engaged, and then execute the punch of a

---

[8]Shakespeare, *Hamlet* V.ii.306–307.

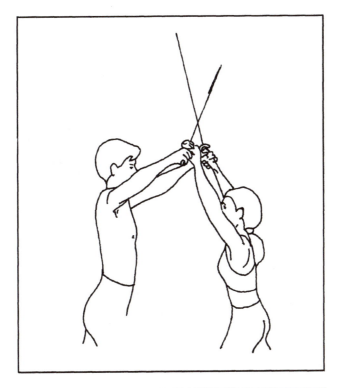

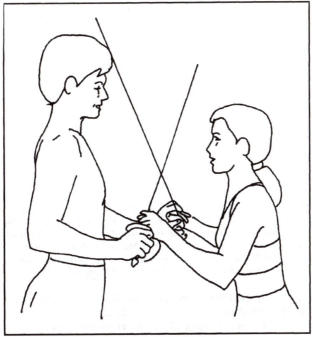

Figure 208. The "rabbit ears" grasp.

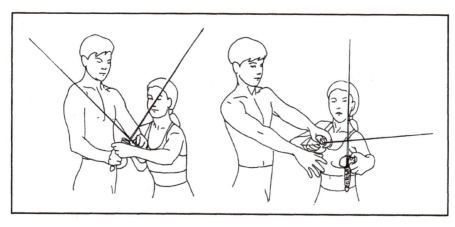

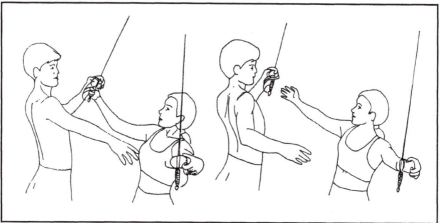

Figure 209. The Hamlet/Laertes switch.

beat away against your partner's forte. The action should not actually disarm your partner. The disarm is acted. Your partner should release the sword into your unarmed hand as your hilt "beats" it away.

The Wrap-n-Trap

> "*Yf he strike aloft at the left syde of yor hed, and run in wt all to take the Cloze or grype of you, then ward it gardant & enter wt yor left syde puting in yor left hand, on the insyde of his sword Arme, neere his hylte, bering yor hand our his Arme, & Wrape in his hand & sword undr yor Arme, as he cometh in, Wrestling his hand & sword close to your bodye turning back yor right syde from him, so shal he not be able to reach yor sword, but yo shall styll have it at lybertye to stryke or thrust him & endanger the breakinge of his Arme, or the takinge away of his sword by yt grype.*" [Silver][9]

The *wrap-n-trap* disarm, also known as the *serpentine,* is a secured disarm that uses the left arm and hand to grasp the sword. Although George Silver's description is difficult to read, it is one of the earlier versions of a disarm that developed with the art of swordplay and found a place in the

---

[9]Silver, p. 101.

works of eighteenth century fencing masters such as those of Domenico Angelo. The action is the combination of a demi-volte and grasp on the opponent's attack, and is executed as follows:

From a right dominant position, Combatant A shows a thrust to B's left shoulder. Combatant B reacts with a standing or demi-volte and a parry of High 1. A completes their attack, lunging inside measure with a grand lunge. B meets the attack with a detached parry and then carries their left hand and arm above A's blade and out to the left. (Fig. 210.a) A holds their blade in place for the completion of the disarm. The action of B's hand and arm continues around A's blade in a counterclockwise circle. (Fig. 210.b) The hand snakes around the blade and comes up on the inside near A's hilt. The inside of the upper arm then presses the foible into the armpit and the hand grasps the hilt from above. (Fig. 210.c) The arm is wrapped around the blade like a serpent, trapping it under the arm and in the grasp. From this position the sword can be secured and disarmed. (Fig. 210.d)

The grasp of the hilt was important in this disarm because without the sword it could be pulled from the arm, injuring the unfortunate combatant.

The wrap-n-trap is a fast, effective disarm that plays well on stage and screen. It must however, be practiced slowly to make sure the opposing point is not accidentally carried into the body and that your partner has time to remove their finger from the hilt. When properly executed, the action up to the grasp should be quite quick and fluid. If you are going to take the action directly into the disarm, it advisable for the victim to remove their index finger from the ricasso of the sword prior to executing the attack. This guarantees that it will not be jammed in the hilt. Just as in the other secured disarms, the wrenching of the sword from the hand must be acted. The sword is passed from one combatant to the other, not taken.

Grasping the Blade

> *"Therewithall take holdfast of the enemies sword, nere the hiltes thereof, yea though his hand were naked . . . All the hazards will be, if the enimie should drawe backe his sword, which causeth it to cutte."*
> [di Grassi][10]

Disarms are also possible by grasping the opposing blade rather than the hilt. As di Grassi points out, this action carries with it a certain hazard with the edge of the rapier. Historically the action could be considered, even with a naked hand, because the risk of injuring the hand was taken to avoid possible serious injury. On stage however, the naked hand should not touch the blade in order to help maintain the illusion that it is a sharp, dangerous, deadly weapon. If you are wearing gloves, however, the action can be justified as long as the blade is not pulled through the hand.

Loosing the Sword

To loose the sword is to wrench or beat it out of the hand with an action of the blade such as the bind over or *heavy parry*. In this type of disarm the weapon is freed from the hand, falling loose to the stage. Loosing the sword is the more complex of the disarms because there is a moment where the blade is in free fall and uncontrolled. This is where the disarm can become dangerous, and where you must pay close attention to exactly how you place the sword as it is freed from the hand. In these examples is not thrown or "whipped" out of the hand. These actions are random, and can send a blade bouncing or flying across the theater if not properly staged. A loosed blade must be controlled, sent to the same place, the same way, each and every time. If the blade is just dropped or tossed, it can possibly bounce back towards you or skid into another fight, the crowd, through scenery, into the orchestra pit, camera crew or the audience. For these reasons, the loosed disarms covered in this text are handled in the following manner.

To control the blade on a loosed disarm, the point of the blade needs to be secured on the floor prior to releasing the grip. The sword must be dropped onto the hilt without pushing or sliding the blade on the ground. It cannot be knocked or beaten out of the hand. The drop must be clean, separate from any of the acted actions of the disarm. (Fig. 211) This action should be practiced prior

---

[10]di Grassi, p. 150.

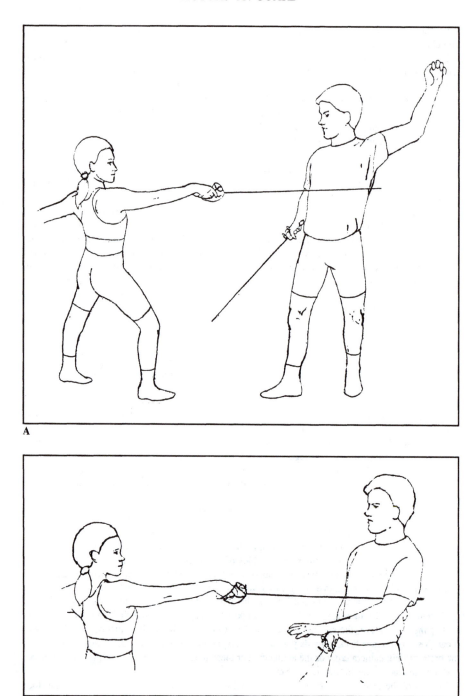

Figure 210. The wrap-n-trap disarm. **A**-Volte with left hand and arm raised; **B**-Bringing the hand and arm down.

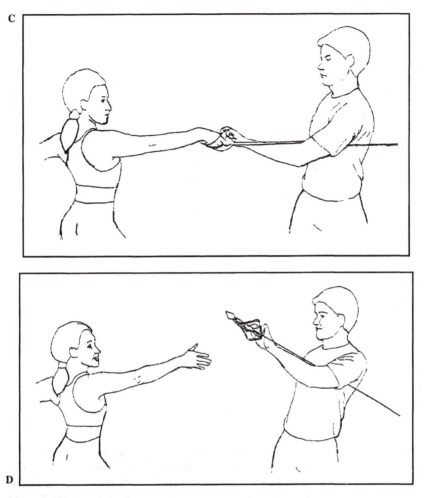

Figure 210. The wrap-n-trap disarm. **C**-Wrapping the arm around the blade and grasping the hilt; **D**-Securing the sword and disarming the opponent.

to working on the disarms. You need to be sure that the blade is controlled to the floor and that it does not bounce or travel from the place that it is dropped.

Disarming on the Bind Over

A loosed disarm can be executed on a bind over taken inside measure. The action of the bind over is executed in the same manner as described in Chapter 11, only for the disarm you move inside measure as the blade is taken over and to the floor. If the blade is taken over to your left, complete the action inside measure with the right foot dominant or vice versa. In this position you should either be to the hilts, or forte to forte with your blade on top of your partner's. Once in this position, you have two options for loosing the sword. You may either bear down on the blade, forcing it out of the hand, or you may use a beat away to "knock it" from the hand. If you are disarming by bearing down on the blade, the push on the opposing blade cannot be enough to bend the blades. Opposition between the blades is fine, actual tension and force is unnecessary. The press can be

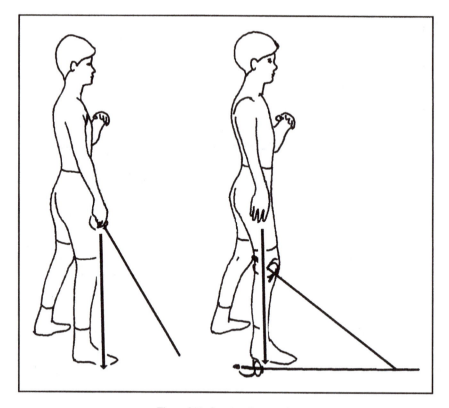

Figure 211. Loosing the sword.

played in an infinite number of ways, the extremes being either a slow strenuous struggle or a quick press of the sword into the floor. The sword may also be loosed with the action of a beat away. Once the bind is complete, immediately draw your blade back about six inches, remaining engaged, and then execute the punch of a beat away against your partner's forte. (Fig. 212) These actions should not actually disarm your partner; the victim should act the impact, and then release the sword in a separate action.

Disarming by Heavy Parry

The heavy parry is an action similar to the croisé, only taken to the floor inside measure. The action travels from a high line parry such as 3 or 4 down to the floor like a bind over, only on the same side of the body. The parry is executed as a step-in parry, but instead of coming to the hilts, you take the opposing blade to the floor. From this placement the disarm is executed in the same manner as the bind over.

Pummel Attacks

The other form of gripes to be offered in this chapter is the *pummel attack*. In medieval and Elizabethan swordplay, the sword's counterweight also served the purpose as an offensive weapon when in the close. The hilt of the sword and the heavy metal pommel made an effective bludgeoning weapon, hence, the term "to pommel" or "pummel" someone is still used today to represent pounding, beating or striking someone repeatedly, especially with the fists.

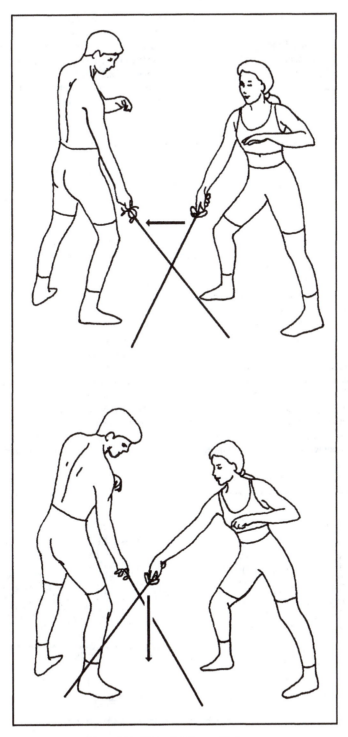

Figure 212. Disarming from a bind over.

The attempted pummel is an offensive action executed in close quarters where the pommel or hilt of the weapon is used to attempt an attack at the opponent's body. This action is referred to as an attempt because none of the pummel attacks offered herein actually land on the body. Each attack is stopped prior to reaching its goal. Some pummel strikes can be choreographed to hit the body, but these actions, like most of the gripes, fall under the hand to hand discipline of stage combat.

Pummel attacks are executed at the close where the combatants are roughly two to three feet apart. This distance is necessary because the threat of the attack must be immediate, and a greater distance between the combatants nullifies the intent of the pummel strike. If the attack does not appear as if it can reach its target, the reason for the action is unclear to the audience. Therefore, these actions are executed inside measure where normal fencing action is impossible.

The delivery of these attacks is actually fairly simple, using mechanics that you already know. The cues for the pummel attacks are those of the shoulder cuts offered in Chapter 7. You may also use the cues for descending diagonal attacks covered in Chapter 9. In close quarters, the large arm wind up of these actions presents the base of the hand and pommel to your partner. The path of the attacks matches those of the cuts, only the action stops at the completion of the first third of the cutting arc. The attack is not "pulled," the arm is stopped by its own muscles as it is reached forward. The pummel attacks can be executed to all twelve targets to which standard cuts are delivered. At close quarters, the stop of the hand and arm at the first third of the cutting arc keeps the blade away from your opponent and ensures control of the attack. (Fig. 213) The fundamental principles of safe cutting attacks are also applied to the pummel attacks.

The defensive action of a pummel strike is executed with the unarmed hand. Responding to the cue, the defendant brings their hand through their center and reaches out towards the attack. The hand must be open with its thumb against the hand in line with the fingers. Do not reach forward with the thumb open, away from the hand. This hand position could possibly jam or break the thumb if it accidentally meets the opposing arm at the wrong angle. The unarmed hand is reached forward and meets the attacking arm. The hand meets the attack in the middle of the forearm. You should not reach for the wrist because the hilt and pommel are close by, and the wrist itself has little musculature to protect it from any hard impact. Reaching for the center of the arm also insures that you don't accidentally hit your partner's elbow. The middle of the forearm has a strong muscle grouping, protecting it from accidental impact. This does not mean that there should be a percussive impact in this block. Aiming for the center of the forearm merely works as an added safety in case a blow accidentally comes in hard. The hand meets the arm, it does not stop it or knock it back. (Fig. 214)

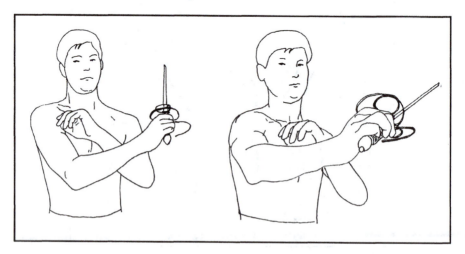

Figure 213. The pummel attack.

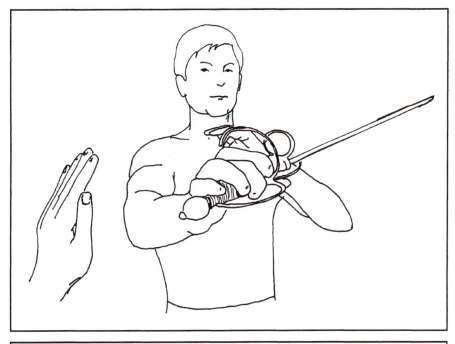

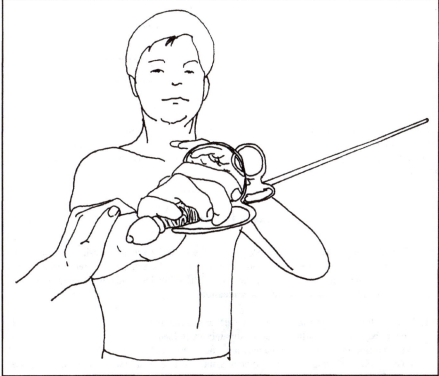

Figure 214. Blocking a pummel attack.

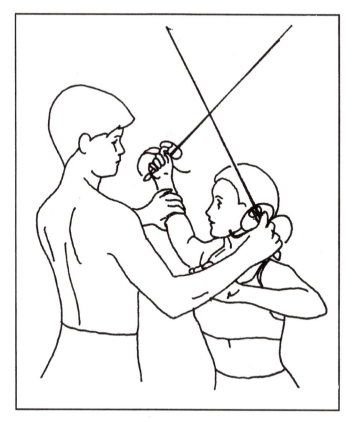

Figure 215. A corps-à-corps from successive pummel attacks.

Once an attack is stopped, you may then take hold of the arm with the thumb and act a struggle or throw. You may also deliver a counter pummel strike that your partner catches, locking the two of you in a corps-à-corps. (Fig. 215) In all these actions remember that the victim is in control and that stage combat is acted aggression.

Closes in Review

In a dramatic conflict the characters can come to the close by accident, design or confines of fencing space, but they must be choreographed to do so and the actions executed inside normal measure must be suited to the confines of the space. The following guidelines should be applied whenever two combatants come inside proper measure.

1. Measure for blade-play in the close is with torsos roughly four feet apart, your blade extending beyond your partner by approximately three inches.
2. When closing measure the combatants must be aware of their feet and knees.
3. When inside or closing measure, the combatants must be aware sword point and hilt placement. Do not bend or reach forward when inside measure. This can cause an accidental collision of hands or swords.

4. Cutting attacks delivered inside measure (generally shoulder and elbow cuts) must be directed twelve to fourteen inches outside the body.
5. Offensive preparations and cues should be clear and outside the body, and any action of the blade that crosses between combatants must stay within a foot of the body.
6. In-distance thrusts are cued from a withdrawn position of the blade. All thrusts must be delivered off-line. When inside measure, the point of the weapon must never travel towards the body.
7. In-distance parries are executed in the same manner as standard parries, only with the forte of the blade against the middle of the opposing blade.
8. When in a grasp, there is no real struggle. Combatants must not manipulate the placement of their partner's weapon.
9. Do not take hold of the opposing weapon before it is set. This could possibly knock or redirect the weapon when executing a grasp or disarm.
10. The naked hand should not touch the blade. Gloves must be worn if the blade is to be grasped.

Disarms

1. A secured disarm keeps the weapon in the hands of the combatants; it is never free or loose on the stage.
2. A loose disarm has a moment where the blade is free, released by both combatants.
3. All loose disarms must be controlled: sent to the same place, the same way, every time.
4. No disarms are thrown or "whipped" out of the hand.
5. In all disarms the victim must remove their index finger from the ricasso prior to surrendering the sword.

Hand to Hand

1. All armed or unarmed hand to hand techniques must be safe, controlled, choreographed, and rehearsed.
2. In all physical encounters on stage, the victim must be in control of their actions.
3. No unarmed techniques taught herein actually land on the body. Attempted pummel strikes are stopped by the aggressor prior to reaching their "goal."
4. When blocking a pummel strike, the defending hand must be open with its thumb in line with the fingers in order to prevent a possible jam or break the thumb. The hand meets the arms; it does not stop it or knock it back.

Chapter 14

Coming to the Point

*"Thrusts, though little & weake, when they enter but iii fingers into the
bodie, are wont to kill."* [di Grassi][1]

An armed encounter usually had two possible ends, disarm or death. A disarm could complete a
duel, the victor retaining their honor while showing mercy on their opponent. Such an action would
be common on a field of honor where both swordsmen are rational and in cold blood. The disarmed
opponent could admit their fault, ending the fight without injury, or they could press the point. If
the point were pressed, or if the encounter were impassioned and hot blooded, the fight could end
by a thrust or cut with the sword. Even if the wound received was not itself fatal, the lack of proper
medical techniques could allow infection to slowly take the swordsman's life. This could be one
reason why over 40,000 French gentlemen died by the sword in single combats in a span of less than
two hundred years.[2]

Like the armed encounters of the sixteenth and seventeenth century, the theatrical duel can end
in a draw, disarm, wound or kill. The disarm, although effective, generally is not the terminating
point in a dramatic encounter. Blood boils on stage and emotion drives the blade forward. When
conversation ceases to resolve the internal contention between characters, words fail and the conflict
comes to the point: the point of the sword.

THRUSTING HOME

The idea of thrusting at your partner was first explored in Chapter 9, where you worked with the
on-line attacks. Measure and proper technique were your safety barriers. Here, however, thrusts that
hit home close measure and actually make contact with your partner's body. This presents a whole
new series of concerns. The idea of closing measure and hitting your partner with a thrust seems
contradictory to all established safety rules. To avoid actually "hitting" one's partner, the old school
of stage combat either made an actual touch with fencing blades or had the sword slapped up under
the victim's arm. With fencing foils the touch is possible, however the blade is not serviceable for
theatrical swordplay and on the thrust home, it bends on impact. In this, there is no illusion of

---

[1] di Grassi, p. 40.

[2] *"The latter half of the sixteenth century saw, with the disuse of the judicial duels, the rise of that extraordinary mania for private duelling which cost France in 180 years the useless loss of 40,000 valient gentlemen,
killed in single combats which arose generally on the most futile grounds."* [Castle, p. 55.]

Plate XXI: A thrust offered from a grand volte, piercing the opponent's head. Cappo Ferro (1610)

penetration or of injuring the character. The second solution, the old "armpit kill," is a standard cliché of bad stage combat. Most actors have seen productions where at the crucial moment in the fight the aggressive blade is placed under the arm of the victim, somewhat akin to the wrap-n-trap, with the point sticking out the back several inches. The blade is obviously along side the body, yet the victim coughs, sputters and falls to their death. Despite everything that has happened before, at this point the fight is safe, but completely ineffective. If the climax of the fight fails, the fight fails. A laugh from the audience as Hamlet kills Claudius destroys the culmination of the piece. From the onset of the play Hamlet has been driven to this tragic moment, if there is no payoff, or if the payoff is humorous in delivery, the essence of the tragedy is lost. Kills must be safe, but they also must be effective.

Misdirecting the Point

The thrust home delivered on stage today is rooted in the idea, but not the mechanics, of the old "armpit kill." The blade needs to be taken off-line, to the side of the body to safely execute a kill. The idea of thrusting on-line, like the thrust of the foil, is completely uncalled-for and extremely dangerous with the weapons used on stage today. Dulled and buttoned stage weapons can still penetrate flesh; therefore *none of the thrusts at the body presented in this text will land on the point.* Kills and wounds with the point of the weapon will always be directed off-line, outside the body.

For effective thrusts to the body, a technique called *misdirecting the point* is used. Misdirecting the point gives the illusion of the blade traveling forward towards the victim, while safely angling the point outside the body. This presents the illusion of a forward stab or thrust without actually threatening the target. The hand and arm travel in a straight line toward the victim, but the wrist turns the blade off-line, directing the tip of the weapon about three to six inches outside the body. (Fig. 216)

Before moving on in the mechanics of the thrust home, you should take some time to practice misdirecting the point. First you should try this at standard measure (at full extension, six to ten inches from your partner's chest). From a rocked back position, extend your hand and arm on-line towards your partner's belly. Your hand is in the middle/vertical position. This is done so that the flat of the blade is presented to your partner and not the edge. The tip of the sword is directed to your partner's left flank (the fleshy area between the ribs and hip bone), three to six inches outside the body. The point of the weapon is always off-line. It does not flick out during the extension, the

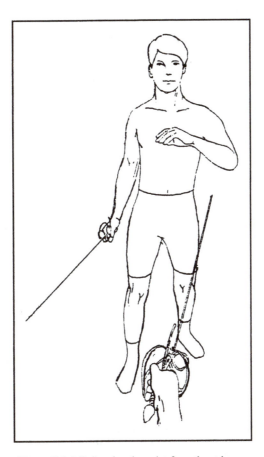

Figure 216. Misdirecting the point for a thrust home.

extension begins with the point off-line. The show, or cue of the thrust should complete with your arm at full extension, directed on-line, at your partner's center. The tip of the sword must be at the level of your partner's flank, three to six inches outside their body. Practice this action until both you and your partner feel confident with the technique.

Proper Measure

Once the technique of displacing the point is practiced, it needs to be moved inside measure. For our purposes, this will be done with the execution of a demi-lunge. Unlike the closes in the previous chapter, the point of the weapon should not pass the body. The problem with the armpit kill is not in the attack to the side, it is in the weapon's placement and the masking of the technique performed by the victim. When a blade is seen protruding out from under the arm, it tells the audience the blade is not inside the body. Therefore, the thrust home must be executed in such a way that the foible of the blade is placed in line with your partner's flank, without letting the tip travel past their body.

To effectively find this placement, start at standard measure and execute a demi-lunge. From the demi-lunge check measure by extending the sword arm and placing the flat of your blade on your partner's flank. The foible should rest on the muscles on the side of the body, with the tip free and to the rear. (Fig. 217) The point of the weapon must not be directed into the side. This generally happens when you are not close enough to your partner, or when you are working with a thinner

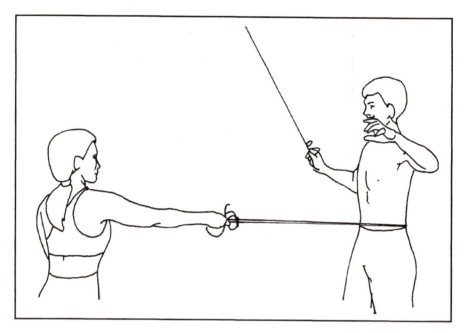

Figure 217. Correct measure for a thrust home.

combatant. If you have a thin partner, it is best to err on the side of safety. To avoid the possibility of the point hitting the flank, the thrust may be taken deeper, extending roughly an inch past the body.

The exact depth of the demi-lunge will vary between combatants. The reach of your arm and size of your feet affect the size of the step. The size however, is not the issue. Because the kill eventually needs to be executed from any variety of distances, the placement of the blade is the focus of this exercise. Where the blade is placed never changes. After you have found the correct placement of the blade, work the attack in conjunction with the demi-lunge.

Starting at standard measure, rock back and extend your hand and arm into the cue placement of a thrust home. Your partner reads the cue and reacts by making sure their left flank is open and that their left hand and arm are outside or above the intended target. Once their reaction is perceived, you may continue with the attack, executing a demi-lunge inside measure, with your hand and arm on-line towards your partner's belly and the tip of your sword at the level of your partner's flank, three to six inches outside their body. Your partner does nothing during this. They should not try to "act" the hit while you are still practicing the placement of the point. Unexpected movement of their body can be dangerous. Make sure they keep still. After completing the lunge, bring your foible in to check measure. This should be practiced slowly at first, but it eventually needs to become a seamless progression of action-reaction-action like the standard thrusting attacks. Because the reaction is not the beginning of a parry, eye contact is crucial to this technique. Be sure to get the "O.K." signal from your partner's eyes prior to focusing on the target. Communication is one of the key elements to safety, and is crucial in techniques where the blade makes contact with the body.

Reacting to the Hit

If a reaction is weak, the action loses its validity no matter how well the attack is executed. Such a reaction is the second failing of the old "armpit kill." In actuality, a stab or thrust with a rapier would hit the body like a punch to the stomach. The reaction would be immediate and violent. The blade does not easily push inside the body, it forces its way in. For this reason you need to work the mechanics of the reaction alone before putting the entire piece together. Although the blade is placed on your side, you must act as if the hit were in the center of the belly. To do this you need to first work on contracting your mid-section.

Standing in the On Guard stance, take your left hand, make a fist and place the palm side of the fist in the middle of your stomach right around your belly-button. Now, take your right hand and place it over the left fist. Relax your stomach muscles, and then apply pressure, pushing your fist into your stomach. (Fig. 218) Do not resist the action, but let the push of the hand drive the stomach and your mid-section backward. The body remains directed forward, erect and in proper placement. You will find that you do not bend over in this exercise as some people are wont to do when acting stabbed. The pressure point of the hand hinders the action of bending forward. To break at the waist and bend forward, the pressure of the hands would need to be lower, and pushing up rather than back. This is also true of a thrust with the rapier. The blade, like your hands, pushes the mid-section back while holding the torso up. It would be almost impossible to bend forward with six inches of steel pushed horizontally into the belly.

After pressing into your stomach several times and getting a feel for the physical contraction of your mid-section. Try working the reaction without applying pressure with your hands. Now you may open your left hand and place its palm lightly on your stomach and allow your muscles to draw your mid-section back. Do not shoot your butt out, draw your stomach backward. The action must still originate at the stomach. Practice this slowly at first, making sure that your body remains erect while your mid-section contracts. If your body responds in the same manner as when you pushed, you may move on. If you are having difficulty contracting the body without pressure from the hands, go back to pushing. Here you can slowly transfer the control of the action from the hands to the body by decreasing the effort of the push each time you repeat the action.

After you have practiced the contraction several times, you need to practice the movement as a reaction to a hit. To do this, stand ready in an on guard position with your left hand at roughly chest level, outside the body to your left. When you are ready to take the hit, bring your left hand down and lightly slap it onto your belly. The slap is the hit of the sword and the reaction should be immediate. Your left hand will remain on your stomach, cradling the wound. Be sure that your technique does not become sloppy as you pick up the speed of this action. Your body must remain erect. Aside from being anatomically incorrect, if you bend at the waist during a sword hit, you have the potential of hitting your head on your partner's sword hilt. Keep your head and torso up, eyes

Figure 218. Practicing contractions.

on your partner. Dramatically, this is also a better picture—featuring the relationship between the combatants rather than focusing on the floor. Also, be sure you are centered as you do this. If you waiver or shift in your feet you have the potential of moving into the path of your partner's blade. Stay balanced and grounded.

Working the Kill

Now that all the mechanics are understood and practiced you may move on to executing the thrust home. Although the hit can be delivered to either side of the body, you have practiced the action for a take on the left so the kill will be described in this manner. If you wish to take the hit on the right after practicing the one on the left, the mechanics are simply reversed.

The attack is executed in the same manner as described above. From a right dominant position Combatant A rocks back and gives the cue for a thrust home. Combatant B reacts, clearing their left hand and arm out of the path of the thrust. A perceives the reaction and continues their attack, executing a demi-lunge inside measure. (Fig. 219.a) This is where the energy of the attack is passed from the aggressor (Combatant A) to the victim (Combatant B). Immediately after the lunging foot is secure on the floor, A lays the foible of their blade in against B's flank. At the same time B brings their left arm down against their side, resting their forearm on A's foible while bringing their left hand into their stomach for the contraction. (Fig. 219.b) B's left hand now cradles A's blade, catching the weapon on the cup of the hand; thumb above, fingers below. (Fig. 219.c) B can apply pressure onto the blade to take it into their center. The flat of the blade should be against their side, thus allowing a slight give in the foible. (Fig. 220) Here the blade appears to be in B's mid-section, and the blade can be withdrawn without having to move B's hand or arm. This gives the illusion of the blade being drawn out of the center of the body and not from the side.

The timing of the thrust home must be painstakingly practiced. If the action is rushed, the victim could possibly carry the point of the attacking weapon into their stomach. Once mastered, however, this "kill" can be performed in the round without giving the trick away. The victim's left arm hides the blade as it rests on the flank, completely masking it from the audience. To further help in the illusion, the victim can release the shoulder opposite of the hit, accentuating the opposite side of the body. By releasing the shoulder forward the body turns slightly, allowing the blade to appear more centered in the mid-section. Do not turn in the hips and pelvis, however, as this is an incongruous reaction to the projected hit. A straight thrust into the center of the body would not turn the pelvis.

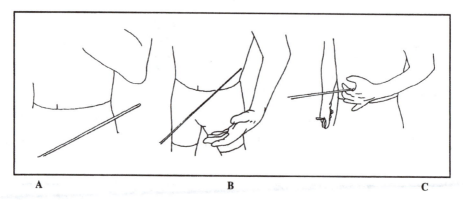

Figure 219. The Thrust Home. **A**-Point off-line, at correct measure for a kill; **B**-Bring the arm down to mask the sword; **C**-Cupping the blade in the unarmed hand.

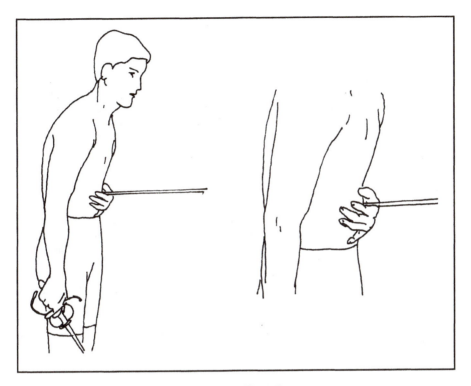

Figure 220. The Thrust Home.

Retracting the Blade

In order to maintain the illusion of hitting home on a thrust, the blade should not be left in the body for an extended period of time. This does not mean it must be an instantaneous in-and-out, but it should be quick. If you are the aggressor, be sure that the blade is withdrawn in the same path that it went in. A straight line thrust must be retracted in a straight line, or it becomes a cut. This is also important so that the point of the weapon does not flip up toward your partner's face. The action should be slightly akin to the withdrawal of a piston thrust. The withdrawal of the blade must also appear difficult. The victim's muscles have grabbed onto the blade, thus requiring effort to retract the blade. A thrust must never look as though the blade travels in and out of butter. It is a violent action against a living organism and it takes effort. Because of this the victim must also react to the withdrawal of the weapon. If you are the victim, your left hand must stay in place, allowing the sword to slide along your side and out from your hand. As the blade is withdrawn, the contraction is reversed and your stomach and mid-section are violently jerked forward.

Falling to the Floor

If the wound is a "kill," it will not take you instantly to the floor. Do not run a wonderfully safe and dynamic sword fight and then haphazardly throw yourself to the ground. Aside from being dramatically ineffective, your knees, wrists and other joints could easily be hurt from the fall. The "death" should be a comfortable collapse, a fade to black where you are in control of every action. A free-fall is not a controlled action and can prove dangerous. If you fall and are injured, the first words out of your mouth will probably not be in character. Stay in character, stay in control.

The Wounding Thrust

"But a small pricke of a rapiers pointe maie either kill, or at least maime." [Saviolo][3]

Because there is no real resistance on the thrust, and no actual push from the blade, the severity of the thrust can be increased or decreased depending on how it is played. The dynamics of the hit and the reaction of the victim tell the audience the gravity of the blow. Conversely, the severity of the wound determines the size of the reaction. The degree of the thrust, to kill or maim, must be established by both combatants prior to executing the action. The presentation of proper physics is important in the hit with a sword as it is in all stage combat. Actions and reactions must match in value. Remember, to every action there is an equal and opposite reaction.

Working the Wound

After you have practiced the thrust home and are comfortable with its mechanics, try working it in with variable blade-play. Start stationary, working a few cuts or thrusts before launching the thrust home. Do not improvise this pattern. Use an exercise like playing the numbers and end the routine with a hit. You may also try combining the thrust home with an attack on the blade or pris d'fer. Try different ways of removing the opposing blade to create an opening for the hit. It is important that you get a feel for executing the thrust home out of a series of moves, because that is the way it will generally be presented to you in choreography. Once you have practiced this, try working the routines with footwork, practice the hit from different measures and from different planes of footwork. Be sure to work everything slowly to ensure control and safety before picking anything up in speed.

CUT TO THE QUICK

Unlike the thrust, there are two ways of delivering an edge blow. The cut can be drawn like a razor or hacked like a knife. Each of these can be delivered in any number of ways, striking various parts of the body. Although the drawn cut was more common in Elizabethan rapier play, both types can be used to good effect on stage.

Draw Cuts

"It is to be understoode, that all edgeblowes ought so to be delivered, that they may cut: for being directly given without any drawing, they cause but a small hurt." [di Grassi][4]

Most of the treatises on the science of fence written during the sixteenth and early seventeenth century advocate that when a cut is used, it should be drawn. To be hit outright with the sword did not guarantee that the blade would cut. A pulling action after the blade landed better insured severing of the opponent.

". . . In delivering of a great edge-blowe . . . [one should] *drawe or slide his sword, thereby causing it to cute: for otherwise an edge-blowe is to no purpose, although it be verie forcibly delivered, especialy when it lighteth on any soft or limber thing: but being drawen, it doth every way cute greatly."* [di Grassi][5]

---

[3]Saviolo, p. 96.
[4]di Grassi, p. 50.
[5]di Grassi, pp. 150–151.

The *draw cut* on stage is a combination of the standard cutting attacks offered in Chapter 7, coupled with the closes offered in the previous chapter. Although the cut is executed inside measure, the mechanics of the piston cut are used to guarantee that the blade does not strike the body.

The most common form of draw cut is executed from the elbow, although there is a form of wrist cut executed inside measure called a *flick cut*. The large action of the shoulder cut will be covered later under the *swashing blow*. Although the draw cut does not strike the body, it does make contact. Because of this, it can only be delivered against targets that support large muscle groupings. These would be the shoulders, hips (at the flank), and knees (at the quadriceps). Do not attempt a contact blow to the head.

When you close measure for a draw cut it is generally with a lunge, full pass, active advance or pass forward. For most draw cuts you will come to the close in the same manner as the close quarter combat of Chapter 13. Measure is set with your blade extended beyond your partner by roughly three inches and your torsos no closer than four feet. Starting at standard measure cue the attack, perceive the correct reaction and close measure. Inside measure continue the piston cut. The blade stops three to six inches outside your partner's body. Immediately after the energy of the cut is sent forward with the piston, lay the foible against the body in the same manner as the home thrust. In this attack however, bring the edge and not the flat of the blade against the body. By separating the action of the cut from the movement that contacts the blade with the body, your partner is not struck by the attack. The placement of the foible on the body is then accompanied by the instantaneous drawing of the sword across the target. This is the draw cut.

The cut of the blade should be pulled back or across the body, away from the target. For example, if a cut is delivered to the right shoulder, draw the cut back to your left or across your body, back to your right. If the cut is made to the left knee, the sword is drawn back to your right or across the body to the left. In either case the edge of the blade needs to be drawn along the target in a straight line. (Figs. 221–222) This is done to show the action of the cut. Like the retracting of a thrust, the drawing of the cut requires effort. The bite of blade into flesh should have the pull of a dull steak knife on under-cooked meat. The victim's muscles resist the cut, making the action more of a rip than a slide of the blade. Because of this the victim must also react just as that under-cooked steak would react to the pull of the knife. If you are the victim, the part of the body being cut is jerked forward with the cut of the blade. Be careful that following the cut does not take you off balance. Remain in control so that you can effectively play the moment. If you over-react and stumble towards your partner, you run the risk of toppling onto the withdrawn point of their sword.

Working the Draw Cut

The timing on the draw cut is what makes the action read as a hit. The transition from the piston cut to the placement of the blade and its following pull must be one seamless action. It should be practiced first with the victim remaining neutral as the cut is executed. This means that the focus of the first practice session is not placed on the acting of the cut, but on the delivery of the mechanics. Until the cut can be safely delivered with some speed, the victim must not react to the pull of the cut. Only after constantly working the action can the victim respond to the jerk of the blade.

After you and your partner have practiced the cuts on all six targets, try working it in with variable blade-play. Like the thrusts, start stationary. Use an exercise like playing the numbers. Make the final action of the pattern a feint attack. From there you can deceive the parry and close in for the cut. You may also try executing the cut after opening a target with an attack on the blade or pris d'fer. Once you have practiced this, try working the routines with footwork. Be sure to determine exactly what actions you will use in these exercises. Do not improvise movement. Set a pattern of blades and footwork and practice it.

Flick Cuts

The *flick cut* is basically the same action as the draw cut, only the cut is delivered with wrist. This cut is less brutal and can be used to startle or intimidate an opponent rather than cripple them.

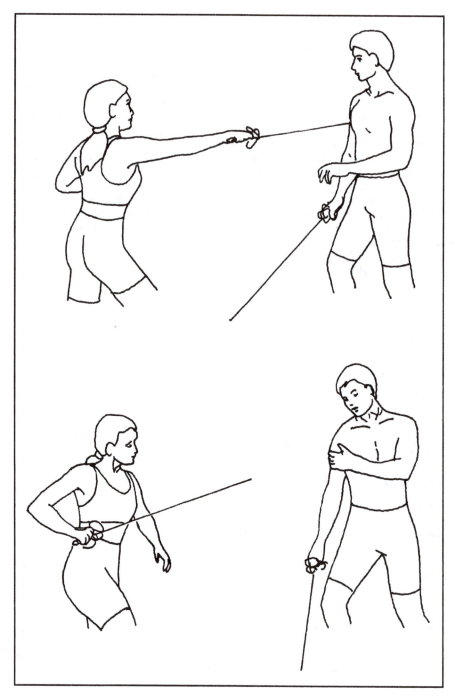

Figure 221. Drawing the cut, from left to right.

Figure 222. Drawing the cut from right to left.

Because of the ''delicate'' nature of this cut, it is an action more often used in transitional rapier play. The procedure of executing the flick cut follows the same steps as the draw cut. The cue is given at standard measure and then the attack is moved inside, stopping the cut roughly three inches outside your partner's body. The draw of the cut is executed in the same way, only the emphasis is much smaller. These cuts move much more quickly than the draw, scratching the opponent rather than cutting into them. Because of this the blade does not pull the body forward, but the body pulls away from the cut in a relaxed action like the startled response to a paper-cut. These cuts can safely be delivered to the six body targets covered above and should be practiced in the same manner as the draw cuts.

Soft Parries

Soft parries are defensive actions against the standard thrusting attacks, executed on an evasion, that meet the arm of the aggressor instead of the "hard" steel of their blade. This action is sometimes also referred to as a flick cut, but the defensive nature of the move has made the term soft parry more widely accepted. The "parry" places the foible or middle of the blade onto the middle of the aggressor's forearm, usually on the inside. The movement of the defensive hand is an exaggerated execution of a standard parry, much like the extended parry used in the beat attacks of Chapter 11. The arm is extended forward in that manner, and the foible or middle of the blade is placed on the arm with a turn in the wrist similar to the placement of the draw or flick cuts. The blade is not cut into the arm, the parry carries the arm and blade out, and then the action of the flick cut is executed at the completion of the extended parry. Although the soft parry can be expected against any standard thrusting attack, the following two examples should serve to represent the mechanics of the action.

A soft parry defending the left shoulder: From a right dominant position at standard measure, Combatant A shows a thrust to B's left shoulder. Combatant B reacts with a diagonal avoid backward (SE) on the right foot, and an extended parry of High 1. A completes their attack with a grand lunge. At the completion of the extended parry, Combatant B flicks their blade up under A's arm, meeting the middle of A's extended forearm. (Fig. 223) The extended parry must place the blade close enough to A's arm that the flick does not strike the arm, but places the blade safely on the arm on the muscles between the wrist and the elbow. From this position A can freeze (for fear of being cut) and B can force A to hand their sword over. Due to the measure of this action, the grasp

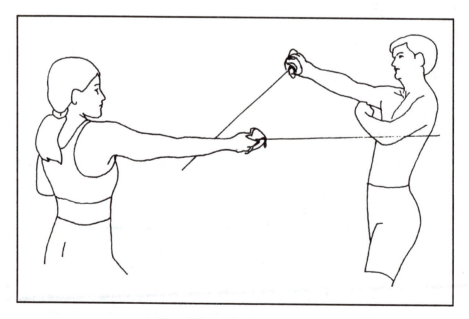

Figure 223. A soft parry of High 1.

Figure 224. A soft parry of 2.

of the sword should be executed on the blade and not the hilt. With or without the disarm, B may then execute a draw cut on A's arm. The cut may be executed instantly after contact, in the manner of the flick cut, or a pause may be played after the blade placement for dramatic tension. When the arm is cut, A must not react and drop the sword from this height. The sword could bounce or skid as it hits the floor.

A soft parry defending the right hip: From a right dominant position at standard measure, Combatant A shows a thrust to B's right hip. Combatant B reacts with a backward lunge, a traverse left (W) on the left foot, or possibly a diagonal avoid forward (NW) on the left foot and an extended counter parry of 2. A completes their attack with a grand lunge. At the completion of the extended parry, Combatant B flicks their blade out to the right, meeting the middle of A's extended forearm. (Fig. 224) As in the previous example (and in *all* soft parries) the extended parry must place the blade close enough to A's arm that the flick does not strike the arm, but places the blade safely on the arm. From this position B has the same options as above.

Soft parries may safely be executed against all standard thrusting attacks. Feel free to work these parries with a variety of evasive actions. The displacement of the body in conjunction with the extended arm and soft parry can be quite dynamic and surprising on stage. The parry cannot be used against a cutting attack because of the possibility of striking the hand or wrist as the offensive hand moves into place. The timing for such an action would need to be exact, and would have little margin for error.

Swashing Blows

"Draw if you be men. Gregory, remember thy swashing blow."[6]

The "swashing blow" (also *washing*) is a remnant of the attacks delivered with broad bladed swords. These were large, sweeping strokes or blows delivered with great force, intended more to

---

[6]Shakespeare, *Romeo and Juliet* [I.i.59–60].

batter than cut the opponent. The big, broad swipes used in Chapter 10 for evasive actions are examples of swashing attacks. These cuts are from the shoulder and travel through the entire plane of attack rather than being sent forward beyond your partner. The force of the attack causes the blade to whistle or swash the air as in the following example from *Romeo and Juliet*.

> *"He swung about his head and cut the winds, Who nothing hurt withal, hiss'd him in scorn."* [I.i. 109–110]

The cutting of the wind and "hissing" or swashing sound of the blade is a distinguishing characteristic of the forceful swashing blow. The force of the arm and wrist is magnified in the blade, savagely cutting the winds. Due to the dynamics of this action, the swashing blow (whether delivered with or without footwork) must never be executed inside measure. The cut forcefully crosses the plane of the victim's body and variance of good distance can prove dangerous. Timing therefore must be exact. The cut uses the same mechanics and execution as that of the horizontal swipes offered in Chapter 10. The preparation and execution of the cut are identical, and it is the reaction of the victim that transforms the miss into a hit.

The most common form of swashing blow on stage is the belly cut. The attack is cued from either the right or left in the same manner as a cut to the left or right hip. The victim reacts by clearing their hands, arms and weapons from the path of the blade and then the cut is released. The blade travels across the belly, in a horizontal plane. The victim physically reacts to the "blow" of the blade as it crosses the belly. Immediately after the attack has cleared the plane of the body, the hands are brought down to cradle the wound. The victim must physically anticipate the hit, or the body will react after the apparent cut landed. Do not however, anticipate the cradling of the wound. If the hands or arms react early, they have the potential of traveling forward into the path of the attack and being struck. The wound can only be cradled after the cut has taken place. Less severe "cuts" can also be delivered to the forward leg.

The swashing blow is generally delivered either on an up stage/down stage diagonal, or in a plane perpendicular to the proscenium arch. This is done to help mask the gap between the blade and the body and to hide the "wound" from the house. The action of the cut and the reaction of the victim tell the story without having to deal with blood bags and technical gore. If the timing of the attacks is tight, however, the sweep of the cut blurs the tip of the sword, making it possible to present the cut parallel to the proscenium. This must be practiced and presented to an outside eye before consideration in a production. The basic rules in wounds are: if we believe what we don't see, keep it; but if we don't believe what we do see, change it.

Working the Wound

Practice the swashing blow stationary, working the attack at standard measure. Once this is comfortable from both the right and left, use an exercise like playing the numbers and end the routine with a swashing blow. You may work these wounds in the same manner as the thrust home and draw cuts. Try combining them with an attack on the blade, pris d'fer and other ways of removing the opposing blade to create an opening for the hit. Just work everything slowly to insure you are in control and at the appropriate measure. Remember, "better too slow than two pieces!"

The Need to Bleed

When it comes to blood, the difference between stage and film is amazing. In a movie, blood is commonly used to help tell the story of the action. This is because the camera can close in and show the details of the hit while special effects presents the graphic reality of the wound. The camera steers your eye to the injury and then to the physical effects of the wound. On film, the audience can be shown the wound and then the action moves on. Here, seeing is believing. On stage however, blood is generally a problem more than an aid. The distance between the audience and the actors makes the focusing on that specific point difficult. The chaos is heightened with the movement of other characters on stage. Therefore, a great deal of blood often needs to be used in order to make the wound visible to the house. This can cause problems with costumes and with further action on stage. Stage blood can make props and costumes sticky or leave wet, slippery patches on the stage floor. Blood may also make the grips of weapons slippery, making it possible to lose the sword during a fight. Blood bags and other technical devices often detract from the scene rather than add to it. Blood devices can break early, or not break at all. They can leak inside the costume or onto the stage, shifting focus from the elements of the scene to that of the blood.

The focus on stage is not the wound, it is the sensation and response to the wound. On stage, blood does not make the wound more believable; it generally acts as a prop to lessen the need for better acting. This of course is not always true; sometimes blood is called for in the script. As a general rule, however, if the characters on stage believe the injury, and respond accordingly, the scene can effectively move forward. Blood does not make the wound real; the cast's continued physical and emotional acknowledgment of the wound tells of its validity and severity.

If you feel blood is essential to the scene, an easy trick is the preset a "bloody handkerchief." A white hanky, pre-stained with a permanent "blood-stain," can be preset on the stage or with a particular character. After the hit is made, the hanky can be used to blot the wound. In this action the blood can be shown to the audience without further technical concerns from the cast or crew. If the need to bleed is specific, and nothing else will do, your fight director will present a variety of options to the production staff in order to make the effect work, while keeping everything safe. Blood effects add a great many variables to a fight. They should be staged by a professional and properly rehearsed.

Plate XXII: A killing thrust executed inside measure with a grasp. Capo Ferro (1610)

A Variety of Violent Actions

These are the most common forms of landed cuts and thrusts used in the theatre, but they are by no means the only ones. These are only a few examples of the types of wounds and kills that can be executed safely with a sword. Each fight director has a few personal favorites and a stock of variations in reserve. Despite the variety of violent actions available, there are a few rules that all professional fight directors follow. These are as follows:

1. The point of the weapon is never used to land on the body.
2. No wound or kill ever sends the force of the actual attack into the victim.

3. No wound or kill is ever delivered to the face, neck or head.
4. Although wounds and kills are a surprise to the character, no wound or kill can be a surprise to the artist.
5. All wounds and kills must be safe and controlled in execution, but dynamic and ''real'' in presentation.

Chapter 15

Adding the Dagger

"That which I have heretofore shewed you, is but small in regarde of that
I meane to teach you hereafter, so that having delivered you the manner
of the single Rapier, you may the better conceive my discourse of the
Rapier and Dagger . . ." [Saviolo][1]

Although historically the practice of *double fence* came before the practice of *single fence* with the rapier alone, the process of training was usually reversed. As exemplified by Saviolo above—now that you are familiar with the mechanics of the single rapier, you may better understand the techniques of the rapier and dagger. Before adding the dagger, however, it is best that you understand the significance of this weapon and the role it played in Elizabethan swordplay. Now that you are practiced and familiar with the techniques of the single rapier, you are ready to move on to the addition of the dagger.

In the grand scheme of armed conflict, the addition of a second weapon to the science of fence is actually a recent development. The concept of using the left hand is as old as the shields of primitive man. The practice of using an offensive and defensive weapon in the left as well as the right hand, however, was not developed until the Italian Renaissance. The art of *double fence,* where the dagger is used in conjunction with the sword, had a short, but important role in the history of swordplay. The addition of the dagger marked the transition from the old practice of sword and shield combat to the effective use of the sword as a weapon both offensive and defensive.

Although the use of the dagger as a weapon flourished in the Middle Ages, it was never a noble weapon. Even though almost everyone carried a knife or a dagger in their belt, they were more eating and utility knives than weapons.

When used in combat, little imagination seems to have been displayed in the manner in which the dagger was employed. It was held beneath the hand (gripped with the thumb at the pommel) and managed as a stabbing weapon. The reversed grip probably served the combatant in punching through mail or unprotected openings such as joints between plates in their opponent's armor. Although used as an offensive weapon in combat, seldom was the dagger used in conjunction with the sword. It was generally held in reserve, being drawn and used in the right hand if a sword were lost, broken or if they needed to dispatch their fallen foe.

The Quillon Dagger

During the mid-thirteenth century a form of dagger developed which resembled the hilt and quillon configuration of contemporary swords. The term *quillon dagger* is now used by arms

---

[1]Saviolo, p. 52.

Plate XXIII: German dagger fighting. Combatants in the gripes, daggers held in reverse grip (1531).

historians to classify this type of dagger. Many of the daggers in this class not only mimic the hilt configuration of swords, but are diminutive copies of the sword in all respects. The earliest forms of the quillon dagger had quillons that curved away from the grip. The blade was short, diamond-shaped in cross-section and single or doubled-edged, tapering evenly from forte to point.

The Dagger in the Age of the Rapier

In the opening years of the sixteenth century the dagger was still uniformly carried. For many people it was their only weapon. The most widely popular of all daggers were those with quillons. Throughout the sixteenth century they were carried over all of Europe. They were worn by the gentry and by the middle class, when in armor or civilian dress. By the mid-sixteenth century, however, the sword also had become a common part of civilian attire. For knights and gentlemen, the dagger, when carried, had become primarily an accessory to the sword. The attack with the reversed grip remained predominant for the greater part of the century, but about mid-century a new fighting technique brought forth a different method of employment.

The Poniard

During the sixteenth century there was little uniformity in the form of quillon daggers. As the hilt of the sword developed, the similarity to contemporary sword hilts disappeared. Of the various hilt configurations developed for the dagger in this period the most noted is that of the *main gauche* ("left-hand") dagger or *poniard*. These daggers were designed to be held in the left hand with the point above, like a sword. This placement allowed the dagger to function as both an offensive and defensive weapon on the left while the sword was held in the right.

The first written record of double fence, where the dagger is used in conjunction with the sword, can be found in Paris de Puteo's *Duello* (1521).[2] De Puteo's treatise on the customs and conventions of dueling speaks of the practice of the *con spada e pungnale* (sword and dagger fencing), suggesting that the sword and dagger were used together as early as the second decade of the sixteenth century.

Serving as a fighting weapon along with the sword, the left-hand dagger needed stout quillions that could receive the full weight of an opponent's blow used to block an attack. These came in a variety of shapes and sizes with the quillions usually equal in length to that of their companion sword. Although many dagger hilt configurations matched those of their companion sword, not all left-hand daggers were made "en suite." It is better to assume that most swordsmen chose their weapons, not due to their looks, but for their effectiveness in combat.

The earliest known illustration of a parrying dagger, and the first description of techniques for double fence appears in Marozzo's *Opera Nova* (1536).[3] The illustrations show a left-handed dagger with a hilt formed by curved quillons and a side ring. The ring was placed on one side of the quillons as they crossed the grips, serving as protection for the knuckles when the dagger was held in the proper position. This side ring could also be a small shell or plate bent towards the blade. Without such supplementary guard, it would strike directly into the holder's knuckles, possibly injuring the hand.

Sword-Breakers

> *"There be othersome, whome . . . have daggers of purpose, which beside their ordinary hilts, have also two long sterts of Iron . . . into which distance, when it chaunceth the enimies sword to be driven, they suddenly straine and hold fast the sworde . . . but I holde it for a thing rather to be imagined than practiced"* [di Grassi][4]

As the rapier's companion weapon developed, some ingenious ways were devised to enable the combatant to catch the enemy's sword blade. Aside from working as simple parrying daggers, these "daggers of purpose" were provided with special contrivances such as the "long sterts of Iron" mentioned by di Grassi that were designed to entangle the opponent's blade and with a strong turn of the wrist, snap it off or wrench it out of their grasp. The most effective of these are now usually called "trick daggers" or *sword-breakers*.

Further Developments of the Parrying Dagger

Despite the variety of daggers developed in this period, the left-hand dagger as those shown in the woodcuts illustrating Marozzo's treatise, proved to be the most practical in the practice of double fence. The left-hand daggers with a symmetrical, arched cross-hilt and side ring provided the fencer with suitable hand protection. An additional reason for the widespread popularity of this dagger was

---

[2]Paris de Puteo, "Duello" (Venice 1525, 3rd Edition) f.G (VI):

[3]Achille Marozzo, a Bolognese fencing master with a school in Venice, published his *Opera Nova* in 1536. This treatise offers the reader a good idea of the practice of swordplay in the late fifteenth and early sixteenth century.

[4]di Grassi, pp. 59–60.

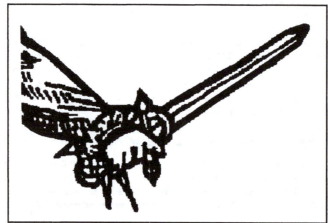

Plate XXIV: **A-**The parrying dagger. From Marozzo (1517). **B-**Close up of dagger with side ring.

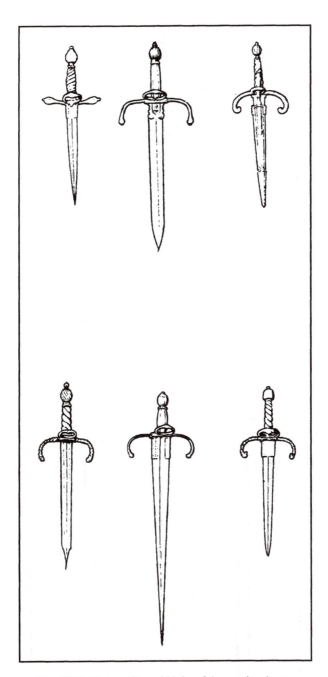

Plate XXV: Various hilts and blades of the parrying dagger.

that the symmetrical guard could be handled with equal convenience in both the right and left hand. This dagger reached its height about 1590 and continued with little or no change during the first quarter of the seventeenth century.

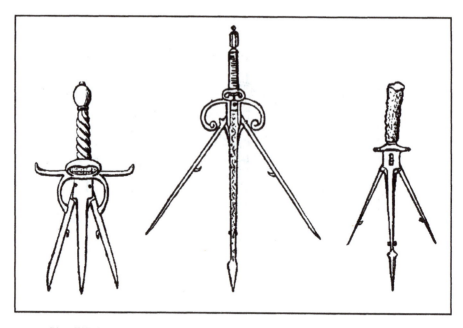

Plate XXVI: Sword-breakers with spring-loaded struts for catching the enemy's blade.

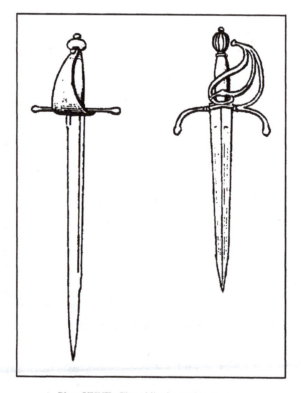

Plate XXVII: Close-hilted parrying daggers

As the dagger advanced, the side ring and shell were enlarged to better protect the dagger hand. The ring when enlarged was often covered with a metal screen to keep the opposing blade frompassing through its center. Such protective devices were mentioned as early as the last decade of the sixteenth century. In the *Combat de seul e seul* (1608), the author mentions "advantageous poniards" with shells that effectively cover the hand.[5] Even in the works of George Silver daggers with extensive hand protection are mentioned. In his *Bref Instruction* he wrote of a *"close hylt vpon yor daggr hand."*[6]

The Dagger in the Transitional Age

As the sword became a weapon of offense and defense, the dagger began to lose its significance. The seventeenth century brought a further decline in the importance of the dagger. The dagger had ceased to be an important adjunct of civilian dress for everyday use in England, France and Germany. In Spain and Italy, however, daggers remained a strong part of civilian dress and the science of arms. The left-hand dagger had gone out of fashion everywhere except Spain and southern Italy, where in the 1650s it developed into a highly specialized and very distinctive weapon which went on being used until almost the middle of the eighteenth century.

The Spanish Daggers

Like their companion cup-hilt rapiers, the Spanish form of left-hand dagger appeared in the second quarter of the seventeenth century, reaching its peak of development in the third quarter, and thereafter entering a period of decline. Both the cup-hilt rapier and the Spanish dagger developed out of the need to protect the weapon-bearing hand. Although the practice of double fence lapsed in most parts of Europe, the use of the left-hand dagger continued in Spain, and in the Spanish kingdom of Naples, until the late eighteenth century. This developed into a bigger weapon, with a longer, heavier blade and very long straight quillons. The quillons were normally cylindrical, and often reached eleven inches or more from tip to tip. Their blades were long and stout with total lengths of nineteen inches or even slightly more. Most characteristic of all, however, was the wide triangular guard that curved from the quillons to the pommel, protecting the combatant's knuckles.

For practical purposes, the Spanish dagger was the most effective ever designed for the rapier and dagger style of fighting. The stout blade and quillons allowed for greater assurance of a parry with the single weapon. The broad quillons made tight feints and deceptions difficult around the weapon's guard and the defensive shell placed around the knuckles allowed the combatant to commit to defensive actions without fear of injury to the dagger-bearing hand. The reason why they were not adapted and used elsewhere in Europe was that by the time they appeared in the 1650s the rapier was in transition and the use of the left-hand dagger had lapsed.

The Eighteenth Century

By the eighteenth century the huge spread of firearms, the advancements in swordplay and the appearance of the bayonet caused the dagger's use to dwindle and then fade away from battlefield and dueling ground. In the cities and among most of the sophisticated areas of western Europe the small sword was the gentleman's weapon. The carrying of daggers as popular items of dress or as customary weapons for personal defense was primarily confined to Scotland, Spain, Italy and the frontiers of America.

THE STAGE DAGGER

In the art of stage combat and theatrical dagger play, the dagger of the stage is merely a representation of the weapons of the past. The needs of actual combat versus the needs of theatrical

---

[5]Marc de la Beraudiere, *Combat de seul e seul.* 1608.
[6]Silver, p. 107.

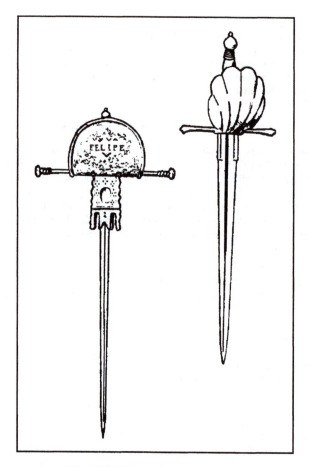

Plate XXVIII: Spanish parrying daggers

swordplay are completely contradictory. A stage dagger, like a stage sword, needs to be designed and constructed for the specific demands of a stage fight.

Sound Weapons Help Safe Technique

To be sure that your dagger is safe for stage combat, apply the rules of selecting a safe stage rapier offered in Chapter 2. The blade must be dulled at the edge and at the point. The tip of the weapon should be rounded, making penetration difficult. The edges must be flat and dull, free of any nicks and burrs. The blade must be stiff, and its shoulders must meet flush and flat with the dagger's hilt. There should be no gaps, shims or wedges to make the blade fit. The weapon must be able to be disassembled so that you may inspect the tang and all its housings. If the tang is thin or weak, and the fittings allow movement, the weapon is unsafe. The grip of the dagger should be constructed of a good hardwood or polycarbonate plastic. It should fit snugly to the tang and sit flush to the base of the quillon block. The grip should also fit well in the hand and be covered in some no-slip material like leather or wire wrap. The pommel should be of solid steel and screw snugly onto the tang. For further security it can be drilled completely through, and threaded at the upper end. This allows for a lock-nut to be placed on the end of the tang, securing the pommel in place and preventing the pommel from loosening during use.

The Anatomy of a Stage Dagger

The theatrical dagger like the rapier is made up of three parts; the guard, the grip and the pommel. The shape and design of these vary depending on the manufacturer, but they almost all fit with this outline of components. This is because although there are a vast variety of hilt configurations, they are almost all based on the parrying dagger first seen in Marozzo's *Opera Nova*.

Types of Blades

Like the theatrical sword, there are a surprising number of suppliers of "stage daggers" that offer decorative wall hangers that are in no way designed, engineered or constructed for stage combat. Their blades are often constructed of soft metal that will easily bend or break. Other daggers are sold or rented with their blades honed close to sharp with a definite point. These daggers are generally comprised of a cheap hilt and handle haphazardly stacked onto the tang of the blade and wrenched together with some generic pommel. When the pommel loosens even a little, the grip and the guard can turn and spin, misaligning the blade and the hilt and allowing for metal fatigue of the tang. These types of daggers are all too often billed as "combat serviceable," but in reality are unsafe and should be avoided. Remember, no matter how safe the practice of stage combat, if the weapons are unsound, the combat is still dangerous.

The dagger, although generally a weapon of defense in double fence, is designed to both cut and thrust. Because of this, a flat-edged blade is best. A wide, flat blade generally provides strong shoulders on which to mount the hilt and an ample tang on which to seat the grip and pommel. It is important to be sure that these blades are of a good temper. There are blades that can easily be bent against the flat by applying very little pressure with the hands. These "putty" knives can shoulder well on the dagger hilts, be provided with ample tangs and appear quite solid, but they will still break or interfere with the blade-play due to the malleability of the metal.

Although the wide, flat dagger blades are generally more historically accurate, there are very few that serve the needs of the stage dagger while remaining in scale with the standard blades of the theatrical rapier. Daggers of historical size and proportion generally dwarf theatrical rapiers making the stage swords look like toys in comparison (except when used with a full-size rapier). To solve

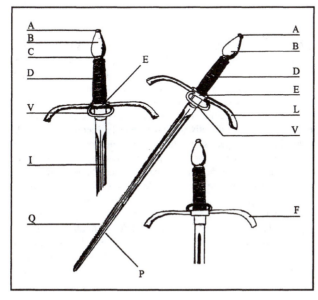

A.	Lock-nut or Capstan Rivet
B.	Pommel
C.	Grip or Handle
D.	Quillon Block
E.	Upper Quillon or Back Quillon
F.	Lower Quillon or Back Quillon
G.	Side-Ring or Shell
	(not on all stage daggers)
H.	Blade
I.	True Edge
J.	False Edge
K.	Shoulders of the Blade
L.	Ricasso (not on all blades)
M.	Forte
N.	Middle Section
O.	Point or Tip
P.	Fuller or Fluting
	(not on all blades)

Figure 225. The Anatomy of the Parrying Dagger

this problem some sword-cutlers have fashioned blades from one-quarter inch bar stock to about the width of a schlager blade. These blades are generally cost effective, serviceable and durable, but they tend to balance and handle like a steel club. Other suppliers cut down actual schlager blades for use in daggers. These blades, while meeting every technical and safety need of theatrical daggers, are not cost effective and can look like bar stock in their shortened form. To be effective on stage, the blade needs to appear to taper to a point, representing both a cutting and stabbing weapon.

Because the "wide" dagger blades do not read well in conjunction with the theatrical rapier blades, many theatrical sword-cutlers provide their daggers with reduced epée blades. Although the epée blade is not suitable for stage swords, its forte, when properly fitted and mounted on a dagger hilt, can function as an effective stage dagger. The reduced blade removes the flexible foible and middle of the triangular blade, and mounts only the stiff forte. This makes the reduced blade sturdy and solid when mounted on the smaller weapon. The epée has the added benefit of tapering from forte to tip, making the blade appear more like a pointed weapon rather than a clunky steel club. It is important, however, to have a professional cutter shorten the blade and round the point. Because of the tapered blade, you must be sure that it, and any stage dagger, does not come to a point.

Blade Length

"Let thy Rapier or Sword be foure foote at the least, and thy Dagger two foote, for it is better have the Dagger too long then too short" [Swetnam][7]

Another point of concern in theatrical dagger blades is the length. Historically the poniard could be anywhere from ten inches to over two feet long. For the purposes of safe stage combat, a theatrical dagger cannot be of such a length. It should be roughly ten to twelve inches long. The length of the blade is quite important in the execution of offensive and defensive actions to be discussed later. If the blade is too short it can prove dangerous because there is a limited forte to effectively meet an attack. This can bring the unprotected hand closer to the offending blade or the offending blade closer to the point of the dagger. In one direction the hand may be struck, in the other, the combatant. Although longer blades provide a better defense, their length becomes a problem as the dagger is forced to navigate around the rapier and sword arm. Eleven inches seems to be a standard and effective length.

The Theatrical Dagger Hilt

The hilt of the left-hand dagger is usually a simple cross-hilt with straight or drooped quillons. On the outside of the hilt, mounted on the quillons or quillon block is a ring or small shell. For theatrical weapons this is an important part of the dagger. The ring is your added safety for hand protection. There is no knuckle bow, counter guard or cup to protect the hand. The ring or shell is the barrier that prevents the offensive blade from angling around the quillons and striking the hand. If the opposing blade slides down the blade, it will come to rest on the ring or shell and stop there. Without such supplementary guard, it could strike directly into your knuckles, cutting your hand.

In order to further protect the hand, some daggers sweep the lower quillon down towards the hand, functioning as a partial knuckle bow. Others curve both quillons towards the point. These daggers seem to be more popular on stage because the symmetrical guard can be used by both a right- or left-handed fencer, where the dagger with the partial knuckle bow is intended to only be used in the dagger hand.

Now that you have had a chance to work the rapier, it is important that you remember for what the dagger will be used. No matter which hilt you decide to work with, it must withstand the constant abuse of theatrical swordplay. Although the dagger is a smaller, lighter weapon, it is still beaten against other swords and daggers and needs to withstand being dropped in a loose disarm or after a kill. Brass and brittle metals cannot stand up to this rigorous abuse. Dagger hilts should be of cast,

---

[7]Swetnam, p. 184.

or welded, low carbon steel. They should be free of sharp corners, points or barbs. There should be no spikes, spears or points with which you could possibly puncture the skin. The side ring or shell should be free of burrs and rough edges that may catch or tear the hand. The hilt should fit snugly to the tang and sit flush between the shoulders of the blade and the grip.

Sword-Breakers

Some suppliers of ''stage'' weapons have parrying daggers with extra quillons and branches that curve around the hilt and up towards the blade. Many of them are quite attractive in design, but dangerous in practice. These added baubles can catch and trap the opposing blade. Although this is the intended feature of some Elizabethan parrying daggers, it can prove awkward and possibly dangerous in a theatrical sword fight. This is also true of actual sword-breakers. Although these daggers have an interesting look and allow for added variety in a stage fight, they should not be used on stage. Modern audiences have no idea what the daggers can do, and their actions are too small to be seen in the theater. With this, the design and effectiveness of the sword-breaker is based partly on chance and does not allow for the specifics of theatrical swordplay. Even in di Grassi's age the effectiveness of such daggers was in question. In his example, he felt that the catching of the blade was a thing to be imagined rather than practiced. If trick daggers and sword-breakers are to be used, they are best used in film where a ''catch'' can be guaranteed, and where the camera can tell the audience what is happening. Such actions are difficult to control, and are lost to the audience when performed on stage.

Holding the Dagger

''Let every man therefore holde his dagger with the edge or flatt towards the enimie, as it shall most advantage him . . . But let every man hold it as he will . . .'' [di Grassi][8]

The historical fighting dagger often had a strong ricasso with a depression for the thumb on the side opposite the ring guard. The hand grasped the hilt of the dagger, knuckles below the ring, thumb placed on the blade, directed towards the point. The ricasso was wide enough to protect the thumb from the edge of the opposing blade. Theatrical daggers generally do not come with the wide blades of the Elizabethan parrying daggers, and placing the thumb on the blade can be dangerous.

There are two ways to properly hold the dagger when working on the stage: the first is with the thumb bracing the blade, the other is with the thumb in opposition to the blade. To brace the blade with the thumb, take hold of the dagger and lightly wrap your fingers around the grip, so that you have a firm, but relaxed hold of the dagger. Adjust the blade in your hand so that the side ring rests above the second knuckle of your index finger. Now, place the pad of your thumb onto the grip, on the side directly opposite the side ring. This places the thumb in line with the flat of the blade working against the grip of the index finger. Your last three fingers lightly grip the handle, bringing it to bear against the palm of the hand.

If the thumb is uncomfortable bracing the blade, try readjusting it to where it is in opposition to the blade. Adjust the dagger so that the side ring rests between the first and second knuckle of your index finger. Now, try placing the pad of your thumb onto the grip, directly in line with the back edge of the dagger's blade. This places the thumb in line with the blade, in opposition to the defensive edge. Here, as before, your last three fingers lightly grip the handle, bringing it to bear against the palm of the hand. (Fig. 227)

Do not put your thumb through the side ring. The ring is not intended to house the thumb, and by placing the finger inside the ring you run the risk of having it broken if the dagger is accidentally torqued during a parry. The ring can also jam on the finger and possibly skin the thumb if the dagger is displaced during swordplay.

---

[8]di Grassi, p. 60.

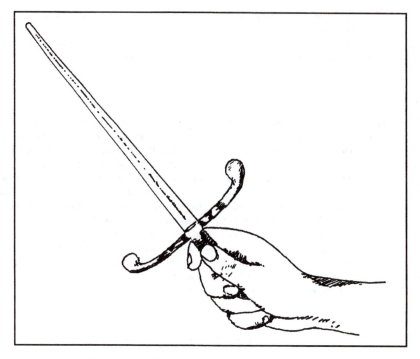

Figure 226. Holding the dagger, thumb bracing the blade.

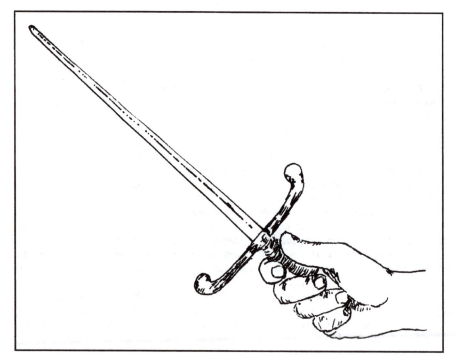

Figure 227. Holding the dagger, thumb in opposition to the blade.

Take Care of the Dagger Hand

As in the handling of the rapier, you should wear a comfortable glove on your dagger hand for your own comfort and protection. If you do not yet have gloves, it is advisable that you now purchase a pair. Although you will practice the actions of the dagger in the same slow, controlled manner as you did with the rapier, accidents can happen. It is always better to be prepared and never get hit, than to expose the hand when learning and run the risk of injury.

Getting the Feel of Steel

Now that you have a dagger and a good set of gloves, you may give the dagger a whirl. First make sure that the area around you is clear, on all sides. Once the area is clear, you may try moving the dagger about. Get a feel for its weight and balance. Try working it through the various doigté exercises of the blade offered in Chapter 4. Practice the vertical and horizontal blade movements, the circles in the air and so on. Get a sense of manipulating a weapon in the left hand.

THE GUARDS OF THE SINGLE DAGGER

"Concerning the dagger, that which is to bee done therewith, it is to be noted, that for great advantage, it would be holden before with the arm stretched forth & the point respecting the enemie, which although it be far from him, yet that it hath a point, it giveth him occasion to bethink himself."
[di Grassi][9]

Before learning the guards of double fence, it is important that you master the manipulation of the dagger by itself. Generally the dagger was never used alone against a rapier or rapier and dagger, but the movement and mechanics of the weapon are better learned when you do not have to concentrate on the manipulation of a second weapon. So for starters, work with the dagger alone. These guards are eventually used to complement the rapier in double fence, but you must first be comfortable with the dagger in the left hand before you attempt to join it with the rapier.

The guards of the rapier and dagger are for the most part variations on the guards of the single rapier. The body remains in the On Guard stance covered in Chapter 3—with your weight centered evenly between your legs. The sword-bearing hand is maneuvered and placed in the same manner as practiced in Chapter 4. The dagger-bearing hand moves and mimics these placements and is covered by the same rules of technique and safety.

The Weapon-Bearing Side

For clarity in movement and placement when working in double weapon play, references are not made to right or left, but to the specific weapon-bearing side. What this means is the right-handed combatant fighting with the rapier in the right-hand refers to their right side as their *sword-bearing* side; and with the dagger in their left-hand, the left is the *dagger-bearing* side. The reason for this is because the terms Prima, Seconda, Terza and Quarta are not used in reference to the side of the body, but the relationship between the body and the specific weapon.

The Dagger's Inside and Outside Lines

In Chapter 5 you learned the correct placement of guards in relation to the sword-bearing hand only. The dagger-bearing hand is a direct mirror image of the sword hand. di Grassi's inside, outside, high and low "lines" are applied to the weapon and not specifically to your right or left. If you remember, di Grassi spoke of the lines in regard to the weapon-bearing hand and its placement, and in regards to the rapier inside and outside. These lines were to the inside and outside of the weapon,

---

[9]di Grassi, p. 59.

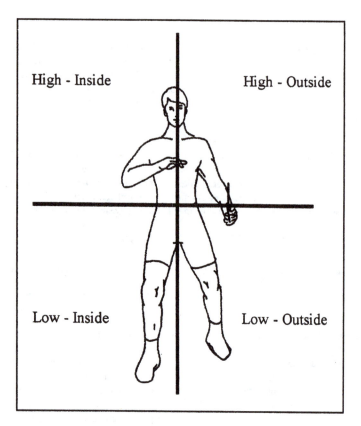

Figure 228. The dagger's lines of attack and defense.

not to its right or left. Hence those parts above or below the specific weapon-bearing hand and on the inside or the outside of that hand define their lines of attack. An attack coming above either hand is still in the "high line"; and below, in the "low line"; but now the area between the two hands, is the "inside line"; and the exterior of the hands, is the "outside line." (Fig. 228)

Dual weapons give the fencer the ability to close more lines of attack, and keep certain lines closed both during offensive and defensive play. Just as in single rapier play, the placement of either blade masters all attacks in the closed line unless your adversary takes some means to displace the guard and force the blade aside.

Dagger Prima

Unlike Prima in single rapier, Dagger Prima is not the first guard that one can safely assume upon drawing the dagger, whether from the right or the left. In fact, Dagger Prima is a guard that is seldom assumed as there is limited hand protection and the length of the blade makes the point of the dagger of little threat to your opponent and little defense for yourself. This guard, however, can be used to good effect with Rapier Prima or Rapier Seconda.

To come to Dagger Prima, bring the weapon to your dagger-bearing side (your partner's right), with the tip directed outside your partner's body. When the dagger is safely outside your partner's body, raise your hand above your head, in front of and outside your body. Turn your knuckles toward the ceiling (thumb down), with the quillons straight up and down, vertical with the floor. The blade of the dagger is directed forward and down towards your partner's right shoulder. Remember, even with the blade of the dagger removed from your partner, the point of the weapon is not pointed at your partner but in a line forward outside your partner's body. The blade is parallel to and outside the imaginary lines on the floor that you and your partner are standing upon. The arm forms a slight curve from the shoulder up and forward. (Fig. 229)

Dagger Seconda

To assume Dagger Seconda, the tip of the daggers directed outside your partner's body, at shoulder level. The dagger hand and arm travel to the level of your shoulder. The hand stops at the level of your dagger-bearing shoulder, with the hand in pronation, quillons horizontal to the floor.

Like Single Rapier Seconda, this guard extends straight from the shoulder and is completely horizontal to the floor. The arm is fully extended, but the body remains square to your partner. The dagger arm forms a slight curve from the shoulder out and forward. Along with the tip being directed straight forward in Seconda proper, the tip of the dagger may also be angled up or down like High and Low Seconda, but it always remains outside your partner's body. (Fig. 230)

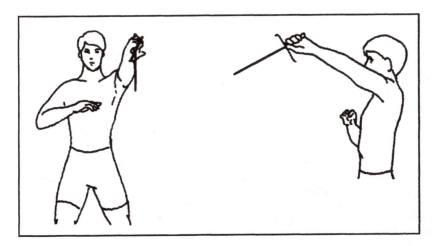

Figure 229. The Single Dagger guard of Prima.

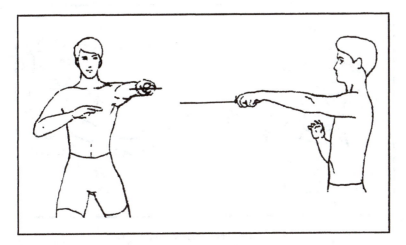

Figure 230. The Single Dagger guard of Seconda.

Dagger Terza

Dagger Seconda and Dagger Terza are the positions of the dagger most often assumed in double fence. This placement of the dagger theoretically closes the high outside line, (providing suitable, but not complete, protection to the torso on the dagger side). To assume Dagger Terza bring your dagger hand and arm in towards you on the left side of your body. Angle the tip of the dagger towards your partner's right shoulder. Your hand is placed in front of your body just above the level of your waist. Your arm is outside the body with the elbow bent at roughly ninety degrees. There should be at least a four-inch gap between your elbow and your side, just as in the guard of Terza with the single rapier. This widening of the arms allows the point of the dagger to travel straight forward while avoiding an actual threat to your partner.

While in Dagger Terza the hand may be held in either pronation (palm down) or the vertical/ middle position (palm to the inside, towards your body). There is no reason to hold the hand in supination as some people do in single rapier. The tip of the dagger may also be dropped to the level of your partner's belly (as in Low Terza in single rapier), but this opens the high line and makes the dagger's defensive capabilities less effective in this guard. If the point is dropped to a Low Terza, the arm should be extended forward roughly six inches. (Fig. 231)

Dagger Quarta

Because the dagger has a much shorter blade than the rapier, it has a limited reach that poses less of a threat to one's opponent and less defense for the bearer, thus the single guard of Quarta is seldom used. In double fence, the outside line on the rapier-bearing side is generally closed by the rapier and the dagger is used to protect the inside lines above the knee and the outside lines of the dagger-bearing side, thus the guard of Dagger Quarta is seldom used in single or double fence. When used, Dagger Quarta is placed below Rapier Prima or Seconda, and not in complement to Rapier Quarta. This would cross the arms and pin either the sword or dagger arm beneath the other, making offensive or defensive movements difficult.

When coming to Dagger Quarta, although the blade is short, still be sure that the tip of the dagger is carried low as you cross the body. As you cross your body (from left to right) turn your hand to supination. Stop with your hand about three inches outside your body with the dagger angled down from your waist toward your partner's knees. Once outside your body, extend your arm forward about ten or twelve inches and raise the tip of your dagger so that it is directed up and towards the outside of the notch in your partner's left shoulder. Your hand is supinated, with your knuckles

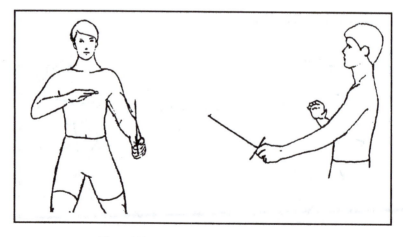

Figure 231. The Single Dagger guard of Terza.

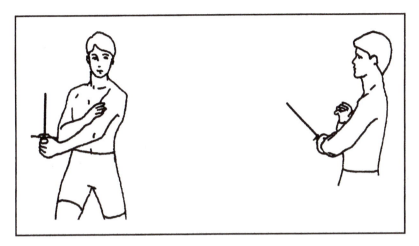

Figure 232. The Single Dagger guard of Quarta.

towards the daggers inside (right). Quillons are horizontal to the floor and your arm is across your body and in front of it. Unlike the rapier guard of Quarta, the dagger arm is about twelve inches out and in front of your body. While in Dagger Quarta, the tip may be lowered to the level of your partner's belly (as that of Rapier Low Quarta), but be sure the tip is still directed forward, outside your partner's body. (Fig. 232)

Cross Body Guards

In dagger play, cross body guards follow the same practices as in the single rapier. The principal variance between rapier and dagger guards is that you may assume a cross body guard with the dagger both on- and off-line. This is due to the length of the dagger's blade. A dagger may be held safely on-line when working at proper rapier measure because its length keeps it at a safe distance from your partner's body. When measure is closed, however, the dagger's guard must be off-line and generally held straight forward in standard placement to avoid directing its point at one's partner. When working inside measure the rules of rapier guards are applied.

Application and Practice

Like those of the rapier, each of the dagger guards must be practiced and understood before moving on. It is easy at first to assume that guards only refer to the sword or are direct reference to the sword-bearing side of the body, but that is not the case with the dagger. Remember that it is a separate weapon, its inside and outside lines are not those of the rapier. Do not try to hurry the process, as incomplete understanding leads to severe difficulties when the two weapons must move in unison. Become quite comfortable working the dagger hand before moving on to the practice of double fence.

Chapter 16

The Guards of the Rapier and Dagger

". . . The several difference of guards are more in number then there are
several kindes of hands in writing, yea many more then any Fidler can play
lessons upon his instrument . . ." [J. Swetnam][1]

Like the wards and guards of the single rapier, the rapier and dagger had a great number of fantastical postures designed to keep the enemy at bay and facilitate the most effective attack or counterattack. Many of these wards may have worked well for their inventor and some of their students, but in the practical science or "true art" of defense it is hard to believe that they served any great purpose. Many of these postures only defended against a specific attack, not really closing any lines, but rather making the sword ready for voiding one attack in order to launch a counter.

The Rapier and Dagger Had Many Guards

A predominant philosophy of the day was to know more wards than one's opponent possibly could, so that you would eventually assume a posture they did not know how to oppose and thus gain the advantage. This philosophy is exemplified in Joseph Swetnam's treatise on the "Noble and Worthy Science of Defence."

". . . For at some times, and for some purposes, one guard may better serve than another: for change
of guards may crosse some mens play, whereas if you use but one guard, may in often play be worne
threed-bare, therefore learne as many fashions of lying with thy weapons as thou canst . . ." [Swetnam][2]

The problem with this philosophy was that each ward generally countered only one other, and that by knowing each and every ward and its "contra postura" you would have mastered the "True Art of Defence." But each of these wards was limited to a small number of offensive or defensive moves which in practice would have greatly restricted the combatant. In the heat of a duel or quarrel it is easy to imagine the confusion of some of the umpteen wards and their specific slips and counters. In fact, the confusion caused by the limitations of each of these wards could prove painful or even lethal to the miscalculating combatant.

---

[1]Swetnam, p. 46.
[2]Swetnam, p. 104.

Plate XXIX: Examples of the variety of guards and contra posturas with the rapier and dagger. Fabris (1606)

> "... You may frame your selfe, sometimes into one guard, and sometimes into an other, taking heed always, that you observe the same defence which belongeth to the guard; for if you are in one guard, and you use the defence of another, so you may deceive your selfe (for everie guard differeth in defence and offence)" [Swetnam][3]

---

[3]Swetnam, pp. 45–46.

Reducing the Number of Guards

It was Agrippa who first noticed the problems with the practice of numerous guards. He felt that each guard should provide the combatant with the greatest number of attacks and defenses possible. He reduced the number of guards to four, and proceeded to show how one guard could facilitate the offensive and defensive actions of many of the restrictive wards. His work, however, was not immediately accepted, and many masters of fence did not hear or heed his advice. di Grassi on the other hand, either had heard of Agrippa's philosophy or had come upon the same idea in his own practices. He, however, found that the great number of wards could be reduced not to four, but three principal guards. In his teachings there is no mention of a ward comparable to Agrippa's Quarta.

> *"In the handling of these weapons, men use to frame manie wards, all which, because many of them carrie no reason, for that they are ether out of the streight line, either under them a man maie easilie bee stroken, I will cast aside as impertinent to my purpose, & restrain my self unto those three with the which a man may safelie strike & defend, whereunto all the rest maie be reduced."* [di Grassi][4]

di Grassi, however, is not the only master to heed Agrippa's advice. In the works of such masters as Saviolo, Fabris and Capo Ferro there also developed the practice of minimizing the amount of practical guards with the rapier and dagger to a small number that facilitated a great array of both offensive and defensive actions. It is interesting to note that although each of these masters offered their students a variety of names for their guards, the placement of the blades and postures of the bodies at times are quite similar.

Using the Numerical System

Capo Ferro used the numerical system originally suggested by Agrippa, and Saviolo's "High Ward" is set in the same placement and principal as Agrippa's Prima, that of a ward where the combatant could draw and be on guard in one swift and simple action. di Grassi's three wards "high, broad or wide, and lowe" (also base ward or lock) are similar to Capo Ferro's Prima, Seconda and Terza. Capo Ferro actually taught six guards with the rapier and dagger, three more than Saviolo or di Grassi, but he along with the others believed that Terza was the most practical.

> *"For this warde* [the low warde, Terza] *doth oppose it selfe against all others . . . Besides, every man doth naturally more accustom himself in it, than in any other."* [di Grassi][5]

And so, as in single rapier, Terza is the guard of choice for the rapier and dagger.

Dagger As Defense

Unlike the early guards of the single rapier, the guards of the rapier and dagger offered more defense for the combatant. Before the rapier was light enough to facilitate both offensive and defensive actions, the dagger was used to guard the left side of the combatant. Its placement forced the adversary to regard the dagger as an obstacle that must be removed or maneuvered around in order to hit home. Fencing manuals speak of the placement of the dagger, not as in closing lines, but in regards to proper placement so as not to be struck either above or below the weapon by the opponent. Thus, by placing the dagger as an obstacle to the attack, even without using it to parry, it became a defensive weapon.

Although di Grassi's lines of attack were for the most part applied to offensive actions, the placement of the dagger in his guards, as well as Saviolo, Fabris and Capo Ferro's, certainly helped close certain lines from attack, literally guarding the body. Because the dagger closed these lines and proved an obstacle for one's opponent, it made the practice of voiding an attack easier, as there were

---

[4]di Grassi, p. 58.
[5]di Grassi, p. 68.

only so many targets available to one's opponent. Being somewhat certain what line the opponent would strike in, the dagger could then be used to "break" an offensive thrust or block a cutting attack, while the combatant voided their body, redirecting the opponent's blade with the dagger and simultaneously launching a counterattack with the rapier. The dagger added to the assurance that a void or slip would be an effective defense freeing the rapier to execute the offensive actions.

Contra Posturas

Although Terza was generally considered the best of all possible guards against any other, and that the dagger helped provide a barrier between the combatant and their opponent, the idea of the "contra postura" or "contra guardia" of Fabris was still applied to the guards of the rapier and dagger. Like the multiple guards of other schools and masters of fence, each of the simple guards had its counter guard or opposite. This generally consisted of the placement of the dagger in opposition to the opponent's rapier. This was the barrier the rapier had to penetrate. The trick to these counter guards was to observe the placement of the dagger, and if it was either too high or too low, the opening was seen and a thrust home made. Thus, the guards were only effective if the weapons were perfectly placed.

Using Capo Ferro's Guards

Of the numerous guards of the rapier and dagger from which offensive or defensive actions can be launched, we only use six defensive positions, and some simple variations. We use the numerical system originated by Agrippa, with the guards and their "contra posturas" based on the six taught by Capo Ferro. Because many of these guards are similar to those of Saviolo, di Grassi, Fabris and others, complementary text is offered whenever possible.

The rapier and dagger guards are theatrically applicable to the popular styles from the mid-sixteenth century through the eighteenth century. As in the use of the single rapier, for reasons of safety and theatricality, alterations are made in the guards of the rapier and dagger. They have been made larger for the audience, and very specific in their position and target for the safety of the actor. The concept of the guard and the reasoning of the placement of the weapons is maintained whenever possible.

Working with Two Weapons

Before you jump into double fence technique, take some time to feel two weapons. Take both weapons in your hands and in an open space, where you can strike no one and nothing, swing the blades about. Get a feel for holding a weapon in each hand. To some people this transition comes naturally and to others it is difficult to handle two weapons. Take a few minutes and practice a few molinellos, try cutting with the rapier and transferring guards with the dagger. You will find that the dagger can get in the way of the rapier or that the placement of the dagger can hinder offensive actions of the rapier. This is a trait of double fence technique, an understanding of which will be helpful as you move on.

Drawing the Rapier and Dagger

The right handed man carries his dagger by the side of his right thigh, and the left handed man by his left: they draw this weapon the moment they have sword in hand.'' [Angelo][6]

The idea of drawing and being "on guard" in one action is a tad more difficult with two weapons. Despite the philosophies of double fence and the active role the dagger played in the offense of

---

[6]Angelo, p. 87.

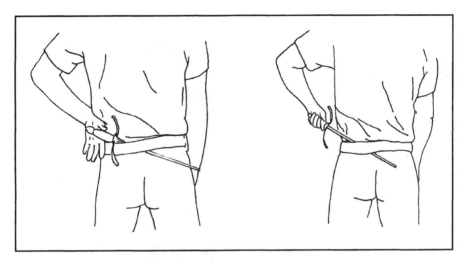

Figure 233. Drawing the Dagger. **A**-Reaching back and taking hold of the grip; **B**-drawing the dagger from the belt or sheath.

blade-play, single rapier Prima was generally the first guard a swordsman came to when called to draw and fight. The dagger only came after they knew the enemy was a foot or two further off.

Thus, in single fence and double fence the drawing of the sword remains the same. For our purposes, draw the sword as it is described in Chapter 5. The left hand holds the scabbard and sword carriage in place as the right hand draws the sword. Once the sword clears the scabbard, the left hand releases the sword carriage and attends to the dagger.

For theatre the dagger is generally carried in the sword belt diagonally across the back, with the hilt toward the left elbow. To draw the dagger you will reach back with your left hand, almost brushing along side your body, fingers down, thumb to the inside. The palm of your hand will come in contact with the grip of the dagger and you will take hold of it in the manner described in the previous chapter. (Fig. 233.a) Once you have hold of the dagger, you will draw it out to your left until it clears the throat of its sheath or is freed from the belt. (Fig. 233.b)

The Guards of the Rapier and Dagger

Joining of the dagger to the guards of the rapier solves many problems of the single rapier guards. With the single rapier, unless the blades are cross body, there is a large opening on the left side of the body, the rapier's inside line. This line is closed or partially defended by the addition of the dagger.

Prima (Double Fence)

In double weapon play, Prima closes the high outside line with the rapier and the dagger. Once you have drawn your weapons, your rapier continues to the placement of single rapier Prima (Standard or Across). As the rapier moves safely to Single Rapier Prima, the dagger hand moves to Dagger Terza. While in Dagger Terza the hand may be held in pronation or vertical/middle position. (Fig. 234)

Seconda (Double Fence)

In double fence, Seconda is the extended guard of the sword-bearing hand. The rapier hand assumes Seconda proper with the hand in pronation and the sword held out from the shoulder,

Plate XXX: Agrippa's Prima Guardia, executed on a pass with the left foot dominant (1553).

parallel with the floor. This guard is generally assumed in standard Seconda, but it may also be safely assumed with the rapier across the body.

The dagger is held in Dagger Terza with your dagger hand placed roughly ten to twelve inches in front of your body just above the level of your waist. As before, the hand may be held in either pronation or the vertical/middle position. (Fig. 235)

Terza (Double Fence)

Whether in single or double fence, Terza is considered the most practical of the guards. Because of this, Terza is the attitude most commonly assumed by the theatrical combatant when called "on guard" after drawing the sword and dagger.

The rapier hand may assume Terza proper (Standard or Across) as in single fence, only with your hand held roughly ten to twelve inches in front of the body just above the level of your waist. The elbow is still outside your body, to the right, and just a touch forward. The blade placement remains the same, directed up and forward roughly three inches outside your partner's body, with the point of the sword at the level of their armpit. The sword hand may be held in pronation, supination or vertical/middle position.

The dagger is also held in Terza, with your dagger hand placed roughly ten to twelve inches in front of your body just above the level of your waist. Unlike the guard of Terza in single rapier, the hand may only be held in either pronation or the vertical/middle position in Dagger Terza.

Figure 234. The Rapier and Dagger guard of Prima (Double Fence).

Both weapon hands are outside and in front of the body, held at approximately the same level and placement. With both arms and weapons out in front of the body be sure not to lean forward when learning this guard. Remain in correct placement. (Fig. 236)

Quarta (Double Fence)

The double fence guard of Quarta is the jumping off point of parallel guards. In Prima, Seconda and Terza the rapier is held in approximately the same placement in both single and double fence, but in double fence Quarta the rapier is held in what would be Terza proper. The placement of the dagger is then used to close the rapier's high inside line.

The rapier hand assumes Terza proper (Standard or Across), the hand held in pronation, supination or vertical/middle position. Unlike Quarta proper, in double fence Quarta the sword hand is seldom held in supination.

In this guard, the placement of the dagger also jumps from comparative guards to a placement closer to what will be a dagger parry of High 3 (to be covered in Chapter 17) than any guard we've explored so far.

From the level of your waist move from your wrist and describe a counterclockwise circle with the tip of the dagger. When the tip reaches one o'clock, turn your palm towards your partner, knuckles slightly up and to the dagger outside (left). As the dagger reaches one o'clock bring the hand up and forward so that it is at elbow level, outside (left) of the body and roughly ten to fourteen inches in front of it. Your palm remains towards your partner, knuckles slightly up and to the dagger outside (left) and angled up at roughly forty-five degrees. The blade of the dagger does not angle

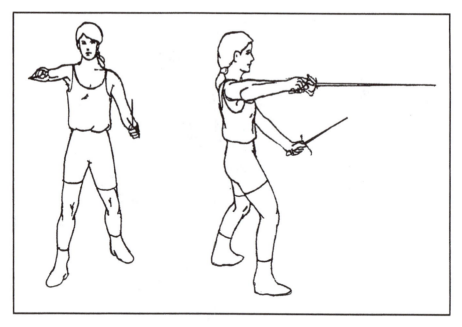

Figure 235. The Rapier and Dagger guard of Seconda (Double Fence).

Plate XXXI: A German guard with the rapier and dagger, similar to the double fence guard of Terza. (1570)

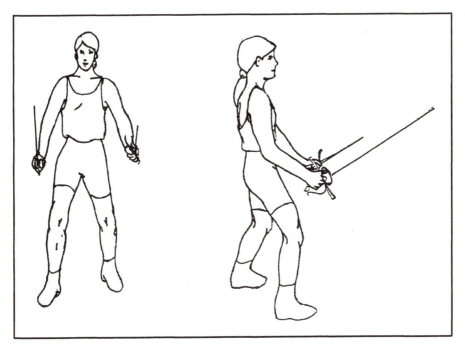

Figure 236. The Rapier and Dagger guard of Terza (Double Fence).

Plate XXXII: Swetnam's "True Guard" of the Rapier & Dagger. Similar to the theatrical double fence guard of Quarta.

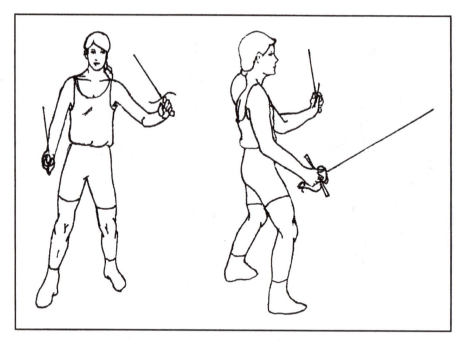

Figure 237. The Rapier and Dagger guard of Quarta (Double Fence).

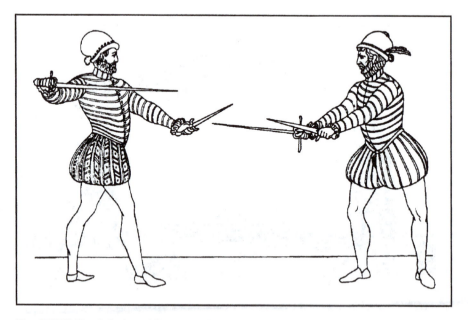

Plate XXXIII: French Rapier and Dagger guards. One is similar to Saviolo's broad ward (a type of drawn back Seconda) and the other is that of Quinta.

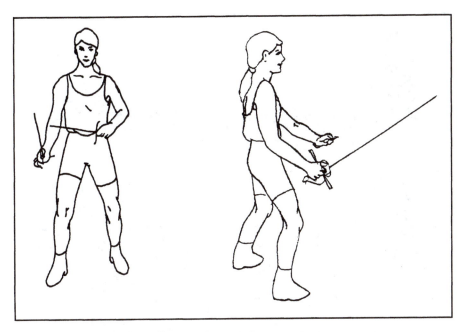

Figure 238. The Rapier and Dagger guard of Quinta (Double Fence).

off behind you, but may be angled slightly forward towards your partner. If you choose to do this, be sure that the blade is not turned towards them, but remains outside their body.

Quinta (Double Fence)

In order to assume the double fence guard of Quinta the rapier hand takes on Low Terza (Standard) as in single fence, only with your hand held roughly ten to twelve inches in front of the body just above the level of your waist. In this guard the sword hand may be held in pronation or vertical/middle position but not in supination.

For the placement of the dagger in the guard of Quinta, bring your dagger to waist level on your dagger-bearing side. From the level of your waist pick the tip of the dagger up so that it is directed to twelve o'clock. Once this is done bring your dagger hand and arm in front of you about twelve to fourteen inches and move it across your body towards your rapier. Leading with the wrist, the hand and dagger begin to travel across the body. As you move the dagger towards the rapier (right) begin to rotate the wrist clockwise, turning the tip of the dagger to two o'clock. Stop the hand and dagger about mid torso (right around your belly-button), and about twelve to fourteen inches in front of your body. The hand remains about waist level, the tip of the dagger placed over and above the forte of your rapier. The weapons are crossed but not touching. The palm of the dagger hand is toward the floor, your knuckles turned towards your partner, the tip of the dagger towards the rapier-bearing (right) side and angled slightly forward. (Fig. 238)

Sesta (Double Fence)

In the double fence guard of Sesta (sixth) the rapier hand assumes the placement of Low Terza (Standard) in single rapier, only with the hand drawn back to the side of the body at waist level. The arm is still outside your body on the right with the elbow bent and directed straight behind you. The blade placement remains the same as Low Terza. The sword hand may be held in pronation or vertical/middle position, but supination in this guard proves awkward and uncomfortable.

Plate XXXIV: Saviolo's guard with the Rapier & Dagger, similar to the theatrical double fence guard of Sesta.

Plate XXXV: The guards and contra posturas of Capo Ferro. Showing Quarta Guardia (D) countering Prima Guardia (A).

Plate XXXVI: The guards and contra posturas of Capo Ferro. Showing Seconda Guardia (B) countering Sesta Guardia (F).

Plate XXXVII: The guards and contra posturas of Capo Ferro. Showing Terza Guardia (C) countering Quinta Guardia (E).

Plate XXXVIII: Swetnam's "Castle-Guard" with the Rapier & Dagger.

Like the guard of Quarta and Quinta, the placement of the dagger in Sesta is different than in any of the single dagger guards. To place your dagger correctly for Sesta, bring the dagger to Dagger Terza with the hand in middle/vertical placement. The guard is then carried up and forward to where the dagger hand is at mid-chest level, on the dagger-bearing side. The arm is stretched forward, but not straight.

The blade of the dagger can be either in a flat plane or pointed towards your partner and over their left shoulder. If the blade is to be angled forward, be sure that the blade is not turned towards the face or head, but that it is safely directed across their body, up and forward over their shoulder. (Fig. 239)

Contra Postura

As mentioned earlier, each guard or ward had its "contra postura," or opposing guard. This opposition was also called keeping "proportion." Keeping correct proportion was one of the three fundamental rules of Elizabethan fencing and is referred to in many fencing manuals and plays of the period. To keep time, distance and proportion were the elements that made up the science of fence.[7] Thus, for each of these guards there is a counter guard that most effectively matches it. For

---

[7]To keep "time," was first to minimize the offensive and defensive motions of the body to those strictly necessary, both in number and in extent; second, to balance those motions carefully with those of the opponent, in order to seize instantly any opportunity while minimizing the possibility of being struck.

"To take time, that is to say when opportunity is profered thee . . . I mean it must be done upon the very motion of his profer, thou must defend and seeke to offend all at once, for thou must not suffer thy enemy to recover his guard, for if thou do thou loosest thy advantage." [Swetnam, p. 83]

To keep "distance," is mainly to keep out of easy reach when on the defensive, and to be in reach while on the offensive.

"To observe distance, by which is meant that thou shouldest stand so far off from thine enemy, as thou canst, but reach him when thou dost step foorth with thy blow or thrust." [Swetnam, p. 74]

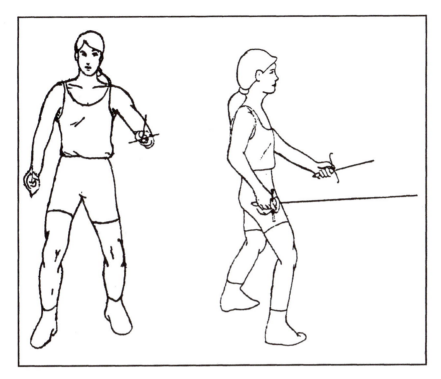

Figure 239. The Rapier and Dagger guard of Sesta (Double Fence).

the guard of Prima it is best to assume Quarta, putting the dagger in opposition to the offending rapier. (Fig. 240) For Seconda one assumes Sesta, and for Terza, the opposite is Quinta. (Figs. 241–242) These are the counter guards suggested by Capo Ferro, offering the greatest amount of defense with the dagger while allowing the greatest freedom to the rapier. Of course, any combination can do, and as long as it's safe and looks convincing on stage, it's completely acceptable.

Engaging the Rapiers

Like the guards of the single rapier, Prima, Terza and Quarta may be engaged. The guards of Seconda, Quinta and Sesta, due to the nature and placement of the blades, generally cannot. It is important to note that whether rapiers are joined or not, the dagger guard is always directed to the same shoulder. The point of the dagger is not aligned across the body when rapiers are joined. The point remains directed forward towards your partner's shoulder except when otherwise specified such as in Quarta and Quinta.

Although Prima, Terza and Quarta may be assumed across the body, the common practice in

---

To keep "proportion," was to move with the opponent, assuming the corresponding wards and positions of assault, and thus never giving them an opening.

"But if you finde your enemye with his poynt down, you must stand upon a low warde, and carrie your body very well, leaning upon the lefte side, and when you have got him within your proportion, you may give him a stoccata or thrust." Saviolo, p. 38

To keep time, distance and proportion, was to master the three basic elements of Elizabethan swordplay. Tybalt is said to have mastered these in Shakespeare's *Romeo and Juliet* (11. IV. 22).

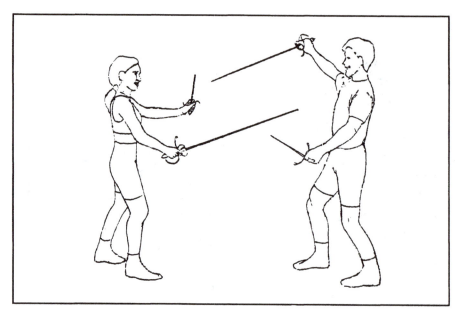

Figure 240. The contra posturas for the Rapier and Dagger; Quarta against Prima (after Capo Ferro).

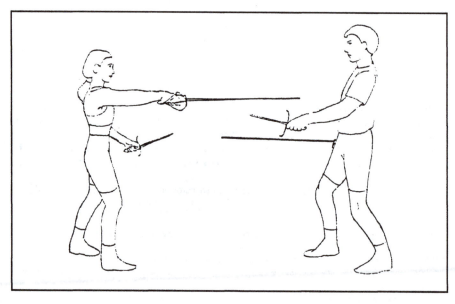

Figure 241. The contra posturas for the Rapier and Dagger; Seconda against Sesta (after Capo Ferro).

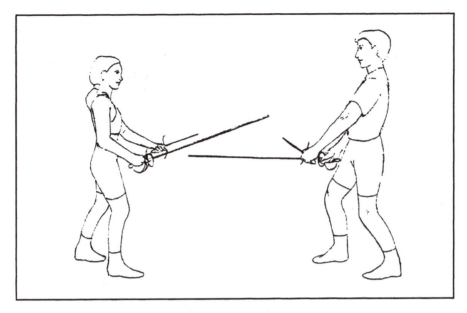

Figure 242. The contra posturas for the Rapier and Dagger; Terza against Quinta (after Capo Ferro).

double fence is to assume the standard guard placement. This is due in part to the fact that the dagger helps close the line a cross body guard would protect and because historically joining the blades was less common in rapier and dagger play. This is, however, no hard and fast rule. Double fence guards can and often are joined on stage. Generally, anything is acceptable if it is safe and reads well to the audience. For this reason, the double fence guards should be practiced both standard and across. This develops a fuller sense of the possibilities in double fence.

Variations

Like the masters of the past, the Elizabethans had a great variety of wards and guards to choose from. Each master offered up their idea of the best offensive and defensive positions, pointing out what was right with theirs and what was wrong or foolish about the others. The above listed guards are based on those of the Italian school, and most directly on those of Capo Ferro. For the most part, the English gentry learned the Italian method, either by foreign masters in England or when abroad. There are, however, many other guards and schools to choose from and any combination of guards is viable on stage if it appears to be effective to the audience.

What is important to the actor is understanding the function of the guard, and what is important to the audience is seeing that understanding.

Changements

As you work through the variety of double fence guards, you will discover that the placement of your partner's dagger now limits the effective choices you have for changements. What were once open lines in single rapier are now closed by the addition of the defensive dagger. The second weapon also provides another barrier around which to manipulate your rapier. Because of this, it is important to review the changement exercises of Chapter 5.

In Chapter 5 you worked the changing of guards with a series of changements that passed the point of the weapon around the opposing rapier. Try working the same techniques, only now work around the dagger. Although cross body guards may be assumed in double fence, the movements of the rapier have already been covered in earlier chapters and our focus in now placed on the dagger. In double fence the dagger forms the barrier that must be removed or manipulated around before an attack can effectively be launched.

Work all the exercises so that the passage of the point is practiced both over and under the defending dagger. Try the change over, under, disengage, coupé and half-disengage around the dagger. Although the rapier and dagger are seldom engaged in the various guards and contra posturas of double fence, try working the changements both engaged and free. Also try practicing counter changements, double changements, and refusing the blade with the dagger. This helps you develop a feel for the opponent's blade. Acquiring a sentiment de fer with the dagger is quite beneficial to you as you learn further skills of double fence. Unlike the single rapier, many of the parries in double fence require combinations of the two blades. In the execution of these double parries you may not always have the opportunity to look at the blades and you must trust your sense of steel.

Engaging the Dagger

The joining of the dagger with the opposing rapier may be initiated by either of the weapons. Unlike the joining of rapiers, however, the dagger does not reach across the body a cross body guard can, so its engagements are limited to its standard placements. Also, because the rapier is seldom carried to single Quarta in double fence, there are almost never cross body engagements between the rapier and dagger in the exchanging of guards.

The blades are engaged with the foible of the rapier crossing the middle of the dagger. Because in double fence the dagger is generally carried on the dagger-bearing side, and the rapier on the rapier-bearing side, the cross of the joined weapons is most commonly formed on the outside of the body where the tip is shown. The same is true if an across guard engages the dagger. If a cross body single rapier Quarta (tip directed to the left shoulder) engages the dagger in double fence Seconda, the cross of the blades is still outside the dagger on the dagger-bearing side.

Taking it Moving

As in Chapter 5, almost all of these exercises may be worked with footwork. After you practice them for a while, and are comfortable with both the transitions and passages of the rapier around the dagger and the workings of the dagger, try adding footwork to the exercise. Like before, the objective is to maintain correct distance and proper control of the blade. Be sure that you review the application of footwork to these exercises before taking them moving.

Trouble Shooting

If you have trouble turning your torso or reaching with the dagger in these exercises, or if your shoulders stiffen and tense up, you may try Sitting This One Out. The exercise offered in Chapter 4 for helping develop a sense of when the body leans, bends or turns, works well with the addition of the dagger. It may also be used to shift focus solely to the upper body, relaxing the On Guard stance.

If you have trouble executing the separate movements of the rapier and dagger in conjunction with one another, you are not alone. At first these demands can be as aggravating as patting your head and rubbing your stomach at the same time. This problem, however, can and will be overcome with time and practice. To help achieve independent movement the following exercise has been provided. Add a few minutes of these to your warm-ups each day and the subtlety, strength and freedom of movement in your hands and arms will definitely be increased.

The arms: Starting with your elbows out to your sides, about chest level, and your hands in front of you, pronated. Keeping your shoulders relaxed, begin to move your hands back and forth through space as if you were wiping off a counter. The hands are moving anywhere from a foot to two feet in their horizontal path. The movement is only from the elbows. After thirty counts of moving back and forth in a horizontal path let the left arm move to another path. The right arm must continue in the horizontal path while the left does thirty counts in each of the other paths.

- horizontal path
- diagonal path
- vertical path
- circular path

Once the left arm completes its cycle and returns to the horizontal path, the right arm moves through the cycle ten to thirty counts on each path. It is important to keep the shoulders relaxed, and to move the arms only from the elbow. Be sure that your body maintains correct placement and that the focus on the exercise does not affect your stance or posture in any way. The arms should be moving independent from the body. Do not hold your breath as you do this exercise.

The exercise can then be repeated with the hands in supination and middle/vertical position.

The Hands: The arm exercises can also be done with only the hands. The arms are held in place with the movement confined to your wrists. You will find this exercise much more difficult than the arm exercise, but it will prove quite beneficial in the long run.

A variation on this exercise is to add the patterns of the figure eight and four-leaf clover point work exercises offered in Chapter 3. These can be added to the other paths, or be worked opposite one another.

Adding Footwork: To further help independent movement, these exercises may be run with someone calling random footwork. Not fast, maybe two or three moves per path. This splits the focus even more and forces you to work both hands and feet at the same time. At this stage in your training, however, footwork should be second nature. It is a little problematic, remember to "think" and then "do." Never commit to an action if you are unsure whether it is the right action.

Do not neglect these exercises as you move forward in technique, they are designed to help build the skills necessary for better blade management when working with two weapons.

APPLICATION AND PRACTICE

Like the guards of the single rapier, each of the six double fence guards must be practiced. Do not rush yourself. It is important that the two weapons move in unison, starting at the same time and ending at the same time.

After you are comfortable with each guard position and can assume them with some proficiency, try stepping through either of the footwork drills, (as coveredin Chapter 3). Now that you are armed with two weapons, either foot may be placed forward with the guard. Generally, however, Prima, Seconda and Terza are still assumed with the right foot forward, and the other three can be assumed either way.

Once you feel comfortable working with the two weapons, you are ready to move on to the parries of double fence.

Chapter 17

The Parries of the Rapier and Dagger

"The Dagger serveth well at length to put by a thrust, and at the halfe Sword to crosse the Sword blade, to drive out the Agent, and put him in danger of his life, and safely in anie of these two actions to defend himself." [Silver][1]

Although we took time in Chapter 6 to look at the ideas and philosophies of the parry, we did not fully explore the function of the dagger. The long and slightly awkward rapier of the sixteenth century could not move quickly enough to parry an attack in the modern sense of the word, thus it needed a second weapon to respond defensively to an oncoming attack. It is true that the modern idea of the parry was not realized until the mid-seventeenth century, but in double fence the dagger served more exclusively as a defensive weapon and therefore provides us with a better example of the parry.

The weight and length of the early rapier made it quite difficult to parry with the sword itself. The awkward weapon restricted the fencer from blocking an attack with any advantage or speed. Previous to Capo Ferro, the parrying dagger fulfilled this aspect of swordplay. Thus, in the sixteenth and early seventeenth centuries, the rapier and dagger always went together. Both weapons were capable of offensive and defensive actions, although the dagger functioned primarily as the defensive weapon. Until the rapier lightened enough to serve as its own defensive weapon, the dagger's intervention was absolutely necessary for the complete defensive action.

The Evasion as Part of the Dagger's Defense

The defensive action of the dagger, however, was still not what we would consider a parry to be today. The dagger was used to help deflect the offending blow as a counterattack was launched with the rapier. As discussed in Chapter 10, it was common practice to remove or "void" the body as a routine part of a defensive action. With the dagger this was done to decrease the chance of injury and diminish the force of an attack taken on the smaller weapon. In regards to the parry with the dagger, Saviolo tells his readers:

"All stoccataes comming under the Dagger, & imbroccataes above the Dagger, are to bee beaten outward toward the lefte side, but an imbrocata by a riversa either in the belly or in the face, should be broken inward toward the right side, with a little retiring of the bodie." [Saviolo][2]

---

[1]Silver, p. 34.
[2]Saviolo, p. 54.

The Dangers of Parrying with the Dagger

The dagger served as a great defensive weapon against any number of point attacks, allowing the combatants to *break* or beat the offensive thrust aside and launch a counterattack without having to engage the sword. Even a large number of cutting attacks could be parried by the dagger. This could be done if the parry was made as a step in parry at "halfe sword," near the middle or forte of the attacking blade, where the force of the cut was less powerful. The dagger alone did not prove a great defense for strong "down right blows" or cutting attacks outside measure where the force of the cut was greatest.

> As Joseph Swetnam points out, *"if the blowe doe chaunce to light neare the point of your dagger . . .*
> *the blow may hap the glance over the point of your dagger, and endanger your head"* [Swetnam][3]

If the parry was made too close to the point of the dagger, the attacking blade could *cut through* the parry. This would force the defending wrist to give, allowing the attack to push through the parry and strike the defender. There was also the variable of intercepting the cut on the defending hand. The dagger, therefore, was not generally used to "stop" or block an attack, but rather to beat an offending blade aside.

What the Dagger's Beat Parry Defends

Although the definition of the dagger parry is unclear, most treatises on rapier and dagger play describe the action as a beat or break of the attack. In di Grassi's text he tells his reader that the attacks must be "beaten" away, and even gives instruction to these defensive actions.

> *"All blowes,"* he says, *"shalbe beaten outwards toward the side or parte of the bodie which is least to the end it may sooner avoide danger. And those blowes that come on the right side must be beaten towards the right side: and those on the left side must in like manner be voided from the same side."* [di Grassi][4]

As well as describing these defensive actions, he also informs his reader of the targets best defended by the dagger.

> *"So that to the Dagger, by reason of his shortness, is assigned the left side to defend downe to the knee: and to the sword all the right side, & the right and lef side joyntly downwardes from the knee."* [di Grassi][5]

This is supported later by Domenico Angelo in his discussion concerning Italian fencing.

> *"The Italians defend all the inside, and the lower part of the body, with the dagger."* [Angelo][6]

Thus, by use of beating or knocking the offending blade aside, the dagger had the responsibility to defend that portion of the body to the inside of the rapier. Through the process of evasive actions and quick reflexes, the Elizabethan fencer depended on their dagger for a great deal of their protection.

The Jam Parry

> *"There be othersome, whome it pleaseth to carrie their Dagger with the flatt towardes the enimie, using for their defence, not onely the Dagger, but also the guardes thereof with which (they saye) they take holdfast of the enimies sword:"* [di Grassi][7]

---

[3]Swetnam, p. 88.
[4]di Grassi, p. 61.
[5]di Grassi, pp. 56–57.
[6]Angelo, p. 90.
[7]di Grassi, p. 59.

There are some indications that seem to point to a third type of parry for the dagger. Depending on the construction of the weapon, some parries seem to have been executed like a block parry taken on the guard of the dagger. If the attack was a thrust, the offending weapon would be intercepted by the blade of the dagger and then guided to its guard or hilt. If a cut, the combatant would close measure and jam the dagger forward towards the offending blade, stopping the attack on the dagger's guard or hilt. Both these practices are now referred to as *jam parries*. The idea of such parries must have been to avoid the possibility of giving in the wrist and being struck through an ineffectual parry. A parry with a straight arm provided much greater strength than one against the wrist.

Trapping the Blade in the Hilt of the Dagger

Performing such a parry, the dagger needed to have an effective side ring and sturdy quillons. Without this protection the jam parry just forced the offending blade directly onto the left hand. Many of the guards of these daggers seem to have had drooped quillons and often some sort of sword-breaker. If the parry was successful the combatant could then simply turn their wrist, locking and trapping the offending blade between the upper or lower quillon and the forte of the dagger. If the offending blade were caught in one of the special contrivances designed to entangle the opponent's blade, it too was trapped. A hard turn of the wrist in either case was supposed to break the tip off the trapped sword.

Checking the Blade

If a jam parry or blocking parry was successful, the swordsman could then command the opposing blade, keeping it in *check* while initiating a counterattack with the rapier. *Checking the blade* is the process of curbing, or restraining the offending blade while freeing the other weapon for a counter strike. By not quitting the blade the dagger can feel where the offending blade is and use that to both offensive and defensive advantage. di Grassi exemplifies this in his work, discussing the finding and keeping of the enemy's blade and the immediate counterattack.

> *"When one wardeth with the Dagger onely, he shall encrease a pace, and beare his arme forwards, and having found the enimies sworde, he shall (with the encrease of a pace) strike him with a thrust underneath, alreadie prepared."* [di Grassi][8]

Over two hundred years after this description by di Grassi, checking the blade was still recognized as an effective part of double fence with the rapier and dagger. In Domenico Angelo's brilliant treatise on fencing he tells his readers:

> *"on any parade made with the dagger, you ought not to quit the blade, if you have a mind to return the thrust."* [Angelo][9]

An essential part of sentiment de fer, the checking of the blade was to great advantage if the parry was executed correctly.

The Problem with the Jam Parry

The problem with these parries is that the fencer executing them had to be quite practiced in the technique. Catching an attack on the guard of the dagger takes more care and timing than on the blade, and the trap is never guaranteed. If successful, the combatant must know how to use the trap to their advantage. The fencer needed to know how to keep the opposing blade in check while launching a counterattack, how to release it without endangering themselves if their counter failed,

---

[8]di Grassi, p. 64.
[9]Angelo, p. 90.

and how to avoid having their advantage reversed by allowing their dagger to be wrenched out of their hand by the trapped blade. Because of the need to master the jam parry and the trapping of the blade, most period treatises dealt with the beat parry as the primary defense with the dagger. Sword-breakers and blade traps were more tricks of the fencing school and the fancy of a few fencers; most swordsmen preferred daggers of simple designs, with straight quillons and side ring.

The Parries "Double"

Although the dagger served quite well as a defensive weapon, it had its limitations. Beat parries seemed to work most effectively on thrusts and light cuts, but such a parry often proved ineffective against strong cutting attacks. For these reasons the practice of the double parry developed. These parries were made with both the rapier and dagger for defense: the rapier providing the strength and length to stop the attack, the dagger to keep the offending blade engaged so the rapier could be removed for offensive play.

Some schools of fence believed that such parries were dangerous, tying up both weapons and delaying the counterattack. Although dedicating a large portion of his treatise to rapier and dagger play, di Grassi mentions these parries only in the negative.

> "No man ought to accustome himselfe to defende blowes with the Rapier and Dagger both together, which manner of defending is now commonly used because men beleeve, that they stand more assuredly by that means, although in trueth it is not so." [di Grassi][10]

Despite his words against such parries, he also tells us that the action was "commonly used." Common practice, however, does not mean that it was practical. In fact, di Grassi's words were not heeded until the age of Capo Ferro. In Saviolo's treatise he seems to favor the double parry in some instances. In describing a defense for an attack to the head Saviolo says, "you may take it upon your rapier & dagger."[11] Even in the early seventeenth century and the age of the single rapier, Joseph Swetnam teaches the use of the rapier and dagger and the practice of the double parry.

> "For defence of a blow double, is sure, and yet you may answer your enemie so soone, and with as much danger to him as if you did defend it single"[12]

Like all parries of this period, the definition of the double parry is extremely vague. There are few illustrations depicting any type of parry from this period and the explanations leave a great deal to speculation. Some manuals hint towards the blades being crossed, while others imply that the blades are placed beside one another for further support, but none are specific as to what a "double" really is. In Joseph Swetnam's treatise, he mentions to the reader that in defending the head, "put your rapier on the out-side of your dagger, and with your dagger make a cross."[13] The implication is towards a cross parry, however the term "cross" in Elizabethan England is sometimes used to indicate the joining or parrying of the blades. As in "And if the enimie warde it, by the traverse or crosse motion of his Rapier, as many use to do" from di Grassi's text or "yo may cross his sword wt yor daggr, yf yo may conveniently reach the same therwt," from George Silver's Bref Instructions.[14] The idea that Swetnam and others' double parry were crossed blades is, however, supported later in Silver's text. "ward it dubble wt forehand ward, bering yor sword hylt to warde yor right shouldr, . . . crossing yor dagger on yor sword blade" Even this can still be speculated as a joining of the blades, and not a crossing of the blades as we now understand the term, but I find that highly unlikely.

It is my belief that double parries were executed both with the blades crossed, and with them

---

[10]di Grassi, p. 57.

[11]Saviolo, p. 73.

[12]Swetnam, p. 50.

[13]Swetnam, p. 92.

[14]di Grassi, p. 54; Silver, p. 103.

parallel to one another reinforcing a specific target. I believe both are based in truth and were probably practiced side by side, if not in the same school, in the same country. One thing is certain, the double parry is the closest thing the Elizabethan rapier had to what we know as a parry. Such actions could only really be executed in double time; one action for the defense and one action for the counterattack. The manuals that speak of doubles in single time are probably referring to something like the *exchange* or *transfer parries* (covered later in this chapter). These parries could be executed where the rapier begins to intercept the offending blade either breaking the thrust to one side or the other, or slowing the attack of a cut but not completing the parry itself. The dagger would then be used to complete the parry taking the offending blade and freeing the rapier for the counterattack in one time. This, however, is speculation and does not in any event lend itself to the theatre, as such a parry would be too fast and dangerous for the artist to try to execute.

THE DAGGER PARRIES

Like the rapier parries, the description of these parries refers to the position of the blade in relation to the face of a clock. The wrist or hand is always at the center of the clock treating the blade as a hand of that clock. The tip of the blade points towards the designated numbers. The instructions always assume you are facing the clock, and are therefore explained from the perspective of the defender.

All parries, whether executed by the rapier, the dagger, or the with both weapons together must adhere to the rules set forth in Chapter 6. When working with the dagger it is of extreme importance to be aware of the placement of the hand and blade. The decreased length of the blade and limited hand protection in comparison to the rapier means that hand and blade placement must be specific to avoid accident or injury. Like rapiers, the parry is made with the true edge (except when started otherwise) and the planes of the blades must meet at ninety degrees. The foible of the attacking blade must be met with the lower third (forte) of the dagger blade closest to the hand. (Fig. 243) Any higher than this point and the attacking blade has the potential of glancing off the blade and in towards the body; lower, and the blade may strike the defender's hand.

Preparation and Removal of the Body

The process of preparation and removal is the same as that of the rapier. As you "wind up," or travel from one parry preparing for the next, rock forward into the stationary offensive position. As you complete the parry, rock the body backward into the stationary defensive position (as described in Chapter 3). "Rocking" is applied to all the parries except where specific lower body movement is dictated. All safety rules apply here.

Dealing With the Rapier

As you go through the dagger parries, you must remove your sword arm from the plane of the attack and parry. This is necessary on most parries made on the rapier-bearing side. The rapier may be removed by lowering or raising the arm, but do not remove it out into the plane of the oncoming attack. The best result is to lower the arm and carry it slightly back behind you. After each parry the sword arm should be returned to Terza (or any other suitable guard), and remain there until it needs to be moved again.

If the rapier proves to be an obstacle in the preliminary training of the dagger parries, you may momentarily set the rapier aside. In this, however, do not let the rapier hand become inanimate. Hold a playing card or small piece of cardboard in your hand as you did in the footwork exercises in Chapter 3, keeping your hand in rapier Terza. Do this until you feel comfortable with the actions of the dagger, and then pick up the rapier again. Be sure that when working these parries with the rapier that during counter and semi-circular parries the dagger does not strike the rapier or the rapier bearing hand.

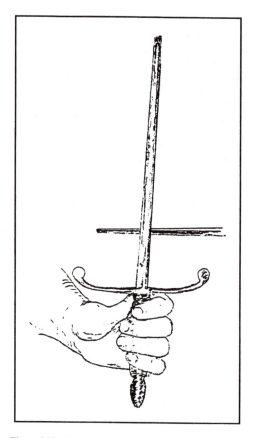

Figure 243. Dagger parry; edge to edge/forte to foible.

Dagger Parry of 1: Defense for an attack to the right hip

From the dagger-bearing side (left), pronate your wrist and guide the tip of the dagger down towards six o'clock. As the tip reaches six o'clock, place the dagger hand just above the level of your waist. Leading with the wrist (the dagger remains hanging straight down at six o'clock) the hand and dagger begin to travel across the body (from left to right). As the motion across the body begins turn your palm clockwise towards your partner, knuckles toward the dagger inside (right). Stop the hand and dagger about six inches outside of, and about ten inches in front of your body on the rapier-bearing side. The dagger hand remains just above waist level with the forte of the blade at the level of your rapier-bearing hip. (Fig. 244)

Dagger Parry of 2: Defense for an attack to the left hip

From dagger parry of 1 roll your wrist so that your palm faces you, knuckles directed toward the dagger outside (left). Angling the tip slightly forward, draw your hand and dagger across your body (from right to left). Stop with the dagger-bearing arm outside the body, extended down and slightly forward, with the dagger closing the low outside line.

Just as in rapier parry 2, your arm should be drawn up and bent at roughly forty-five degrees, with your elbow pointing directly behind you. Your hand just above waist level, the knuckles turned to the dagger outside (left). The blade of the dagger travels straight down, the tip directed at six o'clock. The forte of the blade is at the level of your left hip. (Fig. 245)

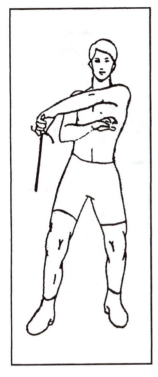

Figure 244. The Single Dagger parry of 1.

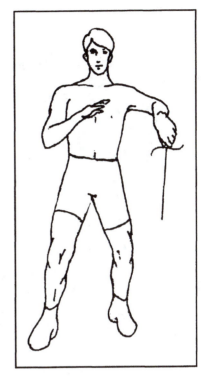

Figure 245. The Single Dagger parry of 2.

Dagger Parry of 3: Defense for a horizontal attack to the left shoulder

Moving from the dagger parry of 2 to the dagger parry of 3, execute a simple semicircular parry from the low to high line. Bring the dagger hand slightly in front of the center of the body and begin to turn the tip of the dagger counter-clockwise to the position of twelve o'clock. As the tip passes three o'clock start to guide the dagger and hand back out across the waist towards the dagger-bearing side. Stop about ten inches outside and in front of the body. The knuckles are turned towards the dagger outside (left), your hand at elbow level (no higher), palm facing your partner and the dagger's tip at twelve o'clock. The forte of the blade is at the level of the notch in your left arm where your deltoid and biceps meet. (Fig. 246)

Dagger Parry of 4: Defense for a horizontal attack to the right shoulder

As in single rapier, the transfer from the parry of 3 to 4 simply involves moving the parry from the high outside to the high inside line. With the dagger this is done by turning your knuckles toward the inside (right) and guiding your arm across your waistline (from left to right). The tip of the dagger is kept at twelve o'clock. The hand and dagger are stopped about eight inches outside, and in front of your body on the rapier-bearing side. The dagger hand is kept at elbow level with your knuckles to the dagger inside (right). The tip of the dagger is at twelve o'clock with its forte protecting the notch in the right arm where the deltoid and biceps meet. (Fig. 247)

Plate XXXIX: Warding with the dagger in the manner of the theatrical dagger parry of 3. di Grassi (1594)

Dagger Parry of 5: Defense for a vertical attack to the head

From dagger parry of 4 turn the dagger clockwise to the position of five o'clock. Extend the arm and drop the hand to the level of your waist. Your palm faces towards you, knuckles towards the floor, with the tip directed down to the right. From this position draw the dagger back across the body to the dagger-bearing side (left), keeping the tip at five o'clock. When the hand is below the left shoulder, stop moving to the left and with your wrist begin to guide the tip in a counterclockwise direction to the position of three o'clock. The blade is horizontal to the floor. As the wrist guides the tip to three o'clock, raise the hand (traveling up in a vertical plane) above your head, keeping the blade horizontal to the floor and in front of your body. Upon completion your hand is just inside your left shoulder, knuckles directed straight up, the tip at three o'clock and the blade above you and in front of you, horizontal to the floor. The arm forms a slight curve up and forward. The forte is in front of and above the center of your head. (Fig. 248)

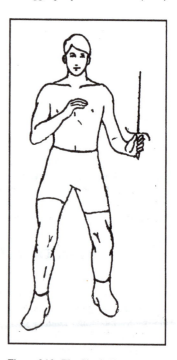

Figure 246. The Single Dagger parry of 3.

Figure 247. The Single Dagger
parry of 4.

Figure 248. The Single Dagger
parry of 5.

Dagger Parry of High 3: Defense for a diagonal attack
to the left shoulder

From dagger parry 5, keep your tip at three o'clock and bring your dagger hand and arm down
to the waist level. From this position, move only the wrist and begin to describe a counterclockwise
circle with the tip of the dagger. When the tip reaches one o'clock, turn your palm towards your
partner, knuckles slightly up and to the dagger outside (left). As the dagger reaches one o'clock bring
the dagger hand up and forward so that the hand is at elbow level, outside (left) of the body and roughly
ten to fourteen inches in front of it. Your palm remains towards your partner, knuckles slightly up
and to the dagger outside (left) and angled up at roughly forty-five degrees. The blade is outside and
in front of your body held at a forty-five degree angle to the floor, the tip at one o'clock, the forte
of the blade protecting the notch in the left shoulder where the deltoid and biceps meet. (Fig. 249)

Dagger Parry of High 4: Defense for a diagonal attack
to the right shoulder

From dagger parry High 3, guide the tip of the dagger to the position of twelve o'clock. Keeping
your hand at elbow level, turn the wrist so that your palm is towards you, knuckles toward the dagger
inside (right). As you reach this placement of the hand, begin to guide the dagger across the body
to the dagger inside (right). As your hand reaches the center of your body, begin rotating at the waist
like you would in rapier High 4 only in the opposite direction, turning your left shoulder slightly

towards your partner. As your hand passes your center line, guide the tip to the position of eleven o'clock. Your hand continues reaching across the body until it is outside your body on the right. The elbow is at approximately the mid section of your torso. The forearm is angled up slightly, with the hand just above the level of your elbow, outside (right) of the body and roughly ten to fourteen inches in front of it. Your palm is facing towards you, with the knuckles turned slightly up and to the dagger inside (right). The blade is at a forty-five degree angle to the floor, the tip is at eleven o'clock, with the forte of the blade protecting the notch in the right shoulder where the deltoid and biceps meet. (Fig. 250)

The Parry of 6: Defense for a thrust to the mid torso

In single dagger, and in double fence, thrusts to the mid torso (directed either to the left or right) are generally parried by dagger 3 or 4 (respectively) or by the rapier. There is no dagger parry 6. The supinated "broken wrist" position is ineffective and awkward with the dagger. In fact the supinated parry of 8 is generally replaced in dagger play by a dagger Low 2, making the following parry of 7 the only supinated parry in dagger play.

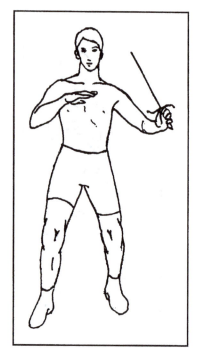

Figure 249. The Single Dagger parry of High 3.

Dagger Parry 7: Defense for an attack to the right thigh

From the dagger parry of High 4, bring your hand to the dagger-bearing side just below the waist line. Lower the tip of the dagger to six o'clock and turn your palm towards your partner as you would for rapier parry of 7 (thumb down, knuckles toward the dagger inside/right). Keeping the dagger at six o'clock, begin to guide the hand across the body (from left to right). As the dagger passes the middle of your body begin the slight rotation of the upper torso as you did in dagger parry High 4. The action stops with the dagger about six inches outside of, and about ten inches in front of your body on the rapier-bearing side. Your hand remains below waist level, your palm facing your partner, thumb down, knuckles to the dagger inside (right). The tip is at six o'clock, the forte at the level of the right quadriceps, just above the knee. (Fig. 251)

Dagger Parry Low 2: Defense for an attack to the left thigh

From dagger parry 7, keep the tip at six o'clock and take the hand back across the body from the right towards the left. As the hand moves across the body rotate the wrist clockwise 180 degrees so that your palm faces you, thumb to the inside, knuckles to the dagger outside (left). Finish moving across the body with your palm turned towards you, stopping with your hand approximately six inches outside of and roughly ten inches in front of your body on the dagger-bearing side. Your arm is almost straight with your palm facing toward you and your knuckles turned toward the outside (left). The blade hangs straight down with its tip at six o'clock and the forte at the level of the left quadriceps, just above the knee. (Fig. 252)

Figure 250. The Single Dagger parry of High 4.

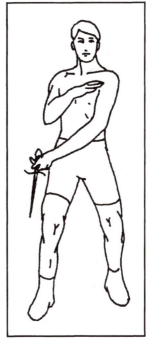

Figure 251. The Single Dagger parry of 7.

Dagger Parry Variations and Modifications

As with the rapier, there are a large variety of variations on the standard parries of the dagger. These variations and modifications provide a greater spectrum of choices for the theatrical combatant and choreographer.

Dagger Parry of High 1: Defense for a horizontal attack to the right shoulder

Although the rapier, or dagger parry 4, is used most often to protect the right shoulder, the dagger parry of high 1 allows for a fast defensive action from the dagger guard of Terza. This parry also allows for a bind over with the dagger after a successful shoulder parry. It is executed in the same manner as dagger parry 1, only the blade is carried across to the dagger inside (right) to defend the right shoulder. Your hand stops at the approximate level of your neck, and about six inches to the right of your body and about ten inches in front of your body. Your forearm runs parallel to the plane of your shoulders, horizontal to the floor, palm turned towards your partner, thumb down, knuckles to the dagger inside (right). The blade is hanging straight down from the hand and hilt, with the tip at six o'clock the forte at the level of the notch in your right shoulder where the deltoid meets the bicep. (Fig. 253)

Dagger Parry of High 2: Defense for an attack to the left shoulder

From dagger Terza, turn your wrist clockwise and guide the tip of your dagger down to six o'clock. As you do this, raise your elbow to the level of your left ear. Your arm should be drawn up and bent at roughly forty-five degrees, your elbow pointing up and to the left. Your hand is just above shoulder level about six inches outside and at least ten inches in front of your body, knuckles

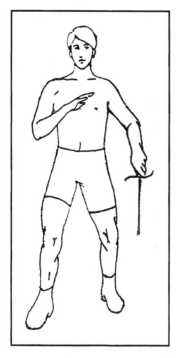

Figure 252. The Single Dagger parry of Low 2.

turned to the dagger outside (left). The tip of the dagger is at six o'clock with the forte of the blade at the level of your left shoulder. (Fig. 254) For best effect, this parry is generally executed as a circular parry—carrying the forte up and out to defend the target.

Dagger Parry of Low 5: Defense for a vertical attack to the groin

Like rapier Low 5, dagger Low 5 is the defensive position to the montante, or a thrust to the low mid torso. To execute this parry begin in Dagger Terza; turn your palm towards you and guide the tip up to the position of twelve o'clock. Guide the tip in a clockwise direction to the position of three o'clock. Extend your arm and lower your hand below your waist line. Keep your hand in front of your left leg. Slightly increase the depth of your plié. This should open your legs just a little wider. Your arm is extended in front of your left leg with your palm towards you and knuckles toward the floor. The dagger is in front of you, horizontal to the floor with the tip at three o'clock and the forte centered below the groin. (Fig. 255)

THE DRILLS

The preceding parries may be taken through the same drills as were offered in Chapter 8, concerning the engagement of the blades. It is important to remember, however, that the dagger parries are offered in a different order in relation to physical targets than the rapier drill. So you must make changes accordingly.

These drills must be worked with the dagger only on the defensive. At this point in double fence we have not learned the proper techniques of offense with the rapier and dagger and therefore must avoid learning things incorrectly. Run the defensive actions first with a partner attacking with the rapier.

Setting Measure

In working these particular drills distance remains the same as established in Chapter 8. Work with a dagger as a defensive weapon does not affect the measure established by the offensive weapon.

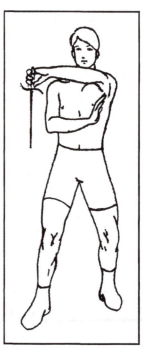

Figure 253. The Single Dagger parry of High 1.

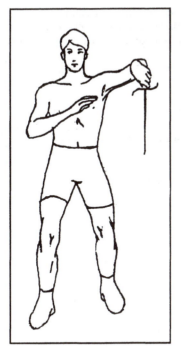

Figure 254. The Single Dagger parry of High 2.

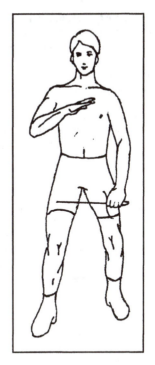

Figure 255. The Single Dagger parry of Low 5.

Stationary Drill

In the stationary drill, if you wish to keep the same attack pattern offered in Chapter 7, the dagger parries must be made in the following order:

Defensive Variation
- Dagger Parry 2
- Dagger Parry 1
- Dagger Parry 4
- Dagger Parry 3
- Dagger Parry 5
- Dagger Parry High 4
- Dagger Parry High 3
- Dagger Parry 4 (defending a stoccata thrust to right chest)
- Dagger Parry Low 2
- Dagger Parry 7

If you wish to run the drill in the correct numerical order of the dagger parries, the attacks will need to be altered in the following manner:

Offensive Variation

- From the guard of Terza, mollinello right to left, Riverso Tondo (mezzo), cut right hip.
- From the right hip, mollinello left to right, Man Dritto Tondo (mezzo), cut left hip.
- From the left hip, Man Dritto Tondo (alto), horizontal cut left shoulder.
- From the left shoulder, mollinello, Riverso Tondo (alto), horizontal cut right shoulder.

- From the right shoulder, mollinello on the inside line, Riverso Fendente, cut to the head.
- From the head, mollinello left to right, Man Dritto Squalembrato, diagonal cut left shoulder.
- From the left shoulder, mollinello from right to left, Riverso Squalembrato, diagonal cut right shoulder.
- From the right shoulder, mollinello on the inside line, Riverso Tondo (basso), cut right thigh.
- From the right knee, mollinello left to right, Man Dritto Tondo (basso), cut left thigh.

Notice there is no thrust to the right chest in this pattern as there is no dagger parry of 6.

Like the stationary rapier drill, this drill may be repeated as many times as you like. At the completion of each series the defender begins the offensive sequence and the offender shifts to the defensive part.

Traveling Drill

In regards to the traveling drill it is best at first to use the previously described defensive variation (2, 1, 4, 3, 5, H-4, H-3, 4, L-2, 7) so that it corresponds to the established pattern of movement in the offensive and defensive footwork drills. You may also take this pattern using the offensive variation. Just be sure that the defensive footwork removes the threatened side of the body and that the offensive footwork is dominant on the side from which the attack is being delivered, i.e., a cut from the right presents the right foot forward; a parry on the left removes the left foot to the back, and so on.

From the final parry (7 or Low 2), A (the attacker) *recovers* back to their original placements. B (the defender) brings their blade back on avoid, and switch sides of the drill. At the completion of each series the defender begins the offensive sequence and the offender shifts to the defensive part.

The same basic rules apply in all other exercises. Either the dagger parries can be ordered to match the targets of the drills established in Chapter 8, or the attacks and footwork must be made to correspond to the parries set in the drills. Either way, or both should be explored in cutting on the circle, thrusting on the circle, practicing the scales, around the clock and playing the numbers to acquire a strong working foundation of the defensive mechanics of the dagger.

Offense/Defense with Rapier and Dagger

The Offensive/Defensive drill may also be run with both the rapier and dagger. In this the offensive pattern remains the same but the parries are altered to accommodate the dagger. As described earlier, the dagger was used to defend the left side of the body. Therefore, the defensive parries are made in the following order:

- Dagger Parry 2
- Rapier Parry 2
- Rapier Parry 3
- Dagger Parry 3
- Rapier Parry 5
- Rapier Parry High 3
- Dagger Parry High 3
- Rapier Parry 6
- Dagger Parry Low 2
- Rapier Parry 8

Of course, you can do any combination of parries. Try as many variations as you can. Get comfortable with the idea of two weapons and double fence.

Working the Parries

The parries of the theatrical dagger may be executed in the same manner as those of the rapier: direct, semi-circular, diagonal and circular. Their placement may be in either standard or transitional

Plate XL: An illustration from Capo Ferro's treatise showing a double fence parry similar to Cross One.

form, just as the rapier. These parries may further be performed as a blocking, beat or detached parry. Because the dagger is used to "break" the attack of the opponent, most dagger parries are either beats or blocks. The detached parry is generally an action of the transitional rapier, a style of blade-play developed after the discarding of the dagger. Just as in the practice of the rapier, however, all three forms of parry can be used to great effect if used to a specific purpose within the choreography. For this reason it is best to become familiar not only with the placement of the dagger parries, but to become familiar with each type of parry as you work the drills.

DOUBLE FENCE PARRIES

As discussed in the introduction to this chapter, double parries generally came in two forms: cross parries and parallel parries. We will look at the cross parry first.

Cross Parries

A *cross parry* (also scissors parry) is a parry executed with two weapons, generally rapier and dagger, where the weapons are crossed at or near the forte, forming an "X" with the blades. The attacking weapon is blocked with the outer portion of the "X," away from the hands. The placement of the rapier and dagger, one in front of the other, is determined by the target being defended and the following counterattack. Whether held in front or in back, the dagger is generally used to hold the attacking blade in check, or to remove it as an immediate threat while the rapier launches a counterattack.

Numbering the Parries

For the purposes of this text a separate numerical system is used for the cross parries. This is done first to keep the mechanics of parries separate from the targets being defended (i.e., the cut is to the head, not to number 5), and second to distinguish these parries from either the single rapier or single dagger parries.

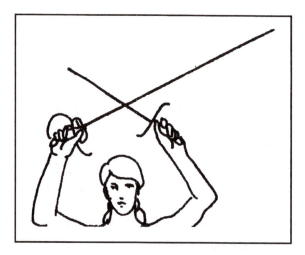

Figure 256. Crossing of the Blades.

Starting from Terza Double

Each of the four basic cross parries, and their variations, are described as executed from the double fence guard of Terza. They may eventually be executed from any guard position like both single weapon parries after the fundamental mechanics have been mastered.

Line the Cross up with the Target

Be sure that in all cross parries that the cross of the blades is directly lined up with the intended target. Just as in single weapon parries, the fortes of the crossed weapons must travel through your center in the same plane as the attack. The cross of the blades must travel out and forward to effectively meet the path of the attack.

In executing these parries, it is important that you remember that these mechanics are guidelines and that everyone's arms are built and move differently. Slight alterations may be necessary to adapt to your physique. Just remember to cross the blades prior to moving towards the attack, to line the cross up with the target and to adhere to all safety rules established earlier in the text.

The Crossing of the Blades

In order to better protect the dagger-bearing hand, the hilt of the dagger should be no closer than four inches from the blade of the rapier in all of the following cross parries. Your hands stop roughly ten inches apart (this distance may vary depending on the blade length of the dagger). The weapons are crossed with the blade of the dagger four to six inches off the hilt of the rapier, and the hilt of the dagger roughly four to six inches from the rapier blade. (Fig. 256) If the dagger hand is placed any closer it runs the risk of being struck by the offending blade. When the instructions call for the joining of the blades, the flats of the blades are joined in this manner.

The Cross of the Blades Must be Firm

When the parry is made the defensive blades should not move. If the attacking blade is knocking or hitting the blades out of place, the attack is coming in too hard. Remember the energy of the attack is sent beyond the target, not into it. The cross of the blades should neither slip down towards the hilts, nor be pushed up the blades towards the points. The defending blades also should not scissor in or out—closing or opening the cross of the blades. The cross remains as it was established until the parry is complete.

Dagger Placement

Unless specifically stated otherwise, the dagger may be placed either before or behind the rapier in the following cross parries. The term "before" refers to the dagger being situated "to the front of the rapier, on the side towards your partner"; and the term "behind" meaning the dagger is "to the back of the rapier, being placed on the side away from your partner." These terms are applied to the dagger's placement in the final position of the parry. Although all of the following cross parries can be executed with either the blade before or behind, only the dagger placements that afford effective counterattacks are discussed herein.

High Cross or Cross Parry Head

The *high cross* or cross parry head (cross parry of 1), is a double weapon defensive action against a vertical cut to the head. This parry may be made one of two ways; either with the dagger before or behind the rapier. The mechanics of the two parries are quite similar to the single rapier and dagger parries of High 5, varying mostly in the angle of the blade and the specific placement of the weapon-bearing hands. (Fig. 257)

Figure 257. Rapier and Dagger Cross Parry One/High Cross.

High Cross

Starting from Terza Guardia lower the tips of both weapons down toward the floor, to the position of six o'clock. Guide both weapons in towards your center line so that they come to rest with the tip of your rapier across your body to the position of seven o'clock, its hand in pronation, palm facing toward you, knuckle bow to the rapier outside (right). Your dagger comes to rest with its point below/above the blade of the rapier, the tip towards the position of four o'clock. The dagger hand in pronation, palm facing toward your knuckles toward the dagger outside (left). Stop the hands when they are roughly ten inches apart and join the blades. The cross is at your vertical center line, positioned below the center line target for a cut to the head.

As the blades come together, turn both wrists (as you would in the parry of 5) so that the palms are toward your partner, thumbs to the inside, knuckles up. This rotation brings the points of both weapons up, but outside your partner's body; rapier point to ten o'clock and the dagger tip to two o'clock. Be aware that the relative position of the crossed blades does not change.

Keeping the hands in this position and the cross of the blades at your vertical center line, raise the hands (traveling up in a vertical plane) above your head and in front of your body. Upon completion your rapier hand is in line with your right shoulder and your dagger hand in line with your left shoulder. The rapier is at ten o'clock with your palm towards your partner, knuckle bow directed up and to the rapier outside (right) the blade above you and in front of you at roughly a forty-five degree angle to the floor. The dagger is at two o'clock with your palm towards your partner, knuckles directed up and to the dagger outside (left), the blade above you and in front of you at roughly a forty-five degree angle to the floor. Both blades are in a plane parallel with the body, or angled slightly forward over the head of your partner.

Low Cross or Cross Parry Groin

The cross parry of the groin *low cross* (cross parry 2) is the double weapon defense for either a montante or a thrust to the low mid torso. Because of the placement of the blades upon completion of this parry there is only one way to effectively execute this defensive action. The parry is generally made with the dagger behind, so the rapier is not trapped between your dagger and your body. (Fig. 258)

Low Cross (Dagger Behind)

Starting from Terza Guardia turn both your points to the outsides, the rapier out to the position of two o'clock, the dagger to the position of ten o'clock. From here, both hands begin an inward rotation of the blades; the dagger moving clockwise, the rapier moving counterclockwise (like the mechanics of the actor's parry of 2). The rapier rotates to the position of seven o'clock; the dagger to the position of five o'clock. As you turn the blades (from the wrists), bring both hands in towards each other. Make sure that the blades do not angle forward toward your partner during this, that the blades travel in a plane flat with your body. As the weapons come to rest in their placement, place the dagger below the blade of the rapier. Join the blades when your hands are roughly ten inches apart. Your palms are towards you, knuckles to the inside and down. The cross of the blades is at your vertical center line, positioned above the center line target for a montante (upward cut to the groin). From the start in Terza through the completion of the parry is one continuous motion.

Keeping the hands in this position and the cross of the blades at your vertical center line, lower the hands (traveling down in a vertical plane) below your groin and in front of your body. Upon completion your rapier hand is in line with your right leg and your dagger hand in line with your left leg. The rapier is at seven o'clock with your palm towards you, knuckle bow directed down and to the rapier inside (left), the blade in front of your body and below your groin at roughly a forty-five degree angle to the floor. The dagger is at five o'clock with your palm towards you, knuckles directed down and to the dagger inside (right), the blade in front of your body and below your groin

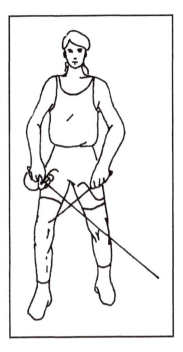

Figure 258. Rapier and Dagger Cross Parry Two/Low Cross.

at roughly a forty-five degree angle to the floor. Your arms are nearly straight with both blades angled slightly forward towards your partner.

The parries of high cross and low cross are often executed in quick succession, one after the other, in theatrical fight choreography. There is a fluid dynamic to this transition both in the offensive action and in the execution of the two cross parries. (Fig. 259)

Figure 259. Transition from the High Cross to Low Cross (frame by frame).

Figure 260. Rapier and Dagger Cross Parry Three/Cross Right.

Cross Right or Cross Parry Right Shoulder

The cross parry right shoulder, also cross parry 3, is the joined double weapon defense against attacks to the right shoulder. (Fig. 260) This parry may be executed with the dagger either before or behind.

Cross Parry Right Shoulder

Starting from Terza Guardia turn your rapier hand toward you, knuckle bow to the rapier outside (right), and drop its point and turn its tip clockwise to the position of seven o'clock. When the blade is at seven o'clock, guide your sword hand across your body, stopping roughly ten inches from the dagger hand. As you do this, you may guide the blade of the rapier over/under the blade of the dagger. When the rapier reaches this position turn your dagger hand toward you, knuckles toward the dagger outside (left), and turn the tip of the dagger towards the rapier to the position of four o'clock. When the blades are in the correct position to join the blades, bring the dagger blade up from below to join the rapier blade.

As the blades come together, turn both wrists (as you had in cross parry head) so that the palms are toward your partner, thumbs to the inside, knuckles up. This rotation brings the points of both weapons up, but outside your partner's body; rapier point to ten o'clock and the dagger tip to two o'clock. The hands and arms do not move during this rotation, keeping the blades outside the body and away from your partner's face. During this action do not let the relative position of the crossed blades change; the blades remain properly crossed as described earlier.

From this placement rotate your hands and blade so that your dagger hand is placed directly above your rapier hand (just above the level of your collar bone) with the dagger point directed at five o'clock and the rapier at one o'clock. This puts the cross of the blades at armpit level, directed out towards your right with the actual "cross" of the blades in line with your vertical center.

Keeping the hands in this position and the cross of the blades at the level of your right shoulder target, move both hands forward and to the right (traveling out together in matching horizontal planes), outside and in front of your body. Upon completion your dagger hand is just above the level of your right shoulder about six inches outside and ten inches in front of the body. The dagger is at five o'clock with your palm towards your partner, knuckles turned slightly down and to the rapier outside (right) the blade outside and in front of you at roughly a forty-five degree angle to the floor. The rapier hand is directly below the dagger hand, just above the level of your waist about six inches outside and ten inches in front of the body. The rapier is at one o'clock with your palm towards your partner, knuckles directed up and to the rapier outside (right), the blade outside and in front of you at roughly a forty-five degree angle to the floor. Both blades are in a plane parallel with the body, or angled slightly forward.

(Note: Some schools have the cross parry right shoulder executed with the hands in reverse placement, i.e., the rapier hand above in a form of High 2 with the dagger below in a form of dagger parry 4. (Fig. 261) This defends the same target in much the same way; however I find it rather dangerous as the elbow of the right arm is brought through the plane of the target and runs the risk of being struck if your partner's timing is off. With the rapier low and the dagger high, only the weapons pass through the plane of the attack, keeping you safe from possible injury.)

Figure 261. Rapier and Dagger Cross Parry Three/Cross Right.

Cross Parry for a Diagonal Attack to the Right Shoulder

The mechanics for a cross parry for the right shoulder or *high cross right* are identical to the cross right shoulder except in the final rotation of the blades. The rotation for this parry stops with the rapier point at eleven o'clock and the dagger hand at chest level, to the left and above your rapier hand, with the dagger point directed at three o'clock. The cross of the blades is at armpit level, directed up and to your right with the actual "cross" of the blades just to the left of your vertical center line.

Keep the hands in this position and the cross of the blades directed up. Matching the plane of a diagonal attack to the right shoulder, move both hands up and to the right (traveling out together) outside and in front of your body. Upon completion your dagger hand is just at the level of your right shoulder and about ten inches in front of that shoulder. The dagger is at three o'clock with your palm towards your partner, knuckles turned down, the blade outside and in front of you parallel to the floor. The blade of the dagger may be placed either in front of or behind the blade of the rapier. The rapier hand is below and outside the dagger hand, just above the level of your waist about six inches outside and ten inches in front of the body. The rapier is at eleven o'clock with your palm towards your partner, knuckle bow directed to the rapier outside (right) the blade outside and in front of you angled just slightly to your left. Both blades are in a plane parallel with the body, or angled slightly forward.

CROSS LEFT OR CROSS PARRY LEFT SHOULDER

The cross parry left shoulder, also cross parry 4, is the joined double weapon defense against attacks to the left shoulder or chest. (Fig. 262) This parry is executed with the dagger either before or behind.

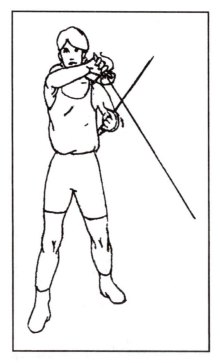

Figure 262. Rapier and Dagger Cross Parry 4/Cross Left.

Cross Parry Left Shoulder

Starting from Terza Guardia guide the dagger hand across the body towards the dagger inside (right). Place the dagger hand so that it faces toward you, knuckles toward the dagger outside (left), the tip of the dagger turned counterclockwise to the position of five o'clock. As you do this, guide the blade of the dagger either over or under the blade of the rapier. Keeping the rapier on the right, turn its hand toward you, knuckle bow to the rapier outside (right), its tip turned clockwise towards the dagger to the position of seven o'clock. Stop the action when your hands and blades are in proper placement to join blades. The dagger hand is eight to ten inches away from the rapier hand, and the cross is in line with the right side of your body, or just to the outside. Once you are in this position, you may join the blades.

As the blades come together, turn both wrists (as you had in cross parry head) so that the palms are toward your partner, thumbs to the inside, knuckles up. This rotation brings the points of both weapons up, the rapier point to ten o'clock and the dagger tip to two o'clock. From this placement rotate the hands and blades counterclockwise until the dagger reaches the position of ten or eleven o'clock and the rapier hand is directly above your dagger hand (just above the level of your collar bone) with the rapier at seven o'clock. The cross of the blades is at armpit level, directed out towards your left with the actual "cross" of the blades in line with your vertical center.

Keeping the hands in this position and the cross of the blades at the level of your right shoulder target, move both hands forward and to the left (traveling out together in matching horizontal planes) outside and in front of your body. Upon completion your rapier hand is just above the level of your left shoulder about six inches outside and ten inches in front of the body. The rapier is at seven o'clock with your palm towards your partner, knuckles turned slightly down and to the rapier inside (left), the blade outside and in front of you at roughly a forty-five degree angle to the floor. The dagger hand is directly below the rapier hand, just above the level of your waist about six inches outside and ten inches in front of the body. The dagger is in front of the rapier, point at eleven o'clock with your palm towards your partner, knuckles directed up and to the dagger outside (left), the blade outside and in front of you angled up at roughly a forty-five degree angle to the floor. Both blades are in a plane parallel with the body, or angled slightly forward.

*Note: There are some schools that have the cross of the left shoulder made with the dagger hand high (in a variation of dagger High 2) and the rapier below (in a variation of rapier 4). This practice however, brings the arm and elbow of the dagger hand through the plane of attack, exposing the arm to possible injury. I prefer the above listed techniques where only the blades are subject to the plane of attack.

Cross Parry for a Diagonal Attack to the Left Shoulder

The mechanics for a cross parry for the left shoulder or high cross left are identical to the cross left shoulder except in the final rotation of the blades. The rotation of this parry stops with the dagger at the position of one o'clock and your rapier hand at a forty-five degree angle off your dagger hand (around armpit level, to the right and above the dagger hand) with the point turned to ten o'clock. The cross of the blades is at armpit level, directed to the left and up with the actual "cross" of the blades just to the right of your vertical center line.

Keeping the hands in this position and the cross of the blades turned up towards the diagonal shoulder target, move both hands up and to the left (traveling out together in matching horizontal planes) outside and in front of your body. Upon completion your rapier hand is at the level of your left shoulder and about ten inches in front of it. The rapier is at ten o'clock with your palm towards your partner, knuckle bow turned up, the blade outside and in front with its tip slightly angled up, almost parallel to the floor. The dagger hand is below and outside the rapier hand, offset by roughly forty-five degrees, just above the level of your waist about six inches outside and ten inches in front of the body. The dagger can be either in front of or behind the rapier, point at one o'clock with your palm towards your partner, knuckles directed to the dagger outside (left), the blade outside and in front of you angled up at slightly to the right almost perpendicular to the floor. Both blades are in a plane parallel with the body, or angled slightly forward in the manner of a transitional parry.

CROSS PARRY RIGHT HIP or LOW CROSS RIGHT

The cross parry right hip or low cross right is the joined double weapon defense for an attack to the right hip. The parry is generally executed with the dagger placed behind the rapier for the same reasons mentioned in the low cross; if the dagger were placed before the rapier, the blade would be unable to counter, being trapped between the dagger and your body. (Fig. 263)

The right leg should be back or removed back away from the attack for this parry.

Low Cross Right (Dagger Behind):

Starting from Terza Guardia raise the tip of your rapier to the position of twelve o'clock (turning your palm towards your partner, thumb to the inside, knuckle bow to the rapier outside) and drop the tip of your dagger to the position of six o'clock (palm

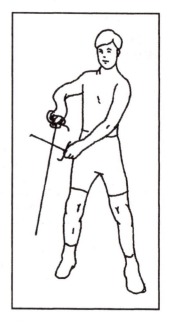

Figure 263. Rapier and Dagger Parry Low Cross Right.

towards you, thumb to the inside and knuckles to the dagger outside). From this position, bring both hands in towards your center and guide the point of the dagger counterclockwise to four o'clock and the rapier clockwise (over the blade of the dagger) to the position of seven o'clock. The palm of your rapier hand is towards you (knuckle bow to the inside, thumb to the rapier outside). Stop the hands when they are roughly eight to ten inches apart with the cross of the blades at your vertical center line. When the blades are in correct placement, join the blades with the dagger blade beneath the blade of the rapier.

From this placement rotate the hands and blades counterclockwise placing your dagger hand directly below your rapier hand. This puts the hand below your waist and in front of your right leg, palm towards you, knuckles turned slightly up and to the rapier outside (right), the dagger's point directed at one or two o'clock. The rapier hand and arm are in normal placement for a transitional parry of 2 (with the point at five o'clock). The cross of the blades is at waist level, directed out towards your right with the actual "cross" of the blades in line with the target of your right hip.

Maintaining the same relative position of the hands and blades, move the parry forward and to the right (traveling out together in matching horizontal planes) outside and in front of your body. Upon completion your dagger arm is almost straight, in a line down and across your body from the left shoulder to below the right hip. Your hand is just below your waist line about six inches outside and ten inches in front of the body. The dagger is at one or two o'clock, the blade outside and in front of you at roughly a forty-five degree angle to the floor. The rapier hand is directly above the dagger hand, just above the level of your waist about six inches outside and ten inches in front of the body. The rapier hand is in the placement for a transitional parry of 2 (tip is at five o'clock), the blade outside and in front of you at roughly a forty-five degree angle to the floor. Both blades are in a plane parallel with the body, or angled slightly forward

Because the weapons are outside the body on the right it is possible for the parry to be made with the dagger to the front. The rapier is not actually trapped between the dagger and the body and can theoretically be removed behind for the counterstrike. Such a removal, however, generally proves more awkward than effective.

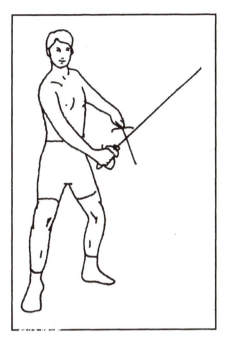

Figure 264. Rapier and Dagger Parry Low Cross Left.

CROSS LEFT HIP or LOW CROSS LEFT

The cross parry left hip or low cross left is the joined double weapon defense for an attack to the left hip. (Fig. 264) The parry is most often executed with the dagger placed behind the rapier for the same reasons mentioned in the low cross.

The left leg should be back or removed back away from the attack for this parry.

Low Cross Left (Dagger Behind):

Starting from Terza Guardia move your hands in towards your vertical center. The rapier is placed over the dagger, its hand towards you, palm facing in (knuckle bow to the inside, thumb to the rapier outside), its tip across your body to the position of seven o'clock. The palm of the dagger hand is towards you (thumb to the inside, and knuckles to the dagger outside), its point at four o'clock. As you rotate the wrist, carry your dagger hand across your body towards your rapier hand. When the blades are in this position, join the blades with the dagger blade beneath the rapier blade.

From this placement rotate the hands and blades clockwise until the rapier hand is directly below the dagger hand (below your waist) with the rapier point now directed at eleven o'clock. The dagger hand rotates its point clockwise from its place at five o'clock to the position of seven o'clock. This rotation puts the cross of the blades at waist level, directed out towards your left with the actual "cross" of the blades in line with the target of your left hip.

Keeping the hands in this position and the cross of the blades at the level of your left hip target, move both hands forward and to the left (traveling out together in matching horizontal planes), outside and in front of your body. Upon completion, your rapier arm is almost straight, in a line down and across your body from the right shoulder to below the left hip. Your hand is just below your waist line about six inches outside the body and ten inches in front. The rapier is at eleven o'clock with your palm towards you, knuckle bow to the rapier inside (left), the blade outside and in front of you at roughly a forty-five degree angle to the floor. The dagger hand is directly above the rapier hand, its arm in normal placement for a transitional dagger parry 2, about six inches outside and ten inches in front of the body. The dagger is at seven o'clock with your palm towards you, knuckles directed to the dagger outside (left) the blade outside and in front of you at roughly a forty-five degree angle to the floor. Both blades are in a plane parallel with the body, or angled slightly forward. The dagger must be behind the blade of the rapier.

What of the Thighs?

There are no cross parries specifically for the thighs. Cross parries of this sort force the torso forward at an awkward angle taking the body off balance. The low cross left or right may, however, be used to effectively parry a cut to either the right or left thigh if you are in a grand lunge. The lowering of the body by the lunge puts the blades in such a place that the body does not have to contort to make these parries.

Ripostes and Counter Attacks from the Cross Parries

The Counter Made with the Dagger in Front: Cross parries made with the dagger placed in the front allows for the counterattack to be delivered above the dagger hand and from the right side while the offending blade is held in check or removed out of harm's way. As soon as the parry is complete the rapier may be removed from the parry by carrying it backward. Once free of the offending blade it may then issue a riposte or counterattack over the dagger or around the body to the right. The rapier may be moved to the right side of your body by a mollinello and used in an offensive manner either for a cut or thrust. During this action the dagger commands your partner's rapier. The command of the blade may be used by simply keeping their rapier in check, or by removing the blade with a croisé, bind or other blade taking action. Just be sure that the blade is not removed into the path of your rapier attack.

The Counter Made with the Dagger Behind: Cross parries made with the dagger placed behind the rapier allow for counterattacks to be delivered below the dagger or from the left side while the offending blade is held in check or removed from the lines of engagement. Once the parry is completed the rapier may be removed from the parry by carrying it forward and below the dagger or across the body to your left. The rapier can then be used in an offensive manner either for a cut or thrust. Cutting attacks seem to be the best counter launched from this type of cross parry, although the ferma, punta rovescio or any other thrust to the opponent's left may also prove effective. During this action the dagger commands your partner's rapier. The command of the blade may be used by simply keeping their rapier in check or by commanding it with a beat, pressure or pris d'fer. As mentioned earlier, any command of the blade is acceptable as long as the blade is not removed into the path of your rapier attack.

Parallel Parries

In rapier and dagger play, there are a great many combinations or types of parries. As we discussed before, the rapier may be used to defend the entire body, the dagger may be used to defend the entire body, and the blades may now be used together to defend the body. Originally the dagger was used to defend the left side of the body from knees up, leaving the lower legs and the right side of the body to the rapier. The weapons, however, may be used jointly to defend certain targets. This idea was exemplified earlier with the cross parries and may now be applied to the parallel parries.

Parallel parries are dual weapon parries where the blades are placed in parallel planes to one another, without touching, to defend the same target. Unlike the cross parry, this technique provides two distinct walls to defend the body.

Be Sure to Allow Room for Both Weapons to Move

When executing parallel parries it is important to give way to the movements of the blades. As the arms and weapons move together toward the same targets, there is the possibility of the blades striking your own arms. More often than not the dagger has a tendency to strike the inside of the rapier arm. Be careful as you mark through these techniques. The mechanics of the parries do not change, but timing may have to be altered slightly in order to allow both weapons to move freely without hindering one another.

Placement of the Blade

When executing these parries, be sure that the blades are placed in planes that are parallel to one another. Although the parries of the rapier and dagger are two separate actions, both defending blades must meet the offending blade at the same time. At the completion of the parry, the blades should be no closer than six inches apart.

In executing a parallel parry, you may use any combination of parries that defend the same target. For example, the right shoulder may be defended from a cutting attack with a parallel parry of rapier 3, dagger 4 (dagger before). (Fig. 265) The same target may also be defended with a parallel parry of rapier 3, dagger High 1 (dagger before); rapier High 2, dagger 4 (dagger before); or rapier High 2, dagger High 1 (dagger either before or behind). The same process is applicable to all targets that can be defended by both the rapier and dagger. These include the head, left shoulder, right thigh, left thigh, groin, right hip and the left hip. (Fig. 266) Any variation is plausible as long as it is safe for the artist and appears effective to the audience.

Figure 265. Rapier and Dagger Parallel Parry right shoulder. Rapier parry 3, Dagger parry 4 (Dagger before).

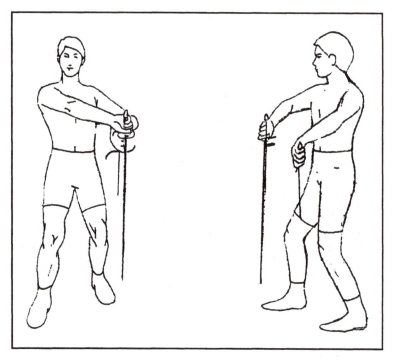

Figure 266. Rapier and Dagger Parallel Parry left hip, Rapier parry 1, Dagger parry 2 (Dagger behind).

Exchange/Transfer Parries

"As soone as he hath . . . found the enimies sworde, he ought to staie [command] *it with his Dagger, and therewithall, withdraw his owne sworde, to discharge a thrust underneath."* [di Grassi][15]

Exchange or *transfer parries* are a form of double weapon parry that use both weapons to deflect and control the offending blade. Unlike the cross parry and parallel parry, the two weapons do not meet the offending blade at the same moment. One blade begins the parry, usually the rapier, either breaking a thrust to one side or the other, or slowing the attack of a cut but not completing the parry itself. The other weapon, usually the dagger, is then used to complete the parry, "staying" the offending blade and freeing the rapier for a counterattack.

Maintain Control of the Offending Blade

In the execution of these parries it is important to remember that the goal is to maintain control of the offending blade. There is a split second of mutual contact as one blade transfers the parry over to the other. For example, a transfer parry could consist of a primary parry of rapier High 1 and the secondary parry of dagger 3 (dagger front). The transfer places the dagger in front to allow the rapier to be removed behind and conduct a counterattack off a mollinello. Once the dagger takes over the parry, the rapier is removed by carrying it backward over and behind the head. (Fig. 267) The continual contact with the opposing blade as the rapier parry is replaced by the dagger maintaining control of the offending blade. The dagger puts the blade in check while freeing the rapier to offer

---

[15]di Grassi, p. 64.

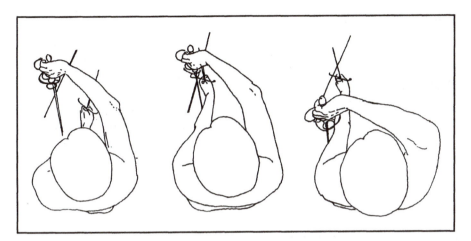

Figure 267. Rapier and Dagger Transfer Parry right shoulder, Rapier parry High 1 transferred to a Dagger parry of 3.

a counterattack from the right. The primary defending blade does not leave the offending blade until the secondary weapon is in contact with that blade. It is an exchange or transfer of the parry, not two separate parries executed on the same blade.

Be Sure There is Enough Room to Manage the Blades Safely

If the dagger is placed behind the rapier on these parries, be sure that the primary parry is executed far enough away from your body that the dagger has enough room to effectively execute the secondary parry. If the dagger is placed in front of the rapier, execute the primary parry correctly and begin to draw it back on the opposing blade, making room for the secondary parry. This sliding movement, in addition to clearing for the secondary parry, starts the rapier in motion for its counterattack.

"Staying the Enimie's Sword"

The secondary parry keeps the offending blade in check, or commands it in some way during the exchange parry. It is important, therefore, for the person controlling the offending blade to keep their blade there for the entire parry. Do not recover your blade after the initial contact of the primary parry.

The Primary Parry

Either weapon may be used for the primary parry. Generally, however, the rapier is used to stop the attack and the dagger to control it. This allows the greatest maneuverability of the major offensive weapon while commanding the opponent's blade.

The Parries

Like the parallel parries, there are any number of combinations and variations of transfer parries. There is no limit to what can be done with the two weapons, any variation is plausible, as long as the weapons can be maneuvered safely around one another (two examples are offered in Figs. 268 and 269). It is only important to remember that whatever combination you use, that it appear effective to the audience.

Transfer Beat Parries

A *transfer beat parry* is a successful primary parry completed with one weapon, followed with a secondary beat parry. Any rapier or dagger parry may be executed as a transfer beat.

Transfer Pris d'Fer

A *transfer pris d'ger* is the instant execution of a pris d'fer by the secondary weapon after the primary weapon has successfully completed the parry. Any rapier or dagger parry may be executed as a transfer pris d'fer.

Dagger Reinforcement Parries

The reinforcement parries covered in Chapter 9 may also be executed with the rapier and dagger. Instead of using the unarmed hand to hold the blade, the dagger braces the sword at the foible in

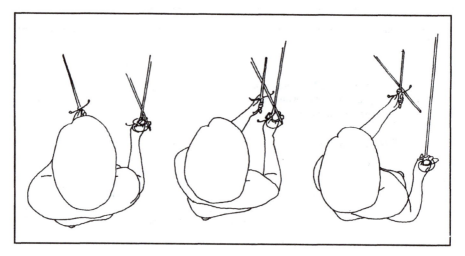

Figure 268. Rapier and Dagger Transfer Parry left shoulder, Rapier parry of 3 transferred to a Dagger parry of 4.

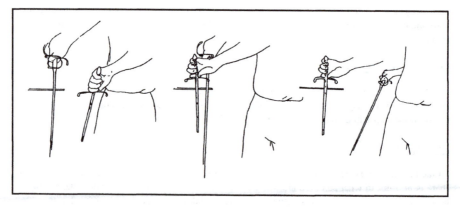

Figure 269. Rapier and Dagger Transfer Parry right hip, Rapier parry of 2 transferred to a dagger parry of 1.

order to strengthen the parry. The placement and mechanics of the sword hand and sword do not change from the reinforcement parries taught earlier, the hilt or blade of the dagger is merely placed against the rapier's blade approximately one third of the way from the tip, and then both hands push the parry out to meet the attack.

APPLICATION AND PRACTICE

As you practice the double parries, try working them from all six of the double fence guard positions. It is possible to go from any guard or parry to any other. As with the parries of the single rapier, have someone call out the parries in any order, and see how smoothly you travel to and from each parry. With the large variety of parries available, do not rush yourself. Remember, "think" and then "do"; know what you are doing and then slowly move from your present guard or parry to the next one called.

THE DRILL

All double parries may be applied to the Offensive/Defensive drill set out in Chapter 8. It is important that you decide what parries will be executed during each run of the drill so as to avoid confusion. The offensive portion of the drill is designed to attack specific targets, not numbers, so you can work a variety of different parries while working the routine. This is one of the best ways of practicing the parries as it runs them against a partner. Once you are comfortable with running the pattern stationary, try adding the appropriate footwork.

Measure

All drills working double fence parries are worked at correct distance for rapier play. Measure does not change in these exercises from that set in Chapter 8.

What About the Non-Defending Weapon?

Do not let either weapon become inactive or removed from the play of the weapons. If the rapier or dagger are not used in a particular parry, they should return to an effective guard position and wait for the appropriate cue before going into action. Neither hand should hang relaxed at the side or become uninvolved in the offensive/defensive play of the drill. You may know the pattern, but the swordsman is always on guard.

MOVING ON

When mastered, rapier and dagger play is one of the most intriguing forms of swordplay to be used on the stage and screen. The various parries presented in this chapter provide you with the framework on which double fence techniques are built. The two weapons work together to help the combatant achieve their objective. Neither weapon is an accessory; they are part of a fighting style quite different to that of single rapier play. As you practice these parries and move on to the techniques in the following chapter, be sure you are not merely performing single rapier techniques with the rapier and a dagger, but that you are truly fluent in the art of double fence.

Chapter 18

Offensive Actions of the Dagger

"You may give him a riversa upon his legge with your Rapier, and stabbe him with your dagger in the bodie." [Saviolo][1]

Although primarily a defensive weapon, the dagger can be used quite effectively for offense as well. The great debate concerning cut or thrust, however, doesn't really affect the use of the dagger. Prior to the introduction of the parrying dagger, knives were generally held in a reverse grip, with the blade below the hand, and were used for stabbing. The parrying dagger is one of the first instances of the blade being held above the hand (like a sword), but its primary function was still to stab. Most treatises concerning the use of the dagger have some reference to its use as an offensive weapon, but very few of them make use of the edge for cutting. In fact, more manuals make reference to throwing the dagger at the opponent than cutting them with it. di Grassi tells his readers to *"fling the dagger in deede at the enemies face,"* and Joseph Swetnam offers similar advice to a combatant who has lost their rapier, suggesting they *"take thy dagger by the point, and make offer to throw it, for that will so dare thine enemy, that he will stand until thou hast taken up thy weapon again."*[2] Be that as it may, in the theatre the dagger may well be used in close measure as an offensive weapon to both cut and thrust, but it is seldom thrown.

STAGE TECHNIQUES

When working with a dagger, remember that the blade is smaller than that of the rapier and that its actions are harder to see by the audience and your partner. Don't forget the mechanics of effective physical dialogue. The illusion of reality needs to be created while still providing the audience with proper points of focus. As mentioned in Chapter 6, actions the audience can see help give the physical conflict sub-textual nuance and character motivation. Don't change the mechanics of the technique because it is a different weapon. The process of Action-Reaction-Action still applies. Remember, "think" and then "do."

DAGGER MEASURE

You will find that it is ineffective to make an attack with the dagger while working at rapier measure. The distance, although safe, completely devoids the action of any real "threat" or intent

---

[1]Saviolo, p. 79.
[2]di Grassi, p. 153; Swetnam, p. 7.

and makes it impossible for your partner to parry. When working offensively with a dagger you must change your measure to suit the weapon. Dagger-play, like rapier-play, is executed out of distance, so that the weapon cannot make contact with your fellow combatant. Correct distance, or dagger measure, is comparable to that of the rapier, being a distance of at least six to ten inches from the chest of one combatant to the furthest extension of the dagger. (Fig. 270) This measure is usually achievable in the same manner as close measure, by one pass forward or an advance inside rapier measure. Do not assume this is the case, be sure to check and confirm measure in the same manner as the rapier. All attacks with the dagger, in this section, must be completed at safe dagger measure.

Of the Thrust

Since the dagger was primarily a stabbing weapon, we will start with point work attacks. The mechanics here are the same as those established in Chapter 7.

- Start each action with eye contact with your partner.
- When beginning all dagger thrusts are off-line. On-line attacks should only be practiced after aquiring proficiency in off-line attacks.
- All dagger thrusts are delivered in a straight line as opposed to an arching strike.
- There must be an effective ''cue'' or showing of the point as a preliminary to the attack.
- The proper response must be perceived prior to the continuation of the attack.
- The attack must be executed at the proper distance for dagger-play.
- Point attacks may only be directed to the seven targets established in Chapter 7. (These are the right and left shoulders, right chest, right and left hips, right and left thighs.)

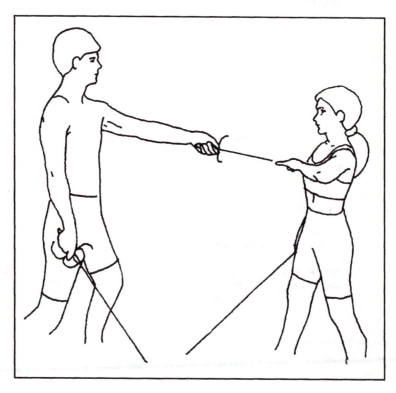

Figure 270. Dagger measure.

- All thrusts are completed with the hand in the same placement (supinated, pronated, etc.) as the cue.

Any of the thrusting exercises described in Chapter 8 may be performed with the dagger. They may be executed against the parries of the rapier, dagger or comparable double parries. Be aware, however, that some parries travel out in front of the body and may feel awkward as you close distance into dagger measure. Although no parries should travel out, towards the aggressor, it is always best to look at a parry prior to closing distance.

Footwork

To become comfortable with movement on the dagger attack, keep your thrusts at rapier measure, show the thrust and then execute either a full pass into a demi-lunge with the left foot or a standard demi-lunge on the right. Thrusts to your partner's right can be executed with the full pass, and thrusts to their left with the demi-lunge (be aware: you need to check distance with your partner to be sure dagger measure is correctly established). Be sure to make eye contact with your partner to see them respond to the cue, then look at the target of the attack.

The Cue and the Reaction

As in the exercises in Chapter 7, start off your dagger attacks with a verbal reaction to the cue. When your partner sees the correct cue, they say "YES," and if there is something wrong, they say "NO." As you are now competent in blade-play you may engage blades during the initial part of practice, but you must still listen to your partner.

Of the Cut

Although most period fencing manuals neglect the use of the dagger's edge, the theatre makes good use of it. By employing every possible offensive action of the weapon the dynamics of the fight are greatly enhanced. There are more dangers, more unknowns, more surprises—and that is what keeps the audience on the edge of their seats.

The cutting attacks of the dagger are primarily those of the rapier. Being a light weapon, however, the attacks are more often delivered from the elbow than from the shoulder. Therefore, the rules and mechanics of the attack are those established in Chapter 7, but the actual technique of the cut are those of the elbow cuts from Chapter 9.

Do not be fooled by the size and relative weight of the dagger, it can still do damage and injury. The smaller weapon is still driven by the strength of the arm and can develop a great deal of force by the time it reaches its target. The mechanics of a safe stage cutting attack still need to be applied.

- Each action must be started with eye contact with your partner.
- The "cue" or wind up is given from the rocked back position.
- The proper response must be perceived prior to the continuation of the attack.
- All attacks must be pistoned (from the elbow) sending the energy of the edge beyond one's partner.
- All cutting attacks must be made with the true edge of the blade (knuckles towards the target.)
- All cutting attacks are delivered to specific, predetermined targets.
- Always know the position and placement of the dagger's blade and point.

Methods of Practice

The cutting attacks with the dagger, although similar in mechanics to the cuts of the rapier, sometimes take longer to master than the thrust. This is due, in part, to the process of developing the mechanics in the less dominant arm. With slow repetition, the technique will come.

If you learn the dagger attacks in the same order as they appear in Chapter 7, you will have developed a pattern of attacks that are a mirror image to the offensive drill. You may have trouble working this pattern with the defensive drill of the rapier, but it works quite well with the numerical parries of the dagger. The pattern may also be adapted to the rapier defensive drill or the defensive drill may be patterned to the dagger attacks. In any event, once you are proficient in all the dagger cutting attacks, you should take them through some variation of the offensive/defensive drill, stationary and then moving.

Footwork

In executing the offensive/defensive drills, check your distance and run the routine at dagger measure. If the routine is taken moving, attacks to your partner's right should be executed with left foot dominant, and attacks to their left with the right foot dominant. You may want to randomly check distance as you begin this process to see if dagger measure is correctly maintained. Be sure to make eye contact with your partner to see them respond to the cue, then look at the target of the attack.

The offensive/defensive drill with the dagger may be executed against the parries of the rapier, dagger or comparable double parries. Just be aware that some parries travel out in front of the body and that it is always best to look at a parry prior to closing distance.

The Cue and the Reaction

Like the above exercises in thrusting attacks, and the exercises in Chapter 7, you should start off your dagger attacks with the "yes/no" reaction to the cue. This practice is important because it focuses on effective communication within the mechanics of the fight.

The Dagger on the Riposte

Other exercises in offensive actions of the dagger include a parry with the rapier and riposte with the dagger. Like the parries discussed in Chapter 17, many of the double parries are easily altered to allow the rapier to check the blade and the dagger to launch the counterattack. In these exercises the person who has the counter must command the offending blade so that it is not a hindrance during the change in measure or to the counterattack.

Evading the Dagger

The evasive actions offered in Chapter 10 are easily applied to the attacks of the dagger. All the mechanics of the techniques must be executed in proper dagger measure. The nature of the attack should be taken into account. Generally, the cut under the feet does not work well with the dagger due to its inability to "reach" the feet. Other such evasions are also subject to this difficulty. The best rule is to practice the action until it is comfortable to do at a performance speed and show it to an observer. If they buy it, it works. No matter how "impractical" the action is.

The Dagger in Evasions

> *"there are many who in avoiding with their bodies, lose their daggers, and put themselves in great danger."* [Saviolo][3]

Remember, your dagger is a defensive weapon, and although you are voiding an attack, the dagger should be removed from the threat, not from the fight. Don't let the weapon drop to your side when not in use. The actor knows there is no need for the dagger for several moves, but the character

---

[3]Saviolo, p. 112.

has no idea what will happen next. Keep your guard up. Don't, however, take this to an extreme. Be sure that when you are working evasions that the dagger guard does not get in the way of the attack.

Dagger Attacks on the Blade

The attacks on the blade and blade-taking actions offered in Chapter 11 can be executed with the dagger as effectively as with the rapier. The beat attacks, pressures, glides and pris d'fer are easily adapted to the dagger. All the mechanics of the techniques remain the same, although most dagger actions tend to be passive rather than active in execution. This is due in part to the length of the dagger's blade, and the effective reach of the dagger-bearing hand. Generally, attacks on the blade and blade-taking action executed with the dagger are used to open lines of attack for the rapier and not to initiate a dagger attack. Dagger attacks may be launched from these actions, but this is not a common practice on stage.

Actions may be performed by the dagger alone, or jointly with the rapier. As described in the last chapter, the rapier or rapier and dagger can be used to defend an action and then the dagger can be used to check the blade or command it with one of the blade-taking actions. Croisés, binds and envelopments may also be executed from parallel parries, commanding the opposing blade with the efforts of both arms. The dagger may also be used to counter a blade-taking action offered by the opponent.

Intercepting the Bind

Intercepting the bind or *stealing the bind* is a form of pris d'fer, executed against a pris d'fer. As Combatant A begins a bind, with rapier to rapier, Combatant B follows the action with their dagger and engages A's rapier during the bind. Once the dagger is engaged, B executes a bind on A's blade, turning the bind back on the aggressor. B's dagger takes control of A's rapier blade and binds it back to the action's point of origin. B's rapier is removed once the dagger intercepts. This action can be executed against any bind with rapier to rapier.

Dagger Deceits and False Play

The rules that define simple and compound attacks of the rapier are also applied to the offensive actions of the dagger. The actions of the disengage and coupé are more actions of the rapier, but they can be used to good effect with the dagger. False attacks and feints with the dagger are generally used to provoke a reaction that opens a line for attack with the rapier. The length of the dagger's blade and the extremes in measure make it difficult to false an attack and close for hit without being parried. False attacks may, however, be used by the rapier to create openings for an effective dagger attack.

Closes and Gripes with the Rapier and Dagger

In theatrical rapier and dagger fight, coming to the close means moving into dagger measure. In this placement the combatants can safely use both the rapier and the dagger for offensive and defensive actions as long as all attacks are directed off-line. The actions of the rapier are the same as those established in the close in Chapter 13. The dagger is handled in the same manner as those described earlier concerning offensive and defensive actions at dagger measure. Both the rapier and dagger can execute standard defensive parries, but no cross parries can be executed while at dagger measure. The actions of the blades travel too close to the opponent, making the actions unsafe and possibly dangerous in close quarters.

To the Hilts

With four weapons instead of two, locking up the blades in a corps-à-corps is a more difficult proposition. Previously, any attack met by a parry could be taken to the hilts. In double fence, however, this action still leaves two weapons free and unencumbered. Thus, in double fence there are generally two ways of coming to the hilts and locking the blades in a corps-à-corps. The first is to execute one parry, close to their hilts and then execute an attack with the free weapon inside measure, parried by the opponent's second weapon. An example of this follows:

From a right dominant position, Combatant A shows a cut to B's left shoulder. Combatant B reacts with a dagger parry 3, and A completes their attack meeting B's parry. Immediately upon making contact with the parry, A initiates an active crossover step forward, passing left then right. The blades remain engaged and A's blade glides from foible to forte as they move forward, where A's rapier hilt comes to rest against the forte of B's dagger. Once in measure, A shows a withdrawn arm dagger thrust to the right hip. Combatant B reacts with a rapier parry 2, and A completes their attack, meeting B's parry. Immediately upon making contact with the parry, A glides their blade in from foible to forte pressing their dagger hilt against the forte of B's rapier. After the second parry the combatants lean in towards one another in the manner of the rabbit ears grasp. (Fig. 271)

The second example of coming to the hilts is to have all weapons engaged prior to coming to the close. This can be done in the following manner. From a right dominant position, Combatant A shows a thrust to B's left shoulder. Combatant B reacts with a dagger parry 3, and A completes their attack, meeting B's parry. Keeping A's rapier engaged, B executes an immediate riposte and shows

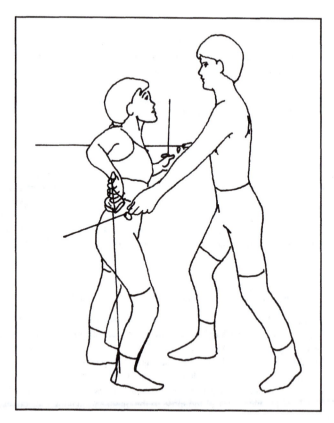

Figure 271. To the hilts in double fence.

a thrust to A's left hip. Combatant A reacts with a dagger parry 2, and B completes their attack, meeting A's parry. (Fig. 272A) As soon as A completes their dagger parry they initiate an active crossover step forward, passing left then right. (Fig. 272B-C) All blades remain engaged and A's rapier blade glides from foible to forte as they move forward, where A's rapier hilt comes to rest against the forte of B's dagger. At the same time A's dagger blade glides down B's rapier from foible to forte, pressing their dagger hilt against the forte of B's rapier. The two combatants can then lean in against one another applying controlled pressure. The controlled pressure allows the bodies to work against each other without overpowering one another.

These are only examples of closing to the hilts with the rapier and dagger. The combinations are numerous. Just be sure to walk through the movements to make sure that the footwork safely carries the body to the close and that the path of the weapons does not interfere with the physical movement or cross the plane of the face.

The Grasps

The process of grasps and securing the swords is a technique for swordsmen with a free hand. With the dagger in the left hand, grasping the opponent's hilt or blade proves awkward. In double fence, these actions are seldom used because there is a possibility of accidentally dropping the dagger or the opposing weapon. If the grip is not sure, the grasp is weak and the action potentially dangerous. This does not mean the actions cannot be done, it merely means that they must be approached with caution and thoroughly practiced.

Double Weapon Disarms

Because the opposing sword cannot easily be grasped or secured in double fence, disarms are generally loose, the blade falling to the stage in the manner described in Chapter 13. Although there are a great variety of disarmaments in double fence, the following examples assume that the opponent is fighting with the single rapier and cannot offer attack with their dagger. If both combatants are equally armed with rapier and dagger, the bind over and heavy parry can be executed with one weapon (usually the rapiers) while the daggers come to the hilts in a corps-à-corps. In this position the disarm can be achieved with a beat away or pressure.

Disarm by Beat Away

The beat away can be an effective way of loosing the opposing sword from a bind or heavy parry. The rapier can execute these actions, taking the opposing blade to the floor, and then the dagger can be engaged with a beat away to loose the sword. The bind or heavy parry may also be executed from a parallel parry where both weapons take the opposing blade to the floor. If both weapons are joined in the placing of the opposing blade on the floor, the dagger can also be used to hold the sword down while the rapier executes the beat away. In each case, the disarm is acted. Your partner should react to the beat, and then safely drop the sword to the floor.

Assisted Heavy Parry

The *assisted heavy parry* is the action of a dagger parry, joined by the rapier into a heavy parry. The action of the heavy parry is executed in the same manner as that of the single rapier, only now both weapons take the opposing blade to the floor. There is also the *transferred heavy parry*, which is a dagger parry transferred to a heavy parry with the rapier. The mechanics are identical to those of the transfer parry offered in the previous chapter except as the rapier joins the opposing blade, it instantly takes it to the floor in the manner of a heavy parry. The disarm in both these actions can be either by joined pressure, bearing down on the opposing blade or with a beat away.

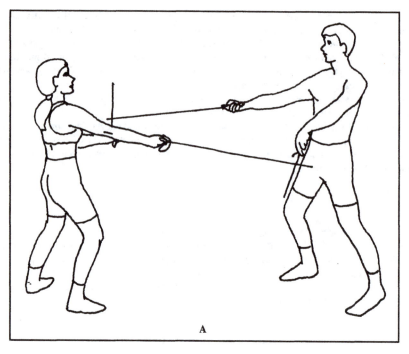

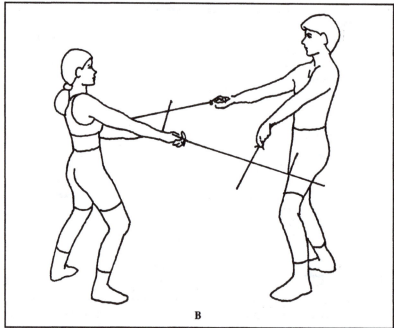

Figure 272. To the hilts in double fence.

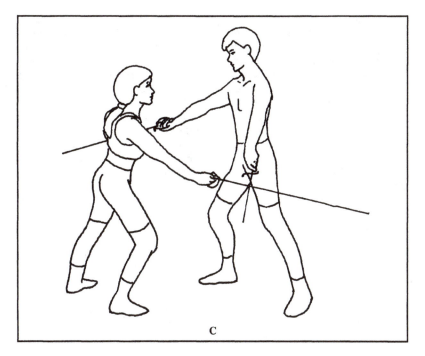

Figure 272 (Continued). To the hilts in double fence.

Pummel Attacks

Pummel attacks can be executed with the dagger in exactly the same manner as with the rapier. The action is not often used in double fence when both combatants are armed with both rapier and dagger. This is due to the fact that the action cannot safely be stopped by an armed hand. To safely execute the type of pummel attack described earlier in the text, the defending combatant must have a free hand to catch the attacking arm. Pummel attacks are rare with the dagger because it is usually an action executed with the sword in close quarters. The sword cannot be used effectively at that measure and so the weapon is turned to club the opponent. The dagger however, can be used effectively in close quarters, thus the idea of using the pommel is not the best offensive choice. Depending on the situation and the character, however, turning the hand to cuff the opponent, rather than stab them, can represent an act of contempt or reckless desperation.

Hitting Home with the Dagger

The Dagger Thrust Home

Because the dagger has a shorter blade than the rapier, and the thrust is executed with the combatants in closer proximity to one another, the technique of misdirecting the point does not present the illusion of the blade traveling forward towards the victim. Holding the hand and arm in a straight line toward the victim, while angling the point outside the body only looks like an attempt to miss with the dagger. To present the illusion of a forward stab or thrust without actually threatening the target, the dagger attack needs to be made off-line, directing the hand, arm and tip of the weapon about three to four inches outside the body.

The measure for the dagger thrust home is the same as that of the rapier. The last third of the dagger rests on the muscles on the side of the body, with the tip free and to the rear. Because of the length of the dagger, it is best to make sure that the point of the weapon is not directed into the side. The footwork used to find this measure varies, but the placement of the blade does not fluctuate.

The execution of the dagger thrust home is the same as that of the rapier, only coming from the left rather than the right. Although the thrust home can be delivered to either side of the body, the attack is generally executed to the left so that the rapier hand does not need to mask the blade. For the purpose of this exercise, the victim should first practice taking the hit with nothing in their left hand. (Fig. 273) Once the technique is practiced, the victim may then try catching the blade with the dagger in the hand. (Fig. 274) In this case the blade is not caught in the cup of the hand, but held to the body with the dagger-bearing hand and wrist. Be careful not to whip the dagger into the opposing blade or aggressor's arm. It must travel below the attacking blade without posing a threat to the opponent. Also, be careful that the quillons of the offending dagger are not dragged into the body or arm of the defendant. Taking the hit with the dagger in hand should be practiced with both the rapier and dagger.

As always, these actions should be practiced with gloves in order to avoid scratching the hand.

Dagger Cuts

The landed cutting attacks of the dagger are executed in the same manner as those of the rapier. They can be executed as draw, flick and swashing cuts. The draw cut is executed at the same measure as the home thrusts listed above. The draw and flick cuts can safely be delivered to the six body targets covered earlier and should be practiced in the same manner as the draw cuts. Because of the limited reach of the dagger blade, the soft parries need to be executed inside measure. This allows for the edge of the dagger's blade to be safely placed on the opponent's arm. The swashing blow with the

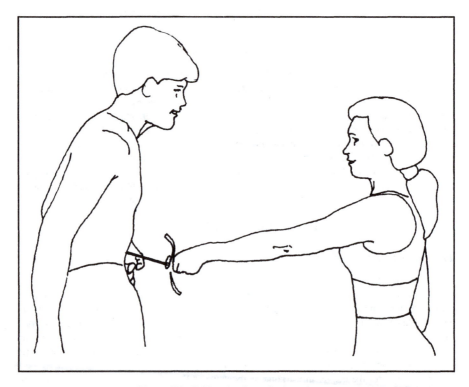

Figure 273. Taking the dagger's thrust home.

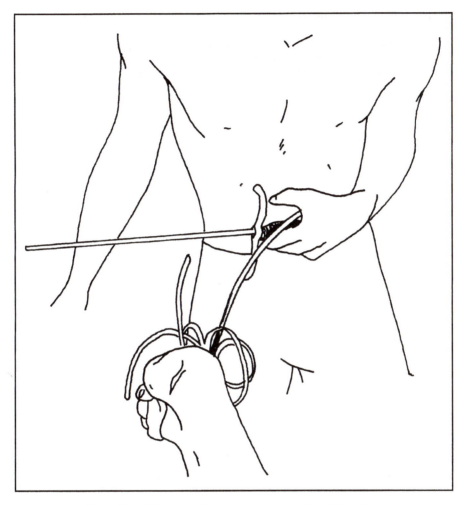

Figure 274. Taking a thrust home with a dagger in the cradling hand.

dagger is executed at proper measure for dagger attacks (six to ten inches from the chest at full extension). All the precautions offered in Chapter 14 still apply in these attacks.

Work these wounds in the same manner as the rapier thrusts and cuts. Try combining them with an attack on the blade, pris d'fer and other ways of removing the opposing blade to create an opening for the hit. Just work everything slowly to insure you are in control and at the appropriate measure for hits with the dagger.

WORKING THE RAPIER AND DAGGER

The art of double fence combines the techniques of the rapier and dagger in an endless number of ways. The possibilities of individual and combination actions are immeasurable. The only boundaries are those of safety and your own imagination. Before you move on in your training, take the time to fully explore the techniques of double fence. Knowing how to move the weapon is completely different than having experienced the movements. At this point in time you should be familiar enough with the standard safety rules to practice the variable techniques in the exercises offered throughout this text. With the two weapons you should try playing the numbers or working around the clock. Evasions, disarms, simple and compound attacks can effectively be worked into these exercises. Plot out the movements with your partner and slowly explore the number of activities available to you. Take the time to master the technique and develop a neutrality from which choices can be made effectively. Do not try to make a scene or act a fight. Explore the movements of the weapons and become comfortable with the actions before trying to perform them.

Chapter 19

Setting the Fight

"All movements—instead of being as small as possible, as in competitive fencing—must be large, but nevertheless correct. Magnified is the word. The routine should contain the most spectacular attacks and parries it is possible to execute while remaining logical to the situation. In other words, the duel should be a fight and not a fencing exhibition, and should disregard at times classically correct guards and lunges. The attitudes arising naturally out of fighting instinct should predominate. When this occurs the whole performance will leave an impression of strength, skill and manly grace." [Fred Cavens][1]

The process of taking the techniques of stage combat and arranging them into a fight is a procedure more difficult than it might first appear. It is not a random series of offensive and defensive actions strung together like the numbers exercise. A choreographed fight is the artful blending of character and technique designed to tell a specific story. Random movement patterns work well for training exercises, but they say nothing about the character or the play. No matter the size or relative importance of the conflict, the actions must come from the play and fit the structure of the character. The process of setting a fight is not to dazzle the audience with a display of your best "tricks" and "feats," but to say what needs to be said about the characters and their situation as clearly and effectively as possible.

A fight is usually a climactic moment in a scene, if not the entire play. Yet the fight itself seldom lasts more than a few seconds to a few minutes. The combatants on the other hand have been, or will be the focus of the audience's attention for the duration of the show. The play cannot stop for the spectacle of a sword fight or an exhibition of fencing. The fight must be set to support what the audience sees and hears about the characters involved in the conflict.

The neutrality of the techniques and exercises offered in the preceding chapters are as merely the foundation of theatrical swordplay. The mechanics are specific. The posture, stance and placement exacting. Yet, that is not how it should appear in a theatrical routine. No two people move or react the same way. The personality of each of the characters determines their posture, stance and placement, and governs everything they do during the fight. The comic cowardice of Andrew

---

[1] Richards, Jeffrey. *Swordsmen of the Screen*, pp. 44. Fred Cavens, a graduate of the Belgian Military Institute, entered films by staging the duels for Max Linder's Fairbanks spoof *The Three Must-Get-Theres*. He has worked with all the great swashbuckling stars: Douglas Fairbanks, Sr., Douglas Fairbanks, Jr., Errol Flynn, Louis Hayward, Cornell Wilde and Tyrone Power.

Aguecheek in Shakespeare's *Twelfth Night* prompts completely different actions than the comic cowardice of Oswald in *King Lear*. The calm, composed confidence of Rostrand's Cyrano de Bergerac produces a fight wholly dissimilar to that of the calm, composed confidence of George Walker's Zastrozzi. A fight is the external manifestation of the character's inner attitude of aggression coupled with their skill with a weapon. The moves of a theatrical fight will only be convincing to an audience if they come from the character who executes them.

Definite Business

In setting a character-specific fight the fight director first turns to the facts offered by the playwright. The facts are referred to as the fight's *definite business* or *obligatory actions*. These are the external actions that define the plot events of the play, such as Macduff killing Macbeth in the last act. These stage actions are described in dialogue or text; and are clear statements, exacting in description of what happens. They are concrete things that a *writer* provides about the characters, their situations and surroundings. All too often the facts of the playwright are muddled with the notes provided in an acting edition of a play. When the majority of people get hold of such editions, they feel that these instructions are imperative, and that somehow the details of the sword fight up and down the staircase, over and around the table, and into the fireplace are all vital to the presentation of the play. They are not. The directorial notes and commentaries are one person's interpretation of the manuscript, not the facts provided by the writer. The "physical blocking" noted in most plays is usually how that rendition was staged and not how it must be staged. "Definite business" is set in the spoken dialogue, all else is left to interpretation. Shakespeare wrote [*they fight*]—and that's it. What is definite is that they fight; what is indefinite is how they fight.

Indefinite Business

After the facts of the play have been explored, the fight director starts investigating how the characters might achieve their obligatory actions. It is definite that Tybalt must hit Mercutio under Romeo's arm (*"Why the devil came you between us? I was hurt under your arm." Romeo and Juliet* III.i), but how this happens is unclear. The actions that tie the facts of the fight together are *indefinite business*. It is the product of deductive reasoning based on the fight choreographer's knowledge of theatre and stage combat coupled with their reading and research of the play. Indefinite business evolves into the fight choreography and establishes how the character goes about achieving the specific actions described in dialogue or text. In acting this is the process of completing the puzzle and developing a complete picture of the character, their situations and surroundings. In stage combat it is the process of taking what has to happen and completing the picture by deciding how it will happen, such as how Tybalt kills Mercutio or how Hamlet delivers the wound that kills Claudius in the last act of *Hamlet*. Unlike the choices made by the actor specifically about their character, these are decisions generally reached between the director and choreographer and given to the actor in the fight choreography.

By analyzing the facts of the text, the fight choreographer, in collaboration with the director, decides on the physical dialogue to take place between the characters. The definite business of Mercutio being stabbed under Romeo's arm, the character information provided by the text, and the opinion of the director leads to the choreographer's "How" this happens. When the "How" is established and set in choreography, the indefinite business becomes definite business by prescribing *what* happens within the fight. As a ghost writer, the choreographer sets the actions to paper, turning them into text and definite business for the artist. This physical dialogue needs now to be treated as definite business, and needs to be analyzed by the artist as intently as any of the text originally presented by the playwright.

Hence, the process of flushing out character is applied to the fight as a given. There will, of course, be some changes in choreography made during rehearsal. Once the fight is set, however, it is definite, a fact of the play. The actor's job is to then look at the fight and determine what must happen so that they can explore how it can happen.

By-Play

Although the definite business of the play is facts, as a general rule, these are flat and boring. They are information that is fatuous if stressed, explained or rationalized, and yet they cannot be ignored. The definite business of the text must be presented by the artists because they're obvious and an audience would resent it if they were missing. If Mercutio says he was struck under Romeo's arm—it must happen. How it happens is decided by the director and choreographer, but it's all the little things that you, the artist, discover that thrill the audience and make them want to pay to see you again.

By-play is the development of character that fills time and space with energy and intent without stepping outside the strict boundaries of choreography. These are decisions made on the part of the actor that include vocalizations, facial expressions, preparation and anticipation of attacks that never come to fruition and personal character traits that make the actions truly their own. It is the choices within the movement, the exploration and expression of the character within the definite business that make a choreographed routine appear spontaneous and real.

The Facts of the Production

The procedure of setting a fight cannot be taken lightly. The collaboration between the director and fight choreographer moves beyond the scope of definite and indefinite business to the elements of theatricality, concept and stage pictures. The set, costumes, lights and so on all play an intricate part in establishing fight choreography. They also must take into account the facts of the actors as well as the characters. Bad knees, bad backs, physical shape and condition and hundreds of other factors about the artists can limit the scope of possibilities within any particular fight. Yet, all things considered, the fight choreography must still support the intentions of the author and truthfully represent the characters in conflict.

Aside from knowing the play and its characters inside and out, a fight choreographer must also know things such as:

- Type of weapons being used
- Limitations and possibilities of the weapon
- Limitations and possibilities of the actors
- The type of theatre (thrust, round, proscenium, etc.)
- Size (height, width and depth) of the playing area
- Placement of levels, furniture, props and people during the fight
- What props or furniture may and may not be used during the fight
- Where the fighters can and cannot go
- Limitations and possibilities of the costumes
- Limitations and possibilities of the lights and special effects

As well as the director's overall theatrical concept;

- View of characters within the play:
- View on theatrical significance of fights;
- View of movement themes within the fight;
- Definite blocking just before, during and after the fight.

To accomplish their task, a fight director must work closely with the director and become an intricate part of the production team. Aside from knowing a variety of armed and unarmed combat techniques, an effective fight choreographer must have a strong knowledge and understanding of directing, dance and dramatic movement, as well as scenic design, costuming and the overall theatrical medium. With this knowledge, a skilled choreographer makes the physical conflict an integral and dynamic part of the drama. Without this knowledge climactic moments can become pallid, comic or even deadly due to ineffective stage violence. A professional fight director makes it possible for the director to stage all physical conflicts convincingly for the audience and safely for the artists.

Notating the Fight

Once all the factors of the production are determined, the fight director maps out the fight. This is sometimes called the *fight plot* or *fight arrangement* and it is the written description of the whole fight. Most fight directors have a cryptic form of short-hand notation to mark the choreography of the fight, but there is no universal form of notation. Each choreographer develops a system of notation based on what they were originally taught and what they have developed throughout their career. This can make it quite difficult for the actor or fight captain to work from different choreographers' notes. The choreographer should, however, provide legible copies of the choreography to all concerned.

When in Doubt, Write it Out!

In the process of notating a fight the best advice is "when in doubt, write it out." There are very few forms of short-hand notation that can take into account all the variables of a fight. Most notation systems employ symbols for cuts, parries, thrusts and simple footwork, but this is very limiting because most fights contain a lot more than simple swordplay. The Laban and Benesh systems of movement notation used by professional dance choreographers and companies seem to be the only exceptions to this rule. Learning these notation systems, however, requires a serious time commitment in training, and then it is completely illegible to anyone who hasn't studied it. Invented notation systems have the same problem in legibility and can't possibly cover everything that might happen in a stage fight. The development of a symbol for "leaping from a table to swing from a chandelier" or to "take hold of a chair and fling it across the room" will take longer to develop and then decode than it would to write it down in plain English.

As actors, you should never assume that the Fight Director's notes will make sense or assist you if a crisis should arise. Even if their choreography is written out in "English," their terms for many of the moves can be different from that with which you are familiar. Therefore it is best for you to take your own notes on a fight, just as you are responsible for taking notes on your own blocking. The basic rule for blocking notation can be applied here: if you can read it and remember it, it is right.

What Needs to be Seen

No matter the form of the notation, the choreography must be clearly and cleanly notated, and must not be vague. From the simplest crossing of swords to the mass brawl that opens *Romeo and Juliet*, the plotting of the fight requires careful step by step documentation. At any stage of a fight, the performers should always be able to tell:

- where they are on stage;
- where they are in relation to their partner;
- their physical relationship with other actors, furniture, props and scenery;
- their foot placement;
- what they have just completed;
- what their partner is about to do;
- what they are about to do; including
    —footwork, and the exact direction it takes them
    —weapon-specific offensive or defensive actions
    —body-specific offensive or defensive actions
    —specific use of furniture, props and scenery

The Fight Plot

Because many actors are unfamiliar with how to jot down a fight, here is a variation on a common form of fight plot, the side-by-side chart. As most fights are combinations of two or three combatants, even in mass battle scenes, this type of chart works well. When working with two combatants the page is divided into five columns. The second, fourth and fifth column are of roughly the same width, the first and third are quite small. This can be seen in the example from Shakespeare's Twelfth Night (III.iv) given below.

Twelfth Night—III.iv

	Viola (Stage Left)		Aguecheek (Stage Right)	NOTES
I	Coming On Guard at Demi-Lunge measure; Right dominant; Terza Guardia Across, with both hands holding the sword.	**-I-** **PHRASE**	Coming On Guard at Demi-Lunge measure; Right dominant; Terza Guardia Across	Phrase I moves parallel to the proscenium; in the "courtyard" below the SR fountain. Sir Toby & Fabian stand aside UL.
1	Slowly move to engage blades	→	Remain On Guard, body carried well back	
2	React to movement; *Pass Back Right:* release Rapier with left hand, Counter Parry 2; Pass Back Left; Rapier Counter Parry 2; Stop, realize there is no threat	←	React to engagement; Instantly draw blade back	Fabian reacts, moves SR ending UC, between Viola & Aguecheek.
3	Come On Guard in Seconda, Left hand supporting Right arm	—	Return to Terza Guardia	

Line Numbers

The first column features the "line" or move number of the fight, presenting the choreographer and artists with specific points of reference within the routine. This can be used to note specific blocking placement; moves 4–18 are executed on the Stage Right (SR) stair unit on the top two steps, or for clarifying movement patterns, 6–11 move counterclockwise on the circle. Numbering is also beneficial in setting a fight to music. Although it is not a process of counting the fight, it is helpful in notating where certain moves take place in the score. This process is also valuable in teaching choreography to a class by specific moves and in easily locating and correcting errors.

Character Columns

The second and fourth column are the Character columns. These are used to place the movements and actions of each character. If there were more combatants, there would simply be more columns. Located inside these columns are each choreographed move of the character. This includes every fight-specific movement they make including their guard positions, footwork, blade work, etc. Acting notes are generally not listed in these columns because how the actions are played should be developed by the actor, not dictated by the choreography.

In order to avoid excessive long-hand, some abbreviations are used in these, and other columns. The most common abbreviations are in stage directions. These include Up Stage (US), Down Stage (DS), Stage Right (SR), Stage Left (SL), Center stage (C), etc. Because these are used in most theatrical blocking notation there is no need to go into them further. In footwork "right" and "left" are usually used to denote feet, except in actions such as Circle Right. If this is the case, the term "right foot" follows the action. To denote active or passive actions, both in footwork and blade-play, an *underline* is used. If the action is Passive it appears in standard print. If it is Active, the action is underlined, as in Viola's first *Pass Back* on Line 2.

When describing offensive actions the body targets are specific to the victim. Cutting attacks that are evaded are described from the aggressor's point of view. For the sake of brevity, choreography notation assumes proper safety technique on the part of the artists.

The Column of Conflict

The third, or middle column is used to indicate the Phrase number of the choreography. Fights, like music, are broken into phrases. A phrase in a fight is an uninterrupted section of choreography, offering a definite beginning, middle and end. This could be a single move or an extended series of moves that has an unmistakable first action and an ending, such as a hit or any other definite break in the action. Some fight directors name their phrases to encapsulate the mood or feeling of the phrase, but this is not necessary.

The middle column is, however, mainly used to indicate the direction of action between the combatants. The arrows in that column on line 2 and 3 in the above example shows the direction of movement in the fight. This does not mean that the fight actually moves in the direction of the arrows, but that the choreography reads from either right to left, or vice versa depending on who initiates the offensive action. For example, on line 1 the choreography reads from left to right as Viola moves to engage Aguecheek; however, on line 2 it reads from right to left as Aguecheek pulls his weapon away and Viola responds by passing backward and parrying. The dash "—" on line 3 indicates that neither combatant is making an aggressive action towards one another at that time. Thus, this type of choreography does not read like a book, but in the direction of the aggressive intention.

Column 5: Fight Notes

The fifth column is for choreographic and staging notes. This can include references to furniture, props, scenery or other actors on stage during the fight. It may also be used to note the direction of a series of moves as in "Phrase I moves parallel to the proscenium," or movements that span several moves such as "the footwork in 34–36 is executed as a Balestra." This column also can be used when a fight is set to music to make notes as to where in the score certain actions should be taking place.

The Focus Herein

Because of the plethora of variables involved in staging a fight for an individual production, this book cannot deal with the scope of offering stock fights. Even if the variables of sets, lights and costumes can be agreed upon, there is no ready-made fight that fits every Director's views and concepts of a production. Remember, a fight must not only come from the facts of the play, but from the Director's interpretation of those facts.

This chapter then, focuses on the process of setting the fight, not the process of choreography. A chapter on choreographic process would assume a great deal of knowledge on the part of the reader and take a book much larger than this.* Setting the fight is the fundamental process of moving through a fight rather than an exercise. In other words, it is the first few readings of a new script that eventually need to be memorized and performed.

Work Slowly Through the Routine

Before jumping into a fight routine, there are a few things of which you should be aware. Despite the training you have had so far, plotting a fight is still a slow process. Although you are now comfortable with the mechanics of the rapier and dagger and with working a number of drills and exercises, it is not the same as a routine. Learning a fight for the first time is like trying to tackle period verse with only a knowledge of contemporary prose. Although they are in a similar language, the rhythms and patterns are completely different.

Although the desired result of a fight routine is spontaneity in performance, as well as an illusion of violence or death, you cannot have the real thing in rehearsal without risking the real thing in performance. What this means is that when you are plotting out the fight you must pay close attention to the safety rules and techniques established earlier in this book. Fight choreography does not notate the exact movements of the blades. For this reason you must work slowly at first, checking the path of your weapons, your distance, targets and so on. If this care is not taken in the beginning stages of plotting the fight, accidents can occur as it is brought up to speed.

A general rule of thumb in plotting out a fight is to allow at least one hour of rehearsal for each twenty seconds of combat. This rule can be affected by a number of factors: if the combatants are untrained fighters; if they are learning techniques that are completely foreign to them; if the fight is being set to music; or if the fight involves more than three people. When any of the above are involved, the rule changes to one hour of rehearsal for each ten seconds of movement. These, of course, are general rules, and there are exceptions on both sides. No matter the situation, however, you should work at a slow pace and take the time to make sure everything is clear and safe.

Take the Time to Get it Right

In a real fight the movements are largely spontaneous and unplanned. Conversely, the movements of the theatrical fight are planned as meticulously as any other part of a production. Because of this, it must also be rehearsed as meticulously as any other part of a production. Thus, once the movements of the fight have been plotted, they must be rehearsed.

In a play it is absolutely essential that the fight be given priority when rehearsals are scheduled. Stage swordplay, even when worked slowly and safely, is one of the most dangerous things actors are asked to do, and they *must* be allowed adequate time to rehearse. If a trained actor can still drop a line, or forget a section of blocking, they can quite possible forget fight choreography. No one gets hurt, however, if a line is dropped. "Early and Often" is a good, safe rule to fight rehearsals. This is true of a fight for a play, film or simply for practice. The process cannot be rushed.

As you work on a fight, your work sessions must be scheduled as closely together as possible. If the fight is being set for a production, it must be set within the first two weeks of rehearsal time. Rehearsal must be consistent. Daily, or every other day, rehearsals or classes are necessary in order to build the kinesthetic links required in learning the movement sequence. If the production has understudies, adequate rehearsal time for them must also be scheduled. All combatants must be allowed adequate time to develop a physical understanding of the fight for obvious safety reasons.

*For further reading and research see Hobbs, William. *Fight Direction for Stage and Screen.* (1995) London: A & C Black and Suddeth, J. Allen. *Fight Direction in Theatre.* (1996) Portsmouth, NH: Heinemann Press.

Walking Through the Fight

After plotting out the moves of the fight you are ready to rehearse it in a *walk through*. This is the process of carrying out all the moves in slow motion. Initially, the walk through establishes whether the moves in the fight safely work when linked together. Later, after addressing all safety issues, repeated walk throughs not only develop your skill in executing the moves, but also help fix them in your memory.

In the preliminary stages of learning a fight it is important that you do not go beyond the walk through stage. At this point, speed and dramatization are not the goal. The idea is to get comfortable with the plot of the fight and not to enact it. That comes later.

LEARNING THE FIGHT

In many cases the process of ''learning'' a stage fight consists of strict memory and repetition of data, like street directions, or historical dates. Fight choreography is not something which you have to commit to memory, it is a thing of which you need to gain a full understanding in order to be able to fully bring it to life. As you are now probably aware, move to move memorization can prove to be a difficult process. A string of actions, many quite similar in execution and sequence of presentation, can prove maddening to remember and easy to get lost within. This is why many fights seem to be separate from the production for which they were staged. The focus of the actor shifts from the continuity of character in their moment to moment circumstances to trying to get through the fight. Everything they have worked on in all the preceding scenes is set aside in order to remember the moves of the fight routine, thus missing the point.

Setting the Character Free

The thought process of ''learning'' a fight needs to be changed. The fight is learned, not as a series of technical actions, but by exploring the character's feelings, thoughts, objectives and finally arriving at performing the fight choreography. This provides the artist with a full understanding of the fight and realization that no other action or actions serve quite the same purpose. A fight is not, and should not appear to be, choreography. It is a dramatic confrontation that must be taken from thought to thought, not from move to move. It is for these reasons that we now move from walking through the fight plot to the process of acting the fight. The process of knowing a fight is much less reliable than understanding the fight.

Chapter 20

Acting the Fight

"We shall get empty, superficial, formalistic, mechanical acting if in our technical training we forget for a moment that the actor's duty is to portray living people." [Bertolt Brecht][1]

STAGE COMBAT AS A SECOND LANGUAGE

It is interesting to notice that in many acting training programs stage combat is taught as a separate subject from acting—as a technique that the actors should, after a semester or two, be able to integrate into their pool of skills and work into their craft. This is like giving an actor one or two semesters of beginning Russian and then assuming they can now mix this knowledge with their craft and do Chekov in the original language. This assumption is unreal. The artist, if they studied well, may be able to struggle through the text, but they will be so overpowered by the language that their craft will be suppressed as they try to master the intricacies of the foreign tongue. Because the process of acting a fight is similar to acting within a foreign language, the final product is often the same, ungrounded and shallow.

Stage combat first needs to be mastered as a skill so that it may be more easily integrated into the acting craft. Having carefully gone through all the fundamental moves and mechanics in a neutral state, we now can explore character within the conflict. Once the skills are understood and the artist is comfortable with the mechanics of the weapon, then they can start a process of working the acting craft into a stage fight. The artist needs to develop an acting process for combat that, after the physical skills have waxed, still provides a system of dissecting a physical encounter and making it an integral part of the acting process, the character and the production.

BLENDING THE TECHNIQUES OF ACTING AND ACTION

This chapter is offered to introduce the artist to the idea of merging the technical skills of stage combat with the artistic process of the actor. It has been my experience that actors, of just about any system or program, have little or no practical training in the process of analyzing and presenting a staged fight. Generally, their primary concern is the memorization and presentation of choreographed material. Their focus is on the creation of a completed product without having any developmental process. The following pages are designed to help develop a bridge between the techniques of acting and action.

---

[1]Brecht, B. *A letter to an actor.*

433

THE CIRCUMSTANCES

"Knowledge itself is power." [F. Bacon][2]

As any actor knows, to read a play and memorize a character's lines is not enough to portray a well-rounded, believable character. The same is true of a fight. Without proper reading and research a great deal of information about the character, their situation and surroundings is neglected. In order to better prepare for playing a particular character and combatant, time must be taken on the part of the actor to identify the specific information or *circumstances* provided by the playwright.

What Are Circumstances?

Circumstances are specific facts or data found in the script either in spoken text or notes. The actor's job is to locate the given circumstances and to fill out the provided information in order to create a whole picture of the character, their situation and surroundings.

Circumstances are particular to the character and their environment, not to the actor themselves. The script simply says "long-sword." This is a fact of the play. If no further information is provided, the actor has to use their knowledge and imagination to fill in the rest of the details, being as specific as possible:

- Rusty or polished?
- Nicked or sharp?
- Comfortable or awkward in the hand?
- A personal or borrowed weapon?

The given circumstances of the play provide the actor with specific information concerning persons, places and things. This information, although specific, should not inhibit the acting process, but rather enhance it. Circumstances merely narrow the point of focus from general to specific for the actor. Every moment, every beat on stage has specific circumstances. Some circumstances are constant, while others are generated by the environment of the scene and the people who enter and exit that scene. Every action has circumstances and is surrounded by larger circumstances. This information is the knowledge on which the choices in the production are based.

The Five W's

In the development of a character the first question the actor must answer is "Who" is the character? This question is the first of the "Five W's" (Who, What, When, Where and Why) of scene study. Each of the five questions should be probed and answered by the actor in order to clarify the character's purpose in the fight. In each scene the actor should answer:

- Who is the character?
- What is the character doing?
- When is this happening?
- Where is this happening?
- Why is the character there?

The actor should know from where the character is coming to arrive at the place they are now. They should be aware of what happened there and if what happened still influences them. Understanding who the character is means knowing their desires, aspirations and goals. It means knowing

---

[2] "Nam et ipsa scienta potestas est." F. Bacon. "Of Heresis." *Religious Meditations.*

why they are where they are and where they are going when they leave. It means knowing what they are planning to do later that day, tomorrow, next week and later on in their lives.

WHO

It is important that the actor finds the traits and characteristics of the character, and understands them before stepping into a fight sequence. A fight is an intimate part of the production and puts the character in a situation, whether they like it or not, where lives may be at stake. There are very few other situations that bring an entire spectrum of emotions to the surface like that of mortal combat. A fight should erupt from the circumstances of the play, not interrupt the play. It should be an insight into the character that can be shown in no other way, and must be approached as an acting challenge that tests the artist's knowledge and portrayal of the character in a way that no other scene can. Thus, the first stage of acting the fight is to understand **who** it is that is fighting.

In exploring the **who** of the fight, it is important to remember that the techniques that have come before are only guidelines and not law. As you explore the character you should investigate all the possibilities of the movement. Not every character or every situation allows for perfectly executed swordplay. The actions must always remain safe, but they also must come from the character. All the techniques offered in this book are the process of learning how to fight—not the finished product. As exemplified by Joseph Swetnam, perfect stance, posture, movement and execution are an ideal, not a constant.

> *"Some will be setting their foote upon their weapons, as if it were to stretch him when hee was right before, but they do it of a foolish custome that they learne of themselves: likewise, some will puffe and blow like a broken winded horse when they are at play, and some will daunce and keep a trampling with their feete, and some will whistle, and some will be blabbring of spittle in their mouthes, and putting out their tongues, and some again will runne about as though they could stand on no ground . . ."* [Swetnam][3]

The famous English fight director William Hobbs says that *"one cannot make rules regarding creativity, but only regarding technique and safety."*[4] This is quite true, and while there are no "rules regarding creativity" in stage combat, you must still adhere to those concerning safe, effective blade-play. Remember, as you change your posture and stance to explore the physicality, age and persona of your character, you also affect technique and measure. A physically awkward or limited, sloppy, or desperate character may use passive or active footwork, a wide or narrow stance, or bend at the waist in an over-committed lunge. Every change in physical presentation of the character can affect measure, visible target areas and range of motion of the body and blade. The physical handicaps of Shakespeare's Richard III are given within the text and must be maintained through each scene and carried into battle. This, and every other character's physical and mental makeup must be explored slowly within the fight to be sure that there are no breaches in the general rules of safety outlined in this manuscript.

In exploring the text, it is important to remember that the "who" is not only the combatant you portray, but also who else is in the production, in your character's world and life. Each person in the play affects your character directly and indirectly. You cannot ignore the other characters within the play. Thus, in the process of understanding who it is that is fighting, you should be aware of:

- who you are fighting
- who you may be fighting for
- who will be affected by this
- who will be opposed to this action
- who will support this action

[3]Swetnam, pp. 46–47
[4]Hobbs, *Stage Combat,* p. 65.

All these "who's" affect your character in this situation. Therefore, when researching your character, it is best to become aware of the people who surround them, friends and foes.

Character Background

Part of the research and reasoning process is to find not only what specifically is said about the character, but also how that character differs from another. Every character is the result of their history and the energy of their dreams. Their individual pasts fueled by their personal goals is what makes each character different and distinct. A warrior king, an Italian duelist, a royal prince all believe in specific things. They hold themselves differently, walk, talk, think, arm themselves and fight differently. Their life experiences, education, physical mannerisms, morals and beliefs are completely different. It is important to think through how a character lives and interacts in their social and political surroundings. When the research and reasoning of the given circumstances are fleshed out, the background of the character falls into place. The background should lead the actor to their character. The ability to understand these differences and identify with them allows the actor to see the fight from the character's perspective.

When looking at a character combatant in a production, questions you should put to the text concerning their background should include:

- What, if any, violent encounters has the character experienced in the past?
- What was the outcome of this/these event(s)?
- What other positive events and episodes are mentioned by them or others?
- What other negative events and episodes are mentioned by them or others?
- What is the social situation of the character?
- What is the character's class or rank in society?
- What is the character's profession or occupation?
- What is the character's history (emotional, physical, philosophical, family, social, etc.)?
- What formal training have they had with a weapon?
- What other forms of training would be available to them within their class, rank and profession?

WHAT

Another portion of the circumstances is the **what** of the play. In its simplest form the **what** of the situation is the fight. A fight, however, can happen for a variety of reasons, and it is important to know what the fight is. Is it:

- a cold blooded duel?
- a hot-blooded brawl?
- a fencing lesson?
- an exercise?
- a battle?
- a drunken encounter?
- a show of skill?
- a civil formality?
- a childish game?

You must know the nature of the fight before you can explore the facets of its actions. The facets of the fight include **what** all is involved in the fight. In analyzing the text the **what** is any definite fact that is not specific to the time or place, or immediate to the character. These include:

- what you are thinking
- what you are fighting with

- what you are wearing
- what you are feeling
- what your objectives are
- what you are doing
- what you are fighting for
- what you are trying to do
- to what end you are fighting
- what obstacles lie in your path

Simply, the ''what's'' of a scene could be that you are fighting (A) with a rapier; (B) to the death; (C) for an insult suffered to your reputation; (D) against an accomplished swordsman, etc. These are all facts of the scene that tell what is happening. Each development in a scene creates new circumstances that provide new facts. Moment to moment, beat to beat, the facts of the scene are constantly changing, constantly developing.

WHEN

The next phase of the five W's is the **when** of the circumstances. In analyzing the **when** of a play or scene many actors stop at the basic information of era and whether it is morning, noon or night. The playwright may have only provided you with that information but there is so much more that needs to be addressed. The **when** of the play is not just the date and time of the scene, it is the social and political backdrop as well.

It is important to remember that in Elizabethan England the sword is the most terrifying and deadly weapon imaginable. A drawn sword is like a loaded gun with a hair-trigger. A sword fight is not a sport to watch like modern fencing. It is life or death. It is very real to the character and an integral part of their everyday life. More than likely, every character in a Greek, Roman, Medieval, Renaissance and Restoration drama had a close friend or loved one die by the sword.

This is **when** the play takes place, this is **when** your character lived, acted and interacted, and this period can affect all their choices in some way. The more information you have the more accurate your choices. What is not provided by the playwright can be developed through reading, research and reasoning. A weak foundation can only support a weak structure.

WHERE

Another of the circumstances to be considered is the setting of the scene, its overall environment, the **where.** Where you are should affect what you see, hear, smell, touch, taste and feel. It cannot just be a setting, it should be a sensory overload. When exploring where you are, these are some of the questions you should be asking yourself:

- Is it familiar to you?
- What does the air smell like?
- What is easily overlooked?
- How much room is there to move?
- What is the temperature?
- Is it light, dark or shadowy?
- How does the ground feel beneath your feet?
- What is its visible texture?
- What instantly catches the eye?
- How does it make you feel?
- What is its physical texture?

- Can you taste the environment?
- Is it wet or dry?
- What noises and sounds are in the air?

Remember, nothing is constant. New information constantly changes your perception of your environment. Sounds, smells, light and atmosphere can come and go. The more you know about where you are, the more you can act in, and react to, that environment.

WHY

The **why** of a scene and play is like the layers of an onion. As each layer is exposed, a new layer can be discovered underneath. Each layer always supporting those above it, but solid on its own merits. The job of the actor is to discover each layer of the onion, peel it away and then explore the next. Like a small child you must constantly ask "WHY?" and "WHY?," again and again. To start off with, Why is Romeo wandering the streets instead of with his new bride? She had to return home. Why? She was only given leave to be away for a short time. Why? Because her parents are restrictive to her activities outside the house. Why? Because she is young and the town is prone to outbursts of violence. Why? And so on. Peel away the layers and develop strong understanding of the overall thought process. The reasoning for choices made by the character is based on the information they perceive to be true. You must delve into their reasoning to understand why they do things. Knowing and understanding "why" a character does something is essential in acting a fight.

Why something is done has many strata. The simplest form is why the action took place: for love, want of money, greed, etc. But the **why** covers many more bases. It is the reasoning for every action the character takes, and is based on all the other circumstances in one way or another. There is a reason for **why** we do anything, if that reason is only known at the split second we do something. It may not even be a conscious form of reasoning, or something that can be explained later—it is simply justification at the moment of the action.

The actor should look to the script to discover why the fight is there, both on a dramatic and character level. Why is it necessary? Pull the violence from the scene and try to discern what, in its simplest form, is missing. Be sure to explore the entire play, and not just the scene in which the violence takes place. The circumstances of the play should make the matter clear.

When exploring the text the actor should be asking themselves questions like:

- What must happen in this conflict to satisfy the basic needs of the character?
- What must happen in this conflict to satisfy the basic needs of this scene?
- What must happen in this conflict to satisfy the basic needs of scenes to come?
- How do the character's actions in this encounter affect their relationships with other characters throughout the production?
- Why now?
- Why at this point in the scene, act and play?
- Why not earlier or later?
- Why this person? This place? This time? This moment?
- Why to this end? (wound, kill, disarm, etc.)
- Why do they, or do they not, remove themselves from conflict?

When probing a fight, like probing text, it is important to remember that the circumstances always come first. It is important to look at what has happened before. The audience cannot tell one sword move from another so it is important that the actor can. A pause between phrases is a telling moment for the audience. The winner and loser can be told in a brief pause linking the action. What is happening now must reflect what has already happened and must carry the characters into what happens next. The strength of the bridge you make from spoken dialogue to physical dialogue is up to your creative imagination. Anything is possible, as long as the text and the given circumstance of your character truly support your choices.

BELIEVING THE CHARACTER IN CONFLICT

"The test of a man or woman's breeding is how they behave in a quarrel." —G. B. Shaw

Actions Speak Louder Than Words

A fight cannot be a series of ambiguous moves tossed into a production to fill the slot where the playwright says "they fight." A stage fight can, and should, tell the audience a great deal about the characters involved in the struggle. It can confirm suspicions about certain characters and support the status of others. Depending on the character "back stabbing," "hitting below the belt," or "kicking someone when their down" may, or may not, support what the playwright had intended. The actions chosen by the character during a fight reflect a true part of their moral fiber that may not be revealed anywhere else in the play. What would the audience think if Romeo cruelly toyed with Tybalt, repeatedly kicked him after tripping him from behind and then stabbed him several times in the back? Would the audience sympathize with his plight or cheer when the violent youth is banished? Violent actions change the situation, the aggressor, the victim and the audience's perception of all three. After an act of violence, no relationship is quite the same again.

The Physical Dialogue

The job of the actor is to look at a fight as they would written text. Look at the moves and discern how and why the fight operates in conjunction with the plot. Explore the through energy of the fight, phrasing of thought and movement, and the overall structure. The actions chosen, then opportunities overlooked, the intensity of the battle is based on text but comes from the characters as they develop. How the actions, thoughts and phrases are broken up is directly related to the emotional state of the character. The actor has to be aware of how all these parallel the text and contribute to the cohesive whole.

The Fight Must Erupt from the Play, Not Interrupt the Play

All the visual impact of a play must be motivated by the author's words and their aim as understood by the director. The production design, sound, lights and fights are all pieces of the picture envisioned by the director. The choreography must fit the director's concept of text, theme, and plot and the characters in the fight, like in all other scenes, must act and interact within the director's overall concept. The aspects of developing a character and investing a character in combat are clearly interrelated. Each part of the character affects the others, and is in turn affected by the others.

A fight makes its impact not only through its end, nor only by seeing and hearing the people who are performing the fight, but by seeing them in contrast and relation to each other and to the place in which the fight is carried out. In other words, the story of the fight is conveyed to the audience through the presented circumstances. The information presented prior to a fight, the things that happen between phrases in a fight and what happens directly afterward create the impact of the encounter. Just as the words of a script do not make a play, the swordplay does not make the fight. The actor must accept the circumstances given by the playwright as the truth and be in the moment, not in the choreography.

Objectives

Once the actor understands the circumstances of the play they can effectively begin to explore the physical dialogue of the fight. With this understanding the idea of choreography is lost and the concept of the fight being the character's thoughts in action can be developed. The rehearsal process is the time for you to explore the fight and to discover the reasoning behind the actions. Everything you do in a fight has its reason. In order to be truthful in the presentation of a fight you must know the nature of what you are doing and you must commit to doing it.

Many actors rant and rave, grunt and groan during fight choreography trying to play a fight rather than concerning themselves with the nature of the conflict. The aim of the characters is not to look as if they are fighting, but to fight. It is not the external shape and presentation they should be pursuing. Their concern should not be with form but with feeling.

Each actor has their own way of working, and therefore of finding the reason for the actions within a fight. The method of understanding the fight, and not just presenting, it varies according to their personal process, but no matter the process, the actor must continually refer to the Five W's.

During a fight you must know what you want. With each action you are trying to do something; the specific something is your *objective*. Objectives are specific, achievable goals of the character that can easily be expressed by using the verb form. You must know exactly what that is. All objectives are either attained, thwarted or abandoned. If you do not reach an objective, you must change to another. If you can complete your objective, continue with it and then find another objective. You must always have an objective. It is what moves you forward.

In the process of finding and setting objectives, they should be strong. In order to be strong, an objective needs an end, a goal. For example, *"I am going to run him through the eye."* The eye is the end of the objective and the ending makes it strong. *"I am going to fight,"* is an objective without an end and is therefore weak. If your objective is *"to run away,"* it is a weaker objective than *"to run to safety."*

Weak Objective:	Strong Objective:
• I'll fight	• I'll fight at dawn
• I'll stab him	• I'll stab him in the back
• I'll kill him	• I'll kill him by slitting his throat

Each fight generally has one main objective, but there are many different qualities and movements within that objective. The main objective of a fight might be *"to make them hurt like they hurt me."* In the course of the fight there can be profound changes in substance and weight,yet it has but one drive, one motive, one objective.

The main objective of the fight must be broken down into smaller objectives or steps. Whether the action is premeditated or immediate to the moment, there are steps to reach the end. For example, in the objective of *"I'll kill him by slitting his throat,"* there are a number of steps, such as acquiring a sharp knife, placing yourself in hiding, cornering or entrapping him, etc. If your objective is to acquire a sharp knife, you can do it. If your objective is to place yourself in hiding, you can do it. You cannot, however, complete the objective to fight at dawn, to stab someone in the back, or to kill someone by slitting their throat unless you break it down into steps that build up to the overall objective.

In all objectives within a fight, you must know:

- What you do
- Who you do it to
- When you do it
- Where you do it
- Why you do it

But you don't know "how" you do it. The **how** is spontaneous and unexpected. There is no such thing as a foolproof plan, something unexpected will always come between the character and their objective. Thus, no matter how you may intend to do something, the situation at the moment of execution offers variables that are not planned for and therefore lead to spontaneous solutions designed to reach the objective. The objective can include how it is intended to be done, but never includes the **how** it is done.

Actions

An objective is reached during a fight through the numerous movements of the sword and body. These movements are called *actions* and can be simple, compound, progressive or combined movements of the blade and body. In the process of exploring the fight, actions cannot be judged in regard to their outcome. The ensuing action of an objective is always correct at the time it is executed. Even if afterwards the consequences of the action should prove unsuccessful, for the moment itself, the action is sensible.

Justification

The choreographer provides you with the specific actions of the fight, but they do not always give you the rationale behind them. With the actions in hand, you must find the character's reason for doing it: the reason is called *justification*. Finding reasons for everything you do during a fight keeps your actions truthful.

The justification is not in the choreography, it is in you. You execute a croisé to remove an offensive blade and create an opening for a counterattack. Justification must go on all the time; it is the prime source of awakening you to the moment to moment interaction of the fight. In this sense the fight is no longer a series of movements to be superficially acted, but rather a series of motivated actions used to reach a specific objective.

Values

Each action, whether simple, compound, progressive or combination movements of the blade and body, has a specific *value* or significance to the character executing them. Not every action has the same commitment, quality or purpose and therefore its value is different to the character. The justification, or reason for the action and the character's commitment to the action establish its value. A feint attack has a different value than a thrust intended to hit home.

Seldom do fights have a single steady beat where each action and reaction have the same regulated weight and speed. Rather, the fight should be as variable as the emotions that drive it. It should be at times fast, at times slow, at times predictable and at times sporadic and unpredictable. But it should never be dull. The variables within the pattern of a fight are established by the emotions and the objectives of the character and set out in their actions. The values of the actions are what establish the tempo and rhythm of the fight.

Tempo: The value of the movement is directly linked to its manner. Not only does one have a reason for moving from point A to point B, but the action may be carried out at different tempos—fast, slow or any variable of speeds between. Actions that are desperately important are generally executed at a much faster speed than those of less value. The value of the actions within a fight directly affects the velocity or rate at which a fight is moving.

Tempo may also be affected by the limitations of armor, costumes, space or physical setting of the conflict, and the weight, or intensity, of the action. Value, however, is a constant within all these variables and still directly affects the tempo of movement, both of sword and body.

Rhythm: As the value of the actions within a fight directly affects tempo, values and tempo directly affect the rhythm of a fight. They, in variable amounts, affect the fight's visible and audible structure of movement patterns. Since not all actions have the same value, and different values offer different rates of speed and commitment, these variables provide the fight's rhythm. A feint attack is executed at one tempo, a real attack at another. The real attack may be parried and then followed by an immediate riposte cutting to the head. The head parry may be deceived and the blade thrust home into the chest. Each of these actions has a different value, and so a different tempo. A feint or deception of parry is not going to have the same value as an attempt to kill. They are actions toward the same objective, but with different values. These variables of rate within beats and phrases of a fight establish the routine's rhythm.

Value also affects rhythm in an audible sense. In the execution of progressive or combination attacks, the actions that are done to set the opponent up have a different connection with the defending weapon than the intended kill shot. For example, two cuts to the opposing shoulder designed to open the low line for a belly cut might be heard as light and soft, light and soft, hard and loud; or "ding, ding, pow." When these values offer abrupt changes in the rhythm, they are *syncopated* to the natural rhythm of the routine.

Syncopation is an abrupt or sharp change in the rhythm of a choreographed routine. This may be done by such means as clipping, abbreviating or stressing certain movements in order to heighten the physical dialogue. These rhythms, when found within swordplay, can help set the mood of the fight as well as help the audience follow the physical dialogue.

A stage fight is like a scripted argument performed physically for the audience. Just as in a vocal argument, if you start off yelling and screaming at the top of your voices with no variance, it's difficult for us to understand; you have nowhere to go but down. Not everything that is said or done has the same value, although it may have the same objective. The value of what you are doing is just as important as the value of what you are saying. The rhythm of your delivery can help convey your meaning.

Obstacles

In analyzing a fight, you will find that most objectives cannot be immediately reached. Anything that prevents a direct path to the objective is called an *obstacle*. A fight is a series of objectives and obstacles constantly checking and counter-checking each other. In a fight, as in other stage business, obstacles can be broken down into three categories: immediate, general and external.

- *Immediate Obstacles:* Those which face the combatant now! The obstacle is directly in front of you and must be overcome or you will be diverted from your objective. If you make an attack to reach your objective, and it is parried and riposted, the riposte is an immediate obstacle to your objective.

- *General Obstacles:* Those obstacles that are undetermined. These fall into the tactical and strategic portion of the fight. Both experience and emotion play a role in a fight's general obstacles. If your objective is to *"cleave their head in two"* and they are armed and on guard, that is a general obstacle. A parry of their head followed by a counterattack or a direct attack at you would be immediate, but actions on the part of your opponent that are not specific and have a variety of options are general. From an on guard position, open invitation, unarmed stance, etc., what your opponent can possibly do or what might happen is general. There is definitely an obstacle but the choice is not immediate.

- *External Obstacles:* Those which are outside the combatant's conscious or subconscious train of thought. This would be any obstacle beyond the perception of the character that somehow affects their immediate or overall objectives. External obstacles can be as simple as uneven terrain that can trip you up to an unknown or unexpected third party getting involved in the fight (i.e., Romeo in the Tybalt-Mercutio fight). These obstacles can also be taken as far as acts of God, king or country, nature or the environment. An example of this would be the objective to *"blind the opponent by getting the sun in their eyes."* If you were to manipulate them accordingly, only to have a large cloud block out the sun; such an obstacle to your objective is external. If, however, the sun comes out and blinds you during the fight, that is an immediate obstacle.

Obstacles do not change the objective, they only prevent a direct path to the objective. If your objective is to *"pin your opponent's shoulder to the wall,"* a counterattack or parry and riposte are an obstacle. It does not stop or change the objective, it is merely something that needs to be overcome to reach the objective. Once they are pinned to the wall this completes the objective and moves you on to another; such as *"to wrench the sword in the wound."* Or if they beat you, and disarm you, your objective is thwarted (if only momentarily) and your new objective may be to *"beg for mercy."*

Through Energy

Each action moves the character towards an objective's end. Commit to that action completely and its end prompts the next action. This is called the *through energy* of the fight. It is the process of identifying the objectives, actions and justifications of the fight and being aware of how each of those three contributes to the fight's movement forward.

Pursue the objective, and know that whatever is done to that end changes the moment and provokes the next thought, and requires more. You cannot afford to take any action for granted. Everything contributes to the texture of the thought and is part of the whole objective. You should notice particularly how the actions are linked, and how they shift the direction of the character's thoughts to bring about the next action.

When you get the sense of the through energy, how one action leads to another, the actions become cumulative. They are not a series of actions that are self-serving, they always build towards an objective. It is important, therefore, that you know the circumstances of your character well, or these connections will not be made.

Beats

In analyzing a fight, like analyzing text, the series of emotional changes that a character goes through are generally referred to as *beats*. Each beat of a fight has an emotional significance. Acting the fight is going from emotion to emotion in a theatrical manner, not as you would, but as your character would.

Beats do not have to follow a logical progression. The emotion that provokes a thought, and in turn an action, is always correct at the time it expresses itself. Even if afterwards the consequences of that action should prove unfortunate, at that moment, the emotion and its actions are justified. People's emotions are not chosen. They are responsive to circumstances, situations and surroundings. They do not systematically move the combatants toward the end of the fight. It is the actions made during each beat that bring about the fight's end. Emotions can, and do, override logic. Despite the character's objectives their own emotions can prove to be devastating obstacles. It is the gut level emotions of the characters, and the thoughts and actions they engender that are the keys to spontaneity, truth and passion within a fight.

The actions of a fight are the physical manifestation of the thoughts and feelings that prompt them. The actions cannot be overlaid with emotion. They must be discovered by penetrating into the action. It is your creative exploration of the fight that should discover the most dramatic physical manifestation of the series of emotional changes (beats) contained within the encounter. The writer wrote the words, and the choreographer set the moves, but it's up to you to find the beats within the fight and make them your own.

During the process of exploring the character's physical dialogue you can almost certainly plot their emotional state by how their thoughts are broken up. A combatant who is calm and tactical generally is more reserved in movement, executing sequences of blade-play that are designed to set their opponent up to a predestined end. Combatants who are emotionally involved have shorter patterns of attack or intend each offensive action to hit. Their focus is scattered, less cunning and more sporadic. A nervous character is more than likely on the defensive rather than the offensive. In each of these cases the character still goes through a variety of beats or emotions: hate, indifference, anger, envy, despair, pity, pain, torment, pride, fury etc. Knowing, understanding and playing these emotions gives the fight and character extra variety, extra interest.

PHYSICAL DICTION

Up until this point, the focus of this chapter has been placed on knowing and understanding the character and the circumstances of their situation and surroundings. This knowledge, in turn, has led to the proper understanding of the objectives and obstacles within the fight. All this, however, is only half the process of acting the fight. Knowledge and understanding are useless if that information cannot be communicated to the audience. Thus, equally important to understanding is the ability to tell the story effectively. The actor needs the language of the fight to be presented in a way that the audience sees what the character is feeling.

The "words" of the fight must be clearly enunciated so that the audience witnesses something that appears natural while communicating feelings and images and generating aesthetic responses. *Physical diction* is the clear, accurate and engaging delivery of the thoughts, emotions and intentions of a character without verbal support. This gives the movements greater clarity and precision. All too often actors have brilliant ideas that never leave their head. This "self-editing" keeps the thought disconnected from what is actually taking place. The actor needs to find ways of releasing the energy of the thought, making them part of the whole physical self, releasing them from the confines of the mind. We have to be continually balancing our need to be truthful with a way of presenting that truth to an audience through the language of swordplay.

Once the thoughts are freed from the mind, time should be given for the actions of the fight to clearly define their intentions. The unguided release of thought is as detrimental to an effective fight as restrained thought. Thoughts lead to actions, and actions move towards an objective. When the audience gets the sense of one thought leading to another, the fight becomes cumulative. The actions are not a series of statements that are end-stopped, they always build.

The actor should not comment on each action. They should move from one thought, one moment, to the next. Each thought needs to be played to its end. So often the clarity of the fight is lost because time is not given to developing the motivating thought. A fast and flashy fight is generally a spectacle providing little in moment to moment objectives.[5] The major objective is played throughout, with little attention to the process of reaching that goal. Each action and its reaction should prompt thought, each thought leading to further actions and reactions designed to reach the major objective. If thoughts are not given enough room to play within the actions of the fight, the thought drops in energy and commitment. This may cause the viewer to lose the end or intent of the thought. A common example of this is where a combatant does not fully extend their arm on an attack so that it may be immediately withdrawn for the following parry. If the thought was to hit, there should be no thought of parrying until the action is thwarted. Time needs to be allowed for the action to be sustained to the end of the thought. Knowing that it is active and asking for a response or further thought, the commitment will not fall away.

No matter the character, situation or surroundings, the thoughts, emotions and intentions of the actions must be clearly expressed to the audience. Just as a character who has an accent or speech impediment must be understood on stage, so must the actions of a combatant. No matter how sloppy a fighter should appear to be, the thought and the intention must still be expressed clearly. For this

---

[5]"Fast and flashy" fights, reminiscent of the old swashbuckling film fights, are still common in the theatre today. These fights are staged more for spectacle than for dramatic content, featuring amazing sword tricks rather than character-specific movement.

reason each and every action needs to be clearly understood by the actor. So that even if the character must move awkwardly or uneasily, their intention is clear.

This does not mean that only the specific movements of the fight need to be made clear and all else can remain vague. Physical expression is as important in the stillness as in the movement, and no less meaningful. Whether in movement or at rest, physical expression must grow out of the nature of the character. The pauses and breaks in action are the time for the character to reflect on what has just happened, plot their next action and anticipate the actions of the opponent. There is no choreographed movement, but the moment is active. It is active in thought, active in energy and active in intention.

THE SOUNDS OF VIOLENCE

"The illusion of 'the real thing' is best achieved when not only what the audience sees but what it hears and feels carries a ring of truth; when not only the look of the staged fight but the music *of that fight—the held and released breaths, the running steps, the clang of metal, the voluntary and 'involuntary' vocal sounds, the lines and dialogue, the responses to injury—combine to produce a vivid and believable impression."* [Bonnie Raphael][6]

As you begin to work on the fight, exploring the circumstances, beats, objectives and obstacles, remember that the voice is a strong part of the dramatic instrument. Accordingly, in most fights you use the voice along with the body. This does not mean that every action should have an accompanying sound, it means that the voice is either working or silent. It is neither forced, nor restrained during a fight. When working the voice should emerge naturally, and in any form: sighing, groaning, grunting, laughing, screaming, growling, crying, etc. If the natural release of these sounds is suppressed, the physical and conscious effort used to restrain them also restrains the body. Tension in the voice restricts the body's freedom of expression. On the other hand, when the voice is silent and does not need to be released, there is no need to force a vocal response. Forced sound has the same effect on the body as suppressed sound, creating physical tension and restricting bodily movement. Therefore, it is important to explore the possibilities of the voice in a fight and to find the natural sounds that arise from the situation moment to moment, not to create them artificially.

Center

The voice, like all action within a fight, must be built from the ground up. It cannot be superficially laid onto an action or it will sound artificial and unconvincing. The actor must be grounded and centered in order to command force or energy. If you are relaxed and properly centered in the execution of your actions, allowing your energy to come from the ground up and support from the diaphragm, you should find the voice naturally freed with the action. If the action and the sound originate from your center, then the response will be spontaneous and organic.

Many actors fight the urge to phonate during a fight, restraining the natural voice. Time, therefore, must be allotted in rehearsal to let the actor breathe into their center and release the sound. This practice must be started from the beginning of the rehearsal period so that the actor learns the movements with the accompanying sounds. The longer they wait to add the voice, the more difficult it will be to find the connection.

Breathing

There is a habit among many new combatants to hold their breath while fighting. The brain and muscles, however, need oxygen to function, and by holding the breath the body tenses up and the

---

[6]Raphael, Bonnie, "The Sounds of Violence, Part I: The Real Thing." *The Fight Master,* Winter '89, Vol. XII, #1. p. 12.

mind starts to cloud. Good, sustained breathing allows the body to relax and move more fluidly, and supports the voice.

During a fight, try to breathe in through the nose and out through the mouth. This keeps the air intake from drying the vocal folds. The breathing should be kept low in the body, in the center. Avoid breathing high and into the chest. High breaths are shallow and do not provide ample oxygen for the actions of the fight or enough breath to support the necessary vocals. The jaw should be relaxed, with the teeth separated approximately a quarter of an inch. The tongue should also be relaxed inside the mouth, not held with tension, blocking the air way. Tension in the jaw and shoulders affects the neck and in turn affects the overall productivity of the voice.

Just as breath is necessary to support the delivery and conviction of the lines, it is also necessary in sustaining a physical dialogue. While a held breath creates tension in the working body, little or no breath can remove the necessary support for the actions and uncenter the actor. Without good breath, the actions become disconnected from their base and become artificial and empty. As text lacking good breath drops off at the end, so physical actions not supported with good breath lack commitment and tend to lose energy and drive as they are executed. Without proper breath the actions are disconnected from the center, and therefore whatever sound is generated from the breath is not connected to the action but is artificial and inorganic. Be sure you breathe deeply during the routine and especially prior to the delivery of lines or the execution of any action.

Tension and Relaxation

Physical tension does nothing but provide obstacles that work against the body and the voice. A tense body does not project dramatic tension, it restricts dramatic sound and movement. In the attempt to relax and remove tension from the body many actors put the strain into their jaw, neck, shoulders and throat. With the tension focused on that portion of their body, the more sensitive muscles, the vocal folds, are affected first. The tautness in the vocal folds caused by physical tension adversely affects the health, stamina, flexibility and responsiveness of the vocal instrument. The actor should relax completely. The strain and the tension of the fight should be entirely acted, even in the vocal instrument.

To avoid this tension, be sure that you allow ample time in your physical warm-up to work the head, neck and shoulders. Within you warm-up, you should also allow adequate time to warm the voice prior to working the fight. In doing this, you not only improve the health, but the sound and clarity of the voice.

Natural sound, supported by good breath and projected by a relaxed voice, reduces the chance of strain and fatigue. The principles of the actor's vocal warm-up should be carried into the fight. A good vocal warm-up is only as good as its techniques in practice. Understanding the principals of the technique are not enough, you must actively use them in rehearsal and performance. The head, neck, shoulders and voice should be relaxed and limber throughout rehearsal and performance, not just in exercises. In order to do this you should rehearse the voice with the fight from the beginning until the technique becomes second nature.

Vocal Orchestration

The idea of orchestrating a fight is not to develop a "grunt per move ratio." Rather, it is to explore sound patterns which reinforce the movement of the fight. The sounds must be character, not actor, specific; supporting the action, the situation and the circumstances of the character and the conflict.

I mentioned earlier that breath and center play a strong role in effective vocal support for a fight. But in the process of exploring the sounds of violence and developing vocal orchestration for a fight, there are a few more standard vocal terms you should know.

- *PITCH:* The highness or lowness of a particular sound on the musical scale.
- *RHYTHM:* The temporal pattern produced by the grouping and balance, or imbalance and

unpredictability, of sounds and dialogue during a fight. The strong and weak elements in the flow of sound and silence.

- *DURATION:* The length of time which the sound or silence is sustained.
- *VOLUME:* The degree of magnitude or loudness of a sound.
- *QUALITY:* The essential character or distinguishing attribute of the sound. The color or timbre of the actor's voice; the features of the sound; rough, voiced, screamed, whispered, etc.
- *INTELLIGIBILITY:* The identification and understandability of the sound. The ability of the sound to convey a certain meaning or message; joy, pain, effort, strain, etc. Pitch, rhythm, duration, volume and quality will be dull attributes of sound within a fight, unless they convey to the audience the range of feelings, the variety of thought, the clarity of the imagination and the powerful spectrum of emotions. Sound for the sake of sound is ineffectual; intelligible sounds tell a story.

All these variables contribute, not compete with one another to orchestrate the overall sound of the fight. These are the essential features of the sounds of a fight, and can be used to refer to the clash of the weapons against each another or against the floor or set, the sound of body striking body or the floor or set, props and furniture falling, smashing, cracking within the battle and, of course, the cries, hollers, screams, grunts, groans and dialogue of the combatants and observers of the fray.

Voluntary Sounds

There are generally two types of vocal sounds within a fight, *voluntary* and *involuntary*. Voluntary sounds are those which the combatant releases by choice. These include lines of dialogue as well as nonverbal sounds, (aggressive, threatening, challenging, taunting); and intentional moments of silence. Moments of silence can be quite intentional, especially when stifling an involuntary sound created from pain.

All voluntary sounds are done by design or intention, they are not accidental. Because of this you generally find voluntary sounds to emanate from the aggressor. These are more predictable and controlled than involuntary sounds and can vary a great deal in pitch, volume and quality. Voluntary sounds are controlled and manipulated by the character. Consonants are generally used to break up the open vowel sounds, creating a more logical series of sounds.

Involuntary Sounds

Involuntary sounds are reactive, springing from accident or impulse rather than a conscious exercise of the will. These can be the natural sounds of the working body including grunts, groans, sighs and other unintentional phonations on the exhalation. They can also be reactive or reflex responses to unexpected stimuli. This can include wounds to the body, strikes or hard physical contact, startling or aggressive actions on the part of the opponent, or anything that catches the combatant by surprise. Because of this you generally find involuntary sounds to come from the victim.

Involuntary sounds are unpredictable, spontaneous resonances not subject to control of the will. Their great diversity in pitch, volume and quality along with their erratic spontaneity often makes them feel detached from the combatant's center, but this is not the case. The abrupt release of breath and sound comes quickly from the center without thought or preparation making the sound seem detached or illogical . Without proper breath, however, there is little or no reactive sound possible. Because these sounds are quick physical responses, the sounds are generally open. Open vowel sounds are more spontaneous, carrying instinctive, primitive undertones.

Reactive Physical Vocal Range: In a perfect world, all sounds would be organic and truthful to the action being presented. Unfortunately, this is not a perfect world and not all sounds are honestly created. We cannot, for example, honestly react to a cut wrist if no cut wrist exists, or a blow to the stomach, or a sword in the chest if these actions have not honestly taken place. These are all actions that stimulate involuntary sounds that we must create voluntarily. For this it is important to under-stand the *reactive physical vocal range*. This is the process of identifying the relative vocal pitch to the part of the body being affected.

Like the rings of a tree, levels of pitch circle outward from the body's center. The body's lowest vocal register starts at the diaphragm or center and builds in pitch outward from that point. Like a stone dropped in a pond, the vocal register (pitch) of the voice raises in degrees as it emanates from the center, like ringlets undulating from that stone. When we stub our toe or receive a paper cut on a finger, the involuntary sound emitted is in our higher vocal register, but when we are struck in the stomach or hit in the crotch (men and women alike) the pitch drops. Simply put, as the stimulus for the involuntary sound moves away from the center, the pitch rises.

The Comic Inversion: The basics of dealing with comedy in a fight are covered later in this chapter's *Comic Fights,* but I will note here how the reactive physical vocal range is used in comedy. One of the basic elements of comedy is to set a specific pattern, and then break it. This pattern can be familiar situations or events, established character icons, or serious actions or actions. These patterns are usually totally believable and real to the characters, with the incongruity or break perceived only by the audience. Although not a tangible pattern, the reactive physical vocal range is established both in the audience's subconscious from personal memory, and from its effective presentation in dramatic film and stage fights. *Comic inversion* is the process of offering contra-dictory vocal reactions to real and believable physical injuries. Cartoons are classic examples of this process showing characters hit in the head with a frying pan or anvil responding in a slow deep vocal register while other characters being kicked in the groin react with a sharp high pitch, and others who are hit quite hard in the stomach don't respond at all. The juxtaposition in vocal response can be quite humorous if used selectively, unpredictably and specifically.

Dealing with an Injury: All too often on stage and in film, we see a character receive a substantial blow or wound accompanied by a great physical and vocal reaction, and then it magically heals three or four moves further into the fight, not affecting the combatant in the least. This is due, in part, to the actor's focus being placed on the choreography and not the circumstances of the character and the fight. The audience, however, saw the event take place and cannot deny its existence. Remem-ber, what happens before has a direct influence on what is happening now, and what happens next. You cannot ignore past events within a fight when moving into the future.

In dealing with an injury, there is an involuntary sound created from pain at the time of impact, but that is not the only effect of the injury. Continued or specific movement could aggravate the hurt, the beat of the heart could cause the wound to throb, loud sounds could besiege an injured head or ear, heavy costume or armor could afflict a bruised or battered body, etc. All of these generate involuntary sounds created because of the injury. The pitch of the sound is determined by its location on the body, its volume and duration depend on the intensity of the hit and its quality and rhythm generally relate to the nature of the injury. Rhythm is most apparent in the breath and vocal patterns established after the injury.

It is important to be as specific as possible about the location and nature of the injury and your character's circumstances at that moment. Not everyone responds in the same way or to the same extent. Remember, involuntary sounds can be deliberately stifled, making the silence a voluntary sound. You should be aware of:

- how off guard the character was when they received the blow.
- the state of mind of both the victim and the aggressor.
- how much the injury actually hurts.
- how serious or detrimental the injury is.
- what the continuance or duration of the injury is. (i.e.—a blow to the stomach has a short duration and little continuing affect, whereas a cut to the arm or leg has an extended duration and has a continuing affect on the character.)
- how willing the character is to let the opponent, or observers know the degree of the injury.

- how this particular blow or wound affects the character's breathing. (i.e.—gasping, wheezing, panting, coughing)

Although these sounds are voluntary creations of involuntary sounds, they still need to be truthful in the playing and their reasoning still needs to be intelligible to the audience. The sounds cannot be disconnected from your center. The primary impulse for the sound must seem to come from the imaginary injury. Because these sounds are not organic, it is important to experiment with them and then let the fight director help shape the final sounds.

Even though the reaction will not be real, it must be truthful to the action. It is important to take the time to find the correct vocal response because we have all experienced and heard the involuntary sound created from pain. If the sound chosen is not truthful to the action, the audience, if only on a subconscious level, knows something is wrong. This affects the overall perception of the fight, diminishing the audience's response to the situation.

Rhythm

The actor's goal is to find the contrasting voluntary and involuntary sounds within the structure of the fight and to explore the many variables of these sounds. By understanding the nature of the sound, active or reactive, you can develop a better and more dynamic presentation of the character in conflict.

The rehearsal process allows you to work with the variables of the sounds. Pitch, duration, volume and quality are generally related to the specific actions of the fight, but rhythm (and volume to a lesser extent) is an independent, artistic variable. Changes in breath, sound, silence and delivery of lines can make a critical difference in the presentation of the fight. Correctly and skillfully-developed vocal orchestration can create the illusion of spontaneity and real danger.

Playing the Pauses

Throughout this process of discovering the sounds of the fight, we have focused on the sounds in specific regard to actions and reactions, but we have not looked at the sounds between the actions; these activities, beats and phrases of a fight, that are moments of pause. These, however, are not necessarily moments of vocal rest. The immediacy of the situation is still quite predominant whether the blades are engaged or not. The effects of any injury sustained can be heard. The fear, tension and composure of the characters may be audibly present. Their physical strain and fatigue are perceived by the listener in the rhythm and sound of their breath. These breaks in the physical action must maintain the tension of what has come before and carry the listener into what happens next. The sounds during a pause in the action are the bridge in understanding for the audience. They should sum up the results of the previous actions, and inform the audience who is in control, losing control, out of control or being controlled. The audience should not feel the danger of the situation is over until the actors chooses to convey such a message.

Specialized Vocal Techniques

The harsh screams and yells of a fight are a variety of sounds known as *specialized vocal techniques*. These sounds put a specific demand on the vocal instrument above and beyond the standard vocal techniques of the actor. They are also something, I believe, that cannot be learned from a book. Specialized vocal techniques are something specific to each actor's instrument and don't fall into any simple or standard technique. They are something that if done correctly can add great depth, variety and passion to a performance, but if done incorrectly can seriously strain and fatigue the vocal instrument.

Although these techniques should not be taught in a book, they should not be ignored. Screams, yells, grunts and groans are an intricate part of the vocal orchestration of a fight. It is for this reason that you should seek out a vocal coach or the fight choreographer and work the techniques under their supervision. Do not, under any circumstance, just start adding specialized vocals to the fight. This is the easiest way to damage your instrument.

When working with a voice coach it is important that you first work on the sounds out of context of the fight. You should work on the vocal technique as a specific skill that must be mastered prior to being introduced to the fight. This means that the techniques should be second nature, and not a conscious effort. If the process of creating sound causes a tenderness or rawness in the throat, or a degeneration in voice quality, the technique is not safely being achieved and you should consider healthier techniques. Do not "tough it out." These problems can be serious and continuing to practice unhealthy techniques can prove quite detrimental to your voice. Remember, you are creating the "illusion" of effort, and not trying to survive its reality. Work with a trained professional on specialized vocal techniques; your voice is a large part of your career and you need to maintain its health, stamina, flexibility and responsiveness.

Vocal Variety

The orchestration of a fight consists of the sounds of the weapons, armor, costumes, props, set, scenery, crowd and combatants. These sounds mingle with one another to help the audience further understand the characters and tell the story of the fight. Each sound must be arranged and blended with the others, complementing, not competing, with one another. The arrangement of the fight's sounds should be so clear that if it were recorded on an audio cassette and played back, or observed with the eyes closed, you could still follow the story of the fight. Much of the orchestration is handled by the fight choreographer, but there are things that you should be aware of in rehearsal.

When working with your partner you should be aware of the differences and similarities in your voices. Your differences make you stand out in the orchestration, similarities blend you together. You want to achieve the greatest difference in sound while still remaining truthful to the character and their circumstances. Your voices should differ enough in pitch, rhythm, volume and quality that the audience can identify your actions and reactions by sound as much as sight.

In this process just be careful not to over-orchestrate the fight. Be sure that you don't upstage your sounds with the actions of the fight, or vice-versa. Remember that all the other sounds and actions take part in the audio plot of the fight and your sounds are a part of the whole, not independent from it. Action takes focus, and sound intensifies and clarifies the action, not the other way around. You are creating the "sounds *of* violence," not sounds with violence.

COMIC FIGHTS

"Dying is easy, comedy is hard"[7]

The above quote is attributed to the comic actor Edmund Gwenn, as the final words given on his death bed. The quote is easily applicable to stage combat. A death scene amidst a violent confrontation is somehow less of a challenge to some actors than finding the laughs in physical conflict. Many combatants are fooled by the idea that if a fight is comic it needs less exploration and commitment. Comic fights generally take as much, or more, focus and concentration than regular knock-down drag-outs. Hapless buffoonery removes a routine from the realm of a comic fight and places it into foolish clowning. The element of danger and the possibility of accident or injury must be maintained during a comic fight. It is the events that surface out of this dramatic situation that make the routine comic.

These are some of the guidelines for a comic fight:

- The situation must be believable (even if a little far-fetched).
- The circumstances of the scene must be established and generally maintained.

---

[7]Edmund Gwenn (1875–1959)

- Tension must be built with the blade-play before it is released with a gag.
- Gags can be
    —incongruous to the specific situation or event;
    —something serious and profound taken in a light, familiar or satirical manner;
    —a complete break from the event, situation or scene;
    —a series or pattern of actions that terminate in a comic or exaggerated picture;
    —serious actions taken with a humorous implement or object.

In actuality there are no hard and fast rules to comedy except that if it gets a laugh, it's funny.

Working on a routine or scene that is comic can be a difficult business. Usually the actors feel that certain actions or movements are silly and they find themselves working in the dark, until they feel the response of the audience on opening night. This is a dangerous trap for the actor because the comic actions of the routine have to be completely real and believable within the realm of the production or the gag is lost. They cannot comment on the action, they must commit to it.

It is important that if a fight is comic, or has comic moments, that the artist get several chances to work the routine in front of an audience. In both comedy and stage combat timing is everything, and to be caught off guard by a comic response from the audience may throw the routine off as one artist pauses to play the laugh and the other tries to move on.

The advantage of working on comic routines in a classroom or group situation is that the routines may be tested on the group to see what comes across and what does not. It also enables them to test timing and helps the group to feel the comedy inherent in good teamwork.

IN CONCLUSION

Without adequate rehearsal the actor is generally excited, or sometimes nervous, about doing a fight sequence and when the moment comes, their reality, and not the circumstance of the character, is carried into the blade-play. This is where so many stage sword fights go awry. The truth of the situation is lost because the circumstances of the character are either abandoned or founded in fancy rather than fact. The actor does not choose to ignore the circumstances but ill-preparedness can cause them to fall back upon what they know as a person, rather than what the character knows. Thus, a fight should be addressed and rehearsed in the same manner as spoken text. Time must be allowed for the process of exploration and discovery or the fight becomes adorned with superficial acting and devoid of the characters and the production. Rehearsal is the key, not just in movement and memorization but in properly understood motivation.

Better Too Slow, Than Two Pieces

As all the preceding chapters come together and you truly begin to rehearse and develop a fight, remember that speed is not the essence. Like beginning actors trying to tackle Shakespeare, many artists new to stage combat feel they've "done" it if they have raced through and made it to the end. Not until later in their training do they discover the rhythm, meter and endless nuances in Elizabethan verse.

There are two separate time-scales in the presentation of a fight; execution and intention. The actions of the fight move through time, continuing from one moment to the next. A fight cannot be seen all at once (like a painting). It is witnessed as it moves through time, taking the audience from one action to the next, one thought to the next. Thoughts, however, are instantaneous, whereas the time needed to execute the actions and play their value is not. The trap actors generally fall into is not to develop thoughts that motivate the actions. The secret of effective swordplay is to merge the two, reaching a theatrical, dynamic end. The actor has to bring together the character's need to express, with the art of expressing. They need to "be" and "present" at the same time.

If the sequences in a fight are rehearsed only for rapidity, the actions become tight but unclear in purpose. Thus, the performed fight is fast, flashy and totally without context. Therefore, the actor's energy and focus should be to find swiftness, but never at the expense of the language of the sword fight. In the same vein, the actor must not, through lack of trust either in themselves or in the movements, over-control the actions of the fight. The actor should not try to explain a fight in its performance.

Speed is relative. A fight should go as fast as it possibly can while remaining true to the circumstances and clear to the audience. The audience must not just see the fight, they must actually understand it as fully as they are able. The actor needs to be continually balancing their need to be truthful with a way of presenting that truth to an audience through the actions of the fight. This comes from understanding; understanding the play, its characters and the circumstances of their situation and surroundings; and from an understanding of the actor's instrument; and all this is communicated through the art of stage combat.

Chapter 21

Fighting Through the Production

"I think an actor, even a successful actor, has to come to terms with the fact that employment is eternally temporary and can come to an end at any time. Any part can be your last part. If you are badly hurt or disfigured or become unable to walk without a limp or to see or hear voices or if you even have a serious heart attack, in fact [you] become unviable." [Charlton Heston][1]

The test of a safe stage fight is not to perform it once without injury, but to perform it night after night without accident while keeping the audience on the edge of their seats. Fight rehearsal and performance are a different beast than training in stage combat, but the premise of safety must never be set aside or forgotten. Everything that has come before must be taken into account when a fight is staged, rehearsed and performed whether on stage or screen. One accident can in fact make you "unviable." For this reason the following guidelines have been arranged to help in the process of taking your technique out of the classroom and onto the stage.

Your Rights as an Actor

The rehearsal process of a fight for a production is often the last thought in a director's or producer's mind. It encompasses no more than a few minutes of the entire show and seldom involves more than a couple of actors. Many times it is an afterthought and the actors are then given a few minutes to come up with a fight. You should know by now that this is not the proper way to do things. First, if you are cast in a production that involves stage combat, even a simple tussle or comic encounter like the Viola/Aguecheek fight, ask if it will be professionally staged. Find out who will be staging the fight, what their qualifications are and what the tentative rehearsal schedule will be. By asking questions prior to beginning rehearsal you can attune the director and producer to the needs of setting the stage fight. If a qualified professional is setting the fights, you can rest assured that they are asking the same questions you are. If, however, a local fencing coach or student has been recruited to put the fights together, you may want to reconsider the role. Remember, no part is too special, no role too dear to be worth endangering yourself in any way. Therefore, it is best that you review your rights as an actor before you begin rehearsal.

---

[1]Charlton Heston, quoted by Bates, Brian. *The Way of the Actor,* p. 140.

Extraordinary Risk

> *"The term 'Extraordinary Risk' shall be defined as any portion of a performance or rehearsal which entails any form of high risk feat exposing ARTIST(S) to possible injury . . . "* [AGMA][2]

> *"An Actor also shall be deemed to be engaging in Extraordinary Risk if the staging or choreography require the Actor to execute movements which depart from the accepted techniques of movement and support as used in contemporary theatre dance . . . "* [AEA][3]

Both AGMA (American Guild of Musical Artists) and AEA (Actor's Equity Association) have clauses in their basic production agreements that deal with what is called *extraordinary risk.* Just about anything that falls under the heading "swordplay" is considered extraordinary risk. In fact, anything that you might potentially be injured in performing can be covered under this heading— even scenery that is out of the ordinary, such as raked platforms, steep stairs without railings, and so on.

The union contracts offer a few examples of extraordinary risks, but preface them with "including but not limited to any of the following." Because of this there is a lot of gray area under the heading, and it is up to the union, as well as the management, the fight director, and the combatants to ascertain if the fight involves extraordinary risk. Once this is established (and never *assume* that it is) then you should sign an Extraordinary Risk Rider. This rider is set up by the unions to protect you, the artist. If you are hurt, and have not signed the rider, you might not be eligible for complete coverage by workman's compensation and AGMA/AEA insurance. Partial coverage will be provided, but the rider ensures that you receive full benefits until the contract is complete or you are able to work again. The rider simply says that everyone involved has acknowledged the possible risk and that the union will cover you completely if you should by chance be injured.

Be sure you check your local union contracts. Many of the contracts now used by AGMA/AEA require that you be paid an additional fee (usually $10 to $50 per performance) for extraordinary risk. For this reason producers sometimes sit on the rider, not mentioning it unless it is specifically addressed. If there is a risk, however, it *must* be addressed.

AGMA—Regulations for Safety with Swords and/or Props as Weapons

As of the summer of 1994, AGMA has a new ruling under their Extraordinary Risk clause that governs the use of weapons and props in a staged physical encounter. According to "Exhibit 2," an amendment to AGMA's "Basic Agreement," the company is required to engage a professional fight director *"who shall be thoroughly familiar with the proper use and maintenance of the weapons required in the production."* The fight director may be engaged by the company to stage the conflict, or they may be used as a consultant to determine the safety of the artists and the routine staged by another party. In either case, Exhibit 2 states that *"Where a question of safety exists in the opinion of the Fight Director, the Choreographer or Stager may not overrule the Fight Director's expert judgment."* To qualify the fight director's "expert judgment," and to avoid the false claims of would-be "Professionals," AGMA has accepted the qualifications of fight director established by the Society of American Fight Directors. Subparagraph 9 clearly states that *"the Fight Director must hold current certification from the Society of American Fight Directors."* As this is a new ruling, be sure you check your theatre's AGMA contract. Not all company contracts reflect the rulings of Exhibit 2. For this reason it is best to consult the AGMA office before making any decisions in the matter. Just because the production staff, general or artistic director aren't familiar with the ruling does not mean it does not exist. Take the time to be sure.

---

[2]*AGMA National Opera Basic Agreement;* Exhibit 2—Extraordinary Risk.
[3]*Actors' Equity Association Agreement and Rules Governing Employment Under the Production Contract.* June 29–June 30, 1992. p. 46 (B)

British Actor's Equity

In England, the Society of British Fight Directors (SBFD) works in conjunction with the union. British Actor's Equity has a fight directors' committee and a register of professional fight directors. Like the requirement of certified fight directors in the AGMA contract in the United States, the British Register provides a list of qualified fight directors for work in union theatres. As a form of quality control and from a concern for the actor's safety, the register negotiated a contract for fight directors with the Theatre's National Committee. This Committee sets the safety requirements and conditions of rehearsal and performance in professional theatres. As a result, only qualified SBFD Fight Directors can work in union houses in England.[4] This protects the actor while allowing for safe, effective swordplay.

Actor's Equity and American Theatre

"It is not the intent of Equity to interfere with proper artistic judgments of the Producer but only to protect the Actor from injury which may jeopardize or terminate a professional career." [AEA][5]

These rulings are important to you, even if you are not a union actor. As stated above, the unions have developed these standards in order to protect the artist, and they would not be necessary if there was not a potential risk. Just because a theatre is not union does not mean that it has the right to neglect the safety of the actor. The following guidelines established by Actor's Equity should be followed in any production where a fight takes place. These should not be viewed as luxuries of big theatres, but as practical rules of common sense.

STAGE FIGHTING

"The ensuing regulations shall be followed whenever a production requires two (2) or more Actors to engage in stage fighting.

"The Actor agrees in a contract rider to participate in stage fighting."[6]

Anything that you do on stage must be agreed upon and done of your own free will. There is no physical price to be paid for acting, and although the show must go on—it should not go on at your expense. You must feel comfortable with the fight director and with the choreography you are being given. AGMA tells their artists that *"No ARTIST shall be required or permitted to handle any weapon in either rehearsal or performance until the ARTIST feels confident that he/she has received adequate instructions."*[7] In other words, if anything feels wrong or dangerous, you have the right to say "NO!"[8] Out of all the techniques and mechanics offered in this text, you are the ultimate safety device. In any given situation you have the power to ask questions and explore options if anything ever feels dangerous or unsafe. When in doubt, you must always err on the side of safety.

---

[4] *"For a production which involves a fight, the manager shall engage a suitably qualified F.D.* [Fight Director]. *Membership of the Equity Fight Directors' Register shall be regarded as proof of qualification. If the F.D. is not on the Equity F.D. Register, the Manager shall inform Equity prior to the commencement of rehearsals."* Theatres' National Committee and British Actors' Equity Association Agreement for Fight Directors. January 25, 1995. (1-d) p. 1.

[5] AEA "Agreement" (62-H-1) p. 89.

[6] AEA "Agreement" (58-L-1) p. 78.

[7] AGMA "Agreement" Exhibit 2-2.

[8] "You have the absolute right to say "NO" to any stunt or scene you think might be dangerous." *Safety Bulletins for the Motion Picture and Television Industry.* Safety Rule #2

The Fight Captain

"A Fight Captain shall be assigned from the company and so designated by a rider to Actor's contract."[9]

A *fight captain* is an actor in the company who works as an assistant to the fight director. Generally the captain is one of the production's combatants, but this is not a requirement. The need for a fight captain is critical. The fight director seldom stays through the run of a production and someone who has worked the fights directly with the choreographer and knows and understands not only all the actions of the fight, but also the choreographer's intentions is important once the choreographer leaves. After the fight choreographer has gone their merry way, the captain must faithfully see to it that the actors warm up prior to each show, as well as keep a wary eye on the integrity of the fight over the run of the production. Without the outside eye of the fight captain, fights can go unchecked and become sloppy and dangerous.

Within the multiple variables of live performance, a great many incidents can take place. A sprained ankle received in a friendly game of basketball, nausea from flu, problems with equilibrium due to a serious head cold, as well as tour fatigue can all seriously affect a fight. These variables, along with replacement artists and understudies going on at the last moment, cannot be totally planned for by the choreographer and often take place after they are no longer at the theatre. Each of these instances, along with the plethora of other variables, can prove dangerous to the artists if not handled correctly. Since the fight captain is the only member of the company who worked with the fight director and understands the intricacies of the fight and all its nuances, they should be the only other member of the company allowed to change the fight.

This does not mean that the fight captain has the authority to re-choreograph the routine, but rather that they are more acutely aware of what can be edited in order to guarantee the safety of the performers while retaining the integrity of the choreography. To avoid the possibility of error, it is advisable to contact the choreographer with the suggested changes. What may seem to be a "simple" edit to the director or producer, may inadvertently create a dangerous situation. If the fight director cannot be reached or if the change needs to be made at the last moment, the fight captain makes the edit.

Fight-Call

"All actors who participate in a fight shall run through the routine before each performance. Any exception to this rule shall be at the express discretion of the Fight Captain." [AEA][10]

In the course of a production there is always the possibility of an actor dropping a line or "going up" in performance. Because this type of human error is a factor in live theatre, it is important to take precautions to minimize its occurrence. When a line is dropped, someone else on stage can pick it up and keep the scene moving with little discomfort. If choreography is forgotten, however, there exists the possibility of accident or injury. For this reason there must be a *fight-call* prior to each performance.

The basic idea behind the fight-call is twofold: (1) to physically warm up the actors, and (2) to provide them with a feeling of "security" by reviewing the fights before the performance. Both are equally important, but the psychological element in particular must be stressed. If the actors are secure in the fights before the curtain, the chances of someone "going up" during the fight are greatly reduced, and the actors will be able to better handle the little things that always seem to go wrong.

---

[9]AEA "Agreement" (58-L-2) p. 78.
[10]AEA "Agreement" (58-L-3) p. 78.

Understudies and Covers

"Whenever possible, performing members of the company shall rehearse fights with Understudies during regular rehearsal hours." [AEA][11]

It seems that a great many theatres bank on the health and stamina of their artists. Many companies today do not cast understudies or covers for many of their roles, some having no understudies at all. If, however, you are working in a situation where there are understudies, or you yourself are an understudy, it is important to note that there is no guarantee of adequate rehearsal time. Professional and non-professional theatres only tend to schedule the understudies "whenever possible."[12] The term can be misleading, and you should see to it for your own safety and peace of mind that you be allowed to rehearse the fights with the performing artists. As you are now aware, stage combat is a delicate blend of technique, team work, trust and timing. A fight is not a series of moves where any Combatant "A" can be paired to Combatant "B," even when both combatants know the choreography. Whether principal or understudy, it takes hours of practice to develop the partnering necessary for a fight to mature into a safe and effective part of the dramatic production. Therefore, the best advice for an understudy or cover is to see that "whenever possible" is as often as possible.

Rehearsing the Fight

Now that you are aware of your rights, you can begin the rehearsal process. Because of the time necessary to set a fight and to develop good partnering techniques and dramatic nuance, the rule for fights is "Early and Often!" As you discovered in Chapter 19, learning a stage fight is a slow process. Fight rehearsals should begin early in the play's rehearsal process and should be conducted often. As you learn the fight you must pay close attention to the safety rules and techniques provided by the choreographer, as well as those established in this book. You must work through the choreography, checking the path of the swords, distance, targets and so on. Despite previous training in stage combat, you must still work at a slow pace in order to make sure everything the choreographer gives you is clear and safe. This is supported by AGMA in a ruling that states that *"at the commencement of each rehearsal involving weapons, performance tempos shall be modified to facilitate a proper warm-up and orientation prior to rehearsing at a performance-level tempo."*[13]

As mentioned in Chapter 19, the process of learning fight choreography takes at least one hour of rehearsal for each twenty seconds of combat. This time table is only for plotting the fight, a great deal more time is needed for you to become comfortable with the routine and to effectively explore it as an actor. The more complex the fight is either in length or number of people involved, the earlier you should begin working on it in the rehearsal period. Even the simplest of violent business should be worked out in detail no less than three weeks before opening, and then rehearsed daily. If the fight is very complex, it should be learned in the beginning of the rehearsal process and given as much time to mature and develop safely as is necessary.

A fight captain should be present at all fight rehearsals. The fight director usually selects this person after a meeting with the cast. They are the choreographer's assistant, helping notate the fights and running any fight rehearsals when the choreographer is not present. If the captain is one of the combatants, there should be a stage manager at all rehearsals to notate fight choreography and to

---

[11]AEA "Agreement" (58-L-4) p. 79.

[12]It is interesting to note that AEA understands the safety issues of handling weapons on stage, yet in 58-K of the "Agreement" they still use the term *"When possible"* to preface the issue of adequate rehearsal for the Understudy *"on the set with such props, lighting effects, mechanical or pyrotechnical devices, weapons, costumes and other cast members as shall be deemed necessary to insure the safety of both the replacement or Understudy and the other performing members of the cast."* p. 78.

[13]AGMA "Agreement" Exhibit 2–4.

work as an outside eye for the captain. In fact, AEA requires that a stage manager be present at all rehearsals, whether a fight captain is present or not.[14] Although both the captain and the stage manager are present at rehearsals to notate the choreography, it is recommended that the combatants do likewise. This will be of great benefit to you as you review the choreography outside of rehearsal.

As you learn and practice the fight, it is important that you take the time to explore and understand the character within the movement. In the process of rehearsing for a production there is seldom rehearsal time for deep exploration within a fight. The melding of your acting process with the techniques offered herein must be firmly in place to effectively use the provided rehearsal time. Avoid the urge to fight fast and apply surface acting techniques. You must control the fight, it cannot be allowed to control you.

The increase in the fight's speed must never be at the expense of accuracy in movement. The fastest speed at which any fight should be fought is never more than that at which the movements can be executed with complete accuracy. The tension and excitement of a fight arises more from the relationship between the characters and quality of the acting than from an energetic display of blade-play. Speed beyond a certain point makes the actions of the fight incomprehensible to the audience.

When you have rehearsed a fight many times, the moves and their timing become familiar to you. Because of this, the speed of the fight can be picked up through repetition and rehearsal. This, however, can mislead you. Becoming accustomed to the fight, what is slow to you may actually be incredibly fast to the audience. Remember, they have never seen the fight before; you do it daily. Good physical diction is always important within a fight. It is for this reason that you must trust the eye of the fight captain and stage manager after the choreographer has left. What you see may not be what the audience gets.

As you begin the rehearsal process, it is advisable that you review the basic rules of safety outlined at the end of Chapter 1. As these have served as guideposts in your training in stage combat, so do they prove beneficial in the transfer from studio to stage. Following are further pieces of information that are also important in the rehearsal and performance of a production fight.

First-Aid

> *"First-aid kits stocked with adequate supplies shall be available and easily accessible at all times whenever the Actor is required to rehearse, dress or perform."* [AEA][15]

Because accidents do happen, it is advisable to have a "fight-specific" first-aid kit readily available in your rehearsal hall. Along with the normal stock of a first-aid kit you will need ice-packs, ACE-type compression bandages, antiseptic, aspirin and non-aspirin pain relievers, liniment, extra foam padding, athletic-type adhesive tape, butterfly bandages, gauze compresses, etc. It has been said that an ounce of prevention is worth a pound of cure, and when dealing with personal safety this is quite true. Because of this AEA insures that *"First aid information and equipment will be made available to the Fight Captain."*[16] Whether you are working in an Equity house or not, you should check to see if the fight captain or stage manager has had basic first-aid training. The American Red Cross offers courses in first aid/CPR which can prove helpful if someone is injured.

Weapons in Rehearsal

It is very important that you have the actual weapons to be used in the fight from the first day of rehearsal. If you practice a routine with one weapon and then are suddenly given another, the

---

[14] AEA "Agreement" (68-A) p. 100.

[15] AEA "Agreement" (62-F) p. 88.

[16] AEA "Agreement" (58-L-5) p. 79.

difference in weight or balance could prove awkward if not dangerous. It is both unsafe and unreasonable to expect you to adapt to such replacements at the last moment. Each sword is a little different and takes time to get used to. Never change to different weapons without proper rehearsal time.

In different theatres the responsibility of the weapons falls on a variety of different people. In some theatres (IATSE houses) the props department handles the weapons, in others it is the stage manager or the fight captain.[17] They are responsible for cleaning and maintaining all weapons and fight props during the duration of rehearsal and performance. No matter who is responsible, however, you must always see that it is done. Accidents in stage fights can often be traced to the weak link, someone who did not do their job. This does not mean that you should be scrubbing, cleaning and de-burring the weapon if it is someone else's job. It merely means that you should look your weapons over and never assume that they are being properly maintained. Check the weapons as a regular part of your pre-show routine. Be sure that they are not broken, loose or damaged. If a weapon is not combat serviceable, it should not be used, for any reason, at any time. If you are responsible for cleaning and maintaining the weapon, follow the guidelines offered in Appendix C in the back of this book.

Props and Costumes

". . . Nor shall any Actor be required to perform in a costume or upon a set which is inherently dangerous." [AEA][18]

Any prop or costume piece used in a fight must be incorporated into rehearsals as soon as possible. Whatever you wear or handle during a fight must have top priority when pulling or building costumes or acquiring props for the production. The importance of wearing and carrying the actual costume pieces or using the actual stage prop, not a facsimile (unless an exact replica), during the rehearsal process cannot be overstressed. *Do not* take chances with your safety by assuming you will be able to adapt to unfamiliar costume pieces or a totally new stage prop at the last moment. This is a completely unnecessary risk!

Conversely, the sooner the choreographer knows the attributes of the costumes and props, the greater the likelihood of safely adapting the fights to the costumes, and not the other way around. If props and costumes are introduced early in the rehearsal process the fight can be choreographed around them. Once the moves are set, however, it is sometimes safer to have the set and costume altered than change the fight. The earlier fight-specific props and costumes are provided, the greater chance that the fight can be molded to their attributes. Costume alterations can be expensive—fight moves are not!

Rehearsing on the Set

The move from the rehearsal room to the set can be a tricky transition. The longer the actors train in one space, the more difficult it becomes to adapt to another. For this reason, rehearsal on the actual set must be scheduled as soon after plotting the choreography as possible. This allows the fight director to make whatever necessary adjustments are needed before the routine is "set" to the rehearsal space. The time on the set also determines the size of movement in the fight. It makes you and the choreographer aware of exactly where stairs, ramps, risers, furniture and scenery are located. Fight rehearsals must then be scheduled on the set as often as possible. This should be at least twice a week. If the choreography is intricate to the set, or if the set is raked or multi-level, rehearsal should take place there as often as possible. This is quite important in fights with three or more

---

[17]*"All weapons will be thoroughly inspected, cleaned and inventoried by the Stage Manager/Property Master and stored for safe keeping."* AGMA "Agreement" Exhibit 2-5.

[18]AEA "Agreement" (62-H-1) p. 89.

people or crowds. Work on the set, with all involved cast members, insures that you have enough room for the movement required in the choreography.

Fighting the Lighting

It is very important that you work the fight under the lighting conditions planned for the performance well in advance of opening. Certain lighting effects can seriously affect how you fight on stage. Strobe light or dim, shadowy light can make seeing cues and determining measure difficult, while bright lights can blind you or make the blade seem to disappear. Time must be allotted to adjust the fight to the lighting. The angles and paths of your footwork may be changed so that you no longer look directly into the side lights, techniques may be enlarged to ensure communication between you and your partner and so on. This time is necessary and cannot be rushed. This is also true of stage effects such as fog and snow. Each new element of the production can have a detrimental or advantageous effect on the fights depending on the time allotted.[19] If you start early, and work often, time will be on your side and the quality of the fight will reflect your efforts.

Fight-Call

For any show involving combat, there must be a fight-call before *each* performance. If you are working a two-show day, one rehearsal will suffice, provided it is before the first show. The fight-call is not a ''rehearsal.'' It is a physical and mental warm-up and review of the fights. If problems have developed in the fight, you should notify the fight captain in order to have a separate rehearsal scheduled. The fight-call should take place at half hour, or fifteen minutes prior to half hour. You will find that anything earlier than this is a burden, and gives you too long a ''cooling off'' period, losing the point of running the fights. The fight-call should last no more than fifteen minutes. Even for heavy fight shows like *The Three Musketeers* or some of Shakespeare's histories the fight-call should last no more than fifteen to twenty minutes.

If you are the fight captain and also in the fight, have the stage manager watch the fight for changes or inconsistencies. You must have an outside eye watch the fight. Any time you, as captain, work a fight in which you perform, you cheat yourself in two ways. If you are running the fight as the fight captain, you lose the point of warming into the fight as a character. If you warm the fight as an actor and combatant, you lose the critical eye that helps keep the routine safe and effective. All fight-calls must have an active observer to ensure that the fights remain safe and the choreographer's intentions are fulfilled.

It is important that all actors directly involved in the fight scene be called for the fight rehearsal. Of course, if an actor is truly only a ''spear-carrier'' or crowd-person and in the judgment of the choreographer completely out of the action, they may be excused from the fight-call.[20] But, if they are at all involved in blocking or business with those on stage handling weapons, they must, for their own safety, attend the rehearsal. Stages tend to be smaller than actors think in the odd instance where something goes awry. Any situation on stage during a fight is potentially dangerous to everyone on stage, but especially to the ''innocent bystander'' who is careless and perhaps unaware of the routine and when it varies.

Running Fight-Call

Prior to running any fight-call it is suggested that the fight captain and all combatants walk their space and look for anything that may have changed, shifted or been added. This is quite important

---

[19]AGMA insures that the staging of the fight be coordinated by the fight director. ''*The Fight Director will be present for at least one on-stage technical rehearsal to observe and to supervise the actual staging of the fight sequence.*'' AGMA ''Agreement'' Exhibit 2-7.

[20]AEA puts the decision of excuse from fight-call on the fight captain. ''*All Actors who participate in a fight shall run through the routine before each show. Any exception to this rule shall be at the express discretion of the Fight Captain.*'' AEA ''Agreement'' (58-L-3) p. 78.

because set and scenery can shift slightly in their placement from night to night, nails and screws can loosen and furniture and spike marks can accidentally be removed or moved during a run or tour. In an AGMA house this check is the responsibility of the company, but it is advisable that you check as well.[21] No one is more familiar with where you go and what you do than you—take a moment to assure yourself that the performance area is safe and clear of any hazards. If there are any hazards, let the fight captain or stage manager know so that the problem may be remedied prior to beginning fight-call. Do not begin fight-call until the area is safe and secure.

The fight-call is not a rehearsal, and it is also not a performance. It must, however, have as many elements of a performance as possible. The first run of the actual fights should be on-stage with fight-specific costume, set and prop pieces. It should be a walk-though or mark-through, which is a one-quarter speed rehearsal of the fights. You and your partner may call out cues, "marking" falls, stopping to fix problem spots, etc. Next, work a one-half speed run-through with lights, sound and one-quarter acting value. This means that you are now in character and there should be no ad-libbing or out-of-context movement. Although you are in character, you are not completely in the scene, you are focused and in control in case any problems arise. Finally, you should work a three-quarter speed, full-acting value rehearsal. This means that acting-wise it's "for-real," but that physically there is something held in reserve. Never foolishly "spend" yourself with a full-out run-through before curtain. Remember that you need a "cool down" period before curtain time if you happen to get behind schedule.

The fight-call is your safety net during the run of a show. You must never move on from one speed to the next if you are uncomfortable with any portion of the fight. Remember that the fight-call is a crucial safety measure, and that injuries, even fatalities can occur. No matter how much you think you "know" the fight, accidents can happen. Make sure that the proper time is taken to warm up the routine.

Trouble Shooting

Mental Blocks

If questions concerning moves arise, the fight captain's copy of the choreography is your path around mental blocks. You would be surprised at how often crucial moves or phrases are forgotten, and only the written notes allay dissension. This tends to be a particular problem about one-third to one-half way into the run, so watch for it. In this instance, no matter what you think a move is, the word of the fight captain is considered the word of the choreographer. It is important that you and your partner support the captain, as they are your outside eye and have your best interest at heart.

Going Up in Performance

The mental blocks you may encounter in fight-call may also surface in performance. Your partner's eyes tell you immediately if they are lost or uncertain as to the next action in the choreography. That look of confused panic is unmistakable. If you are lost or your partner is giving you "the stare," do not improvise in order to get back on track. No matter how good your intentions, no one can read your thoughts and "know" what you have in mind. Also, it is best not to go back and try to fix what went wrong. For, just as no one can read your mind, there is no way for you to know why your partner has gone up, and going back may well be more problematic than you surmise. It is best then, to have a predetermined backup plan. If there is a problem, following are two options, both of which are preferable to improvisation and injury. First, you may tell your partner the next move or beat of the fight. This works well in operas and other productions with

---

[21]"*After each setting of the stage, it shall be checked for loose nails, splinters and firmness of sets. The EMPLOYER agrees to be responsible for such a check and shall instruct the proper persons to eliminate any hazards that may exist.*" AGMA "Agreement" (31-d) p. 30.

music underscoring the fight. Usually words shared between combatants are lost or distorted in the music. A simple vocal cue in this situation can get your partner back on track without the audience hearing you.

Or, as another solution to going up in a fight, you may give a vocal cue that is specifically assigned to represent a cry for help. A common cue for help is to call your partner a "Villain." This term is agreed upon prior to performance and may also be randomly rehearsed during choreography rehearsals. When "Villain" is called, the other combatant must get eye contact with their partner, make sure there is not a serious injury, and then issue a cut to the head. The lost fighter parries High 5, and then the two combatants slip into a tight corps-à-corps. In this position the two may act a struggle while they discuss what the problem is. Once the two are in agreement as to what to do next, they break from the hold and move on with the fight. This action can also be used if there is a physical problem (dizziness, nausea, twisted ankle, etc.) or an external problem (missing essential prop or person, or a costume problem that prevents certain choreographed movements) in the fight. The grapple allows for the dynamics of the scene to continue as the combatants safely solve the immediate problems. At no time should you improvise choreography. The corps-à-corps is a pre-planned action and the on stage solution can only be a continuation in the choreography or a cut to the end of the fight.

Broken Blade Rehearsals

It is a fact in live theatre that accidents do happen. No matter how practiced and safely choreographed a routine, something can go wrong. The above example for using the word "Villain" takes into account a great deal of potential problems and solves them safely. The one problem with the technique is that it does not allow for a broken blade. It is important to have a rehearsed solution for this possible problem. In rehearsal a cue word like "Rascal" or "Rogue" can be assigned to represent cutting to the last move of the fight or a specialty ending. This alleviates the corps-à-corps which may be impossible if one combatant's blade is broken, or they are disarmed. The specialty ending is something that the Choreographer takes into account in order to avoid "killing" someone with a broken blade. Once a blade snaps, it is sharp and can cut or pierce the skin quite easily. In no event should you continue a fight with a broken or damaged weapon.

Another solution to a broken blade in performance is to have a spare sword placed somewhere on the set. Such a placement must be accessible, but not appear as an obvious "safety" to the audience. It could be the weapon of a bystander, a wall decoration, and so on. The retrieving of the weapon must be preplaned and rehearsed by the combatants. The transition from choreography to back-up choreography must appear seamless and remain fitting to the characters and their circumstances. To do this the spare sword scenario must be rehearsed.

Rain Fights

If you are working in an outdoor Shakespeare festival or Renaissance faire, the elements play a key role in your performance. For this reason it is important for you not only to rehearse the production fights, but to have specific choreography in reserve for bad weather days. Working in such an environment, your choreographer will give you specific choreography for such instances. This is usually an abbreviated version of the fight with limited footwork. Dew, drizzle and rain can instantly turn a previously safe performing environment into a slip-n-slide of death. Boots and shoes that previously held firm can randomly shoot out from underneath you, making even simple stage combat techniques difficult and dangerous. There is no way of knowing exactly how safe a wet stage is, and therefore you must assume that it is dangerous. Don't be a hero, play it safe. To err on the side of safety is to allow yourself a chance to perform again tomorrow.

When the Understudy Goes On

In a perfect world the understudy has a chance to practice and rehearse the fights with the principal company members. As mentioned earlier, however, this is not a perfect world. Generally the understudy has a basic working knowledge of the fights and has only had an opportunity to practice the routine with the other understudies or the fight captain. For this reason, the understudy cannot be expected to go on and perform a fight at a moment's notice. It may be necessary to edit the choreography. If the choreographer provided you with rain fights, you're in luck. These fights are safe, short and still say what the choreographer intended in the scene. If there are no rain fights, call the choreographer and ask for recommendations.[22] If they cannot be reached, or if the change is made at the last moment, it is up to the fight captain to edit the fight. The simplest solution is to do the first and last phrase, or just the last phrase. Just be sure the fight is edited and not re-choreographed. Changes in choreography without ample rehearsal time are accidents waiting to happen. Here, as in any part of stage combat, safety comes first.

GUIDELINES CONCERNING REHEARSING AND RUNNING A STAGE FIGHT

The following guidelines are provided as a reference to the rehearsal and performance process. Although many of these guidelines have been developed from union rules and regulations, they should be followed in any production where fights take place. Practices for safe, dramatic swordplay should not be viewed as luxuries of big theatres, but as practical rules for any theratrical production. Remember, no part is too special, no role too dear to be worth endangering yourself in any way. If you are working in a union theatre, be sure to check your local union contracts and review your rights as an actor before you begin rehearsal. When in doubt, always err on the side of safety.

Before Signing a Contract

1. Read the script and discern if you will be called upon to participate in a staged fight.
2. Find out if the production's fights will be professionally staged. Ask who will be staging the fights, what their qualifications are.
3. If the production involves a long or complex fight, be sure adequate rehearsal time is being allotted from the beginning. Ask what the tentative fight rehearsal schedule will be.
4. If you are working in a union house, check the local Agreement to see if you should be signing an Extraordinary Risk rider.
5. Do your homework. Just because the production staff isn't familiar with current stage fighting rulings does not mean they do not exist. Take the time to be sure.
6. If you are understudying or covering a fight role, see to it that you are assured, in writing, adequate rehearsal time to safely learn all fights.

Setting the Stage for Rehearsal

1. As you begin the rehearsal process, review the basic rules of safety outlined at the end of Chapter 1.
2. Do not try to "tough" anything out. If anything feels wrong or dangerous, you have the right and responsibility to say 'NO!'
3. No matter how qualified the fight cirector, you must feel comfortable with the physical business you are given. Remember, anything that you do on stage should be done of your own free will.

---

[22]In AGMA houses the Fight Director must be notified and supervise restaging of any fights. *"In the event that the performance parameters change (by way of example without limitation: where a smaller stage diminishes individual ARTISTS' parameters of safety necessitating fewer ARTISTS, fewer weapons, or revised choreography), the Fight Director will supervise restaging."* AGMA "Agreement" Exhibit 2-8

4. Before rehearsal begins, report to your fight cirector any and all physical injuries or limitations that may, *in any way,* affect your performance of a staged fight. It is also wise to mention whether you are right or left handed.
5. At the top of rehearsal a fight captain should be appointed.
6. A "fight-specific" first-aid kit must be readily available in the rehearsal hall and backstage.
7. Identify who among the company has first-aid training. It is advisable for the fight captain to have basic first-aid training.
8. All fight-specific weapons and props must be made available as soon as possible. Ideally, at the first day of rehearsal.
9. The fight captain should be present at all fight rehearsals.
10. A stage manager should be present at all rehearsals.

Rehearsing the Fight

1. In almost all cases, fights must be rehearsed "Early and Often!" Stage swordplay should be worked out in detail no less than three weeks before opening, and then rehearsed as often as possible.
2. The more complex a fight (either in length or numbers of people involved), the earlier it should be scheduled in rehearsal.
3. It takes roughly one hour of rehearsal to stage approximately twenty seconds of fight movement.
4. Any fight-specific prop or costume piece (i.e., hats, shoes, boots, wigs, doublets, corsets, breeches, dresses, skirts, etc.) must be incorporated into rehearsals as soon as possible.
5. To ensure safety, dynamics and spacing, rehearsal on the actual set must be scheduled as soon after plotting the choreography as possible.
6. Fight rehearsals should be scheduled on the actual set (once available) at least twice a week.
7. Fights must be rehearsed under the lighting conditions planned for the performance well in advance of opening.
8. Time must be allotted to safely adjust a fight to any special lighting or stage effects (such as fog, snow and so on).
9. All relevant company members (fight captain, stage manager, combatants) should write down the fight choreography in a manner discernible to them.
10. After a fight has been set, it should be rehearsed as often as possible. Daily rehearsals are ideal.
11. Prepare for problems. Rehearse solutions to unforeseen incidents such as going up in performance, broken blade, missing essential prop or person, or a physical, environmental or costume problem that prevents the execution of certain choreographed movements. Always have a back up plan.
12. If you are working in an outdoor theatre, have specific choreography, such as "rain fights," in reserve for bad weather days.
13. Make it a habit to always check your weapons prior to rehearsal and performance, no matter whose job it is. Be sure that they are not broken, loose or damaged.
14. If a weapon or prop is not combat serviceable, it should not be used in a fight, for any reason, at any time.
15. Never change to different weapons without proper rehearsal time.
16. Be sure to allot time to review fight choreography outside of rehearsal.
17. Understudies and covers must be allowed to rehearse the fights with the performing artists.

Run-Throughs and Production

1. A Fight-Call is mandatory prior to each run-through and performance. This is necessary to physically warm up the actors, and to provide a feeling of "security" through review.

2. The Fight-Call is generally at half-hour, or fifteen minutes prior to half-hour.
3. The Fight-Call should be on-stage with fight-specific costume, set and prop pieces.
4. All actors directly involved in the fight scene must be called for the Fight-Call.
5. No one is excused from Fight-Call without the express consent of the Fight Captain.
6. Prior to beginning Fight-Call the set must be checked for any possible hazards.
7. Fight-Call should be run in three stages: (1) a one-quarter speed walk-through or mark-through; (2) a one-half speed run-through with fight-specific lights, sound and one-quarter acting value; (3) a three-quarter speed, full acting value rehearsal.
8. Fight-Call is a warm-up, not a performance. Do not foolishly "spend" yourself with a full-out run-through before curtain.
9. Never move on in the Fight-Call if anyone is uncomfortable with any portion of the routine.
10. There must always be an outside eye watching the Fight-Call to ensure that the fights remain safe and the choreographer's intentions are fulfilled. If the fight captain is in a fight, a stage manager familiar with the routine must observe the fight for inconsistencies.
11. Be sure there is a "cool down" period from the Fight-Call before curtain time.
12. It is important that all combatants support and trust the fight captain after the choreographer has left. They are the informed outside eye and have the fight's best interest at heart.

When Problems Arise

1. To alleviate argument, if a question of choreography arises, the fight director's notes must be followed. If they left no notes, the fight captain's copy should be addressed and treated as the word of the choreographer.
2. If problems should arise in performance, use pre-rehearsed solutions. Never improvise choreography.
3. If an understudy or cover with inadequate rehearsal time goes on it may be necessary to edit the choreography or have them perform the fight in slow motion. Never let an underprepared combatant do a fight at performance speed.
4. No changes should be made in the choreography without first consulting the choreographer. If they cannot be reached, or if the change is made at the last moment, it is up to the fight captain to edit the fight.
5. Changes in choreography without ample rehearsal time are accidents waiting to happen.

Closing Note

As you step out of the classroom and into the rehearsal hall, it is important for you to remember your rights. Not everything is guaranteed in writing, and written agreements can change. Safety must come first whether you are working in a union theatre or a local community playhouse. Apply these guidelines to your rehearsals, speak out to protect your rights and yourself. If you are in a union house, before confronting anyone, consult your local office to verify any information provided herein. If you are a union member, it is recommended that you contact your local office and acquire a complete copy of the contract and amendments for more detailed reference.

Please understand that the specific rules and regulations provided in this chapter are only as current as the Agreement's last date of publication. Also, it is important to note that the preceding notes from the AEA and AGMA Agreements are not complete. Due to the scope and topic of this chapter and book, only those sections most applicable to the actor/combatant were selected. To better know your rights as an actor, take the time to read your union agreements. After all, "knowledge is power"!

Epilogue

"Be not wise in thine owne conceit, in thinking that thou hast learned all the skill which is possible to be learned already, farre deceived art thou if thou thinke so, for if thou live till thou art olde, yet thou mayest learne still."[1]

The art of stage combat is changing and growing at a considerable rate. From the time that I began this book, until now, there have been a great many changes in its application. It's hard to believe that what is written today can become dated material tomorrow. I have, however, made all attempts to bring the text up to date prior to its printing.

In your classes or on stage, you may encounter new and different approaches to what you have learned herein. If they are safe, embrace them. Remember that this is what makes stage combat an art form. It grows, changes and develops as its participants creatively merge their knowledge with the ideas and knowledge of others. Just remember that not every style is worth embracing. Be sure that what you are doing makes sense both in execution and presentation. As you move on, here are three questions that I use to evaluate new techniques and information. Use them in good health.

1. Is the victim in control of the action?
2. Is there clear communication between the combatants and between the combatants and the audience?
3. Is the technique safe and effective?

Stay *ON GUARD*, remember, you are the ultimate safety device. If the answer to all the questions is not "YES," you have the power to say "NO!" No part is too special, no role too dear that it is worth endangering yourself in any way. Protect yourself, and enjoy the art of safe stage combat.

---

[1]Swetnam, ff. xix.

Appendix A

Societies of Stage Combat

Many components ultimately influence the relative success and believability of any staged fight: the director's concept, the choreography, the choreographer's style and teaching techniques, the performers' acting abilities, and their movement skills and understanding of stage combat, the intrinsic value of the fight in advancing the plot, and the costumes, to mention only a few. Because the actual performance of a stage fight is a culmination of all these ingredients, no book can impart the precise, detailed understanding of stage combat that study with a skilled master instills. This book serves as a valuable introduction and guide to the areas of technique, safety and theatricality, but it cannot completely assure success. The primary intention of this book is to serve as an auxiliary source, augmenting the guided study of stage combat and acting. In America, Britain and Canada there are established societies of professional fight directors whose goals are to make the physical conflict in the theatre as safe and exciting as possible. If you are not presently studying with an acknowledged teacher of stage combat, or if you are interested in furthering your training and skills I recommend you contact any of these prestigious organizations at the below addresses.

THE SOCIETY OF AMERICAN FIGHT DIRECTORS
1834 Camp Avenue
Rockford, IL 61103
United States of America
Phone: (800) 659-6579

THE SOCIETY OF BRITISH FIGHT DIRECTORS
To better accomodate the needs of students of the dramatic arts, and those of the professional actor, as of 1996 the SBFD has changed its name and divided into two separate organizations. Both of these organizations are only concerned with the teaching of stage combat in the academic realm. All professional fight directing matters are being dealt with by the British Actors' Equity Fight Directors register.

The British Academy of Stage
  & Screen Combat
Contact:
Richard Ryan
10 Cranbrook Park
Wood Green
London
N22 5NA
United Kingdom
Phone: (0144) 181 881 1536

The British Academy of
  Dramatic Combat
Contact:
Steve Wilshire
20 Lincoln Street
Canton
Cardiff
CF5 1JX
United Kingdom
Phone: (0122) 223 8428

FIGHT DIRECTORS CANADA
Robert Seale, President
39 Wheatsheaf Crescent
North York, Ontario M3N 1P7
Canada
Phone: (416) 667-1346

NEW ADDITIONS TO THE SOCIETIES OF STAGE COMBAT

In the past few years, several countries have started forming stage combat organizations to better promote safe and effective stage violence within their dramatic community. Following are some of the fledgling organizations.

Society of Australian Fight Directors
Marcus Hogan, President
127 Charlotte Street
Brisbane, Queensland 4001
Australia
Phone: 011-61-732296930

The New Zealand Stage Combat
  Society
Attn: Tony Wolf
P.O. Box 38046
Wellington Mail Centre
Wellington, New Zealand

The Nordic Stage Fight Society
Peppé Ostensson, President
Nya Tannesforsv. 26C
Linkoping, 58252
Sweden
Phone: 011-46-13-12611

Appendix B

Swordcutlers and Suppliers

Twenty years ago the only vendor of theatrical weapons was a fencing equipment supplier. Foils and epée blades were mounted on a variety of "hilts," and set on stage as swords. Since that time the art of stage combat and its weapons have grown and evolved. There are, however, still a good deal of "fencing" weapons used on the stage, but among these relics are weapons specifically designed for the repetitive abuse of stage combat. Chapter 3 deals with the specifics of choosing a safe stage weapon, mentioning that although some swords are billed as "combat serviceable," they may in reality be unsafe. The following list of swordcutlers and suppliers of theatrical swords offer a great variety of hilt configurations and types of blades, finish and decorations. What you are looking for and the range of your budget will determine the quality and appearance of the weapon you receive.

No matter what you choose, whether for personal or production use, the sword must meet the fundamental safety criteria set in Chapter 3. Although there is no perfect stage weapon, you must take as few chances as possible in order to lower the risk of accident and injury. Catalogues and sales personnel can be deceiving. A sword is both a financial and a personal investment, CHECK OUT THE WEAPON.

Price should not be the governing concern in renting or purchasing a sword. Durability, dependability and stability are three key factors in ordering a sword. Ask if there is a guarantee on the hilt, blade or craftsmanship of the weapon. If you are ordering by catalogue, be sure there is a money back guarantee if the weapon received is not the "safe" weapon advertised. No matter how safe the practice of stage combat, if the weapons are unsound, the combat is still dangerous.

ALAN MEEK, *SWORDCUTLER*
  180 Frog Grove Lane
  Wood Street Village
  Guildford
  Surrey GU3 3HD United Kingdom
  Tel. 01483-234084

ARMS and ARCHERY
  The Coach House
  London Road
  Ware
  Herts. SG12 9QU United Kingdom
  Tel. 01920-460335

ART of the SWORD
  761 Calusa
  El Cerrito, CA 94530
  (415) 526-3755
  No catalogue

ELLER ROBERT COOK
  P.O. BOX 188
  Etowah, NC 28729
  (704) 692-0323
  Catalogue available: $2.00 fee

LUNDEGAARD ARMOURY
  P.O. BOX 287
  Crompond, NY 10517
  Catalogue available: $1.50

RAMSHEAD ARMOURY
  P.O. BOX 653
  Champaign, IL 61820
  (217) 351-7232
  Catalogue available: $2.00

THE ARMOURY
American Fencers Supply Co.
1180 Folsom Street
San Francisco, CA 94103
(415) 863-7911
Catalogue available: $3.00 fee

ARMS and ARMOR
1101 Stinson Blvd. NE
Minneapolis, MN 55413
(612) 331-6473
Catalogue available

BELLE & BLADE
124 Penn Avenue
Dover, NJ 07801
(201) 328-8488
Catalogue available

THE COLLECTOR'S ARMOURY   INC.
800 Slaters Lane
P.O. BOX 1061, Dept. CA
Alexandria, VA 22313
(703) 684-6111

DENNIS L. GRAVES,
  SWORDCUTLER*
255 South 41st Street
Boulder, CO 80303
(303) 494-4685
Catalogue available

MUSEUM REPLICAS LIMITED
ATLANTA CUTLERY CORP.
2143 Gees Mill Rd.
BOX 840
Conyers, GA 30207
1-800-241-3664
Catalogue available: $2.00

STAGES UNLIMITED INC.
635 Dee Road
Park Ridge, IL 60068
(312) 698-6545
No catalogue

TRIPLETTE COMPETITION
  ARMS
162 West Pine Street
Mt. Airy, NC 27030
(919) 786-5294
Catalogue available

VULCAN'S FORGE*
3013 Shannon Drive
Baltimore, MD 21213
(410) 325-2046
FAX: (410) 727-4366

TUDOR ARMOURY
Tudor Lodge, Salmon Lane
Annesley Woodhouse
Nottinghamshire NG17 9HB
United Kingdom

WEAPONS of CHOICE
4075 Browns Valley Rd.
Napa, CA 94558
(707) 226-2845

STEVE VAUGH
800 Vernal Road
Attica, NY 14011
USA
(716) 591-3673

---

*Over the past twelve years I have worked exclusively with Dennis L. Graves and Vulcan's Forge. I feel comfortable and confident with their swords. I have not had the opportunity to use the weapons of all the listed suppliers and suggest that you put every weapon to the test. If the supplier is truly manufacturing weapons for stage combat, there should be no problem. Each supplier offers a variety of designs and styles, and you may well find exactly what you want from any of these armories.

Appendix C

Maintaining the Weapon

Once you have selected a stage weapon, it is important to know how to keep it clean and rust free. It must be properly cared for in order to insure a long and productive life. Although there are no perfect stage weapons, an awareness of your sword's limitations and its correct use and maintenance will help make it last a long time. The techniques in this book deal with the proper handling of the sword, so here I deal with the everyday maintenance and storage of the sword.

Everyday Care

It is hard to imagine that there is much to the maintenance of a sword. There are no moving parts, no wires, and no batteries necessary. It's a sword. This attitude, however, is the reason that many good stage weapons die long before they should have. The weapon needs to be checked and properly attended to every time it is used.

Oiling the Sword

The most common problem with swords is rust and corrosion. These are things that appear minor at first, but can destroy a blade or hilt. Rust eats away metal, and once a portion is eaten, it does not come back. The damage may not be visible to the eye, but the structural integrity of the metal is diminished. This weakens the blade and can lead to its breaking. Rust must be treated before it appears on the sword.

Climates with a high humidity level seem to affect blades the most. High humidity combined with fluctuations in temperature create condensation. This forms a thin layer of moisture on the sword which can start the process of corrosion overnight. For this reason make it a habit to wipe your sword down with a lightly oiled rag each day after you are finished with its use. A silicone gun cloth will do, or you may use a natural fiber rag (cotton, wood, etc.) lightly doused in Marvel Mystery Oil®.[1] Other oils that also form a strong barrier against corrosion are Rig, Zep, 3 in 1, and any gun oil. WD-40, although good for cleaning a sword, does not protect it from corrosion. The "WD" stands for "Water Displacement," and the oil contains kerosene. This helps in removing water and condensation from the blade, but its protective qualities tend to evaporate.

If you live in a dry climate with steady temperatures, you should still oil your sword. Despite the lack of moisture in the air, swords can still rust. Every time you touch the hilt and blade with your hands you leave skin oil on the sword. This oil can be corrosive, having the same effect as humidity

---

[1] Marvel Oil Company, Inc. Port Chester, NY 10573.

and condensation. Therefore, in order to avoid rust and corrosion it is best to wipe down the entire sword each day after it is used. Do not oil the grip, however, even if it is wrapped in wire, unless the sword is going into storage.

If your sword has a highly polished hilt or blade, it is doubly important to keep it oiled. Once the metal starts to tarnish, the finish is damaged and can only be regained through buffing. Continued polishing on a buffing wheel, however, weakens the integrity of the weapon. The process of re-polishing the sword brings its shine back, but each new buffing removes metal.

Basic Cleaning

If the sword begins to tarnish, or rust does manage to form, an oil wipe is no longer sufficient. You must take the time to clean the sword. Aside from being unsightly and destructive to the weapon, rust can cause infection if someone is even scratched with the blade. If cleaned in the early stages of discoloration the process is fairly simple.

Steel wool used to be the right tool for the job, but there are now much better products for cleaning a tarnished sword. A wonderful device is the "steel eraser," or Kraytex. This is a rubber bar, much like the red rubber erasers from school, laden with small particles of metal. When rubbed on the sword the Kraytex literally erases the discoloration. It comes in a variety of textures, much like sandpaper, and can be purchased at your local hardware store. Also available at the hardware store are Scotchbrite pads. These also come in a variety of grades, gray for finer parts of the sword, green for the tougher spots. Kraytex works well dry, Scotchbrite cleans better when used with an oil. It is best to oil the blade first, let the steel absorb the oil, and then clean the sword. Afterwards, the sword should be wiped off with a dry rag, and re-oiled with a coat of Marvel Mystery Oil or the like.

For those swords that are highly polished, it is best to clean with a very fine grain Kraytex. The Scotchbrite pads tend to scratch and damage the finish of the sword. Of course, it is best to avoid the tarnish altogether. Oil the sword. A few minutes a day can prevent a longer and messier session in the future.

If you have a sword with a complex hilt configuration where it is difficult to get inside all the tight nooks and crannies with the Kraytex or Scotchbrite pads, emery cloth may also be used. A fine grain, cloth "sandpaper" can be cut into small strips and pulled through the tighter sections of the hilt. Then, in a process much like buffing a shoe, the cloth is briskly pulled back and forth to sand away the corrosion. Because of the abrasives of the emery cloth, this process is not recommended for swords with highly polished hilts.

Checking the Blade

No matter how careful you are in swinging the sword, some nicks and burrs are generated through repeated use. These are incisions in the edge of the blade created through compression of the metal. Most of the time they are not harmful to the blade, but some can lead to stress fractures and blade breakage. It is best to keep an eye on your blade, watching for any deep nicks or incisions. If the indentation is more than 1/10 of an inch deep, especially on an epée or the foible of the blade, you should concider replacing the blade.[2] The blade may be fine, but it is not worth risking accident or injury.

If you are working with a Musketeer blade, the edge to edge play in this manual could be nicking the blade. As mentioned in Chapter 3, the blade is not designed for repetitive edge-play. Be careful, and check your blade often, especially the foible.

---

[2] If you need to replace your blade, be sure it is fitted to your hilt and has the correct threading for your pommel. The most common threadings are: 12 × 24"; 1/4 × 20"; 5/16 × 18"; and 6 × 1 mm.

Although schlager blades are incredibly durable, there are bad blades. Also, a heavy hand or bad technique can gouge even the toughest blades. Do not assume that because you have a schlager, the blade will not nick. It merely means that the blade is less apt to nick or break. Check it. It's always better to be safe than sorry.

Removing the Burrs

Although you should inspect your blade often, it is generally clothing or your oil rag that finds burrs first. Small splinters of metal snag and catch fabric, telling you there is a need to de-burr the blade. This is easily done with a fine grade sandpaper or metal file. If you are using a file, be sure that it is a metal file, as wood files have different teeth. The sandpaper can be lightly rubbed on the blades edges to remove the burrs. With the file, first fit the blade in a vice, and then work down the edge of the blade. Each stroke carries the file roughly one-third of the way down the blade. Keep the file at an angle of roughly 20–30 degrees to the blade. Work both sides of the edge in this manner. This keeps the file from scratching the flat of the blade and sharpening the edge. Don't pull the file back on the blade, its teeth only cut on the forward stroke. If filing seems to be "sharpening" the blade, you can blunt the edge with the file.

Don't get overzealous in these actions. Just remove the nicks and splinters. Leave as much of the blade intact as possible. A good test to check if the major burrs are removed is to run an old nylon stocking down the edge. If there are any burrs left, the nylon will snag.

Periodic Check-Up

It is advisable to give your sword a check-up once a month. This, of course, varies depending on the amount you use your sword. If it is being used at least twice a week in class or rehearsal, strip it, and check its components each month. To do this you need to remove the pommel of your sword. In most cases you will need a vice or vice-grips to unseat the pommel. Be sure to check with the weapon's manufacturer, as some pommels are only hand tight. If a vice is needed to unseat the pommel, be sure that the teeth or metal surface is covered with leather or some other yielding material. This prevents the vice from scarring the pommel. Once unscrewed the weapon should be disassembled. If the weapon is well crafted, it may take a few taps with a rubber mallet to unseat the components.

Check the grip for any disfiguration. Both ends should be flat, square to the pommel and the hilt. The hole through the center should snugly fit the tang with no slop or play from side to side. If you have a plastic grip there probably are no problems. Wood grips, however, should be checked regularly. Constant use and wear and tear can compress and misalign the ends. This misalignment affects the arrangement of the other parts of the sword and can lead to tang damage or breakage. If the grip is crooked or deformed, it's time to get a new grip.

Be sure to also check the hilt and tang. You should first look for signs of rust, stress or metal fatigue. That means bends, fractures, cracks or light-colored distentions at points of stress. If you find any cracks or fractures on the tang, replace the blade. If cracks or signs of stress appear on the hilt, contact its manufacturer concerning repair or replacement. Be sure to also check for bending, collapsing or breakdown of the hilt. Too many disarms can cause the guard to bend or collapse. This is most common on the quillons and knuckle bow. Hilts constructed of low carbon steel can generally be bent back into shape without snapping.

When reassembling the sword, be sure that all the pieces are put back in the same way they came off. Some hilts and grips only fit together on the tang in one way. Parts should be snug, but they should not need to be forced together. When reattaching the pommel, be sure to follow the manufacturer's directions concerning tightening. They should be snug, but never wrenched down.

Storing the Sword

If you are putting your sword away for more than a few days, you need to do more than oil the blade. First, dismantle and inspect the weapon, then clean and oil all its metal parts. Then reassemble the weapon and lightly tighten the pommel by hand. This allows for possible expansion or contraction of the components while in storage. All exposed metal should then be coated with Canuba wax. The wax seals the steel from the elements and protects the sword from condensation and corrosion. Other forms of wax that work well are butcher's wax and good old "Turtle Wax." You may also coat the blade with a layer of grease. The sword can then be placed in a gun sock, sword bag or even wrapped in a towel and put away. When the blade is removed from storage, a dry cloth can easily buff out the wax, or remove the grease.

Appendix D

The Language of Swordplay

The following glossary offers some of the most common terms used in this text, as well as by professional Fight Directors and Choreographers.

Absence of Blades A state in which the sword blades are not in contact. See *Free*.

Abstraction The process of reducing a fight sequence, style or form down to its most essential characteristics.

Academic Combat A mechanical, technically correct fight, performed move for move with little or no acting intent.

Accent Stressing of one particular action or sequence, either greater or lesser than previous actions.

Acquired Parry Another name for the *Circular* or *Counter Parry*, reflecting the practice necessary to master the action.

Across Any guard position that has the weapon's blade directed across the body.

Acted Percussion: The illusion of force and rebound where two bodies/objects collide with much less force than it appears.

Action-Reaction-Action (Also *Cue-Reaction-Action* and *Preparation-Reaction-Action*) The process of giving and taking focus during physical conflict. The first "action" is the aggressor's cue and control point for the attack. The "reaction" is that of the victim, who, upon reading the cue, responds accordingly. In the final "action" the two combatants complete the offensive/defensive action together.

Actions Simple, compound, progressive, or combined movements of the blade and/or body used to accomplish the combatant's objectives within a fight.

Active Bind See *Bind*.

Active Footwork (Also *Grand Footwork* and *Traveling*) A process of amplifying the distance a standard or *Passive* piece of footwork covers to create dynamics within a fight.

Active Movement Any movement executed in an amplified, more dynamic fashion.

Activities Simple movements or actions taken by a character that serve no specific dramatic purpose.

Actor's Parry of Eight The Actor's Parry completed in a parry of 8 rather than 2. See *Actor's Parry*.

Actor's Parry A large sweeping circular parry of 2, so called because although appearing difficult, it is rather easy for the theatrical swordsman to master.

Actor/Combatant a.) The first category of the four skill levels dictated by the Society of American Fight Directors. **b.)** Any actor involved in a fight sequence or scene.

Ad Lib Extemporaneous movement that does not appear in the fight choreography.

Advance-Lunge See *Patinando*.

Advance (also *Fencing Step*) Footwork carrying the body forward by moving the lead foot first, followed with the lag foot (without crossing them). The opposite of *Retreat*.

After-cut A cut on the riposte. See *Riposte*.

Agrippa, Camillo Sixteenth century Milanese author of the first treatise to reduce the vast number of fencing guards advocated by the masters of his day (1568). He recommended the use of only four guards, which correspond roughly to prime, seconde, tierce and low quarte of modern fencing. Agrippa is also the first swordsman known to stress the value of the thrust as opposed to the cut.

Aids (Also *Last Fingers*) The last three fingers on the sword hand which assist or aid the manipulators (thumb and forefingers).

Alignment Essentially good posture, where the various parts of the body are all in correct relative position to one another.

Alto (It.) Used in reference to the target at the upper part of the opponent's body; at the shoulder or chest level.

477

Angelo, Domenico (Also *Domenico Angelo Malevolti Tremamondo*) An Italian-born author whose "School of Fencing" (1763), considered the foremost text on small sword play, contains some of the best plates on the topic.

Answer a.) A *Riposte*. **b.)** To meet an aggressor in a fight; to return a hostile action.

Answering Beat See *Return Beat*.

Appel A stamping or slapping of the floor with the sole of the lead foot, generally executed immediately before an attack or feint with the blade, often accompanied by a loud shout.

Armpit Kill a.) A cliché "kill" seen in bad stage fights where the blade is laid under the victim's arm and cradled in their armpit. **b.)** A kill, like a *Boar's Thrust*, delivered upward under the victim's arm and appearing to pierce the chest.

Arms of the Hilt See *Pas d'Ane*.

Around the Clock An exercise in offensive/defensive blade-play that runs cutting or thrusting attacks on the exchange, in either numerical order or around the body like the numbers on the face of a clock.

Arranger See *Fight Arranger*.

Arrebatar (Span.) A cutting attack from the shoulder with the entire arm. See *Shoulder Cut*.

Articulation of Movement To form or fit individual actions into a systematic whole while maintaining the clarity of their individual purpose.

Assisted Heavy Parry The action of a parry, joined by a second weapon into a *Heavy Parry*; both weapons taking the opposing blade to the floor.

Asymmetry A lack of proportion or balance in time, space or energy, opposed to conventional balance.

Attack into the Attack To attack one's opponent as they are attacking.

Attack on Preparation An offense that is made as the opponent prepares their attack, whether the preparation is made with the sword or footwork, separately or together.

Attack on the Blade (also *Attacks of Force*) Actions used to remove or displace the opponent's blade before an effective offensive action can be launched. Attacks on the Blade are generally broken into three major categories, *Beats, Pressures,* and *Flowing*.

Attack with Opposition An attack maintaining a strong controlled contact with the opponent's blade which may deflect it out of line.

Attack a.) A simple or compound offensive action intended to hit one's opponent. **b.)** An assault.

Avancés (Fr.) The targets of one's opponent nearest to you; the sword arm and lead leg.

Avantage The slight bow or bend in the foible of a fencing blade which "trains" the blade to give on a hit rather than pierce.

Avoidance A movement of the body and/or feet designed to dodge an attack.

Back-Edge See *False Edge*.

Back a.) The "back" or false edge of a blade. **b.)**

The rear or dorsal part of the human body. Generally used in reference to the rear portion of the upper torso. **c.)** To go, or cause to go, backward or in reverse. See *Backpedal*.

Backpedal To travel backward from an opponent, or opponents, through passing steps or consecutive retreats, though still facing them.

Backsword A popular eighteenth-century contesting sword similar in style to a basket-hilted claymore, with a single cutting edge where the false or back edge is blunted except for a few inches at the tip, where it is double edged. Also sometimes referring to a stick with a basket-hilt used instead of the sword in practice.

Backswording a.) The practice of the backsword. **b.)** Cutting attacks delivered from the elbow or wrist, made with the false or back edge of the blade.

Backward Diagonal Avoid An evasive action taken to the rear onto either the SE or SW diagonal plane of footwork. See *Diagonal Avoid*.

Backward Lunge (also *Echappement*) An evasive by distance which removes the body from cutting attacks across the belly or chest with grand lunge straight backward.

Balance a.) A state of equilibrium where the combatant's weight is equally divided between both feet. See *Center*. **b.)** The total composition of a scene so that it is esthetically pleasing to the observer.

Baldric A belt or girdle of the Baroque period, usually of leather and richly ornamented, that supported the wearer's sword and scabbard.

Balestra (also *Jump-Lunge*) **a.)** A compound piece of footwork designed to quickly cover a great deal of ground by combining a jump forward and the grand lunge. In some schools the *balestra* refers to the jump forward proceeding the lunge and not the compound action of the jump and lunge.

Balloon Walk An exercise designed to help the actor/combatant keep their feet on track while traversing linear footwork by having them carry an inflated party balloon between their inner thighs.

Basket-Hilt a.) The most common cavalry sword of the seventeenth century whose hilt was curved into a shape resembling a basket, designed to provide defense for the combatant's hand. **b.)** Used as a term of contempt, suggesting a swordsman whose sword, and hence style, were old-fashioned.

Basso (It.) Literally "low" or "lowered." Generally used in reference to the lowest immediate target on the opponent's body; at the thigh or knee.

Bastard Sword (Also *Basterdsword* and *Hand-and-a-Half Sword*) A contemporary term, now used to describe a sword that may be wielded by one or both hands.

Battement (Fr.) A beat attack. See *Beat*.

Battle-Axe Grip (Also *Battle-Ax Grip*) See *Conan Grip*.

Battre de Main (Fr.) To parry with the hand. See *Hand Parry*.

Beat Attack (also *Battrement*) A controlled tap with the forte or middle part of one's blade against the middle or weak part of the opponent's blade to remove a threat, open a line for attack, or to provoke a reaction.

Beat Away Disarm A disarm executed by using the mechanics of the beat away. The disarm may be secure or loose, but is more frequently secured.

Beat Away (also *Quillon Bash*) A type of beat attack that knocks the opposing blade away after the successful completion of a blocking parry by punching the hilt of the sword towards the parried blade.

Beat Out See *Beat Parry*.

Beat Parry A parry made by striking the opponent's blade sharply aside, removing the attacking blade and allowing for a immediate riposte.

Beat-Aside (also *Rising Parry* or *Intercept Parry*) A defensive action that beats the offensive blade aside during the execution of an attack.

Beat A sharp, controlled tap against the middle or weak part of the opponent's blade to open a line of attack or to provoke a reaction.

Beating the Bind (also *Change Bind*) A beat attack executed by the victim of a bind by disengaging around the aggressor's guard, in the same direction as the bind, and then instantly snapping the blade against the middle or foible of the opponent's blade, beating it aside.

Beats a.) Attacks on the blade that utilize percussive shock to laterally remove the opposing weapon. **b.)** The series of emotional changes that a character goes through during a scene or fight.

Before Referring to the dagger placement in a cross parry where the dagger is situated to the front of the rapier, on the side towards the other combatant. Opposite of *Behind*.

Behind Referring to the dagger placement in a cross parry where the dagger is situated to the back of the rapier, being placed on the side away from the other combatant. Opposite of *Before*.

Bell-Guard The cup or bell-shaped guard of the Spanish rapier.

Belly Cut See *Belly Swipe*.

Belly Swipe A theatrical cutting attack not intended to land, but to slash through the air (from either right or left) outside measure and across the belly, in a plane parallel to the floor. Usually executed with an evasion by distance. See also *Horizontal Swipe* and *Swipe*.

Besnard, Charles Seventeenth-century French teacher and master of the "Academie Royale d'Arms," best known for his introduction of the "reverence," the practice of formally saluting one's opponent before a bout.

Bind Away (also *Throw Off*) An active bind that throws or flings away the opposing blade.

Bind Over An active bind that carries the blades up, over and down to the floor on the opposite side used to disarm the opponent or to pin their weapon.

Bind A pris d'fer that carries the opposing weapon from a high line to a low line, and vice versa, diagonally across the line of engagement. The Bind can be executed both in a passive and active form.

Blade The essential part of a cut and/or thrust weapon that covers its entire expanse. The basic blade is broken down into the following parts: *tip, foible, middle, forte, shoulders*, and *tang*. Many blades, like the rapier, have a *ricasso* between the forte and tang. The cutting edge is divided into the *true* and *false edge*.

Blank Choreography Any sequence of choreography, fight or fight scene presented without any given circumstances or text.

Block a.) A defensive action used to stop or deflect an oncoming attack. **b.)** A parry. **c.)** To lay out action or movement in a scene with actors and/or camera.

Blocking Parry (also *Standard Parry, Opposition Parry* and *Parry by Opposition*) A parry made by moving the sword to close the opponent's line of attack, stopping the attack from landing.

Blood Groove (Also *Blood Gutter*) A misnomer created to explain the grooving and/or fluting of a blade, which falsely supposed these grooves were devised to allow the blood to drain from one's opponent. See *Fuller* and *Fluted Blade*.

Boar's Thrust A violent thrust punched upward into the body after the sword hand is suddenly dropped to the level of the knee.

Body Blow Any attack, armed or unarmed, that is landed, or appears to land, on the body of a fighter.

Botta Dritta a.) A pronated thrust from the right; the straight thrust. **b.)** In theatrical rapier play, a pronated thrust, from *Seconda* or *Terza*, to either the opponent's right or left shoulder/chest.

Botta Lunga (also *Grand Lunge*) Classical movement which replaced passing (as a means of reaching an opponent and attacking them) early in the seventeenth century.

Botta Segrete The "secret attack." Most masters of the sixteenth century Italian school claimed to have developed a secret attack to which there was no possible defense. No such attack ever existed, or has been discovered, but the secret attack was often sold, for a great price, to "select" students.

Botta An attack from its beginning to its completion; a blow or thrust.

Bout The spell of activity between two fencers engaged in personal combat.

Box Target A target system in on-line swordplay with four body targets that when joined with imaginary lines form a box.

Break a.) A pause between beats, phrases or sections of a fight. A space in the action. **b.)** A term for the sudden or violent separation or splitting of bones. **c.)** A quarrel or fight.

Breakaway (Also *Break-away*) Props and/or set pieces that are specially designed to safely fall apart on impact, such as bottles, chairs, windows, etc.

Breaking Ground Any action of footwork that surrenders ground to the opponent.

Broadsword a.) A term now apply to almost all swords of the Medieval period. Most often applied to the *Armying Sword* of the Middle Ages. **b.)** A style of theatrical swordsplay representing combat with a "broadsword" (*armying sword*) spanning European history from the tenth century to the end of the fifteenth century.

Brochiero A variety of hand shield or buckler.

Broken Time When two movements are deliberately made to not follow immediately one upon the other.

Buckler (Also *Bokeler*) **a.)** A small round (sometimes square) shield generally used in conjunction with the broad bladed swords of the Middle Ages and early Renaissance. The buckler and the short sword were the national weapon of England until the late sixteenth century. **b.)** See *Target*.

Business Any small movement or action used by an actor in a scene to further the action and/or add color to the interpretation of their character. See *By-Play*.

Button The round flat metal disk used to blunt the tip of the competitive fencing blades of the foil and epée.

By-Play Decisions made by the actor (including objectives, obstacles, beats, vocals, facial expressions, etc.) that fill time and space with character-specific energy and intent without stepping outside the strict boundaries of choreography.

Cadence The rhythm of a sequence of interrelated movement with a definite beginning and end. A fencing tempo.

Capo Ferro, Ridolfo Sixteenth century Italian master, who, with the development of the *bota lunga* ("elongated blow" or the lunge) changed the manner of fencing from the round, circling style of his predecessors to that of the direct linear style now mandated in competitive fencing.

Capstan Rivet A small rivet forged from the tang of the blade, crowning the top of the pommel and joining and locking the hilt of the sword to its blade.

Carranza, Commander Jeronimo de "Father" of the Spanish science of fence, a fantastical style basing its principals on seemingly irrelevant mathematical principles (1569).

Carriage a.) The manner of carrying one's body, bearing, mien. **b.)** The sword carriage. The complicated waist belt and suspension rigging for the Elizabethan rapier. **c.)** The loop attached to the sword-belt, through which one passes the sword.

Carte See *Qaurte*.

Case of Rapiers Twin rapiers. A slightly decedent style of rapier play involving the use of a rapier in each hand. The case of rapiers were generally of a special design so they could be carried in the same scabbard.

Cavatione di Tempo Fabris' term for the *Time Disengagement*.

Cavatione (also *Cavazione*) Literally "drawing away." Fabris' term applied to the disengage. Today it is applied to the semicircular motion of the point around the opposing guard. See *Disengage*.

Ceding Parry See *Yield Parry*.

Center Line a.) An imaginary vertical line that bisects the body. **b.)** An imaginary vertical line that bisects the stage.

Center of Percussion See *Middle*.

Central Guard (Also *Neutral Guard*) Misleadingly called a "guard," the central guard places the hand and the blade at mid body along the center line, thus opening both inside and outside lines to possible attack. See also *Lines*.

Cercle Late seventeenth century term for a half circular parry generally ending in the parry of seven. See *Circular Parry*.

Certified Teacher (Also *Certified Instructor*) The second level of the four levels of advancement as recognized by the Society of American Fight Directors. An individual who has extensive educational training and has passed tests in the following areas: teaching techniques, historical styles, weapons theory and practice, and theatrical choreography.

Change Beat (also *Indirect Beat*) Beat attack executed after the successful completion of a Changement. The Beat, accompanied by a Changement, allows the initiator of the action to manipulate the direction their partner's blade is knocked.

Change Bind An changement (disengage/coupé) executed by the victim of a bind. The action consists of a bind, changement and counter bind.

Change Down Half-disengage executed from the high line into the low line.

Change of Engagement The act of engaging your opponent in a new line.

Change Over Changement executed from a free guard position that passes the point up and over an opposing weapon into a new line.

Change Parry See *Circular Parry*.

Change Under Changement executed from a free guard position that passes the point down and under an opposing weapon into a new line.

Change Up Half-disengage executed from the low line into the high line.

Changement The practice of changing, joining, freeing, removing and replacing the blades. Any action of the blade, from a free or engaged guard position, that moves the blade to a new line of engagement. Each type of changement has a particular name and function.

Character Columns The vertical columns (usually the second and fourth) in a side-by-side fight plot used to place the movements and actions of each character.

Check Action in armed or unarmed combat that follows a block or parry with one hand by an immediate second action that curbs, or restrains the attacking arm while freeing the original arm for a counter strike.

Checking Distance The process of confirming measure during training and rehearsal. The combatant with the longer reach generally sets the measure. See also *Distance, Correct*.

Checking the Blade (also *Check* or *Check Parry*) The process of curbing, or restraining, the offending blade while freeing another weapon for a counter strike.

Cheek Cut A descending diagonal cut, generally executed from the wrist or elbow, directed at the opponent's cheek. Actual cheek cuts are dangerous and seldom used on stage.

Chest Swipe Theatrical cutting attack not intended to land, but to slash through the air (from either right or left) outside measure and across the chest, in a plane parallel to the floor. Usually executed with an evasion by distance. See also *Horizontal Swipe* and *Swipe*.

Chest a.) Target in fencing and in stage combat, on either the right or left side of the body at approximately rib or arm-pit level, below the top of the shoulder and above the flank. Often used in theatrical broadsword-play so as not to confuse its parries with the numerical parries of the rapier's shoulder targets. **b.)** On-line target in swordplay, generally referring to the center of the upper torso at the level of the zyphoid process.

Chicken-Wing Parry Slang for the parry of High Two.

Choreographer (Also *Fight Choreographer, Fight Director, Fight Arranger*) The individual who creates and supervises the fight sequences in a film, television and/or stage production.

Circle Left Passing action in footwork that carries the combatant clockwise around the imaginary circle.

Circle Right Demi-lunge to the right that advances a combatant counterclockwise on the imaginary circle. Used in conjunction with the demi-volte in order to move the combatant continuously around the circle while keeping the sword arm to the inside towards one's opponent.

Circle Steps See *Circular Paces*.

Circles in the Air A dexteriy exercise with the sword that has the combatant draw circles with the point of the sword in both a clockwise and counterclockwise direction.

Circular Feint a.) Offensive movement of the blade where the point of the weapon describes a complete circle, made to resemble a disengage-coupé on an attack. **b.)** Taking a circular step either to the left or right with a feint attack, then springing from the advanced foot and reversing with a step and attack from the opposite direction of the circle.

Circular Paces (also *Circle Steps*) Ninth and tenth direction of footwork determined by the ten directions of movement in theatrical swordplay; these are the *Circular Pace Right* and *Circular Pace Left*. They match the pattern of the theatre's *Mysterious Circle*, crossing the eight angular planes of movement returning to the point of origin.

Circular Parry (also *Counter Parry* and sometimes "*Twiddle*") Any parry in which the point of the

weapon describes a complete circle with the hand and weapon finishing in the position in which they started.

Circular Halfe Pace Giacomo di Grassi's term for the *Demi-Volte*.

Civil Salute See *Salute*.

Civilian Sword Any sword worn by someone not in the military. The rapier was one of the first swords to be considered primarily a civilian weapon.

Clinch a.) Struggle or scuffle at close quarters. See *Corps-à-Corps*. **b.)** In unarmed combat, where fighters have locked onto one another while fighting in close.

Cloak and Sword Sixteenth century alternative to rapier and dagger, the cloak being used in the left hand for defense while the rapier was used in the right hand for offense.

Close Measure Fencing measure used when working offensive/defensive blade-play in the close. The blades extend beyond the combatants by roughly three to four inches.

Close Quarters a.) When two combatants are inside normal measure, by accident or design, but can still wield their swords correctly. **b.)** Immediate contact with the foe. **c.)** Said of a battle or combat where the participants are close enough for hand to hand combat.

Close a.) To cover or shut a line of engagement (by the defender's weapon) against an attack. **b.)** (also *The Close, Foot-to-Foot, At the Half-Sword*, and *Close Quarters*) Rough and tumble portion of swordplay when two combatants are inside normal measure, but can still wield their swords correctly. In this position they can strike with the unarmed hand, kick and punch their opponent.

Closed Line Line of engagement where the defender's weapon covers or blocks the line to an attack.

Closing Lines Act or placement of the weapon(s) where one or more of the lines of attack open to the adversary are blocked off, or "closed."

Cobb's Traverse Euphemism for running away from a fight, running backward, or back-pedaling from an encounter, named for an Elizabethan fencer and brawler.

Coin Carrier An exercise designed to help the combatant develop fluid horizontal movement in footwork by placing a coin either on or under the initiating foot and then carrying the coin forward with that foot.

Cold Steel (Also *Cold Iron*) Slang for a cut and thrust weapon. Now generally applied to any sharp sword.

Colichemarde (Also *Conichemarde* and *Konigsmark*) A blade that came into fashion between 1680 and 1690, first in France, then in Germany and England. The blade was characteristically wide at the forte, for about eight inches from the hilt, then it narrowed quite suddenly, being extremely light and flexible for the remainder of its length. Used between 1680 and 1720, when it seems to have been replaced by the small sword.

Column of Conflict The third, or middle, column of

a side-by-side fight plot, used to indicate the *Phrase* number of the choreography and to indicate the direction of offensive and defensive action between the combatants.

Combatant a.) One who fights; a warrior. **b.)** One who is armed and ready to fight. **c.)** Actor/combatant or any performer involved in a fight.

Combination Delivering of two or more offensive actions in quick succession to one another.

Comic Inversion Process of offering contradictory vocal reactions to real and believable physical injuries for comic effect. Such a juxtaposition in vocal response can be quite humorous if used selectively, unpredictably and specifically.

Coming to the Close Angelo's term for getting within distance and seizing the opponent's blade.

Command (Also *Commanding the Blade*) Controlling the opposing blade during the execution of a pris d'fer and remaining engaged upon completion. Opposite of *Expulsion*.

Commanding (also *Commanding the Sword*) **a.)** See *Command*. **b.)** Manipulation of the opposing blade for a disarm or offensive advantage. A beat, pressure or pris d'fer. **c.)** Coming to the close and seizing the opponent's blade.

Communication a.) Give and take of focus during a fight; the cueing, responding, eye contact and partnering of an effective fight. See *Action-Reaction-Action, Eye Contact, Cueing* and *Partnering*. **b.)** The successful projection of story line and character in physical dialogue.

Complementary Footwork Footwork in a fight that complements that of the opponent, keeping correct distance as they move across the floor.

Composed Attack See *Compound Attack*.

Compound Attack Any attack that requires the combined movements of at least one feint attack and a changement before the execution of the direct attack.

Compound Footwork Execution of two or more simple elements of footwork as one complete action, such as the patinando (An advance followed immediately by a lunge).

Compound Pris d'Fer Uninterrupted succession of blade taking actions.

Compound Riposte Riposte consisting of one ore more feints.

Conan Grip Slang for an improper and tight hold on the sword, locking the hand about the grip as if it were the sword of "Conan the Barbarian."

Connotation Suggestion of a meaning to an action apart from any common significance the movement possesses.

Contained Movement Controlled or confined action, dictated by space, character or style.

Content Central concern or intent that guides the movement in a physical dialogue.

Contra Cavatione (also *Contra Cavazione*) Fabris' term for the Counter Changement.

Contra Guardia Giganti's term for a covered engagement of the blades.

Contra Postura (also *Contra Guardia*) A placement of the body and weapon(s) that compliments or counters the guard assumed by the opponent. This idea, first presented by Fabris, is the beginning of the modern meaning of "guard." See also *Postura* and *Proportion*.

Contre-Parade See *Counter Parry*.

Control Point Built-in safety in armed and unarmed combat that reads as a cue to the victim and also allows the aggressor to look for the proper reaction before committing to the attack.

Controlling the Point Sixteenth-century term for commanding or displacing the opponent's point.

Corps-à-Corps (literally "body-to-body") An action in which there is body contact or where the blades are locked together and distance is closed so that normal fencing action becomes impossible. There are two forms generally used on the stage today: the corps-à-corps to the *Hilts* and to the *Grasp*.

Correct Distance The correct or prescribed measure for the execution of a particular action, sequence or fighting style.

Coulé (Fr.) Literally "flowed." (Also *Gissade* and *Glide*). A thrust in the line of engagement while keeping contact with the opponent's blade, gliding along its side.

Counter Attack To take an action that will hit the opponent before the final movement of the opponent's attack is executed. See *Stop Hit, Time Hit* and *Stop Thrust*.

Counter Changement Changement executed in response to a changement executed by the opponent. The counter is executed during the opponent's changement, carrying their blade back to their point of origin.

Counter Disengagement Simple offensive action that deceives a change of engagement or counter parry with a disengage or coupé.

Counter Guard Bars or rings placed on the inside of the hilt of sixteenth and seventeenth century rapiers to help protect the combatant's hand and wrist. Sometimes used for the *Contra Postura*.

Counter Offensive Actions An attack into an attack. See *Stop Hit, Stop Thrust,* and *Time Hit*.

Counter Parry From the seventeenth century French *Contre-Parade*, meaning a counter or circular parry.

Counter Press A Press attack offered in resistance to the opponent's initial Press on the blade.

Counter Riposte The offensive action which follows the successful parry of a riposte.

Counter Time Initiating an action that provokes a stop hit or stop cut from one's opponent, parrying it and seizing time on the counter attack and landing with the second intention.

Counter a.) Sixteenth and seventeenth century term for an attack delivered into the opponent's attack, which deflects the attacking weapon and hits the opponent. The stronger attack taking the advantage. Not to be confused with the *Counter Attack*. **b.)** A *Riposte*. **c.)** Sometimes applied to the *Circular Parry*.

Counterpasses The counter movements in footwork that maintain the distance between the combatants by either passing forward or back in response to the footwork initiated by one's opponent. See also *Complimentary Footwork*.

Coup Derived from the Latin *colpus*, meaning a blow with the fist, a knockout blow. The French term came to represent the actual blow or hit delivered to one's opponent, and finally to the "touch" made in a fencing bout.

Coupé (Also *Cut-Over* and *Cut Over*) A changement associated with the French school executed from an engaged guard position and carrying the blade around the point of the opposing weapon.

Court Sword a.) A somewhat impractical, practically useless imitation of the small sword, worn on rare occasions, by very few men, as an ornament with official court dress. **b.)** Often misapplied to the *Small Sword*.

Covered See *Closed*.

Coward's Parry (Also *Ninth Parry*) An ignoble term given to the avoidance of an attack by displacing the body. See also *Cobb's Traverse*.

Croisé (also *Twist* or *Cut Down*) A blade taking action that carries the opposing weapon from a high line to a low line, and vice versa, on the same side of the body as the engagement.

Croked Pace See *Slope Pace*.

Cross Body Guards Guard positions that angle the blade of the weapon across the body, with the hand and hilt on one side and the point on the other. Generally associated with transitional rapier play.

Cross Five Sometimes applied to the double fence parry, *High Cross* or *Cross Parry One*, defending a descending vertical cutting attack to the head.

Cross Four (Also *Cross Parry Four*) **a.)** See *Cross Left*. **b.)** (also *Cross Low Five*) Sometimes applied to the last of four cross parries, protecting the crotch. The standard term for this parry is *Cross Two* or *Low Cross*.

Cross Left (also *Cross Parry Left Shoulder* and *Cross Parry Four*) The joined double fence parry against attacks to the left shoulder or chest made with the rapier hand above the dagger in a placement similar to rapier parry high one and the dagger hand beneath that of the rapier, held in a fashion similar to the dagger parry of three (made with either the dagger before or behind the rapier).

Cross One (Also *Cross Parry One* and *Cross Parry Five*) See *High Cross*.

Cross Parry (Also *Scissors Parry* and *X-Parry*) A parry executed with two weapons, generally rapier and dagger, where the weapons are crossed at or near the forte, forming an "X" with the blades. The attacking weapon is blocked with the outer portion of the "X", away from the hands.

Cross Right (also *Cross Parry Right Shoulder* and *Cross Parry Three*) The joined double fence parry against attacks to the right shoulder made with the rapier hand beneath the dagger in a placement similar to parry three and the dagger hand above that of the rapier, held in a fashion similar to the dagger parry of high one (made with either the dagger before or behind the rapier).

Cross Three (Also *Cross Parry Three*) See *Cross Right*.

Cross Two a.) Common for the cross parry used to defending a rising vertical attack to the groin. See *Low Cross*. **b.)** (Also *Cross Parry Two*) Sometimes used for the cross parry that protects the left shoulder. Generally referred to as *Cross Four*.

Cross-Hilt a.) (Also *Cross-Guard* and *Cross-Bar*) A very simple form of sword guard, consisting of straight quillons set a right angles to the weapon, thus forming a cross with the handle and blade. **b.)** A term applied to a sword with a cross-hilt.

Cross-Step See *Pass*.

Cross a.) Sometimes used for the pass or crossover step in footwork. **b.)** A cross parry in double fence. **c.)** A term for the parry as used by Elizabethan Fencing Masters such as George Silver. Joining of the blades.

Crossing Eighteenth century term for the croisé. The technique was not popular with most fencing schools in this period, but it was advocated quite strongly by Angelo.

Crossover Step Backward A double pass back in footwork which increases the distance from the opponent at a very quick rate.

Crossover Step Forward A double pass forward which closes distance on the opponent at a quick rate.

Crossover Step A double pass forward or back, that enables the combatant to gain or break ground quickly, ending with the same foot forward as when the action began.

Crowd A tactic in armed and unarmed combat where one deliberately closes quarters with an opponent in an effort to enable them from delivering effective or strong blows, then applying specific offensive pressure prepared for such in-fighting.

Cue-Reaction-Action See *Action-Reaction-Action*.

Cue a.) A placement of the arm and/or weapon that reads as a specific attack to a specific target, leaving no question as to the direction of the attack from its point of origin to its intended target. **b.)** A pre-arranged signal for someone to perform a specific action.

Cup-Hilt a.) (Also *Cupped-Hilt* and *Bell-Guard*) A cup or bell-shaped guard that offers almost complete protection to the sword hand. **b.)** Often applied to the entire sword when fitted with a cup-hilt. The cup-hilt rapier.

Cuscinetto (Literally "little cushion") A small circular leather cushion placed on the inside of a cup-hilt to prevent the fingers from jamming against the guard.

Cut & Thrust Said of a weapon suitable for attacks both with the edge and point.

Cut Down Sometimes used for a croisé executed from the high to low line.

Cut the Air (Also *Cutting the Air*) Cutting attacks where the energy is not pistoned forward, but carried through the entire plane of attack.

Cut to the Quick Edge blows, or cuts that land or appear to land on the body. Such cuts can be drawn like a razor or sliced as with a knife.

Cut Up Sometimes used for a croisé executed from the low to high line.

Cut A stroke, blow or attack made with the edge of the blade; distinguished from a thrust, made by driving the point forward.

Cutlas (Also *Cutlass*) A short sword with a flat, wide and slightly curved blade, designed more for edge-play than for point work.

Cutover (Also *Cut-Over* and *Cut Over*) The English term for *Coupé*.

Cutting Edge a.) The sharp, true or fore edge of any blade. **b.)** (Also *True Edge*) That edge of the blade which, when the weapon is held correctly, is naturally directed towards one's opponent.

Cutting on the Circle A drill in blade-play that takes the combatants through a series of cuts, parries and ripostes while executing circular paces on the tracks of the imaginary circle.

Cutting Stroke A blow or attack delivered with the edge of the blade. See *Cut*.

Cutting the Lines Said of circular parries that cut across the line of engagement. A Circular Parry that does not begin and end in the same line but cuts across the center line of the body, starting in one line, ending in another.

Cutting Through Steel Used in modern sabre fencing when, due to the flexible fencing blades, an attack strikes the opponent around a successful parry.

Dagger Grip a.) The method of holding the dagger. **b)** In theatrical swordplay, the dagger is held either with the thumb in line with the flat of the blade, in opposition to the grip of the index finger, bracing the blade or with the thumb in line with the blade, in opposition to the defensive edge of the blade. **c.)** The handle of a dagger.

Dagger Measure A Distance of at least six to ten inches from the chest of one combatant to the furthest extension of the dagger at the completion of any aggressive action.

Dagger Parry Any parry executed with the dagger.

Dagger Reinforcement Parry A defensive action of the rapier braced by the hilt or blade of the dagger being placed against the rapier's blade approximately one third of the way from the tip.

Dagger a.) A short stout weapon, like a little sword, with a blade designed for both cut and thrust; a *Poniard*. **b.)** The offensive and defensive weapon used in the left hand, "*main-gauche*," along with the sword or rapier.

Deceive Avoiding blade to blade contact with the opponent's weapon as they attempt to parry, engage, or attack your blade.

Deception of Parry (also *Deceive of Parry* and *Tromper*) A form of refusing the blade where the aggressor avoids blade to blade contact with the opponent's parry, or parries, during the final stage of a feint attack.

Deception of the Blade (Also *Deceive of the Blade*) An action that consists of removing one's blade from an opponent's attempt to make contact with it. See also *Refusing the Blade*.

Defense (UK *Defence*) **a.)** The action or position of keeping off or resisting an attack. To take action against attack, injury or threat; shielding; guarding; warding off; protecting. The practice, art or "science" of defending oneself with or without weapons; self-defense. **b.)** Readiness for combat, means or practice of fighting.

Defensive Box An imaginary box that encloses the combatant (theoretically leaving no portion of the combatant unprotected), its walls being created by the placement of the blade when parrying. In theory, eight parries are needed to protect every portion of the combatant's body, creating a defensive box.

Definite Business (also *Obligatory Actions*) Stage actions that a writer provides about the characters, their situations and surroundings.

Dégagé See *Disengagement*.

Delayed a.) Generally refers to a riposte which does not follow immediately after the parry. **b.)** Said of any action that is not executed at first opportunity.

Démarches Sixteenth-century term used by the French master Sainct-Didier to represent the gaining and surrendering of ground. These could be advance and retreat or passing movements of footwork.

Demi-Circle Half circle. A *Semi-Circular Parry*.

Demi-Lunge (also *Punta Sopramano*): A half, or short lunge where the lead foot is extended slightly forward on the attack while the lag foot is held in place.

Demi-Plié A partial or half bending of the knees.

Demi-Volte (also *Circular Half Pace*) A method of removing the body from the line of attack by swinging the lag foot back, generally to the right, along the outer track of an imaginary circle turning the body parallel to the line of attack.

Demi Meaning partial or half.

Dérobement Blade movements executed with an extended arm which evade the opponent's attempts to beat or take the blade. See also *Refusing the Blade*.

Désarmement Removing the opponent's weapon from their hand by either force or leverage. The *Disarmament*.

Descendente (Literally "descending" or "downward") **a.)** A cutting attack delivered from the high to the low line. **b.)** In theatrical swordplay, a cutting attack delivered from the high line, from either the right or left, downward on a diagonal to either the opponent's right or left shoulder. A *Squalembrato*.

Detached Parry (also *Detachment*) A crisp defensive action of the blade (generally in the transitional style) that merely taps a thrusting attack to confirm the parry and then immediately leaves the parried blade to move on to the next action.

Deux Temps (En Deux Temps, "in two actions") The practice of the late seventeenth-century French school to separate the parry and riposte into two distinct and separate actions. See *Double Time*.

Development The combined actions of the extension of the sword arm and the lunge.

Diagonal Attack Any armed or unarmed attack that travels from a high line to a low line, or vise-versa, at an angle of roughly 45 degrees.

Diagonal Avoid (also *Diagonal Evasion*) **a.)** An evasive step used against vertical and diagonal swipes, removing the body with a sloped pace or lunge onto either the NE, NW, SE or SW diagonal, roughly forty-five degrees of the standard north-south tracks of linear footwork. **b.)** An evasive action that removes the body from the plane of a diagonal attack by leaning or displacing the torso. See *Slip*.

Diagonal Parries (also *Half Counter Parries*) Any parry where the hand and blade travel diagonally across the body from the high to low line or vice versa and the parrying movement of the blade follows a semicircular path from one line to the other and from one side of the body to another.

Diagonal Swipe A theatrical cutting attack not intended to land, but to slash through the air from either right or left, in either a descending or ascending plane roughly 45 degrees to the floor. See also *Swipe*.

Diamond-Grind Schlager A German fencing blade, diamond-shaped in cross-section, used in theatrical rapiers. One of the most durable blades available.

Dig A angular thrusting attack in epée fencing, generally delivered at the wrist and forearm from the extended arm position.

Dimension The apparent size of a movement, relative both to previous movement and to the stage space.

Direct Attack An attack or riposte delivered in one blade movement without changing the relative positions of the blades.

Direct Beat (also *Simple Beat*) A beat attack delivered to the opponent's blade without changing their relative position.

Direct Parry (Also *Instinctive Parry* and *Simple Parry*) Defensive actions of the blade where both the hand and blade move from one position to another along the shortest possible route in either a horizontal or vertical plane; that is, remaining in the same line (High, Low, Inside or Outside) but moving to the opposite side.

Direct Riposte A riposte delivered as a direct attack.

Direct Thrust-Cutover Attack A false thrust delivered in the line of engagement, followed by a coupé as the final action of the attack.

Direct An attack or riposte delivered in the line of engagement.

Direction a.) Instructions given by the director, or by the writer in the script, or by the assistant director to the background, as to the action, the mood, or rhythm of a scene, as well as how the scene is to be shot, etc. **b.)** Relative lines of movement, such up stage left to down stage right or counter clockwise.

Disarm An action of the blade or body that forces the weapon from the hand of one's opponent in combat. Stage disarms can be done in two ways, either by *Securing the Sword* or by *Loosing the Sword*.

Disarmament The action of disarming. See *Disarm*.

Disengage A changement executed from an engaged guard position by passing the point either over or under the hilt of the opposing weapon.

Disengagement The action of a disengage executed from free guard position. See *Disengage and Change Under*.

Dish-Hilt A shallower "cup" than that of a cup-hilt or bell guard. Common among small swords and still in use on the modern fencing foil.

Displacement See *Evasion by Displacement*.

Distance, Correct The specified distance for the safe execution of blade-play. The distance between two combatants engaged in armed combat, where, after the execution of any attack and/or footwork, the point of the weapon is six to ten inches from the opponent's chest.

Distance, In a.) Said of any combatant who can hit their opponent by merely fully extending the sword arm. **b.)** At a measure where the combatants can reach one another with their weapons without the aid of footwork. At *Close Measure*.

Distance, Out of a.) Being outside correct distance for any reason. **b.)** In unarmed combat, when a combatant cannot be hit or kicked without closing measure.

Distance a.) See *Distance, Correct*. **b.)** The Elizabethan term for remaining out of easy reach when on the defensive, and to be in reach while on the offensive.

Distortion A change from the normal or average, whether by abruptness, complexity of movement or some other means. To alter the shape or style of movement without destroying continuity.

Dodge To change or vary one's position or alter one's ground to elude a pursuer or an attack, or to get a sudden advantage on one's opponent. See *Avoid*.

Doigté (also *Doigté*) The technique of directing the sword's point in all sorts of movements, circular or lateral, without the stiffening of the arm's muscles. The point is directed by the manipulators (thumb and forefinger), with the other fingers giving the blade steadiness, power, and support in the various actions of blade-play.

Dominant a.) Indicating the lead foot or hand. **b.)** Said of a portion or side of the body that is more dexterous and better developed.

Double Beat Two beats delivered in quick succession on the same side of the opponent's blade.

Double Change Beat A change beat being executed, the blade again changes its line of engagement and delivers a second beat from the original side.

Double Changement Counter changement executed against a counter changement, allowing the combatant who initiated the action to continue with their original intent.

Double Fence The practice of using an offensive and defensive weapon in both hands, (including but not limited to the sword and dagger, the rapier and dagger and the case of rapiers).

Double Intention See *Second Intention.*

Double Parry (Also *Parries Double*) Double fence defensive actions made with both weapons. These may be a *Cross Parry Parallel Parry, Transfer Parry* or *Reinforced Parry.*

Double Pris d'Fer A succession of takings of the blade where contact is lost between each one.

Double Time A parry and riposte executed in two separate actions or "times." Not meaning twice as fast, but rather twice the time. See *Dui Tempi.*

Doublé (also *Double Deception*) A compound attack in any line which deceives a direct parry and a counter-parry.

Draw Cut A cutting action made by a pulling or slicing action of the blade, rather than chopping or hacking. On stage all draw cuts are controlled placements of the blade executed against large muscle groupings—the shoulders, hips (at the flank), and thighs (at the quadriceps).

Draw a.) To remove or pull one's sword, or other weapon, from its scabbard or holster for the purpose of either offense or defense. **b.)** A call or challenge to fight.

Drawing Diamonds A doigté exercise of point work that focuses on the diagonal rather than circular paths of the point by drawing diamonds in the air with the point of the blade.

Drills Specific choreographed routines in footwork and the positions and movements of the hands and/or blade, designed to educate combatants in style and form through repetition.

Dritta (also *Dritto*) Literally meaning "right." Generally referring to the right hand (the sword hand), the fencers sword arm or sword arm side.

Dritto Filo Right edge. The true, or fore-edge of the blade.

Duck The instantaneous lowering of the head and torso vertically towards the floor to avoid a horizontal attack at the head.

Duel of Chivalry A meeting in single combat between two knights, generally on horseback and always with great public ceremony, to settle a difference of law, possession or honor.

Duel of Honor An armed conflict fought for personal reasons.

Duel a.) A formal fight between two persons; a single combat. A private fight, prearranged and fought with deadly weapons, with the intent to wound or kill, usually in the presence of at least two witnesses, called seconds, having for its purpose to decide a personal quarrel or to settle a point of honor. **b.)** A trial by wager of battle; judicial single combat.

Dueling Punctilio The strict rules that governed all aspects of a duel from the issuing of the challenge to the fight and or reconciliation.

Duellist (Also *Duelist*) One who is an expert in the rules and practice of dueling. See also *Duel.*

Duello The established code and convention of duelists.

Dui Tempi To parry and riposte in two distinct actions. See *Double Time.*

Dynamics The energy of movement, expressed in varying intensity, accent and quality.

Echappement See *Backward Lunge.*

Edge a.) The thin sharpened side(s) of a cutting blade, opposed to the *flat* or broad side of the blade. See *Cutting Edge.* **b.)** The sharpness given to a blade by whetting; to sharpen.

Effort An attack on the opposing blade that travels from its foible to forte. See *Glissade.*

Eight, Parry of The defensive position for a thrust or horizontal attack to the weapon bearing leg or thigh, closing the low outside lines. The hand is supinated with the point lower than the hand.

Elbow Cuts A cutting attack that generates the scope of its cutting arc from the articulation of the elbow rather than the shoulder or wrist.

En Finale Generally applied to a parry deliberately executed at the last or "final" moment possible. By waiting as long as possible, the parry has the least chance of being deceived and allows for a quick execution of the riposte.

En Garde The basic position assumed by a combatant when fencing.

En Guarde See *On Guard.*

En Marchant An attack on the march, extending of the sword arm while simultaneously passing forward.

Engage a.) To cross swords; to interlock weapons. **b.)** To entangle, involve, commit or mix up in an undertaking, quarrel or fight.

Engaged Coupé A Changement executed over the point of the opposing weapon where contact of the blades is maintained until the blade clears the point of the opposing weapon, and then it is brought to rest at its intended target.

Engaged a.) Said of two crossed or joined weapons. **b.)** To be committed to, or locked in a fight.

Engagement The crossing, joining or touching of blades.

English Fight See *True English Fight.*

English Guard (Rapier) Foreign fencing masters dominated the schools of rapier play in England, and an Englishman, depending on their taste and training, would assume either an Italian, Spanish, and sometimes even German guard; or an Anglicized version thereof.

English Masters of Defence A guild of professional swordsmen established in 1540, under a patent granted by Henry VIII. See *Master's Prize*.

Enunciation of Movement To make each action of physical dialogue a clear and definite movement. To give definite expression to each movement in a choreographed routine; to move clearly and effectively.

Envelopment (also *Wrapping it Up*, or the *Wrap Up*) An attack on the opponent's blade which, by describing a circle with both blades in contact, returns to the original line of engagement. The Envelopment can be either *Passive* or *Active*.

Epée Blade a.) A triangular blade (fluted on three sides for lightness) approximately 35 inches in length, tapering evenly from forte to tip, generally provided with a button and narrow tang used in competitive fencing. **b.)** A blade often inappropriately and unwisely used in "inexpensive" stage weapons, to represent a wide variety of "blades."

Epée The modern "dueling sword," taken from the eighteenth century small sword, and evolved during the nineteenth century as a sport weapon designed to reproduce, as closely as possible, an actual small sword duel. The blade of the modern fencing epée. See *Epée Blade*.

Escrime The French word for fencing.

Espada Ropera Literally "dress sword". A civilian sword; a sword to be worn with common dress. See *Rapier*.

Espée Early spelling of epée.

Evade Back a.) Compound footwork that joins the action of a pass back with that of a backward lunge to avoid a horizontal attack across the chest or belly. **b.)** See *Jump Back*.

Evade To escape or avoid a blow or attack by contrivance. See *Evasion*.

Evasion To escape or elude an attack by cleverness or stratagem. The action of avoiding or escaping a blow or attack by artifice or contrivance; dodging.

Evasions by Displacement The most common form of avoiding a thrust, by safely and effectively removing the target from the path of the intended attack.

Exchange Parry See *Transfer Parry*.

Expulsion Using the energy of a blade taking action to throw or fling the opposing blade aside. Opposite of *Command*.

Extended Parry A parry executed with a fully extended arm. The action is generally used as type of a beat attack removing the point of the opposing weapon.

Extension a.) The reaching of the sword arm forward. **b.)** The position of the sword arm when straightened to its full length. Any obstacle beyond the perception of a character that somehow affects their immediate or overall objectives.

Extraordinary Risk A clause in some union Production Agreements that deals with potentially dangerous situations and staging.

Eye Contact The process of looking into your partner's eyes to acknowledge mutual awareness and readiness to perform the techniques.

Eyes of the Hilt See *Pas d'Ane*.

Eyes An expression used by combatants for the establishing of eye contact during a particular action or phrase of movement.

Fabris, Salvator Italian master of the late sixteenth and early seventeenth century whose treatise (1606) was the introduced and defined. *contra postura,*

False Art The process of using tricks and misleading movements of the sword and body to dupe the opponent into unwittingly opening a line for attack. The opposite of *True Art*.

False Attack An attack which is not intended to land, but is delivered to distract one's opponent, test their reaction, or to draw a parry. See *Feint*.

False Balestra A balestra performed with the jump in place, gaining no ground, designed to draw an attack on the preparation from one's opponent so as to hit on the second intention.

False Cut See *Feint with the Edge*.

False Edge The edge of the blade turned away from the knuckles of the sword hand. On the rapier, the back edge was generally sharp for at least the uppermost third of the blade, and would often be sharp from the point to forte like the true edge.

False Ricasso A part of some theatrical rapier guards situated between the pas d'âne and the quillon block that replaces the ricasso of historical blades.

False Thrust See *Feint with the Point*.

Falso Dritto (It.) A cutting attack from the right with the false or back edge of the blade. See *Backswording*.

Falso Filio (It.) See *False Edge*.

Falso Manco (It.) A back-handed cutting attack from the left with the false or back edge of the blade. Sometimes referred to as *Backswording*.

Feder (Ger.) Sixteenth-century term for the rapier.

Feeble See *Foible*.

Feeling-Out Process The initial period of a fight between two combatants where both appear tentative, executing moves that help them learn more about the opponent, before deciding on a particular stratagem to the fight.

Feint Attack See *Feint*.

Feint with the Edge (also *Falsing the Cut, False Cut and Feint Cut*) Offensive movements made to resemble cutting attacks or the beginning of an attack with the edge. In theatrical rapier play there are two types of Feint Cuts: the *Stop Short* and the *Set Up*.

Feint With the Point (also *Falsing the Thrust* and *False Thrust*) A feint of a thrusting attack where the arm commits to the action, but there is no footwork executed to land the point. When footwork accompanies this action, the arm is withdrawn prior to completing the attack.

Feint (also *Feint Attack*) **a.)** Any action (movements of the arm, body, legs, or various actions of the blade) susceptible to misinterpretation by the opponent as to the nature and sincerity of its intentions. **b.)** In stage combat, any action of the body or blade choreographed not to be met by a parry, avoided or land on the body. These include the *Feint With the Body, Feint With the Edge* and *Feint With the Point*.

Feinte de Degagement see *Circular Feint a.*).

Feinte See *Feint*.

Fence a.) The action, practice, art or science of offensive and defensive swordplay. Fencing. **b.)** The action of defending; warding; to defend. The attitude of self-defense.

Fencer a.) A skilled swordsman or combatant. **b.)** One who fights with a sword or foil. **c.)** One who practices the modern sport of fencing; with a foil epée or sabre.

Fencing Master A teacher or coach who has been accredited and licensed to instruct competitive fencing in three weapons—foil, epée, and sabre. A fencing master is not a stage combat instructor or choreographer and has not been trained in the complexities and demands of the theatrical/historical fight.

Fencing Measure Correct distance between combatants when performing in stage combat. The common rule of correct fencing measure is a distance of six to ten inches from one's opponent at full extension from a lunge. See *Measure*.

Fencing Step See *Advance*.

Fencing Tempo See *Tempo*.

Fencing a.) The term derived from the practice of offensive and defensive swordplay. It now represents the action or art of using the sword scientifically as a weapon of offense or defense. **b.)** The practice or competition of all swordplay with blunted and rebated weapons. **c.)** An outdated term in theatre, film, TV, and opera sometimes still applied to any staged swordplay.

Fendente Literally "slash." **a.)** A cutting attack delivered downwards in a plane vertical to the floor. **b.)** In theatrical swordplay, a cutting attack, with the true edge, from either one's right (*Man Dritto Fendente*) or left (*Riverso Fendente*), traveling in a vertical plane downward, to either the opponent's head (parried in the high line) or continuing downward toward the floor outside the body (*Vertical Swipe*).

Fente see *Grand Lunge*.

Field of Honor The established or set location for the duel of honor. Sometimes applies to the lists of the judicial duel.

Field of Play The area in which the bout is contained. The boundaries can be determined by rules, regulations or the availability of space.

Fight Call A physical and mental warm-up and review of fights prior to performance designed to physically warm up the actors, and provide them with a feeling of "security" by reviewing the fights before the performance.

Fight Captain The Choreographer's assistant (generally an actor in the company) who works directly with the Choreographer and knows and understands not only all the actions of the fight, but also the Choreographer's intentions and desired effect.

Fight Director a.) A theatrical fight choreographer who also coaches the dramatic presentation of a fight sequence. **b.)** The third level of recognition within the ranks of the Society of American Fight Directors. **e.)** The name of the professional journal of the Society of British Fight Directors.

Fight Master a.) Anyone who has established themselves as a leader in the science and art of armed combat whether historical or modern. **b.)** The fourth and highest level of recognition within the ranks of the Society of American Fight Directors. **c.)** The professional journal of the Society of American Fight Directors.

Fight Notation Any form of short-hand notation used to mark the choreography of the fight. At present there is no universal form of notation.

Fight Plot (also *Fight Arrangement*) The written description of the whole fight.

Fight a.) To contend in arms; to combat; to battle. **b.)** Single combat. A duel. **c.)** A brawl or fray. **d.)** A quarrel.

Fighter a.) A combatant, a warrior. **b.)** A swordsman or duelist.

Figure-Eight Drill a.) A doigté exercise with the sword that has the combatant trace the pattern of a figure-eight in the air (horizontally or vertically) with the point of their weapon. **b.)** Sometimes applied to the *Wrapping the Eights* drill.

Filo Dritta The true or fore-edge of a blade.

Filo Falso The false or back edge of a blade.

Filo a.) The edge of the rapier blade. See *Filo Dritta* and *Filo Falso*. **b.)** Sometimes used for the *Glissade*.

Find In stage swordplay; when a cut or thrust is met by a parry. The defender "finds" or meets the attacking blade in a designated parry.

Finger Fight Sometimes used for the marking of a fight with the combatants using their fingers in place of weapons.

Finger Flexing Exercises used to develop the hand and finger finesse necessary for proper point control.

Finger Loop A small metal ring, found in some sixteenth-century German weapons, through which a fencer could pass one finger of their sword hand. The loop was situated in the crook created where one of the quillons meets the blade.

Finger Play a.) A method of manipulating the sword with the fingers. See *Doigté*. **b.)** See *Finger Fight*.

Finger Waving Exercises used to develop strength and agility in the base of the fingers or palm. There are three Finger Waving exercises, the *Flying Wing* (where the motion of the hand and fingers looks like a bird waving its wing), the *Finger Wave* (where the motion of the fingers look like an ocean wave) and the *Finger*

Roll (where the fingers roll in towards and out away from the palm).

First Counter-Riposte The initial riposte of the attacker.

First Intention An offensive action, with no "testing" the opponent or exploratory actions, in which one intends to be entirely successful.

Fishing-Line Throw A metaphor for the mechanics of sending the energy of a cutting attack beyond one's opponent, much like casting or throwing a fishing-line. See *Pistoning*.

Five A, Parry of (Also *Five Alternate* and *Window Parry*) **a.)** A variation of the parry of high five placing the hilt and sword hand on the left side of the body, the point to the right and the blade parallel to the floor, above the head and in front of the body. **b.)** A defensive position used by some instructors and choreographers for a diagonal cutting attack to the left cheek or temple. The parry is similar to that of High 3.

Five W's See *W's, The Five*.

Five, Parry of (also *High Five* and *Muscle Beach*) **a.)** Defense for a vertical attack to the head with the blade held above the head, parallel to the floor, the hand and hilt on the weapon bearing side. The forte is in front of and above the center of the head. **b.)** A defensive position used by some instructors and choreographers for a diagonal cutting attack to the right cheek or temple. The parry is similar to that of High 4.

Flanconnade Any attack to the flank (usually a thrust) preceded by a bind of the opposing blade.

Flank Muscle mass situated between the ribs and the hip. Often applied to a hip or waist cut.

Flash Cards Exercise in swordplay designed as a training tool for cueing and cue response. One combatant assumes various cue positions while others are given a limited amount of time to respond with the corresponding parry.

Flash see *Flèche*.

Flat The wide portion of the blade, in comparison to the narrow edge.

Flèche (Literally "arrow") Offensive action in footwork that swiftly propels the combatant forward in a sprint or run. A running attack.

Fleuret Late seventeenth-century term for the protective leather cap placed over the point of the foil blade. Referred to as a fleuret because of its resemblance to a flower bud; eventually representing the entire foil.

Flick Cut a.) The mechanics of the hand and wrist used in the execution of a wrist cut. See *Wrist Cut* **b.)** A light wounding cut generally delivered with the foible of the blade to a major muscle group.

Flourish a.) A showy brandishing of a weapon. **b.)** A fast and graceful exchange of blade-play.

Flowing Attacks Attacks on the blade that use a sliding or grazing action down the opposing blade in order to displace it. The most common form of Flowing Attack is the *Glissade* or *Coulé*.

Flute The groove, channel or furrow found in blades such as the small sword and modern epée blade that removes precious ounces from the blades weight without jeopardizing its structural integrity.

Fluted Furnished, or ornamented with grooves, channels or furrows resembling the half of a flute split longitudinally, with the concave side outwards. See Flute.

Flying Lunge A jump forward that, instead of terminating in the on guard position, extends forward into a grand lunge.

Foible (Seventeenth-century French for "weak") The uppermost, and weakest, third of the exposed blade closest to the tip. Modern fencing weapons—foil, epée, sabre—all have flexible foibles designed to give, or bend, on a hit to avoid penetration.

Foil a.) A light weapon used in modern fencing; a type of small sword with a blunt edge and a button on the point. **b.)** Elizabethan for any rebated, blunted or dulled weapon. **c.)** A term in wrestling for a throw not resulting in a flat fall, hence; to defeat.

Foot-to-Foot Fighting in close combat where the combatant's feet can touch.

Fore Edge (Also *True Edge*) The edge presented towards one's opponent when the weapon is held correctly. On the rapier it was generally sharp from the tip to the forte.

Fore-Cut A cutting attack with the fore or true edge of the blade.

Forte to Foible The basic principal of defense in swordplay; the strongest section of the defending blade (forte) against the weakest point (foible) of the offending blade.

Forte The widest and strongest third of the exposed blade closest to the hilt. The portion of the weapon most often used by the combatant to block and parry attacks.

Forward Diagonal Avoid An evasive action taken with a forward lunge or pass onto the NE or NW diagonal tracks of footwork. See *Diagonal Avoid*.

Forward Foot See *Lead Foot*.

Four, Parry of The defensive position for a thrust or horizontal attack to the non-weapon bearing shoulder, closing the high inside lines.

Four-Leaf Clovers Exercises in point control or doigté that draw four circles in the air that make a patter similar to the leaves of a clover.

Four-Point Stance The fencing stance that places the feet equally apart in width and depth as if standing on two opposite corners of an square upon the floor.

Foyning Elizabethan for puncture play. See *Foin*.

Free A common practice of Elizabethan rapier fence where the blade was kept from touching the opponent's weapon.

Froissé See *Pressure Glide*.

Froissement Attack on the opponent's blade that combines the action of a beat and press attack, accentuated by a quick glide along the blade to displace it. See *Pressure Glide*.

Full Cut See *Shoulder Cut*.

Full Pass (also *Pass Forward-Lunge*) A compound action in footwork that combines a pass forward with the extended leg position of the lunge. Often completed with the upper torso extended beyond the lead leg with the non-weapon hand used for support.

Fuller A groove, channel or furrow made in the flat of the blade, designed to lesson the weight of the blade without jeopardizing its structural integrity. See also *Fluting*.

Gaining Ground Any step forward that purchases ground from the opponent.

Gaining (Also *Gaining on the Lunge*) An alternative to the balestra where the lag foot is brought up against the lead foot with a half pass, just before the execution of a lunge.

Gauntlet a.) An iron glove intended to protect the weapon bearing hand(s). **b.)** Leather fencing gloves or similar hand protection for the theatrical combatant.

General Obstacles Obstacles to the character's objective that are undetermined.

German Guard (Rapier) The on guard position in the German school of rapier play was based on, and thus resembled, that of the Italian school. See *Italian Guard*.

Giant Epée (also *Musketeer Blade*) A form of epée blade that has been widened severely at the forte and tapers to a much stiffer foible. A triangular, fluted blade used to represent a transitional rapier blade designed mostly for point work (the foible and tang not being sufficiently enlarged to handle much edge-to-edge-play).

Giganti, Nicoloetto Sixteenth-century Italian master whose treatise on fence (1606) is noted mostly for having first clearly explained the techniques of the *stoccata lunga* ("elongated thrust" or the lunge).

Glide (also *Graze*) Thrust in the line of engagement that displaces the opponent's blade by maintaining contact and applying pressure while sliding down the blade. See also *Glissade*.

Glissade Feint Feint of a flowing attack on the blade meant to draw a parry against which an attack may be made with a redirection of the point.

Glissade (Also *Glizade*, *Glide* or *Coulé*) Flowing attack on the blade, executed from an engaged guard position, that displaces the opposing blade by gently sliding down the opposing weapon foible to forte. The most common form of flowing attack used in stage combat.

Golden Age of Swordplay The peak of the evolution and practice of the sword and swordplay spanning the sixteenth to eighteenth century, from the introduction of the rapier to the eventual retirement of the civilian sword.

Grand Lunge Offensive action which replaced passing as a means of reaching an opponent on the attack by extending the lead leg forward as far as the

combatant can conveniently manage (about thirty inches) while straightening the lag leg.

Grand Volte (also *Bum in the Face*) Large evasive step that removes the body from the line of attack by compassing the lag foot back and around the lead foot approximately one-hundred and eighty degrees.

Grapple a.) To wrestle, to contend in close fight. **b.)** The securing of ships with hooks and rope and then pulling them together in battle.

Grasp a.) (also *Gryps*) Sixteenth and seventeenth century term for closing measure and seizing and wrenching the opponent's hilt or arm in order to take their weapon or break their wrist in the attempt. **b.)** A wrestling term for coming to close quarters; body to body. To come to the grasp; to grapple. **c.)** See *Grip a.*)

Grasping the Blade A seizure, or disarm of the opponent's weapon by grabbing the blade rather than the hilt. The action is often used on stage by combatants with gloved hands.

Grassi, Giacomo di Sixteenth-century Italian master whose chief contribution to the science of fence was the consideration and definition of lines of attack, which became indispensable parts of later fencing treatises, modern fencing and stage combat terminology. He also favored a freer employment of the point against the older theories of swordplay.

Graze Feint A glide executed only with the extension of the arm (no attack or lunge). This action is meant to draw a parry with which a hit may be made upon its deception.

Graze See *Glissade*.

Grip a.) The manner in which the weapon is held, which can vary depending on the weapon, school, period and personal preference. **b.)** The part of the sword situated between the guard and the pommel. Also referred to as the handle. **c.)** See *Grype*.

Gripes (also *Grappling*) Techniques of swordplay that favor the locks, holds, grips and throws of wrestling.

Grunt Per Move Ratio The forced, primitive sounds created by some actors as they attempt to superficially vocalize during a fight. Sound for sounds' sake.

Grype (Also *Gripe* and *Grip*) To wrestle or grapple at close quarters.

Grypes Sixteenth and seventeenth century technique of seizing and wrenching the opponent's hilt or arm in order to take their weapon or break their wrist in the attempt.

Guard a.) Originally a position from which to initiate an offensive or defensive action. Nowadays, however, a guard is a posture of defense; a placement of the blade that closes one or more lines and allows a fencer to deliver every possible attack and come to every possible parry while expending the least possible amount of energy. **b.)** Often applied to the hilt of the sword. **c.)** Sometimes used as a loose synonym for "on guard," or the on guard stance.

Guarde (Fr.) See *Guard.*

Guardia (It.) The fencing position that allowed for the best *offensive* move in relation to whatever guardia was assumed by one's opponent.

Guiding Hand Exercise designed to break the habit of bending forward at the waist during blade-play by placing a fencing glove upon the combatant's head.

Half Counter Parry A parry that travels diagonally across the body from a high to a low line and vice versa. See *Diagonal Parry.*

Half Disengage (also *Meggia Cavatione*) A form of changement executed to the same side of the body as that of the engagement. If the opposing guard closes the high inside line, the changement lowers the point to the low inside line, and vice versa.

Half Pass (also sometimes *Cheat Step* or *Paused Step*) Simple form of footwork that carries the foot forward/backward in the same manner as a pass, only bringing the foot to rest parallel to the opposing foot rather than one foot length passed it; generally executed in conjunction with a similar action of the foot that completes the pass.

Half Stance (Also *Two-Point Stance*) On guard position, suggested by the early twentieth-century fencing master Professor Leon Bertrand, in which the body was turned so as to expose as little of the chest as possible.

Half-Sword a.) (Also *Close* and *In-Fighting*) Being in close quarters; fighting inside measure where the blades cross at their middle, at half the swords length. **b.)** A small sized sword; a sword roughly twice the length of its counterpart; a dagger.

Hamlet/Laertes Switch A mutual securing of the swords from a corps-à-corps, disarm and exchange of weapons by combatants, named from the characters and stage directions in the final Act of Shakespeare's *Hamlet.*

Hand Parry A method of defense with the unarmed hand that beats or swats the opposing blade aside. Such actions are only used against thrusting attacks.

Hand to Hand (Also *Hand unto Hand* and *Unarmed Combat*) **a.)** Unarmed combat at close quarters where the only weapons are the combatants' hands, feet, etc. **b.)** One of the two mandatory styles of stage combat required by the SAFD and FDC for recognition as an Actor/Combatant.

Handle See *Grip-b.).*

Hang Left The hanging parry for the left shoulder. The hand over the head, the blade below the hand, sloping down with the tip at roughly eight o'clock. The middle of the blade in front of and above the notch in the left shoulder.

Hang Right The hanging parry for the right shoulder. The hand and hilt over the head on the left, the blade below the hand, sloped down and to the right with the middle of the blade in front of and above the notch in the right shoulder.

Hanging Parry (also *Sloped Parry* or *Waterfall Parry*) A defensive action against a diagonal or vertical swipe that presents a sloped or angled blade that meets the attack and causes it to sheer or ricochet off to the side, deflecting rather than blocking or intercepting the offending blade.

Happy Feet Used to describe inconsistent footwork that tends to dance about rather than adhering to the specifics of technique or choreography.

Head Swipe A theatrical cutting attack to the head not intended to land, but to slash through the air (from either right or left) where the head *was*, in a plane parallel to the floor. Usually accompanied by a duck or another form of low-line evasion on the part of the victim.

Heavy Parry An offensive action made from a successful high line parry which closes measure and carries the opposing blade to the floor in an action similar to the croisé.

High Cross Left A defensive action in double fence for a diagonal cutting attack to the left shoulder. Generally made with the rapier hand above the dagger in a placement similar to rapier parry high one. The dagger hand is below that of the rapier, held in a fashion similar to the dagger parry of three (either before or behind the rapier).

High Cross Right A defensive action in double fence for a diagonal attack to the right shoulder. Generally made with the rapier hand below the dagger in a placement similar to parry three. The dagger hand is above that of the rapier, held in a fashion similar to the dagger parry of high one (either before or behind the rapier).

High Cross a.) (also *Cross Parry Head, Cross Parry of One* and sometimes *Cross Five*) A double fence defensive action against a vertical cut to the head. The cross may be made either with the dagger before or behind the rapier. **b.)** A cliché, and completely theatrical attack on the blade where both combatants cut to the space directly above and inbetween them, engaging in the high line and crossing the swords. This action is often followed by a corps-à-corps or offered in succession with the *Low Cross.*

High Eight A supinated parry used to defend the sword bearing hip or shoulder. The point is down with the blade roughly perpendicular with the floor. Sometimes referred to as a *Hanging Parry.*

High Five See *Five, Parry of.*

High Four, Parry of The parry of four executed in such a manner as to defend the non-weapon bearing shoulder from a descending diagonal cutting attack. Hilt just below the elbow, knuckles to the outside, blade angled at roughly 45 degrees, tip up and above the head.

High Line The area of attack and defense located above the sword hand in a neutral guard, roughly waist level and up.

High One, Parry of (also *Watch Parry* and sometimes *Hanging One*) The standard parry of one raised to defend the non-weapon bearing shoulder. The hand

and hilt are on the non-weapon bearing side of the body at roughly neck level, the blade is below the hand, its forte at the level of the notch in the non-weapon bearing arm where the deltoid meets the biceps.

High Seconda (also *Low Prima*) The single rapier guard assumed with the arm extended forward, the hand and hilt at approximate ear level. The hand is pronated, the quillons are horizontal with the floor, the tip lowered to the level of the opponent's chest. The guard may be formed either Standard or Across.

High Three, Parry of Defense for an descending diagonal attack to the weapon bearing shoulder. The parry of three executed with the hilt just below elbow level, knuckles to the outside, blade angled at 45 degrees, tip up and above the head.

High Two (Also *Chicken-Wing Parry*) Defense against an attack to the weapon bearing shoulder. The arm is angled up, elbow at roughly ear level, the hand just above shoulder level, the blade is below the hand, its forte at armpit level.

High-Low Attack Compound attack where the first action is a feint in the high line to draw a parry. The second action deceives the parry and moves the blade into the low line to complete the attack.

Hilt, To the a.) Thrusting attack that is delivered and lands in one's opponent and, is further, driven into the victim's body all the way up to its hilt. **b.)** A metaphor, derived from the old meaning, for going all the way or all out.

Hilt (Also *Guard*) **a.)** A portion of the weapon comprised of three parts: the guard, the grip, and the pommel. **b.)** Often applied to the guard of the sword itself, as in cup-hilt, cross-hilt, and the like. **c.)** The haft or handle portion of any weapon.

Hip A target in swordplay that generally refers to the muscle mass located on either side of the body, above the waist and below the rib cage. See *Flank*.

Hole in the Parry Slang for an incorrect or unsuccessful parry through which a hit is made.

Home a.) The intended target or mark. **b.)** To strike or hit the intended target. See *Thrust Home*.

Horizontal Attack A cutting attack that travels in a plane parallel to the floor.

Horizontal Swipe A theatrical cutting attack not intended to land, but to slash through the air from either right or left, in a plane parallel to the floor. See also *Belly Swipe*, *Chest Swipe* and *Head Swipe*.

Hour-Glass System The most common system of on-line body targets (compared to the *Box Target* and *Triangle Target* systems). It offers five on-line body targets; right and left chest, center line at waist level and the right and left thigh.

Imaginary Circle (Also *Mysterious Circle*) **a.)** Seventeenth-century Spanish school's *Lines Infintas*. The geometrical basis from which all footwork and distance was to be calculated and executed in Spanish rapier play. **b.)** Used in stage combat footwork for the two parallel lines that join one's lead and lag foot to one's

partner's lead and lag foot, respectively, on a circle. See the *Ten Directions of Footwork*.

Imbroccata (It. & Ger.) **a.)** Downward thrust, generally delivered from the right with the hand pronated, over one's opponents sword arm. **b.)** Pronated thrust delivered from *Prima* to either of the opponent's shoulders, or chest.

Immediate Obstacles The obstruction which is directly in front of the character and must be overcome.

Immediate Generally refers to a riposte which follows a parry without a pause in the action.

In Distance See *Distance, In*.

In Fighting (Also *In-Fighting*, *Infighting* and *Inside Fighting*) **a.)** When two combatants have closed distance and are inside normal measure, but without the blades being locked as in a corps-à-corps, and any normal swordplay is impossible. See *Close Measure* and *Closes*. **b.)** The practice of moving inside fighting measure, getting up close to one's opponent to deliver a blow with the hand or hilt of a weapon. **c.)** Fighting or boxing at close quarters, hand to hand.

In Line a.) (Also *On-Line* and *On Point*) Having the sword arm extended straight forward, with the point threatening the opponent. **b.)** See *On-Line*.

Indefinite Business The actions that tie the *Definite Business* of the play and fight together and establishes how the character goes about achieving the specific actions described in dialogue or text.

Indirect Attack Aggressive action that in its execution does not immediately threaten the body, but is directed towards the opponent's blade (such as beats, pressures or pris d'fer), not the opponent.

Indirect a.) Attack not delivered in the line of engagement. **b.)** See *Indirect Attack*

Inquarta (It.) (Also *Inquartata* and *Inquarto*) See *Demi-Volte*.

Inside Line The area of attack and defense on a combatant, delineated by their vertical center line, which is furthest from their weapon bearing side. Opposite of *Outside Line*.

Inside Measure See *Close Measure* and *Closes*

Inside Mollinello (Also *Inside Moulinet*) Mollinello executed on the inside (non-weapon bearing side) of the body.

Insistence The continuation of an attack in the same line after being successfully parried. See *Remise*.

Instance Narvaez's term for the corresponding footwork of two combatants traversing the imaginary circle; maintaining their relative position to one another. See *Complimentary Footwork*.

Instinctive Parry see *Simple Parry* or *Direct Parry*.

Intelligibility Used to describe the identification and understandability of sound during a fight.

Intensity Presence of a greater or lesser degree of energy; relative level of energy concentration.

Intercepting the Bind (Also *Stealing the Bind*) Form of pris d'fer, executed against a pris d'fer in double fence techniques where the victim of a bind uses their second weapon (usually the dagger) to catch the opponent's blade and bind it back to its point of origin.

Interna Linea (It.) See *Inside Line.*

Invitation Any movement of the blade/arm intended to tempt the opponent into an attack.

Involuntary Sounds Reactive sounds, springing from accident or impulse rather than a conscious exercise of the will. Natural sounds of the working body including grunts, groans, sighs and other unintentional phonations made on the exhalation.

Italian Guard (Rapier) Theatrical on-guard positions for the sixteenth and seventeenth century Italian school are that of Terza, low Terza and Seconda (high, low and proper). Capo Ferro, however, advised the use of Terza proper.

Jam Parry (Also *Stop Parry*) **a.)** Blocking parry thrust forward (often inside measure) towards the middle or forte of the offending blade, taken on the guard or hilt of the parrying weapon. **b.)** Head parry in broadsword play where the defender closes measure while pushing their sword up and forward (either to the right or the left), bringing the attacking blade to rest on the hilt of the defending blade. The blades meet true edge to true edge; forte to forte.

Joining Blades To engage weapons. Practiced early in the development of swordplay, it was not a common practice until the mid-seventeenth century. See *Engagement* and *Sentiment De Fer.*

Joining a.) The action of meeting in combat. Engaging in a fight or conflict. **b.)** To engage weapons. **c.)** The *Disarmament.*

Jug, String & Stick Hand and wrist strengthening exercise that uses an empty milk jug fastened to the middle of a rod by a piece of string. The jug is partially filled with water and the combatant repeatedly winds and unwinds the string around the rod.

Jump Backward (also *Active Retreat*) Evasive action, removing the body backward with an exaggerated retreat where the lag leg is kicked backward.

Jump Forward (also *Active Advance*) Forceful hop or glide forward made with an exaggerated advance where the feet travel forward two or three times that of a standard advance. The action is executed quickly, remaining close to the ground.

Jump Up (Also *Jump*) Leap over a horizontal attack to the feet.

Justification The tangible rationale for every action within a fight and the prime source of awakening the actor to the moment to moment interaction of the fight.

Kill a.) To deprive of life, to put to death by some means or action. **b.)** The finishing stroke or blow in a stage fight.

Kinesthetic Learning The process of physically memorizing patterns of movement through slow and constant repetition.

Kinesthetic Muscle sense basic to movement awareness.

Kissing Steel Describing the gentle and controlled meeting of blades during offensive/defensive bladeplay.

Knuckle Bow Branch of the sword guard that sweeps from the hilt to the pommel in a bow shape offering protection to the sword-hand.

Lag Foot The foot in the rear or back position at any time during footwork.

Last Fingers See *Aids.*

Lateral Parry See *Simple Parry.*

Lead Foot The foot in the forward position at any time during footwork.

Leading a.) To have the weapon bearing hand and/or foot forward. See also *Dominant.* **b.)** (Also *Showing Point*) The extension of the swordarm towards the target, leading the body in the attack. **c.)** A beat, feint or attack accompanied by a step forward.

Left Dominant Leading with the left side of the body, usually implying a left lead foot.

Level(s) (Sometimes *Horizontal Planes*) Aspect of space dealing with height from the base or floor to the greatest altitude accessible from the performing area.

Linas Infinitas (Sp.) (Literally "Infinite" or "Never-ending" Lines) Imaginary lines on the floor that join the combatants' feet in Spanish rapier play. See *Imaginary Circle.*

Line of Direction a.) The bearings of a combatant, or combatants, and the course the fight takes. **b.)** The set of "railroad tracks" a combatant is traveling upon. See *Ten Directions of Footwork.* **c.)** The path which anything travels. (Right to left; upstage to downstage; camera right to camera left; high line to low line; etc.)

Line of Engagement The area in which the point or blade is threatening. See *Lines.*

Line of Gravity Imaginary vertical line that joins the ears, shoulders, arms, ribs, hips, knees, and instep in correct relative position to one another.

Line a.) The specific area of the body to be defended or attacked. See *Lines of Attack.* **b.)** Referring to the imaginary planes that bisect the body, one vertical (delineating Inside and Outside) and one horizontal (delineating High and Low).

Linea (It.) The lines of engagement; alta (high), bassa (low), esterna (outside), interna (inside).

Lines of Attack The areas of offense and defense determined by placing the armed hand in a *Central Guard* (*Neutral Guard*). An attack coming above the hand is in the *High Line*; below, in the *Low Line*; on the weapon bearing side, in the *Outside Line*; on the non-weapon bearing side, in the *Inside Line*. See also *Lines.*

Listening (Also *Physical Listening*) The technique of responding to the immediacy of the moment within a fight.

Locking Nut (Also *lock-nut*) A small nut screwed onto the tang of some modern stage weapons which locks the pommel in place.

Long-Sword A sword with a simple cross-hilt and a long cutting blade.

Loosing the Sword Type of disarm where the weapon is freed from the hand and falls loose to the stage.

Low Cross Left (also *Cross Parry Left Hip*) The joined double fence defense for an attack to the left hip made with the rapier and dagger crossed. The left leg is generally removed away from the attack for this parry.

Low Cross Right (also *Cross Parry Right Hip*) The joined double weapon defense for an attack to the right hip made with the rapier and dagger crossed. The right leg is generally removed away from the attack for this parry.

Low Cross a.) (also *Cross Parry Two* and sometimes *Cross Low Five*) The joined double fence defense for either a montante or a thrust to the lower middle torso. The parry is usually executed with the dagger behind, so the rapier is not trapped between the dagger and the body. **b.)** Attack where both combatants cut to an ambiguous space in-between them (about knee level), crossing the swords in the low line. Opposite of *High Cross*.

Low Five, Parry of a.) The single weapon defensive position for an ascending vertical attack to the groin (*Montant*) made with the hand and hilt outside the weapon bearing leg, and the blade parallel to the floor at about knee level with the forte protecting the groin. **b.)** Sometimes applied to the *f Low Cross* in double fence.

Low Line Evasion See *Passata Sotto*.

Low Line The area of attack and defense located below the sword hand in a natural guard position (at roughly waist level). See *Lines* and *Lines of Attack*.

Low Quarta (also *Quarta Guardia Bassa*) The single weapon guard (rapier or dagger) assumed with the hand supinated, knuckles towards the inside, quillons horizontal to the floor, the arm in front of the body (about three inches away from the belly). Formed either Standard or Across.

Low Seconda (also *Seconda Guardia Bassa*) The single weapon guard (rapier or dagger) assumed with the arm horizontal to the floor and fully extended from the shoulder, the hand supinated, with the tip of the blade lowered to the level of the opponent's waist. Formed either Standard or Across.

Low Terza (also *Terza Guardia Bassa*) The single weapon guard (rapier or dagger) assumed with the hand just above the waist with the elbow outside the body (roughly three inches forward) and bent at roughly ninety degrees with at least a four inch gap between elbow and flank. Formed either Standard or Across, held in pronation, supination, or vertical/middle position.

Low Two; Parry of Defense for an attack to the weapon-bearing thigh made with the hand and hilt just below waist level. Blade is below the hand with its forte at the level of the weapon bearing leg's quadriceps, just above the knee.

Lower Side-Ring (Also *Lower Port*) The larger of the two side-rings found on the two-ring and swept-hilt rapier hilts, situated the closest to the weapon's pommel. See *Side-Ring* and also *Upper Side-Ring*.

Lunga (It. "elongated") See *Lunge*.

Lunge a.) Forward movement executed by advancing the leading foot toward the opponent while the rear foot remains stationary (usually following the extension of the weapon arm). **b.)** Forward movement of the body toward the opponent that elongates the combatant's reach without advancing the lag foot. There are three distinct types of lunges: the *Standing* or *Stationary Lunge*, *Demi-Lunge*, and *Grand Lunge*. **c.)** A thrust with a rapier, epée, foil, or any other weapon.

Maestro (It.) An eminent master in the art. See *Master*.

Magnified Fencing A term coined by film fight choreographer Fred Cavens for the exaggerated actions used in dramatic fencing matches.

Main Gauche (Fr. "left hand.") (Also *Main Gauche Dagger*) Name for the parrying dagger used in the left hand in conjunction with the rapier. Now applied to the dagger, whether used in the left or right hand.

Making Ground To move forward. See *Gaining Ground*.

Man Dritto Squalembrato (It.) Descending diagonal cutting attack delivered from the weapon bearing side.

Man Dritto Tondo Supinated horizontal cutting attack delivered from the sword bearing side. *Man Dritto Tondo Alto* is directed to the opponent's shoulder, *Mezzo* to the hip and *Basso* to the thigh.

Man Dritto (It. Man = "hand;" "Dritto = "Right") (Also *Mandritto* or *Mandritta*). **a.)** Literally meaning "right handed" or "forehand." Said of a cut or thrust delivered from the right side of the body. **b.)** Refers to any supinated cutting attack delivered from one's right to the opponent's left in theatrical rapier play. See *Man Dritto Tondo*.

Manipulators The index finger and thumb of the hand that holds and manipulates the movements of blade and point of the weapon.

Mark of Zorro A doigté exercise where the point of the blade describes a "Z" in the air.

Marozzo, Achille Bolognese fencing master who presented the first sound treatise on handling the sword in personal combat (1536). His treatise represent the development of double fence and the general practice of swordplay in the late fifteenth and early sixteenth century.

Master a.) Teacher and choreographer of stage combat of the highest rank and standing. **b.)** The highest level of achievement, and most revered rank in the SAFD, SBFD and FDC. **c.)** Celebrated maestro of the old science and school of fence.

Measure a.) The controlled distance of one combatant from another when engaged in stage combat. See

Distance, Close Measure and *Closes.* **b.**) The distance between combatants when on guard, determined by the length or reach of the fencers lunge or thrust.

Meeting Angle The opposing planes of swords that allow the blades to be joined. These planes must cross forming an "X", "T" or open "V" with blades or they cannot be engaged.

Meggia Cavatione (It.) Fabris' term for the Half-Disengage, which is still used by the Italian school of fencing. See *Half-Disengage.*

Mesure (Fr.) See *Measure.*

Meter Systematically arranged and measured rhythm for movement.

Mezza Cavazione (It.) Attack on a half disengagement from a high to a low line on the same side of the opponent's body. See *Half-Disengage.*

Mezzo-Tempo (It.) Literally meaning "half-time," the mezzo-tempo consists of two actions, a parry and a riposte, executed in the time it would have taken to complete the initial attack.

Mezzo (It. "middle.") Used in reference to the target at the middle of the opponent's body, at the hip or waist-line.

Middle (also *Center of Percussion*) The name given by most schools for the portion of the blade that links the weaker foible to the stronger forte. As the *Center of Percussion* it is the mediator between the percussive attacks of the foible and percussive blocks of the forte.

Misdirecting the Point To guide the blade off-line (to the side of the body) to safely execute a stage kill.

Mixed Meter Rhythmic pattern made up of irregular or regular units of different meters.

Mollinello (Also *Moulinet*) Literally "like a little wind mill." The action of pivoting the blade (from the shoulder, elbow or wrist) in a circle, in either a clockwise or counter-clockwise direction.

Montant Literally meaning "rising." Cutting attacks generally delivered upward to the groin or under the arms.

Montante Literally "rising," "mounting"; an "uppercut." A rising vertical cutting attack, with the true edge, to the groin executed from either the right side of the body (*Man dritto*) or from the left (*Riverso*).

Moulinet Derived from the word *moulin*, meaning "wind mill"; applied to the circular swinging of a sword, like the blades of a wind mill. See *Mollinello.*

Movement Theme The basis for development of the story line and physical dialogue. The central concern or intent behind the action of the piece.

Movement Transition(s) A movement, or sequence of movements, serving to connect phrases of movement.

Multiple Feints A combination of two or more single feint attacks.

Muscle Beach (also *High Five* and *Five, Parry of*) A nick name for the parry of High Five attributed to American Fight Master David Boushey.

Muscle Mass Referring to any major muscle group.

Musketeer Blade A nick name for the theatrical epée blade. See *Giant Epée.*

Mysterious Circle The Spanish *Lines Infinta.* The infinite circle that joined the combatants at the feet and formed the basis of all footwork and distance in the complex geometrical style of sixteenth and seventeenth century Spanish swordplay. See also *Circle Steps.*

Narvaez, Don Luis Pacheco de Student of Carranza who became the master of the Spanish school in the later part of the sixteenth and early seventeenth century. He offered his own reproduction of Carranza's work, basing his system on the *imaginary circle.*

Neutral Guard See *Central Guard.*

Neutral a.) (Also *Neutral Placement*) Well balanced and centered placement of the physical instrument, devoid of character or circumstances and charged with a relaxed but powerful energy ready to be discharged in a highly focused way. **b.)** The position of the sword hand with the thumb on top and the palm turned toward the inside (left); halfway between supination and pronation.

Nine, Parry of See *Coward's Parry.*

Objectives Specific, achievable goals of the character that can easily be expressed by using the verb form. Actions within a fight must always have an objective.

Obstacles Anything that prevents a direct path to the objective. These may be *Immediate Obstacles, General Obstacles* and *External Obstacles.*

Octave (also *Eight*) The guard and parry used in small sword and modern fencing that closes (protects) the low outside line. The hand is supinated, with the point lower than the hand. This parry is close to the parry of eight used in theatrical rapier play.

Off-Line Fencing (Also *Off-Line Technique*) Any blade-play consisting of attacks that are directed safely outside the body. The safest form of theatrical point work.

Offense (UK *Offence*) To be on the attack or assault.

Offensive-Defense Counter attack by means such as a *Stop Thrust* or *Stop Cut.*

Offensive/Defensive Footwork Drill Exercise of complimentary footwork that may be repeated without having to readjust position or stance. The pattern of this drill compliments the Offensive/Defensive drill of blade-play.

On Guard a.) The fundamental position of the combatant preparatory to actions of an offensive or defensive nature. Most commonly the guard of Terza. **b.)** Being consciously aware and prepared for any event or happening.

On the Exchange Series of attacks, parries, ripostes, parries, counter ripostes, etc. Exchanging offensive and defensive actions between combatants.

On-Line Fencing (also *On-Line*) Mode of theatrical swordplay where attacks are aimed at specific body targets on the combatant.

One Card Shuffle Exercise designed to help the

combatant develop fluid horizontal movement in footwork by focusing on a playing card held in the sword hand.

One, Parry of Defensive action for a thrust or horizontal attack to the non-weapon bearing hip with the hand at roughly waist level, knuckles to the inside, blade below the hand closing the low inside lines.

One-Two Attack Compound attack consisting of a disengage designed to draw a direct (lateral) parry and a second changement, deceiving the intended parry.

Open Invitation Deliberate placement of the blade which exposes the entire body, intended to draw a offensive reaction from the opponent.

Open Line(s) Area(s), position(s) or parts of the body unprotected.

Opening The area on one's opponent that is unprotected. See *Open Line(s)*.

Opposition Grip Holding a sword or dagger with the pad of the thumb placed in line with the back edge of the blade (or on the ricasso), in opposition to the grip of the index finger.

Opposition a.) Movement of engaging and not releasing the opponent's blade. **b.)** The art of closing the line of engagement to the opponent's blade while attacking, preventing them from striking with a counter attack. **c.)** See *Opposition Parry*.

Orchestration The arrangement of vocal and physical sound with the story line of the fight in order to achieve the maximum effect in the composition of physical dialogue.

Out of Distance See *Distance, Out of*.

Outside Line The area of attack and defense on a combatant, delineated by their vertical center line, which bears the identifying weapon. The weapon-bearing half of the body. Opposite of *Inside Line*.

Outside Mollinello (Also *Outside Moulinet*) A moulinello executed on the weapon bearing side (outside) of the body.

Overhand Grip Holding a sword or dagger with the point above the hand. Opposite of *Reversed Grip*.

Pace Elizabethan for a pass or walking step. See *Pass*.

Parade (Fr. & Ger.) See *Parry*.

Parallel Parry Double fence parry executed with the blades placed side by side rather than crossed.

Parry by Distance Evasive action that removes the body backward out of the reach of the attack, while remaining in the line with the attack.

Parry a.) Defensive action of a bladed weapon where the forte opposes the foible of the attacking weapon stopping the attacking blade at its weakest point with the strongest point of the defending blade. These may be *Direct Parries*; *Semicircular Parries*; *Diagonal Parries*; and *Circular Parries* and may be executed as an *Opposition Parry*, *Beat Parry* or *Detached Parry*. **b.)** To ward off or turn aside an offensive blow or weapon by opposing one's own weapon, hand or other means of defense; To take such an action.

Pas d'âne (also *Arms of the Hilt*) Literally "donkey step" or "mule foot." The two horseshoe-shaped half rings branching up from the quillon block that help protect the index finger of the rapier hand when placed over the cross guard of the sword.

Pass Back a.) (also *Walking Step Backward*) Simple action of footwork that moves a combatant backward by passing their lead foot to the rear beyond their lag foot into a new lag position. Opposite of *Pass Forward*. **b.)** Used by some to represent the *Crossover Step Backward*.

Pass Backward-Demi-Volte/Grand Volte Compound step that allows the lead foot to shift backward and into a demi or grand volte.

Pass Forward-Circle Left Compound circle step that allows the right foot, when in the lag position, to shift to the lead position both forward and to the left on the inner ring of the imaginary circle.

Pass Forward-Circle Right Compound step that allows the right foot, when in the lag position, to shift to the lead position both forward and to the right on the inner ring of the imaginary circle.

Pass Forward a.) (also *Walking Step Forward*) Simple action of footwork that carries a combatant by passing their lag foot to the fore, into a new lead position. Opposite of *Pass Back*. **b.)** Used by some for the *Crossover Step Forward*.

Pass Traverse Passing steps executed to the combatant's immediate right or left. See *Traverse* and *Ten Directions of Footwork*.

Pass a.) (also *Passata*) The chief means of gaining and breaking ground prior to the seventeenth century consisting of passing one foot by the other, changing the placement of the lead and lag foot. See *Passing*. **b.)** A round, bout or tournament of swordplay. A course of fencing, until one of the combatants is hit. **c.)** A thrust or lunge with the rapier. To make a push in fencing.

Passado An English spelling of either the Spanish *Passada* or the Italian *Passata*; a forward thrust with the rapier, accompanied with a pass (which was not always the case with the actual passada and passata).

Passata Sotto to the Rear Low line evasion that vertically removes the body from the plane of attack by propelling the lag leg straight backward, bending of the lead leg's knee, placing the left hand on the floor (for stability) and angling the pelvis and trunk directly forward in line with the extended lag leg.

Passata Sotto to the Side Low line evasion that vertically removes the body from the plane of attack by extending the lag foot backward and across the path of the lead foot (traversing to the right), bending of the lead leg's knee, placing the left hand on the floor (for stability) and angling the pelvis and trunk forward and to the left in line with the extended lag leg.

Passata Sotto (Literally "pass beneath") Low line evasion that vertically removes the body from the plane of attack by expanding the base and lowering the physical center. Executed in two ways, the *Passata Sotto to the Side* and the *Passata Sotto to the Rear*.

Passing Jump Back Compound action of footwork initiated with the action of a pass back and propelled backward with the completing action of a jump back.

Passing the Point The movement of the tip of the weapon from one line of engagement to another executed either under (*Change Under*) or over (*Change Over*) the opposing weapon. See *Changement*.

Passing The chief means of gaining and breaking ground in fencing, facilitating the greater part of footwork before the introduction of the lunge by simply passing one leg by the other.

Passive Bind See *Bind* and *Passive Movement*.

Passive Defense a.) To run away; to remove one's body from the line of attack, or threat of attack, without execution of any offensive action. Defensive actions that protect the body without harming or endangering the aggressor. **b.)** See *Parry by Distance*.

Passive Footwork Standard footwork that when executed carries the combatant the length of one foot either forward or back. Opposite of *Active Footwork*.

Passive Movement Contained or controlled movement. A standard or normal scope of movement that can be enhanced or made active for dramatic effect.

Patinando (Advance-Lunge) Compound piece of footwork involving a quick succession from an advance to the grand lunge. Generally ending with an attack.

Pattern The organization of individual movement into distinguishable relationships.

Percussion The sharp impact of one object with or against another, producing on contact a perceivable shock or sound.

Percussive Movement Quality of movement in stage combat characterized by sharp starts and stops.

Personal Body Habits Physical mannerisms that have been conditioned into the body through years of repetition.

Peso (Span. & It.) The balancing point of a sword. See *Point of Balance*.

Phrase (Also sometimes *Phase*) Uninterrupted section of choreography (a single move or an extended series of moves), offering a definite beginning and ending.

Physical Dialogue The thoughts and feelings of the characters when manifested in a physical rather than verbal form.

Physical Diction Process of expressing, not explaining, the actions of the character. The clear, accurate and engaging delivery of the thoughts, emotions and intentions of a character without verbal support.

Physical Inventory The process of trusting the body instead of the eyes to correct technique. To look internally and feel what is right and what is wrong with specific techniques or placement.

Physicality The physical orientation of the character including the size, shape and build of the body; the way in which it is carried in motion and at rest; and the prevalent manner in which the character bears their physical being.

Piste The strip used in modern fencing.

Piston Cut See *Pistoning*.

Piston Thrust Thrust delivered from an exaggerated windup (usually on the weapon bearing side) rather than from a standard guard position.

Pistoning a.) (Also *Piston Cut*) The forward stroke of energy that channels the attack *beyond* the opponent during a cutting attack in theatrical swordplay. **b.)** See *Piston Thrust*.

Pitch The highness or lowness of a particular sound on the musical scale.

Placement, Correct a.) The proper posture used in assuming a neutral fighting stance which allows the combatant safe and effective movement. **b.)** The neutral stance from which all techniques can be safely executed and character choices can be added.

Plane Perfectly straight, imaginary line that an armed or unarmed attack can travel upon, from any one point to another, at any angle (horizontal, vertical, diagonal).

Planes of Movement The path in which any action can be said to travel (including horizontal, vertical, diagonal and circular planes).

Playing the Numbers Blank choreography exercise that uses random patterns of numbers to establish a series of offensive and defensive blade-play.

Plié (Fr.) The bending movement in the knees required for almost all footwork in swordplay. A shallow or half-bend is called a *Demi-Plié*, a deep bend, a *Grand Plié*.

Point Control a.) The safe and correct execution of blade movements in theatrical swordplay. See *Doigté*. **b.)** In modern fencing, keeping the point on-line to threaten the opponent's target.

Point of Balance The point on a sword, located on the forte of the blade about two to three inches from the hilt, that will maintain its equilibrium when balanced on a finger.

Point of View Character's overlying philosophy on life; their set of motivating beliefs. The sum of the character's ideas and convictions; their personal attitude.

Point a.) The sharp end of a sword or dagger. **b.)** The tip of the blade, generally sharpened to a point in an actual sword.

Pointing the Way Exercise in swordplay that focuses on directing the blade effectively towards the intended target by placing a cardboard "arrow" or a triangle on the foible of the blade.

Pommel (also *Pummel* (Fr.)—meaning "little apple") **a.)** The metal fixture that locks together the different parts of the weapon and acts as a counterweight to the blade. **b.)** To strike, beat or attack with the pommel of a weapon instead of with its blade.

c.) To beat or strike repeatedly with the hands or fists as with the pommel.

Poniard (also *Parrying Dagger*, and *Main Gauche Dagger*) Form of quillon dagger developed during the sixteenth century designed to be held in the left hand with the point above, like a sword. The guards of these daggers were provided with a hilt formed by curved quillons and a Side-Ring, serving as protection for the knuckles.

Poop-Deck Fighting a.) Patrick Crean's term for fighting inside measure; derived from the confined space on a ships deck (the "poop-deck") and the restrictions dictated by the frame of a camera in the swashbuckling films of the 1930's and 40's. **b.)** Often applied to any close quarters combat.

Postura (It.) The position of the body and the weapon; preceeding the modern definition of guard.

Posture a.) The particular position of a weapon in drill or combat. Most likely derived from the Italian "postura." **b.)** The placement and carriage of the limbs and the body as a whole; attitude, alignment, pose.

Preparation of Attack Blade, body, or foot movement which opens the way for the attack.

Preparation-Reaction-Action See *Action-Reaction-Action.*

Presentation of Cutting Edge The turning of the true edge towards the target to be attacked.

Press Attack on the opposing blade that pushes it aside to open a line of attack.

Pressure Attacks Attacks on the blade that utilize consistent lateral pressure to displace the opposing blade. The contact with the blades may utilize more than one point on the opposing blade.

Pressure Glide (also *Ruffling, Scrape, Effort* and *Froissement*) Attack consisting of a strong beating or pressing of the blade in conjunction with a fast graze or glissade from forte to foible.

Pressure a.) The application of force to something by something else in direct contact with it. **b.)** Attacks on the blade that utilize lateral pressure to displace the blade. There are two common forms of Pressure Attacks; the *Press*; and the *Froissement*. See *Press* and *Pressure Attack.*

Prima (also *Prima Guardia*) (from the Latin *Primo*—"firstly") **a.)** Agrippa's term for the first guard position that can safely be assumed upon drawing the sword. **b.)** The single weapon guard that closes the high outside line with the hilt above the head and in front of the body, the blade below the hand, tip directed toward the opponent's shoulder (either Standard or Across) **c.)** (Double Fence) The first guard that can safely be assumed upon drawing the rapier and dagger. The rapier assumes the placement of single weapon Prima (standard or across); the dagger in single weapon Terza.

Prime (also *One*) **a.)** The transitional rapier and small sword (also modern fencing) parry that closes (protects) the low inside line, the hand is across the

body, with the blade below the hand. This parry is close to the parry of one used in standard theatrical rapier play. **b.)** The cross body guard used in transitional rapier and small sword to close the high, outside line. See *Prima.*

Principle of Defense The opposition of forte to foible.

Pris d'Fer (also *Pris de Fer* and *Controlling the Point*) Attacks on the Blade that catch the opposing blade, master it, and hold or remove it in preparation for an attack. These actions command the opposing blade and may retain it or remove it with the action of an *Expulsion.*

Progressive Attacks Method of delivering certain compound attacks as one fluid action.

Projection The communication of the story line to the audience, guided by the choreography and fight direction and made possible through the abilities of the actor/combatants.

Pronation The position of the hand where the palm is turned down, nails of the sword hand facing the floor.

Proper Alignment Posture where the various parts of the body—head, shoulders, arms, ribs, hips, legs, feet—are all in correct relative position to one another. See also *Line of Gravity.*

Pummel Attack Offensive action executed in close quarters where the pommel or hilt of the weapon is used to attempt an attack at the opponent's body.

Pummel a.) To attack, strike or bludgeon with the pommel of a sword. **b.)** To pound, beat, or strike repeatedly with the fists as with the pommel of a sword. [*LLL*—V.ii.618]

Punta Dritta (*punta* = point, *dritta* = right) **a.)** Attack with the point, hand in pronation, delivered from one's right. **b.)** In theatrical swordplay; a pronated thrust from the right, from either *Terza* or *Seconda*, to either of the opponent's hips or thighs.

Punta Rovescio (Also *Punta Reversa*) (*punta* = point; *rovescio* = turned over; upside down.) **a.)** Thrust made from the reverse side of the cutting circle, from the left with the hand often in supination. Opposite of *Punta Dritta* or *Mandritti.* **b.)** In theatrical swordplay, a supinated thrust from the left, usually from, or passing through, the guard position of *Quarta.*

Punta Sopramano (also *Demi-Lunge*) (It. = "thrust over the hand") **a.)** Attack introduced by Viggiani (1575) in which the lead foot is extended forward, about eighteen inches, accompanied by a supinated thrust with the sword arm and a slight turning in the torso. **b.)** A demi-lunge, whether or not it is accompanied by an attack.

Punta Literally "point" or "tip." The point of a weapon, hence, a thrust or attack with the point.

Punto Reverso English rendering of the Italian *Punta Rovescio*; a thrust from the left with the hand in supination.

Punto Literally "point." The point of the weapon; stroke or thrust with the point of a sword.

Quality a.) The characteristics of movement determined by the way energy is used, such as swinging, percussive, suspended, sustained and vibratory movement. **b.)** Term used for the essential character or distinguishing attribute of sound. The color or timbre of the actor's voice; the features of the sound; rough, voiced, screamed, whispered, etc.

Quarrel a.) Dispute or contest that can not be settled by words; private difference as well as dissension and combat for a public cause and on a larger scale.

Quarta (also *Quarta Guardia*) **a.)** The single weapon guard assumed with the arm across the body to the inside (about three inches away from the belly), the hand supinated, the tip at roughly armpit level (Standard or Across) closing the high inside line. **b.)** The double fence guard assumed with the rapier in single rapier Terza (Standard or Across), and the dagger in a placement similar to its parry of High Three, closing the rapier's high inside line.

Quarte Outside Seventeenth and Eighteenth Century term sometimes given to the parry or guard of sixte because the supinated hand position of sixte did not become common until the late eighteenth century.

Quarte Over the Arm Seventeenth Century term for a disengage from the guard of quarte with a supinated thrust delivered in the high line over the opponent's arm.

Quarte (also *Four*) **a.)** The small sword, transitional rapier and modern fencing guard that closes (protects) the high inside line. Close to the guard of Quarta and the parry of four in theatrical rapier play with the point higher than the hand, which is supinated. **b.)** The transitional rapier and small sword parry executed with the point higher than the hand, which is supinated, closing the high inside line.

Quillon Bash (also *Beat-Away*) Standard parry followed by beating or knocking the attacking blade up, out or down with the cross guard of the defending weapon. See *Beat Away*.

Quillon Block Study block of metal from which the branches, quillons, knuckle bow, as well as the variety of other loops and rings of the rapier hilt extend.

Quillon Dagger (Also *Poniard*) Form of dagger developed during the mid thirteenth century and used in various forms through the eighteenth century, which resembled the hilt and quillon configuration of contemporary swords. See also *Poniard*.

Quillon(s) (Fr.) One or both of the arms or branches forming the cross guard of a sword, providing the sword-hand with a protective barrier and preventing the opposing blade from sliding down the sword and striking the hand. See also *Rudder of the Blade*.

Quinta (It.) (also *Quinta Guardia*) The fifth guard position in Double Fence technique assumed with the rapier in Low Terza (Standard) with the hand held roughly ten to twelve inches in front of the body and the dagger held across the body above the rapier, the hand pronated and in front of the body at mid torso, the blade placed over and above the forte of the rapier.

Quinte (Fr.) (also *Five* or *Fifth*) **a.)** The modern sabre parry that closes the high line and protects the head, much like the theatrical parry of five. **b.)** The fifth thrust, or parry of eight taught in the French school.

Rabbit Ears Grasp (also *Scissors Grasp*) Corps-à-corps where both combatants grasp hilts and create an ''X'' with the blades.

Railroad Tracks Term used to describe the two imaginary parallel lines that a combatant's feet are said to travel upon. These tracks keep the feet at the correct distance apart, and the torso traveling straight forward.

Rain Fights Abbreviated version of the fight with limited footwork set as a safety in case of foul weather in outdoor performances.

Range The relative scope or extent of movement.

Rapier and Dagger (Also *Rapier & Poniard*) **a.)** The fashionable style of swordplay during the later half of the sixteenth century and into the early portion of the seventeenth century where the rapier was held in the right hand; used chiefly for offensive purposes, and the dagger was held in the left for warding or deflecting blows. See *Rapier*. **b.)** One of the two mandatory combat styles required in a skills test with the SAFD and FDC.

Rapier Blade A long, flat, and heavy blade with several parts: *Tip, Foible, Middle, Forte, Shoulders, Ricasso,* and *Tang*. The flat of the blade tapers to two edges (the *True Edge* and *False edge*) and was often grooved or channeled (*Fullers* or *Fluting*) to lessen the weight without jeopardizing its structural integrity.

Rapier Hilt The protective guard (consisting of a variety of bars, rings, branches and arms) placed between the swords grips and exposed blade in an attempt to shield the sword hand from the opposing blade. In stage rapiers, there are three types of guards; the *Two-Ring Hilt, Swept Hilt* and *Cup-Hilt*.

Rapier, Age of (*Circa* 1550–1625) The beginning of the *Golden Age of Swordplay* when armor began to be abandoned, the sword became a part of the attire of every gentleman, and schools and masters of the science of fence became established in most western countries.

Rapier Long, thrusting sword developed in Italy in the 1480's. Originally used for both cut and thrust attacks (actually being poorly designed for either), the rapier became a weapon chiefly used for thrusting. In an attempt to protect the sword hand from a thrust, over a hundred distinct hilt configurations were developed (including the *Two-Ring Hilt, Swept-Hilt* and *Cup-Hilt*).

Reactive Physical Vocal Range The layers of vocal pitch that emanate from the body's center in relation to the part of the body being affected during activities within a fight.

Reactive Sounds Vocal sounds emanated as reflex

responses to anything that catches the combatant unprepared or by surprise.

Rear Foot See *Lag Foot*.

Rear Lunge See *Backward Lunge*.

Rearing Lunge Lunge where the combatant rears back before they spring forward.

Recover Backward To move back into the on guard stance.

Recover Forward To move forward into the on guard stance.

Recover Return to the on guard position.

Recovery The action of returning to the on guard position.

Redouble a.) To reengage in combat with twice as much effort, energy or attacks. To strike twice as hard and fast as before. **b.)** To repeat an attack or blow.

Redoublement New attack made against an opponent who has failed to riposte. Generally made while still in the lunge from the previous attack.

Refusing the Blade To avoid crossing or engaging swords with the opponent by means of a *Change Under, Change Over, Vertical Change* or other Changement.

Reinforced Parry (also *Split Parry*) Defensive action of the sword and unarmed hand where the unarmed hand takes hold of the rapier's blade (approximately one third of the way from the tip) to strengthen and brace the parry against the opposing blade. See also *Dagger Reinforcement Parry*.

Relaxing the Cut Exercise that works the mechanics of the flick or wrist cut by executing several cuts in quick succession.

Relevé Literally "relifted." Rise to the ball (or demi-pointe) of the foot. The rise is sometimes called *elevé* when it is made without the benefit of a preceding plié.

Remise (Fr.) A parried attack that is renewed without withdrawal of the weapon arm.

Renvers Literally to "reverse," "to turn upside-down," "to turn the wrong way," "to turn back." **a.)** A cutting attack delivered from the left side of the body. **b.)** A cutting attack made with the back or false edge of the blade.

Replacement Beat (Also *Replacement Beat Parry*) Double fence replacement parry where the primary parry stops the attacking blade and the secondary parry engages the attacking blade and beats it away.

Replacement Parry Double fence parry where the attacking blade is stopped with a single weapon parry and then a second weapon engages the attacking blade and takes the place of the first parry.

Replacement See *Remise*.

Reprise The process of renewing a parried attack by drawing the arm back to the cue position when the opponent fails to offer a riposte.

Respost See *Riposte*.

Resting Guard Variation on the single weapon guard position of Terza where the pommel is placed on the right thigh allowing the sword arm a moments rest.

Retire a.) To retreat or surrender ground; yielding ground. To retreat from battle or danger. **b.)** See *Retreat*.

Retreat a.) Action in the footwork of fencing used to step back, moving the rear foot first and then the lead foot (without crossing them). Opposite of *Advance*. **b.)** To withdraw in the face of opposition; retiring or moving backward from danger. See *Retire*.

Return Beat Beat attack executed in immediate reply to the opponent's beat.

Révérence (Fr.) See *Salute*.

Reverse (Sometimes *Reverso*) **a.)** Cutting attack delivered from the left side of the body; a backhanded stroke or cutting attack. **b.)** To suddenly change the direction of an action of the blade, body, footwork or any other action within a fight or fight sequence.

Reversed Grip See *Underhand Grip*.

Rhythm a.) The visible and audible variables of rate within beats and phrases of a fight. **b.)** The strong and weak elements in the flow of sound and silence.

Ricasso The thick portion of a blade's tang situated between the pas d'âne and the quillon block in the hilt of a rapier. See also *False Ricasso*.

Ricavatione (It.) **a.)** Fabris' term for the *Double Changement*. **b.)** (Also *Ricavzione*) See *Doublé*.

Riposte Counterattack launched by the combatant after successfully completing a parry.

Rising Parry (Also *Intercept Parry* or *Beat-Down Parry*) See *Beat-Aside*.

Riverso Squalembrato (It) Descending diagonal cutting attack delivered from the non-weapon bearing side.

Riverso Tondo (It) Pronated horizontal cutting attack delivered from the non-sword bearing side. Riverso Tondo Alto is directed to the opponent's shoulder, Mezzo to the hip and Basso to the thigh.

Rocking a.) Back and forth movement of the body during the execution of stationary footwork. **b.)** In active footwork; a partial advance or retreat on the part of the combatants.

Rompre (Fr.) See *Breaking Ground*.

Round Parry See *Circular Parry*.

Roversi (It.) **a.)** Sixteenth Century term for a cutting attack delivered from one's left to the opponent's right side. **b.)** In theatrical rapier play, a cutting attack delivered from the left side, the hand in pronation, delivered to the opponent's right.

Rovescio (It.) (Also *Punta Rovescio*) Thrusting attack delivered in supination from one's left to the opponent's right side.

Rudder of the Blade Nick-name given to the quillons, which can be used by the combatant to determine where the blade is directed, and help "steer" the blade to its correct placement. See *Quillons*.

Run a.) Continuous series or succession of parries and ripostes. **b.)** To pierce or stab a person; to run them through. **c.)** To take flight; to retire rapidly. See *Cobb's Traverse*.

Sabre (Also *Saber*) **a.)** Heavy sword with a curved blade (very effective for cutting attacks), and a simple hilt configuration used by the cavalry of all European nations in the eighteenth and early nineteenth century. **b.)** The only cut and thrust weapon in modern sport fencing.

Sabreur (also *Sabrer*) One who fights with a sabre. Often applied to a soldier in the cavalry who is distinguished for bravery in war rather than skill.

Safety The first of all priorities in a stage fight. If a prescribed action cannot be done safely, it should not be done in that manner!

Salle Literally a "hall" or "room". Used in reference to the *salle d'armes* ("room of arms"), the school or studio where lessons are given, skills practice and bouts held.

Salute (also *Révérence*) **a.)** The formal exchange between combatants prior to a duel or fencing bout. **b.)** Formality in modern sport fencing which displays good sportsmanship between the competitors.

Saviolo, Vincentio Sixteenth Century Italian fencing master who introduced the art of rapier-play to the court of Queen Elizabeth. His book in 1595 was the first text on swordplay originally written in English.

Sbasso (It.) See *Low Line Evasion* and *Passata Sotto*.

Scabbard Case or sheath which protects the blade of a weapon when not in use.

Schlager Blade (Ger.) Light, long, flat and strong sword blade with a rounded point, thick shoulders and a substantial tang, designed specifically for edge to edge play that is now used in theatrical rapiers. See also *Diamond Grind Schlager*.

Schlager (Germ.) **a.)** Weapon that replaced rapier play of German students in the early 1830s. **b.)** See *Schlager Blade*.

Scissors Parry a.) Term generally used to describe double fence cross parries. See *Cross Parry*. **b.)** (Also *Scissoring*) Sometimes used to describe a double fence cross parry where the cross of the blades has closed like a pair of scissors.

Scooping the Parry (also *Scooping*) Increased arc in the blade's path (especially in semicircular parries) that carries the hand through the plane of the intended attack; placing the hand where it may accidentally be struck.

Scrooge British slang for the *Froissement*.

Second Intention Tactical attack designed to score on the counter riposte.

Seconda (It.) (also *Seconda Guardia*) Considered the "Spanish" guard in theatrical swordplay. **a.)** (Also *Seconda Proper*) The single weapon guard assumed with the arm and blade held completely horizontal to the floor, the hand in pronation with the arm fully extended, the body square to the opponent, tip at shoulder level (Standard or Across). **b.)** (Also *Double Fence Seconda*) The extended guard of the sword-bearing hand where the rapier hand assumes Seconda proper and the dagger is held in Dagger Terza with the dagger hand placed roughly ten to twelve inches in front of the body just above waist level.

Seconde (also *Second*) **a.)** The guard and parry in small sword, transitional rapier and modern fencing that closes (protects) the low outside line, taken with the point lower than the hand, which is pronated. The parry of seconde is close to the parry of two in theatrical rapier play. **b.)** Often applied to the Transitional Rapier Parry of Two.

Secured Disarm Disarm executed where the weapon stays in the hand of the aggressor and is never free or loose on the stage.

Securing the Sword To wrench the opponent's sword out of the hand from a physical action such as the gripes. See *Secured Disarm*.

Self-Awareness Knowing and understanding of one's self physically, mentally, emotionally and morally.

Semicircular Parry Defensive action of the blade where the hand maintains its same relative placement and the blade moves from one position to another in a semicircular path; changing lines but remaining on the same side of the body.

Sensing the Steel (also *Sentiment de Fer*) Kind of intuition, or "sixth-sense," that warns the fencer of the intentions and the will of their opponent, allowing the fencer to anticipate them.

Septime (also *Seventh*) **a.)** The guard and parry of small sword and modern fencing that closes (protects) the low inside line, with the point lower than the hand, which is in supination. The parry of septime is close to the parry of seven in theatrical rapier play. **b.)** Often applied to the Transitional Rapier Parry of Seven.

Sesta (It.) (Also *Sesta Guardia* and *Double Fence Sesta*) The Double Fence guard where the rapier hand assumes the placement of single rapier Low Terza (Standard), the hand drawn back to the side of the body at waist-level and the dagger in a variation of single weapon Terza (Standard) with the arm extended forward, the hand at roughly chest level.

Set Up a.) Feint attack with the edge aimed at a target on the opponent other than that which is the real object of the attack. **b.)** Returning to, recovering to, or assuming the correct position and placement for a specific sequence or a particular move. **c.)** Moving or manipulating an opponent into a particular position or place for the execution of a preplanned move or sequence.

Seven, Parry of Defense for an attack to the non-weapon bearing thigh. The hilt and hand below waist level, palm towards the opponent, blade below the hand, its forte at the level of the non-weapon bearing leg's quadriceps, just above the knee.

Sgualembrato (It.) Descending diagonal cutting attack.

Sharps Non-theatrical weapons. Swords not rebated, buttoned or blunted.

Sheath Case or covering, for the blade of a weapon when not in use; usually close fitting and conforming to the shape of the blade. See *Scabbard*.

Shell-Guard Portion of a sixteenth century sword hilt named for its resemblance to an open sea shell. The shell was seated below the shoulder of the blade, atop the pas d'âne, and could be affixed to one or both sides of the hilt.

Short Sword (also *Short-Sword* and *English Short Sword*) **a.)** Common term for the traditional English single-handed broadsword. A sword with a stout, short blade, roughly the length of a man's arm, furnished with a simple cross hilt, pas d'âne, side-ring and often a knuckle bow. See *True English Fight* and *Sword and Buckler*. **b.)** Term often mistakenly applied to the short bladed Roman Gladius.

Shoulder Cuts (also *Full Cut* and *Standard Cut*) **a.)** Large, sweeping, cutting attacks delivered with the whole arm from the shoulder. See also *Piston Cut*. **b.)** Any cutting attack delivered to the shoulder.

Shoulders a.) Step or notch in the blade of the sword where it narrows from forte to tang designed to meet flush and flat to the hilt of the sword (on the quillon block and often the pas d'âne) to minimize torque and strain on the tang of the weapon. See *Tang* and *Slop*. **b.)** The target in cutting and thrusting attacks situated on the arm at the notch where the deltoid and biceps meet (at roughly chest level where).

Showing Point (also *Showing the Point* and *Show and Then Go*) The underlying principal of all theatrical puncture play where the arm is extended towards its target as a cue and control point prior to executing the final action of the attack.

Side-Ring (Also *Side Ring*) Ring or rings placed on the side of the hilt intended to protect the knuckles and the back side of the sword hand. See *Parrying Dagger, Upper Side-Ring* and *Lower Side-Ring*.

Sidestep Evasion See *Traverse Evasion*.

Silver, George Champion of traditional English "cut and thrust" swordsplay. His text "Paradoxes of Defence" (1599) was a sarcastic airing of extreme English views on swordplay and the art of defense.

Simple Attack Action comprised of two separate attacks; an *Indirect Attack* (such as a changement, attack on the blade or pris d'fer) removes the opposing blade and opens the line for an immediate *Direct Attack*.

Simple Beat See *Direct Beat*.

Simple Changement Blade movement made from one guard position to another that does not require manipulation around, over or under the opposing blade.

Simple Footwork Base elements of footwork that involve the execution of one component, such as the *advance*.

Simple Parry Parry made by a simple lateral movement carrying the blade horizontally across the body.

Simultaneous Attacks Two attacks launched at the same time.

Single Feint Attack (Also Simple *Feint Attack*) Feint of a direct attack, followed by a deception of parry and ending with an actual direct attack in a different line.

Single Fight Fight or combat consisting of two participants; a duel.

Single Rapier The rapier alone. In many sixteenth and seventeenth century schools of fence, the single rapier was considered the foundation of the science of arms and the best possible style to introduce to a novice.

Single Sword a.) Any sword light enough to be used in one hand, generally wielded with a second weapon such as a dagger or buckler, but is used alone to function both offensively and defensively. See *Transitional Rapier* and *Single Rapier*. **b.)** A combat style in Skills Testing recognized by the FDC and SBFD.

Single Time a.) Where the parry and riposte are one action. **b.)** The time it would take to complete one simple attack.

Single Weapon a.) Working with only one weapon, be it rapier, sword, dagger, etc. Mechanics or techniques concerned with the management of a solo weapon. **b.)** The handling of a weapon in a solo manner whether or not there is a second weapon in the other hand.

Sitting This One Out Exercise that allows the combatants to relax and place their focus on the movement of the hand and wrist instead of on maintaining correct stance and placement by sitting both combatants in chairs.

Six, Parry of Single weapon defensive action for a thrusting attack to the mid torso, the hand supinated (picking up the attacking blade with the false or back edge) with the blade above the hand.

Sixte (also *Sixth*) **a.)** The guard in small sword, transitional rapier and modern fencing that closes (protects) the high outside line; taken with the point higher than the hand, which is supinated. Sixte is closely related to the guard of Terza and the parry of six in theatrical rapier play. **b.)** The parry in transitional rapier and small sword executed with the point higher than the hand, which is supinated, closing the high outside line.

Size Relative magnitude, established by enlarging, maintaining, or limiting the amount of space used for a movement within a given area.

Slinging Steel Slang for crossing swords in offensive and defensive play whether as an exercise or for rehearsal. Swordplay.

Slip Backward Evasive action that removes the body with a sloped pace backward on a diagonal, roughly forty-five degrees off the parallel tracks of linear footwork.

Slip Forward Evasive action that removes the body with a sloped pace forward on a diagonal, roughly forty-five degrees off the parallel tracks of linear footwork.

Slip Evasive action executed either to the right or left used to avoid both ascending and descending diagonal cuts. The feet remain stationary and the torso leans away from the attack, straightening the leg and creating a diagonal at roughly forty-five degrees to the floor.

Slop a.) Careless swordplay with uncertain attacks and parries; dangerous stage combat. **b.)** Poorly fitted or manufactured parts of a sword or poorly assembled weapons with gaps, shims or wedges to make it all fit.

Sloped Pace a.) (also *Croked Pace*) Footwork executed on the four diagonal planes that run at a forty-five degree angle to linear tracks of straight pace footwork. See also *Ten Directions of Footwork*. **b.)** Side steps on the imaginary circle, to either the right or the left, where the feet do not cross one another.

Small Sword The last form of the rapier. A sword with a light, triangular, fluted blade (used only for thrusting) with a very simple hilt consisting of two half shells, or an elliptical plate, and a smaller guard for the hand and fingers.

Society of American Fight Directors (Also *S.A.F.D.* or *SAFD*) The worlds' largest professional, non-profit organization created to promote the art of fight choreography and combat safety as an integral part of the theatre, film and television industries. See *Actor/Combatant, Certified Teacher, Fight Director* and *Fight Master*.

Soft Parry (also *Short Parry*, rarely *Flick Cut*) Defensive actions against standard thrusting attacks that meet the arm of the aggressor instead of the ''Hard'' steel of their blade.

Space a.) Possibility for space and dimension; an environment essential for any movement. **b.)** The amount of room available for any action or activity. **c.)** The final frontier.

Spada Sola Literally ''Sword alone.'' See *Single Rapier*.

Spada Literally ''Sword.'' Generally referring to the rapier.

Spanish Blade a.) Superior blade; one of the best blades available. Toledo, Spain was considered to be one of the best manufacturers of sword blades during the Elizabethan era. **b.)** Rapier furnished with a blade manufactured in Spain. See *Spanish Sword*.

Spanish Dagger Form of parrying dagger that appeared in the second quarter of the seventeenth century, consisting of a bigger weapon, with a longer and heavier blade, long straight quillons (often reaching 11 inches or more tip to tip), a long and stout blade (with total lengths of 19 inches or more) and a wide triangular guard that curved from the quillons to the pommel, protecting the combatant's hand and knuckles.

Spanish Guard (Single Rapier) The theatrical on guard position for the sixteenth and seventeenth century Spanish style of fence is Seconda Proper with the legs practically straight, the upper torso upright and the left hand outside the body at about waist level.

Spanish Sword Term for the rapier used by Englishmen exposed to the Spanish weapon in the court of Mary Tudor, preceding the introduction to the Italian weapon and school.

Spatial Design The interrelationship of combatants to each other and to the space through which they are moving. This refers both to the floor area, to the space around the combatants, to the picture they make in space, and to the space they had just occupied.

Specialized Vocal Techniques Harsh screams and yells that need coaching to avoid seriously straining and fatiguing the vocal instrument.

Spectacle a.) Fight that draws attention to itself instead of enhancing and furthering the dramatic intent of a play or film. A stage display, as contrasted to real drama. **b.)** A specially arranged or prepared exhibition, especially on a large scale, designed to impress those viewing it; a grand display; an entertainment of marvelous scale and proportion.

Speed Velocity or rate at which a fight is moving. The degree of quickness of movement, both of sword and body, usually as a result of exertion, clarity, swiftness; also the power or rate of progress.

Spin (also *Full Turn*) Extended grand volte that turns the combatant 360 degrees on the foot as a single axis, like a drafting compass.

Squat Duck (Also *Duck*) Deep bend in the knees that lowers the torso, displacing the head from target of a horizontal attack.

Staccato Clear-cut detached or disconnected engagements of the blades.

Stacking (Also *Stacking Actors*) Placing one or more actors directly upstage (or up-camera) of one another for masking or specific blocking purposes.

Stage Combat (also sometimes *Staged Combat*) **a.)** All physical conflict, armed and unarmed, that takes place in a staged performance. A choreographed confrontation highlighted with acted aggression. **b.)** Distinct dramatic movement discipline where dramatic integrity is essential and the artist's safety is paramount.

Stance The specific positioning of the feet and body as part of correct physical placement for a particular technique or form of combat. See *Postura*.

Standard Cut See *Shoulder Cut*.

Standing Lunge Thrust with the sword arm punched forward by a weight shift onto the lead leg and a slight turning in the torso.

Standing Volte Evasive action of the body where the upper body pivots ninety degrees as the lower body ''rocks'' away from the attack without moving the feet.

Steccada (Also *Stoccata*) (It.) Thrusting attack under the opponent's sword arm, much like McBanes *Boar's Thrust*.

Steccado Thrust or thrusting attack with the rapier.

Steel Generic term for the blade, or the entire weapon, nondescript to any period or weapon.

Step Out (also *Traverse*) Evasion to the side. See *Side Step Evasion*.

Step-in-Parry (Also sometimes *Jam Parry*) Defensive action against a cutting attack that combines the mechanics of a standard parry while moving into the close.

Stesso Tempo (It.) Common practice of the sixteenth century Italian school of executing the parry and riposte in one action.

Stoccado The point of a sword or dagger, or, a thrust with this point.

Stoccata Lunga (Literally "Elongated Thrust") Gigantti's term for the lunge. See *Grand Lunge*.

Stoccata (It.) **a.)** (Also *Stucatho*) Thrust in fencing. **b.)** In theatrical rapier play; a pronated thrust from *Terza*, to either the right or left shoulder (on or off-line).

Stop Cut a.) Counter offensive cut designed to strike the opponent before the final movement of the opponent's attack is executed. **b.)** Sometimes applied to the *Stop Short*.

Stop Hit Counter offensive action, cut or thrust, designed to strike the opponent before the final movement of the opponent's attack is executed.

Stop Parry See *Jam Parry*.

Stop Short a.) Feint with the edge of the blade that resembles a proper full arm cut, this attack is abruptly brought to a halt, prior to executing the final two-thirds of the cut. **b.)** To suddenly halt during or immediately after gaining ground for offensive or defensive reasons.

Stop Thrust Counter offensive thrust designed to strike the opponent before the final movement of the opponent's attack is executed.

Straight Attack Attack executed from an open guard position where the opposing blade is neither an immediate threat nor closes the immediate line of attack. A *Direct Attack*.

Straight Pace Backward Any footwork straight backward.

Straight Pace Forward Any footwork straight forward.

Straight Thrust Direct and simple form of attack.

Stroke Attack or blow with a weapon or the hand, inflicted on or aimed at another person. Sometime applied to the thrust of a weapon. See *Cutting Attack*.

Style a.) Personal or characteristic manner of choreographing or executing a fight. **b.)** Esthetic creative choice based on the actual mechanics of the weapon or form of combat.

Sub-Text The character's inner dialogue. What a character is thinking while they're listening to, talking to, or fighting someone else.

Successive Parries Several unsuccessful parries following one another until the attacking blade is found.

Super Objective What a character wants overall.

Supination The position of the hand when the palm is turned up, with the nails of the sword hand pointing up towards the ceiling.

Sustained Movement Quality of movement that is smooth and unaccented. There is no apparent stared or stop, only continuity of energy and flow.

Swash a.) To fence with, or to make the sound of clashing swords or of a sword striking a shield; to bluster with, or as with weapons. **b.)** Heavy forceful blow, usually sounded with a crash. **c.)** The whistling sound created as a heavy or forceful blow as it "cuts the air." **d.)** A swaggering bravo or ruffian; a swashbuckler.

Swashbuckler [*swash b.*) + *buckler* = the striking of a buckler with a "crash."] one who makes a noise by striking their own, or their opponent's shield with their sword. **a.)** Elizabethan term for a reckless swaggering bully much given to dueling with their sword and buckler; a swaggering bravo or ruffian. **b.)** Stylized sword swinging cinematic adventure. **c.)** Gallant swordsman and gentleman.

Swashbuckling Acting like, or characteristic of the conduct of a swashbuckler.

Swashing Blow (also *Washing Blow*) **a.)** Large, sweeping stroke or blow delivered with great force, intended more to batter than cut the opponent. **b.)** In theatrical swordplay; cuts from the shoulder that travel through the entire plane of attack causing the blade to whistle or swash the air. Often used for a kill or wound, especially to the belly.

Swept-Hilt Guard consisting of several curved branches and side-rings interconnecting with one another. There are generally at least two side-rings on the guard sweeping down from the pas d'âne with branches stemming to the knuckle bow.

Swetnam, Joseph Seventeenth Century English fencing master and tutor to the Prince of Whales. Although his treatise (1617) provides no new or innovative developments in the science of fence, it is the first book penned by an Englishman dealing with rapier and dagger fence.

Swipe Theatrical cutting attack not intended to land, but to slash through the air over an opponent's head, across their belly, etc.

Sword & Buckler (*Sword and Buckler*) **a.)** Armed with, using, or pertaining to a sword and buckler. **b.)** The traditional weapons of England: in most popular use from around the beginning of the sixteenth century until the turn of the seventeenth century. **c.)** The weapon of servants, fools and oafs on stage. **d.)** The traditional weapon was, by the turn of the century, identified only with the lowest class of men, ruffians and soldiers, thus when identified with a gentleman, considered an insult.

Sword & Dagger a.) Style of swordplay where a sword is carried in the right hand for offense, and a dagger carried in the left for warding, parrying or deflecting the adversary's attacks. See also *Rapier and*

Dagger. **b.)** Armed with, using or pertaining to the sword and dagger.

Sword & Lantern Style of swordplay where a combatant would use their lantern as a defensive weapon for warding, parrying or deflecting the adversary's attacks.

Sword Cane Hollow cane or walking stick housing a steel blade which may be drawn and used as a sword.

Sword Carriage Waist belt and suspension rigging for the Elizabethan rapier.

Sword of Fashion Civilian sword, most often the small sword, but sometimes the rapier. See *Small Sword.*

Sword, Age of the (*Circa* 1450–1550) Period where the sword became the paramount weapon above the heavy cutting and crushing weapons of the Middle Ages.

Sword-Arm Protect (also *Sword-Arm Protect Parry*) Hanging parry executed to protect the sword baring side of the body. The hand and hilt are on the right side of the body at roughly ear level, palm back, away from the opponent, the blade is below the hand, sloped down with the tip at roughly four o'clock.

Sword-Arm Arm with which the sword is wielded; generally the right arm.

Sword-Blade See *Blade.*

Sword-Breaker a.) Any type of dagger provided with special contrivances designed to entangle and entrap the opponent's blade. **b.)** Device designed to catch a sword blade and break it; a notch, hook, etc. on a dagger, buckler, etc. manufactured for breaking the blade of an adversary's sword.

Sword-Hilts The portion of the sword comprised of the guard, grip and pommel. The handle of the sword. See also *Hilt.*

Sword a.) Weapon, generally carried at one's side, used by hand, adapted for cutting and/or thrusting. Comprised of a handle or hilt and a straight or curved blade with either one or two sharp edges and/or a sharp point. **b.)** See also *Broadsword, Rapier, Short Sword, Small Sword* and *Transitional Rapier.*

Swordbelt (Also Sword-Belt) Wide, tight waist-belt with vertical straps ending in snaphooks, used in the nineteenth century to carry sabers and officers' swords.

Swordplay The exchange of offensive and defensive actions (cuts, thrust, blows, strikes, parries, etc.) with swords, whether in practice or in combat; fencing.

Swordsman (Also *swordman & swordmen*) Person skilled in the use of a sword; a man of the sword; a sword fighter.

Swordsmanship Skill in the use of the sword.

Syncopation Clipping abbreviating or stressing of certain movements of a choreographed routine in order to heighten the physical dialogue.

Taking the Blade (also *Taking the Opponent's Blade*) See *Pris d'Fer.*

Tang (Originally referred to as the "tongue" of the blade) Portion of the blade that extends from the forte and shoulders, passes through the guard and grip of the sword and fastens in some way to the pommel.

Tap Parry a.) See *Beat Parry.* **b.)** Sometimes applied to a *Detached Parry.*

Targe (It.) (Also *Target*) Round or squarish shield, fitted with two enarmes, one strapping across the forearm and the other held in the left hand.

Target a.) That part of the body an attack is directed towards. See also *Box Target, Hour-Glass System, Triangle Target, On-Line* and *Off-Line.* **b.)** See *Targe.*

Technique a.) The mechanical or formal part of stage combat; the manner of execution or performance of specific details in stage combat. **b.)** A person's skill, ability or style of execution, choreography or instruction of stage combat.

Temper a.) To bring steel to a suitable degree of hardness and resiliency by heating it to the required temperature and impressing it while hot. **b.)** The degree of hardness and elasticity imparted to steel, namely to a sword. The quality of a sword.

Tempo Indivisable Literally "indivisible time." When the parry and riposte follow one another with no pause whatsoever.

Tempo a.) (Also *Fencing Tempo*) The amount of time required to execute one simple fencing action. **b.)** The pace or speed at which movement progresses; relatively slower or faster.

Ten Directions of Footwork The variable directions that any piece of footwork can take a combatant during a stage fight. Generating out from a central position below the combatant, like the points on a compass, with the chest and torso always facing "North."

Terza-Bassa (It.) See *Low Terza.*

Terza (also *Terza Guardia*) (from the Latin *Tertio*—"thirdly") **a.)** The standard single weapon On Guard position in historical and theatrical rapier fence assumed with the hand just above the waist (held in pronation, supination, or vertical/middle position), the arm bent at roughly 90 degrees, the blade angled up with the tip at roughly the opponent's armpit level (Standard or Across) **b.)** The double fence guard assumed with the rapier in single weapon Terza (Standard or Across) with the dagger also held in single weapon Terza (Standard).

Three, Parry of Defense for a horizontal attack to the weapon bearing shoulder with the hand and hilt at roughly waist level on the weapon bearing side, knuckles toward the outside, the blade above the hand, its forte at the level of the notch in sword bearing arm where the deltoid and biceps meet.

Three-Point Stance Stance in swordplay with an increased depth and reduced width than that of the standard four-point stance, narrowing the parallel tracks of linear and circular footwork from shoulder width to approximately one foot.

Through Energy The process of identifying the objectives, actions, and justifications of the fight and being aware of how each contribute to the fight's movement forward.

Throw Off a.) Term for the *Bind Away*. **b.)** Strong blade taking action that upon its completion propels the attacking sword, and its bearer, off in the direction the defending sword sends it.

Thrust The action of thrusting. An attack with the point of the weapon, opposed to a blow with the edge.

Thrusting Home a.) Attack with the point that closes measure and lands, or intends to land on the opponent. **b.)** Term for the "kill" or killing thrust.

Thrusting on the Circle Drill in blade-play that takes the combatants through a series of thrust, parries and ripostes while executing circular paces on the tracks of the imaginary circle.

Tierce (also *Third*) **a.)** The small sword, transitional rapier and modern fencing guard that closes (protects) the high outside line; taken with the hand in pronation and with the point higher than the hand. Tierce is closely related to the guard of Terza and the parry of three in theatrical rapier play. **b.)** The transitional rapier and small sword parry taken with the hand in pronation and with the point higher than the hand, closing the high outside line.

Tight a.) Said of two or more combatants fighting inside measure. **b.)** Said of any cramped space or performance area. **c.)** A routine or sequence that has reached a highly effective tempo and timing.

Time Action Stop hit executed by closing the line in which the attack is to completed.

Time Disengagement Action to deny the opponent an engagement of the blades. "Time" refers to timing the action so that it is executed at the last possible moment prior to engagement and therefore gaining the advantage. See also *Absence of Blade* and *Refusing the Blade*.

Time a.) The practice of Elizabethan and modern fencers that minimizes the offensive and defensive motions of the body to those strictly necessary, both in number and in extent; and also balances those motions carefully with those of the opponent, in order to seize instantly any opportunity while minimizing the possibility of being struck. **b.)** The period of time taken to execute any one action of the blade, arm, or foot.

Timing To acknowledge an opportunity or opening and execute the correct action at the best possible moment.

Tip Control See *Point Control*.

Tip a.) The pointed or rounded end of a sword blade or dagger. See *Point*. **b.)** To give a slight blow, knock or touch to; to tap lightly.

To the Hilts Active form of coming to the close where the offensive and defensive weapons join and meet guard to guard as the combatants close measure.

Toledo a.) Spanish town renowned for its rapier blades during the Elizabethan era **b.)** A modern manufacturer of cheap replica arms, non-combat serviceable. See *Wall-Hanger*.

Tondo Literally "around" or "compass." Circular cutting attack delivered in a horizontal plane. See *Man Dritta Tondo* and *Reverso Tondo*.

Touch & Go Exercise designed to work on wide attacks and parries where at each target the attack is checked, the parry executed, the blades lightly touch, and the combatants move on.

Touch a.) Very light hit, knock, stroke or blow. **b.)** Valid hit in fencing, scored within the prescribed target area.

Touché (Fr.) Rather outdated vocal acknowledgment to a touch or hit received in fencing practice.

Tournament a.) Originally a martial sport or exercise of the Middle Ages in which a number of armored and mounted combatants divided into parties or teams, fought with blunted weapons under certain restrictions for the prize of valor; **b.)** Encounter or trial of strength in combat; a prize fight.

Tournaments of Champions Public exhibition developed in the twelfth century where knights would come together to display their skills at arms. See *Champion*.

Tourney a.) To take part in, or to tilt in a tournament. **b.)** A *Tournament* or *Tournament of Champions*.

Tracking Practice of following one's opponent with the attacking blade during the execution of an evasive maneuver (duck, side step, etc.)

Tracks The two imaginary parallel lines or *Railroad Tracks* that a combatant's feet are said to travel upon.

Transfer Beat Parry Form of transfer parry where a successful primary parry is completed with one weapon, followed with a secondary beat parry.

Transfer Heavy Parry Transfer parry where the primary parry is executed with the dagger and as the parry is transferred to the rapier it instantly takes the offending weapon to the floor in the manner of a heavy parry.

Transfer Parry (also *Replacement Parry*) Double fence parry that uses both weapons to deflect and control the offending blade.

Transfer Pris d'Fer (also *Replacement Pris d'Fer*) **a.)** Variation on the transfer parry where a pris d'fer is instantly executed by the secondary weapon after the primary weapon has successfully completed the parry. **b.)** Double fence technique that uses both weapons, one after the other, in the execution of a pris d'fer on the opposing blade.

Transition, Age of (*Circa* 1625–1675) The second phase of the *Golden Age of the Sword* (following the *Age of the Rapier*) where the rapier decidedly tended towards simplification, but had not yet assumed the definite shape of the *small sword*. The weapon became lighter and faster, and the dagger had, for the most part, been abandoned, forcing the fencer to trust solely in the rapier for defense. See also *Transitional Rapier*.

Transition Moving of the blade from one line or placement to another. See also *Changement*.

Transitional Footwork a.) Footwork executed

from the narrower base of the three-point stance, allowing for the style of gaining and breaking ground generally associated with the quick exchange of point work of the Transitional Rapier. **b.)** Any footwork used as a shift between two specific pieces of choreography.

Transitional Parries (also *Transitional Rapier Parries*) Parry angled slightly forward as a threat to one's opponent and to facilitate the quick pointwork of the transitional rapier.

Transitional Rapier a.) A rapier with a smaller, lighter blade designed mostly for point work, a razor sharp point (the edges were kept sharp only to prevent the opponent from seizing the blade), and a less complex hilt configuration then that of the earlier rapiers. See *Transition, Age of.* **b.)** A lighter, faster stage weapon generally fitted with a cup-hilt and mounted with a *Musketeer Blade* or *Giant Epée Blade*.

Transport Parry a.) Defensive maneuver with a bladed weapon that lifts or lowers the opposing blade to a different line than that being attacked. **b.)** Parry executed with a pris d'fer.

Transport (Hung.) See *Pris d'Fer.*

Traveling Footwork See *Active Footwork.*

Traverse Evasion (also *Traverse Right* and *Traverse Left and Sidestep Evasion*) Evasive action that removes the body from the cutting plane of a vertical or diagonal swipe by lunging either to the left (west) or to the right (east) and leaning the torso into the lunge, displacing the body from the plane of attack.

Traverse a.) Any footwork executed directly to the right/East (*Traverse Right*) or left/West (*Traverse Left*) instead of movement forward or backward on the linear tracks. See *Ten Directions of Footwork.* **b.)** To run a weapon through something; to pierce, stab.

Trial by Combat Legal dispute settled through personal combat.

Triangle Target One of three systems of body targets in on-line fencing. The targets, when joined with imaginary lines form a triangle; one center chest (at the sternum) and the other two located on opposite thighs at approximately groin level.

Triplé (Fr.) Compound attack in any line that deceives a direct parry and two counter parries.

Trompement The deception of the opponent's parry or parries in the course of executing a compound attack. From the French *tromper* meaning "to deceive, delude or cheat."

True Art Elizabethan philosophy of superior practice and skill in the techniques of striking the opponent while safely defending one's self.

True Edge Part of the blade which, when the weapon is held correctly, is naturally directed towards one's opponent. It is with this edge that most cutting attacks on stage are delivered, and most parries received.

True English Fight a.) Sword and Buckler play. **b.)** English practice of traditional weapons and the rough, "manly" methods of fighting, scorning the tricks and

dodging style of the rapier's subtle, "mathematical" craft. See also *Short Sword* and *Sword and Buckler.*

Twiddle (Also *Twydle*) **a.)** To lightly or delicately rotate, or describe a circle with, the tip of the blade in a manner where one can parry an attack and return to the original position of the blade; a circular parry. **b.)** An endless series of parries and deception of parries; so that the blades move about one another much like the action of twiddling thumbs.

Twist See *Croisé.*

Two, Parry of Defense for an attack to the weapon bearing hip where the hand and hilt are just above waist level on the weapon bearing side of the body, knuckles turned to the outside, the blade is below the hand, its forte at the level of the weapon bearing hip.

Two-Hand (also *Two-Hander*) Said of a weapon wielded with two hands [*H6/2*—ii.I.46]

Two-Ring Hilt One of the earliest guard configurations of the rapier developed from the medieval cross-hilt, having an upper and lower side-ring to protect the back of the sword-hand, counter guards, pas d'âne and a knuckle bow.

Uncovered Position where the line of engagement is not closed. See *Open Line(s).*

Under Stop Thrust Low line evasion executed with a stop thrust. See *Passata Sotto.*

Underhand Grip (also *Reversed Grip*) Way of holding a dagger or knife with the blade held beneath the hand (gripped with the thumb at the pommel) and managed as a stabbing weapon. Opposite of *Overhand Grip.*

Upper Side-Ring (Also *Upper Port*) The smaller of the two side-rings found on the two-ring and swept-hilt rapier hilts situated the furthest from the weapon's pommel. See *Side-Ring* and also *Lower Side-Ring.*

Value The significance of each action within a fight to the character executing them. The justification, or reason for the activity and the character's commitment to the action establishes its relative worth or value.

Variable Planes of Footwork The multiple directions of movement within a stage fight. See also *Ten Directions of Footwork.*

Vault Spring or jump into the air in order to avoid an attack at the feet. See *Jump.*

Vertical Attack Any cutting attack that travels from a high line to a low line, or vise-versa, in a plane that is perpendicular to the floor.

Vertical Changement Changement executed from a free guard position by passing the point to an open line by moving either up or down.

Vertical Jump (Also *Jump*) **a.)** The classic cliché for the dashing swordsman to jump over an adversary's attack at the feet. **b.)** To leap up onto a structure above that which the combatant leapt from (such as a table, chair, platform, etc.)

Vertical Swipe Theatrical cutting attack not intended to land, but to slash through the air from either right or left, in either a descending or ascending plane perpendicular to the floor. See also *Swipe*.

Viggiani, Angelo (Also *Vizani, Angelo*) Italian master of the sixteenth century, who first proclaimed the superiority of the thrust over the cut (1560). He developed the *punta soporamano* (A "thrust over the hand" or the demi-lunge) which was an advancing of the right foot with the sword arm fully extended and the left arm lowered backward to provide a counter balance.

Vocal Cue a.) Any vocalization that is used to key in one's partner to a specific technique or sequence when eye contact or a physical cue is impractical. **b.)** (Also *Verbal Cue*) The use of a rehearsed word or catch phrase to help get combatants back on track if there is a problem in performance.

Vocal Orchestration a.) The development of sound patterns which reinforce the movement of the fight. **b.)** The sounds supporting the activity, the situation and the circumstances of the character and the conflict.

Vocal Warm-down Process of allowing the voice to relax from the vocal demands of a fight, helping avoid strain and fatigue in the instrument.

Vocal Warm-Ups Process of preparing the voice for the diverse demands placed on the instrument during a staged fight.

Vocalized Rhythm The quaint sounds omitted by actors and choreographers to exemplify the particular rhythm set by the values of the actions in a routine.

Volte Sudden and dexterous method of removing the body from the line of attack by swinging the lag foot back and to the side along the outer track of an imaginary circle, turning the body more or less parallel to the line of attack. See *Demi-Volte* and *Grand Volte*.

Volume The degree of magnitude or loudness of a sound.

Voluntary Sounds Sounds during a fight which the combatant releases by design or intention.

W's; the Five The fundamental questions asked to discover the circumstances of a play: *Who* is the character?; *What* is the character doing?; *When* is this happening?; *Where* is this happening?; *Why* is the character there?

Walk Through The process of carrying out all the moves of a fight at a slow, comfortable pace.

Walking Foot Exercise designed to help the combatant develop fluid horizontal movement in footwork by moving the initiating foot with a walking or 'rocking' action.

Walking the Line Exercise designed to help the combatant keep his feet on track while traversing linear footwork by following actual lines on the floor.

Walking the Plank Exercise designed to help the combatant keep his feet on track while traversing linear footwork by having the combatant perform linear footwork on two 2×4 planks.

Wall Bound Blade-play exercise that helps maintain measure and places the combatant's focus on the management of the point by working a series of stationary drills with their back up against a wall.

Wall-Hanger Decorative sword, that is made only as decoration and is in no way designed, engineered, or constructed for stage combat.

Ward a.) Archaic term for the guard when it was a position of observation for the purpose of discovering the approach of danger and effectively launching a counter attack. **b.)** Defensive posture or movement; to parry, repel, fend off, turn aside a stroke or thrust, blow, attack, weapon. **c.)** The part of a hilt of a sword that protects the hand; the guard.

Watch Parry Slang for the parry of High One and sometimes the standard parry of one; where the hand and wrist are placed as if the combatant was looking at their watch.

Water Works Exercise designed to help the combatant develop fluid horizontal movement in footwork by carrying a full glass of water in the sword hand.

Weapon-Bearing Lines a.) Lines of attack as determined by the weapon-bearing side of the body. **b.)** In double fence techniques lines are determined by the *sword-bearing* and *dagger-bearing Lines of Attack.*

Window Parry (also *Parry 5A*) Reversed Parry of High 5. A nick-name for the reversed parry of 5 given by American Fight Master David Boushey because the position of the right arm and blade form a frame around the face.

Wrap-n-Trap (also *Serpentine, Silver's Disarm* and *Angelo's Disarm*) Secured disarm taught by George Silver that has the unarmed-hand snake around the opposing blade, coming up on the inside near the hilt, wrapping the arm around the blade, trapping it under the arm and in the grasp where the sword can be secured and disarmed.

Wrapping It Up Slang for the *Envelopment*.

Wrapping the Eights Exercise in blade manipulation that has the combatant execute a series of full arm molinellos on both sides of the body in the pattern of a large figure-eight.

Wrapping (also *Wrapping the Cue*) Misaligned cue that is carried around and behind the body. Such an action makes the cue difficult to read and places the blade and tip in a gray area outside peripheral vision.

Wrist Cut (also *1/3 cut*) **a.)** The fastest and tightest cut delivered in theatrical swordplay made only from an action of the hand and wrist. **b.)** Cutting attack delivered to the wrist.

Yield Parry (also *Ceding Parry*) Parry executed against a flowing attack without separating the blades.

Yield To give up or surrender, the action of giving in; submission.

ZA Term coined by Patrick (Paddy) Crean, for the charismatic allure and charm of the gallant swashbuckler.

Bibliography

Anderson, Bob. *Stretching*. Bolinas, California: Shelter Publications, 1981.

Angelo, Domenico. *The School of Fencing*. London: Printed for S. Hooper, at Ceaser's Head, the East Corner of the New Church in the Strand, 1765.

Ashdown, Charles Henry. *An Illustrated History of Arms & Armour*. Hertfordshire: Wordsworth Editions Ltd, 1988.

Aylward, J.D. *The English Master of Arms*. London: Routledge and Kegan Paul, 1956.

Aylward, J.D. *"Playing a Prize." Notes and Queries*. 196 (1950).

Baldick, Robert. *The Duel*. London: Chapman and Hall, 1965.

Billacois, Francois. *The Duel: Its Rise & Fall in Early Modern France*. New Haven, CT: Yale University Press, 1990.

Blakeslee, Fred Gilbert. *Sword Play for Actors: A Manual of Stage Fencing*. New York: M.N. Hazen Co., 1905.

Burton, Sir Richard. *The Book of the Sword*. London: Chatto and Windus, 1884.

Castle, Egerton. *Schools and Masters of Fence*. London: George Bell & Sons, Chiswick Press; Charles Whittingham & Co., Tooks Court, Chancery Lane, 1885.

Cohen, Robert & Harrop, John. *Creative Play Directing*. (2nd ed.) Englewood Cliffs, N.J.: Prentice-Hall, Inc., 1984.

Craig, Horace S. *"Duelling Scenes and Terms in Shakespeare's Plays." University of California Publications in English*. 9 (1940).

Crosnier, Roger. *Fencing with the Foil*. New York: Barnes and Co., 1962.

Dessen, Alan C. *"The Logic of Elizabethan Stage Violence: Some Alarms and Excursions for Modern Critics, Editors, and Directors." Renaissance Drama*. New Series #9, (1978).

Diehl, Huston. *"The Iconography of Violence in English Renaissance Tragedy." Renaissance Drama*, n.s. II (1980).

di Grassi, Giacomo. *His True Arte of Defence*. London: 1594.

Edge, David and Paddock, John Miles. *Arms & Armor of the Medieval Knight*. Bison Books Corp., 1988.

Editors of Sports Illustrated. *Sports Illustrated: Book of Fencing*. Philadelphia & New York: J.B. Lippincott Co., 1962.

Featherstone, Donald F. *Dancing Without Danger*. South Brunswick and New York: Barnes, 1970.

Garret, Maxwell R., and Poulson, Mary H. *Foil Fencing.* The Pennsylvania State University Press, 1981.

Graves, Thorton S. *"The Stage Sword and Dagger." South Atlantic Quarterly,* 20 (1921).

Hammond, Sandra Noll. *Ballet Basics.* 2nd ed. Mayfield Publishing Co., 1984.

Hartnoll, Phyllis, edited by. *The Oxford Companion to the Theatre.* 4th ed. Oxford University Press, 1985.

Hobbs, William. *Techniques of the Stage Fight.* London: Studio Vista, 1967.

Hobbs, William. *Stage Combat: The Action to the Word.* New York: St. Martins Press, 1980.

Holmes, Martin. *Shakespeare and His Players.* New York: Charles Scribner's Sons, 1972.

Hotson, Leslie. *"The Adventure of the Single Rapier." Atlantic Monthly,* July, 1931.

Hutton, Capt. Alfred. *Old Sword-Play.* London: H. Grevel & Co., New York: B. 1892.

Jackson, James L. *"The Fencing Actor-Lines in Shakespeare's Plays." Modern Language Notes,* 57 (1942).

Jonson, Ben. *The Selected Plays of Ben Jonson: Volume I,* edited by Johanna Procter. Britain: Cambridge University Press, 1989.

Jonson, Ben. *The Selected Plays of Ben Jonson: Volume II,* edited by Martin Butler. Britain: Cambridge University Press, 1989.

Lukovich, Istvan. Translated by Butykay, Istvan. *Fencing.* Debrecen, Hungary: Alfoldi Printing House, 1986.

Martinez, Joseph. *Combat Mime: A Non-Violent Approach to Stage Violence.* Chicago: Nelson-Hall Publishers, 1982.

Linda McCollum, *The Fight Master, "To Cut or Thrust?,"* Sept. 1986, Vol. IX, num. 3; p. 8.

Minton, Sandra C., and Genoff, Karen. *Modern Dance: Body and Mind.* Morton Publishing Co, 1984.

Morton, E.D. *Martini A-Z of Fencing.* London: Queen Anne Press, a division of Macdonald & Co (Publishers) Ltd,

Norman, A.V.B. *Rapier and Small Sword: 1460–1820.* UK: Lionel Leventhal, Arms and Armor Press.

Onions, C.T. *A Shakespeare Glossary.* Oxford, at the Clarendon Press, 1988.

Oxford English Dictionary, The. Compact edition; complete text reproduced micrographically. Vol. I & II: A-Z, Vol. III: Supplements 1–4. USA: Oxford University Press, 1987.

Penrod, James, and Plastino, Janice Gudde. *The Dancer Prepares.* 2nd ed. Palo Alto, California: Mayfield Publishing Co., 1980.

Pollock, W.H., Castle, E., and others. *Fencing, Boxing, Wrestling.* The Badminton Library. Longmans, Green, London, 1890.

Reid, William. *The Lore of Arms: A Concise History of Weaponry.* New York: Facts on File, Inc., 1984.

Richards, Jeffrey. *Swordsmen of the Screen.* London: 1977.

Saviolo, Vincentio. *His Practice in Two Books: the first intreating of the use of the Rapier & Dagger, the second of honour and honourable quarrels.* London: 1595.

Schmidt, Alexander. *Shakespeare Lexicon and Quotation Dictionary.* New York: Dover Publications, Inc., Third Edition, 1971.

Shakespeare, William. *The Riverside SHAKESPEARE.* Boston: Houghton Mifflin Company, 1974.

Sievers, W. David, et al. *Directing for the Theatre.* 3rd ed. Dubuque, Iowa: Wm. C. Brown Co. Publishers, 1982.

Sievking, A. Forbes. *"Fencing and Duelling."* In *Shakespeare's England.* General Editor, Sidney Lee. Volume 2. Oxford: Clarendon Press, 1917. 2 vols.

Silver, George. *Brief Instructions on My Paradoxes of Defence.* London: 1600. Reprinted in: Jackson, James L. *Three Elizabethan Fencing Manuals.* Delmar, New York: Scholars, Facsimiles and Reprints, 1972.

Silver, George. *Paradoxes of Defence.* London: 1599.

Simkins, Michael. *Warriors of Rome.* London: Blandford Press, 1988.

Soens, A. L. *"Tybalt's Spanish Fencing in 'Romeo and Juliet.'"* *Shakespeare Quarterly.* 20 (1969).

Soens, A. L. *"Two Rapier Points: Analysing Elizabethan Fighting Methods."* *Notes and Queries.* (1968).

Swetnam, Joseph. *(The) Schole of the Noble and Worthy Science of Defence.* 4°. London: Printed by Nicholas Okes, 1616(17).

Szabo, Laszlo, and Kiado, Corvina. Translated by Gyula, Gulyas. *Fencing and the Master.* Budapest, Hungry: Franklin Printing House, 1982.

Tarassuk, Leonid & Blair, Claude, edited by. *The Complete Encyclopedia of Arms and Weapons.* New York: Simon and Schuster, 1982.

Thimm, Carl A. *A Complete Bibliography of Fencing & Duelling.* Bronx, New York: Benjamin Blom, Inc., 1968.

Wise, Arthur. *The Art and History of Personal Combat.* Greenwich, Connecticut: Arma Press, 1972.

Wise, Arthur. *Weapons in the Theatre.* New York: Barnes & Noble, Inc., 1968.

Wright, Louis B. *"Stage Duelling in the Elizabethan Theatre."* *Modern Language Review.* 22 (1927).

CPSIA information can be obtained
at www.ICGtesting.com
Printed in the USA
LVHW050418050821
694513LV00005B/214